NEW OXFORD HISTORY OF MUSIC
VOLUME V

THE VOLUMES OF THE
NEW OXFORD HISTORY OF MUSIC

THE PROLOGUE OF LULLY'S *ALCESTE*

Scene from the open-air performance in the Cour de Marbre, Versailles, 4 July 1674, three months after the original performance in Paris.

Engraving by Le Pautre.

OPERA AND CHURCH MUSIC
1630–1750

EDITED BY

ANTHONY LEWIS

AND

NIGEL FORTUNE

LONDON

OXFORD UNIVERSITY PRESS

NEW YORK   TORONTO

1975

Oxford University Press, Ely House, London W.1

GLASGOW NEW YORK TORONTO MELBOURNE WELLINGTON
CAPE TOWN SALISBURY IBADAN NAIROBI LUSAKA ADDIS ABABA
BOMBAY CALCUTTA MADRAS KARACHI LAHORE DACCA
KUALA LUMPUR SINGAPORE HONG KONG TOKYO

ISBN 0 19 316305 5

© *Oxford University Press 1975*

PRINTED IN GREAT BRITAIN
BY EBENEZER BAYLIS AND SON LTD
THE TRINITY PRESS, WORCESTER, AND LONDON

GENERAL INTRODUCTION

THE *New Oxford History of Music* is not a revision of the older *Oxford History of Music,* first published in six volumes under the general editorship of Sir Henry Hadow between 1901 and 1905. It has been planned as an entirely new survey of music from the earliest times down to comparatively recent years, including not only the achievements of the Western world but also the contributions made by Eastern civilizations and primitive societies. The examination of this immense field is the work of a large number of contributors, British and foreign. The attempt has been made to achieve uniformity without any loss of individuality. If this attempt has been successful, the result is due largely to the patience and co-operation shown by the contributors themselves. Overlapping has to some extent been avoided by the use of frequent cross-references; but we have not thought it proper to prevent different authors from expressing different views about the same subject, where it could legitimately be regarded as falling into more than one category.

The scope of the work is sufficiently indicated by the titles of the several volumes. Our object throughout has been to present music, not as an isolated phenomenon or the work of outstanding composers, but as an art developing in constant association with every form of human culture and activity. The biographies of individuals are therefore merely incidental to the main plan of the history, and those who want detailed information of this kind must seek it elsewhere. No hard and fast system of division into chapters has been attempted. The treatment is sometimes by forms, sometimes by periods, sometimes also by countries, according to the importance which one element or another may assume. The division into volumes has to some extent been determined by practical considerations; but pains have been taken to ensure that the breaks occur at points which are logically and historically justifiable. The result may be that the work of a single composer who lived to a ripe age is divided between two volumes. The later operas of Monteverdi, for example, belong to the history of Venetian opera and hence find their natural place in volume v, not with the discussion of his earlier operas to be found in volume iv. On the other hand, we have not insisted on a rigid chronological division where the result would be illogical or confusing. If a subject finds its natural conclusion some ten years after the date assigned for the end of a period, it is obviously preferable to complete it within the limits of one volume rather than to allow it to overflow into a second. An exception to the general scheme of continuous chronology is to be found in volumes v and vi, which deal with different aspects of the same period and so are complementary to each other.

The history as a whole is intended to be useful to the professed student of music, for whom the documentation of sources and the bibliographies are particularly designed. But the growing interest in the music of all periods shown by music-lovers in general has encouraged us to bear their interests also in mind. It is inevitable that a work of this kind should employ a large number of technical terms and deal with highly specialized matters. We have, however, tried to ensure that the technical terms are intelligible to the ordinary reader and that what is specialized is not necessarily wrapped in obscurity. Finally, since music must be heard to be fully appreciated, we have given references throughout to the records issued by His Master's Voice (R.C.A. Victor) under the general title *The History of Music in Sound*. These records are collected in a series of albums which correspond to the volumes of the present work, and have been designed to be used with it.

J. A. WESTRUP
GERALD ABRAHAM
ANSELM HUGHES
EGON WELLESZ
MARTIN COOPER

CONTENTS

CONTENTS

ILLUSTRATIONS

INTRODUCTION TO VOLUMES V and VI

By J. A. WESTRUP

LA Fontaine, having related the fable of the frog and the ox, pointed the moral:

> Le monde est plein de gens qui ne sont pas plus sages:
> Tout bourgeois veut bâtir comme les grand seigneurs,
>   Tout petit prince a des ambassadeurs,
>   Tout marquis veut avoir des pages.

Apart from the rhyme he might equally well have written 'musiciens' instead of 'ambassadeurs'. It was an age of 'conspicuous expenditure', restricted only by limited resources, not by any lack of ambition. Patronage was not new, but in the seventeenth century it cost more. The principal reason for this was opera, which involved not only the expense of singers and orchestra but also paying for scenery and costumes. The spectacle was all-important. Except in the relatively few places where commercial opera flourished it was an aristocratic entertainment which enhanced the prestige of the ruler. In France in particular it was a means of glorifying the king, whose praises were sung in a prologue.

Opera and ballet were mainly responsible for establishing the orchestra as a standard ensemble. But their influence on music in general went further. The idioms of the opera aria were transferred to oratorio and in Germany to the church cantata. The dance movements of the ballet found their way into instrumental suites and concertos. Opera also left its mark on instrumental movements in the form of pointed rhythms which recall the feminine endings of Italian verse, of broad and expressive melodies in the style of the slow aria, of dramatic programme music, and poignant slow movements which reflect in their intensity the idioms of accompanied recitative. Instrumental music in turn had its influence on opera, particularly in the lengthy ritornellos which often introduce an aria; and there was much in common between the *da capo* aria and the solo concerto. Instrumental music reached a wider public than opera, since it was performed outside court circles. There were no concert halls until the Holywell Music Room was opened in Oxford in 1748. Concerts were given in any convenient building— in a church, in a theatre, in a coffee house or a tavern, in a private house, and in the open air. There was also a growth of amateur or student activity—in private circles, in universities, in the Italian conservatories.

The sheer mass of music produced during this period is staggering: hundreds of operas, oratorios, cantatas, concertos, and sonatas. Composers were prolific not from a persistent itch to write music but in order to satisfy a demand, even if it meant setting the same libretto more than once. Both the courts and the public, where there was one, wanted a constant supply of new operas, just as the Lutheran church needed an ample repertory of cantatas. The very fact that composition was their daily bread gave composers a reliable technique which enabled them to write quickly, quite apart from the fact that they were ready to adapt earlier works if it would save time and labour. Since they were all practical musicians, active as conductors or performers, they must have led very busy lives; yet many of them were not averse to social intercourse, and some of them wrote books.

Opera and instrumental music, in particular, called for and encouraged virtuosity. Though travel was slow and often uncomfortable, singers and players sought positions anywhere in Europe where their talents could be rewarded. Alternatively impresarios went to find them, as Handel did when he was organizing opera in London. Sometimes the virtuosos were merely birds of passage. At other times they settled in an adopted country, making money not only by performing but by teaching. Kusser (or Cousser), born in Bratislava and trained in Paris, held posts in several German cities before he visited England and finally settled at Dublin, where he died. Geminiani, a pupil of Corelli and one of the most distinguished violinists of his time, also established himself in Dublin after Kusser's death, though without any official appointment. Tartini, equally distinguished, spent a few years in Prague; but for most of his life he stayed in Padua, where his school of violin-playing was famous and attracted pupils from all over the Continent.

In this way Italian music became widely known, though it had little success in France. But familiarity did not depend on personal contacts. Operas and church music more often than not remained in manuscript: the sumptuous editions published in Paris were on the whole an exception. But a considerable quantity of instrumental music was published, frequently in sets of six or twelve works, and composers or their publishers began to adopt the practice of labelling the sets with opus numbers. No doubt many of the concertos and *sinfonie* were bought for performance by court orchestras; but they may also have been played by amateurs, who certainly found plenty of scope for their activity in what is now known as chamber music. Instrumental resources differed widely. Few court orchestras in the eighteenth century had more than thirty players, and many had less. Outside court circles directors of music had to make do with what they could get. Even in a thriving city like Leipzig Bach was seriously embarrassed by the difficulty of finding adequate players and would have been even more embarrassed if he had not been able to call on pupils at the school and university students, with the addition of members of the *Stadtpfeifer*. The *Stadtpfeifer*, or city waits, were members of a professional gild which maintained a traditional standard of wind playing. They taught younger musicians, and their art was often handed down from father to son through several generations.

The 120 years covered by these two volumes form the greater part of what is currently known as the 'Baroque' period. The word, though allegedly derived from the Portuguese *barroco*, a rough or misshapen pearl, is of uncertain origin. In the eighteenth century it was used, like 'Gothic', in a derogatory sense. Hasse, in his old age, told Burney that he found the music of Durante 'not only dry, but *baroque*, that is, coarse and uncouth'. Rousseau defined 'une musique *baroque*' as 'celle dont l'harmonie est confuse, chargée de modulations & de dissonances, le chant dur & peu naturel, l'intonation difficile, & le mouvement contraint'. In the late nineteenth century, largely through the work of Heinrich Wölfflin, who published his *Renaissance und Barock* at the age of 24, it was applied to a particular style of Southern European architecture, which in its addiction to elaboration and ornament was a reaction against the Classical or Palladian style of the sixteenth century. The term was not adopted by historians of music until the early part of the twentieth century, apparently in the belief that there were parallels between the architecture and the music of the same period. As a sort of code name for the period it is harmless enough: as a description of the music it is virtually meaningless. It is true that there are certain features which are common to most of the composers of the time: contrasts of texture and dynamics, vivacious rhythms, the use of a definite key centre, and extended melodies. But there are also many differences. It would be difficult to see anything in common between the recitatives in Handel's operas and Bach's harpsichord suites. The chief impression made by the music of this period is its astonishing diversity.

This is true even of the works of individual composers. The contrapuntal elaborations of *Die Kunst der Fuge* and the cheerful ditties of the *Peasant Cantata* seem to belong to different worlds. Historians often speak of the firm establishment of tonality in 'Baroque' music, but lingering evidence of modality is not hard to find, particularly in the frequent use of the flattened seventh of the key, which is often introduced at the very beginning of a movement, e.g. the Minuet of Bach's

First Brandenburg Concerto. In accompanied recitative key is often abandoned in favour of unpredictable modulations, and the same thing may happen in purely instrumental music, e.g. in the second movement of Vivaldi's *L'Autunno* (Op. 8, no. 3), which begins and ends in D minor but migrates through several keys in the course of 45 bars. In movements of a more regular construction modulation was generally more strictly controlled and served in fact as a structural element in a composition.

The music of this period rested on a firm diatonic basis. In the sixteenth century, chromaticism tended to be used as a melodic device which might incidentally result in unusual harmonic progressions. In the seventeenth and early eighteenth centuries it still had melodic significance, notably in the chromatic ground bass; and there are traces of older methods in Purcell's fantasias and even as late as Bach, e.g. in his harmonization of the chorale melody 'Mach's mit mir, Gott, nach deiner Güt" (to the words 'Durch dein Gefängnis, Gottes Sohn') in the St. John Passion, or the final cadence of the three-part Invention in D minor (BWV 790), where the independent movement of the parts results in an unpredictable harmonic progression. But for the most part chromaticism was treated as a logical harmonic process within a diatonic framework, and some its procedures, e.g. the Neapolitan sixth (originally a melodic alteration), became regular formulas.

Among the technical features of the period were the regular use of a *basso continuo* and what in Italy was called the concertato style. The *basso continuo* could either serve as a support for the full harmony of voices or instruments or both, or provide the harmonic background for a texture consisting merely of melody and bass. In the former case it was sometimes dispensed with, e.g. in the aria 'Patrii numi' in Alessandro Scarlatti's *Il Mitridate Eupatore,* where its absence is still striking. As a harmonic background it served to supply all that was necessary without distracting attention from the strong melodic character of the two principal parts. So important was the bass line that it was often used to provide the ritornello for an aria. The concertato style was one in which clear contrasts were established between voices and instruments, between groups of instruments, or between one or more solo instruments and the main body of the orchestra. Apart from the trombone, which was reserved for the accompaniment of church music, and the double bass, which did not emerge into the limelight until later in the eighteenth century, there was hardly a single instrument of the period which was not used as a soloist, either in concerted instrumental music or as an obbligato in vocal works. The term concerto, though widely used for instrumental compositions, with or without soloists, was also still used, like symphonia, as the title of a work for voices and instruments, e.g. Bach's cantatas. Though the concertato style invaded church music everywhere, the older contrapuntal forms without independent accompaniment also survived, particularly in Germany, though in a harmonic language firmly founded on the bass.

Ornamentation was an essential element in 'Baroque' music, as it had been in the preceding period. It was sometimes written into the text but more often was left to the performer to improvise. No doubt it was used most lavishly in the theatre, where singers were competing for applause, and by instrumental soloists. It would be a mistake, however, to suppose that it was merely a way of showing off. The English word 'grace' indicates that it was regarded as a refinement. Its execution was a matter of taste, for which there was no universal criterion. An enterprising publisher (Roger of Amsterdam) issued an edition of Corelli's violin sonatas (Op. 5) in which the solo part of six of the slow movements was furnished with an ornamented version, allegedly representing what the composer played. Roger North roundly condemned it: 'Upon the bare view of the print any one would wonder how so much vermin could creep into the works of such a master'. Though much of the ornamentation consists of little more than superficial decoration, there is some justice for North's criticism in those places where there is excessive elaboration. In fact the edition did little service to interpretation since it presented in a stereotyped form what should have been the natural expression of the player's personality. Some writers of the period expressly warn against excessive ornamentation. Where taste was the guide, there were bound to be lapses. The positive value of improvised ornamentation was that it prevented any performance from being hidebound. The same applies to modifications of rhythm, both rubato within the bar and the lengthening or shortening of notes within the beat. When Couperin observed that French composers did not write what was actually played he was affirming the principle that performance must not be rigid and that the niceties of a fluid interpretation cannot be notated.

Purcell, in his contribution to the twelfth edition of Playford's *Introduction to the Skill of Music* (1694), recommended that the two upper parts in simple three-part harmony should run in thirds. He added: 'I'm sure 'tis the constant Practise of the *Italians* in all their Musick, either Vocal or Instrumental, which I presume ought to be a Guide to us'. Mattheson put it more bluntly when he said of the English: 'Itziger Zeit *imitirt* diese *Nation* platterdings den Italiänischen *Stylum*'. He was writing in 1713, by which time there were some grounds for his criticism. It would not have been true in Purcell's day, when French music exerted a considerable influence, particularly on instrumental music. In Germany, French and Italian music for long held equal sway: composers like Georg Muffat handled both styles with equal assurance. Italy, on the other hand, was impervious to outside influences: Corelli is reported to have failed to play an overture of Handel's as the composer wanted because it was in the French style. Throughout this period musicians were fully aware of the differences between French and Italian music. A dialogue in Lully's *Ballet de la Raillerie* (1659) is an amusing parody of the two styles. François Raguenet in 1702 published what professed to be a reasoned comparison between the music of the two countries, but after initial praise of Lully it proved to be heavily weighted in favour of the Italians.

Mere imitation cannot reproduce a style. It is hardly surprising that Corelli is said to have expressed a poor opinion of Purcell's sonatas: their English ancestry was too clearly marked. Nor would the so-called 'Italian airs' or *ariettes* in eighteenth-century French opera have deceived anyone who was acquainted with the genuine article. Composers such as Purcell, Bach, and Rameau were not only men with a local tradition behind them: they were individuals, who are now seen to have been among the élite of their time, however little they may have been known when they were alive. But even with individuals there were cross-currents. Domenico Scarlatti might reasonably be claimed as the most original composer of the period; yet he is recognizable as belonging to the same century and the same race as Vivaldi. There were other cross-currents: the same idioms served both the church and the chamber, however different the words might be. Baron Pöllnitz said of the Venetians: 'They spend half of their time in committing Sin, and the other half in begging God's Pardon'. Suitably adapted, it might well do as a motto for the period.

One cannot help admiring the sturdiness of composers who continued their work in spite of the chances and changes of this mortal life. Vivaldi suffered from asthma all his life and never went out of doors on foot. Handel faced bankruptcy. Bach produced thirteen children during his time in Leipzig, in addition to the four who survived from his first marriage. They showed an equal resilience in the face of political changes. Purcell served three very different monarchs with apparent unconcern. Schütz might lament the setback that church music had received from the Thirty Years War, but between 1631, when Saxony was involved, and 1648, when the war ended, he managed to publish five substantial works. In general musicians were too busy to have time for other activities. But Steffani managed to be not only a composer but a bishop *in partibus* and a diplomat as well. In the latter capacity he seems to have shown the courtesy expected from ambassadors. 'He was', says Hawkins, 'perfectly skilled in all the external forms of polite behaviour, and, which is somewhat unusual, continued to observe and practise them at the age of fourscore.'

The musical literature of the time was considerable. Of the books listed by Bukofzer in *Music in the Baroque Era* some 380 were published between 1630 and 1750. They range from polemical pamphlets and elementary instruction books to the voluminous works of Mattheson and Rameau. There was clearly a desire among the educated public to learn about music and musicians. Works like Brossard's *Dictionnaire de musique* (1703), Walther's *Musicalisches Lexicon* (1732), and Mattheson's *Grundlage einer Ehrenpforte* (1740) supplied information in a convenient and accessible form. Many of the books were didactic and therefore have something to offer to the present-day performer, provided he accepts what they have to say as an expression of opinion and not as the voice of God. The tone of these works was not necessarily pedantic. Couperin advised learners not to make faces when playing the harpsichord. Heinichen explained that if the intermediate cadences for the harpsichord in recitative were delayed the singer would be left in the air with nothing to do. Rameau said: 'One can judge music only through the medium of hearing: reason has authority only inasmuch as it agrees with the ear'; and again: 'Fugue is an ornament in music whose only principle is good taste'. Mattheson held that practice was more important than absorbing dusty doctrines from the past.

The division between Vols. V and VI of the *New Oxford History* is purely a matter of practical convenience, designed to ensure that the material is more or less evenly distributed between the two. For that reason Vol. VI, the bulk of which is devoted to instrumental music, begins with chapters on English Ode and Oratorio and Solo Song. These subjects are clearly related both to opera and to church music, but they can hardly be said to fall within either category. No apology is needed for devoting two volumes to a period which was so rich in the production of music and in musical activity and from which so much that is memorable has become a necessary part of our existence today.

PUBLISHER'S NOTE

THIS volume was planned by Sir Jack Westrup and edited by Sir Anthony Lewis; Nigel Fortune acted as text editor.

As is usual in publications of this kind, there has been a considerable gap between the final establishment of the text and the volume's appearance. Thus it has not been possible to incorporate references to the most recent publications and numerous reprints of older ones.

We record with regret the death of Paul-Marie Masson prior to the publication of this volume; also of two valued members of the editorial board of the *New Oxford History of Music*: Dom Anselm Hughes and Egon Wellesz.

Chapters I, II and VI(*a*) have been translated by Marina Branscombe, Chapter IV by Norma Deane, and Chapter VII(*a*) by J. W. Jolliffe.

The Bibliography was edited by David Scott, and the Index compiled by Frederick Smyth.

I

ITALIAN OPERA FROM THE LATER MONTEVERDI TO SCARLATTI

By HELLMUTH CHRISTIAN WOLFF

GENERAL

OPERA was the dominant art form of the baroque era in Italy. In it all the arts—literature, music, painting, architecture, and the theatre—were combined to express the ideals of the baroque world. Ever since *musica reservata* and mannerist painting in the mid-sixteenth century, the representation of heightened emotion had been an essential aim of Italian art. From the beginning of the seventeenth century this came to include even the fiercest passions, and the changing state of the human soul was faithfully portrayed. 'Truth' became more important than beauty, as Monteverdi expressed it in the preface to his Fifth Book of madrigals in 1605.[1] At the same time there was an artistic striving towards the miraculous and the transcendental: gone was the serene feeling of reality characteristic of the Renaissance, to be replaced by elements of fantasy, surprise, enchantment, and sharp contrast; the moderation, restraint, and humility of the Italian Renaissance and of humanism were discarded in favour of ecstasy, extravagance, and an increasingly sensuous artistic portrayal of every human emotion.[2]

It is impossible to reach a proper understanding of baroque opera without some knowledge of this artistic evolution. One of the main problems is that Italian opera from 1630 to 1750 has no uniformity of style—in fact it went through a most remarkable process of development. The declamatory recitative style of the early operas was soon broken up by closed forms such as songs, choruses, and dances, thus drawing attention again to purely musical elements. However, recitative and the expressive declamation of the text remained an essential requirement of Italian opera until the end of the eighteenth century—a fact often overlooked up to now in performances which treat recitative as nothing more than a necessary evil. In Italian opera of the seventeenth

---

[1] '... the modern composer builds upon the foundation of truth.' Translation from Oliver Strunk, *Source Readings in Music History* (London, 1952), pp. 411–12.

[2] A notably good English account of the years of transition in the arts in Italy is John Shearman, *Mannerism* (Harmondsworth, 1967).

and eighteenth centuries, primary importance was attached to the libretto and to the emotional interpretation of the action, and this importance cannot be measured by literary standards alone. A form of dramatic art evolved here which cannot be dismissed as crude sensationalism depending for its effect on mere public appeal. It was not only that human passions had to be presented on the stage; they had also to be aroused in the listener. He should feel himself wholly involved and caught up in the action.

Seventeenth-century Italian baroque opera must be considered in close relationship to the plays of Calderón, Lope de Vega, and Shakespeare, for only then will the many complexities, surprises, and contrasts of the action be clearly understood. It is impossible to judge baroque opera from a purely musical standpoint. The development of the sciences, the growing knowledge of distant lands—these, as well as the bold enterprise of merchants and seafarers in those early days of capitalism, were reflected in the opera librettos. Political events and personalities, and social conditions, all found their way into the texts. Moral and ethical concepts were combined with the latest innovations in aesthetics, literature, and music. A particularly important factor was man's increasing knowledge of history, which was turned to good account in the librettos. Librettists—Apostolo Zeno, for example—were frequently both scientists and historians. Outstanding figures from the past served either as heroic models or as terrifying examples; and each character's behaviour was determined by feelings and passions which were shown in every possible degree of intensity. A character's emotions are best depicted in affairs of the heart, and it is for this reason that love plays such a decisive role in the librettos of Italian operas right up to the present day.

The imitation of classical dramas provided an important source of inspiration but was generally restricted to external form, especially solo recitative. Originally the choruses of classical drama had also been adopted, but these were later replaced by arias. Calzabigi stated clearly that the arias in Italian opera—especially later on, in the works of Metastasio—fulfilled the same purpose as did the antique chorus, that is to say they were lyrical meditations of universal significance.[1] Taking all this into account, one must consider the aria operas of the seventeenth and eighteenth centuries in quite a different light, despite their exploitation by virtuoso singers. The well-known term 'concert opera', once widely used to describe the operas of that era, can no longer be applied—it has led to a completely false conception of all the old Italian operas. One has only to look at opera scores by Legrenzi, Leo, Vinci,

[1] See Ranieri Calzabigi, 'Dissertazione su le poesie drammatiche del Sig. Abate Pietro Metastasio', in Metastasio, *Poesie* (Turin, 1757), i, pp. xvii ff.

Gasparini, Bononcini, Vivaldi, or Caldara to realize what powerful dramatic elements they contain.

Insufficient attention has been paid to works written between 1630 and 1750, and a great deal of important research remains to be done. An incomplete knowledge of Italian baroque opera precludes a deeper understanding of the instrumental music of the day, for it was in opera that most of the musical forms first developed, and its symbolism and sensitivity of expression found their way into instrumental music; as for formal principles, it is generally accepted that the symphony evolved from the operatic overture and that the concerto also traces its origins back to the overture and the *da capo* aria.

OPERA IN ROME

Something has been said in the previous volume about early Roman opera, but a little more needs to be said here to supplement that account.[1]

After 1630 two events occurred that were to have a far-reaching effect on the fate of early opera. In 1632, through the initiative of Cardinals Antonio and Francesco Barberini, a theatre, capable of holding 3,000 people, was established in the Barberini Palace in Rome. Later, in 1637, the first public opera-house, San Cassiano, opened in Venice, where for the price of a ticket anyone could gain admittance. A large number of similar opera-houses quickly sprang up in Venice, so that here for the first time opera was launched as a public concern, and the prototype of today's multifarious and demanding opera audiences was formed. This coincided with endeavours to affect and influence the common people: the opera carried on in the theatre an art-form which had its beginnings in the festivals and pageants of the courts and in early baroque church art.

The distinguished architect and sculptor Lorenzo Bernini designed the sets for the opera chosen to inaugurate the new Roman theatre: *Il Sant' Alessio* (1632), with text by Cardinal Giulio Rospigliosi. Angels flew singing through the air, and a huge cloud floated down and opened; the same effects might be seen in the religious paintings of Tintoretto, Pontormo, Orsi, Vasari, and Titian. Miraculous elements were presented on the stage, necessitating the construction of flying machines and trap-doors, all part of the stock-in-trade of baroque opera, which demanded from the outset a highly sophisticated stage technique. Printed text-books, such as the one by Nicola Sabbatini,[2] gave instruction on the technical equipment of the baroque opera stage.

[1] See Vol. IV, pp. 837–42.
[2] *Pratica di fabricar Scene e Machine ne' Teatri* (2nd ed., Ravenna, 1638

The theme of *Il Sant' Alessio* is one of religious conversion, based on an incident which took place in Rome in the fifth century. Alexis, a rich young man, forsakes home and family in order to follow the religious life. The opera deals with his return, disguised as a beggar. Living under the steps of his old home, he is forced to endure the taunts of the servants and laments of his wife, who are unaware of his true identity. The music by Stefano Landi (*c.* 1590–*c.* 1655) gives prominence to solo recitatives, clearly derived from church music and oratorio. The compass of the recitatives is for the most part very restricted, though fourths are used for dramatic effect (Ex. 1, i, bars 2, 8–9 and 10), and there are single high notes (Ex. 1, ii, bar 5) in parts sung by castratos:[1]

Ex. 1 (i)

(i) (Alexis, what will you do? Will you be cruel to one to whom, as you well know, gods and men would have you show pity? What shall I do? Must I make myself known? Or shall I conceal myself?)

[1] Act II, scene 5; taken from Hugo Goldschmidt, *Studien zur Geschichte der italienischen Oper im 17. Jahrhundert,* i (Leipzig, 1901), pp. 226 and 228. The appendix to this book (pp. 153 ff.) contains substantial excerpts from Roman and other operas from the early and middle years of the seventeenth century.

(ii)

(ii) (Pity, now cease to torment my breast. Ah! How fierce the struggle on the battlefield of my heart!)

Presumably the actual written notes were supplemented by improvised appoggiaturas and other embellishments. The second part of the recitative in this example has a certain symmetry with the first: the two opening phrases are identical, and the bass line is almost the same—a not unexpected unifying feature in the work of a composer who wrote so many strophic variations.[1]

The operas staged in Rome generally had choruses, which continued the tradition of the madrigal. Groups of three to eight singers, portraying demons, angels, virtues or servants, provided with their march and dance rhythms a secular contrast to the recitatives. Here and there Alexis himself sings songs in saraband rhythm—'O morte gradita', for instance,[2] in Act II, scene 5. From the beginning, dance rhythms played an important part in the short arias of the principal characters; this remained true over the whole history of the baroque aria. The manner in which they were performed in the theatre emphasized the dance element, the origins of which are to be found in the visual arts of the age—witness the swaying lines of the statuary inside and outside baroque churches.

[1] Cf. Vol. IV, pp. 168–9.   [2] Cf. Goldschmidt, op. cit., pp. 230–1.

Cardinal Rospigliosi (later Pope Clement IX) also wrote secular opera librettos such as *Chi soffre, speri* (Rome, 1639), a *commedia musicale* concerned with the love story of an impoverished nobleman. Realistic crowd-scenes at a fair and the discovery of hidden treasure in a ruined tower (ideas borrowed from Boccaccio's *Decameron* and Tasso's *Aminta*) gave scope for lively recitatives, duets, and choruses. Marco Marazzoli (1619?–62) and Virgilio Mazzocchi (1597–1646) collaborated in writing the score. Mazzocchi, choirmaster of the Cappella Giulia at St. Peter's, was the originator of the baroque 'massive' style, which he used in the double choruses of *Chi soffre, speri*. These are unskilful and mostly homorhythmic, though relieved by the frequent interpolation of short solos:[1]

Ex. 2

Act II, scene 9: cf. ibid., pp. 319–20; the duet 'Ombra lieve lampo' is on pp. 323-4.

(Sop: Who'll buy rare ribbons, combs, mirrors, fine mantles? Bring your pennies!
Ten: Now that the May song calls me abroad . . .)

The duet 'Ombra lieve lampo' is in the form of a passacaglia, which opera borrowed from instrumental music; it is specially important in the operas of Monteverdi and Cavalli.

The polyphonic style of the older Italian madrigals was continued by Loreto Vittori (1604–70) in the choruses of his opera *La Galatea* (1639), and by Michelangelo Rossi (*c.* 1600–*c.* 1670) in *Erminia sul Giordano* (1637),[1] where frequent hunting scenes, storms, and seascapes gave the composer the opportunity to introduce several charming effects, including echoes.[2] To some extent, however, the choruses of the Roman operas already anticipate the later ensembles of *opera buffa*, as for example in this quartet from *Dal male il bene* by Antonio Maria Abbatini and Marazzoli (1653):[3]

Ex. 3

---

[1] See Vol. IV, pp. 840–1, including two musical examples.
[2] See Goldschmidt, op. cit., pp. 258, 265, and 270, for example.
[3] Act I, scene 2: cf. ibid., pp. 329–30.

(L: Follow this servant; she will lead you to a safer place. Begone, all tarrying
is dangerous. Delay could bring dire consequences. T: Well said, and avoidance
of conflict will lessen fear. A plague on the courtesies! This venture is inauspicious.
F: I, eternally indebted to you . . . M: Come . . .)

Here already are the rapid *parlando* and the dactylic rhythms which
abound in Venetian opera from Pietro Andrea Ziani to Vivaldi. The
librettist of *Dal male il bene* was once again Cardinal Rospigliosi, who
this time took his inspiration from the Spanish theatre. Rospigliosi had
lived for some years in Madrid, where he became acquainted at first
hand with that blend of tragedy and comedy typical of Calderón and
his contemporaries. This compound of tragic and comic elements served
as a model for Italian opera until about 1700. *Dal male il bene* takes as

its theme a love story of the time, showing aristocrats in the grip of the prevailing Spanish code of honour. The action is extremely complicated and varied, and, as in the plays of Calderón and Shakespeare, comic servants play a key role. The servant Tabacco, in his lighthearted arietta 'Il più bella dell'età',[1] sings a refrain on the solmization syllables. His music makes free use of dance rhythms, and he joins in ensembles with the main characters, as in the sextet finale of Act III, which ends with the moral 'Dal male il bene'.[2] This style of writing, with its carefree moralizing, reappears in Mozart's *Così fan tutte*. The role of the soubrette Marina in *Dal male il bene* was another innovation which was to become a model for many later Italian operas.

Opera in Rome was subject to the highest papal authority, which had to enforce the old ruling that no women might perform on the public stage. Consequently all the female parts in these operas were sung by castratos, a convention that proved a great drawback to any convincing attempt at realism in the theatre. There was indeed a marked tendency towards stylization of the type existing today in many Chinese opera companies, where the singers are all male or all female. One result of this stylization in the seventeenth century was that some composers and singers left Rome and migrated to Venice, where women were allowed to perform in opera and greatly added to its artistic impact on the stage.

VENICE 1630–1700

The opening of the first public opera-house in Venice in 1637 was a real milestone in operatic history. As a commercial venture it had to take public taste into account, whereas up to then opera had been performed for the personal amusement of individual princes, who graciously allowed the public to attend free of charge. This practice continued well into the eighteenth century in all the court opera-houses. In Venice the first public opera-house was quickly followed by a series of others, in which the leading families, the moneyed aristocracy, not only rented boxes but even bought them: they thus became part-owners of every opera-house. The great demand for opera in Venice was largely created by the constant stream of foreign visitors to the city, and for many years, until the end of the eighteenth century, there were six, eight, or even more opera-houses giving performances at the same time. This did not go on all the year, of course, but happened at certain seasons, especially at the spring carnival. Venice was an important centre for trade, diplomacy, and politics, and merchants, princes, officers, and ambassadors flocked there from the four corners of the earth. It was estimated that in the seventeenth century the spring

[1] Act II, scene 6: cf. ibid., pp. 335–7.   [2] Ibid., pp. 341–8.

PLATE I

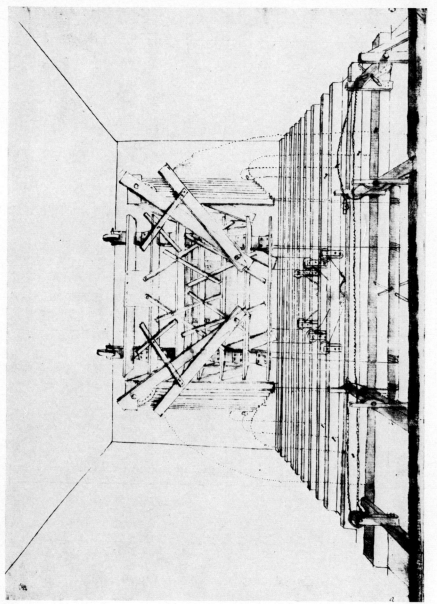

VENETIAN OPERATIC SCENERY: DESCENDING CLOUD MACHINERY

From the designs for Legrenzi's opera *Germanico sul Reno*, produced at the Teatro Vendramino di San Salvatore, Venice, 27 January 1676. (Cf. Plate II.) The designs are now in the Bibliothèque de l'Opéra, Paris.

carnival attracted some 60,000 visitors to Venice, all of them ready to plunge into a whirl of masked balls, dancing and gaming, matching their *joie de vivre* with that of the courtesans. Opera was therefore only one of the many delights offered by the carnival, and devotees often attended performances masked and in fancy dress. The opera-house was in addition a social meeting-point, where diplomatic or business affairs might be discussed. From time to time the Venetian aristocracy, the princes and diplomats, would place their numerous boxes at the disposal of foreign guests, as Rousseau describes in his *Confessions*. Rousseau thought he had arrived in Paradise, so carried away was he by the beauty of the music and of the singing.[1]

Venice, as a republic, permitted a greater degree of freedom in public life at this time than states ruled either by princes or by the church. Even though behind the scenes the Council of Ten jealously watched over the fortunes of the republic, lest her already disintegrating colonial empire be further weakened, a spirit of freedom, non-existent in other great cities, pervaded the world of entertainment and the theatre. Opera audiences were made up of people from all walks of life, from the scions of the noblest families in Europe down to the Venetian *barcaiuoli*, simple gondoliers, who had free right of entry to the opera-house and acted as its claque.[2]

MONTEVERDI'S LATE OPERAS

The Venetians regarded their city-state as the successor to the old Roman republic, whose bacchanalian orgies they sought to emulate in their carnival celebrations. Opera absorbed its share of the spirit of profanity and paganism, and the cult of outward beauty and uninhibited passion finds expression in Claudio Monteverdi's last opera, *L'incoronazione di Poppea* (Venice, 1642; different version, Naples, 1656).[3] Nero, flouting every convention, repudiates his lawful wife, Octavia, in order that Poppea, wife of his general Ottone, may become his concubine and later his empress. The libretto, by Giovanni Francesco Busenello, is certainly neither quite as good nor quite as bad as has been variously claimed. Instead of the traditional legends of the early Daphne and Orpheus operas Busenello used historical material and took up a problem of modern love and marriage that was particularly relevant to the

[1] See Jean-Jacques Rousseau, *Confessions*, vii: 1743–4 (see pp. 294–5 in the translation by J. M. Cohen, Harmondsworth, repr. 1967).

[2] See Hellmuth Christian Wolff, *Die venezianische Oper in der zweiten Hälfte des 17. Jahrhunderts* (Berlin, 1937), pp. 17 ff.

[3] Monteverdi, *Tutte le opere*, ed. Gian Francesco Malipiero, xiii (Bologna, 1931). The many other editions of this opera are listed in Denis Arnold and Nigel Fortune, *The Monteverdi Companion* (London, 1968), p. 307.

many conventional marriages of the time: the right to true love. Thus when the forsaken wife attempts to provoke the murder of her rival (Octavia urges Ottone to kill Poppea) it was entirely in accordance with the Venetian philosophy of life that Octavia should be banished. It has been suggested that this episode probably derived from an actual incident in the life of Duke Vincenzo Gonzaga of Mantua;[1] at the same time, however, it was quite in keeping with the prevailing conception of love.

Further evidence of the authors' intent to glorify true love is provided by the allegorical figures who appear in the opera. They derive, it is true, from the world of the humanist theatre, but they are by no means as unimportant or unnecessary as has sometimes been thought. In the prologue to *L'incoronazione di Poppea,* Fortune, Virtue, and Love are quarrelling as to which of them shall rule the world. Love asserts that he will prove himself the strongest; in this way the significance of the opera is made clear from the outset and the characters shown in their true colours. Octavia does not really love Nero but is filled with hatred and cunning and must therefore resign herself to her fate. At the end of the opera Venus gives Poppea her blessing, thus making her love appear worth the winning and the whole question more than just a matter of morality in ancient Roman history.

Monteverdi's power of dramatic characterization has always been the object of admiration, and *Poppea* is full of magnificent examples of it. In the episode that has already been mentioned, for instance, he suggests Ottone's indecisiveness and contrasts it with the brutal violence of Octavia as she tries with every manner of intrigue to induce him to murder his wife:[2]

Ex. 4

[1] Cf. Claudio Sartori, *Monteverdi* (Brescia, 1953).
[2] Act II, scene 9: cf. Monteverdi, op. cit., pp. 157–8.

(Oct: I want your sword to settle my account with Poppea's blood; I want it to kill her. Ott: Kill whom? Oct: Poppea.)

Octavia's character is conveyed by disconnected and reiterated words, as well as by octave leaps (bars 7–8), while Ottone's agitation is shown in short sequences and, again, word repetition (bars 9–11 and 13–15). Recitatives of this kind are a very prominent feature of *Poppea*, for Monteverdi uses far fewer closed forms than in his earlier opera *Orfeo*, and these are for the most part very short and in the manner of ariosos. The comic scenes, involving servants, are of special importance in *Poppea* and often follow closely on moments of dramatic tension, as in Spanish plays at that time. Such contrasts are of the very essence of baroque theatre, and they should never be omitted in modern productions. There should also be as rapid a delivery as possible in the recitatives and dialogues, since these were originally performed at high speed; the recitatives were certainly delivered in the later *secco* style, accompanied only by a harpsichord, possibly with violoncello, but no other instruments.

Three of the operas Monteverdi wrote for the Venetian stage are lost: *Proserpina rapita* (1630), *L'Adone* (1639, only the libretto is extant), and *Le nozze di Enea con Lavinia* (1641); but we do have the score of *Il ritorno d'Ulisse in patria* (1640),[1] another notable landmark in the musical theatre of the time, if not quite so consistently fine as *Poppea*. *Poppea* itself is the first great 'human' opera and an astonishingly modern one. Even so, some commentators have gone too far in seeing Monteverdi as the precursor of Gluck and Wagner; and admiration for his achievement should not be allowed to obscure the high qualities of other important Italian composers of opera—such men as Legrenzi, Leo, Vivaldi, Pollaroli, and Gasparini.[2]

THE LIBRETTOS

All opera at that time was based on the librettos, which were usually specially printed for each production, and read by the audience during the performance; little wax candles were sold at the entrance to the theatre together with the libretto. Opera was regarded until well into the eighteenth century as an imitation of classical tragedy. Close attention must therefore be given to the librettos, though they should not be judged by the same criteria as the spoken drama, since their aesthetic premises were fundamentally different. In opera the sung word determined the text, which was necessarily more succinct and more concentrated than that of a stage play. This is clear from the stage adaptations of baroque opera texts such as *Il Giasone*, by Giacinto Andrea Cicognini, whose opera texts and plays single him out as Italy's chief exponent of the Spanish-influenced literary style of the seventeenth century. His libretto for *Giasone*, together with Cavalli's music (Venice, 1649), was such a success that Cicognini later adapted the text as a straight stage play. He expanded the short lines of the opera libretto into lengthier discussions and soliloquies in prose.[3] The opera libretto evolved from the beginning its own stylistic rules, which were based on the close relationship between music and text. In Goldoni's day it would still have been unthinkable to set one of his dramatic texts to music, as was commonly done from the end of the nineteenth century onwards.

Venice saw the development of a specific type of libretto which com-

[1] Monteverdi, op. cit., xii (Bologna, 1930).

[2] The literature on Monteverdi is considerable; further on the stage works in particular see Anna Amalie Abert, *Claudio Monteverdi und das musikalische Drama* (Lippstadt, 1954), and Wolfgang Osthoff, *Das dramatische Spätwerk Claudio Monteverdis* (Tutzing, 1960).

[3] See Abert, 'Schauspiel und Opernlibretto im italienischen Barock', *Die Musikforschung*, ii (1949), p. 133.

PLATE II

VENETIAN OPERATIC SCENERY: DESCENDING CLOUD, CLOSED AND OPEN

From the designs for Legrenzi's opera *Germanico sul Reno* (cf. Plate I). The designs are now in the Bibliothèque de l'Opéra, Paris.

bined successfully the peculiarities of the Spanish baroque theatre with the demands of the operatic stage. Great store was set by well-made and striking stage sets, which could be rapidly and frequently changed by means of movable flats. Since new scenery could hardly be provided for each new opera, there were some eleven or twelve stock scenes which recurred in every opera: temples, gods (in clouds), the sea, palaces, gardens, dungeons, flights of steps, streets, and caves. In 1681 Claude François Menestrier gave a detailed catalogue of these types of scenery, only slightly modified.[1] Among the special effects there were floating and rotating clouds with their complement of gods, angels, and spirits; there were ships that moved, vehicles, animals, and trap-doors. The purpose of all of these was to intensify the elements of wonder and surprise in the action. Librettists had to bear all this very firmly in mind, as well as all the other devices that gave their plots the greatest variety and tension—disguises, mistaken identities, unmaskings, dream sequences and ghost scenes, misdirected letters, murders and suicides. It was not until the eighteenth century that these peculiarities came to be regarded as superficial and decadent. The nineteenth-century romantics were the first to rediscover the true poetry of the dream sequences and slumber scenes in baroque opera; they could appreciate them as attempts to cross the frontiers of the unconscious mind and come to grips with its complexities. Today a reappraisal of those operas reveals the special qualities that set them apart from everything that classicism stood for.[2]

Usually these operas are concerned with several pairs of lovers, who are involved in every kind of mix-up and cross-pairing, in order to prove their love—or not, as the case may be. Serious and comic situations directly follow each other, as in Cicognini's *Il Giasone*, where the hero, Jason, pays a nocturnal visit to a beautiful woman whom he takes to be a lady's maid—in fact she is Medea, herself in love with him. This was a favourite comic theme in the seventeenth century: similar incidents had already been used by Giovanni Battista Porta in his comedy *Cintia* (Venice, 1628) and by Shakespeare in *Measure for Measure* (1604). Exaggerated heroics are also mocked in *Il Giasone* when Medea, in a scene with the infatuated Egeo, throws at his feet the dagger with which she is supposed to kill him. Similar situations recur persistently in Venetian operas until the end of the century. Another popular comic

---

[1] See Menestrier, *Des Représentations en musique anciennes et modernes* (Paris, 1681), pp. 171–4; also see Wolff, op. cit., p. 200. Simon Towneley Worsthorne, *Venetian Opera in the Seventeenth Century* (repr., Oxford, 1968), *passim*, is especially useful on the visual element.

[2] See Gustav René Hocke, *Die Welt als Labyrinth: Manier und Manie in der europäischen Kunst von 1520–1650 und in der Gegenwart* (Hamburg, 1957), *passim*.

device in these operas is the mad scene, likewise typically baroque. One master of such grotesque situations was Matteo Noris, in whose *Totila* (Venice, 1677) a Roman consul goes mad with grief over the supposed death of his wife. They provided opportunities for writing parodies of death scenes, outpourings of grief, and the invocations of spirits.[1] Poisoning is another way of sending people mad; they quickly returned to normal after swallowing an antidote. In Cavalli's heroic opera *Pompeo Magno* (1666) a mad ballet was performed as an entr'acte. None of this was in any way exceptional; it merely reflected a general desire to express the unusual, the exaggerated, and the grotesque—such scenes were placed within and directly beside heroic deaths and scenes of genuine despair. Noris was regarded as a specialist in his field, and he even rewrote earlier librettos in this style, such as, for example, *La Semiramide* (Venice, 1671), based on a text by Giovanni Andrea Moniglia.[2] In its new form, with music by Pietro Andrea Ziani, *La Semiramide* became a superbly grotesque comedy of disguise and mistaken identity; it deserves to be recognized as a pure comic opera which even today would have a powerful effect on the stage.

As regards subject-matter, three types of opera were created in Venice: heroic-comic (*eroicomico*), pure heroic, and pure comic. Almost all these operas deal with historical material, with the result that the various characteristics of each have only recently been determined.[3] Behind historical titles such as *L'Annibale in Capua* (1661) by Niccolò Beregan, *Il Candaule* (1679) by Adriano Morselli, *Messalina* (1680) by Francesco Maria Piccioli, or even *Agrippina* by Vincenzo Grimani (set to music by Handel in 1709 for the Venetian stage), we find comic operas—or at least an abundance of comic scenes.

In the field of heroic opera one of the leading librettists was Nicolò Minato, whose *Pompeo Magno* and *Seleuco* (1666) and the double opera *La prosperità di Elio Sejano* and *La caduta di Elio Sejano* (1667) glorified the courtly ideals of magnanimity and selflessness, loyalty and constancy. In such works he was to a large extent inspired by the tragedies of Corneille and Racine. The conflict between love and duty also raged in the hearts and minds of operatic heroes, as in *L'Adelaide* (1672) by Pietro Dolfin.[4] Minato's development was remarkable; he later produced a great quantity of comic material (in librettos written for Antonio Draghi in Vienna), with, for example, ancient Greek philosophers—Diogenes or Socrates—as central characters.[5] After 1700 Zeno

[1] See Wolff, op. cit., pp. 76 ff.
[2] See ibid., pp. 116 ff.
[3] See ibid., pp. 107 ff.
[4] See ibid., pp. 43 ff.
[5] See Max Neuhaus, 'Antonio Draghi', *Studien zur Musikwissenschaft*, i (1913), p. 104.

and Metastasio cut out the many smaller roles and comic scenes in the librettos in order to attain a simpler classical style.

In seventeenth-century librettos the main characters were fixed and recurrent types: the true lover, the faithful servant, the wise king, the scheming villain, the comic nurse (always played by a man). Once again, this standardization derived from the Spanish theatre, though it was developed and extended to include new figures: thoughtless or unscrupulous queens, soubrettes, vacillating lovers. Metastasio achieved a degree of psychological refinement by limiting the number of characters involved, greatly simplifying the plot and transferring the element of complexity from the action to the mind of the characters. It should be stressed that the standardization that took place in the seventeenth century is really a stylization, and not a fault; it emphasized a universal truth that transcended individuality, a super-reality—and these were characteristics of the baroque theatre in general.[1]

FRANCESCO CAVALLI

With an output of forty-two operas (of which twenty-seven are extant in the Biblioteca Marciana in Venice) Francesco Cavalli (1602–76) was certainly the most notable composer of opera in mid-seventeenth-century Venice.[2] The development of his operatic style reflects the evolution of opera in general at that time. In his early works he still favoured mythological themes, as in *Le nozze di Teti e di Peleo* (1639) and *Gli amori di Apollo e di Dafne* (1640). But it was not long before he turned to historical material, in *L'Egisto* (1643, with libretto by Giovanni Faustini), *Il Romolo e il Remo* (1645, libretto by Giulio Strozzi), *La prosperità infelice di Giulio Cesare dittatore* (1646, libretto by Busenello) and *Xerse* (1654, libretto by Minato), to which he added some comic ingredients, as in *Il Giasone*. In his late operas Cavalli turned to high tragedy with his *Muzio Scevola* (1665) and *Pompeo Magno* (1666), both with librettos by Minato. The special importance of Cavalli may be gauged from the fact that Louis XIV commissioned him to write one of the first great Italian-language operas for the Parisian stage. This was

[1] See Hermann Abert, 'Wort und Ton in der Musik des 18. Jahrhunderts', in *Gesammelte Schriften und Vorträge* (Halle, 1929), p. 182.

[2] On Cavalli in general see Egon Wellesz, 'Cavalli und der Stil der venezianischen Oper, 1640–1660', *Studien zur Musikwissenschaft*, i (1913), p. 1; Henry Prunières, *Francesco Cavalli et l'opéra vénitien au XVIIᵉ siècle* (Paris, 1931); Raymond Leppard, 'Cavalli's operas', *Proceedings of the Royal Musical Association*, xciii (1966–7), p. 67; Goldschmidt, Wolff and Worsthorne, all op. cit., *passim*; and Anna Amalie Abert, *Claudio Monteverdi*, *passim*; nearly all these works contain musical examples, some of them extensive. Specifically on a single opera, not mentioned here, see David Swale, 'Cavalli: the "Erismena" of 1655', *Miscellanea Musicologica*, iii (1968), p. 145, and Harold S. Powers, '*L'Erismena travestita*', *Studies in Music History: essays for Oliver Strunk*, ed. idem (Princeton, 1968), p. 259.

Ercole amante (1662). The interpolation of ballet music by Lully detracted from Cavalli's sense of achievement and he returned to Venice a disappointed man.[1]

Initially Cavalli carried on the recitative style of his teacher, Monteverdi; but in his first operas he still wrote choruses in the fashion of Roman opera too. It was not until 1643 that he began to abandon them in favour of dialogues and monologues, with the addition of short song-like passages. Cavalli, to a far greater extent than Monteverdi, made use of purely musical structures, such as sequences in the recitatives, repeated motives, variations, and *ostinato* basses in songs and arias. He was a born composer for the stage and would sometimes provide short orchestral interludes to heighten the effect of a specific stage set, as for example the *sinfonia navale* in Act II, scene 5, of *La Didone* (1641), where a few bars of broken triads suggest the gentle rocking of the waves.[2] Cavalli's arias[3] are always short and often written to dance rhythms, as in this aria of Medea's in the first act of *Il Giasone*:[4]

Ex. 5

[1] See *infra*, pp. 192–4.

[2] Quoted in Janet E. Beat, 'Monteverdi and the opera orchestra of his time', in Arnold and Fortune, op. cit., p. 296.

[3] See B. Hjelmborg, 'Aspects of the aria in the early operas of Francesco Cavalli', *Natalicia Musicologica Knud Jeppesen* (Copenhagen, 1962), p. 173.

[4] Taken from the edition of this act in Robert Eitner, *Publikationen älterer praktischer und theoretischer Musikwerke*, xii (Berlin, 1883), p. 29.

gio - ia   d'a - mo - re   Si   strug-ge il   mio   co - re,   La

(If the sharp arrow of a dazzling look wounds my breast, if my heart melts in the joy of love . . .)

The saraband rhythm is maintained almost throughout, sustained by chords on the strings.[1] Jason similarly has songs based on dances, and there is even a farcical duet between Orestes and the stuttering Demo which recalls the *commedia dell'arte*.[2] A wider use of decorative coloratura effects is apparent in Cavalli's music, not as yet in the arias, but in recitatives, to highlight single words—for instance, 'grandinate' (hailstorms) in the prologue to *Eritrea* (1652)—or to embellish his graphic musical descriptions of the painted ice and snow in stage storms. Another device was to draw on the techniques of strict counterpoint in order to achieve a stage effect; an example of this is the four-part prayer chorus of *Ercole amante*, beseeching a goddess to safeguard the union of two lovers.[3] Then there are the great lamentation scenes invariably written over a passacaglia bass, a feature that Cavalli extensively developed as a musical means of conferring unity on large scenes. In *L'Ormindo* (1644) a descending bass theme of this type, written in long notes in 3/2 time, is repeated thirty times to endow Ormindo's deathscene with due solemnity and impressiveness, and the vocal line unfolds over it with notable resource:[4]

[1] A similar dance rhythm, the Venetian *forlana*, occurs in the duet 'Musici della selva' in *Egisto*, recorded in *The History of Music in Sound*, v.

[2] In Eitner, op. cit., pp. 41–54.

[3] In Goldschmidt, 'Cavalli als dramatischer Komponist', *Monatshefte für Musikgeschichte*, xxv (1893), pp. 105–11.

[4] The original manuscript is in Venice, Biblioteca Marciana. A vocal score of *L'Ormindo*, by no means following the manuscript, has been published, ed. Leppard (London, 1969); the scene ('Prison scene') from which Ex. 6 is taken is also available separately (London, 1966).

Ex. 6 (i)

((i) E: Ah, Ah, this . . . (ii) O: Don't grieve. (iii) E: Yes, yes, yes, tonight through Love our souls will see the dawn of an everlasting resplendent day. O: Yes, yes, don't grieve.)

Another conveniently available example illustrating this distinguished genre comes from *La Didone*.[1] These passacaglia scenes of Cavalli's greatly influenced French opera, which shared his predilection for strict forms such as this—the passacaglia appears again and again in the works of Lully, Campra, and Rameau.[2]

Lastly one must mention Cavalli's dramatically pointed recitatives. These are often rapid exchanges of dialogue and are full of rising intervals, broad, pathetic cadences and recurring melodic formulae, as the following excerpt from *Pompeo Magno* (II, 5) shows:[3]

Ex. 7

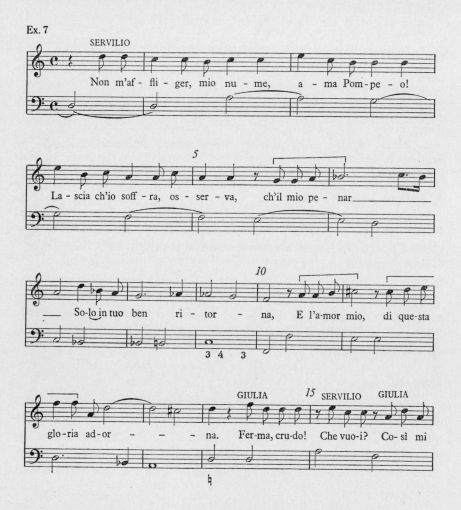

[1] In Robert Haas, *Die Musik des Barocks* (Potsdam, 1928), p. 136.
[2] Cf. *infra*, Chap. IV, *passim*.
[3] Ansbach (Bavaria), Regierungsbibliothek, MS. VI.g.37.

(S: Do not aggrieve me, great Deity, love Pompey! Let me suffer; see how my grief but redounds to thy good, and to my love adds glory. G: Stop, heartless one! S: What's the matter? G: Do you leave me thus? S: Because I love you! G: Ungrateful one, is this love? S: Yes. G: Cruel one, for you I scorn the love of Pompey, I disdain majesty and . . .)

In the opening section for Servilio a single motive appears three times (bars 5–6 and 10–12), while a different motive dominates the words of Giulia (bars 19 and 21). In this way the *secco* recitatives maintain a formal unity, a device followed by Lully in France.[1] Italian opera composers on the whole preferred a less rigid treatment of the *secco* recitatives; though these follow the rhythm of the text, melodically they conform to the expression demanded by the individual words in speech and in declamation.

ANTONIO CESTI

With Cavalli, Antonio Cesti (1623–69; baptized Pietro)[2] has always been considered to be one of the most important opera composers of the era. Born at Arezzo and destined for the priesthood, he was composing operas for the Venetian stage from the middle of the seventeenth century. The first of his works to be performed in Venice was

[1] Cf. *infra*, pp. 210 ff.

[2] On Cesti see, among other literature, Hermann Kretzschmar, 'Die venezianische Oper und die Werke Cavallis und Cestis', *Vierteljahrsschrift für Musikwissenschaft*, viii (1892), p. 1. There has so far been no comprehensive study of his operas; studies of individual operas are referred to in subsequent footnotes; and see Nino Pirrotta, 'Le prime opere di Cesti', *L'Orchestra* (Florence, 1954), p. 153.

L'Orontea (1649 or soon after);[1] some dozen operas by him survive. He increased the number of arias in the opera, with particular emphasis on lyrical and vocally rewarding melody. In addition, by linking together several recitatives and arias sung by one character, he created groups of scenes which thus assumed something of the nature of the solo cantata (a field in which he also excelled: see Vol. VI). Kretzschmar insisted on regarding him as the leader of a 'democratic' movement in opera, as opposed to the 'aristocratic' opera, represented by Cavalli. But Kretzschmar overlooked the fact that the innovations introduced by Cesti were only part of a more general development, and that even the heroic operas of this time contained many short song-like arias, as in the works of Antonio Sartorio.[2] Furthermore, Cesti wrote most of his operas for performance at princely courts—in Florence, Innsbruck, and Vienna. It would therefore be more accurate to look on him as representing the court opera of his time. However, the differences are not so very great—at least, not from a purely musical point of view.

Cesti's operas contain an abundance of very varied musical forms, ranging from the dramatic recitative and arioso (as well as accompanied recitative), to song-like arias, ensembles, and choruses. His recitatives were still greatly admired in the eighteenth century, largely on account of their naturalistic word-setting.[3] He was seen as a pupil of Carissimi, whose oratorios he had certainly got to know in Rome before 1650, and Carissimi's expertise in the art of expressive declamation, coupled with his concise and tuneful melodies, had a lasting influence on Cesti.

The libretto for *L'Orontea* (or *Orontea, regina d'Egitto*) was by Cicognini, who has already been mentioned as an example of the Spanish influence in the Italian theatre. The Egyptian Queen Orontea loses her heart to a young slave, who later reveals himself to be a king's son, thus enabling her to marry him. This libretto was so widely acclaimed that in 1688 Michel Le Clerc translated it into French, and the opera was given at Chantilly, with music by Paolo Lorenzani and décor by the celebrated Jean Bérain.[4] One aria from this opera became particularly well known: 'Intorno all'idol mio', which was sung in one of the characteristic slumber scenes generally popular in Italian opera at that

---

[1] See William C. Holmes, 'Giacinto Andrea Cicognini's and Antonio Cesti's *Orontea* (1649)' *New Looks at Italian Opera: essays in honor of Donald J. Grout*, ed. William W. Austin (Ithaca, N.Y., 1968), p. 108; and idem, *Orontea: a study of changes and development in the libretto and music of mid-seventeenth-century Italian opera* (Diss., Columbia University, 1968, unpub.). The opera is ed. idem, *The Wellesley Edition*, xi (Wellesley, Mass., 1973).

[2] See *infra*, pp. 30 ff.

[3] See Charles Burney, *A General History of Music*, iv (London, 1789), p. 60.

[4] See André Tessier, 'L'Oronthée de Lorenzani et l'Orontea du Padre Cesti', *Revue musicale*, ix (1928), p. 169. See *infra*, p. 229.

time, but especially in Venice.[1] In *Alessandro vincitor di se stesso*, set
by both Cavalli (Venice, 1651) and Cesti (Lucca, 1654), the librettist,
Francesco Sbarra, attempted to bring new moral issues on to the stage.
The hero, Alexander the Great, nobly renounces his love for a Persian
slave-girl, knowing that she is loved by one of his own generals. The
girl is ultimately found to be the Greek bride of the painter Apelles,
forcibly abducted to Persia. The fantastic and involved action culminates in the glorification of a prince's magnanimity, as in Cesti's
La magnanimità d'Alessandro (Innsbruck, 1662).[2] These librettos are
clearly influenced by the tragedies of Corneille. His idealized portraits
of human greatness, written only a short time before, were intended also
to be an example to the absolute rulers of the time. True kingliness,
according to Corneille, must be maintained by self-control and the
sacrifice of personal happiness, whether the hero's name was *Rodogune*
(1644), *Nicomède* (1651), *Pertharite* (1652), *Cinna* (1640) or Caesar (in
Pompée, 1641). The effect of these heroic tragedies on Italian opera was
very considerable, as has already been shown with reference to Cavalli.
As a result a whole style of heroic opera developed, represented above
all by Sartorio, which still had an important part to play in Metastasio's
works in the eighteenth century.

To mark a visit by Queen Christina of Sweden, an ardent patroness of
opera who spent the greater part of her life in Rome,[3] Cesti wrote the
opera *L'Argia* in 1655 for the court at Innsbruck (with libretto by
Apollonio Apolloni). A monologue delivered by Argia (Act I, scene 14)
reveals Cesti as a master of declamation:[4]

Ex. 8

[1] See Wolff, op. cit., p. 201. The aria appears in Burney, op. cit., pp. 67–8, and in F. A.
Gevaert, *Les Gloires de l'Italie* (Paris, [1868]), ii, p. 181.
[2] See Osthoff, 'Antonio Cesti's "Alessandro vincitor di se stesso"', *Studien zur Musikwissenschaft*, xxiv (1960), p. 13.
[3] See Adolf Sandberger, 'Beziehungen der Königin Christine von Schweden zur italien-

(Ah, treacherous Selino! Ah, wretched son! Alas, false counsel! Alas, wicked destiny! O demented Argia! O Feraspe, O Dorisbe, O kingdom, O heaven, O God, have pity on my grief.)

Unconnected single notes, pauses, leaps, surprising changes of harmony (bars 3–4, 6–7 and 13–14) show clearly that Cesti had not forgotten Monteverdi's precepts: indeed he even developed them. The preceding lament, also sung by Argia, has dissonant appoggiaturas and passing notes:

Ex. 9

ischen Oper und Musik, insbesondere zu M. A. Cesti', *Bulletin de la Société 'Union Musicologique'*, v (1925).

[4] This and the next example are taken from the manuscript of the opera at Venice, Biblioteca Marciana. There is an arietta from *Argia* in Arnold Schering, *Geschichte der Musik in Beispielen*, (2nd ed., Leipzig, 1955), pp. 256–7.

- re in___ la - cri - mo - si fiu - mi,

(Dissolve, then, in floods of tears.)

The delicate accompaniment of a string orchestra was a new timbre in opera which remained in favour until well into the eighteenth century. An opera that was especially well known was Cesti's *La Dori, ovvero Lo schiavo fedele* (libretto by Apolloni), written in 1661 for Cosimo de' Medici in Florence and repeated in Venice in 1663.[1] Princess Dori, disguised as a man, is searching for her lover and is on the point of killing herself in despair. Orontes is consumed with longing for her and is mocked by his servant Golo, who ridicules his master's lament by taking up the character and melody of this aria:[2]

Ex. 10 (i)

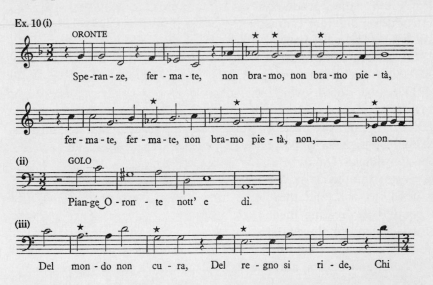

ORONTE

Spe-ran-ze, fer - ma - te, non bra-mo, non bra-mo pie - tà,

fer - ma - te, fer - ma - te, non bra-mo pie - tà, non,___ non___

(ii)   GOLO

Pian-ge O - ron - te nott' e di.

(iii)

Del mon - do non cu - ra, Del re - gno si ri - de, Chi

[1] There is an incomplete edition by Eitner of *La Dori*, together with excerpts from *Le disgrazie d'Amore* (1667), *La Semiramide* (1667) and *La magnanimita d'Alessandro* (1662), *Publikationen älterer praktischer und theoretischer Musikwerke*, xii (Berlin, 1883). The libretto of *La Dori* is one of those discussed in Nathaniel Burt, 'Plus ça change, or, the progress of reform in seventeenth- and eighteenth-century operas as illustrated in the books of three operas', *Studies in Music History*, p. 325.

[2] Taken from the manuscript in Vienna, Nationalbibliothek.

pec-caॄa suo dan-no Fi - ni-taॄè la leg-ge E s'al-tri cor - reg -ge.

((i) O: Cease, hope. I desire no pity. (ii) G: Orontes weeps night and day. (iii) He cares naught for the world. He scorns his kingdom. When the lawgiver is lax, the law is in jeopardy.)

The descending melody sung by Orontes is parodied by Golo in a faster tempo and in a major key (see the notes marked in the example); parodies of this type were then very popular and were known right up to eighteenth-century *opera buffa*. Apart from the scenes of anguish and despair involving the main characters in *La Dori*, much is made of the grotesque comic scenes between Golo and Dirce, a servant couple, who carried on the tradition of the *commedia dell'arte* in ribald quarrelling. Such *buffo* scenes were commonplace in opera at this time; they were often treated as independent episodes inserted in the text, and at the beginning of the eighteenth century they came to be known as *intermezzi*. Duets and choruses of Amazons complete the ingredients of *La Dori*, which also contains an accompanied recitative ('Invitto figlio', Act II, scene 19),[1] a form not first used by Alessandro Scarlatti, as has usually been supposed, since it appears both here, in Cesti's opera, and, still earlier, in Cavalli's *L'Ormindo* (Act III, scene 12) in duet form. For the Venetian production of *La Dori* Cesti wrote a new prologue introducing different characters—Apollo, Deceit, Envy, and Love—all struggling for supremacy.

To celebrate the marriage of the Emperor Leopold I, Cesti wrote his most celebrated opera, *Il pomo d'oro* (probably first performed in December 1666),[2] which was given in an open-air theatre in Vienna before an audience estimated at 5,000 people. Even though contemporary accounts are possibly somewhat exaggerated, they do show that Italian opera now appealed to a considerable proportion of even a foreign public. The twenty-three stage sets for this production became especially famous; large copper engravings of them adorned the libretto printed in 1668, and they have been reproduced several times more recently.[3] In creating them the distinguished stage-designer Ludovico Burnacini had employed the entire resources of baroque stage machinery and architecture. The illustrations reveal the profusion of flying machines and ballets, and the stylized gait affected by the actors.

---

[1] Eitner ed., pp. 170–1.

[2] The Prologue and Acts I, II and V, ed. Guido Adler, *Denkmäler der Tonkunst in Österreich*, iii, 2, and iv, 2 (Vienna, 1896–7) (Acts III and IV are lost). See Wellesz, 'A Festival opera of the seventeenth century', in *Essays on Opera* (London, 1950), p. 54.

[3] See, for example, the frontispiece to the handbook to *The History of Music in Sound*, v (2nd ed., London, 1961), and Wellesz, *Essays on Opera*, facing pp. 58 and 76; they appear complete in the Adler ed. of the music.

4

Though the stage production of *Il pomo d'oro* may for a large section of the public have been more a great spectacle than anything else, Francesco Sbarra's libretto presupposed a close acquaintance with Greek mythology. The thread running through the action is the Judgement of Paris, who awards the golden apple—thrown by Zeus—to the most beautiful of the goddesses: Pallas Athene, Juno, and Venus. These three now scheme against one another (Sbarra is ridiculing the intrigues of the Viennese court), so that finally the apple is reclaimed by Zeus's eagle and offered instead to the Empress of Austria. A great array of gods and mythological characters appear on stage, from Neptune, Pluto, and Mars to Proserpina, Charon, and the messenger Momus, who takes the role of court jester and makes satirical observations on contemporary affairs, such as the faulty administration of justice and the power of money. In contrast to the smaller string orchestras of Venice, Cesti could once more call here upon the large orchestra typical of early baroque opera; it consists of two cornetts, three trombones,[1] regal, three bass viols, and *graviorgano*, in addition to the strings. Besides song-like arias Cesti included many ensembles (trios and quartets), choruses, and ballets in his score. One of the most typical ingredients of Italian opera at that time was the strophic aria with variations from verse to verse. Proserpina's 'E dove t'aggiri' in Act I, scene 1, is an example in which the second verse is a slightly altered version of the first:[2]

---

[1] As in Proserpina's aria 'E dove t'aggiri' (Ex. 11), recorded in *The History of Music in Sound*, v.

[2] Adler ed., iii, 2, pp. 47–8 and 50.

(1. And wherever thou turnest among the mourning souls, thou hearest naught but plaints and sighs. 2. There Tantalus groans for the deceitful bait; here Sisyphus rolls the stone that escapes him.)

The dotting of the second minim in the bar is characteristic of saraband rhythm, which was then very often used in arias. It reappears in Venus's aria 'Ah, quanto è vero' (Act II, scene 9) (Ex. 12),[1] written in all probability by the very man in praise of whom the opera was composed;[2] for the Emperor Leopold I was an industrious composer and made several contributions to Cesti's operas.

Ex. 12

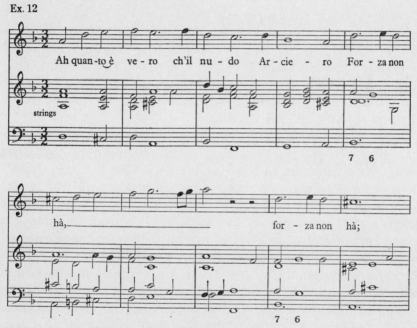

(Ah! how true that the nude Archer has no power.)

The grace and charm of these plunging and soaring melodies are very typical of the Italian music of the period. The combination of dance rhythms and vocal melodies, and their close relationship with the lines of the text, resulted in concise, compact aria forms, revealing as yet no trace of the elaboration later found in *da capo* arias. The string accompaniment in Ex. 12 is especially charming, with the vocal line soaring

[1] Ibid., iv, 2, pp. 50–1.   [2] See ibid., iii, 2, p. vi, n. 1.

above it, in contrast to Ex. 9, where the vocal line lies squarely in the middle of a similar string accompaniment. Both arias provide excellent models for earlier, invariably improvised realizations of the *basso continuo* on harpsichords, lutes, or theorboes.

ANTONIO SARTORIO

The genre of the 'heroic' opera as created by Cavalli in his last works was continued by Antonio Sartorio (*c.* 1620–1681), who composed his most important operas between 1672 and 1681 for Venice. For *L'Adelaide* (1672) the Venetian librettist and historian Pietro Dolfin found his inspiration among the heroines of Corneille (*Médée*, 1635) and Racine (Hermione in *Andromaque*, 1667). The story is taken from medieval history: Queen Adelaide of Burgundy is abducted by the Italian King Berengar II and subsequently freed by the German King Otto I. She defends her liberty with great fortitude and sings of her resoluteness in the most passionate tones.[1] This encouraged Sartorio to extend the scope of her arias by the addition of coloratura passages and by the introduction of concertante trumpets to express her mounting heroism. In her constant efforts to evade her pursuers Adelaide even hurls herself from a tower into a lake; but each time she is rescued by King Otto, unrecognizable in his disguise, and in the end she rewards him with her hand and her kingdom.

It would be impossible to give here a detailed account of the many tense situations in *L'Adelaide*. One particular moment of high drama occurs when Otto tries to kill Adelaide, mistaking her in her youth's clothing for Adalberto, Berengar's son—an incident which shows the continuing influence of Guarini's *Pastor fido*. There is an impressive dungeon scene, and another remarkable episode when Adelaide seeks refuge in a marble quarry. Here, in one of the first crowd-scenes in operatic history, quarry-workers are shown singing as they labour. This scene too ends violently, for the charge placed in the wall of the quarry detonates prematurely, killing several workmen who are standing too close. This libretto caused a sensation in its day. In 1684 the German dramatist Johann Christian Hallmann chose it as the basis for a German-language play, and in 1727 this in turn was rewritten as an opera text (*Adelheid*) for Telemann at Hamburg.[2]

In Sartorio's opera the heroine is contrasted with the soubrette Gisilla, whose songs are set to gay dance rhythms. Here for the first time in opera a line is drawn between the dramatic coloratura soprano and the soubrette, although Sartorio does not carry the distinction too

[1] See Wolff, op. cit., pp. 43 ff.
[2] See Wolff, *Die Barockoper in Hamburg, 1678–1738* (Wolfenbüttel, 1957), i, p. 58.

far—Adelaide has her share of dance songs, and Gisilla sings a touching lament. Berengar is painted as a fierce tyrant, and his aria 'Numi tartarei' (Act I, scene 11) is based on a constantly repeated dactylic rhythm. The purely musical structure of the arias, which are still usually very short, took a further step towards independence with Sartorio, and many of them have either a steadily moving bass line or a lively *ostinato* bass. This style generally gained ground and was adopted by, for example, Stradella (in his *Floridoro*, Rome, 1670s)[1] and then by Legrenzi.

Sartorio conveys Adalberto's vacillation between love and honour (Act I, scene 2) by the spirited interplay of voice and *basso continuo*, punctuated by trumpet calls and dactylic rhythms:[2]

Ex. 13

(With arms they wage fierce war.)

The words 'Fan con l'armi un'aspra guerra Nel mio sen sdegno e l'amore' recall a similar speech by Don Rodrigue in Corneille's *Le Cid*. Adelaide is given much greater scope for vocal pyrotechnics, and her arias already anticipate those of Handel.[3] The adoring King Otto likens himself to lovelorn gods such as Hercules and Zeus in a lighthearted

---

[1] The aria 'Dimmi, amor' from the second act of this opera is recorded in *The History of Music in Sound*, v.

[2] Exx. 13–16 are taken from Wolff, *Die venezianische Oper*, appendix, nos. 7–9 and 16 (the last two more fully than there); the source is Venice, Biblioteca Marciana, Cod. Contarini CCCLXXX. Exx. 14–16 are printed complete in Wolff, *The Opera*, i (Cologne, 1971).

[3] Her first aria, 'Vittrici schiere', with the opening *sinfonia* of the opera, is given complete in Schering, op. cit., pp. 290–3.

arietta (Act I, scene 2) written on a lively ground bass. The bass theme is repeated twelve times; the following are the first three statements:

Ex. 14

(If lovelorn Hercules paraded in women's clothes . . .)

The dance rhythms of Gisilla's cheerful songs are influenced by those of Venetian folk-dances and dance-songs, for example the *villotta* and the *siciliano*-like *nio*:

Ex. 15

(Rejoice, my soul, be glad, my heart.)

Sartorio preferred tragic themes which ended in murder or suicide—a predilection unusual in Italian baroque opera, where the prevailing mood was rather one of cheerful serenity. For the double opera *La prosperità d'Elio Sejano* (1666) and *La caduta d'Elio Sejano* (1667), per-

formed on two successive days, Minato chose as his subject the downfall
of the proud villain Sejanus, who lies and cheats his way into the good
graces of the ageing Emperor Tiberius until in the second part his
villainy is exposed and he takes his own life in a dungeon before the
death sentence can be carried out. In this scene the ghost of Drusus,
whom he has murdered, appears to him (inevitably one is reminded of
Banquo's apparition in *Macbeth*). Another tyrant gets his deserts on the
stage in Sartorio's *Antonino e Pompejano* (1677), in which Antonino,
with his unbridled appetite for women, appears as a forerunner of Don
Giovanni. The allegorical figure of Fame (Act III, scene 2) sings an aria
accompanied by a concertante trumpet which looks forward to the style
of Scarlatti and Handel:

Ex. 16

(Arise, Nymphs of Love!)

No account of Sartorio's work would be complete without some reference to his *Orfeo* (Vienna, 1672; Venice, 1673), in which the librettist Aurelio Aureli gave the classical myth a completely new meaning. Orpheus is here so consumed with jealousy of his step-brother Aristeus that he even pursues Eurydice across the stage with a dagger in an attempt to kill her.[1] Aureli devised numerous sub-plots and comic situations, as in his many other librettos, which are often kaleidoscopes of colour and action appealing strongly to the audiences of the time.

GIOVANNI LEGRENZI

The operas of Giovanni Legrenzi (1626–90) include some of the cleverest and wittiest works written for the Italian baroque theatre. Lighthearted comic scenes predominate, and the character of the soubrette overshadows that of the heroine. In his arias Legrenzi made greater use than ever before of rhythms borrowed from folk-songs and dances, especially the Venetian *forlana*, *villotta*, and *nio*, in addition to the gigue, saraband, and minuet. Stirring songs of battle and outbursts of rage were also well within his scope, and in *Totila* one aria of this type is accompanied by two concertante trumpets. Any sudden contrast or unexpected turn in the action is reflected in Legrenzi's music. Each of his operas contains on average from seventy to eighty arias, all of them, needless to say, relatively short, and mostly of the song type. In constructing these arias Legrenzi made use of the patterns ABBA, AABB, ABB, and ABA; in adopting the last of these he was an early contributor to the emergence of the big eighteenth-century *da capo* aria. The interweaving of serious and comic elements in Legrenzi's operas justifies our describing them as 'heroic-comic'.

Legrenzi came to Venice in 1672 as director of the Conservatorio dei Mendicanti. Previously his main centre of activity had been Ferrara, where his first operas were performed. In Venice he quickly sprang to international fame and was much sought after as a teacher, several of his pupils themselves becoming leading composers of opera in the following generation: Carlo Pollaroli, Antonio Lotti, Antonio Caldara, and Francesco Gasparini. It was largely through their work that the combination of *cantabile* melody with strict form and contrapuntal writing was continued into the eighteenth century. Even in 1720 some of Legrenzi's arias were still well-known show-pieces for singers, and Bach and Handel borrowed and arranged some of his themes. Unfortunately only four scores survive out of some seventeen authenticated operas: *Eteocle e Polinice* (1675), *Germanico sul Reno* (1676), *Totila* (1677), and the best known of all, *Il Giustino* (1683).

[1] See Wolff, *Die venezianische Oper*, pp. 61 ff.

Noris, in his libretto for *Totila*, dealt with the sacking of Rome by Totila, King of the Ostrogoths, here shown in the dual role of conqueror —very like Sartorio's Sejanus—and tender and charming lover. For this reason Totila is not condemned to death. Instead he is subjected to the scornful taunts of the soubrette Marzia, daughter of a Roman senator, who eventually becomes his wife. The martial background to this opera, the burning city, a sinking ship, are all mitigated by Noris's use of scornful irony and grotesque comedy. Totila himself sings furious love-songs. The consul Publicola, who loses his reason because his wife threatens to stab herself and her child (to prevent its capture by the Goths), has already been mentioned.[1] In impassioned parody arias Publicola invokes the furies and sings love-songs to his servant, supposing him to be Narcissus.

Totila the warrior, in his cheerful, lovelorn moments, is characterized by dotted and dactylic rhythms such as those in an aria in Act I, scene 8:[2]

Ex. 17

(I am beauty's warrior; I want no more to wade through surging torrents of foemen's blood; the milk of a fair breast gives nourishment to my heart.)

[1] See *supra*, p. 16.
[2] Exx. 17–20, from Venice, Biblioteca Marciana, Cod. Contarini CCCCLX and CCCCXXVI, are published in Wolff, op. cit., appendix, nos. 20, 26, 29, and 32 (the first more fully than there).

Appoggiaturas and sevenths (bars 6–8) make a striking effect. Marzia mocks her lover (in Act II, scene 5) in the style and rhythm of the *villotta* (in quick 6/8 time):

Ex. 18

(I shall practise false charms to mock a loving heart.)

Particularly noteworthy are Legrenzi's quick-moving arias on ground basses, which develop techniques similar to those we have just seen in arias by Stradella and Sartorio; the tempo even accelerates to *presto* when the infuriated Totila sings (Act III, scene 6):

Ex. 19

(Jealousy is a cruel monster.)

One of the greatest operatic successes of the seventeenth century was Legrenzi's *Il Giustino*, which after its première in Venice was repeated in many Italian towns: Naples, Genoa, Brescia, Bologna, and Rome (several times). Certainly Legrenzi's music made a tremendous impact; but Niccolò Beregan's libretto also contributed to this success and was later set to music by Albinoni (1711), Vivaldi (1724), and Handel (1736).

Il Giustino, with its moral precepts, carried on the traditions of true heroic opera. In his preface, Beregan inveighed against the frivolity of contemporary comic operas (without actually mentioning Pietro Andrea Ziani and Carlo Pallavicino by name he left their identities in no doubt); with his own opera he wanted to 'put a bridle on human error and set spurs to virtue'. The moral of the piece is expressed by Giustino himself in the last act:

> Da Giustino apprende 'l mondo
> Ch'a Virtù l'honor succede,
> E de la Gloria è solo il merto herede.

(Let the world learn from Justin that honour is the reward for virtue and that glory comes only to those who deserve it.)

The example chosen to point the moral was the historical figure of the Emperor Justin I, born the son of a peasant. Summoned to the aid of the Roman Emperor Anastasius in his struggle against the oriental prince Vitalianus, Justin is more than once instrumental in saving the emperor's life and his throne. The theme was particularly apposite at the time, in view of Venice's own conflict with the Turks. But an even greater impression was created by the glorification of loyalty and stead-fastness, and Justin, the country lad who embodied these ideals, became a paragon of the age. Not only the Venetian Republic, but the princes of that time had need of such dedicated supporters who despised intrigue. The notion of introducing a farmer's boy on the stage in the mantle of such heroism may well have interested Handel in the subject too, in that it was a representative of the common people, not a prince or a noble-man, who here personified the highest moral attributes.

Justin first appears (Act I, scene 7) ploughing in the fields. In his lament the voice and bass line are in canon, and Legrenzi also lets him sing a lullaby recalling well-known Italian children's songs but skilfully elaborated by his use of chromaticism. Lyrical passages dominate the whole score of *Il Giustino*, even the arias sung by Anastasius, whose role (like that of Justin) was sung by a castrato. One of the outstanding moments occurs in the leavetaking between Anastasius, who is going off to war, and his wife Ariadne. Legrenzi wrote this aria in the form of a chaconne, in which the theme has the rocking rhythm of the *forlana*, later popularly known as 'barcarolle' rhythm:[1]

[1] Also published in its entirety in Wolff, *The Opera*, i, pp. 74 ff.

Ex. 20

(My love, I leave you my soul as a pledge if I leave you. A sign of my ardour . . .)

The voice takes up the bass theme, and guides it through a series of strict variations. The reiteration of the seventh D–C sharp (bars 8 and 11) accentuates the impression of grief. Legrenzi's music is not so devoid of tensions as first impressions might suggest. Closer examination reveals an addiction to dissonances and chromatic basses (especially in the arias), which effectively express sorrow and anguish. The Empress Ariadne is given more extensive dramatic coloratura passages, instrumental in character (e.g. in her aria 'Caderà, chi mi fa guerra', Act II, scene 13), while Euphemia, Justin's sister, is identified as the soubrette by the brisk 6/8 rhythms of her lighthearted arias. A Turkish spy, Andronicus, goes about disguised as a woman and, having fallen in love with Euphemia, matches the mood of her arias with cheerful love-songs of his own, as for example 'Baciami, baciami, o bella bocca' (Act I, scene 14), in 3/4 time.

Legrenzi's lost *La divisione del mondo* (Venice, 1675) is a parody on the life of the gods (anticipating Offenbach). The librettist, Giulio Cesare Corradi, personified in Zeus, Neptune, and Pluto the 'splendour and power of the Venetian aristocracy', as he says in the introduction to his libretto. But these gods squabble in a most ignoble fashion over their love for Venus, just as in the parodies of heroes and gods written by Tassoni, Bracciolini, and Dottori. For the Venice production vast sums were expended on stage sets, with clouds, storms, sea-monsters, and the like. The opera *L'Odoacre* (Venice, 1680), at one time attributed to Legrenzi, but indisputably the work of his pupil Giovanni Varischino, is a direct antecedent of the later *opera buffa*.[1]

PIETRO ANDREA ZIANI AND COMIC OPERA

In the seventeenth century Venetian comic operas were almost without exception based on historical material, and their titles are for the most part hardly distinguishable from those of heroic and heroic-comic operas. The demarcation lines separating the three genres were ill-defined, for unexpected contrasts of every kind were characteristic of the baroque theatre. Comic operas often contained some serious scenes and arias, and this blending of the two elements is an important reason for the comparative neglect of this type of comic opera. Who would guess from the titles that *Annibale in Capua* (1661) is really a rollicking farce, full of sorcery and witchcraft, that *La Semiramide* (1671) is a brilliant comedy of errors or that *Messalina* (1680), far from being a gory drama of ancient Rome, presents a satirical portrait of seventeenth-century Venice? Two of the foremost composers responsible for settings of this kind were Pietro Andrea Ziani (1620–84) and Carlo Pallavicino (*c.* 1630–1688). It is clear from letters written by Ziani that he felt the public had lost interest in long soliloquies and much preferred canzonettas.[2] This may have been one of the reasons why Ziani, who had previously been a church musician in Bergamo, Vienna, and Naples, preferred lightweight opera librettos. He thus played a greater part in developing the resources of popular song within the structure of opera than did Cesti, who has previously, though mistakenly, been given the credit for this.

Between 1654 and 1679 Ziani composed fifteen operas for Venice, often sending them to the city piecemeal from elsewhere, usually to Marco Faustini, then director of the Teatro SS. Giovanni e Paolo. In

---

[1] See Wolff, *Die venezianische Oper*, p. 95; the manuscript is in the Biblioteca Marciana, Venice. Further on Legrenzi in general see Piero Fogaccia, *Giovanni Legrenzi* (Bergamo, 1954).

[2] See Kretzschmar, 'Weitere Beiträge zur Geschichte der venetianischen Oper', *Jahrbuch der Musikbibliothek Peters*, xvii (1910), p. 64.

Annibale in Capua Hannibal is presented less as a hero, and defender of Carthage, than as a lover who falls under the spell of a captured Roman maiden. Growing jealous of a young Roman, he finds that sleep eludes him and he is shown lying on his bed (like so many other operatic heroes of that time) in a typical slumber scene. Scenes of this nature played down the heroic aspect of the piece, in sharp contrast to the heroism of Corneille and its offshoot, heroic opera. Even the ghost of Hannibal's father Hamilcar mocks his son in cheerful dance rhythms. The scenes between the Roman Florus and his slave Gilbus are almost all parodies of scenes invoking the furies, appearances of ghosts, or episodes from mythology. Also involved in the goings-on are an old serving woman, who is usually disguised as a soldier, and a witch who wakes the dead, flies through the air, changes people into negroes, and so on. This is the style of the 'magic farce', which reached a new high point with Ferdinand Raimund in nineteenth-century Vienna and has its origins in the baroque theatre.

Songs with gay dance rhythms feature in two more of Ziani's operas: *L'amore guerriero* (1663, with libretto by Cristoforo Ivanovich) and *La Semiramide*, which was described by Noris as a *mascherata*. He based his text on a somewhat older libretto by Moniglia. The Assyrian Queen Semiramis changes places with her son Ninus, who resembles her closely—a deception which leads to the most fantastic confusion and complications. The dauntless queen, dressed in her son's clothes, sallies forth to war, leaving the son at home to reign in her stead (suitably garbed in woman's clothing). Only a slight indication can be given here of the ensuing comedy of errors, the confusion over letters and lovers.[1] Love duets are sung which are in fact not love duets at all, and the exactly paralleled actions of two pairs of interchanged lovers, in the style of Calderón, reveal a highly skilful dramatic technique where the composer's function was often the least important.

For scenes such as these Ziani evolved a style of recitative which, with its short interjections, contrasts, and echoes, anticipates the eighteenth-century *opera buffa*:[2]

Ex. 21

[1] A more detailed account may be found in Wolff, op. cit., pp. 116–20.
[2] This example is from *La Semiramide*, Act II, scene 9; for more of this recitative, with further extracts from the same opera, see ibid., appendix, nos. 57–61.

(Isi: And I love you! Ir: And I adore you, beautiful rosy mouth! Isi: Beloved face! N (*aside*): Beloved face? Ir: Sweet lips! S (*aside*): Sweet lips? N: What lascivious talk is this? S: What dalliance, what madness? D: I will flee the uproar.)

In *Il Candaule* (1679, libretto by Adriano Morselli) Ziani again uses classical dramatic material to create a comic opera. The drunken servant Brillo is the central character who tangles up the plot through his clumsy ineptitude. The climax is a succession of incidents which take place in a dark corridor with several doors leading off it. These are real *buffo* scenes, not generally encountered until much later in the works of Galuppi and Cimarosa. But Ziani's *Candaule* also contains touching lovers' laments, such as the *adagio con viole* 'Che ti feci, idolo mio' (Act II, scene 2).[1] At times the arias need a particular kind of delivery, as in the following rather 'instrumental' duet between Candaule and Alinda (Act I, scene 8) marked 'aria allegra affettuosa e bizarra':[2]

[1] In Wolff, op. cit., appendix, no. 65; new edition in idem, *The Opera*, i, pp. 68 ff.
[2] Idem, *Die venezianische Oper*, appendix, no. 63.

Ex. 22

(Yes, beautiful lips, I shall wound you with passionate kisses, and all the honey, cruel one . . .)

P. A. Ziani's carefree style was emulated by his nephew Marc'Antonio Ziani in his *Damira placata*, an opera for marionettes (produced at the Teatro San Moisè, where Rossini's first opera *La cambiale di matrimonio* had its première in 1810), and in *L'Alcibiade* (1680). In the latter, the Greek sculptor Praxiteles falls in love with the courtesan Phryne, a lady 'as lascivious as she is charming', who is also loved by Alcibiades. The details of the plot are derived more from everyday life in Venice, and the carnival celebrations there, than from classical antiquity.

CARLO PALLAVICINO

Venetian manners and morals also form the background to Carlo Pallavicino's[1] opera *Messalina* (dated 1680 on the title-page, but possibly first performed in December 1679), for the Roman empress Messalina, as she appears here in Francesco Maria Piccioli's libretto, bears a stronger resemblance to the pampered, scheming wife of a Venetian aristocrat than to the historical Messalina, to whom murder was commonplace and no crime too black. The similarity to Venice is emphasized by the presentation of a great carnival on stage, during which all the characters run through the streets masked and in fancy

---

[1] On Pallavicino see the introduction to his *La Gerusalemme liberata*, ed. Hermann Abert, *Denkmäler deutscher Tonkunst*, lv (Leipzig, 1916), pp. v–lx, and Julian Smith, 'Carlo Pallavicino', *Proceedings of the Royal Musical Association*, xcvi (1969–70), p. 57.

dress (Act I, scene 6). The Emperor Claudius is in love with Floralba, who for her part doubts the fidelity of her lover Tullius. A hotchpotch of tense and grotesque scenes carries the action along. One particular moment of high comedy occurs when two men disguised as women gain entry to a ladies' bathing establishment. Claudius, in a fit of jealousy, attempts to stab a man, but tears at the other's clothes so violently that his breast is bared and finds himself face to face with a woman. There is also, in one of Tullius's arias, some political criticism levelled at royal despots. Messalina deceives her husband at every turn, and towards the end of the opera announces its ironical and satirical moral:

> Dalle donne, infidi amanti,
> Imparate ad adorar . . .
> Apprendete dalle donne
> Ad amar con fedeltà:

(Faithless lovers, learn from women how to adore . . . learn from women how to love faithfully.)

Handel's *Agrippina* (Venice, 1709) ends on a similar note.[1] Rhythms borrowed from dances and from military bugle calls are an attractive feature of Pallavicino's arias, as is his use of syncopation, illustrated by this aria of Messalina's in Act II, scene 1:[2]

Ex. 23

(I want to enjoy to the full, so as not to regret one day.)

[1] Cf. the aria 'Se vuoi pace' (Act III, scene 14). All Handel's operas are in the complete edition of his works ed. Friedrich Chrysander. Some have so far appeared in the *Hallische Händel-Ausgabe. Serie II* (Kassel and Basle, 1955–).
[2] In Wolff, op. cit., appendix, no. 70.

Pallavicino, who also lived for some time in Dresden, wrote at least twenty-two operas. After *Messalina* one of the most interesting of these works is his *Bassiano, ovvero Il maggior impossibile* (1682), based on Calderón's well-known comedy *El mayor imposible* (1682).[1] *Vespasiano* (1678) seems to have been the most widely performed one. Another well-known one was his last opera, *La Gerusalemme liberata* (Venice and Dresden, 1687),[2] although it was officially commissioned as a gala opera for the court at Dresden and is by no means representative of his operas as a whole. In *La Gerusalemme liberata* the capture of Jerusalem by Godefroi de Bouillon is linked with the stories of Rinaldo and Armida, and Tancred and Clorinda. All are episodes in Tasso's famous epic; but as material for an opera one of the themes should be singled out to dominate the other two. The abundance of characters and stage effects—invocations, ghost scenes, the transformation of Rinaldo's knights into animals—weighs down the main thread of the action, which ends happily with Armida's conversion to Christianity and her marriage to Rinaldo. Giulio Cesare Corradi clearly planned his libretto with all the devices of the Venetian stage in mind, just as Sbarra had done when Cesti's *Il pomo d'oro* was commissioned for Vienna. The music of *La Gerusalemme liberata* reveals the mature style of Pallavicino's arias. He often wrote long roulades that made great demands on the singers, though virtuoso performers were admittedly as plentiful in Dresden as they were in Venice. The best and most expensive Italian singers were engaged; if they showed any reluctance to come, forcible abduction was not unknown, a procedure which had political repercussions.

Dresden's connection with Italian opera was of long standing. As early as 1662 Giovanni Andrea Bontempi (1624–1705), having transferred his allegiance from Venice to Dresden, organized there a performance of his opera *Il Paride*. The score of this work was immediately printed with a German translation of the text. This was the only complete printed edition of an Italian opera from the period 1630–1750 —all other scores were only manuscript copies. After 1700 a few printed scores of Italian operas appeared in London, published by Walsh, but containing only the arias; they will be dealt with later. Bontempi's *Il Paride* is based on the same material as Cesti's *Il pomo d'oro*, that is to say, the Judgement of Paris; presumably Sbarra and Cesti drew their inspiration from Bontempi's opera. Bontempi kept to the forms used by Cavalli and Cesti.[3]

---

[1] A German version of this libretto, set to music by Johann Philipp Förtsch, was given in Hamburg in 1684. See Wolff, *Die Barockoper in Hamburg*, i, p. 67.

[2] Edited complete in *Denkmäler deutscher Tonkunst*, lv (see p. 42, n. 1).

[3] See Richard Engländer, 'Die erste italienische Oper in Dresden: Bontempis Il Paride in musica', *Svensk Tidskrift för Musikforskning*, xlii (1961), p. 119.

MELANI AND STRADELLA

Jacopo Melani (1623–76)[1] and Alessandro Stradella (1642–82) may be taken together, since both of them, working outside Venice, introduced simple, ordinary people into their operas. Although in the second half of the seventeenth century Venice was acknowledged to be the leading centre of Italian opera, new opera-houses had also been established in most of the other Italian cities, and these often followed trends of their own, as in Rome, Florence, and Bologna, where everyday characters—noblemen, citizens and country folk—appeared in leading roles. Operas such as these must be regarded as forerunners of the middle-class *opera buffa* of the eighteenth century. The Roman operas of Cardinal Rospigliosi had on occasion dealt with impoverished aristocrats and gentlefolk drawn from contemporary life. The Teatro della Pergola in Florence opened in 1657 with a performance of Melani's opera *La Tancia, ovvero il podestà di Colognole*, in which the central character is a country girl who is loved by one of the landed gentry. Tancia's father, the local mayor, opposes the match from sheer avarice. Giovanni Andrea Moniglia, a doctor and man of letters living in Florence, was influenced in writing the libretto by the old rustic comedy *Tancia* (1612) by Michelangelo Buonarotti (the younger), which he adapted by the addition of serenades, disguises, stage-fights, and grotesque parodies of spirit-raisings (reminiscent of Carlo Porta's earlier comedy *Carbonaria*).[2] Moniglia called *La Tancia* a *dramma civile rusticale*, stressing the novelty of this rustic bourgeois drama, which, like Molière's *L'Avare*, culminates in a satire on middle-class greed. In the music for *La Tancia*, strophic arias and arias in dance-rhythms predominate, and duets appear side by side with very lively *recitativo secco*. A loyal and cunning servant helps his master in his amorous adventures; and farcical stuttering-scenes, not to mention imitations of animal noises, mingle elements of the *commedia dell'arte* with the madrigals and dance-songs of the early baroque period.

The action of Alessandro Stradella's[3] comic opera *Il Trespolo tutore*

[1] See Arnaldo Bonaventura, 'Jacopo Melani e la prima opera buffa', *Il Pensiero musicale*, ii (1922), p. 129.

[2] See Goldschmidt, *Studien zur Geschichte der italienischen Oper*, i, pp. 107 ff., and R. L. Weaver, *Florentine comic operas of the 17th century* (University Microfilms, Ann Arbor, 1959).

[3] The literature on Stradella is extensive. The following items may be mentioned here: Heinz Hess, *Die Opern Alessandro Stradellas* (Leipzig, 1906); Gino Roncaglia, 'Il "Trespolo tutore" di Alessandro Stradella, "la prima opera buffa" ', *Rivista musicale italiana*, lvi (1954), p. 326; J. A. Westrup, 'Stradella's "Forza d'amor paterno" ', *Monthly Musical Record*, lxxi (1941), p. 52; Carolyn Gianturco, *The Operas of Alessandro Stradella (1644–1682)* (Diss., Oxford, 1970, unpub.; and idem, 'Caratteri stilistici delle opere teatrali di Stradella', *Rivista italiana di musicologia*, vi (1972), p. 211. There is a vocal score of *La forza d'amor paterno*, ed. Alberto Gentili (Milan, 1930).

(Genoa, 1677?[1]) again unfolds against a background of humble people. Trespolo is a guardian in love with his ward, an original situation subsequently copied in many other comic operas up to Donizetti's *Don Pasquale*; but he is also a loutish peasant, whose clumsiness and violent temper are skilfully used to ridicule baroque poetry. Poetic similes were very popular at that time, and at one point (in Act II, scene 2) Trespolo likens his body to a kitchen, in which Love is the fire roasting his heart:[2]

Ex. 24

(Ah, Despina, you kindle a furnace in my body, where Love roasts my heart on a trivet.)

The role of Trespolo is written for bass, contrary to the usual practice, for leading male parts were generally taken by soprano or alto castratos. Comic dream sequences and mad scenes, the use of nonsense words,

[1] See Gianturco, 'A Possible Date for Stradella's "Il Trespolo tutore"', *Music and Letters*, liv (1973), p. 25.
[2] Taken from Hess, op. cit., p. 86.

and pointless coloratura passages emphasize the absurd side of this opera, in which the fool Ciro and the fever-ridden Nino outdo one another. Another comic opera by Stradella is *Floridoro, ovvero Il moro per amore* (Rome, 1670s?). Here the young Queen of Sicily is loved by Prince Floridoro of Cyprus, disguised as a Moorish slave. Stylistically, the music was for the most part based on the forms currently popular in Venice.[1]

Probably the most widely known fact about Stradella concerns his mysterious death. He was murdered, not by the Venetian nobleman Contarini, whose mistress Stradella had certainly abducted, but by the brothers of an actress whom Stradella had betrayed with her own pupils in Modena. Flotow's opera *Alessandro Stradella* (1844), which at one time enjoyed considerable success in Germany, gives the old, fictitious version of the tale, according to which the hired assassins renounce their murderous intent after listening to Stradella's new Marian motet.

OPERA IN VIENNA IN THE SEVENTEENTH CENTURY

The Habsburg emperors turned their court theatre in Vienna into a centre of Italian opera. The Habsburgs were closely linked both politically and culturally with Italy, since, besides the Tyrol, Naples, Milan, Mantua, Parma, and Piacenza were at one time or another after 1700 under Habsburg domination. Italian poets and composers, among them the best and most progressive artists of the day—for example, Zeno and Metastasio—were more or less permanently engaged to collaborate in productions in Vienna. The sumptuous public presentation of Cesti's *Il pomo d'oro*, which has already been described, was but the first tableau in a glittering pageant of Italian opera that was to play its part in the life of the Imperial capital for more than a hundred years. In the second half of the seventeenth century the leading figure in the world of Viennese music was the composer Antonio Draghi (*c.* 1635–1700).[2] From 1663 onwards he produced more than 170 operas, festival works, and serenades (also operatic in character) and more than forty oratorios. The most outstanding of his librettists was Nicolò Minato, whose name has already been mentioned several times, and his stage designer was Lodovico Burnacini. Together these three built up the impressive artistic edifice that was the Viennese baroque theatre.

Draghi made his mark initially as a writer of comic operas, the plots

[1] Two arias and a recitative from Act II are recorded in *The History of Music in Sound*, v.
[2] On Draghi see Wellesz, 'Die Opern und Oratorien in Wien von 1660–1708', *Studien zur Musikwissenschaft*, vi (1919), p. 5, and Neuhaus in *Studien zur Musikwissenschaft*, i (unfortunately only a small part of the latter is devoted to the operas). A complete catalogue of Draghi's operas is given in *Die Musik in Geschichte und Gegenwart*, iii (1954), cols. 735–7.

of which were borrowed from Greek legend and history, as in *La
lanterna di Diogene* (1674), *I pazzi Abderiti* (1675), *Il silenzio di Harpo-
crate* (1677), and *La pazienza di Socrate con due moglie*[1] (Prague, 1680).
The characters in *La mascherata* (Vienna, 1666)[2] were taken from the
humdrum world of peasants and servants. Most of Draghi's historical
operas are cast in the mould of the Venetian operas, and his musical
idiom, as far as may be judged from what is known of it, follows the
pattern set by the Venetian composers, with short arias, strophic and
song-like, and frequently recurring dance rhythms.

The earliest of Draghi's operas to have come down to us, *Achille in
Sciro* (1663), still provides examples of the onomatopoeic treatment of
single words, as is commonly found in madrigals. The musical high-
lighting of various key words provides great scope for contrast in
Comedy's aria, but breaks it up into short, quite distinct fragments:[3]

Ex. 25

[1] Act I, scene 2, printed in Schering, op. cit., pp. 296–301.
[2] Five excerpts printed by Neuhaus in *Studien zur Musikwissenschaft*, i, pp. 186–9.
[3] In ibid., p. 176 (together with six other excerpts from the same opera, pp. 174–5 and
177–85).

(On life's stage, each one of us plays his part in comedy or tragedy, depicting peace or war.)

This aria lacks the musical unity achieved by contemporary Venetian composers, to whose example Draghi now began to turn. Not content with the small-scale Venetian string ensembles, he incorporated other instruments into his orchestras, and in his double opera *Creso* (Vienna, 1678) several times uses three flutes, a *zuffolo* (small flute), three violas, and an organ. One rustic scene is written as a five-part canon,[1] and elsewhere he shows a fondness for three- to five-part writing. His arias contain symmetrical sections made up of groups of two or four bars, with a bass line which is definitely vocal in contour. Both of these characteristics are in sharp contrast to the operatic idiom of German composers in Hamburg at this time, who preferred freer, more lively and purely instrumental bass lines.[2] Absolute clarity of external form was the guiding principle adopted by Draghi and the Italian composers, whereas the Germans often disregarded symmetry in their emphasis on expression and tended towards more exciting harmonies. *Creso* has as its theme the intended burning of the Lydian king Croesus, whose life is saved when he cries out to the philosopher Solon from his funeral pyre; for his persecutor, Cyrus, at last realizes that no man may be accounted happy in the face of death. This warning against arrogance and tyranny was such an important issue at that time that several different versions of *Creso* were performed in Hamburg up to 1730.[3] Even in Vienna these Italian operas were more than just another form of entertainment and were certainly not as frivolous or trivial as has often been thought. They were closely related to contemporary Viennese oratorios[4] and prepared the way for the work of Zeno and Metastasio.

Unlike Italy, Vienna quickly absorbed the influence of the new French operas, with their large-scale choruses and ballets, which were from the outset destined to play an important part in the Viennese theatre. Moreover, Lully's new style of scoring, using oboes and bassoons, was soon adopted in Vienna. The appreciation of music was particularly encouraged in Austria by the fact that the emperors themselves, notably

[1] Printed in Wolff, *Die Barockoper in Hamburg*, ii, no. 118.

[2] Cf. Wolff, op. cit., i, p. 229.

[3] See ibid., pp. 229 ff., and 269 ff.

[4] See Wellesz in *Studien zur Musikwissenschaft*, vi, p. 6.

Leopold I (1658–1705) and Joseph I (1705–11), were keen composers who often set complete librettos to music, or at least contributed to operas by other composers (as with *Il pomo d'oro*). The whole Viennese court took an active interest in operatic productions, and up to the beginning of the eighteenth century the courtiers would often stage complete performances among themselves.

CARLO FRANCESCO POLLAROLI

Two almost exactly contemporary composers were, together with Alessandro Scarlatti, destined to shape the course of Italian operatic history around the end of the seventeenth century and the beginning of the eighteenth: Carlo Francesco Pollaroli (*c.* 1653–1722) and Agostino Steffani (1654–1728). Pollaroli (or Pollarolo) wrote some seventy operas, sixty-four of them for Venice, and in his time achieved greater renown than either Alessandro Scarlatti or Steffani, who was active in Germany but quite unknown in Italy itself. Pollaroli's contribution remains virtually uncharted territory on the map of operatic history.[1] He radically altered the orchestral accompaniment of the operatic aria in that he often discarded the *basso continuo* and substituted four solo violins or violins in unison. Here is the beginning of one of Termanzia's arias (Act I, scene 12) in *Onorio in Roma* (Venice, 1692):[2]

Ex. 26

(He who really loves gives his heart and can never say 'no'.)

Initially there are two violins to each part; but later each of the four violins has its own part (not shown in Ex. 26). This was a completely new and limpid sound, moving away from the heavy baroque style

---

[1] But see Wolff, *Die venezianische Oper*, pp. 97–102. His operas are listed in *Die Musik in Geschichte und Gegenwart*, x (1962), cols. 1420–2, and Burt in *Studies in Music History*, p. 325, discusses the libretto of his *Gl'Inganni felici* (1695).

[2] Published complete in Wolff, op. cit., appendix, no. 45.

towards the airy gracefulness of the eighteenth century. One of Onorio's arias is accompanied only by a string trio (again *senza cembalo*), for which Pollaroli wrote a purely harmonic type of accompaniment, full of short ostinato figures and devoid of motivic devices:[1]

Ex. 27

senza cembalo

(My kingdom is tottering.)

In other arias Pollaroli's accompaniments have two oboes, or sometimes a single oboe, alternating with strings. The influence of Lully and his orchestra was assimilated in a highly individual way and modified to suit the requirements of the arias. French opera also inspired the fine *ciaconna* at the end of Act III of *Onorio in Roma*, in which the ballet is accompanied by two vocal trios and a quintet.[2] Pollaroli even added a *vaudeville*, in French, echoing the little songs heard in those days at the *comédie italienne* in Paris.[3] Pollaroli emerges as a daring pioneer of new ideas in Italian opera. Among other things he introduced the principle of the instrumental concerto grosso, after the fashion of Corelli. In one scene of *Onorio in Roma*, set in a park, a three-part *concertino* is heard behind the scenes, while the *ripieno* in the front of the house plays the accompaniment to one of Placidia's arias. In this way the old practice of using multiple choirs at St. Mark's in Venice was transferred to the operatic stage, where it created an evocative echo-effect amid the parkland scenery. Similar orchestral effects occur in Pollaroli's *Ottone* (1694).

STEFFANI AND ITALIAN OPERA IN GERMANY

Agostino Steffani's[4] importance lay in helping Italian opera to become

[1] Taken from ibid., appendix, no. 48.
[2] See ibid., p. 177; and printed in part in appendix, no. 80.
[3] Ibid., appendix, no. 49.
[4] A good deal has been written on Steffani. The following are among the most substantial works: Hugo Riemann, 'Agostini Steffani als Opernkomponist', *Denkmäler der Tonkunst in Bayern*, xii, 2 (Leipzig, 1912), pp. vii ff.; W. H. Baxter, *Agostino Steffani: a study of the man and his work* (Diss., Rochester, N.Y., 1957, unpub.); Gerhard Croll, *Agostino Steffani (1654–1728): Studien zur Biographie und Bibliographie der Opern und Turnierspiele* (Diss., Münster, 1961, unpub.); and Philip Keppler, 'Agostino Steffani's Hannover operas and a rediscovered catalogue', *Studies in Music History*, p. 341.

firmly established in Germany. His eighteen operas, written for the court theatres in Munich, Hanover, and Düsseldorf, were also performed at Hamburg (in German translations) between 1695 and 1699. At one time they aroused interest mainly because Handel modelled his operas on them, since he was able to study at close quarters, during his stay in Hanover, the effective combination of vocally rewarding melodies with a contrapuntal bass. Steffani spread throughout Germany the Venetian operatic idiom—especially that of Legrenzi—as well as Corelli's instrumental style. Steffani himself brought vocal and instrumental styles into a much closer relationship, with the result that not only instrumental passages from his operas, but even arias, could be arranged and published as purely instrumental suites and chamber sonatas (also for solo flute with *basso continuo*).[1] Melodiousness and pellucid but strict counterpoint are the most striking features of Steffani's operatic writing, and also of the *duetti da camera* for which he is especially famous.

In composing the arias for his operas Steffani frequently gave the accompanying or concertante instruments themes of their own or treated them as second voice parts; this resulted in a style similar to that of Corelli's trio sonatas. For instance, in the aria 'Piangerete, io ben lo sò' from Act III, scene 3 of *Tassilone*[2] (Düsseldorf, 1709), the voice part is joined by a single oboe in a duet of great charm. Through Steffani's use of melodic variation, each repeated cry of 'Piangerete' differs from the last. Like Pollaroli, Steffani on occasion dispensed with the harpsichord in the arias, leaving only a string accompaniment, as in *Niobe* (1688).[3] In the same opera he used mutes and demanded decrescendos such as *p-pp-ppp-pppp*, which were well in advance of the normal practice of his day. His music shows the influence of French opera even more than does Pollaroli's. Not only did Steffani take over the woodwind (flutes and oboes); he even copied the form of the French overture and introduced marches and dances into his scores. His most popular operas were *Servio Tullio* (Munich, 1685, with libretto by Ventura Terzago) and *Henrico Leone*[4] (with libretto by Ortensio Mauro), written for the opening of the opera-house at Hanover (1689) and based on an incident in German history involving Henry the Lion. Other noteworthy operas include *Alarico*[5] (Munich, 1687), *Arminio* (Düsseldorf, 1707), and his

---

[1] See Wolff, *Die Barockoper in Hamburg*, i, p. 239.

[2] *Tassilone* has been published complete, ed. Croll, *Denkmäler rheinischer Musik*, viii (Düsseldorf, 1958); the aria mentioned is on pp. 118–20.

[3] Extracts from most of Steffani's operas appear as *Ausgewählte Werke*, ed. Riemann, *Denkmäler der Tonkunst in Bayern*, xii, 2.

[4] The aria 'Un balen' in Archibald T. Davison and Willi Apel, *Historical Anthology of Music*, ii (London, 1950), pp. 122–3.

[5] Ed. Riemann, *Denkmäler der Tonkunst in Bayern*, xi, 2 (Leipzig, 1911).

last opera, *Tassilone*. Thereafter Steffani abandoned composition and
was appointed to administrative and diplomatic posts, as a member of
the elector palatine's council at Düsseldorf and later as papal envoy to
northern Germany (where he lived mostly at Hanover).

Steffani's operas contain interesting turns of harmony and a great
deal of chromatic part-writing, which increase and broaden the expressive capability of baroque music. The middle section of the aria 'Scelga
il dardo' from Act II, scene 4 of *Tassilone* gives an example of this:[1]

Ex. 28

(Die with me, my merciless, cruel fate.)

[1] Croll ed., pp. 81–2.

The vocal part is buried in the thick texture of the accompaniment (as in Cesti), with the difference that here the voice part is partly played by the accompanying instruments in defiance of all the rules of counterpoint, though in the following decades this innovation was to become one of the most important tasks of the orchestra in Italian opera. Chromaticism, producing diminished chords, underlines the word 'crudo' (bars 7 and 9).

In Munich, too, the cult of Italian opera was carefully fostered. Next to Steffani, its foremost representative here was Giuseppe Antonio Bernabei (1649–1732), whose thirteen surviving operas (in the National Library in Vienna) from the period 1678–91 have not yet been studied. A little later Pietro Torri (1655–1737) wrote twenty-six operas for the Munich stage (between 1690 and 1736), of which a detailed account is given by Hermann Junker in the introduction to his selection from Torri's works.[1] Torri's style largely conforms to the general pattern of his day, though to some extent he widened the scope of the wind instruments by devising charming and novel effects for them.

ALESSANDRO SCARLATTI

Alessandro Scarlatti (1660–1725) was beyond doubt the most prolific composer of opera around 1700. By his own account he was the author of 115 operas, though this tally probably included adaptations and smaller works. In the preface to the libretto of *La Griselda* (Rome, 1721) Scarlatti refers to it as his 114th opera, and it was followed by *La virtù negli Amori* (1721). The titles (and librettos) of only some eighty of these operas have come down to posterity, and only thirty-five scores are still extant, though recently additional titles have been discovered.[2] Hitherto, consideration of Scarlatti's operas has thus been incomplete, all the more so since the existing scores do not seem to have been thoroughly examined or analysed. Alfred Lorenz confines his attention to those operas written before 1698, while Dent treats only a select few.[3]

It is nevertheless possible to say with certainty that Scarlatti was not the founder of a new Neapolitan style in opera, as has often been claimed in the past. The existence of a separate or predominantly

---

[1] *Denkmäler der Tonkunst in Bayern*, xix-xx (Leipzig, 1920), containing Act III of *Merope* (1719) and excerpts from several other operas.

[2] See Emilia Zanetti and Sartori, 'Contributo a un catalogo delle opere teatrali di Alessandro Scarlatti', *Gli Scarlatti* (Siena, 1940). There is a list of Scarlatti's operas in the article on him in *Die Musik in Geschichte und Gegenwart*, xi (1963), cols. 1486–8.

[3] See Alfred Lorenz, *Alessandro Scarlatti's Jugendoper*, 2 vols. (Augsburg, 1927) (the second volume consists of 400 musical examples, 135 of them of complete pieces); and Edward J. Dent, *Alessandro Scarlatti: his life and works* (new impr., London, 1960). These are the two biggest studies of Scarlatti's works to date. An edition of nine operas by Scarlatti, ed. Donald J. Grout, is in course of preparation (Cambridge, Mass.).

Neapolitan 'school' is in any case questionable, at least in the normal definition of the word. The whole question will be discussed later in more detail. Scarlatti invented neither the *da capo* aria nor the comic opera; he did not create the figure of the soubrette, nor did he write the first examples of accompanied recitative, as Dent supposed.[1] All of these were known at an earlier date, as has been shown above. Again, extensive coloratura passages in arias had already been used by Sartorio, at the same time as Pollaroli in Venice was experimenting with the replacing of the *basso continuo* by short instrumental motives on the strings in the accompaniments to his arias. After 1718 Scarlatti's operas were no longer performed in Naples, as Dent noted, so it can scarcely be assumed that he exercised an influence on composers working there after that date, since printed scores and vocal scores were then non-existent. Care must be taken not to exaggerate Scarlatti's significance. His main contribution was towards the expansion of aria form and the more active participation of a concertante orchestra in the arias. Scarlatti continued the tradition of the late seventeenth century; but he did not himself inaugurate a new epoch in musical style.

Attempts have been made to classify Scarlatti's creative activity into different periods, though these have hitherto been based on superficialities rather than on considerations of style. He wrote his operas not only for Naples, but also for Rome, Florence, and Venice, and on one occasion for London (*Pyrrhus and Demetrius*, Haymarket Theatre, 1708). His very early operas originated in Rome, where the first opera-house (Tor di Nona) had been opened in 1671. In 1679, for the Capranica Theatre in Rome, he wrote *Gli equivoci nel sembiante*, which was an outstanding success and was shortly afterwards performed in other Italian cities. This work was a pastoral comedy for four soloists, with interchanged twin brothers as the central characters—a favourite comic situation since Plautus's *Menaechmi* and Shakespeare's *A Comedy of Errors*. Scarlatti's first *opera seria*, *Il Pompeo* (Rome, 1683), was based on the libretto by Minato already used by Cavalli in his *Il Pompeo Magno* (Venice, 1666). The action revolves around the love of a young Roman, Sextus, for the wife of King Mithridates, who is in captivity. As in Cavalli's opera, Pompey intervenes at the eleventh hour to prevent the wholesale suicide of Mithridates's family. In the end, the only fatal casualty in the opera is a quasi-comic scheming slave-woman, Harpalia.[2]

Of Scarlatti's Neapolitan operas written between 1684 and 1702 the most outstanding is *Clearco in Negroponte* (1686), notable for the short motives used in the vocal and orchestral parts, a practice which became

---

[1] Cf. Dent, op. cit., pp. 45 ff. and 50 ff.
[2] See Lorenz, op. cit., i, p. 90, and Wolff, *Die venezianische Oper*, pp. 34 ff.

widespread in the eighteenth century; the following example is from an aria in Act I, scene 2:[1]

Ex. 29

(no sharp in original key-signature)

(Ungrateful, merciless one! You know that I adore you, that I die for you.)

[1] Taken from Lorenz, op. cit., ii, no. 130.

The sudden change from a mood of excitement to one of contrasting lyricism, achieved here by altering the time, derives from Monteverdi and Cavalli. Scarlatti liked to reflect events taking place on stage in short instrumental pieces, such as the last moments of a dying man (in *Massimo Puppieno*, 1695); but this, too, had already been done at an earlier date in Venice. On the other hand, the nimble interplay of voice and orchestra in short motives, as in an aria in *L'Amazone guerriera* (I, 1) (Naples, 1689), was entirely new:[1]

Ex. 30

(no sharp in original key-signature)

(To peer into your heart is to see a demon from hell.)

[1] Ibid., ii, no. 173.

Carlo Pallavicino, who in 1685 had set the same libretto by Giulio Cesare Corradi for Venice, set the text of this aria to a dance rhythm in 3/8 time,[1] giving it ironic overtones. Scarlatti, by writing a wide-ranging vocal line, sought to create an impression of greater vehemence that looks forward to Handel. The plot of this opera has much in common with Shakespeare's *The Taming of the Shrew*. In Corradi's story the Queen of the Goths, Alvilda, who is determined to yield to no man, is loved, taken captive, and married by Alfo, King of the Danes. Several scenes are almost the same as in Shakespeare's play, notably those in which Olmiro, the young lover, gains entry to the household of the Queen's younger sister as dancing-master.

Now and then Scarlatti built up his arias by adding extensive florid passages, as when he has the soloist imitate the song of a nightingale in *Le nozze con l'inimico* (Naples, 1695):[2]

Ex. 31

[1] Pallavicino's setting is placed conveniently next to Scarlatti's in ibid., ii, no. 174.
[2] Ibid., ii, no. 272.

(O listen to the nightingale alone in that bush; how sweetly he sings 'lio li'.)

The movement of the bass line and the initial dactylic rhythms are still entirely Venetian. Nightingale arias were very popular during the eighteenth century; even Handel included one in the score of his last opera, *Deidamia* (London, 1741, Act I, scene 5), in which the solo violins play a much more independent role.[1]

In Venice a close relationship grew up between Scarlatti and Cardinal Vincenzo Grimani, who in 1707 authorized a performance of Scarlatti's opera *Il Mitridate Eupatore*[2] in his own Teatro San Giovanni Grisostomo. Scarlatti dedicated several of his operas to Grimani: *Il Teodosio* (Naples, 1709), *L'amor volubile e tiranno* (Naples, 1709), and *La principessa fedele* (Naples, 1710).[3] From 1708 Grimani was Austrian Viceroy at Naples, where Handel also made his acquaintance. Grimani himself wrote the libretto for Handel's *Agrippina*, given in Venice in 1709 at the theatre that had previously been used for the production of Scarlatti's *Mitridate*; the young Handel would almost certainly have attended performances of some of Scarlatti's operas, since the two knew each other well, and he may well have known *Mitridate*. Handel, like Scarlatti, used two concertante cellos—unusual at that time—in two of Nero's arias (in Act III, scenes 3 and 8) and in one sung by the heroine Agrippina (Act I, scene 23). The inspiration for one of the finest pieces in *Agrippina*, Ottone's lament, 'Voi che udite il mio lamento', with a fugal accompaniment in slow, regular quavers, was surely drawn from an aria in Scarlatti's *Mitridate*, 'Patrii Numi, amici Dei':[4]

---

[1] See *infra*, Ex. 76.

[2] For a fuller account of this work—of which there is an unreliable vocal score, ed. Giuseppe Piccioli (Milan, 1953)—see Westrup, 'Alessandro Scarlatti's *Il Mitridate Eupatore* (1707)', *New looks at Italian opera*, p. 133.

[3] See Lorenz, op. cit., i, pp. 32 ff.

[4] The Scarlatti example is in Deutsche Staatsbibliothek, MS. Berlin 19641 (now at Marburg).

Ex. 32

(Paternal Gods, friendly deities . . .)

Handel simply chose the key of F minor (as opposed to Scarlatti's
F major) and sought out even more unrelated keys. Perhaps he was even
more affected by the broad, sweeping melodic curves which Scarlatti
used with such artistry in *Mitridate Eupatore* and which must be counted
among the highlights of early eighteenth-century opera—see, for instance, this line in Laodice's lament in the fourth act:[1]

Ex. 33

(Dear tomb of my beloved, take me to your bosom; be a tomb also for me.

The melodic phrases are progressively lengthened by the reiteration of
words, ejaculations, and sequences, and conjunct movement is interrupted, with consummate artistry, by wider intervals and triadic forma-
tions. Melodic lines of this kind demanded a singer of exceptional
virtuosity with some talent for improvisation. This again is an aria that
Handel seems to have remembered—when he wrote 'Cara sposa' in
Rinaldo: not only are there similarities in the vocal lines but textures are
similar too, and both pieces are scored for upper strings only.[2]

The architect and poet Girolamo Frigimelica Roberti had conceived
Mitridate Eupatore as a great classical tragedy in the mould of the
Electra of Euripides. Scarlatti's *Il trionfo dell'onore* (Naples, 1718)[3] is

[1] Loc. cit.
[2] See Westrup in *New looks at Italian opera*, pp. 138–41.
[3] Vocal score ed. Virgilio Mortari (Milan, 1941).

set in quite a different world. Here certain citizens of contemporary Pisa were brought to life on the stage in a comedy setting similar to that of Mozart's *Don Giovanni*. The opera was performed at the popular Teatro de' Fiorentini in Naples, where until then only operas in Neapolitan dialect had been produced. In many of these works the traditional rhythms of the southern Italian *siciliano* were used in the arias, though, as we have seen, the similar rhythms of the *forlana* were already familiar to Venetian opera-goers and were in use in Italian opera long before Scarlatti. Scarlatti refined the harmonies of these dance-forms and gave remarkable harmonic colour to the music; Handel did the same with great success in *Agrippina* (e.g. Nero's aria 'Quando invita la donna l'amante', Act II, scene 12). Many of Scarlatti's operas contain comic scenes with servants that were often so independent of the main action that they could also be performed on their own. These were the direct antecedents of the *intermezzi*, which will be discussed in the next section.

Scarlatti also set a few librettos by Apostolo Zeno, the great reformer of Italian opera after 1700. These were *Gli inganni felici* (Naples, 1699), *Odoardo* (Naples, 1700) and *La Griselda* (Rome, 1721).[1] This last was one of the best-known librettos of the day and was set to music by many other composers, who, apart from Torri, include Antonio and Giovanni Bononcini and Vivaldi, whose respective versions are discussed in the next chapter.[2] Zeno had written at the beginning of the century his libretto based on the story of Griselda, the poor country girl who, after enduring many trials and tribulations, is made a queen as a result of her loyalty and trustworthiness; it was first set to music by Pollaroli for Venice in 1701. It was therefore already well known when Scarlatti decided to use it; he altered various details, adding new aria texts as well as new ensembles and orchestral pieces, without, however, making any basic changes in the work. The textual alterations were the responsibility of Francesco Ruspoli, though they hardly entitle him to be regarded as the author of the libretto (as is claimed in Drechsler's edition). In this late work Scarlatti's melodic construction may be seen particularly clearly. He develops whole arias from a single motive-germ, which he gradually allows to grow, as in Constanza's aria in Act II, scene 9:[3]

---

[1] Ed. Otto Drechsler (Kassel, 1962). The *sinfonia* is in Davison and Apel, op. cit., pp. 155–157, and a recitative scene in Schering, op. cit., pp. 374–7; Schering also has (pp. 371–3) a comic scene from *Gli inganni felici*. See Hermann Junker, 'Zwei "Griselda"-Opern', *Festschrift zum 50. Geburtstag Adolf Sandberger* (Munich, 1918), p. 51 (the other setting referred to in the title is Torri's); and Grout, 'La "Griselda" di Zeno e il libretto dell'opera di Scarlatti', *Nuova rivista musicale italiana*, ii (1968), p. 207.

[2] See *infra*, pp. 79 ff, 99, and 105 ff.

[3] Taken from Deutsche Staatsbibliothek, MS. Berlin 19640 (now at Marburg).

Ex. 34

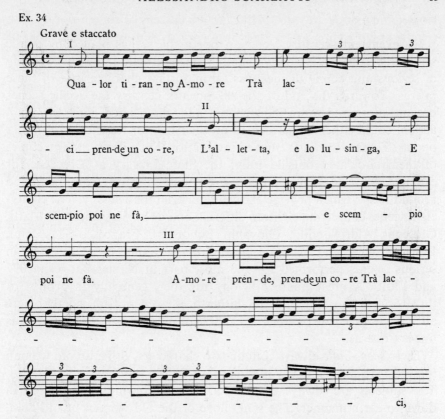

(Whenever the tyrant Love ensnares a heart he entices and deceives it and then destroys it.)

The first motive (I) is built up by degrees to II and III. Syncopations and other rhythmic subtleties are the first signs of the coming 'sentimental' style, for which Scarlatti prepared the way.

In his later operas Scarlatti frequently made use of ensembles (duets, trios, quartets) to round off an act; Dent has already commented on this in some detail.[1] Nor was this feature confined to comic operas. In serious operas, for example *La Griselda*, every act (and many operas had five) culminated in an ensemble of some kind. This became common practice in Italian opera of the eighteenth century, and ensembles of this type occur in many operas by Vivaldi, Leo and others, which by no means consist solely of arias for the soloists. Scarlatti gave one such quartet in his *Tito Sempronio Gracco* (Rome, 1720), 'Idolo mio, ti chiamo', the rhythm of a *siciliano*.[2]

[1] Op. cit., pp. 167 ff.
[2] Recorded in *The History of Music in Sound*, v.

COMIC SCENES

In seventeenth-century Venetian opera the scenes played by comic servants were as a rule closely linked to the main action: the interweaving of serious and comic themes was an important characteristic of these operas. Towards the end of the seventeenth century the comic scenes became more and more independent and, dissociated from the main action, could either be performed on their own or transferred to other operas. These *scene buffe* enjoyed international popularity. Many copies of them circulated outside Italy: the State Library at Dresden, for example, possesses two comprehensive volumes of them from the period around 1700,[1] which provide excellent material for a survey. The eighty-eight scenes come from eighteen different operas by Alessandro Scarlatti, Giuseppe Aldrovandini, Giovanni Bononcini, Francesco Gasparini, Luigi Mancia, and Antonio Severo di Luca and were inserted in serious operas performed for the most part in Naples between 1697 and 1701.[2] A great number belong together, generally in groups of three or five (a point that has hitherto escaped notice), so that here already we have true *intermezzi*, capable of independent performance as one-act operas.

These *scene buffe* always contain two characters, either an old woman (played by a man) and a young man, or an old man and a young girl. The subjects are always erotic, and sex-relationships are treated in down-to-earth manner. The senile love of the old woman or old man, the impecuniosity of the young ones, are the recurring themes, which invariably lead to strife, intrigue, estrangement, and reconciliation. There is no lack of satires and parodies of the love-scenes, pastoral idylls, ghost-scenes, and incantations of serious opera. Popular music of all kinds is employed, mixed with comic speech and sound effects: laughter, stuttering, pauses, rapid speech, and instrumental sounds (e.g. bassoons).

Scarlatti is particularly well represented, with scenes from ten different operas, of which two may be mentioned here. Serpollo and Serpilla, a pair from *Il pastor di Corinto* (Naples, 1701), make fun of pastoral scenes. In one duet Scarlatti uses three oboes without keyboard continuo to imitate the sound of bagpipes playing a *siciliano*:[3]

---

[1] Landesbibliothek, Mus. MS. 1.F.39,1, and 39,2.

[2] See Hanns Nietan, *Die Buffoszenen der spätvenezianischen Oper (1680–1710)* (Diss., Halle, 1924, unpub.).

[3] Exx. 35–6 come from the first and Exx. 37–9 from the second of the two manuscript volumes mentioned in n. 1, *supra*.

Ex. 35

(Serpilla, my love, if you are cruel you will soon see your Serpollo die.)

The duet begins *adagio*, changing abruptly to *presto*. In the five *buffo* scenes from *L'Eraclea* (Naples, 1700) we find already the rapid speech on one note, punctuated by short interjections from the other partner (*nò, nò*), and the many repetitions of words that were favourite devices in eighteenth-century *opera buffa*:

Ex. 36

(A: You are Lilla, tell me, you are she, say, confess. L: No, and again no.)

The myopic old Doctor Alfeo, mistaking the young Livio for a girl named Livia, makes love to him, thus providing opportunities for farcical acting which cannot be appreciated from the music alone. Alfeo is none other than the familiar 'Dottore' of the *commedia dell'arte*, boasting of his wisdom as usual in the aria 'Precipitata filosofia'.

When the dilettante composer Luigi Mancia (b. *c.* 1665) introduces into his *Partenope* (Naples, 1699) some thoroughly realistic bargaining over the purchase-price of a somewhat questionable lady's love, written in the style of an *opera seria* duet, it is clearly intended as a satire on the serious love-duet:

Ex. 37

(A: I am discreet, dear Beltramme, give me a little; oblige me, give me a little
. . . B: There's no money; I haven't a penny, not a farthing; in anything else I'll
serve you!)

The comic scenes in the operas of Francesco Gasparini (1668–1727) were often known by separate titles of their own, usually consisting of the names of the two characters taking part: for instance, *Pollastrello e Parpagnacco* or *Catulla e Lardone*, which were the first comic scenes that can be regarded as independent *intermezzi*. Gasparini's *Melissa e Serpillo* became one of the most famous of these and was also performed under the title *Melissa schernita, vendicata, contenta* as an interlude in his opera *L'amor generoso* (Venice, 1707); this *intermezzo* was heard again in Naples in 1709, this time with music by Antonio Orefice and Francesco Mancini, as well as in many other cities. Serpillo is a typical soldier in defeat, penniless and begging his way from country to country, who swindles an elderly woman out of her money and jewels in order to squander them on another, younger woman: a biting satire on militarism and on the mercenary soldiers of the age.[1] Before coming to Venice in 1700 Gasparini had composed for the Roman stage: for example, his very first opera, *L'Ajace* (Rome, 1697), was a serious work to which he added a pair of comic servants, Gilbo and Lydia. Lydia disguises herself as a negress (under the name of Gloda) in order to tell Gilbo's fortune and predict that he will become her husband. Gilbo, however, rebuffs her on the grounds that she is black, and suddenly, within the framework of the classical world of opera, important racial problems of the time confronted the audience:

Ex. 38

[1] An account of the different versions of this *intermezzo* may be found in Wolff, *Die Barockoper in Hamburg*, i, pp. 120–2.

(L: Give me at least some hope, oh, give succour to her who adores you. G: O, if you were not a blackamoor I would be kind to you.)

None of this was taken too seriously, however, since Lydia is only disguised and is really in love with Gilbo. Gasparini wrote more than sixty operas, most of them for Venice, which have as yet remained in total obscurity. His *Tamerlano* (Venice, 1710) will be discussed in the next chapter.[1]

Finally there is Giovanni Bononcini (1670–1747), whose comic scenes from *Il trionfo di Camilla* (Naples, 1697) must be mentioned. This opera was performed in many other cities besides Naples, including London (1706–28), and brought Bononcini international fame. Kurt Hueber has proved conclusively that *Il trionfo di Camilla* (also known simply as *Camilla*) was written by Giovanni, not by his brother Antonio; the works of these two composers are often confused, and even now not

[1] See *infra*, pp. 93 ff.

all the questions of authorship have been cleared up.[1] The two comic characters in *Camilla* mock the favourite type of love-scene found in seventeenth-century *opera seria* in which a lover addresses a distant beloved who does not appear on the stage. Here it is Tullia who is sighing and longing:

Ex. 39

[1] See Kurt Hueber, *Die Wiener Opern Giovanni Bononcinis von 1697 bis 1710* (Diss., Vienna, 1955, unpub.), pp. 29 ff. Bononcini's operas are discussed more fully in the next chapter; see *infra*, pp. 74 ff.

(T: I languish, I sigh, my beloved! L: But why? I am here! T: I'm not talking to *you*! My beloved! L: I'm here. T: I'm not talking to *you*! Do you long for me? L: Yes, yes! T: Help! L: It's here!

Linco, who loves her, stands close at hand and answers Tullia's cries with brief remarks that he is here, and so on. Throughout, *adagio* (for her languishing) alternates with *allegro* ('I'm not talking to *you*!', etc.), a comic contrast which is seldom found in the set forms of even the later *opera buffa*.

These *scene buffe* and *intermezzi* were very important in setting the pattern for the eighteenth-century bourgeois comic opera, with its ordinary characters and situations; and many of them if performed today would still prove very effective.

II

ITALIAN OPERA 1700–1750

By Hellmuth Christian Wolff

INTRODUCTORY

Italian opera of the first half of the eighteenth century has had to endure the harsh judgements of later generations who branched out in new directions and chose to regard older operas as either imperfect precursors or degenerate latecomers. Most of these verdicts have proved quite unreliable, since they were based on far too superficial a knowledge of the operas themselves. This is true even of Handel's operas, which have received most attention. In the case of Pergolesi much greater difficulties arise, for works have been ascribed to him that he certainly never wrote. The numerous splendid operas by composers such as Gasparini, the two Bononcinis, Leo, Vinci, Caldara, Conti, and Vivaldi, widely admired in their time, are virtually no longer performed; the same is true of the many other composers who helped to create the golden age of early Italian opera. It is high time to make a reappraisal, which can for the most part be based on the original manuscripts.

At the beginning of the eighteenth century Italian operatic style changed radically. In seventeenth-century opera the voice parts had always been supported by the *basso continuo*, which itself enjoyed a certain degree of thematic independence; in the eighteenth century the emphasis came to be placed on the voice alone, and the accompaniment became a purely harmonic support. Melodic elements were brought to the fore, not only the vocal melody as such, but also its character and treatment, which were dictated by the text and its emotional overtones and also by the requirements of musical form. This applied in particular to the art of the *da capo* aria, in which the virtuoso soloist was called upon to sing expressive coloratura passages and, more important still, to increase the emotional content of the music itself through the subtlety of his performance. The 'melody' was not an end in itself but served to intensify the expression of both text and emotion. The artistic purpose was 'the imitation of nature' through the melody alone, by which was meant the nature of the emotional overtones. The singer's task was to provide 'a mirror for the emotions' and to 'touch the heart'.

Thus Arteaga, in the second half of the eighteenth century, described what for him was the essential achievement of the operas of Gasparini, Leo, Vinci, Porpora, Pergolesi, and the rest.[1] He says nothing of coloratura or virtuoso effects, which we are so prone to consider the most outstanding characteristics of the period. It is true that Arteaga represented the ideals of a later generation, one which repudiated the pre-1750 'melodic and harmonic refinements' and for this reason emphasized the 'rebirth of melody'. It is very remarkable, however, that he saw this 'rebirth' in those same masters of Italian opera who were active before 1750 and that it struck him as being the most important attribute of their music. Italian opera in the eighteenth century strove to reproduce 'the natural accents of the passions', both in the arias and in the recitatives, which should not be dismissed as mere bridges from one aria to the next. On the contrary, librettists like Zeno and Metastasio wrote first-class texts whose poetry reached its most expressive heights in the recitatives.

Closer acquaintance with the operas of Gasparini, Vivaldi, Lotti, and other composers reveals that the operatic pendulum was once more swinging back to Venice, which previously, in the years around 1700, had temporarily been overshadowed by Naples. In fact the evidence of the following survey proves that Venice was the real centre of eighteenth-century Italian opera.

GIOVANNI AND ANTONIO BONONCINI

The Bononcini brothers,[2] who hailed from Modena, actively participated in the spread of Italian opera to Austria (Vienna), Germany (Berlin), and England (London). The name Bononcini is perhaps best known from references in biographies of Handel, for Giovanni (1670–1747) was for some years Handel's great rival in London. Early Handel biographers took the view that Bononcini was the superficial 'entertainer' of a pleasure-loving society, a 'reactionary' who tried in vain to imitate Handel's 'noble style'.[3] More recent research has shown that the exact opposite was true and that Handel found in Bononcini's operas a great source of inspiration; these operas had been performed regularly in London since 1706. Dent submitted that Bononcini had been developing the so-called Handelian style from as far back as 1697 and had already made it familiar to London audiences—a theory which

---

[1] See Stefano Arteaga, *Le rivoluzioni del teatro musicale italiano*, 3 vols. (Bologna, 1783–8), *passim*.

[2] There is no general study of their music; references to specific aspects of their work are given below, as appropriate.

[3] See, for example, Friedrich Chrysander, *G. F. Händel*, ii (Leipzig, 1860), pp. 65 and 71 ff.

has recently been more thoroughly investigated and corroborated by Hueber.[1]

Giovanni Bononcini's first work to be written in this style was *Il trionfo di Camilla* (Naples, 1697), which was repeated in London between 1706 and 1728.[2] *L'Etearco*, composed by Bononcini for Vienna in 1707 and subsequently performed in Naples in 1708 and in London in 1711 (where Handel surely heard it), has the strongly dotted rhythms which now seem so typical of Handel's arias:[3]

Ex. 40

(If you ever learn that cruel heaven wished me dead, sigh and . . .)

In this aria, sung by Mirene in Act II, scene 6, Bononcini follows the earlier saraband-style arias of the Venetian opera, though he alters their character by replacing the gentle 3/2 rhythm of the Venetians by a stronger, dotted rhythm, more characteristic of Lully and French opera.

Harmonically, Bononcini was a bold innovator, and his music is spiced with unusual dissonances and rapid modulations which horrified many of his contemporaries. His cantatas are full of such effects,[4] as are his operas; for example, in *Camilla* extensive chromaticism is used to create a gloomy atmosphere. Bononcini, a master of melodic variation, was particularly fond of varying a short basic theme in such a way that a strict and ordered terseness of structure developed in his arias.[5] Burney pointed to the 'clearness and facility' of Bononcini's melodies, further describing them as 'graceful and elegant'.[6] But in the last analysis

[1] See Edward J. Dent, *Alessandro Scarlatti: his life and works* (new impr., ed. Frank Walker, London, 1960), p. 65; for Hueber's work see p. 71, n. 1.

[2] See *infra*, p. 78.

[3] In Vienna, Nat. Bibl., 18267, f. 28v.

[4] See Hellmuth Christian Wolff, 'Bononcini—oder die Relativität historischer Urteile', *Revue belge de musicologie*, xi (1957), p. 3.

[5] Ibid., p. 10.

[6] Charles Burney, *A General History of Music*, iv (London, 1789), pp. 273 ff.

7

what Burney most appreciated in Bononcini were the qualities that linked him with Handel. He took as an example the aria 'Son qual face' from *Griselda*,[1] which in its dignity closely resembles some of Handel's arias; the individual nature of Bononcini's music escaped Burney.

On the whole, Bononcini's operatic arias are much shorter and more concentrated than those of Handel, and indeed in some respects they are similar to Corelli's instrumental music, though they remain essentially vocal; they include arias taken from his *Cantate e duetti* (London, 1721). From 1727 he rejected the lavish use of concertante effects between the orchestra and the solo voices found in Handel's operas, and he deplored the instrumental quality inherent in many of Handel's aria themes. It was not that he was averse to instrumental effects; but he limited their use to appropriate moments such as the following example from his early opera *Polifemo* (Berlin, 1702).[2] Here two flutes alternate with the solo voice:

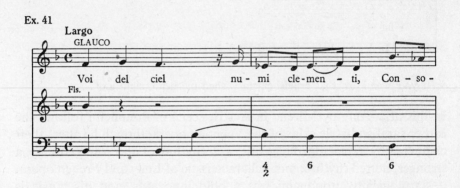

---

[1] Full score of the arias, etc., printed by Walsh (London, [1722]), p. 60.
[2] Berlin (now Marburg), Deutsche Bibl., 2190.

(Console a languishing heart, you benevolent gods in heaven.)

Sighs set to music punctuate the vocal line on the word 'consolate'.

Polifemo was performed privately in the Charlottenburg Palace, near Berlin, by members of the court, under the musical direction of the Prussian Queen Sophie Charlotte. Among those present was the young Telemann, then a student, who from a hiding-place watched and listened to his first Italian opera.[1] The libretto, by Attilio Ariosti, took as its theme the story of Acis and Galatea, which Lully had already used for an opera in 1686: Bononcini's music shows signs of French influence in the French overture, the use of woodwind and the arias in minuet time. The wide vocal leaps in the arias of the comic giant Polyphemus a bass, are derived from the old *scene buffe* with comic servants that were incorporated into serious operas.[2]

From Berlin Bononcini moved to Vienna, where from 1704 he brought out a new opera almost every year.[3] One of these was the already mentioned *L'Etearco* (after Herodotus), staged in Vienna in 1707. At the instigation of his second wife, the Cretan King Etearchos plans to have Fronima, the daughter of his first marriage, murdered. In *Il Mario fuggitivo* (Vienna, 1708), the celebrated Viennese court poet Silvio Stampiglia based his text on the *Fidelio*-like theme of self-sacrificing

[1] See Curt Sachs, *Musik und Oper am kurbrandenburgischen Hof* (Berlin, 1910), pp. 110–14.

[2] See *supra*, pp. 64 ff., including Ex. 36.

[3] See *Giovanni Bononcini: Arias from the Venetian Operas*, ed. Anthony Ford (*The Baroque Operatic Arias*, i) (London, 1971).

conjugal love. Many of these operas were closely bound up with the political events of the times. In Bononcini's *Il ritorno di Giulio Cesare* (Vienna, 1704) a parallel is drawn with the return of the victorious Emperor Joseph I from the War of the Spanish Succession.

Il trionfo di Camilla laid the foundation of Bononcini's reputation in London. The opera is concerned with an incident in Virgil's *Aeneid* in which Camilla fights against Aeneas and dies. By 1710 Bononcini's arias were so popular in London that they were inserted into other operas, and several of his later arias became popular English songs. One outstanding success was *Astarte* (London, 1720),[1] but *Griselda* (London, 1722) became the most famous of all Bononcini's operas. Paolo Rolli wrote a special version of the text for him, which diverged completely from the already familiar libretto by Zeno. However, the basic story was the same—the love of Prince Gualtiero (Walter of Saluzzo) for the poor, faithful country girl Griselda, who, after enduring various trials, becomes his wife at the request of the people. Boccaccio (in the *Decameron*) and Petrarch had already used this story. Human steadfastness and loyalty triumphing over all differences of social standing was one of the ideals of that time and was admired by the middle-class opera-going public both in Venice and in London.

Bononcini built up his arias from the declamation of single words, as in Griselda's farewell[2] in the first act:

Ex. 42

(Farewell, farewell, my gentle love, but remember me.)

The emphatic accentuation of every single word, underlined by rests and dotted rhythms, is combined here with a broad vocal melody. Other arias, such as this one in Act II, demonstrate the close affinities between vocal and instrumental style:

---

[1] As with *Griselda*, Walsh printed a full score of the arias of this opera, *Astartus* (London, [1721]).

[2] This and the two following examples are taken from the Walsh ed., pp. 9, 39, and 12 respectively.

Ex.43

(You come where the inclemency of inhospitable stars will not impose on you a tyrannical fate.)

Similar themes abound in contemporary instrumental music, whether by Corelli or Bach (e.g. the last movement of the Sixth Brandenburg Concerto). Bononcini had taken this aria almost unchanged from his cantata 'Misero pastorello', though the printed version (in the *Cantate e duetti* of 1721) is set a tone lower, to the words 'Sì, si vi rivedrò'.

Griselda represents a triumph for Italian taste. The voice predominates throughout, and even when two oboes or a solo flute appear they generally play *with* the voice and do not have separate solo parts. This should not be regarded as a defect, though it seems so at first, for all of these arias were really designed to show off the vocal expertise of the most famous singers of the day, who, by virtue of their unbelievably refined technique, performed them in a most effective and discriminating way. The written or printed notes were only the framework for the singer's highly individual interpretative skill. A profusion of additional notes was improvised, especially in the repeat of the first part of the *da capo* aria. A duet by Bononcini, 'Sempre piango', written in 1691, has been preserved together with elaborations of this sort by Carlo Antonio Benati.[1] Examples will be given later of original embellishments in arias by Handel and Hasse which give some idea of the lavish use of such improvisations.[2]

One of the highlights of *Griselda* is the following aria of Gualtiero in Act I, sung by the castrato Senesino. Note how the high register of the solo cellos combines with the low register of the castrato (bars 2 and 3), how the vocal melody grows out of the expressive declamation of single words, and how it remains flowing and animated despite the rests—an excellent piece of composition from a technical point of view. The concertante violins complement the voice part in such a way that it is never obscured, but enfolded in a clear three-part texture:

[1] Both versions printed in Ernest T. Ferand, *Improvisation in nine centuries of Western music* (Cologne, 1961), pp. 118–22.
[2] See *infra*, pp. 146 ff. and 158 ff.

Ex. 44

(My face will feign affection, joy and smiles, but my heart will weep and dissolve in tears of grief.)

Bononcini's operas also aroused keen interest in France, and the London opera company was invited to Paris in 1723 to perform his *Erminia*—a very rare honour in those days and one which Handel never experienced.[1] There are still several unfilled gaps in Giovanni Bononcini's life story, particularly the periods 1711–20 and 1733–40. But Hueber has thrown some light on his last years:[2] from 1740 Bononcini was again living in Vienna, where he supported himself on a small pension from the Empress Maria Theresa and where he died in dire poverty on 8 July 1747. In some respects he appears to have had a split personality; earlier in his life he had to resign his court appointment in Vienna as a result of unseemly conduct towards the emperor.

Antonio Bononcini (1677–1726), seven years younger than his brother Giovanni, is often confused with him, especially since he too composed numerous operas. Some of his contemporaries rated him higher than Giovanni, among them Padre Martini, who appreciated the stricter contrapuntal technique in Antonio's writing. As was mentioned in the previous chapter, Giovanni's opera *Il trionfo di Camilla* used to be ascribed to Antonio.[3] Similar confusion still exists in the case of *Griselda*, since Antonio also composed an opera of that name which was first performed in Milan in 1718. No score of this other *Griselda* was known to exist until the present writer discovered what is in all probability the missing opera, in a manuscript in the Staatsbibliothek, Berlin.[4] On the inside cover of this hitherto neglected manuscript there is the following pencilled inscription in an unknown hand: 'Griselda von Buononcini. Aufgeführt in London 1722' ('Bononcini's *Griselda*. Staged in London in 1722'). The title-page is missing. However, not one aria in this manuscript corresponds to any of those in the published arias from Giovanni Bononcini's *Griselda*. It seems natural to assume that this is Antonio's opera, especially since the music, with its numerous strict polyphonic passages in the introductions and accompaniments to the arias, is entirely in keeping with his style. Another point is that this opera is based on the libretto by Apostolo Zeno in its original form, whereas Giovanni, as we have seen, used a version that had been completely altered. The pencilled entry 'Aufgeführt in London 1722' must therefore, it seems, be regarded as erroneous, since the writer clearly did not know Giovanni's work and assumed that this manuscript was his opera.

---

[1] See F. W. Marpurg, *Kritische Einleitung in die Geschichte und Lehrsätze der alten und neuen Musik* (Berlin, 1759), p. 92.

[2] Hueber, 'Gli ultimi anni di Giovanni Bononcini: notizie e documenti inediti', *Accademia di Scienze, Lettere e Arti di Modena: Atti e Memorie*, ser. v, xii (1954), p. 153.

[3] Cf. *supra*, pp. 70 ff., and also p. 75.

[4] Berlin, Deutsche Staatsbibliothek, 2185.

Antonio based his *Griselda* on Zeno's text without changing it in any way, which indicates the high regard it inspired. In the recitatives he painstakingly ensures that the text is declaimed so as to bring out the poetic beauty of Zeno's language—unlike Scarlatti who in his later opera (1721) altered many details of the libretto, as did Vivaldi in *his Griselda* (Venice, 1735). Antonio Bononcini constructed his arias on the principle of expressive declamation of the text, introducing subtle variations, as in these extracts from the aria in Act II, scene 5, in which Griselda looks forward to her return to the countryside:

Ex. 45

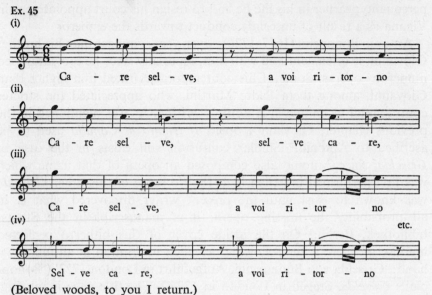

(Beloved woods, to you I return.)

The strictly symmetrical development of this aria through variations on its opening theme is clearly recognizable. Antonio gave the accompanying instruments a far greater degree of independence than did Giovanni. For instance, Ottone's aria in Act II, scene 8, 'La bella nemica', is accompanied by two *corni da caccia* as well as two violins; the horns and strings are given entirely different motives, suited to the character of each, as can be seen in bars 12 ff.:

Ex. 46

(Love will seize the fair enemy who stole my heart.)

Antonio had already written a contrapuntal accompaniment for three obbligato instruments to an aria in his opera *Arminio*, composed in 1706 for Vienna: Segimondo's aria 'Chiedo all'erbe' is accompanied by two oboes and bassoon, in a style somewhat similar to a Corelli trio-sonata —though of course this wind trio derived from French opera:[1]

Ex. 47

[1] Dresden, Landesbibl., Mus. 2209.F.1.

-le___ vi-o-le   Se il mio sol di___ quì pas-sò;

Di - con nò,   nò,   nò,

vio - le,___ vio - le ed er - be.

(I ask the grass and the violets whether my sun has passed this way; the violets and the grass say 'no'.)

The combination of Italian melody with French instrumentation is particularly obvious here. In the older Venetian manner most of the arias in his *Arminio* are accompanied only by the *basso continuo*. But here too he is already employing two concertante solo violins in an aria accompaniment, and there is a virtuoso part for concertante cello in Ismene's aria 'Innocente è chi ben'ama'. The voice parts are written expressly to show off the expertise of the singers—Segesto's bass aria 'Tu da morte' has extensive coloratura passages and leaps of up to a twelfth. The libretto for this *Arminio* was by the Viennese court poet Pietro Antonio Bernardoni and was intended to mark the birthday of the Emperor Joseph I. The old German Prince Arminius (Hermann) was a very popular figure at this time, and both Handel and Hasse also wrote operas called *Arminio*.

ZENO

From about 1700, the history of Italian opera takes a decisive turn with the introduction of a new style of libretto. The first major figure here was Apostolo Zeno, whose manner was developed by Pietro Metastasio; but the new style can in fact be traced back to the creation of a refined language in the circle around Queen Christina of Sweden in Rome and to the establishment of Arcadian academies in many Italian cities in the later years of the seventeenth century.[1] The baroque exuberance of the seventeenth-century librettos, which were full of surprises and complex entanglements, gave way to a simplified style, for which Zeno drew inspiration from classical drama as well as from the tragedies of Corneille and other French dramatists of his time. Zeno discarded all comic scenes and instead re-introduced choruses. His literary forebears were the librettists of the heroic operas in Venice and Vienna, Nicolò Minato and Silvio Stampiglia. The latter, whose aims he also honoured, he succeeded in 1718 as imperial court poet. Zeno's relatively new concept of language was based on those cornerstones of classical Italian poetry, Tasso and Ariosto. Opera librettos in the seventeenth and eighteenth centuries were looked on as literary achievements of the first order and were sometimes more highly regarded than plays and lyric poetry: in librettos all the arts had to be taken into account—a feat demanding extensive learning—and in any case Italian literature was at a fairly low ebb during much of the period. Some of Italy's more notable poets and writers wrote librettos—Giacinto Andrea

[1] See Nathaniel Burt, 'Opera in Arcadia', *Musical Quarterly*, xli (1955), p. 145; Robert Freeman, 'Apostolo Zeno's reform of the libretto', *Journal of the American Musicological Society*, xxi (1968), p. 321; and, for a study of several reworkings of the same libretto (by Silvio Stampiglia), idem, 'The Travels of *Partenope*', *Studies in Music History: essays for Oliver Strunk*, ed. Harold S. Powers (Princeton, 1968), p. 356.

Cicognini, Gabriello Chiabrera, Fulvio Testi, Giovanni Maria Crescim-
beni, and Carlo Goldoni among others. Perfection of language was the
first rule. This has often been overlooked by modern critics too ready to
accept the ensuing judgements of each generation, causing them to play
off the younger writers against the old, such as Zeno against Minato
and Stampiglia, Metastasio against Zeno, and Calzabigi against Metastasio. It was seldom realized how close these authors really were and
that they differed only in individual details.[1]

Zeno was a native of Venice, where he was mainly active as a librarian
and historian (numismatics was his special interest). He scored a great
success with his very first opera libretto and was encouraged by this to
continue writing. In all he wrote thirty-five librettos, fifteen of them in
collaboration with Pietro Pariati[2] (the extent of each writer's contribution to these texts is still uncertain). In addition, Zeno was the author
of seventeen oratorio texts, which had close affinities with the opera
librettos and were epoch-making in their genre. Zeno not only held a
mirror to the courtly baroque world; he also illustrated an ideal code of
duty for both the princes of the age and their subjects, much as Corneille
had done in the French theatre. Not only in style (as we have seen) but
also in content, then, Corneille, and his French contemporaries, were
among the most powerful influences on Zeno;[3] seventeenth-century
Italian librettos were another—a fact that is generally ignored and will
be referred to later. Loyalty and human steadfastness were the moral
requirements of 'virtù' as Zeno so often portrayed it on the Italian
operatic stage. Obedience to the law of the land, the renunciation of
personal desires for the sake of the common good: these were the kind
of moral objectives which Zeno dramatized by using important figures
from history as his examples. In this, his experience as a historian stood
him in good stead: he had a remarkable flair for finding unfamiliar
incidents in history and demonstrating their suitability as operatic
material.

In the second half of the seventeenth century operas, as we have seen,
were made up of a great number of short song-like arias. After 1700,
when composers began to extend the length of the arias, Zeno restricted
their number and varied and deepened the characterization. Arias were
inserted at specific points in the action, generally at the end of scenes,
either as commentaries or as soliloquies. Differences were made between
entrance arias, those sung in mid-scene, and exit arias. Entrance arias

---

[1] See Remo Giazotto, *Poesia melodrammatica e pensiero critico nel settecento* (Milan,
1952), *passim*.

[2] See Naborre Campanini, *Un precursore di Metastasio* (Florence, 1904).

[3] See Max Fehr, *Apostolo Zeno und seine Reform des Operntextes: ein Beitrag zur
Geschichte des Librettos* (Zürich, 1912).

were known as *escite*, since the singer came out on to the stage, and exit arias were *ingressi*, on the principle that the singer went off into the wings. The *ingressi* were not only the commonest but also the most important: they brought the scene to an end and gave the singer the opportunity for a dramatic exit; furthermore, this was the easiest way to break off the action; and even at the time of Metastasio these arias were still regarded as a substitute for the antique chorus, which used to make general observations at such points in the action. The librettos were mostly written for a particular theatre and for a particular group of singers; and an almost geometrical arrangement of the arias was observed. Each soloist was given a certain number of arias, which had to be different in character; in addition, no two arias of the same type might follow each other, even though sung by different soloists. The three main categories into which the arias were divided were: action arias (*arie d'azione*), metaphor arias, where the psychological state is portrayed through comparison with natural phenomena (storms, wind, waves, stars, etc.), and finally 'general' arias. When considered in detail, even finer distinctions can be drawn, and these will be discussed when we come to the work of Metastasio.

The underlying reason for this schematization of baroque librettos was neither self-consciousness nor ignorance, but a strong feeling for form and a judicious sense of economy, both lacking in the work of many later librettists. As in the old pastoral drama, the recitatives had to be strictly composed of seven- and eleven-syllable lines; the arias are a mixture of shorter and more varied verse-forms in which rhyme is an essential feature. Those who describe this formalism as pointless would do well to remember that the great seventeenth-century French tragedies were written in one verse-form exclusively, the alexandrine. The main emphasis in the librettos falls not on the arias but on the recitatives, which are often very long. This is clear from a glance at any of the texts in the beautiful edition of Zeno's complete works.[1] The performance of the recitatives was considered to imitate especially the style of the classical Greek drama. The stresses were laid down by the composer and executed by the singers with the utmost subtlety, even in fast tempi.

Eighteenth-century opinion—even Calzabigi, Metastasio's great admirer and publisher—often rated Zeno's librettos above those of Metastasio. His texts were set to music as often as those of Metastasio, right up to the nineteenth century. His *Griselda* alone was used by twelve different composers between 1701 and 1747. Slight modifications were sometimes introduced, generally cuts or changes in the aria texts;

[1] Zeno, *Poesie drammatiche*, 10 vols. (Venice, 1744).

Paolo Rolli adapted Zeno's *Faramondo* in this way for Handel in 1738.

There is no sign of a 'decline' in Italian opera librettos in the eighteenth century. In Italy, Zeno and Metastasio have always ranked among the great classics of the Italian language.

METASTASIO

If Pietro Metastasio had been nothing more than the poet of superficial beauty and a social culture based on reason for which he is taken today, his enormous overall influence in the eighteenth century would be incomprehensible. His influence can be traced in the classical German dramas of Friedrich Schiller, who derived from Metastasio not only the use of aphorisms but also his penchant for examples of human virtue. In 1786, J. A. Hiller could still praise Metastasio as the 'apostle of virtue, loyalty, obedience, patriotism, and of the duties of every social class'. Only in this light does it seem logical that Metastasio's librettos were on everyone's lips all over Europe and that in Italy, England, and Germany 'there was no man of taste, no well-educated young lady, who did not know them almost by heart'.[1]

Metastasio achieved this by infusing music into language. He generally wrote his librettos at the harpsichord and, unlike Zeno, was himself a trained singer and composer. In this way he not only made the composer's task simple, he also created poetic works which even without music were considered perfect stage plays and linguistic triumphs.[2] Although he frequently drew his inspiration from antique dramas, Metastasio developed these ideas with the means and methods of his own time. The action was concentrated in a mere handful of characters—usually six in all—and he devised an endless flow of tense situations and surprising twists in the plot. Metastasio's recitatives are always short and concise, in contrast to the long-drawn-out dialogues of French tragedy. The arias—or at any rate those at the end of scenes—are to be regarded as interludes taking over the role of the ancient chorus and making general comments on the events. This very important observation was made by Calzabigi;[3] it is of crucial significance for any interpretation of these arias and should be carefully noted by all producers of Handel's operas.

Idealizations always seem rather unreal, wooden, or stylized, and later generations have reproached Metastasio with all these criticisms, since

[1] Johann Adam Hiller, *Ueber Metastasio und seine Werke* (Leipzig, 1786). See Simon Towneley Worsthorne, 'Metastasio and the history of opera', *The Cambridge Journal*, vi (1952–3), p. 534.

[2] See Ranieri Calzabigi, 'Dissertazione su le poesie drammatiche del Sig. Abate Pietro Metastasio', in Metastasio, *Poesie* (Turin, 1757), i, pp. vi-vii.

[3] Ibid., i, pp. xvii ff.

by their standards the psychological development and the delineation of the different characters is apparently lacking. The formal structure of his librettos eventually passed unnoticed, and it was not recognized that Metastasio in fact presented a wide range of characters and that he paid close attention to the nature of the emotions. Today these things will be better appreciated, and the superb architecture of Metastasio's librettos will arouse as much admiration as the beauty of his poetry.[1]

Once again it was Calzabigi who pointed out[2] that Metastasio's heroes are of widely differing types and that they are characterized with great accuracy, from the fiery ambition of Achilles (in *Achille in Sciro*) to Megacles' loyal friendship (in *Olimpiade*) or the gentleness and generosity of Titus (in *La clemenza di Tito*). Metastasio usually shows his heroes faced with the conflict between love and duty, which results in a wide range of tense psychological situations—there is no question of a set pattern in the characterization. He was also criticized for the monotony of his happy endings; this, too, was refuted by Calzabigi, who cited among others the tragic conclusions of *Didone abbandonata* and *Catone in Utica*, two of the most popular opera librettos of the eighteenth century. Calzabigi further showed that Metastasian operas contain more 'truth' and 'verisimilitude' than the 'fantasies' of many French operas of the time, whose spirits, sorcerers, winds, and furies certainly lent colour to the stage performances but did nothing to increase the dramatic effect.[3] For this reason Metastasio's admirers often rated him above Quinault and even above Racine. He was indebted to Racine for many of his ideas, particularly in his oratorio *Gioas*, for which Racine's *Athalie* served as model. His opera librettos must also be seen in close relation to his oratorio texts, where he created similar idealizations, but of a religious nature.

Literary works are usually very difficult to translate into other languages. In the eighteenth century Metastasio's librettos had to endure clumsy, inept translations, as in Germany, and the resulting criticisms were quite false if applied to the originals; an exception must, however, be made for the translations into English by John Hoole.[4] Then again, the different adaptations to which the librettos had to submit did not always enhance them.

Metastasio's first full-length libretto was *Didone abbandonata*, performed in Naples in 1724, with music by Domenico Sarro, and again in Venice in 1725, with music by Tommaso Albinoni. Thereafter new

---

[1] See Rudolf Gerber, *Der Operntypus Johann Adolf Hasses und seine textlichen Grundlagen* (Leipzig, 1925), chap. 1.

[2] In op. cit., *passim*.

[3] Loc. cit.

[4] *The Works of Metastasio*, trans. John Hoole, 2 vols. (London, 1767).

librettos appeared almost every year and were set to music by the leading composers. Most of the earlier ones were set by Leonardo Vinci in Naples; but after Metastasio's summons to Vienna in 1730 to succeed Zeno as court poet, Antonio Caldara, and later Hasse, were his chief composers—Hasse probably set all but one of Metastasio's texts.[1] Apart from the full-scale librettos, usually in three acts, Metastasio wrote many smaller works—serenatas, birthday odes and the like. He continued to live in Vienna until 1782.

Metastasio's reputation, especially in Germany, is that of a formalistic reactionary whose work was superseded by Gluck; but in reality there has never been any basis for such a view. Romain Rolland pointed out that in essentials Metastasio was the direct forerunner of Gluck.[2] Metastasio stood for a culture of refinement and restraint and in him we find the domination of poetry and drama over music, the introduction of choruses at important points in the action, and an increased number of accompanied recitatives in relation to the arias. Metastasio's emphasis on the last of these points is particularly marked after 1749 in the librettos he wrote for Hasse.

NAPLES OR VENICE?

Besides Venice, many other Italian cities were engaged in furthering the cause of opera in the eighteenth century. Chief among these were Rome and Naples, but most of the other cities also had opera-houses whose repertoire was by no means restricted to well-established works— they commissioned new operas of their own. Naples grew into an important centre where many very successful composers worked, including Alessandro Scarlatti, Leo, Vinci, and Pergolesi. Naples was from 1714 to 1738 ruled by the Habsburg emperor, with the result that here, as in Vienna, opera was especially encouraged. Nevertheless, Naples's part in the history of opera has certainly been exaggerated by those who talk of a specifically 'Neapolitan' school which is supposed to have taken over the lead from the older 'Venetian' school. In the first place some of the so-called 'Neapolitan' operas had their premières in Rome or Venice. And their new style, which placed the emphasis on the vocal line so that the accompaniment was reduced to a harmonious background, was practised at the same time and even earlier in Venice, by composers such as Vivaldi, Lotti, and Giovanni Bononcini. It was also to be found in the music of Giuseppe Maria Orlandini in Florence and of Ignazio Conti and Hasse in Vienna and Dresden.

[1] See *infra*, p. 152.
[2] See 'Metastasio: the forerunner of Gluck' in his *Voyage musical au pays du passé* (Paris, 1919), p. 157; Eng. trans. (London, 1922), p. 145.

8

Even in the operatic heyday of eighteenth-century Naples, not more than three or four operas were ever performed in any one year. This is quite clear from Florimo's catalogue of all the operas staged there,[1] though the number of operas actually performed is not in itself decisive proof. However, a more detailed comparison with some of the operas by Venetian composers such as Vivaldi and Lotti reveals that the new style appeared in Venice before 1725, though a special study of the other contemporary Venetian composers would be necessary to corroborate this evidence.

The main centre of Italian opera, not only in the seventeenth century but throughout the whole of the eighteenth, was Venice. Between 1637 and 1800 no fewer than nineteen opera-houses were established there, many of them generally giving performances at the same time, so that in eighteenth-century Venice an average of from twelve to nineteen operas were staged in any one year;[2] the great majority were written specially for Venice. So rich was the crop of new operas that Venice must be acknowledged as a centre of the first magnitude, whose position has probably never been challenged since. The following figures give some idea of the number of operas performed: fifteen in 1709, twelve in 1725, fourteen in 1730, ten in 1760, sixteen in 1780, thirteen in 1791 and thirty-five in 1800. These random statistics set the pattern for all other years between 1700 and 1800. All the titles of these operas are known and their librettos have survived,[3] but in general, despite the fact that some scores are still extant, the composers are known only by their names. Tommaso Albinoni, Francesco Gasparini, Antonio Lotti, Antonio Bononcini, Luca Antonio Predieri, Antonio Zanettini, Giovanni Maria Ruggieri, Antonio Vivaldi, Giacopo Antonio Perti, Fortunato Chelleri, Giuseppe Maria Orlandini, Giuseppe Maria Buini: these are but a handful of the men who provided Venice with so many of her operas, and there are dozens more. This is a rich field that has hardly been touched by modern research.

[1] See Francesco Florimo, *La scuola musicale di Napoli e i suoi conservatorii*, 4 vols. (Naples, 1880–2); also see Helmut Hucke and Edward O. D. Downes, 'The Neapolitan tradition in opera' (two separate articles), *International Musicological Society: Report of the Eighth Congress, New York, 1961*, i (Kassel, etc., 1961), pp. 253 and 277, respectively; and Wolff, 'The fairy-tale of the Neapolitan opera', *Studies in eighteenth-century music: a tribute to Karl Geiringer on his seventieth birthday*, ed. H. C. Robbins Landon in collaboration with Roger E. Chapman (London, 1970), p. 401, extended as 'Das Märchen von der neapolitanischen Oper und Metastasio', *Analecta Musicologica*, ix (1970), p. 94. More generally, see Michael F. Robinson, *Naples and Neapolitan Opera* (Oxford, 1972).

[2] See Taddeo Wiel, *I teatri musicali veneziani del settecento* (Venice, 1897); also in *Archivio Veneto*, i-vii (1891–7).

[3] The Venetian opera librettos are all at Venice, in the Museo Goldoni, in the Biblioteca Marciana, and now in the Fondazione Cini too.

GASPARINI

One of the most celebrated of the Venetian opera composers after 1700 was Francesco Gasparini, who wrote more than sixty stage works. Apart from holding the appointment of *maestro del coro* at the Ospedale della Pietà, he composed twenty-four operas in Venice before 1713. After 1717 he lived in Rome. Most of the texts set to music by Gasparini are by Apostolo Zeno and Pietro Pariati—for example, *Ambleto* (1705), *Engelberta* (1708), *Sesostri* (1709), *Costantino* (1711), *Merope* (1711), and *Lucio Vero* (1719). Of special interest are Gasparini's tragedy *Taican, rè della Cina* (Venice, 1707), set, as the title indicates, in China, his comic operas *Anfitrione* (also 1707) and *L'avaro* (Venice, 1720), and numerous comic *intermezzi* which have already been mentioned.[1] Gasparini was one of the first Italians to have works performed in London, where he made his début in 1711 with the opera *Il più fedel fra i vassalli*, first heard in Venice in 1703 and done in London under the title *Antioco* (and not to be confused with his opera of that name first performed in Venice in 1705). In the following year his *Ambleto* scored a tremendous success, and Walsh published the arias from it.[2] Gasparini taught both Marcello and Quantz, and compiled perhaps the best-known text-book on practical thorough-bass playing, *L'armonico pratico al cimbalo* (Venice, 1708). It was as the author of this book— frequently republished—that his name remained known right through the eighteenth century, long after his operas had been forgotten.

Gasparini adopted the seventeenth-century Venetian style of aria accompanied by a *basso continuo*; but he also used solo instruments such as the oboe, as well as a string orchestra, to accompany the arias— for example in his opera *Tamerlano* (Venice, 1710), from which nine arias are extant.[3] The subject of this opera, a popular one at the time, contrasts the savagery and barbarity of the famous medieval emperor of the Mongols, Tamerlane, with the pride and passion of the equally volatile Turks, their leader Bajazet and his daughter Asteria. Marlowe had already dramatized this material in his play *Tamburlaine the Great* (1586), which was taken to Europe and made familiar in the seventeenth century by groups of strolling players and adapted as an opera libretto in Hamburg in 1690 by Christian Heinrich Postel.[4] Gasparini used a libretto by Agostino Piovene, which was later set by Handel (London, 1724), and other Tamerlane operas were composed by Marc'Antonio Ziani, Leo, Vivaldi, and Porpora. From beginning to end Piovene's

---

[1] See *supra*, pp. 69 ff.
[2] *Songs in the opera of Hamlet* (London, [1712]).
[3] Berlin, Deutsche Staatsbibliothek, 30.330, nos. 17–25.
[4] See Wolff, *Die Barockoper in Hamburg, 1678–1738* (Wolfenbüttel, 1957), i, pp. 51 ff.

libretto is packed with tense situations arising from the captive Bajazet's refusal to buy his freedom by sacrificing his daughter's honour—he prefers death, as does Asteria herself. Ultimately, in Act III, scene 9, Bajazet takes poison, whereupon Asteria comforts her father before he dies; Gasparini's melody here can instructively be compared with Handel's:[1]

Ex. 48
(i)   Gasparini

Pa-dre a - ma to,   vò__ per - do - no, ·   Se__ tra - di - sco

il mio do - ver,__   se__ tra - di - sco il mio do - ver.__

(ii)   Larghetto   Handel

Pa - dre a - ma - to, ·   in me   ri -

- po - sa,   Io quell' om - bra   ge - ne -

- ro - sa   A   mo - men - ti se - gui - rò

((i) Beloved father, I ask your pardon if I fail in my duty.)
((ii) Beloved father, trust in me; I will straightway follow that noble shade.)

Handel altered the text a little, to turn the plea for forgiveness ('Vò perdono') into words of consolation ('in me riposa'). Gasparini's melody relies heavily on conjunct motion, while Handel starts off with a downward leap of a fifth, introducing further sections with balancing leaps of a fourth (bars 5 and 9–10). From the outset Handel's melody is less static, whereas Gasparini builds up his melody gradually until in the last bar of the piece it culminates in an octave leap. A comparison of the two versions of Asteria's aria from Act I, scene 7, 'Deh!

[1] All Handel's operas appear in the complete edition of his works, ed. Chrysander. Some have so far appeared in the *Hallische Händel-Ausgabe*, Serie II (Kassel and Basle, 1955–). For similar comparisons of Handel and Hasse see *infra*, pp. 143 ff.

lasciatemi il nemico', reveals similar differences. Handel's melody is
quicker to reflect changes in mood and is marked by strong rhythms,
for example dotted notes, which make it more poignant than Gasparini's.
A further comparison is possible between the two versions of Asteria's
aria 'Cor di padre e cor d'amante' (Act III, scene 1):

Ex. 49

(i)   Gasparini

Cor___ di pa - dre e cor d'a - man - te, Sal - da fe - de,

o - dio co - stan — — — — — — — — te,

(ii)   Largo e staccato   Handel

Cor di___ pa - dre   e cor d'a-man - te,

Sal-da fe -de,   o - dio co-stan-te,

(Father's heart and lover's heart, steadfast faith, constant hate . . .)

Once again, in his setting as a continuo aria, Gasparini's melodic line moves conjunctly. Handel, setting the same text, uses wide, agitated leaps, given in this case to the accompanying violins, though the voice, too, has an octave leap in the very first bar which is twice repeated by the violins. Handel's scoring for the concertante instruments in the accompaniment, and his chromatically descending bass line, create additional movement and agitation, whereas Gasparini concentrates on bringing out Asteria's irresistible determination, through the use of even crotchets and a firm roulade: his manner here harks back to the seventeenth century.

LOTTI

Venice was also the main centre of activity of Antonio Lotti (1667–1740);[1] between 1692 and 1719 he composed some twenty operas, in which he not only carried on the tradition of his teacher Legrenzi but in addition adapted his music to the new stylistic ideal that put the main emphasis in the arias on solo melody. The climax of Lotti's operatic career came when he was appointed in 1718 to the court at Dresden, where his opera Teofane was performed at the opening of the new opera-house in 1719. The cast included famous singers from Italy such as Senesino, Giuseppe Boschi, Durastanti, and Lotti's wife, the prima donna Santa Stella. Lotti then suddenly returned to Venice, abandoned opera completely and concentrated exclusively on writing sacred choral works, for which he is now best known. Like Gasparini and Pollaroli, he elaborated the tripartite da capo aria, scoring for concertante instruments and providing coloratura passages for the singers.

For his Teofane Lotti used a libretto by Stefano Pallavicino (son of the composer Carlo Pallavicino); it was on this same libretto that only a few years later Handel based his opera Ottone (London, 1722).[2] Handel certainly made considerable cuts and had several aria texts rewritten, but, overall, the texts have so much in common that a comparison of the two works is perfectly legitimate. Lotti broke up Adalberto's love song 'Bel labbro, formato' into small units of two bars each, with the melody rising in the first group and falling in the second.[3]

---

[1] On Lotti see Charlotte Spitz, Antonio Lotti und seine Bedeutung als Opernkomponist (Diss., Munich, 1918, unpub.).

[2] See idem, 'Die Opern "Ottone" von G. F. Händel (London, 1722) und "Teofane" von A. Lotti (Dresden, 1719); ein Stilvergleich', Festschrift zum 50. Geburtstag Adolf Sandberger (Munich, 1918), p. 265.

[3] The manuscript is in the Landesbibliothek, Dresden.

Ex. 50

Bel lab - bro,__ for - ma - to   Per far - mi   be -

a - to,   per far - mi__ be - a - to,   Il   no - me a-mo - ro - so   etc.

(Pretty lips, made for my delight, learn to repeat the loving name)

Here Lotti was aiming at a harmonious rise and fall in the melodic line. By contrast, Handel set the words to a single, continuous eight-bar melody:

Ex. 51

Larghetto

Bel lab - bro,   for - ma - to   Per far - mi   be - a - to,   Il

no - me   di   spo - so   im - pa - ra a__ ri - dir,

(Pretty lips, made for my delight, learn to repeat the husband's name)

In bars 1 and 6 the melody rises by a sixth; these leaps are separated by broad, stepwise descending movement, which is more compactly repeated in bar 7. Such sweeping curves and balanced construction are typical of Handel's melodies.

Adalberto has passed himself off as Ottone in a bid to win the love of Teofane, who does not yet know Ottone; he is pursuing political ends under cover of his projected marriage with Teofane. When she discovers the deception, at a dramatic moment in the action, she sings a long aria expressing her sense of outrage, 'Falsa immagine'—referring to the 'false semblance' by which she has been beguiled. At the beginning of this aria Lotti represents a violent outburst of anger by two leaps in the vocal line, dotted rhythm and emphatic repetition of the second phrase:

Ex. 52

Fal - sa im - ma - gi - ne, m'in - gan - na - sti, m'in - gan- - na - sti, Mi mo - stra - sti Un vol - - to a- - ma - - - - - bi - le,

(False semblance, thou didst deceive me, thou didst show me a kindly face.)

Another symmetrical pattern occurs in the roulade of bars 12–15. Handel's approach to the same aria is quite different:

Ex. 53

Fal - sa im - ma - gi - ne, m'in - gan - na - sti, Mi mo - - stra - sti Un vol - to a - ma - bi - le, E quel vol - to__ m'al - let - - tò,_____ e quel vol - to m'al - let - tò.

(. . . and that face delighted me.)

His opening is calmer, though he does enliven the movement by dotted notes; there is a sudden upsurge of emotion at 'mi mostrasti' which is very similar to the opening of Lotti's aria. Then in the third bar Handel leads the voice slowly upwards, keeping to a dotted rhythm, through a whole octave—a development of the first motive; in this way he succeeds in creating formal unity and a mounting tension. (This was the aria, incidentally, which, so the story goes, Francesca Cuzzoni found lacking in virtuosity and which resulted in the famous scene during which Handel threatened to hold her out of an open window in a successful attempt to make her change her mind.) It should be emphasized that neither Lotti nor Handel was much concerned with vocal virtuosity. Both concentrated rather on interpreting the text in the most expressive way possible, and coloratura passages and embellishments were added purely to heighten the emotional effect. It is clear that Lotti had a preference for shorter phrases symmetrically arranged, while Handel's taste was for sweeping melodic curves and stronger accentuation both in melody and rhythm, still without neglecting symmetry.

VIVALDI

Antonio Vivaldi (1678–1741)[1] must rank as one of Venice's favourite composers of opera, with forty-six to his credit, of which for a long time only the titles were known, and there was even some uncertainty about these.[2] The scores of twenty-two operas are extant and are now in the Biblioteca Nazionale, Turin. They were mostly written for Venice, between 1713 and 1738. Since the manuscripts have not yet been fully authenticated it would be rash to accept them all as being incontestably the work of Vivaldi, though the majority bear his cipher and must be regarded as autographs (he used the letters of his surname to devise a monogram). Comment on the works, therefore, must necessarily be made with some reservations.

Many of Vivaldi's librettos are seventeenth-century texts previously set by other composers: there is nothing unusual in this—indeed it was quite a common practice. For example, *L'incoronazione di Dario* (Venice, 1716) by Adriano Morselli had already been used by Giovanni Domenico Freschi in 1685; *Il Giustino* by Niccolò Beregan, set to music by Legrenzi in 1683, was the basis for Vivaldi's opera of 1724, written for Rome; and Giacomo Francesco Bussani's *Ercole sul Termodonte*, which Vivaldi set for Rome in 1723, had been set by Sartorio in 1678.[3] Others among Vivaldi's librettists are Silvio Stampiglia, Zeno, and Metastasio: *Atenaide* (Verona, 1732), *Griselda* (Venice, 1735), and *Teuzzone* (place and date unknown) have texts by Zeno, *L'Olimpiade* (Venice, 1734) and *Catone in Utica* (Venice, 1737) by Metastasio.

From a musical point of view Vivaldi's operas all reveal the absolute dominance of vocal melody. The accompaniment almost invariably provides nothing more than a pleasant background, though there is a certain amount of imitative writing; often, however, the voice part is also played by the orchestra. Vivaldi also uses concertante instruments: there are, for instance, one horn in *L'Olimpiade* (see Ex. 56), two horns in *Griselda*, and a solo violin (with string orchestra) in *Armida al campo*

[1] There is a large Vivaldi bibliography. See, on the operas in particular, Marc Pincherle, *Vivaldi* (Paris, 1955); Eng. trans. (London, 1958), pp. 200–16; Walter Kolneder, *Antonio Vivaldi* (Wiesbaden, 1965); Eng. trans. (London, 1970), pp. 156–88; and Wolff, 'Vivaldi und der Stil der italienischen Oper', *Acta Musicologica*, xl (1968), p. 179.

[2] See Mario Rinaldi, *Catalogo numerico tematico delle composizioni di Antonio Vivaldi* (Rome, 1945), pp. 243–54.

[3] See Wolff, *Die venezianische Oper in der zweiten Hälfte des 17. Jahrhunderts* (Berlin 1937), pp. 53 and 106 f.

d'Egitto (Venice, 1718). He also wrote a virtuoso flute part, with strings *senza cembalo*, for the aria 'Sol da te, mio dolce amore' in *Orlando furioso* (Venice, 1727).[1] In *Il Giustino* there is even a *salterio* (psaltery or dulcimer), an instrument which since about 1700 was enjoying a return to popularity in Europe; it was of oriental origin and in Venice was played by the women students of the conservatories, who clearly must have taken part in operatic productions. As a rule, these 'concertante' instruments seldom diverge far from the voice part, which they accompany in sixths or thirds or in unison, or lightly embellish: true concertante scoring is rare.

The basis of all the aria accompaniments in Vivaldi's operas is the string orchestra, frequently without harpsichord continuo; in the aria 'Alla rosa rugiadosa' in *Orlando finto pazzo* (Venice, 1714)[2] the entire accompaniment is played pizzicato by the strings. The timbre of Vivaldi's orchestra was quite different from that of Scarlatti, Gasparini and seventeenth-century composers, where with very isolated exceptions the *basso continuo* always accompanies the arias and the writing is invariably in at least two parts. Vivaldi's bass parts support the harmony and are generally non-thematic in character. The timbre and style of what used to be called 'Neapolitan' opera are already fully developed in Vivaldi's operas, most of which were written before the early operas of Leo, Vinci, and Pergolesi.

The orchestral ritornellos to Vivaldi's arias include a certain amount of imitative writing, though this disappears on the entry of the voice. For example, Arianna's aria 'Mio dolce amato sposo' at the end of the second act of *Il Giustino* starts off with imitative entries on the strings, which then quickly move on to take up the voice part and to give it a harmonic accompaniment:[3]

Ex. 54

[1] Turin, Bibl. Naz., Giordano XI (=39b).
[2] Turin, Bibl. Naz., Giordano VIII (=38), ff. 28–9.
[3] Turin, Bibl. Naz., Foà III (=34), ff. 68–71; it is printed complete in Wolff, *The Opera*, ii (Cologne, 1971), no. 7.

(My dear, beloved husband, I shall know how to die content; since I die faithful I die resolute.)

This aria is in no way exceptional—on the contrary, it represents the dominant style found in Vivaldi's operas. By the repetition of words and phrases he stresses the mood of urgency, an urgency which he also builds up slowly by increasingly using wider intervals, as in bar 5, where a downward leap of a perfect fifth is followed at once by an upward leap of a diminished fifth. He renews the tension by inserting a coloratura passage on the word 'costante' (where Ex. 54 breaks off). This aria gives some idea of the wide range of pregnant motives that Vivaldi normally employed. In his own version of *Il Giustino*, thirteen years later, Handel made this aria shorter, with broader, curving melodies, and he gave the orchestral accompaniment independent motives, such as the falling chromatic figure shown in the following example. The similarity between a phrase in bar 3 of Handel's aria and Vivaldi's initial theme is certainly accidental, though it points to the existence at that period of a common style:

Ex. 55

Vivaldi's *L'Olimpiade* (Venice, 1734) is based on one of Metastasio's best-known and most frequently used librettos.[1] The central character is the noble and selfless Greek Megacles, who competes in the Olympic Games on behalf of his friend Lycidas, hoping to win for him the hand of the king's daughter, which is the victor's prize. Megacles does not suspect that the girl in question is Aristea, with whom he himself has long been happily in love. In the ensuing conflict between loyalty to his friend and love for a woman, Megacles chooses the first. He determines to kill himself rather than break his pledge to Lycidas, then to accept the death penalty imposed on him for the deception practised in the games. In the end, however, Lycidas is put to death as the instigator of the crime, and the lovers are united. Calzabigi described Megacles as 'the most virtuous, humane, and amiable character ever presented on the stage'.[2] It is easy to understand the enthusiasm such a story aroused in the eighteenth century, presenting as it did the perfect image of human

---

[1] It is one of those discussed in Burt, 'Plus ça change, or, the progress of reform in seventeenth- and eighteenth-century opera as illustrated in the books of three operas', *Studies in Music History*, p. 325.

[2] See op. cit., p. lxxxii.

loyalty, touchingly and effectively drawn. In the previous year Metastasio's text had received its first performance in a setting by Caldara
in Vienna, and Vivaldi was one of the first to introduce the story to
Italian audiences. These Italian operas are not to be considered
separately from their librettos, as mere stage concerts—the texts were
frequently more important than the music. The first priority in this
opera, then, was that Metastasio's affecting poetry should be heard,
expressively declaimed and acted. The arias were only in the nature of
interludes, as has been mentioned earlier.

At one point Lycidas chances on the sleeping Megacles and wishes
him peaceful dreams, little knowing what terrible thoughts torment the
other's heart. Vivaldi creates the atmosphere of dream-filled sleep by
using a *corno da caccia* in the orchestral accompaniment to this aria,
delicately supported by the strings:[1]

Ex. 56

[1] Turin, Bibl. Naz., Foà I (=39), ff. 44 ff.

-cer de' son-ni tuo-i Con l'i-de -

- - - a del mio pia - cer, del mio— pia-cer.

(While you sleep, may love increase the pleasure of your dreams with the thought of my pleasure.)

Lycidas starts off with the notes of the triad of F major, the basic key of the horn, and thereafter the vocal line moves for the most part sinuously and seductively in conjunct motion. Sequences in bars 3 and 4 lend clarity to the structure, and the word 'idea' is highlighted by an exciting coloratura passage. When Pergolesi set the same libretto the following year, and Leo three years later, they both used two horns in this aria, possibly under the influence of Vivaldi's setting.[1]

[1] See *infra*, pp. 108 and 124 ff., including Exx. 58 and 69.

The story of Roland's madness, well known in Italy since Ariosto's
Orlando furioso, played quite a prominent part in Vivaldi's operatic
career. In addition to the two settings of Grazio Braccioli's *Orlando*
libretto already mentioned – *Orlando finto pazzo* and *Orlando furioso*—
two acts survive of another setting called simply *Orlando*.[1] *Orlando
furioso* includes chorus scenes, and to round off the acts there are duets
and trios; this was to become a common feature of operas by Leo,
Vinci and Caldara. Vivaldi's choruses are not markedly polyphonic: the
voices tend rather to alternate with one another or else move in parallel
thirds or sixths. Short parenthetic interjections enliven the trio at the
end of Act II of his *Griselda*, sung by the three main characters,
Costanza, Griselda, and Gualtiero. Each singer is to some extent
characterized by individual themes, as for instance Gualtiero's bugle-
call motif (bar 6):[2]

Ex. 57

[1] Turin, Bibl. Naz., Giordano XII (=37).
[2] Turin, Bibl. Naz., Foà 36.

(Gr: No longer queen, but a shepherdess, I am not your bride but your servant. C: Pity the poor girl, for her constancy deserves it. Gu: Look on me and tremble, I am yours! C, Gr: Pity, mercy! Gr: Hear me! Gu: Be silent. It is in vain. C: Look at her. C, Gr (then Gu): How harsh a verdict, what terrible sorrow, what outrage I feel . . .)

Points of particular interest here are the initial absence of the continuo and—important for the future—the contrasting motives and the rapid exchange of dialogue, reminiscent of the comic operas of the period. Vivaldi completely altered the words for this trio; but even before this, in 1721, Scarlatti had substituted a different text at the same point in Zeno's libretto, though he too turned it into a trio, whereas Antonio Bononcini had kept strictly to Zeno's original words.[1]

[1] See *supra*, pp. 81 ff. An opera by Vivaldi not discussed here, *La fida ninfa* (Verona, 1732), is available ed. Raffaello Monterosso (Cremona, 1964).

9

LEO

Leonardo Leo (1694–1744)[1] worked in Naples, where he first became known through his sacred dramas, some of which—*La morte d'Abele* in particular—are still known in Italy. It is therefore mostly in the context of church music that his name is known, with works such as his *Miserere* (1739), written for two choirs, through which he restored to favour in Naples the strict style of Palestrina. Leo composed some thirty serious operas, not only for Naples, since some were for performance in Venice, Bologna, Milan, and Turin; however, he wrote practically all of his twenty-five *commedie musicali* and *intermezzi* for Naples and in Neapolitan dialect. With Leo, and Vinci too, the middle-class *opera buffa* of the eighteenth century took on new importance.

In the arias of his *opere serie* Leo firmly established the dominance of the solo voice, following the precedent already set by Vivaldi in Venice. Once again we often find the orchestra simply providing an agreeable background of no thematic importance, though Leo was expert at devising new instrumental figures. A good example of this is Lycidas's slumber aria from *L'Olimpiade* (Naples, 1737), already referred to in the previous section on Vivaldi. In Leo's accompaniment the strings maintain a steady but agitated undercurrent of sound in sextuplets:[2]

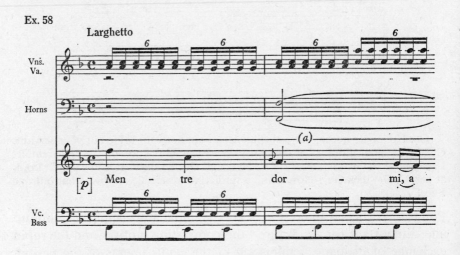

Ex. 58

[1] On Leo see Giacomo Leo, *Leonardo Leo, musicista del secolo XVIII., e le sue opere musicali* (Naples, 1905); Dent, 'Leonardo Leo', *Sammelbände der internationalen Musikgesellschaft*, viii (1906–7), p. 550; and Giuseppe A. Pastore, *Leonardo Leo* (Galatina, 1957). His operas are listed in Hucke's article on him in *Die Musik in Geschichte und Gegenwart*, viii (1960), cols. 625–6. There is a modern edition of a comic opera not mentioned in this section, *Amor vuol sofferenze*, ed. Pastore (Bari, 1962).

[2] Dresden, Landesbibl., 2209.F.1.

(While you sleep, may love increase the pleasure of your dreams with the thought of my pleasure.)

It has been suggested above in connection with Ex. 56 that Leo possibly knew Vivaldi's setting of these words. Nevertheless he shows his individuality in various ways; for instance, his vocal line is much more lively, moving in wide intervals which are almost instrumental in character. Leo also clearly took Metastasio's text as his starting-point, dividing it into three clearly defined sections (*a*, *b*, and *c*), each section containing its own musical motive. In the next section these three elements are varied and developed. Leo gave the middle section of the aria a different tempo and rhythm, thus introducing an element of contrast not found in Vivaldi's aria.

As late as 1782, the aria 'Non sò con dolce moto', from Leo's opera *Ciro riconosciuto* (Turin, 1739), was still regarded by Reichardt as the perfect example of an accomplished and varied melodic structure, and an excellent setting of the text, expressing the grief of 'a resolute father faced with the suffering of his innocent child'.[1] Reichardt comments on the splendid effect created by the break in the vocal line after the first two words, when the instruments take over:

Ex. 59

---

[1] See Johann Friedrich Reichardt, *Musikalisches Kunstmagazin*, i (1782), pp. 39–41.

(I do not know . . . my heart trembles in my breast with gentle movement: I feel a passion never felt before that makes me melt with tenderness.)

The 'broad, rapid and laboured strides' give the vocal line great power, and the coloratura passage on 'fa' creates a 'sublime, excellent, irresistible' portrayal of the 'strongly flowing tears of the resolute father'. After this eulogy, however, Reichardt becomes critical of the 'exaggerated emotionalism' of this aria, whose agitated music is, he claims, on several occasions at variance with the mood of the text, which contains phrases such as 'dolce moto' and 'affetto ignoto'. He puts his finger here on the important element of baroque exuberance, which leads Leo to portray alarm and despair when Reichardt, clearly speaking with the 'reasonable' voice of the late eighteenth century, would have preferred a mood of more restrained grief.

In Leo's operas the striking modulations, skilful contrapuntal orchestral parts and surprising new-style dynamic contrasts were all original features destined to have a decisive influence on the whole field of eighteenth-century opera.[1] These points are illustrated by the following hitherto unpublished examples taken from Leo's *L'Andromaca* (Naples, 1742), for which Antonio Salvi wrote the libretto. This opera, a notable work of Leo's maturity, is perhaps one of the finest achievements in eighteenth-century Italian opera. Vocal music and drama are here brought together in ideal union, and powerful accompanied recitatives interpret the emotions of fear, rage, and despair in an entirely new way. The central figure is Andromache, familiar from Racine's *Andromaque*, whose young son is to be put to death. These scenes have the power and greatness of classical tragedy. In the following extract Leo uses a precisely controlled crescendo to build up the tension:[2]

[1] See Dent in *Sammelbände der internationalen Musikgesellschaft*, viii; also Hermann Abert, *Niccolò Jommelli als Opernkomponist* (Halle, 1908), pp. 116 ff.

[2] This and the next two examples are from Leipzig, Städtische Musikbibl., Mus. 3860. See Wolff, 'Leonardo Leo's Oper "L'Andromaca" (1742)', *Studi musicali*, i (1972), p. 285.

Ex. 60

(You do not pity me in my danger, overbearing mother!)

Leo also integrates into the orchestral accompaniment frequent un-expected contrasts between *forte* and *piano*, a fundamental means of expressing emotion that he uses in, for example, Orestes's aria 'In placida sembianza' at most appropriate words:

Ex. 61

(But an icy fear troubles hope.)

The style of the so-called Mannheim school of instrumental music is clearly prefigured here: its practitioners obviously owe much more to Italian opera than has generally been assumed.[1] Leo's varied, polyphonic orchestral writing can be illustrated from an aria sung by Pylades in the first act in which the brilliance of the vocal writing, the colourful touches from the horns, and the orchestral crescendo (in bars 3–6) are all stylistic innovations:

[1] See Lucian Kamieński, 'Mannheim und Italien', *Sammelbände der internationalen Musikgesellschaft*, x (1908–9), p. 307.

Ex. 62

(Firm rock amid the battering of the waves ...)

Spurred on by Metastasio and by his own preoccupation with classical drama, Leo included large-scale choral passages in his operas, for which he enlisted the services of the women students of the Conservatorio Santa Maria della Pietà dei Turchini in Naples. However, these choruses were not, as in his oratorios, extensive polyphonic movements, but as a rule simple homophonic pieces such as the one in Act I, scene 4 of *L'Olimpiade*. Here a chorus of shepherds and shepherdesses appears on stage singing the introduction to an aria by Argene. Of even greater interest are the duets, trios and quartets with which Leo punctuates serious and comic operas alike: they feature even in quite early works such as *Zenobia in Palmira* (an *opera seria* performed in Naples in 1725) and the comic opera *Lo matrimonio annascuso* (Naples, *c.* 1727), where for the first time he introduced a two-part (slow-fast) form in such an ensemble (previously they had always been written in three-part *da capo* form).[1] A rapid exchange of dialogue highlights these ensembles, a device that Leo also used in his comic Neapolitan-dialect opera *La somiglianza di chi l'ha fatta* (Naples, 1726):[2]

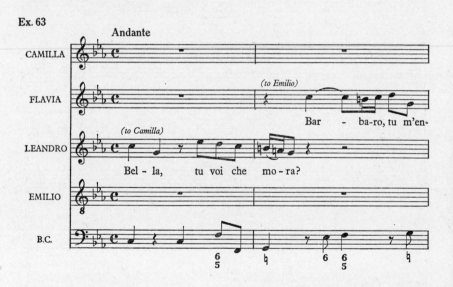

Ex. 63

[1] See Dent, 'Ensembles and finales in 18th-century Italian opera', *Sammelbände der internationalen Musikgesellschaft*, xii (1910–11), p. 112, and Marianne Fuchs, *Die Entwicklung des Finales in der italiënischen Opera buffa vor Mozart* (Diss., Vienna, 1932, unpub.).

[2] Manuscript at Naples, Conservatorio di Musica. Information from Helmut Hucke on this opera and Vinci's *Artaserse* and *Le zite 'n galera*.

L: Fair one, do you want to die? F: Cruel one, you deceive me! C: No, don't die yet! E: Ah! do not cause me more pain. F, L: Ah sad reply, farewell, farewell! C, E: You have my love!)

Quartets of this type revive the old art of polyphonic writing, complete with imitations and strict progressions. For his many comic operas Leo generally chose stories of middle-class love and marriage, though on occasion he turned to parody. Gay dance rhythms and *buffo* motives, popular songs and dances of all kinds, but especially the *siciliano* and the barcarolle, and even the chaconne, are typical of the music of these almost entirely neglected works.

VINCI

Leonardo Vinci (?–1730)[1] composed some thirty-six operas, about two-thirds of them for Naples and most of the remainder for Rome. He is the acknowledged creator of the Neapolitan-dialect opera, but his output also includes a large number of *opere serie*. He was the first composer to set to music in any great number the texts of Metastasio, with whom he evidently had very close affinities: his settings of *Siroè, re di Persia* (Venice, 1726), *Catone in Utica* (Rome, 1727), *Alessandro nell'Indie* (Rome, 1729) and *Artaserse* (Rome, 1730) are particularly noteworthy. Vinci's primary concern was the expressive rendering of Metastasio's verse, whether in recitatives or arias. When we remember what attention Metastasio's contemporaries paid to the recitatives in his librettos it is clear that we too must carefully study both them and the most scrupulous settings of them. The following is an example from Act II, scene 11, of Vinci's *Artaserse*:[2]

Ex. 64

ARBACE

Ec - co-mi, ec - co-mi a pie - di tuoi. Scu - sa i tra - spor - ti

d'un in - sa - no do - lor. Tut - to il mio

[1] On Vinci see Dent, 'Notes on Leonardo Vinci', *The Musical Antiquary*, iv (1912–13), p. 193; Alberto Cametti, 'Leonardo Vinci e suoi drammi in musica al Teatro delle Dame', *Musica d'oggi*, vi (1924), p. 297; Giuseppe Silvestri Silva, *Illustri musicisti calabresi: Leonardo Vinci* (Genoa, 1935); and Ulisse Prota-Giurleo, 'Leonardo Vinci', *Il convegno musicale*, ii (1965), p. 3.

[2] Manuscript at Naples, Conservatorio di Musica, from which this and the next two examples are taken.

san - gue si ver - si pur non me ne la - gno, e in -

-ve - ce di chia - mar - la ti - ran - na, io

ARTABACE

ba - cio quel - la man che mi con - dan - na. Ba - sta,

sor - gi; pur trop - po hai ra - gion di la - gnar - ti. Ma

sap - pi... (Oh Dio!) Pren - di un ab - brac - cio, e par - ti!

(Arb: Behold me at thy feet. Forgive the transports of frenzied anguish. If you shed my blood I bear no resentment, and instead of accusing I kiss the hand that strikes me. Art: Enough, arise. You have good cause to bear resentment. But I know . . . (oh God!) Let me embrace you and go!)

The compactness and economy of the scene are remarkable: Artabace, whom agitation almost robs of speech, breaks off in mid-sentence. In Arbace's anxious pleas there are longer phrases and more conjunct motion than in Artabace's reply, which gains in authority from the shorter phrases and higher proportion of wider intervals. Vinci's accompanied recitatives are also frequent and distinguished.

Semira's aria at the end of Act I of *Artaserse* illustrates how concisely many of Vinci's arias are written. Here Semira likens her state of mind to a river which threatens to depart from its accustomed course. The waves are suggested by roulades. The snatches of imitation in the orchestral accompaniment enhance the effect of compression:

Ex. 65

(Should the river change its flow, it tries to burst forth from its accustomed bed.)

A lavish use of appoggiaturas, especially when associated with dotted rhythms, gives Vinci's melodic writing that sense of increased intensity and sensibility which came to be regarded as one of the most important characteristics of music around the middle of the eighteenth century. It is clearly seen in Arbace's aria from Act II, scene 10, of *Artaserse*:

Ex. 66

(Through that paternal embrace, through this last farewell . . .)

Pergolesi, Hasse, and Graun wrote in this style, which eventually passed
into instrumental music. Basically it is a kind of syncopation, which
appears in another form in Vinci's *Alessandro nell'Indie*, when Cleofide's
grief at parting is conveyed by suitably gentler syncopated rhythms
(Ex. 67(i)).[1] Such rhythms threatened to swamp Italian opera altogether
and properly belong to that era of excessive sensibility known as
'Empfindsamkeit'.

Ex. 67 (i)

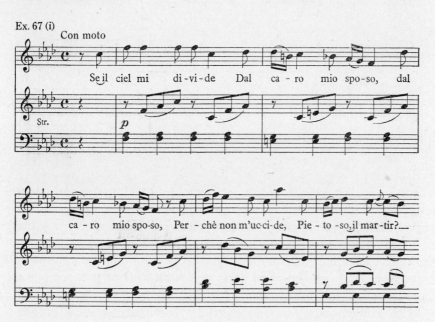

(If heaven separates me from my beloved husband, why does grief in its mercy
not kill me?)

A comparison with Handel's setting of the same text (in *Poro*, London,
1731) is particularly interesting:

Ex. 67 (ii)

[1] Taken from F. A. Gevaert, *Les gloires de l'Italie* (Paris, 1868), ii, pp. 136 ff.

There is a striking contrast here between 'old-fashioned' and 'modern' music, virtually between baroque and rococo styles. Vinci, only five years Handel's junior and writing two years earlier, offers an entirely harmonic accompaniment, whereas Handel writes a strict three-part setting in which the violin and bass go their separate ways; it is true that they keep pace with the vocal part, but at the end of the example the three lines are truly independent.

In his comic operas Vinci adopted the style of the *scene buffe*, broadening it by introducing elements of *opera seria*—longer arias, larger ensembles (more trios and quartets in place of duets) and greater use of the orchestra. The new eighteenth-century *opera buffa* was thus in many respects directly descended from *opera seria*. This is borne out by Vinci's dialect opera *Le zite 'n galera* (Naples, 1721), a comedy of disguises and errors in which the chief characters are a barber and a pirate's daughter.[1] The opera is set, as were most of these Neapolitan comedies, in the streets and squares of Naples itself. Neapolitan folk music forms the basis of the score, elaborated by the use of *opera seria* forms. Now, however important these dialect operas were for Naples and for Italy, their significance should not be overrated: the comic *intermezzi* written in Italian were much more famous and important through their performance all over Europe by pairs of virtuoso singers. Vinci left his mark on this genre too and indeed wrote what was possibly

[1] See Nicola d'Arienzo, 'Origini dell'opera comica', *Rivista musicale italiana*, vi (1899), p. 473, and Andrea della Corte, *L'opera comica italiana nel '700: studi ed appunti*, 2 vols. (Bari, 1923).

the most famous of all early eighteenth-century *intermezzi, Il giocatore* (*Serpilla e Bacocco, ovvero Il marito giocatore e la moglie bacchettona*— Gambling husband and bigoted wife), with libretto by Antonio Salvi. These three scenes were first given in Venice in 1718 and subsequently performed in adaptations and translations in Brussels, Hamburg, London and Paris.[1] As with most of these *intermezzi*, the scenes were originally inserted between the acts of an *opera seria* before being performed as a separate one-act opera. *Il giocatore* is a satire on compulsive gambling, which threatens to destroy a marriage. There are scenes before a divorce lawyer, and parodies of scenes of lamenting and suicide. The composer Giuseppe Maria Orlandini has often been credited with this effective score, but a comparison of the various extant versions reveals that Orlandini merely arranged Vinci's original music.[2] Orlandini transposed Serpilla's part from alto to soprano, augmented the orchestral accompaniment and made a few small changes in the duets; he also wrote one or two new arias for Serpilla. Here is the opening of the final duet from scene 1 of this as yet unpublished score, showing Vinci's use of the babbling *buffo* style:[3]

Ex. 68

[1] See Wolff, *Die Barockoper in Hamburg*, i, pp. 123 ff.

[2] See Georgy Calmus, 'Leonardo Vinci, der Komponist von Serpilla e Bacocco', *Zeitschrift der internationalen Musikgesellschaft*, xiv (1912–13), p. 170, and O. G. Sonneck, '*Il Giocatore*', *The Musical Antiquary*, iv (1912–13), p. 160. Two main sources at Wolfenbüttel, Landesbibl., 257–8, are clearly marked with Vinci's name. The manuscript at Rostock, Universitätsbibl. (Mus. Sacr. XVIII.49,5) is attributed to Orlandini, although, apart from the changes mentioned above, it corresponds to the two Wolfenbüttel manuscripts.

[3] Taken from Wolfenbüttel, Landesbibl., 257.

Dia - vo -lo, Dia - vo -lo, Dia -vo -lo, il Dia - vol con

te, Di - vor — tio, di - vor - tio!

Se più

★ these two notes added by Orlandini

(S: For years I have listened to such promises. No longer I believe thee, no, no, no, devil incarnate. Divorce! B: Serpilla, my sweet, no more I'll play dice and cards. If ever I wrong thee again . . .)

The rapid reiteration of words and notes, the contrasting tempi, the comically excited reproaches and endearments, became permanent features of comic opera: for instance, all of them appear in the works of Nicola Logroscino (1698–?1765), written somewhat later, between 1738 and 1765. Logroscino was for a long time mistakenly held to be the inventor of the *buffo* finale;[1] but this theory was disproved as early as 1910 by Dent, who referred back to the older ensembles of Scarlatti and Leo.[2]

PERGOLESI

The importance of Giovanni Battista Pergolesi (1710–36) is usually vastly overrated. His international reputation stems from the famous performance of *La serva padrona* which took place in Paris sixteen years after his death. The success of this opera caused an upsurge of interest in his other works. Eventually more works were ascribed to him than he could possibly have written before he died in his twenty-sixth year, including a large proportion of the compositions which have become well known under his name. Only since 1949 has a

[1] See Hermann Kretzschmar, 'Zwei Opern Nicolò Logroscinos', *Jahrbuch der Musikbibliothek Peters*, xv (1908), pp. 47–8.
[2] See Dent in *Sammelbände der internationalen Musikgesellschaft*, xii. The aria 'Io non songo bona bona', typical of Logroscino's *buffo* style, is recorded in *The History of Music in Sound*, v.

thorough investigation been carried out, and it is not yet complete.[1] It is
unfortunate that even the modern Italian complete edition of Pergolesi[2]
still contains many such misattributions.

Of the four authenticated *opere serie*, *L'Olimpiade* (Rome, 1735), his
last opera and the one most popular with eighteenth-century audiences,
is also acknowledged to be the most important. It invites interesting
comparisons with the many other settings of Metastasio's text,[3] though
these are not always to Pergolesi's advantage. He was hampered by
having no first-class singers at his disposal, with the result that many of
his arias are more like songs. In Lycidas's slumber aria, Pergolesi chose
the key of F major, and scored for two horns (Vivaldi scored for one
horn in 1734, and Leo for two in 1737, when they set the same words):[4]

Ex. 69

[1] See Frank Walker, 'Two centuries of Pergolesi forgeries and misattributions', *Music
and Letters*, xxx (1949), p. 297; idem, letter 'Pergolesiana', *Music and Letters*, xxxii (1951),
p. 295; and Giuseppe Radiciotti, *Giovanni Battista Pergolesi* (2nd ed., Milan, 1935), rev.
and enl., trans. into German and ed. Antoine-E. Cherbuliez as *Giovanni Battista Pergolesi:
Leben und Werk* (Zürich and Stuttgart, 1954) (the edition used for this chapter). The article
on Pergolesi by Hucke in *Die Musik in Geschichte und Gegenwart*, x (1962), separates (cols.
1054–8) authenticated, and spurious and doubtful works.

[2] Ed. Filippo Caffarelli, 28 vols. (Rome, 1939–43). Ten volumes are devoted to operas in
vocal score. The following are not by Pergolesi: *Il maestro di musica* (which is by Pietro
Auletta), *Il geloso schernito* (by Pietro Chiarini) and *La contadina astuta* (by Hasse) (they
are in vols. xxv, iii and xi, respectively).

[3] Again see Burt in *Studies in Music History*, p. 325.

[4] The opera is in Dresden, Landesbibl. 3005.F.13, from which this example and Exx.
70(i) and 71(i) are taken; this example is in complete ed., xxiv (Rome, 1942), p. 52. Cf.
supra, pp. 102 ff. and 108 ff., for the settings by Vivaldi and Leo.

* only these notes given in original

(While you sleep, may love increase . . .)

Pergolesi set the beginning of the text to an octave leap, and the energy generated through it is expended through syncopated appoggiaturas in the mid-century 'sentimental' style introduced by Vinci in particular.[1] Pergolesi follows Vivaldi's example by having the vocal part played (at least in outline) by the accompanying instruments; in this respect he goes further than Vivaldi, who now and then gives the violins independent motives. Pergolesi's originality and his importance for the coming rococo style lay in his tendency to use short phrases, limited to a few bars, often only to a single bar. An example of this is the theme of the final duet in Act I (Ex. 70(i)), with which Leo's setting (ii) may be usefully compared:[2]

Ex. 70 (i)

Larghetto   Pergolesi

Ne gior-ni tuoi   fe - li-ci,   Ri-cor-da-ti di

me,   ri-cor-da-ti   di   me.

[1] Cf. *supra*, p. 118.
[2] Complete ed., xxiv, p. 63 (transposed into A flat); the quotations from Leo, here and in Ex. 71(ii), are from Dresden, Landesbibliothek, 2209.F.1.

(ii)

(Remember me in the days of your happiness.)

The words are set by Pergolesi strictly according to the number of syllables, accentuated only by appoggiaturas and by the dotted Lombard rhythm (cf. bars 1 and 3) that we are finding increasingly frequently in this study. In contrast to this, Leo treats the text with greater freedom, repeating single words ('ricordati', 'di me') rather than phrases, and writing in longer melodic curves.

A comparison of the vocal lines of the respective arias sung by Lycidas in Act I, scene 3, of *L'Olimpiade* might suggest that Leo was familiar with Pergolesi's opera:[1]

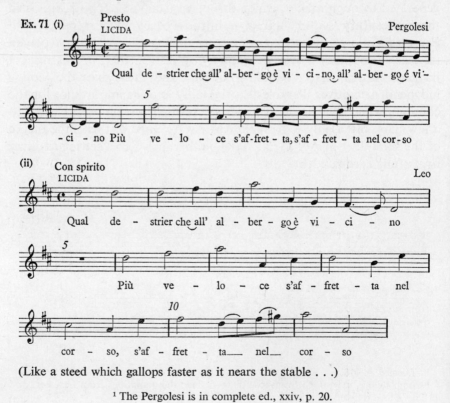

(Like a steed which gallops faster as it nears the stable . . .)

[1] The Pergolesi is in complete ed., xxiv, p. 20.

And yet how differently they are treated. The flourish of Leo's D major triad is weightier and more impressive than that of Pergolesi, who places his first climax at the beginning of the second bar, followed by a downward movement in the melodic line. Leo delays the climax until the beginning of bar 3 and allows the singer a rest to take a break in bar 5, so that the following six bars can be sung in a single breath. These are perhaps mere details; but on such things depends the whole effect of Italian operas of this period, with their emphasis on the solo aria.

In these and similar instances it is unnecessary to cast around for any direct influence. Definite types of aria developed—warlike and storm arias, slumber arias, laments, *siciliano*-type arias—all at times musically closely related and yet allowing plenty of scope for individual treatment by the various composers. Florid coloratura passages generally occur only at points of climax to create a very special effect—not here, there and everywhere, as might readily be inferred from many eighteenth-century writings on opera, satirical and otherwise. A typical coloratura aria from Pergolesi's opera *Adriano in Siria* (Naples, 1734), 'Torbido in volto e nero', was incorporated into the operatic pasticcio *Meraspe* (London, 1742), set to different words ('Tremende oscure atroci').[1] Vocal *tours de force* were popular with all composers at the time, and singers loved them; but they were essentially highlights, exceptions, far removed from the usual style, which concentrated more on interpretation of word and text than is generally realized.

La serva padrona (Naples, 1733), originally interpolated as *intermezzi* in Pergolesi's *opera seria Il prigionier superbo*[2], had a predecessor in Albinoni's *Pimpinone* (Venice, 1708)[3] (Telemann's well-known opera of the same name uses the same libretto). Here, too, a rich old bachelor is inveigled into matrimony by his servant girl. In Albinoni's version she outwits her master, relieves him of his money and proceeds to squander it. It would be interesting to investigate why, instead of the older work, it was the much later version that caught the public fancy. At all events Pergolesi's Uberto is none other than the old Pantalone of the *commedia dell'arte*, the source of many *scene buffe* and *intermezzi*, which were becoming increasingly popular.

New features in Pergolesi's opera are his delineation of old Uberto's quick changes of mood from rage to anxiety, Serpina's rapid dissimulations

---

[1] *Adriano in Siria* is in complete ed., xiv (Rome, 1942). Walsh published *The favourite songs in the opera call'd Meraspe o l'Olimpiade* in 1742. The aria is in *Répertoire français de l'ancien chant classique*, no. 575 (Paris, 1914), and is quoted by C. Hubert H. Parry in *The Oxford History of Music*, iv (London, 1902), pp. 206 ff.

[2] *La serva padrona* is in complete ed., xi (Rome, 1941), and there are several other editions; *Il prigioner superbo* is in complete ed., xx (Rome, 1942).

[3] MS. in Vienna, Nat. Bibl.

and the musical reproduction of her speech, mimicry, and gestures.[1] The timelessness of the theme and its universal application—compared, for instance, with the strictly topical satire on compulsive gambling in Vinci's *Il giocatore*—certainly contributed in no small measure to the tremendous success of *La serva padrona* in the second half of the eighteenth century. Another point in its favour was the memorable simplicity of Pergolesi's music, which after 1750 was used as ammunition against the vocal virtuosity and deep emotion (of lofty and remote historical personages) in *opera seria*, and influenced so strongly the development of the *opéra comique* in France:[2] as has been stated above its great reputation in France dates from the Paris performances of 1752, though the work had already been heard there in 1746—all these performances were in Italian, and the work was not given in French until 1754.

Among Pergolesi's other operas are *Lo frate 'nnamorato* (Naples, 1732), in Neapolitan dialect, and *Livietta e Tracollo*[3] (originally conceived in 1734 as *intermezzi* within the framework of Pergolesi's *Adriano in Siria*), published in Paris in 1753 and widely performed in the eighteenth century. Here two young girls disguise themselves as peasants in an attempt to catch a thief (Tracollo) who is masquerading as a Polish girl. Tracollo falls in love with one of the girls (Livietta) and turns over a new leaf. The mixture of lachrymose moralizing, grotesque satire, and parody strongly appealed to audiences of the time. In this work Pergolesi more or less abandoned the *da capo* aria, replacing it in many scenes with a combination of recitative and arioso.

CREATIVE ABUNDANCE

Of the composers who contributed to Italian opera between 1700 and 1750, only a few—notably those whom we have been discussing in the foregoing pages—are much remembered now. But as well as these there were a host of others, who in their time wrote a great many operas that were not only familiar in Italy but became known in other countries, often through copies which are now scattered among many libraries outside Italy. Such composers include Tommaso Albinoni, Giuseppe Maria Orlandini, Nicola Porpora, Gaetano Latilla, Geminiano Jacomelli. Francesco Mancini, Domingo Terradellas, Gaetano Schiassi, Giuseppe Aldrovandini, Giuseppe Antonio Paganelli, Domenico

---

[1] See Radiciotti, ed. Cherbuliez, op. cit., pp. 168–238.

[2] See *infra*, p. 242.

[3] Complete ed., ii (Rome, 1939) and xi (Rome, 1941), respectively. There are other vocal scores of the latter, ed. Radiciotti (Paris, 1914) and Alceo Toni (Milan, 1920).

Lalli. Giovanni Porta.[1] There are twenty-one operas by Rinaldo da Capua, whose *La Zingara* was at one time so popular.[2] Have all thirty of Giuseppe Maria Buini's scores been lost, as Dent assumed?[3] They would occupy a special place in the history of comic opera, since they were written in Venice for middle-class audiences.

The Venetian Giovanni Battista Pescetti (*c.* 1704–1766), a pupil of Lotti, followed in Porpora's footsteps by working in London from 1737 as musical director at Covent Garden and later at the King's Theatre, during which time he wrote a considerable number of operas.[4] From *La conquista del vello d'oro* (1738) he took not only the overture but also some of the arias and turned them into purely instrumental music for inclusion in his *Sonate per gravicembalo* (London, 1739). With this in mind it would be interesting to analyse the harpsichord sonatas of Baldassare Galuppi, whose instrumental music contains many of the characteristics of contemporary operatic writing.

The Florentine Orlandini was another who built up a reputation outside his native Italy. His operas *Arsace* (a revised version of his *Amore e maestà*) and *Nerone* were performed in Hamburg in German translations by Mattheson in 1722 and 1723, respectively. Here Orlandini was already using the new style of harmonic accompaniment in his arias, with short accompanying motives and frequent exact repetitions of them, generally first associated, as we have seen, with Vinci.[5] Orlandini's adaptation of Vinci's *Il giocatore* has already been mentioned.[6] He was well known as the composer of several other *intermezzi*, among them *Porsugnacco e Grilletta* (1727) and *Grullo e Moschetta* (1732), the latter also being given in London in 1737.

Benedetto Marcello deserves a place here, less as a composer of operas than as the author of an operatic satire in book form, *Il teatro alla moda* (Venice, *c.* 1720).[7] Marcello levelled his biting criticism at the whole fabric of contemporary opera, without, however, significantly altering

---

[1] The operas of all these composers except Lalli are listed under the relevant entries in *Die Musik in Geschichte und Gegenwart*. There is a score of Terradellas's *La Merope*, ed. Roberto Gerhard (Barcelona, 1951).

[2] See Philipp Spitta, 'Rinaldo von Capua und seine Oper *Die Zigeunerin*', in *Musikgeschichtliche Aufsätze* (Berlin, 1894), p. 131.

[3] See Dent, 'Giuseppe Maria Buini', *Sammelbände der internationalen Musikgesellschaft*, xiii (1911–12), p. 329.

[4] Arias from some of them were printed at the time in London. On Porpora see Robinson, 'Porpora's operas for London, 1733–1736', *Soundings*, ii (1971–2), p. 57.

[5] See *supra*, pp. 116 ff., and Wolff, *Die Barockoper in Hamburg*, i, p. 298.

[6] See *supra*, p. 121.

[7] Complete translation by Reinhard G. Pauly in *Musical Quarterly*, xxxiv (1948), p. 371, and xxxv (1949), p. 85; partial translation in Oliver Strunk, *Source Readings in Music History* (London, 1952), pp. 518–31; also see Pauly, 'Benedetto Marcello's satire on early 18th-century opera', *Musical Quarterly*, xxxiv (1948), p. 222.

the course of operatic history in Italy. But his short work provides an important piece of documentation on the situation of opera at the time. Marcello did not condemn it outright, but only criticized certain details with the intention of improving them. The power wielded by the prima donnas, the repression of the composers, the undue emphasis on décor and the appearance of live animals on stage—these were some of the things he attacked. Marcello himself never came to public notice as an opera composer, but almost his only work of any size, *L'Arianna*, was given privately at the Casino dei Nobili in Venice in 1727.[1]

A new flowering of comic opera in Venice began with the advent of the poet Carlo Goldoni, who produced a succession of librettos. Inspired by the Neapolitan *commedie musicali*, Goldoni's *Gondolier veneziano* (1734)—his first work in this genre—brought Venetian dialect to the operatic stage. *La birba* and many more of Goldoni's pieces were performed in Venice, as were his stage plays, which owed at least some of their material to the older *scene buffe*. The external form of Goldoni's opera librettos is quite different from that of his stage plays. In the operas he always uses verse and rhyme and makes a sharp distinction between the sections of dialogue intended as recitatives, and the arias and duets. At that time it was impossible to set spoken comedies to music: their form precluded it; they were much too naturalistic; and the dialogue is for the most part in prose, with no clearly-marked set pieces for arias. It would have been out of the question to set plays like *I quattro rusteghi* or *Le donne curiose* as operas: Wolf-Ferrari was able much later to do so, but the strictness of the aesthetic code in those days forbade it; however, the fine distinctions so sensitively drawn between stylization and naturalism were unfortunately lost sight of later.

Most of Goldoni's librettos were set to music by Galuppi (1706–85), as gifted a composer as Goldoni was a writer, and, like him, a Venetian by birth, from the island of Burano (for this reason he was also known as 'Il Buranello'). Galuppi's activities in Venice date from 1722, and for many years, especially from 1744 to 1773, he dominated the opera-houses of that city,[2] where he also produced a large number of *opere serie*. In one of his comic operas, *Il mondo alla roversa* (1750), based on a text by Goldoni and set in a topsy-turvy world ruled exclusively by love and women, he satirizes the pastoral idylls of the time. In *Il paese della cuccagna* (1750) Goldoni ridicules a land of Cockaigne where everything is allowed except jealousy. Free love is the order of the day and no one needs to work, until eventually an enemy army attacks, compelling everyone to work. This was a satire on the ideals of

[1] See Andrea d'Angeli, *Benedetto Marcello* (Milan, 1940), pp. 107–21.
[2] See Werner Bollert, *Die Buffoopern Baldassare Galuppis* (Diss., Berlin, 1935).

life and love of the eighteenth-century 'galant homme', which were cultivated to a particularly high degree in Venice.[1]

FUX, CALDARA, AND CONTI

The Habsburg court at Vienna was a flourishing centre of Italian culture and music in the eighteenth century. There were always Italian court poets here who were primarily employed as librettists, such as Pariati, Pasquini, Bernardoni, Cupeda, Stampiglia, and above all Zeno and Metastasio, the most celebrated Italian poets of their time. Composers permanently employed there included Johann Joseph Fux, Antonio Caldara, Francesco Conti, Carlo Agostino Badia, Giuseppe Porsile, and many others, whose rich output of operas showed strongly independent traits and were not simply copies of the current productions in Rome, Venice and Naples.

Fux (1660–1741)[2] was primarily a church musician, and the strict polyphony of his compositions led to his being referred to as 'the Austrian Palestrina'. His rigid and carefully cultivated style left its mark on Viennese opera. Of his nineteen operas sixteen are still extant; *Dafne in lauro* (1714) and *Angelica vincitrice di Alcina* (1716) were especially well known, and the latter was given a gala open-air performance on the lake in the park of the Imperial Palace called 'Favorita', before many thousand spectators. In 1723 his *Costanza e fortezza*,[3] written for Prague in honour of the coronation of the Emperor Charles VI, was staged in a specially constructed open-air theatre. Fux adapted his style to suit the acoustics of an outdoor presentation, using longer note-values and weightier orchestral resources. The grandiose style of the music owes something to Lully's operas, especially in the choruses and ballets. The theatre in Prague was illuminated by a thousand candles, and transparent décor was used. The title of the opera is a translation of Charles VI's motto *Constantia et fortitudo*, which was demonstrated on stage through Lars Porsenna's siege of Rome. Mucius Scaevola thrusts his own hand into the fire after he has murdered Porsenna's scribe, mistaking him for Porsenna himself.

The musical structure of *Costanza e fortezza* rests on the expressive declamation of the recitatives, and it would be quite wrong to dismiss the opera as nothing more than a grandiose spectacle. In the arias Fux

[1] See Wolff, 'Die Musik im alten Venedig', *Festschrift Heinrich Besseler* (Leipzig, 1961), p. 291.

[2] See Andreas Liess, *Johann Joseph Fux* (Vienna, 1948); Egon Wellesz, *Fux* (London, 1965); and J. H. van der Meer, *J. J. Fux als Opernkomponist*, 3 vols. (Bilthoven, 1961). A complete edition of Fux is in progress, ed. Hellmut Federhofer (Kassel and Graz, 1959 ff.); the operas are in ser. v.

[3] Ed. Wellesz, *Denkmäler der Tonkunst in Österreich*, xvii (Vienna, 1910), with an important preface and illustrations of the original sets.

carried on the contrapuntal tradition of the Venetians, in the style of composers such as Marc'Antonio Ziani and Lotti, though in contrast to Italian usage he brought in many old-fashioned instruments—cornetts, bass viols, and theorboes—and wrote parts for clarini and ordinary trumpets which made great demands on the players. Basically the music is written in a strict four-part texture, especially the orchestral introductions and interludes. Despite this there was nothing ecclesiastical about the sound—'nicht kirchenmässig' was the verdict of J. J. Quantz, who left the most vivid account of the performance.[1]

A far more important role in the Austrian theatre was that of Antonio Caldara (1670–1736),[2] with a contribution of more than one hundred operas. He lived in Vienna from 1716 until 1736, and twelve of his operas were written for performance in Salzburg. One of these, *Dafne* (Salzburg, 1719), has recently become known again.[3] It is a small-scale work, with only four soloists, and deals with the metamorphosis of Daphne into a laurel tree. The arias are mostly short and are often accompanied by the continuo alone; but there are also sophisticated instrumental effects, as when Phoebus Apollo's aria in Act II, scene 1, is accompanied by a solo oboe and pizzicato[4] strings and without harpsichord continuo. The contrapuntal writing in this opera (which is described as a serenata) is always clear and transparent in texture, so that each part, and above all the voice, is always easily heard. Many of the arias continue the song-like pattern familiar from seventeenth-century Venetian opera and are based on dance rhythms such as the minuet or the *siciliano*. French influence is evident in the instrumentation of Peneo's song in the second act, 'Buon pescatore non è,' for two oboes and bassoons, with continuo.[5]

On a much larger scale Caldara wrote three-act operas such as *La verità nell'inganno* (1717), an adaptation of which was performed in Vienna in 1730 under the title *Tiridate*. The first version has an aria accompanied by a concertante solo cello (in Act II, scene 2), remarkable not only for Caldara's skill in achieving a transparent concertante sound but as an indication of the way in which cellists alone used to improvise the continuo (see bars 3–4):[6]

[1] Printed in Marpurg, *Historisch-kritische Beyträge zur Aufnahme der Musik*, i (Berlin, 1754), p. 210.

[2] There is information about Caldara in Ursula Kirkendale, *Antonio Caldara: sein Leben und seine venezianisch-römischen Oratorien* (Graz and Cologne, 1966), though the oratorios are the main subject of the book.

[3] Ed. Constantin Schneider, *Denkmäler der Tonkunst in Österreich*, xci (Vienna, 1955)·

[4] Ibid., pp. 44–7.

[5] Ibid., pp. 71–4.

[6] This and the next example are from Leipzig, Städt. Musikbibl., III.15.

Ex. 72

(Repentance is a powerful defence when Love is the judge.)

Caldara uses a number of short instrumental figures in Tiridate's aria
'Nella membra lacerate' (Act II, scene 4) to convey mounting rage:

(Broken bones will be the chastisement of the enemy and the liar.)

Here Caldara creates a solid musical structure which, while abandoning broad, linear writing in the orchestral parts, yet preserves the independence of the various instrumental strands in the counterpoint. In this way he cleverly linked the old to the new. For the comic *intermezzo* scenes in this opera, he partly took the music of the preceding serious scenes and let the servants make fun of it, as for instance in Lisetta's aria 'Che bella cosa è una donna' (Act I, scene 14), which takes over the theme of the preceding duet between Arsinoe and Atalo, 'Ah nò, vivi a me' (Act I, scene 13). The gayer, simpler tunes from Caldara's operas became so widely popular in Austria, Moravia and Bohemia that they became 'folk-songs' and were later—at the end of the eighteenth century —taken up as such by Viennese classical composers, thus finding their way back into art music. The process illustrates the tremendous impact of Italian opera in the countries of central Europe.

One of the finest of Zeno's librettos to be set by Caldara was *Orno-spade* (Vienna, 1727). As in many Italian operas dating from this time, the Orient is here transported to the European stage. The action takes place in Mesopotamia, and the real content of the work is the glorification of loyalty in all its aspects—loyalty to one's prince, between friends, between husband and wife. Despite the fact that he has been insulted by his king (Arsaces Artabanus, king of the Parthians), the general Ornospades joins battle with the mutinous general Anileus and overwhelms him (the story is from Tacitus's *Annales*, iv). In the opening scene, Princess Palmide, in soldier's dress, is searching for her betrothed, Ornospades, whom the king has banished since he is himself in love with the princess. She for her part is determined to die rather than prove unfaithful to Ornospades. The scene is 'a blood-stained battlefield before the besieged town of Carre [Qayyarah?], at sunset'—a gloomy setting into which Palmide enters, accompanied by her old servant Vonone, who tries to comfort her in the following tense dialogue:[1]

Ex. 74

[1] This and the following example are from Leipzig, Städt. Musikbibl., III.15/3.

(P: I am resolved. V: To die? P: Yes. V: Does not this field, sprinkled with bones and blood, terrify you? P: On the contrary, I gaze on it to accustom myself not to fear death, the end of my ills. V: Await it with constancy, not anger. Come, live. P: For whom shall I preserve myself? V: For your Ornospades.)

Gone are the long, soliloquizing recitatives of the older operas, and in their place we find a terse, modern-sounding dialogue; Caldara's music follows every slight rise and fall in the text. (Perhaps the reader should be reminded here that in recitatives at this time two final notes of the same pitch were never sung as such: the first one was raised a degree as shown in the bracketed notes in the foregoing example.)

A close examination of Zeno's text reveals that the recitative-dialogues are much more important than the relatively short aria texts. The characters are excellently drawn, especially the magnanimous King Arsaces, who is deceived by Anileus and then becomes a prey to jealousy. There is no question of introducing standardized types either here or elsewhere in Zeno's works or in any of Metastasio's.

Caldara expands the polyphonic orchestral accompaniment in *Orno-spade*, which occasionally results in passages of four-part string writing

pointing the way to the classical string quartet, as in Arsaces's aria in
Act II, scene 10:

Ex. 75

(You indeed gave me your sword.)

Ornospade is full of tense and unexpected situations. Zeno's art is far removed from the detachment of classicism: despite the restricted number of his characters it stands in a direct line of succession from the older Italian opera librettos of the seventeenth century. In the end two happy couples are united: Ornospades and Palmide, and Mithridates and Nisea. All four join forces to sing the final moralizing 'chorus', typifying the gay finales then very common in Italian operas; its message—'the triumphs of deceit are brief and illusory; innocence alone enjoys steady benefits and true pleasures'—underlines the ethical as well as the optimistic side of these operas, which were much more than mere entertainment.

As yet, very little is known of the operas written by Francesco Conti (1682–1732)[1] for Vienna between 1706 and 1732. Some of them were so successful that they were also performed in Hamburg—works such as *Issipile* (Vienna, 1732; Hamburg, 1737) and the comic opera *Don Chisciotte in Sierra Morena* (Vienna, 1719; Hamburg, 1722), with libretto by Zeno and Pariati. *Don Chisciotte* is a perfect example of the satirical parodies of the time. Baroque aria texts are held up to ridicule in the meaningless jumble of phrases strung together by a love-crazed knight, Don Quixote's stage companion.[2] Conti introduced the new *buffo* style into his music, with brief orchestral motives, repeated notes and broken-octave basses, at a time when in Italy itself older styles were for the most part still in use. He had a great influence on German composers living in Hamburg, one of whom, Telemann, took up the lighthearted style of his operas and used it as the basis for his own orchestral and chamber music.

HANDEL: INTRODUCTORY

From the beginning of the eighteenth century, Italian opera had come to hold such a commanding position in European music that many non-Italian composers devoted themselves to it and achieved great success both in Italy and abroad. Chief among these are three German-born composers: Handel (from Halle), Johann Adolf Hasse (from Bergedorf, near Hamburg) and Carl Heinrich Graun (from Wahrenbrück, in Saxony). All three studied Italian opera in Germany and also at first hand in Italy before launching out as composers of Italian-language operas in their own right.

Of all Italian baroque operas those of Handel (1685–1759) have been the most frequently revived in our own time, no doubt because he is the

---

[1] His operas are listed in the article 'Conti' in *Die Musik in Geschichte und Gegenwart*, ii (1952), cols. 1641–2.
[2] Wolff, *Die Barockoper in Hamburg*, i, pp. 292–305.

greatest composer to cultivate the genre: they have been seen especially in Germany since the 1920s[1] and in England since the 1950s. For many people, therefore, the whole conception of early Italian opera is closely linked with Handel's works, though in a number of respects he deviated from the methods of the Italian composers of his time and went his own way. He kept to the older style of contrapuntal writing used by Scarlatti and Steffani, elaborating it by scoring for concertante instruments in the aria accompaniments; such textures are still found in his very last operas, such as *Serse* (London, 1738) and *Deidamia* (London, 1741), though it is true to say that these later operas are of a lower specific gravity and density than their predecessors. He thus tended to resist general developments in Italian opera during those years, never subscribed to the ascendancy of the vocal line over the accompaniment and was sharply criticized by his contemporaries for his lavish use of the orchestra in his arias. The magnificent aria 'Vedrò fra poco', which closes Act II of *Admeto* (1727), offers just one example of a densely imitative and rather old-fashioned string texture that in itself contributes to the aria's feeling of finality and climax appropriate to its position in the opera.

Of his forty-one operas[2] Handel composed all except the first five for London, between 1711 and 1741. In London he could undoubtedly command the services of the most distinguished Italian singers of the era—the castrato Senesino, the prima donnas Durastanti, Cuzzoni, and Faustina Bordoni, the bass Boschi. He could therefore count on expertly improvised elaboration of his arias—one of the most important characteristics of the art of *bel canto*.

Beginning with Burney's general account, histories of opera and studies of Handel in general normally include consideration of his operas in greater or lesser degree, but there has yet to be published a separate full-scale study of the operas.[3] The present pages on these operas consider first of all the general qualities of their librettos and their music, and then the operas are treated chronologically.

[1] See idem, *Die Händel-Oper auf der modernen Bühne, 1920–1956* (Leipzig, 1957).
[2] The total includes *Muzio Scevola* (London, 1721), of which Handel composed only Act III; the pre-London works are *Almira* and the lost *Nero* (both Hamburg, 1705), the lost two-part *Florindo* and *Daphne* (Hamburg, 1708), *Rodrigo* (Florence, *c.* 1707) and *Agrippina* (Venice, 1709).
[3] Details of the general books referred to will be found in the usual bibliographies. Among studies in English see in particular the admirable Winton Dean, *Handel and the opera seria* (London, 1970), and the chapter on the operas by Dent in Gerald Abraham (ed.), *Handel: a symposium* (London, 1954), p. 12. All the operas appear in the complete edition of Handel's works, ed. Chrysander. There are also more recent editions of some of the operas, by no means always reliable, e.g. in the *Hallische Händel-Ausgabe, Serie II* (Kassel and Basle, 1955–).

HANDEL'S LIBRETTOS

Handel wrote his operas almost without exception to Italian librettos. He was thus addressing from the outset the cultured audiences of the day, not the ordinary man in the street. His collaborators in England, Nicola Haym and Paolo Rolli, generally adapted older Italian librettos by men such as Stampiglia, Salvi, Beregan, Minato, and Noris; no particular value was attached to the originality of the material or to linguistic perfection. Even texts by Zeno and Metastasio were revised for Handel and were generally cut to allow more space for the arias, which were the principal feature of his operas. Such alterations, adaptations and supplementary aria texts were common because the operas were written for different casts, whose individual vocal and interpretative abilities had to be catered for. Handel's recitatives were understood probably by only a very small proportion of London opera-goers. The recitatives of the older librettos were ruthlessly pruned for him, but their dramatic content is always at least equal to that of the arias. In common with Italian composers, he paid close attention in the recitatives to the precise inflections and expression of the Italian language,[1] and this presents problems in translation which have not always been overcome.

Handel's librettos normally exclude undue complication in the action, as well as all extraneous comic interludes (though, as we shall see in a moment, there is some integrated comedy). Their content was to some extent determined by Zeno's principles and by those of Metastasio, though Handel set only one text by Zeno (*Faramondo*, 1738) and only three of Metastasio's (*Siroe*, 1728; *Poro*, 1731; and *Ezio*, 1732), all of them altered. The stirring, fantastic plots of seventeenth-century librettos form the basis of Handel's operas, even though in his hands they differ in points of detail and interpretation. French tragedy provided models of particular importance, and in some of the operas most often performed today the moral ideals of Corneille and Racine are clearly discernible: *Rodelinda* (1725) goes back to Corneille's drama *Pertharite*, *Giulio Cesare* (1724, though based on an older libretto by Bussani) was modelled on Corneille's *Pompée*, while *Poro* (1731), a setting of Metastasio's *Alessandro nell'Indie*, had originated in Racine's *Alexandre le Grand*. The libretto of *Teseo* (1713) is basically a translation of Philippe Quinault's libretto for Lully's *Thésée* (1675).[2] The new emphasis on fidelity, honour, and moral duty in these works partially

---

[1] See Wolff, 'Die Sprachmelodie im alten Opernrezitativ', *Händel-Jahrbuch 1963*, p. 93.

[2] See David Kimbell, 'The libretto of Handel's "Teseo" ', *Music and Letters*, xliv (1963), p. 371.

supplants the baroque dramas of intrigue that had their roots in the Spanish theatre. An example of this is Handel's *Il Giustino* (1737), in which a supposed simple countryman becomes Emperor of Rome by dint of his personal ability. (The story had already been adapted as a libretto by Beregan for Legrenzi in 1683.)[1]

For all the seriousness and heroism of many of his operas, Handel does indulge in a certain amount of comedy, involving the principal characters themselves. This was the case with *Agrippina* (1709), whose libretto, by Cardinal Vincenzo Grimani, contains a satire on unbounded and criminal lust for power; many of the scenes in this opera are treated in the style of the future *opera buffa*. *Partenope* (1730), *Serse*, and *Deidamia* also contain fine comic scenes, in which soubrettes generally take a leading role; scenes involving Elviro in *Serse* show too the influence of ballad opera. It is possible that further work on the texts would reveal a few topical allusions. English history provided the theme of *Riccardo I* (1727)—but with the exception of this opera and *Tamerlano*, Handel's plots come from Greek, Roman, or Dark Ages history or from romances based on Ariosto and Tasso.

THE MUSIC OF HANDEL'S OPERAS: GENERAL

The music in Handel's operas shows an extraordinary diversity, ranging from the great tripartite *da capo* aria—with or without concertante instruments—to simple little dance-songs; there are accompanied recitatives, ariosos, and duets, and occasionally trios, quartets, and choruses, many examples of these forms being used at points of climax: this pattern is already familiar in broad outline from the operas of Scarlatti and Steffani. As with them, dance rhythms were an important impetus behind many of Handel's arias: he set many texts as *siciliani*, minuets, gavottes, or sarabands—for instance, Cleopatra's aria 'V'adoro, pupille' (*Giulio Cesare*, 1724)[2] is written in saraband-rhythm, the only difference being that Handel shortened the time-value from the old 3/2 to the modern 3/4, compensating for the change by marking the music '*largo*'. A point worth noting here is the long silence of the bass instruments, a device used by Pollaroli at the end of the seventeenth century which paved the way for the new, more translucent style of eighteenth-century scoring.

Comparisons of the musical style of Handel's operas with that of his contemporaries enable one to acquire a closer knowledge of their individual characteristics. Some comparisons have been made earlier,[3]

---

[1] See Wolff, *Die venezianische Oper*, pp. 84–92, and *supra*, p. 37.

[2] This aria is recorded in *The History of Music in Sound*, v. On the opera see J. Merrill Knapp, 'Handel's *Giulio Cesare in Egitto*', *Studies in Music History*, p. 389.

[3] Cf. *supra*, pp. 94 ff. and 119 f.

and it may be profitable to add to these. Whereas in the Scarlatti aria quoted as Ex. 31 the song of the nightingale is imitated by purely vocal means, Handel in *Deidamia* (1741) places the main emphasis on the accompanying violins, which join with the voice in a concertante duet:

(The nightingale hides its nest in the highest branches from snake and hunter.)

In his mature operas from about 1724 onwards, Handel generally allotted an important role to the accompanying violins and to the continuo, both of which are given a high degree of thematic independence.

In writing for the voice, Handel generally uses, more often than his contemporaries, wide intervals, repeated strong accents and dotted rhythms. The sweeping melodic curves of his *Ottone* (1722) as compared with Lotti's *Teofane* (Dresden, 1719) have already been discussed (see Exx. 50–3). Comparison, too, of the aria 'Mio dolce amato sposo' from *Il Giustino*, set by Handel and Vivaldi—Exx. 54–5—has already given

us a further indication of the more conspicuous part played by the
instruments and of their thematic individuality in Handel, whereas in
Vivaldi's setting the voice part is reflected in the orchestral accompaniment. It is not simply a question of a difference in technique between
the two composers; there is also a difference in interpretation, for
Handel gives the text the overtones of an impassioned lament, while
Vivaldi chooses to bring out the feeling of Ariadne's resolution.

Further comparisons are possible with operas by Hasse, in particular
with his *Cleofide*, which, like Handel's *Poro*, dates from 1731, and both
of which are settings of the same Metastasio libretto. Despite one or two
affinities, the two operas are totally dissimilar. Handel persists with the
dactylic rhythms of seventeenth-century Venice in Porus's aria 'Vedrai
con tuo periglio'. Hasse, on the other hand, uses even at this date the
sentimental appoggiaturas of a later style, also found at the same time
in the music of Leo and Vinci:[1]

(You will see, to your danger, like lightning over the field, the flash of this
sword in the eyes of him who wields it.)

Handel shows a fondness for dotted instrumental rhythms of the type
common in Lully's overtures, and their use heightens the effect of
Alexander's rage. Hasse's syncopations are again more typical of a later
style, and his melodic line, more supple despite a faster tempo, is
certainly easier to sing:

[1] Exx. 77(ii), 78(ii) and 79(ii) are from the manuscript of Hasse's *Cleofide* at Dresden,
Landesbibl.

Ex. 78 (i)

(Those weeping eyes are the cheap trophy of a cowardly soul.)

Handel based Porus's aria 'Se mai più sarò geloso' on a short, striking motive, gradually building up to a climax, in contrast to Hasse's broad, swinging, song-like melody:

Ex. 79 (i)

(If I ever again grow jealous may the sacred divinity that tames the Indies punish me.)

The divergence between the two is even more marked if a comparison is made between Handel's setting of Cleofide's aria 'Digli ch'io son fedele' (Act II, scene 5) and Hasse's version. Handel writes in short, terse motives which emphasize single words in the text—'digli' is treated in this way. The first lines of the text are delivered clearly and distinctly, almost without accompaniment. Not until bar 7 is there concertante writing between voice and orchestra; then the first 'digli' motive reappears in a kind of inversion (bar 13), followed by a quasi-inversion of the original 'non disperi ancor':

(Tell him that I am constant, tell him he is my treasure, tell him to love me, tell him I adore him, tell him to despair no longer.)

Hasse sets the same words in broadly flowing melismas, designed to give outstanding singers the opportunity to express, through brilliant improvisations, the longing and passion of true love (cf. Ex. 85).

IMPROVISED EMBELLISHMENTS IN ARIAS

Handel's operas, like others of the time, also relied on improvisations and virtuoso elaborations by the performers. It is possible to examine a set of these embellishments for some of the arias in *Ottone*, which provide invaluable information concerning the detailed execution of Handel's operatic arias.[1] Slow-moving arias were particularly suited to such elaborations, as for example Teofane's 'Affanni del pensier' (Act I, scene 10):[2]

[1] See James S. and Martin V. Hall, 'Handel's graces', *Händel-Jahrbuch 1957*, p. 25. It is unlikely that these embellishments were probably written for the castrato Gaetano Guadagni in 1751, as the Halls say.
[2] Decorated version from Oxford, Bod., Mus. MS. Don.C.69. It is printed complete in Wolff, *Original Vocal Improvisations* (Cologne, 1972).

Ex. 81

(Cares of my mind, leave me in peace for a moment at least, and then return . . .)

The singer starts off with small variations, but in the course of the aria the note-values become shorter and shorter. Presumably these elaborate decorations were sung in the reprise of the first section of a *da capo* aria, but even the first time through this first section might be slightly altered by the soloist, notably at the final cadence; Handel also wrote out variations for the second sections of this and the other arias which are likewise extensive and demand virtuoso technique.

Such elaborations were not, however, confined to slow melodies: that the livelier arias were treated in the same way may be seen in the aria 'Alla fama dimmi il vero' (*Ottone*, Act, II, scene 6), of which Handel chose to decorate only the first part. Triplets, runs and subtle syncopations were all brought into use both here and in the aria 'Benchè mi sia crudele' in the same opera (Act III, scene 6). Handel no doubt exercised the art of improvisation in his early operas too. Embellished arias, mainly from *Rinaldo*, were published by the harpsichordist William Babell about 1715: his versions are for harpsichord solo, with the result that many characteristics of harpsichord technique were superimposed upon them.[1] Another similar piece, arranged from an aria from *Floridante* (1721), exists in Handel's autograph.[2]

For too long the art of vocal improvisation has been wrongly regarded as nothing more than singers' vanity or as a 'weakness' of the time, whereas it represents a fundamental feature of Italian operas of the period. The adding of brilliance by the execution of rapid 'divisions' had for long been a general principle of musical performance. Even the motets and madrigals of the sixteenth century were generally enlivened by virtuoso embellishments.[3] The virtuoso soloist maintained a preeminent position in the seventeenth century and reached new heights in the eighteenth-century *da capo* aria. The added ornaments, on which several eighteenth-century writers left detailed notes,[4] were an obligatory feature of Italian opera. They lent greater movement and expressiveness to the arias: dissonant, plangent appoggiaturas, especially in slow-moving arias, could certainly intensify the expressive content, which might even be radically altered by the more extreme embellishments.

[1] See Babell, *Suits of harpsichord and spinnet, lessons* . . . (London, *c.* 1715 and 1717); Chrysander reprinted them in his complete Handel edition, xlviii, pp. 210–43, together with Handel's own keyboard version of one of the arias, 'Vò far guerra', pp. 206–9. Also see Robert Haas, *Aufführungspraxis der Musik* (Potsdam, 1931), p. 192, and Wolff, 'Vom Wesen des alten Belcanto', *Händel-Konferenz-Bericht* (Leipzig, 1959), p. 95.

[2] See Terence Best, 'An example of Handel embellishment', *Musical Times*, cx (1969), p. 933.

[3] See Ferand, op. cit., pp. 52 ff., for examples; also see Vol. IV, pp. 147–8 (with further references at p. 148, n. 1).

[4] For example Pier Francesco Tosi: see the translation of his treatise published in London in 1742 as *Observations on the florid song* (repr. London, 1905). See Hans-Peter Schmitz, *Die Kunst der Verzierung im 18. Jahrhundert* (Kassel, 1955), for a good modern work on the subject (though largely concerned with instrumental music).

HANDEL'S OPERAS: A CHRONOLOGICAL SURVEY

Of Handel's earliest operas written for Hamburg, only *Almira* (1705) is extant. The text, whose German parts are by Friedrich Christian Feustking and the Italian by Giulio Pancieri, was set to music at the same time by Reinhard Keiser, who was then at the height of his powers, and his setting is finer than Handel's.[1] Handel's music was still that of a beginner, although he was already making certain experiments, such as greater use of instrumental resources in the arias, and expansion of the arias by means of rather instrumental coloratura.

Of the two operas Handel wrote in Italy, *Agrippina* (Venice, 1709) is specially important: for one thing its themes recur in oratorios such as *Joshua*, *Jephtha*, and *Judas Maccabaeus*. It was also very successful, was given twenty-eight times and gained Handel a wide reputation. In it he continued the style of the Venetian satirical-comic operas which had been common from the time of Pietro Andrea Ziani, Legrenzi, and Pallavicino—thus Pallavicino's *Messalina* (Venice, 1680) was a direct forebear of Handel's *Agrippina*.[2] Characters from ancient history were portrayed as people of the baroque age and were often involved in difficult and unexpected love-affairs. This often implied criticism of the way of life of the princes and nobility of that time; but it was also a way of reducing great characters from history to a normal human level. Handel emphasized this in his music by introducing lively march and dance rhythms, and 'conversational' trios and quartets which already point to the later *opera buffa*. As we have already seen,[3] he seems, now and later, to have been directly inspired by certain of Scarlatti's operas, and he also took themes and even whole numbers from the operas of Hamburg colleagues such as Mattheson and Keiser, and refashioned them.

Handel's first opera performed in England was *Rinaldo* (London, 1711), with libretto by Giacomo Rossi after Tasso's *Gerusalemme liberata*. The performance took place in the Queen's Theatre, and the main parts were taken by famous soloists. Handel's operatic activity in London falls approximately into four periods.[4] The first lasts as far as *Amadigi* in 1715. The climax of the second period comes between 1720 and 1728, when, at the King's Theatre, Haymarket, the Royal Academy of Music performed some dozen operas by him—works such as *Radamisto* (1720), *Ottone* (1722), *Giulio Cesare* (1724), *Tamerlano* (1724), and *Rodelinda* (1725): the last three in particular are a magnificent series

---

[1] On Keiser and on *Almira* see *infra*, pp. 309–14 and 315 respectively.

[2] See Wolff, *Die venezianische Oper*, pp. 107–41, and idem, *Agrippina: eine italienische Jugendoper von G. F. Händel* (Wolfenbüttel and Berlin, 1943), p. 15. Also see *supra*, p. 43.

[3] See *supra*, pp. 59–61 and 62.

[4] For background information cf. George E. Dorris, *Paolo Rolli and the Italian circle in London, 1715–1744*(The Hague, 1969).

of works. The most famous singers of the day took part, such as the castrato Senesino and the prima donnas Durastanti and Cuzzoni. In 1728 the Academy had to close its doors, in spite of its previous successes. Handel was faced, too, with a strong rival in *The Beggar's Opera* (by Gay and Pepusch), which was sung in English, touched on topical themes, ridiculed Italian opera and prompted a large number of other ballad operas.[1]

Handel's music for the Royal Academy operas consists mainly of recitatives and arias; he developed the latter to such an extent that his operas have mistakenly been called 'concert operas'. The term is quite inapplicable, since even his great *da capo* arias are dependent on the expressive rendering of the text. For many of the arias he employed the dance rhythms that we have noted above: particularly notable examples are his arias in *siciliano* tempo through which moods of idyllic peacefulness but also of grief could be evoked (e.g., Asteria's 'Se non mi vuol amar' in Act I and Bajazet's 'Figlia mia, non pianger' in Act III of *Tamerlano*).[2] Handel's gay dance-songs, such as the aria 'Il tricerbo humiliato' in *Rinaldo*, became popular melodies in England. The great dramatic accompanied recitatives must also be mentioned: scenes such as Caesar's lament at the grave of the murdered Pompey in *Giulio Cesare* or the suicide of Bajazet in *Tamerlano* (with its sequence of recitatives, ariosos, and arias similar to the mad scene in *Orlando* (1733)) reach the highest pinnacle of dramatic art.

Orlando is a major landmark of the third main group of Handel's operas for London, written between 1729 and 1736; other masterpieces here are *Poro* (1731), set in ancient India, and *Ezio* (1732), set in late classical antiquity, both with texts by Metastasio. For a time Handel directed his operatic enterprises with the assistance of the impresario John James Heidegger. He had to leave the King's Theatre, however, after *Arianna* in 1734, and from *Ariodante* (1735) he performed in the Covent Garden Theatre. The dance troupe which appeared in this theatre with the French ballerina Marie Sallé was included in one or two of these operas, such as *Ariodante* and *Alcina* (1735). From 1734 Handel had to fight against the competition of a second Italian opera company in London, which moved into the King's Theatre, was supported by the political enemies of King George II and had the gifted Porpora as its composer: because the King's son and many of the aristocracy supported this second company it was known as the 'Opera of the Nobility'.

[1] See *infra*, pp. 300 ff.
[2] See Wolff, 'Der Siziliano bei J. S. Bach und G. F. Händel', *Atti del Congresso Internazionale di Musica Mediterranea* (Palermo, 1954), p. 301.

Handel's last operas form a fourth group, including *Arminio* (1737), *Giustino* (1737), and the comic opera *Serse*. This opera has as its first aria the famous 'Largo' (in reality a Larghetto), 'Ombra mai fù', which is sung by the hero in praise of a beautiful plane tree; it is thus an apotheosis of the beauty and peace of nature and not the dirge which it has later become, often in purely instrumental form. Handel's last opera, *Deidamia* (1741), is a gay comedy of love; everywhere dance rhythms crowd into the score—gavotte, bourrée, minuet, and so on. Here and in others of these last operas, such as *Serse* and *Imeneo* (1740), we see the beginning of a lighter style, though Handel did not go over completely to the 'soloist opera' in which the vocal solo is everything and the orchestral accompaniment only the harmonic support. This new stylistic ideal had been developed to brilliant effect in London in 1734 with the pasticcio *Artaserse* (a reworking of Hasse's score of 1730).[1] Handel on the other hand retained to the last the concertante style and a contrapuntal orchestral accompaniment; and there is even a hint in the splendid aria 'Sorge nell'alma mia' in Act II of *Imeneo* of the grander, symphonic kind of aria found later in Gluck and Mozart. On the whole, though, Handel's operas must by the late 1730s have seemed old fashioned. When he abandoned opera in 1741 he devoted himself more assiduously than he had so far done to the composition of oratorios. These are nearly all dramatically conceived works, in external form very similar to his operas: several have been successfully staged in recent years.[2]

HASSE

The operas of Johann Adolf Hasse (1699–1783)[3] herald the arrival of the sentimental style—the style of 'Empfindsamkeit'—which was to dominate Italian opera, especially in Dresden and Vienna. Hasse was raised in the tradition of the old Hamburg and Brunswick opera and made his first appearances as a singer in the operas of Keiser and Georg Caspar Schürmann. From 1722 he studied in Italy with Porpora and Scarlatti and was eventually summoned to the court at Dresden in 1731, where for thirty years he played a leading role in European opera. The Elector of Saxony made it possible for Hasse, accompanied by his wife, Faustina Bordoni, to go and produce his operas all over Europe, in

---

[1] On the principal versions of this opera see Sonneck, 'Die drei Fassungen des Hasse'schen "Artaserse" ', *Sammelbände der internationalen Musikgesellschaft*, xiv (1912–1913), p. 226.

[2] See Vol. VI and Dean, *Handel's Dramatic Oratorios and Masques* (London, 1959).

[3] On Hasse see Vol. VII, pp. 25–31, Carl H. Mennicke, *Hasse und die Brüder Graun als Symphoniker* (Leipzig, 1906), and Gerber, op. cit. All Hasse's operas are listed in *Die Musik in Geschichte und Gegenwart*, v (1956), cols. 1776–7.

London, Venice, and Vienna. When, during the bombardment of
Dresden by Frederick II of Prussia, all the scores he had prepared for
publication (they were probably already engraved) were destroyed,
Hasse moved in 1761 to Vienna. After more than ten years of activity
there he returned to Venice, his wife's home. These biographical details
show how highly Hasse was regarded in the musical world of his day:
indeed no composer was more popular. A great many of the major roles
in his operas were written for his wife. Since he himself was also trained
as a singer, the voice is, not unnaturally, predominant in his music, and
he was largely responsible for the development of the 'soloist opera' and
the solo vocal style of the period.

Hasse is perhaps best known as the composer who spread Metastasio's
fame—he set all but one of his dramatic works to music;[1] he also wrote
several comic *intermezzi*. In the past there has been a tendency to regard
his operas only as a series of beautiful arias which delighted cultured
audiences all over Europe by their clarity and formal perfection and by
sacrificing everything else to the charm of vocal purity. However, some
contemporary critics, Marpurg for one, singled out Hasse's recitatives,
for the recitatives are the key passages in Metastasio's librettos; Hasse
paid particular attention to the dramatic delivery and the scansion of
the poetry. Marpurg analysed the first recitative in Hasse's *Ezio* (Naples,
1730; Dresden, 1755), as an outstanding example of good Italian
recitative (see Ex. 82(i)).[2] Each section of the text is set within a single
tonality and each new phrase indicated by a change in harmony; these
changes occur at the first stressed word and not at the very first syllable.
Hasse distinguished carefully in his cadences between different sorts of
punctuation in the text, and these cadences could in addition be
strengthened or weakened, with rising or falling melodic lines, dissonant
or concordant harmonies. In the *Ezio* recitative a true close comes only
at the end (at letter x); at other breaks in the text we find only imperfect
cadences, representing semicolons (as at a, d, g, and i). Unwritten commas (at b and c) are indicated by pauses or alterations in the bass. Many
short phrases of the text are 'incomplete' in themselves (as at e, h, k, and
m), so several phrases are run together and treated as a single unit. On
the other hand, many commas are strengthened by changes in the
harmony (t, v) in order to achieve a climax. These and many other
devices occur frequently in recitatives, firmly underlining the linguistic
and declamatory role of virtually every syllable:

---

[1] So he told Burney: see Mennicke, op. cit., p. 440. The exception is *Temistocle*. Mennicke
casts doubt on two others, *Siface* and *Issipile*: however, Hasse set the former as *Viriate* for
Venice in 1739, and he may have set *Issipile* for Naples in 1742.

[2] See Marpurg, *Kritische Briefe über die Tonkunst*, ii (Berlin, 1761–3), pp. 385–9; the music
is in a manuscript at Dresden, Landesbibl.

Ex. 82 (i)

Si-gnor, vin - cem-mo; Ai ge - li - di tri -
- o - ni il ter-ror de mor - ta - li fug-gi-ti - vo ri -
- tor - na; Il pri - mo io so - no che mi-ras - se fi -
- no - ra At - ti-la im-pal - li - dir; Non vi - de il
so - le più nu-me-ro-sa stra - ge; A tan - te
mor - ti e - ra an-gu-sto il ter - re - no. Il san - gue

(Sir, we have conquered; the scourge of men returns fleeing to the frozen north;
I am the first man ever to see Attila turn pale; never did the sun see such carnage;
the battlefield was littered with the dead, blood ran in turbid torrents; threats
and groans were intermingled; and amid fear and anger the brave, the base,
conqueror and conquered wandered in confusion.)

When Handel set *Ezio* he shortened the same recitative text to nine bars
and grouped several phrases together on a single chord (as in bars 5–7
of the following example) but otherwise kept to the same formula as
Hasse (at the end, though, he gave the word 'vincitori' a further telling
change in the harmony).

Ex. 82 (ii)

Examples of Hasse's vocal writing have already been cited.[1] In his
arias he tended to favour melodies in conjunct motion, interrupted from
time to time by isolated wider intervals. For instance, the aria 'Vil
trofeo d'un alma imbelle' from *Cleofide* (Ex. 78(ii)) begins with a
fourth; then comes a descending fifth at the beginning of the second bar,
followed by a rising seventh, and an octave at the beginning of bar 3—an
artfully arranged progression of widening intervals within the framework of a melodic line otherwise proceeding by conjunct motion.

[1] See Exx. 77–9; also see Vol. VII, Exx. 11–16.

Another masterstroke is the beginning of the aria 'Se mai più sarò geloso' (Ex. 79(ii)), where an upward leap of a sixth is immediately followed by a falling sixth, before the conjunct motion resumes its course. Of course, this kind of harmonious balance between rising and falling melodic lines was by no means new—Palestrina is only one of many composers who had practised it—but Hasse increases the size and vigour of the intervals and makes greater use of syncopated and 'Lombard' rhythms. A typical example is a first-act aria for Dido in his *Didone abbandonata* (Dresden, 1743), a work greatly admired in his day; the leaps and rests which punctuate the question give this theme a strongly dramatic flavour:[1]

(Ingrate, has the heart no claim when one who swore faith abandons it?)

Hasse was famous for his orchestrally accompanied scenes, which he inserted at climactic points in the action, after the fashion of Scarlatti and Vinci. In a scene of this kind from the third (1760) version of *Artaserse* he uses a wide variety of motives and introduces flutes, horns, and trumpets. The following few bars from the first scene of *Didone abbandonata* show clearly his manner in such scenes; Aeneas is expressing his embarrassment at leaving Dido without warning:

[1] This and the next example are from the manuscript at Dresden, Landesbibl.

(D: Speak. A: I must . . . but no . . . love . . . oh God! faith! Ah, I cannot speak. Explain it for me: love, faith.)

The powerful scene in Act III in which Dido gives way to despair became very famous indeed: here Hasse wove together recitatives and closed numbers to form a magnificent dramatic scena.

An excerpt from Hasse's *Cleofide* (1731) shows the skill with which
the improvised embellishments in the arias were executed; the aria
'Digli ch'io son fedele' was one of the most brilliant and popular items
in the repertoire of opera singers at that time. For this aria the rather
minimal embellishments of Faustina Bordoni have been preserved,
together with another, more elaborate set written by Frederick the
Great for the Italian castrato Antonio Uberti Porporino. Both versions
are given here below Hasse's notation:[1]

Ex. 85

[1] For (*a*) see n. 1 on p. 143; (*b*) is in Munich, Landesbibl., 2477.F.10; (*c*) is in the collection of Frederick the Great's musical autographs in Berlin, Deutsche Staatsbiblothek. (*a*) and (*c*) and the bass are printed complete in Schmitz, op. cit., pp. 121–4. They are all printed complete in Wolff, *Original Vocal Improvisations*.

- - mi, che m'a - . mi, ch'io— l'a - - -

- - mi, che m'a - mi, ch'io— l'a - - -

mi,_____ che m'a - mi, ch'io_____ l'a -

do - ro, Che non di - spe - ri an - cor,

do - ro, Che non di - spe - ri an - cor,

do - ro, Che non— di - spe - ri an - cor,

(Tell him that I am constant, tell him he is my treasure, tell him to love me, tell him I adore him, tell him to despair no longer.)

Ornamentation carried to this extreme parallels the rococo style in architecture then prevalent in Germany, examples of which may still be seen in the Nymphenburg Palace, near Munich, and Frederick's own Sanssouci at Potsdam: these extravagant decorations and flourishes represent a peculiarly German manifestation of the last vestiges of baroque style.

When Hasse's contemporaries admired his 'naturalness' they meant no artless song-like quality or straightforward realism but rather the naturalness of his portrayal of the emotions. Imitation of this kind, embracing a wide range of emotions and often combined with highly sophisticated forms and techniques, was demanded by eighteenth-century aesthetics: it was described by Boileau and Charles Batteux as imitation of nature, and its application to music was advocated by Mattheson, Johann Adolf Scheibe, and others. These ideals could be artistically realized in literature through similes, in the visual arts through nature pictures; in music an important equivalent is the emotionally highly charged performance of operatic arias that we have been discussing.[1]

[1] There is one opera by Hasse not mentioned in this section available in a printed full-score edition: *Arminio* (1745), ed. Gerber, *Das Erbe deutscher Musik*, xxvii-xxviii (Mainz, 1957–66).

Several operas by Hasse were also performed in Warsaw, especially during the period 1755–61 after Augustus III, with his entire court, had had to flee there following the Prussian occupation of Dresden. The king also took with him the entire staff of the Dresden opera-house, who performed in Warsaw Hasse's *Il sogno di Scipione* (1758) and *Zenobia* (1761)—both new works—and a revised version of his *Siroè, re di Persia*, as well as others of his earlier operas. Over a century before this, under King Ladislas IV (1633–48), it had been the custom on the occasion of court festivities regularly to perform Italian operas, such as *Santa Cecilia* (1637) and *Il ratto d'Elena* (1638), with librettos by the king's Italian secretary, Virgilio Puccitelli, and music by Marco Scacchi.[1]

GRAUN

Together with Hasse, the most significant exponent of Italian opera in Germany was Carl Heinrich Graun (1698/9–1765),[2] who between 1741 and 1756 composed twenty-seven Italian language operas for Berlin. While he, too, set to music the dramas of Zeno and Metastasio, he also collaborated with the court poets writing in Berlin, Tagliazucchi, Botarelli, and Villati. These men adapted well-known French plays as Italian opera librettos, such as *Cleopatra e Cesare* (after Corneille's *La mort de Pompée*), written for the opening of the Berlin Opera House in 1742, *Ifigenia in Aulide* (after Racine's *Iphigénie*, Berlin, 1748), and *Rodelinda* (after Corneille's *Pertharite*, 1748); we have seen that these plays had already been used as sources by earlier librettists. Frederick the Great himself, imbued with the ideals of enlightened absolutism, drafted several librettos in French, which were then translated into Italian verse by his court poets. The best known of these was *Montezuma*, in an Italian version by Tagliazucchi and with music written by Graun for performance in Berlin in 1755;[3] this opera is concerned with the clash between the ideal, benevolent ruler and the brutal conqueror of Mexico, Cortez.

Graun wrote in the same *galant*, sentimental style as Lotti, who had been his teacher in Dresden. He is especially successful in evoking moods of tenderness and pathos, as in Montezuma's first aria, 'Non

---

[1] See Karolina Targosz-Kretowa, *Teatr dworski Władysława IV (1635–1648)* (Cracow, 1965), and Karyna Wierzbicka-Michalska, *Teatr warszawski za Sasów* (*Studia z dziejów teatru w Polsce*, iv) (Wrocław, Warsaw, and Cracow, 1964).

[2] On Graun see Albert Mayer-Reinach, 'Carl Heinrich Graun als Opernkomponist', *Sammelbände der internationalen Musikgesellschaft*, i (1899–1900), p. 446.

[3] Ed. Mayer-Reinach, *Denkmäler deutscher Tonkunst*, xv (Leipzig, 1904), with an important introduction.

saprei curare il vanto di grandezza passaggera,' which can surely be taken as a kind of personal confession on the part of Frederick, admitting the vanity of transitory greatness and advocating the gentle application of sovereign authority. In devising virtuoso ornamentation for the voice, Graun outdid even Hasse, as the following excerpt from *Cleopatra e Cesare* shows:[1]

Ex. 86

(An unhappy soul alone is found in me.)

Here we even have an example of the old *trillo*—the rapid reiteration of one note advocated by Caccini and found in, for instance, Monteverdi's *Orfeo*. One of Graun's main objects was to get away from the form of the *da capo* aria, and in his later operas he turned to a two-part cavatina form. Italian singers and dancers, such as the famous Barbarina, lent a special glamour to the opera performances in Berlin.

DÉCOR AND PRODUCTION

No account of Italian baroque opera would be complete without some more detailed mention of its elaborate external appearance than has been attempted in the foregoing pages.[2] This was not dictated by pomp and luxury but was an attempt to combine all the arts. The sensual and graphic portrayal of the emotions, the presence of the

---

[1] Leipzig, Städt. Musikbibl, III.5.10.

[2] In connection with the present section see the relevant pages in Wolff, 'Oper, Szene und Darstellung von 1600 bis 1900', Heinrich Besseler, Max Schneider and Werner Bachmann (eds.), *Musikgeschichte in Bildern*, iv, 1 (Leipzig, 1968).

elements of surprise and wonder, were fundamental to the baroque theatre: the stage, therefore, was inundated with a spate of constantly changing scenes. The sets were partly architectural designs, conceived by first-rate architects, and in another sense they were pictures, composed strictly in accordance with the rules of perspective, into which the singers were duly placed. The system of wings used in the baroque theatre meant that scene-shifting could be carried out very quickly.

Specialists in operatic stage design and machinery were already emerging early in the seventeenth century, outstanding among them being Giacomo Torelli, whose designs for *La finta pazza* (Venice, 1641), *Il Bellerofonte* (Venice, 1642), *La Venere gelosa* (Venice, 1643), and *Le nozze di Peleo e di Teti* (Paris, 1654) became widely known from copperplate engravings.[1] Venice produced a large number of stage designers— men like Antonio Mauro, Domenico Girolamo, Lodovico del Basso, Giacomo Cipriotti, and Tommaso Bezzi (nicknamed 'lo Sticchino'). In Venice, too, the most astonishing stage effects were quite usual— shipwrecks, conflagrations, clouds that rotated and sank down, pieces of scenery which were transparent, or else made of glass—but there is very little descriptive material available on this subject.[2]

Vienna was the headquarters of Lodovico Burnacini, whose exceptional, extravagant sets for Cesti's *Il pomo d'oro* were mentioned in the first chapter: they should not be regarded as typical of the normal productions of Italian opera. Burnacini wielded a tremendous influence, and his designs were still being copied in Hamburg after 1700.[3] Domenico and Gasparo Mauro worked in Munich, and their engravings for *Servio Tullio* (1685), among other works, are preserved in the libretto. They are as relatively little known as the costume designs by Stefano della Bella for the Teatro della Pergola in Florence towards the middle of the seventeenth century.[4] Printed librettos are in fact the principal source of illustrations showing operatic stage sets.[5]

After 1700 Ferdinando and Francesco Galli Bibiena were largely responsible for giving a new aspect to operatic stage design by erecting their sets obliquely. The result of this use of perspective was a closer relationship between stage and auditorium, and in addition, new and

---

[1] See Worsthorne, *Venetian Opera in the Seventeenth Century* (repr., Oxford, 1968), where several designs are illustrated, and Per Bjurström, *Giacomo Torelli and Baroque Stage Design* (Stockholm, 1961).

[2] But see in addition André Tessier, 'La décoration théâtrale à Venise à la fin du XVII siècle', *La Revue de l'Art ancien et moderne*, liv (1928).

[3] See Wolff, *Die Barockoper in Hamburg*, i, pp. 355 ff. and 362.

[4] Information from Oskar Fischel. See the illustration in Haas, *Die Musik des Barocks* (Potsdam, 1928), p. 176.

[5] See ibid., pp. 146 ff., 151 and 174 ff., and plates viii, xv, etc.; also idem, *Aufführungspraxis der Musik*, plates xiii and xiv.

unexpected visual angles were created. The older 'peep-show' stage had already undergone considerable modifications at that time.[1] It is especially interesting to examine the relationship at this period between stage design and painting. For instance, Francesco Algarotti recommended the study of paintings by Titian, Poussin, and Claude and the application of their landscape technique in stage sets. Conversely, the influence of the theatre on the fine arts was considerable: the highly charged acting of the singers on the stage, coupled with the pictorial quality of baroque stage design, often inspired artists in their landscape painting, interiors, festive scenes and love scenes—this influence is especially noticeable in the work of Bellotto, Longhi, and Tiepolo.[2]

The costumes and gestures of the actor-singers on the stage were in the style of their own time, and not that of the period in which an opera was set. The singers moved with a stylized dancer's gait resembling the steps and positions of early ballet. This fashion was as integral a part of the official code of public behaviour in the baroque age as the wigs and swords. Despite the stylized, dance-like acting, the performances were usually vivid and full of movement, as can be seen from an examination of Metastasio's texts and their stage directions. The singers are given copious instructions covering a wide range of gesture and expression.[3]

OPERA IN SPAIN[4]

Although Italian operatic influence was paramount in Spain during a large part of the eighteenth century, its beginnings—when the first Italian company appeared in Madrid in 1703—were not particularly auspicious. The company was accorded royal patronage, without which it would hardly have maintained its foothold, but it had to compete with a form of native opera, the *zarzuela* (which took its name from Philip IV's palace, Real Sitio de la Zarzuela), created by Calderón (1600–81). Though the alternation of spoken dialogue with songs and dances, characteristic of the *zarzuela*, arose naturally from the Spanish custom of musical interpolations on the stage, it was an increasing emphasis on lyricism in the verse itself that gave musical intervention its

[1] See Paul Zucker, *Die Theaterdekoration des Barock* (Berlin, 1925); Joseph Gregor, *Denkmäler des Theaters*, 12 portfolios (Munich, 1925 ff.), especially portfolio 2; and Franz Hadamowsky, *300 Jahre österreichisches Bühnenbild* (Vienna, 1960).

[2] See Wolff, *Die venezianische Oper*, p. 183 f., and idem, *Die Barockoper in Hamburg*, i, pp. 345–75.

[3] Such as *uscendo frettoloso* (departing hurriedly), *con impazienza* (impatiently), *turbata* (disturbed), *con isdegno* (scornfully), *trattenendola* (restraining her), *abbracciandola* (embracing her), *si alza con impeto* (he rises impetuously), *snuda la spada* (he bares his sword), *piange* (she weeps), etc.

[4] By José Subirá, with revisions and additions by Ann Livermore and Gerald Abraham.

chance to expand. Mythological representations were no new fashion. Gil Vicente, founder of the Spanish-Portuguese drama, provided a musical frame for divine and supernatural actions in the 1520s in his *Cortes de Jupiter*, and in *Dom Duardos* he stopped the action during an entire scene for songs and instrumental pieces to affect the characters; and an *égloga pastoral* by Lope de Vega, *La selva sin amor* (The forest without love), was performed at court in 1629. *La selva* is known to have had a great deal of music, though it is impossible to determine how much of the text was sung; and the name of the composer remains unknown, though he was probably the blind Juan Blas de Castro (*c.* 1560-1631).[1] But it was Calderón who perfected the balance between song and declamation of a poetic text. His earliest *fiesta de zarzuela* actually so called, the one-act *égloga piscatoria El golfo de las sirenas*, was performed on 17 January 1657, and his *zarzuela en dos jornados* ('in two acts') *El laurel de Apolo* was given in the Coliseo del Buen Retiro on 4 March of the following year. But the earliest Calderón *zarzuela* of which any of the music survives is the three-act *Celos aun del aire matan* (Suspicions, even of the air, kill) (5 December 1660), composed by Juan Hidalgo (d. 1685).[2]

The outstanding composers of *zarzuelas* in the early eighteenth century were Sebastián Durón (d. *c.* 1715) and Antonio Literes (*c.* 1670-1747). The latter's masterpiece, *Accis y Galatea* (to a libretto by José de Cañizares), was performed in the royal palace at Madrid on 19 December 1708 with an almost entirely female cast in accordance with the normal Spanish practice in the musical theatre of the period; the music included *recitativos* and ended with a *minué* danced by the whole company.[3] Another *zarzuela* or *comedia de musica*, *Los desagravios de Troya* (The compensations of Troy), with libretto by José Escuder and music by Joaquin Martinez de la Roca, produced at the Count de Montemar's palace at Saragossa on 29 June 1712, has the distinction of being the only Spanish opera to be printed in full score[4] until well into the nineteenth century. But the young Bourbon king, Philip V (1701-46), knew no Spanish, and he gladly permitted the Italian company, the 'Compañia de los trufaldines', as they were popularly nicknamed, to perform operas and other pieces—notably *El pomo de oro para la mas hermosa* (The

---

[1] See Livermore, 'The Spanish dramatists and their use of music', *Music and Letters*, xxv (1944), p. 146.

[2] Act I published by Subirá (Barcelona, 1933). See also idem, *El operista español d. Juan Hidalgo* (*Madrid*, 1934), and Otto Ursprung, '*Celos aun del aire matan*, die älteste spanische Oper', *Festschrift Arnold Schering* (Berlin, 1937), p. 223.

[3] Galatea's *da capo arieta* 'Si de rama en rama' is given complete by Rafael Mitjana in Albert Lavignac and Lionel de La Laurencie, *Encyclopédie de la musique*, I, iv (Paris, 1920), p. 2111.

[4] Copy in Bibl. Nacional, Madrid.

golden apple for the most beautiful: sung in Italian, with a Spanish synopsis for the audience) on 25 August 1704—before the court in the Coliseo del Buen Retiro. The *trufaldines* had to leave the Buen Retiro, but in 1708 they established themselves in a theatre specially built for them, the Teatro de los Caños del Peral, where they remained until 1735. Philip's Italian leanings were greatly strengthened by his second marriage, to Elisabetta Farnese, in 1714, and in 1721 the Parmesan envoy, Annibale Scotti, was actually appointed director of the Italian opera. The immense influence of the castrato Farinelli from 1737 until the end of the reign of Ferdinand VI is well known; it was naturally musical as well as political, and under Ferdinand (1746–59) the superintendence of the court theatres was only one of his offices. Not only Ferdinand but his consort, Barbara of Braganza, were thoroughly Italian in their musical sympathies; her music-master, Domenico Scarlatti, moved to Spain with her when she married.

It was probably Scotti who did more than anyone else to encourage Italian composers to set Spanish librettos. Among the festivities for the wedding of the Prince of the Asturias in 1722 was a *drama musical u ópera scénica en estilo italiano* entitled *Angélica y Medoro*, for which Cañizares wrote the libretto; the composer is unknown but may well have been Paolo Facco, with whom Cañizares had collaborated two years before in a *Jupiter y Anfitrión*. Facco was an Italian composer who had gone first to Portugal, and then because of his reputation was retained at Madrid, where he stayed on as director of the royal chapel. A more important immigrant was Francesco Coradini (Corradini, Coradigni), a Neapolitan who came from Valencia to settle in Madrid in 1730. Here he composed a *melodrama armónica* 'in the Italian style' to a libretto by Cañizares, performed at the Teatro de la Cruz in 1731. This piece, *Con amor no hay libertad* (There's no freedom with love), suggests by the phrase 'in the Italian style' and by being sung in Spanish that full Italianization was not yet firmly established so far as the public —as distinct from the court—theatres were concerned. In Coradini's several contacts with more traditional Spanish centres of theatre music we can see the distinction made in Spain between Parmesan and Neapolitan artists, for the latter came from a state under Spanish rule and were not regarded as total foreigners. Coradini wrote many works for the city theatres; the municipality later commissioned religious plays (*autos sacramentales*) from him, and finally he was engaged as court operatic composer. Pieces like *Con amor no hay libertad* were real contributions to Spanish opera.

Two other Italians who appeared in Madrid at this period were Giovanni Battista Mele, a Neapolitan who arrived *c.* 1735, and a

Parmesan, Francesco Corselli (d. 1778), a few years earlier; both composed Italian operas and serenatas for the court as well as operas to Spanish words. The only outstanding native composer was José de Nebra (*c.* 1688–1768),[1] who was first and foremost a church musician; however, he wrote not only music for *autos sacramentales*, beginning with Calderón's *La vida es sueño* (Life is a dream) in 1723, but a great number of *zarzuelas*, most of them during the 1740s. In 1745 he was commissioned to set a Cañizares libretto, *Cautela contra cautela, ó el rapto de Ganimedes* (Craft against craft, or The rape of Ganymede), for the opening of the Teatro del Príncipe; two years later, for the same theatre, he composed *Antes que zelos y amor la piedad llama el valor y Aquiles en Troya* (Better than jealousy and love, piety excites valour, and Achilles at Troy), with a celebrated comic episode in which Briseis's maid Mademusela and Achilles's friend Melocoton sing seguidillas under the walls of Troy.

On the other hand, Italian opera flourished in the hands of Corselli, who was Nebra's Parmesan colleague in the Capilla Real. Corselli's first work for the stage was Spanish, *La cautela en la amistad y robo do las Sabinas* (Craft in friendship, and The rape of the Sabines) (1735),[2] but he evidently thrived on the opportunities that developed with Farinelli's arrival in 1737. The marriage of the future Charles III was celebrated at the Buen Retiro with Corselli's setting of Metastasio's *Alessandro nell'Indie*, in which the performers were Italian. His *Farnace* was given in 1739, his *Achille in Sciro*, again to a text by Metastasio, in 1744. The printed librettos of these years give Metastasio's titles in Spanish.

The Caños del Peral theatre was rebuilt in 1738 by Scotti; its use was obviously predetermined, and Italian companies played here under royal patronage. Operas by Hasse, Gaetano Schiassi (1698–1754) and others whose names are unknown—six works altogether—were performed, after which the theatre was closed for many years. (To what extent Hasse's *galant* style affected Spanish composers cannot fairly be judged until more scores of this period are available.) The Teatro de la Cruz was activated in 1743, and, as already mentioned, the Teatro del Príncipe was inaugurated in 1745 (on 5 June).

Generally the theatres had to make do with a skeleton orchestra: five violins and a bass viol sufficed for ordinary performances; a guitarist came forward on the stage to accompany the singers. But according to Farinelli's manuscript in the Royal Library,[3] the orchestra of the royal

[1] See Nicolás Solar-Quintes, 'El compositor español José de Nebra', *Anuario musical*, ix (1954).

[2] See Subirá, *La música en la casa de Alba* (Madrid, 1927).

[3] Madrid, Bibl. del Pal. Real, 1.412.

Italian opera at the Buen Retiro consisted of three keyboard instruments, sixteen violins, four violas, four cellos, four double basses, five oboes, two bassoons, two horns, two trumpets, and two drums. Here the musicians who played on the stage were drawn from the Spanish and Walloon guards.

When the royal opera resumed after Philip V's death in 1746, Scotti had been completely superseded by Farinelli. The season was opened in carnival week 1747 with the three acts of Metastasio's *La Clemenza di Tito* set by Corselli, Coradini, and Mele respectively, priority still being given to Corselli. However, the libretto was translated into Spanish by the neo-classicist poet Ignacio de Luzán. On 4 December, Queen Barbara's name-day, Metastasio's *Angelica e Medoro* was given with music by Mele, an honour which shows that he was now in highest favour. For the carnival of 1748 the same three masters set the three acts of Paolo Rolli's *Polifemo*, and for the king's birthday the same year Mele composed *El vellón de oro conquistado* (The golden fleece conquered), to Pico de la Mirandola's text. Mele maintained his ascendancy in 1749. For *Artaserse*, Metastasio's text was reduced, in accordance with a frequent practice, and though the score was by several composers Mele wrote all the recitatives. He also wrote the music for Metastasio's serenata *L'Endimione*; his *El vellón de oro conquistado* was repeated; and for Metastasio's *Demofoonte*, though a certain amount of new music was commissioned from Baldassare Galuppi, part of the score was contributed by Mele.

On the occasion of the wedding of the Infanta Maria Antonia Fernanda in 1750 Metastasio's *L'asilo d'amore* was chosen for the serenata; this time Corselli wrote the music, and it was elaborately staged under Farinelli's direction.[1] Twelve days later a new opera by Mele was given, *Astrea placata* (the Spanish title was *Armida aplacada*— Armida appeased), to Metastasio's libretto. These festivities were marked by Farinelli's being made Knight of the Military Order of Calatrava. However, Mele returned to Italy in 1752.

Another Neapolitan, Niccolo Conforto (1727–65), appeared with settings of Metastasio's *Festa cinese* (1751) and *Siroe* (1752), and a serenata, *Las Modas*, to words by Pico de la Mirandola, in 1754. In the next year he was formally invited to Madrid, and his first work, *La ninfa smarrita* (The bewildered nymph), apparently composed in Spain, was staged at Aranjuez on 30 May 1756 for the king's name-day; the music is lost. Later the same year he set Metastasio's *Nitteti*, 'at the request of his friend Farinelli'. In 1757 appeared his setting of the same

[1] For an account of these festivities and of Farinelli's productions generally, see Ralph Kirkpatrick, *Domenico Scarlatti* (Princeton, 1953), pp. 110–12.

poet's *Adriano in Siria,* and a one-act *La forza del genio, o sia Il pastor guerriero,*[1] with words by Bochechy, was staged on the king's name-day at Aranjuez. But this was the last season of the reign; the queen died on 28 August 1758, and Ferdinand a year later. Side by side with Conforto's operas from 1755 to 1758 the Bolognese Antonio Mazzoni's *Il re pastore* (1757) (to Metastasio's words) and an intermezzo, *L'orfanella astuta* (The shrewd orphan, 1758), by the Catalan composer Nicolás Valenti, known as 'Aulita', had been given. Works by Jommelli, Latilla, and Galuppi interspersed the production of Conforto's operas before his arrival in 1755, so he had stood comparison with some highly popular musicians before he was summoned to court. He appears to have been Farinelli's favourite protégé. Ironically, while all these Italians triumphed in Spain, a native composer, the Catalan Domingo Terradellas (1713–1751), was composing librettos by Zeno and Metastasio for Rome, Florence, Venice, and even London but remained unhonoured and apparently unperformed in his own country.

It should be mentioned that opera in Portugal belatedly followed a similar course. Serenatas and a *zarzuela, En poder de la Harmonia* (By power of harmony), by an unknown composer, were performed at the court of John V during 1711–13. Encouraged by his Austrian queen, John brought in Italian musicians and sent Portuguese to Italy to study, and one of the latter, Francisco António de Almeida, is credited with the composition of the first Italian opera by a Portuguese, the *dramma comico La pazienza di Socrate,*[2] performed in the royal palace during the carnival of 1733. *La finta pazza* followed two years later and *La Spinalba*[3] in 1739. 1733 also saw the production of a vernacular opera, *Vida do grande Dom Quixote de la Mancha,* by a Brazilian Jew, António José da Silva. But in 1735 one of John V's Italian violinists, Alessandro Paghetti, founded an opera company—at first with his own family as a nucleus—which opened with a *Farnace* (probably Vinci's or Giovanni Porta's), and he followed it with various works by Schiassi, Caldara, and Leonardo Leo. The supremacy of Italian opera remained unchallenged for thirty years after.

---

[1] Score in the Royal College of Music, London.
[2] Act III only in Lisbon, Bibl. da Ajuda.
[3] Complete score in Bibl. da Ajuda.

III

THE ORIGINS OF FRENCH OPERA

By MARGARET M. McGOWAN

OPERA has long been regarded as belonging to the 'disordered' tradition in French seventeenth-century theatre—the natural opposite of the decorous, unified form known to us as French classical tragedy. In fact, however, it is precisely at the moment when opera also assumes the barer lines of tragedy—when its action is governed by the rules that gave tragedy its unity and dramatic impact—that the so-called 'disordered' art comes into its own. Lully did not suddenly invent French opera. It emerged through a long and complicated process. Its origins, complex and multiple, are to be found in most musical and theatrical forms elaborated in the seventeenth century. Even those factors that seem to work against the establishment of opera in France paradoxically contain those very elements that will prove to be a necessary part of French opera. We shall see, for example, that court ballet, which seemed for so long a rival of opera, was actually preparing the ground for the new musical form.

It is important to stress that all those forms that went into the making of opera—court ballet, machine plays, pastorals, tragedies, French and Italian musical dramas, *airs de cour*—were often being developed simultaneously; and many continued to be elaborated side by side with French opera. Indeed it is often a difficult task to try to separate these various genres. Seventeenth-century writers were not very particular about nomenclature, frequently entitling the same work *ballet, comédie-pastorale, tragédie lyrique* or *pastorale tragique*, and employing every possible permutation. For reasons of clarity, the evolution of each of these forms will be discussed separately, if somewhat artificially, and it is also necessary to begin a little before the starting-point of the present volume to consider in a little more detail *ballets de cour* mentioned only briefly in the preceding volume.[1]

[1] See Vol. IV, pp. 811–12.

EARLY COURT BALLETS

Music and dancing have always been favourite pastimes at princely courts; they gave particular pleasure to French kings and queens in the sixteenth and seventeenth centuries, when an important tradition of court ballet grew and thrived ubiquitously. The sources of court ballet go back well beyond the famous *Balet comique de la Royne*, conceived by Balthasar de Beaujoyeulx in 1581 to delight Henry III and his favourite the Duc de Joyeuse; and ballets continued to be performed long after Isaac de Benserade received his last call from Louis XIV's court to prepare his *Ballet de l'Amour* in 1681. Not only French monarchs but their courtiers too, trained from early childhood to dance well, revelled in this form of art, and eagerly took part, alongside professionals, in most court performances. By the beginning of the seventeenth century most courts in Europe, recognizing French superiority in the dance, ardently sought to persuade French dancing masters to travel in order that they too might learn the intricacies of this art.[1]

The form of court ballet was usually fairly complex. Simple ballets—that is, dances performed to well-known *airs de cour* played on a handful of instruments—could, of course, be performed in the intimacy of any private salon (princely or bourgeois) with rudimentary décor.[2] Such works, indeed, were frequently improvised and served both to enliven evening entertainments and to satisfy the needs of the courtiers to demonstrate their talents. Probably most of the so-called *mascarades* danced during the reigns of Henry IV (1594–1610) and Louis XIII (1610–43) were of this type. While their large number gives us a clear indication of the popularity of such works, the simplicity of their form makes them less interesting for our purpose than the spectacular ballets organized for special court occasions. These mingled music, dance, verse, and spectacle to form a unified and dramatic whole.

At the beginning of Louis XIII's reign the task of co-ordinating such varied elements was given to the poet. Étienne Durand, for example, conceived the plan of the *Ballet de la Délivrance de Renaud* (1617); verses were then given to Pierre Guédron, who composed all the music for the ballet (with the exception of one *air* written by Gabriel Bataille); and Tomaso Francini undertook the construction of spectacular machines appropriate to the pastoral theme of Rinaldo and Armida, which Durand had borrowed from Tasso. The choice of such a theme ensures a certain degree of unity. Ballet is such an open form that one strong

---

[1] Their popularity was noted by Henri Sauval, *Histoire et recherches des antiquités de la ville de Paris* (Paris, 1724), iii, p. 329. The Duke of Buckingham, for example, commissioned a book on dancing from François de Lauze in 1623. See Margaret M. McGowan, *L'Art du ballet de cour en France, 1581–1643* (Paris, 1963), p. 243.

[2] A list of these can be found in ibid., pp. 251–309.

personality or exceptionally gifted artist could orientate its effect in new directions. Louis XIII's own love of music makes this art dominant in his *Ballet de la Merlaison* (1635); while extraordinary dancing and mimetic ability made some choreographers concentrate on burlesque themes for ballets where mime and acrobatics could develop freely, as, for example, in *Le Ballet de la Douairière de Billebahaut* (1626). The effects of different modes of preparation upon the ballet may be clearly seen by comparing the *Balet comique*, devised, as we have seen, by the choreographer Beaujoyeulx, with Durand's *Délivrance de Renaud*. In the former work the greater glory is given to the dance, to those complicated 'figures géométriques' which the author describes so lovingly and in such detail that their lavishness and harmony remain long in the memory. In the later ballet, however, a sense of drama is uppermost, built up through the combined efforts of poet, musician and choreographer within the romantic setting provided by the scene designer.

It has frequently been argued that Guédron's dramatic gifts were primarily responsible for such an effect of drama. For some years he had been the most sought-after composer of vocal music for court ballets;[1] and it is true that his compositions often heightened the emotional and dramatic content of the work. Yet one must not forget that, equally, the great impact of his songs derives from the dramatic context prepared for them: the form of the ballet largely controls the effect of the music. In the *Ballet de Mgr de Vendôme* (1610), Guédron tried to underline the dramatic nature of both Alcina's triumph and defeat by introducing a kind of recitative (see Ex. 87).[2] The novelty of such a procedure is emphasized by the difficulty that the writer of the official account finds when he tries to describe the exact nature of Alcina's singing: 'elle récitoit (en chantant et sonnant d'une Pandore)'. This musical declamation is further thrown into relief by the fact that two choirs of nymphs repeat the refrain to her song.

For his next extended work, however—the *Ballet de Madame* (1615), designed as a spectacular farewell to Princess Elizabeth before her departure for Spain—Guédron had the help of his son-in-law Antoine Boësset (1585–1643) and of Henry Le Bailly, whose reputation as a

---

[1] See Lionel de La Laurencie, 'Un musicien dramatique du XVIIe siècle: Pierre Guédron', *Rivista musicale italiana*, xxix (1922), p. 445, and André Verchaly, 'Un précurseur de Lully: Pierre Guédron', *XVIIe siècle* (1954), nos. 21–2, p. 383. Other composers were: Antoine Boësset, from 1622, after the death of Guédron, 'surintendant de la musique du roi, et maître de la musique de la Reine', and Gabriel Bataille (see Verchaly, 'Gabriel Bataille et son œuvre personnelle pour chant et luth', *Revue de musicologie*, xxix (1947), p. 1); along with Jean Boyer, François de Chancy, Étienne Moulinié and François Richard. See Vol. IV, pp. 187–94, for the songs of some of these composers.

[2] Taken from Henry Prunières, *Le Ballet de cour en France avant Benserade et Lully* (Paris, 1914), p. 236.

Ex. 87

1. Noi - res fu-reurs,   om-bres sans corps,   L'ef-froy   des vivans

et   des morts,   Trom-peu-se ban - de que j'ap-pel - le,____

____Im - puis-sante ou bien in - fi-de - le.   Al-lés, Dé-mons,

faib-les es - prits,____ Je vous quit-te- et____ tiens à mes - pris.

(Black furies, disembodied shades, terror of the living and the dead, I call on
you, deceitful band, powerless and faithless. Go, demons, witless creatures; I
leave you and despise you.)

singer seemed at its height when, in the role of Night, he sang the
opening verses in praise of the queen. Perhaps as a consequence of this
collaboration, as well as of the nature of the ballet itself, the vocal
music is less strikingly dramatic. Most of the verses are compliments to
the royal family in a pastoral guise: the king is 'notre grand Pan', the
queen is both Minerva and a shepherdess. In the *Délivrance de Renaud*[1]
Guédron selects the most moving moments of the drama to set to
music: the opening scene of enchantment, when Armida's musician-
minions succeed in charming Rinaldo with their three-part song; the
moment when Armida discovers that her slaves have lost their power;
the soldiers' chorus; and their dialogue with the prophet. Armida's
despair is very reminiscent of Alcina's tones of fury mingled with
complaint:

Ex. 88

Quel____ su - bit____ chan - ge-ment!   Quel-les

---

[1] Prunières transcribed all the music for this ballet. In addition to the work of Guédron,
Bataille and Boësset composed one air each, and Jacques de Belleville wrote all the instrumental music. See Prunières, op. cit., pp. 251–65; the following example is on pp. 259–60.

(What sudden change, what harsh news! O gods! what do I see? Do you dare, faithless demons, to appear before me?)

The whole movement of the ballet leads up to this moment of Armida's discovery of the failure of her magic powers; Rinaldo's release follows automatically, and the 'grand ballet'—a solemn spectacular dance, signifying joy and harmony restored—closes the proceedings. In many ways, as far as music for court ballet is concerned, this ballet can be seen as Guédron's masterpiece. He composed a variety of pieces: choral ensembles, *récits*, and dialogues, showing that he could control music for massed voices, even if the harmonies seem a little rigid.

Guédron's most dramatic compositions nearly always coincide with court ballet at its most unified as a form. After 1619 another form of ballet came into prominence and helped to develop the gifts of Antoine Boësset.[1] His talent was primarily lyrical, and his languorous music fitted in well with ballets whose form was simply a theme with variations —either burlesque or serious. His airs for the *Grand Ballet de la Reyne représentant les fêtes de Junon la Nopcière* (1623), displaying his talents as a melodist, provide good examples of his latter style; while the *Ballet de Billebahaut* (1626) shows evidence of the former.

[1] Marin Mersenne and Constantijn Huygens conducted a correspondence about the relative merits of Boësset and the Dutchman Jan Albert Bannius. This is recorded in W. J. A. Jonckbloet and J. P. N. Land, *Musique et musiciens au XVIIe siècle* (Paris, 1882), pp. lxxx ff.

Although one can analyse in some detail the contributions of composers for the vocal parts of many ballets—since their works were subsequently published in collections of *airs de cour*[1]—it is much more difficult to get a clear idea of the scope of instrumental music used in these ballets. André Philidor, Louis XIV's music librarian, left a vast collection of transcriptions; but Prunières demonstrated their unreliability, showing that, while only the treble and bass parts of any composition are given, even these have been tampered with.[2] Often the composers of music for dancing were the choreographers themselves, as was the case with Jacques de Belleville, who directed the dance movements of the *Délivrance de Renaud*; indeed, it was rare, before 1657, for a musician to compose all the music—vocal and instrumental —for a ballet. Choruses for large bodies of singers, often preceded and followed by tiny instrumental symphonies, abound in most ballets of this period (1580–1643). Jacques Mauduit, according to Mersenne, excelled in music involving large numbers of voices and instruments; and, since his time at the Académie de Musique et de Poésie, he had never ceased to experiment with ways of blending voices and instruments together—the opening music for the *Délivrance de Renaud*, performed by sixty-four voices, twenty-eight viols, and fourteen lutes was composed and directed by him. Such musical effects were particularly suited to the theatre, not only to condition the responses of the audience, but also to form a bridge between reality and illusion. The theatrical possibilities of such ensembles were abundantly realized by the composers of the *Ballet de Tancrède* (1619), Belleville and Guédron. Here complicated cloud machines helped to enhance the theatrical power of the music. Twenty-eight angels suspended in the heavens sing the glories of Louis XIII; the incantations of Ismeno, in the dead of night, are accompanied by strange sounds, 'groans and growls, with thunder and light-

---

[1] The principal collections, all published by Ballard, are as follows: Pierre Ballard, *Airs de différents autheurs* (1621), *Airs à quatre de différents Auteurs* (1610, 1613), *Airs de cour* (1615, 1617, 1619, 1621, 1623, 1624, 1626, 1628); Robert Ballard, *Recueil d'airs de Luth* (n.d.), *Recueil d'airs* (1614); Bataille, *Airs de différents autheurs mis en tablature de luth* (1608, 1609, 1611, 1613, 1614, 1615), *Airs de différents autheurs mis en tablature par eux mesmes* (1617, 1618, 1623); Antoine Boësset, *Airs à 4 et 5 parties* (1617, 1620, 1621, 1624, 1626, 1628, 1630, 1632, 1642), *Airs de cour* (1620, 1621, 1624, 1626, 1628, 1632, 1643); Boyer, *Airs à 4 parties* (1619), *Airs* (1621); de Chancy, *Deuxième livre d'airs de cour* (1644); Moulinié, *Airs* (1624, 1625, 1629, 1633, 1635), *Airs de cour* (1637, 1639); Richard, *Airs de cour* (1637), *Airs de cour à 4 parties* (1637); and de Rigaud, *Airs* (1623). On all these *airs* see: Théodore Gérold, *L'Art du chant en France au XVIIe siècle* (Strasbourg, 1921), pp. 1–95; the articles by Verchaly listed in Vol. IV, p. 864; and in particular his edition of 90 *Airs de cour pour voix et luth (1603–1643)* (Paris, 1961); but see also the review of the latter by Daniel Heartz in *Journal of the American Musicological Society*, xv (1962), p. 356.

[2] See Prunières, op. cit., pp. 211–12. Instrumental music for a *ballet à cinq* was published by Jules Écorcheville from the manuscript at Kassel in *Vingt suites d'orchestre* (Berlin, 1906, repr. 1970), no. 2. There are also some helpful comments in Michel Brenet, *Les Concerts en France sous l'ancien régime* (Paris, 1906).

ning sounding, coming from the souls of the departed'. Even the dances in this ballet are extravagant, impregnated with some magic power. Ismeno's actions, for instance, are closely matched and imitated in the music:[1]

Ex. 89

The flames which rose from the enchanted forest seemed a fitting climax to this ghoulish experience. The descriptive powers of music had been awakened, and this was to be exploited in ballet, play, and opera throughout the seventeenth century. The music in burlesque ballets, for example, tried to represent the ridiculous nature of the characters not so much through the musical notation as through strange assemblages of musical instruments, as in the *Ballet du sérieux et du grotesque* (1627), where the instruments were 'vielles, trompes marines, lanternes, grils, jambons et piés de pourceaux'. Cacophony, in fact, often replaced genuine musical composition.

Although it is obvious that many of the essential ingredients of opera are already present in these early court ballets, it must also be stressed that these forms, however protean, had severe limitations musically. The vocal music was frequently composed only for the first verse of a long speech, and the mood of the other verses does not always correspond. A good example is the music for the famous lines of Armida (see Ex. 88), which also does duty for a rather insipid song of praise:[2]

> La présence de ce grand Roy,
> Et tant de beauté que je voy,
> En charmes divins si fertiles
> Ont rendu les miens inutiles.

In addition composers had to put up with the most appalling acoustics, since most of these works were performed in the large, overcrowded auditoriums of temporary theatres, which were accommodated in the

[1] Taken from Prunières, op. cit., p. 216.   [2] See ibid., p. 236.

Louvre and other princely palaces for these exceptional occasions. Bénigne de Bacilly is very eloquent on this particular deficiency;[1] and yet conditions did not improve even when Louis Le Vau, François d'Orbay and Gasparo Vigarani and his sons built the Théâtre des Tuileries in 1658: vast space and a multiplicity of pillars apparently made it impossible to hear vocal compositions at all, though instrumental passages performed there were often praised.

Moreover, the original unified form of works like the *Ballet de Mgr de Vendôme* or *La Délivrance de Renaud* was temporarily lost, and the ballet assumed a form very like a modern spectacular revue, where splendidly clad personages filed past in song and dance, their characters and attributes only loosely linked to the main theme of the work. In a sense, the art of the dance had won its competition with the other arts: ballet merely provided a means to show off one's dancing talent, and the musical possibilities of the genre were temporarily forgotten.

LATER COURT BALLETS

No one was more eager to display his dancing powers than Louis XIV. He was an excellent dancer, and after the troubled years of the Fronde (1648–51) he regularly exposed his considerable talents to the admiration of his courtiers, until he retired from the public stage in 1670. At first (1650–55) the music for the works in which he appeared was mainly instrumental, accompanying the elaborate ballets devised by the celebrated dancer Charles-Louis Beauchamps.[2] Sung *récits* introduced each of the four parts of these rather formalized ballets, a typical, interesting and influential instance being those composed for the *Ballet royal de la Nuit* (1653). Some of these *récits* were contributed by Jean-Baptiste Boësset[3] and Michel Lambert.[4] Others were composed by Jean de Cambefort, including that of Night with its melodic declamation; one for the Hours constructed with special attention to dissonant chords carefully prepared; one for the Moon, showing the influence of Boësset; and another for Venus—a light and gay piece, the first part of which is as follows:[5]

---

[1] See Bacilly, *L'Art de bien chanter* (Paris, 1668), p. 45; English edition, *A Commentary upon the Art of Proper Singing*, trans. and ed. Austin B. Caswell (*Musical Theorists in Translation*, vii) (New York, 1968), p. 22.

[2] Jean Loret, *La Muze Historique* (18 February 1657) describes him as 'l'incomparable Beauchamp / Le meilleur danseur de France'.

[3] Jean-Baptiste was the son of Antoine Boësset; see Norbert Dufourcq, *Jean-Baptiste de Boësset, 1614–1685* (Paris, 1962).

[4] Lambert was in 1661 'maître de la musique de la chambre du Roi'; see La Laurencie, *Les Créateurs de l'opéra français* (Paris, 1930), p. 195, who argues that his music is more dramatic than that of Boësset.

[5] See Prunières, 'Jean de Cambefort', *Année musicale*, ii (1912), p. 205. The four *récits* mentioned are printed at pp. 219–26, the example being on p. 223.

Ex. 90

(Flee far away, flee far away, enemies of joy, miserable objects! Must one see you amid all that is attractive and sweet in love?)

All these words and notes—the complicated dances in which Jean-Baptiste Lully probably made his first public appearance as a talented dancer (and perhaps composer)[1]—were intended to prepare the climax of the ballet, the rising of the Sun, that is the King of France, Louis XIV. Projection of his greatness through a varied use of verse, music, dance, and spectacle became the sole aim of the ballets performed in Louis's reign. He gave them unity; but it was the artists' task to find suitable

[1] This ballet is discussed by Charles I. Silin, *Benserade and his Ballets de Cour* (Baltimore, 1940, 2nd. ed., 1970), pp. 214–28; the reference to Lully is on p. 219, Lully (1632–87), the dominant figure in seventeenth-century French music, was Italian-born; he was taken to France when he was fourteen and was in Louis XIV's service from the age of twenty (when the king himself was only fourteen).

means of diversifying this single theme. After 1655 music began to play a more dominant role: the *récits* were sometimes songs, dialogues, or serenades; and the chronicler Loret starts naming the singers who take part, as though, suddenly, the public has become alive to the importance and emotive power of the music. Mlle. Hilaire, the most popular of all singers, Mlle. de la Barre, and Signora Anna Bergerotti are named; male voices are rarely mentioned, except in the librettos.

As this form evolves so music assumes a larger role until, by the *Ballet de Flore* (1669), the songs seem to overshadow the dancing. It might well be that music could only be given a chance to develop fully when the king's dancing prowess was on the wane. It might also be that Lully, having established himself skilfully in the favour of Louis and the public, gradually managed to impose his own ideas upon those of his colleagues Boësset, Cambefort, Louis de Mollier, and others. He seems to have composed most of the music for the *Ballet des Plaisirs* (1655); and in 1657, for the *Ballet de l'Amour Malade*, he even assumed Boësset's role as composer of the songs. For the first time a composer had the chance to give a unity of tone to a choreographic work.[1] In the following year, on a pastoral theme from Gomberville's novel *Polexandre*, Benserade created his verses for the *Ballet d'Alcidiane*. Boësset and Mollier composed the airs, and Lully himself wrote all the instrumental music, as well as introducing *récits italiens* (I,1), a *marche italienne* (I,7) and a *trio italien* (III,7) into his primarily French score.[2] One remarkable feature about this ballet is its overture. It shows the extent to which Lully tries to preserve the traditions of court ballet while introducing at the same time elements from his own personal inspiration. Slow and pompous instrumental movements traditionally began and ended court ballets, setting the atmosphere of splendour suitable for the occasion; and it was usual to return to these solemn and serious sounds in the final moments—no matter how burlesque and unserious the intervening parts of the ballet may have been. The two-part overture of the *Ballet de Mademoiselle* (1640) is fairly typical. The slow majestic rhythm of the pavane opens the ballet, immediately followed by the same music played at double the speed. Lully retains the two-part structure of a solemn, slow opening followed by a quicker section. The second section, however, is no longer a simple repetition of the first at greater speed, but is, instead, a new composition in complex, lively style, with the dotted rhythm that was to become a feature of most of the instrumental pieces in his operas. Lully's tight control over his orchestral players, forcing

---

[1] Loret, op. cit. (20 January), singles out Lully for special praise: 'Il faut toutes fois, que je die / Que Batiste, en toute façon, / Est un admirable Garçon'.

[2] It is possible that some of the fast speeds in Lully's works are connected with his astonishing skill as a dancer.

them to pay strict attention to rhythm and attack, was another reason
for the success of his instrumental movements. Here is the beginning of
the overture to the *Ballet d'Alcidiane*:[1]

Ex. 91

[1] Most of the music by Lully mentioned in this chapter has been published in the (still
incomplete) *Œuvres complètes*, general editor Prunières, 10 vols. (Paris, 1930–9). The
present example is in *Les Ballets*, ii, ed. André Tessier and A. Dieudonné (Paris, 1933),
pp. 13–14. Further on the French overture see *infra*, pp. 222–3.

The protean nature of ballet allowed all such developments. Yet it is noticeable that these were usually undertaken with considerable caution. Musical contributions tended to vary in the way that the elements of décor, costume, and dance were diversified to satisfy the needs of variety and ingenuity demanded by a court always avid for superficial change. *Récits*, dialogues, choruses, miniature symphonies, all had their established places in the ballet; but their composers—even Lully—did not fully develop their musical possibilities within that genre. The form of ballet was fixed by the desires of the king, while its open-ended structure seemed to allow for much experimentation. But on the whole the innovations were restricted to shortening or lengthening the work, or to juggling with its parts, as in the *Ballet des Muses* (1666), which had three different works of Molière incorporated into its successive performances[1]—a somewhat crude means of catering for the royal taste for novelty.

FRENCH THEATRE: PASTORAL THEMES AND MACHINE PLAYS

Pastoral literature had frequently provided court ballets with themes. This preference for love stories gleaned from the works of Ariosto, Tasso, contemporary novels, and ancient mythology extended to the public theatre. The lyrical expression of feeling, happy or lamenting, became the dominant note in most plays. Orpheus with his lute made more appearances on the stage than any other figure, his musical powers of persuasion being frequently exploited. Authors were quick to seize upon the dramatic and pathetic possibilities of his legend; thus Chapoton's play *La descente d'Orphée aux Enfers* (1640)—a mainly spoken drama—ends with the bard's long sung lament, 'Fidelles tesmoins de mes peines/Arbres sacrez, superbes Chesnes', and his suicide; and in Corneille's *Le Toison d'or* (1660) Orpheus serves as a kind of bridge between earth and heaven, calling down the gods and pleading for their aid.

Basically founded upon a utopian or escapist view of the world, pastoral plays constantly introduced themes concerned with magic, metamorphosis, and the marvellous; for there is no better way of making an emotional impact than through the sung incantations of a Circe or through the persuasive songs of the sirens (cf. Claude Boyer's *Ulysse dans l'Isle de Circé*, 1649). It was thought that, if these magical musical effects could in some way be supported by visual illusion, then the total effect of the love drama might well be even more compelling. Naturally the public wanted to be thrilled by the sight of highly complex stage

---

[1] *Mélicerte* was replaced by a *pastorale comique* on 5 January 1667 and by *Le Sicilien* on 14 February.

machines at work, and scene designers such as Giacomo Torelli, the Marquis de Sourdéac, and the Vigarani family were only too eager to show off their new inventions and demonstrate their increasing technical mastery. Paris theatres were quickly transformed, and the area behind the stage was considerably enlarged to accommodate the machinery necessary to produce the cloud effects of *Le Toison d'or* or the heavenly flights of *Psyché* (1671). Music had a very important role to play in this elaboration of spectacle, for its theatrical possibilities were soon perceived and put into effect.

At first music was used only intermittently; it accompanied the arrival of gods upon earth, as in Jean de Rotrou's *Hercule mourant* (1632) or *Les Sosies* (1636); it accompanied the ballets which had been designed to complicate the intrigue of Jean Gilbert Durval's *Agarite* (1636) or of Rotrou's *Alphrède* (1636); or it served merely to enhance the pompous prologues, where gods or allegorical figures uttered elaborate compliments to France or her king, as in Jean Donneau de Visé's *Le Mariage de Bacchus et d'Ariane* (1672). Boyer's prologue to *La Feste de Venus* (1669) is more ambitious. The soft melodies of pipes and sweet-sounding flutes set the pastoral scene, then gradually give way to the sound of violins playing ritornellos. Their concert is interrupted by trumpets heralding Victory's approach, and the scene finally fades on the dances of the slaves of love performed to the sound of more violins. This festive atmosphere is typical of many pastoral plays where shepherds and their loves—whether in the guise of human beings or gods—play, love, and weep. Their lives are circumscribed by the pattern of their love, and these patterns are the principal matter of the plays. Intrigues, rivalries, feelings of joy, and sometimes of pain, are the elements to be communicated to the audience, as is demonstrated in Charles Dassoucy's *Amours d'Apollon* (1650) and Charles de Beys's *Triomphe de l'Amour* (1655), both of which contained a considerable quantity of songs, dialogues and instrumental pieces.[1]

Little is known of the composers of the music for these plays and instrumental pieces; it is probable that, as in the ballet, different musicians were employed for the vocal and instrumental parts. Perhaps already existing music was used, lifted out of another context; this would not have been too incongruous, since there is often a disturbing sameness about the content of these works. The musical contributions could, nevertheless, be fairly varied in form. For instance, in Boyer's *Amours*

[1] Prunières analyses these works in *L'Opéra italien en France avant Lulli* (Paris, 1913), pp. 333–51; they are also discussed in detail by La Laurencie, *Les Créateurs de l'opéra français*, pp. 166–70. Another important article on opera at this time is Étienne Gros, 'Les origines de la tragédie lyrique et la place des tragédies à machines dans l'évolution du théâtre vers l'opéra', *Revue d'Histoire littéraire de la France*, xxxv (1928), p. 161.

de Jupiter et de Sémélé (1666), where the music is thought to have been written by Mollier, the play opens with the sound of trumpets and the Prologue presents the expected compliments to the city of Paris. Thalia, playing on a drum and accompanied by a consort of viols, comes down from heaven; Euterpe arrives, to the music of flutes and oboes; and then all these instruments together perform a symphony fit for the appearance of Apollo. Each goddess in turn performs a song in praise of the arts, and, appropriately, 'fureurs poétiques' arrive to demonstrate their qualities through a complicated dance. Thus the Prologue ends; but, throughout the rest of the play, music and dancing form a continuous thread, linking the stories of Jupiter's loves, and the proceedings terminate spectacularly with the heavens burning to the sound of music. Music, in fact, lends the necessary unity to this play, as it does in Donneau de Visé's *Le Mariage de Bacchus et d'Ariane*, where the mood of the work is lighter.

Such cohesive power was frequently lacking, since the form of these plays was almost as elastic as that of ballets and permitted—as in Philippe Quinault's *Comédie sans comédie* (1654)—heterogeneous elements from comedy, farce, pastoral, tragedy, and machine plays to stand ostentatiously and awkwardly side by side in the same entertainment. Corneille, on his own admission, felt that music and machines had not been properly integrated into his tragedy *Andromède* (1650), though the composer, Dassoucy, did try to multiply the use of choruses to enhance the spectacular and emotional moments of the drama: the choruses of the people and of Andromeda's nymphs provide a kind of sensitive audience on the stage itself. We seem a long way from French opera, it is true, in these plays. Yet it must be stressed that it is through such performances as these that the public at large became conditioned to having musical elements in their plays and that Lully and his associates understood the theatrical power of music and the emotive force of spectacle, which could so quickly establish a world of wonder for the spectator. Once a sense of the dramatic in word and music was integrated with a unified conception of a work then the real conditions for opera would be achieved.

COMÉDIES-BALLETS

Lully gained further experience of the possibilities of music in drama through his collaboration with Molière.[1] This began in 1661 when Fouquet, who wished to surprise Louis XIV when he received him at his country seat at Vaux le Vicomte, asked Molière to provide some

---

[1] The only work on Molière's *comédies-ballets* is out-of-date: Maurice Pellisson, *Les comédies-ballets de Molière* (Paris, 1914).

suitable entertainment to delight the king. Molière conceived *Les Fâcheux*, a rapid-moving farce whose comic effects all derive from the unexpected, haphazard arrival of a large variety of beings who sing and dance their way importunately around a pair of lovers, who strive to meet but fail to do so until the end of the piece, when their union is celebrated with general festivities.[1] The usual pains and laments of a lovelorn couple are here totally dominated by the verve and gaiety that this irrational revue exudes. Molière liked singing, and both he and Lully were excellent dancers; and, in such a kaleidoscope of activity, they both gave virtuoso performances, which won the favour of the king. For some time Molière remained the dominant partner in the collaboration: he amused Louis XIV and was free to dictate to Lully the kind of music he wanted—and gaiety from songs and dances, communicating enjoyment or satire, was what Molière required.

But the court demanded a certain restraint, a certain elegance and decorum in its pleasures. The gargantuan banquets they absorbed needed to be tempered by a sense of the noble and the refined. Molière catered for these tastes with *La Princesse d'Élide* (1664), writing light, well-modulated verse, which was easy to set to music; and Lully wrote *récits*, dialogues, and extended instrumental movements to accompany the many dances devised to soothe the princess. In 1670 the king himself suggested the lofty theme of *Les Amants magnifiques*, to which Lully's contributions were even more numerous.[2] In this atmosphere of the best of all possible worlds, in the Valley of Tempe where musicians and poets can sing at will, the good genius of Lully orchestrates symphonies for a 'quantité d'instruments', songs of Æolus and Tritons, and music for innumerable dances (prologue). He composes choruses and an extended 'petite comédie en musique', entirely sung (second interlude); and finally his most ambitious musical composition to date: the last interlude, which opens with a magnificent chorus of four Greek heroes, whose song alternates with that of a massed choir and an instrumental symphony and leads to a trio sung by the priestess and her two helpers. Opera will not make any greater musical demands than this.

Such works as *La Princesse d'Élide* and *Les Amants magnifiques* illustrate only one of the two strands that held the Molière-Lully collaboration together. The festive occasion always demanded laughter, and, although there are some pastoral scenes in these other works, as in the interludes for *George Dandin* (1668), where Lully experimented with large vocal ensembles, he was more often forced to develop the more

---

[1] Lully composed the courante sung and danced by Molière as Lysander (I, 3).

[2] The music survives in the Bibliothèque du Conservatoire, Paris, in a manuscript entitled 'le divertissement royal 1670'.

impish side of his gifts and to extend his repertoire. Farce is the co-ordinating principle that fully integrates music, dance and speech. At first, apart from *Les Fâcheux*, the harmonizing was not quite perfect: in *Le Mariage forcé* (1664), for example, the ballets were felt to be a little unnatural and were removed when the play was put on again in 1668. But by the time Molière came to write *Monsieur de Pourceaugnac* (1669) he had come to realize the comic and dramatic advantages of integrating music and ballet more thoroughly into his work.[1] Laughter is the anti-dote to the menace of doctors and their tribe, as he noted in 1665 in *L'Amour médecin*, where Comedy, Ballet and Music sing together at the end of the play:

> Sans nous tous les hommes
> Deviendront mal sains,
> Et c'est nous qui sommes
> Leurs grands médecins.

Lully did not take much persuading, and in *Le Bourgeois Gentilhomme* (1670) he surpassed himself both as composer—with the mock-solemn overture that begins the proceedings, his *chansons à boire* (of which 'Buvons, chers amis, buvons', composed as part of the entertainment for the banquet in Act IV, always remained his favourite song), and the symphonies he wrote to accompany the innumerable dances that gave M. Jourdain the impression that he was a genuine 'gentilhomme'—and in his role as 'le grand Mufti', which he danced and mimed with such dazzling panache that he virtually stole the show. The 'Ballet des Nations', composed as a glorious supplement to the ridiculous Turkish ceremonies, was again used by Lully in the following year as the prologue to his first opera, *Les Fêtes de l'Amour et de Bacchus*. Lully had triumphed over his greatest artistic rival in the favour of the king, and even in the eyes of the public; and he could now begin to evolve a style which was his own, dictated neither by poets nor by comedians. He would organize, direct, and command; he would be subservient to no one.

TRAGEDY[2]

Corneille's long preface to *Andromède* (1650) shows how far he was worried by attempts to write tragedies that have to do with music. For him it was the word that was of paramount importance, and he allowed music only at moments when no important fact or idea needed to be

---

[1] See Friedrich Noack, 'Lullys Musik zu Molières "Monsieur de Pourceaugnac"', *Festschrift für Johannes Wolf* (Berlin, 1929), p. 139.

[2] Romain Rolland has a very interesting discussion on opera and tragedy in his *Histoire de l'opéra en Europe* (Paris, 1895), pp. 259 ff.

communicated.[1] Obviously the word always had priority over music—except when it did not matter. This view was shared by many of his contemporaries: Madame de Motteville was persuaded of the emotive power of the word when it was declaimed dramatically from the stage; Madame de Sévigné went into ecstasies over La Champmeslé's declamation of Racine's verses;[2] even Mersenne, that erudite musical enthusiast, stated that the word was the very soul of music;[3] and Menestrier thought that only certain moments of the drama should be set to music.[4] The most eloquent views on the subject of music and tragedy were expressed by St.-Evremond. He admired enormously the tragedies of Corneille and therefore argued with much prejudice.[5] His arguments against opera, and music in drama, are nevertheless very revealing for our purpose. His main complaint is that one gets quickly bored because the mind is not sufficiently engaged and in consequence even the senses languish. Sense and sensibility lie behind his criticism; he clings obstinately to the first, and his attempts to justify this position lead to remarks such as: 'the structure of operas is an extravagant mixture of poetry and music'; he points out that it is incongruous for heroes to sing or for an entire domestic action to be sung from one end to the other, while only diminutives, such as 'Nanete' or 'Brunete', sound well in music. His prejudice thus leads him to the conceiving of opera as comic. Behind all these comments, however, lurks the fear that opera might spoil tragedy, and spoil it precisely because of the power of music upon the mind. In a letter of 4 February 1676 he writes to Anne Hervaert: 'Because of the way operas are conceived one loses all track of the performance through the dominance of the music'.[6]

In a sense St.-Evremond had reason to be afraid. He is concerned about tragedy and opera at a time when opera has absorbed significant elements from tragedy. They share many characteristics.[7] They develop the same themes and show similar heroic characters in similar predicaments,

[1] Per Bjurström points out the inappropriate nature, too, of many of Torelli's machines in his *Giacomo Torelli and baroque stage design* (Stockholm, 1961), pp. 154 and 156.

[2] La Champmeslé created many of Racine's leading female roles: see Sévigné, *Lettres*, ed. Gérard-Gailly, 3 vols. (Paris, 1953–7), i, pp. 229, 242, 249, 264, 266, 267, 456, 494, 497 and 507; iii, pp. 332, 344, 392 and 514.

[3] Mersenne, *Harmonie Universelle* (Paris, 1636–7) (facsimile ed. François Lesure, Paris, 1963; partial English translation by Roger E. Chapman, The Hague, 1957); see the chapter entitled 'Des Chants'.

[4] Claude François Menestrier, *Des représentations en musique anciennes et modernes* (Paris, 1681), p. 191.

[5] Noted at the beginning of his letters on opera, where he adds: 'Je n'admire pas fort les Comédies en musique', *Œuvres en prose*, ed. R. Ternois, iii (Paris, 1966), p. 149.

[6] Quoted by Ternois in ibid., p. 140.

[7] The same writers worked on both forms. See Racine's preoccupations as described by Jacques Vanuxem, 'Racine, les machines et les fêtes', *Revue d'Histoire littéraire de la France*, lxi (1954), pp. 295 ff.

and the interest in both is centred upon love. The aim of each is to move the spectator profoundly, the one through carefully balanced speeches, harmonious phrases, and a rigorous logic, the other through words harnessed to music. Both are solemn and majestic, belonging to the courts of princes, where elaborate ceremonies are performed. Both work according to a clearly established ritual, within a formal pattern which concentrates attention. The fussy incongruities and imbalance of moods of some earlier dramatic forms have been pared away: only the essential moments of communication and conflict between individuals remain, the spectacular setting serving to magnify their problems and to give them added status and more universal applicability. Music can at one and the same time develop the dramatic and emotionally charged moments of the story while not neglecting its own force as spectacle. Lully was very conscious of these similarities—he even sent his singers to the theatre with orders to study actors' styles of declamation; and his first major operatic success, *Cadmus et Hermione* (1673), through its concentrated dramatic form acknowledges opera's debt to tragedy.

ITALIAN INFLUENCE

Italian music had been heard regularly in France since the beginning of the seventeenth century, when Giulio Caccini and Ottavio Rinuccini had accompanied Maria de' Medici there.[1] Eighty years on, Menestrier was still aware that both these men had shown how words and music could be made to work together to produce the most poignant expressions of feeling so that men might, in Caccini's phrase, 'speak in tones'.[2] Giambattista Andreini resided in Paris from 1614 to 1622, and it is clear from his two published pastorals, *La Ferinda* and *La Centaura*, that he made a serious attempt to incorporate recitative into drama.[3] Not only did Italian theatre companies and musicians visit France, there was also much traffic in the opposite direction. Singers of the calibre of Bacilly, Lambert, and Nyert all went to study their art in Italy and returned having discovered how to embellish their songs, convinced of the need to pronounce words distinctly and to breathe and speak according to the rhythm of the verse.[4]

By the late 1630s there were official attempts to establish Italian music

[1] See Ferdinand Boyer, 'Giulio Caccini à la cour d'Henri IV (1604–5)', *Revue musicale*, vii (1926), p. 241: also Angelo Solerti, 'Un viaggio in Francia di Giulio Caccini (1604–1605)', *Rivista musicale italiana*, x (1903), p. 707.

[2] Menestrier, op. cit., p. 164, and Caccini, preface to *Le nuove musiche* (1602), ed. H. Wiley Hitchcock (Madison, 1970), p. 44.

[3] See analyses of these works in Prunières, *L'Opéra italien en France*, pp. xxxviii-ix.

[4] Tallemant des Réaux reports these facts in his 'historiette' on Nyert in *Historiettes* (ed. Paris, 1960–61), ii, pp. 521–3. Italian influence on French song is discussed by Gérold, op. cit., pp. 80 ff., and by Verchaly, 'Les airs italiens mis en tablature de luth dans les recueils français du début du XVIIe siècle', *Revue de musicologie*, xxxv (1953), *passim*.

in Paris. Richelieu, who appreciated the political advantages of lavish spectacle, encouraged artists to come to France from Italy. Indeed, he sent André Maugars to Rome in 1639 specifically to write a report on the state of music in Italy.[1] After the great minister's death in 1642, Mazarin, the successor he had trained, accelerated the process of drawing singers out of Italy. Mazarin had spent much time in Italy and had grown passionately fond of Italian music; moreover, many of his friends were music-lovers, men such as the powerful Barberini brothers, who had built a theatre in their palace in Rome capable of holding 3,000 people. It was as much in an attempt to satisfy his own musical desires as to dazzle Europe with lavish spectacles at court that Mazarin expended such energies on the search abroad for singers of quality.[2] At carnival time in 1645 a 'comédie italienne' (which cannot be identified) was given to entertain the court, and it had a musical prologue, arias, and dialogues accompanied by two violins and a bass instrument. No doubt some parts were sung by the extraordinary soprano Leonora Baroni (said to have been loved by the Pope, her talents sung by Milton), who had arrived in Paris in the spring of 1644 at the same time as the tenor Atto Melani and who had rapidly won the favour of the queen mother.[3]

This tiny pastoral was merely intended to whet the appetite for a more important work that was being prepared for the end of the year. Already in June 1645 Giacomo Torelli had come from Parma to create magnificent machines for the opera *La finta pazza* (words by Giulio Strozzi, music by Francesco Sacrati).[4] By command of Anne of Austria, Jean-Baptiste Balbi had set to work to compose ballets to be introduced at the end of each act. The singers were all Italian: Margherita Bertolotti, who played Aurora in the Prologue and whose sweetness of voice was praised in the official account; Louisa Gabrielli Locatelli, who played and sang the role of Flora with great vivacity; and Giulia Gabrielli, a passionate singer who took the part of Thetis. The opera was a success, not so much because of the music but rather through the astonishing spectacular effects achieved by Torelli. February 1646 witnessed yet another Italian opera, *Egisto* (presumably, but not certainly, Francesco Cavalli's), this time intended to please the Barberini brothers, who had

[1] See Maugars, *Response faite à un curieux sur le sentiment de la musique d'Italie* (Rome, 1639), ed. Ernest Thoinan (Paris, 1865, repr. London, 1965); English translation in J.S. Shedlock, 'André Maugars', in Robin Grey (ed.), *Studies in Music* (London, 1901), p. 215.

[2] Prunières gives a detailed analysis of his correspondence; see his *L'opéra italien en France, passim*.

[3] Leonora stayed in France only one year, much to the queen mother's regret. Melani was to be a faithful servant to Mazarin in his dual role as singer and spy.

[4] The opera had already been performed in Venice in 1641. The French preface and synopsis are published in Marie-Françoise Christout, *Le Ballet de cour de Louis XIV, 1643–1672* (Paris, 1967), pp. 195–204.

arrived in Paris a month earlier. Their presence gave an extra impetus to Mazarin's obvious determination to flood the Paris musical scene with Italian compositions. Anne of Austria loved melancholy songs, and the opera was full of such languid solos. Although no one else seems to have particularly liked the work—Madame de Motteville thought she would die of cold and boredom—plans went ahead for one of the most ambitious opera productions of the time.

Luigi Rossi had come to Paris at Mazarin's request in June 1646. He immediately began to gather together a group of artists capable of singing his opera *Orfeo*: Marc'Antonio Pasqualini (a castrato, to sing Aristeus), another castrato, in the service of the Bentivoglio family, to be Eurydice's nurse, Atto Melani (Orpheus), Anna Francesca Costa, known as 'La Checca' (Eurydice), and Rosina Martini (Venus).[1] The librettist, Francesco Buti, had added numerous ballets, to be inserted in each act; and Torelli was again in charge of the machines, the first performance being considerably delayed, since the stage of the Palais Cardinal necessitated considerable modifications.

Dramatically the work is very poor. A prologue in which Victory sings the triumph of French arms is followed by a multitude of scenes where the serious and the burlesque are unhappily thrown together and where the high points of emotional tension are immediately undermined by dances of satyrs or dryads. Musically, however, the opera is highly significant. It is melancholy music, admired by the French. St.-Evremond writes of its charm and lyrical expression of feeling—an impression confirmed by the Florentine representative living in Paris, who notes the extent to which the instruments charmed the audience. The *Gazette* goes so far as to state that the singing, joined to the playing of the instruments, 'drew the soul through the ears of the spectators'.[2] The king went three times. The public, however, seem to have been more impressed by the scenery than by the music.

The composer, who admired the French way of singing,[3] was especially gifted in the writing of purely lyrical airs. This was undoubtedly his preferred mode of composition, and he was often prepared to sacrifice the dramatic potentialities of the text to such lyrical expression. His melodic writing is nearly always beautiful and it becomes particularly

[1] Full discussions of this work are given in Romain Rolland, *Musiciens d'autrefois* (Paris, 1919), pp. 55 ff., and in Prunières, *L'Opéra italien en France*, chap. 3. Music from the opera is contained in Hugo Goldschmidt, *Studien zur Geschichte der italienischen Oper im 17. Jahrhundert*, i (Leipzig, 1901), pp. 295–311. See also Donald Jay Grout, 'Some forerunners of the Lully opera', *Music and Letters*, xxii (1941), p. 1, which touches on several other matters discussed in the present chapter.

[2] Quoted by Christout, op. cit., p. 50: 'Selon la Gazette, le chant joint au jeu des instruments tire "l'âme par les oreilles de tous les auditeurs"'.

[3] St.-Evremond, *Œuvres*, iii, p. 124, notes that Rossi was actually responsible for the admiration accorded Antoine Boësset's airs.

poignant in the very last scene of the play, when Orpheus utters his despair in a three-verse aria based on the principle of strophic variations over a bass moving mainly in crotchets. The beginning is as follows:[1]

Ex. 92

(I, who in life was left without my soul, do not come to see so shadowy a realm.)

The following example shows the still greater pathos of the close, when, as at the end of the first two verses, the bass becomes chromatic, and the repetition of words now makes the effect even more intense:

Ex. 93

[1] This and the two following examples are taken from Goldschmidt, op. cit., pp. 307–8, 309, and 303–4 respectively.

Deh!   ren - de - te-mi, o dei,   l'a - ma - to___ be - ne.

(. . . where yet at the last hour every mortal comes, O gods, give me back my beloved.)

By contrast, Eurydice's melancholy seems more voluptuous and less strained. To introduce variety into his vocal writing Rossi intersperses his solos with duets, trios, quartets, and even choruses for from six to eight voices. Here he shows his greatest ingenuity and grace with the use of homophonic writing varied with more imitative sections emphasizing his polyphonic gifts, as in the Prologue. Trios of voices calling to each other, echoing each other and the instruments, are elegantly handled and seem to anticipate many passages in Lully. The sweet-sounding dissonance of the trio in Act II, scene 9, provides a good example:

Ex. 94

(Fair eyes, go to sleep.)

Sometimes, in his search for descriptive effects, Rossi introduces an incongruous note, as in the first scene of Act III, when the 'fileuses' are suddenly revealed. On the other hand, the power of the instrumental music accompanying Eurydice's refusal to abandon Orpheus in spite of Venus's threats makes that moment very dramatic. The weakest part of the opera is the recitative. The disappointing impression that it gives can perhaps be explained by the wordiness of Buti's text. The knowledge that the librettist is at fault does not, however, relieve the monotony. This comment nevertheless seems a detail compared with the success the opera enjoyed: a success which aroused Mazarin's critics to complain about the expense lavished on such luxuries while the people of France starved. Such criticism culminated in the Fronde, which was to keep Italian singers silent until 1654.

In *Le Nozze di Peleo e di Teti*—libretto again by Buti, music by Carlo Caproli—performed for the first time on 14 April of that year, a careful attempt to balance French and Italian elements was made.[1] French

---

[1] The synopsis is published by Christout, op. cit., pp. 205–11.

singers appear side by side with the Italians Vittoria Caproli (the composer's wife), Antonio d'Imola, Girolamo Pignani, and Giuseppe and Filiberto Ghigofi, who took the major roles. Carlo Caproli had been called to Paris with his troupe specially for this occasion. Except for the ballet music,[1] the music of the opera is lost; the official account refers only to its sweetness. In any case, it is probable that the Parisians were drawn not so much by the singing as by the dancing, since the king took several roles alongside the professionals Beauchamps, Mollier, Vertpré, and Lully. Mazarin was delighted with the opera-ballet's success,[2] and he immediately began making plans for getting Italian singers over every year so that he could form a permanent company.[3] Unfortunately his dream was never realized. For the marriage of Louis XIV a company of Italian singers was hurriedly brought together —Giuseppe Melone, Atto Melani, Francesco Tagliavacco, and Anna Bergerotti—to sing on 22 November 1660 Cavalli's opera *Xerse*, first produced in Venice in 1654.[4] A number of ballets had been composed by Lully to please the king. These fitted very awkwardly into a work which was already somewhat diffuse. The whole effect of the drama, dominated by long stretches of recitative and impressive to the French only in details (such as the more moving parts of the role of Xerxes himself), was monotonous. Even the extraordinary agility and virtuosity of Lully and his dancers could not redeem a work in which neither the king nor his court had taken an active part.

Mazarin was dead by the time another work by Cavalli, *Ercole amante*—his only opera composed specially for Paris—was performed, on 7 February 1662. Cavalli had been called from Venice to take charge of rehearsals and probably had some difficulty in integrating the ballets, which were devised and composed by Beauchamps and Lully so that the king and his courtiers might make a magnificent entry into the Théâtre des Tuileries.[5] The singers had to sustain a libretto which made no attempt to explore the psychological depths of any of the characters. Hercules is a brute, his wife is merely jealous, and the two lovers are insignificant. The only character with a developed personality is Lykos, and this is largely because we see him in a burlesque light. Buti, who

[1] It is not known who composed the ballet music, which is preserved in the Philidor Collection.

[2] As a recompense Caproli was made 'maître de la musique du cabinet du Roi'.

[3] The French ambassador in Rome—De Lionnes—vetted the singers found by Italian agents.

[4] Fossard, the king's music librarian, apparently made a copy of the score of this opera in 1695; it is preserved at the Bibliothèque Nationale (MS. Um 4/2). See Prunières, *L'Opéra italien en France*, p. 251.

[5] The music, in an autograph score, is preserved in Venice, Bibl. Marciana, MS. 9883. See Prunières, op. cit., p. 278; the following example is taken from the musical appendix to this book, pp. 27-9.

again wrote the libretto, had obviously not thought of Cavalli's particular talents; he wrote the words as though he were still working with Rossi, arranging everything for airs, duets, trios, and so on. Cavalli could achieve a certain rhythmic vigour and grandeur of conception in his songs, as is evidenced in Pasithea's lullaby to sleep:

Ex. 95

(Murmur, streams; rustle, breezes . . . Rest, O sleep, in Pasithea's arms; you could not find a nymph more sympathetic to you.)

Nevertheless, his great strength was in his recitative, which takes on an imposing, expressive, and natural character. He accompanies some of his extended recitatives by the orchestra, producing both dramatic and emotional effects; striking contrasts of vocal and instrumental textures are a major characteristic of his work. Furthermore, what is most remarkable about this opera is Cavalli's ability to offer, through such variety, a much more massive conception, with broad, simple harmonies, than anything so far attempted in France in the seventeenth century. His achievement stands in great contrast to Lully's music for the ballets in the same opera: here rhythmic precision and elegance are the dominant features, whether in the sudden abrupt movements of the Shades or the tumbling of quavers to match the Winds. For once the official account of the opera in the *Gazette* was complimentary to the music, praising both the orchestral music and the choruses.[1] Yet this was the last Italian opera performed in Paris in the seventeenth century.

[1] Quoted by Charles Nuitter and Thoinan, *Les Origines de l'opéra en France* (Paris, 1886), p. lix.

Italian opera was not an unqualified success in France. In this last, most extravagant, performance even that part of the action which had consistently astonished and pleased the Parisians—the machines—had not functioned smoothly, and the acoustics in the vast theatre were so terrible that hardly any of the songs could be heard.[1] However, the whole experiment, extending over fifteen years, was not wholly un-rewarding. Lully and others had participated in these events and had observed the disadvantages of long recitatives and their unsuitability to French taste. They had also seen the emotional and dramatic effects that could be achieved by mingling voices and instruments, by sudden contrasts of textures and dynamics, and by allowing primacy to melody at moments of pathos. Lully must have noted and absorbed all these points and was ready to use them when he had his own chance to compose opera.

ITALIAN AND FRENCH RIVALRY

Probably one of the most cogent reasons against the easy establish-ment of Italian opera in France was the sense of rivalry between the two countries. This rivalry persisted in many spheres and on many levels throughout the century, and in particular—as has already been indicated above—in quarrels concerning their respective singing techniques. In 1639 Maugars claimed that the Italian style was more varied and more scientific; at the end of the century François Raguenet[2] maintained the same point of view, arguing that the Italians were possessed of greater virtuosity than the French. On the other hand Le Cerf de la Viéville[3] opposed Raguenet's reasoning, striving manfully to support the singers of his own country.

There were, of course, political reasons for French dislike of the Italians. A long tradition, dating back to the political activities of Catherine de' Medici and her Italian servants in the mid-sixteenth century, had conditioned such an attitude. The complaints at the expense of *Orfeo* in 1647 were not really because such luxuries should not be afforded but that the money was spent on 'Italian machines and Italian musicians'.[4] No doubt one must make a distinction between the opinion

[1] In 1665 Bernini claimed that no one could hear anything in this theatre, which could accommodate an audience of 7,000; see his *Journal de voyage*, ed. Marie Lalanne (Paris, 1885), p. 210.

[2] *Parallèle des Italiens et des François en ce qui regarde la musique et les opéras* (Paris, 1702); anonymous English translation, London, 1709, reprinted by Oliver Strunk, *Musical Quarterly*, xxxii (1946), p. 411, and (without the translator's copious notes) in idem, *Source Readings in Music History* (London, 1952), p. 473.

[3] *Comparaison de la musique italienne et de la musique française* (Paris, 1704-6); partial translation in Strunk, *Source Readings*, p. 489.

[4] Nicolas Goulas complained of 'l'horrible dépense des machines et des musiciens italiens'. See his *Mémoires*, ed. Charles Constant (Paris, 1879), p. 212.

of the public and that of court circles, where personages such as Anne
of Austria could indulge their love of song in the privacy of their own
salons; for in spite of the criticism Italian singers continued their sojourn
in France. There is evidence too that, for the general public, interest in
their music did not altogether diminish: the letters of René Ouvrard
show that he had a large collection of Italian pieces,[1] and those of
Huygens show that the musical activities of Anna Bergerotti and her
circle were greatly appreciated by many Parisians and foreigners, including himself.[2] It was not until 1667 that Italian musicians were
officially ordered to leave Paris.

It was, more precisely, the Italian bombastic style of singing to which
the French objected when Anna Bergerotti first arrived in France.
Everyone thought her style extravagant, the sounds she produced harsh
and strange: 'a kind of shrieking more suited to the vast space of a
church'. The Italian style of singing communicated strong emotions,
and, although St.-Evremond claimed that the Italians exaggerated
feelings and that the sounds they produced were more like laughing than
singing, Bacilly seems to admire the variety of feelings they could
convey, particularly the more dramatic and theatrical.[3] A long tradition
of ornamentation and improvisation had existed in Italy, giving singers
a versatility unknown north of the Alps. St.-Evremond, and many
Frenchmen with him, hated the long and often monotonous recitatives
of operas and felt uncomfortable at the blatant display of passions that
these works encouraged. There was a fundamental clash of national
temperaments as well as of styles. The most characteristic features of the
Italian style of singing ran exactly counter to the decorous, timid,
delicate, and refined art that had developed in France.

The French excelled in short songs and languorous and melancholy
sounds. Rossi was an exception to the rule among his countrymen when
he found the singing power of Lambert or Nyert so extraordinarily
moving that he wept.[4] Mersenne prefers these melancholy strains,[5] and
Menestrier claims that the French have perfected the art of singing
sweetly by the most discerning and exact control of the voice. But
Menestrier himself is too discriminating not to realize that the French
language is hardly suited to dramatic or passionate statements of feeling
set to music. It cannot sustain the variety that is required.[6] The mute 'e'

[1] Ouvrard was 'maître de musique de la Ste. Chapelle'. For his interest in Italian music
see Prunières, *L'Opéra italien en France*, p. 313.

[2] See his letters in Jonckbloet and Land, op. cit., *passim*.

[3] Bacilly, op. cit., pp. 91–4; Eng. ed., pp. 42–3.

[4] Ibid., in the 'Discours', p. 10, inserted in later editions (1671, 1679, and 1681) only; not
in English edition.

[5] See op. cit., 'Des Chants', p. 172.

[6] See op. cit., pp. 107–8 and 136–7.

provides a further source of difficulty, according to Bacilly, since it has so softening an effect that it is hard to produce sounds that are striking and deeply moving.[1]

Such were the problems that Lully had to solve. How could he so manipulate the delicacy of the language that he might create opera in French? His first attempts are interesting. Into the sixth and seventh entries of his *Ballet de la Raillerie* (1659) he inserts a dialogue between Italian and French music—the former sung by the celebrated Anna Bergerotti, the latter by Mlle. de la Barre. The episode could therefore not go unnoticed. Lully acknowledges the problem but does not solve it. Each singer praises the style of singing in her own country, and their debate neatly divides the honours between the two. As Lully gains more confidence, however, he begins to climb down from his fence of impartiality: Italian styles are more frequently matter for laughter, as they are by 1669 in his *Monsieur de Pourceaugnac*,[2] while French styles predominate in his ballets and later in his operas. The quarrels of a century help him to come to terms with the problem.

PATRONAGE

Patrons play a far more dynamic role in the elaboration of French opera, destructive as well as constructive, than one might at first suspect. Obviously, large sums of money must be available to lavish upon such enterprises. Apart from the king only the most eccentric of noblemen, such as the Marquis de Sourdéac[3] (whom Tallemant appropriately puts in his chapter 'Extravagans, visionnaires, fantasques, bizarres'), and the most wealthy of ministers, such as Fouquet, could afford to indulge such pleasures. State spending on such occasions was of course justified by the prestige propaganda which traditionally attached to such ceremonies; ambassadors reported its magnificence; and Louis XIV was pleased to bestow millions on projects which he knew would for the most part enjoy only an ephemeral existence.

Such patronage might have advantages in that expensive forms of art such as opera could not be realized without it; it also had serious disadvantages. Mazarin liked Cambefort and encouraged him; Colbert

[1] Bacilly, op. cit., p. 96; Eng. ed., p. 44. This reference occurs in a section dealing with the problems of the French language when set to music. Further on differing French and Italian attitudes to singing, earlier in the century, see Nigel Fortune, 'Italian seventeenth-century singing', *Music and Letters*, xxxv (1954), pp. 211–12 and 214.

[2] See also the burlesque Italian trio composed by Robert Cambert for Guillaume Marcoureau de Brécourt's comedy *Le Jaloux invisible*, put on at the Hôtel de Bourgogne in 1666. The music is contained in an appendix to Arthur Pougin, *Les Vrais Créateurs de l'opéra français: Perrin et Cambert* (Paris, 1881), pp. 281–97.

[3] See Armand Jardillier, *La Vie originale de M. de Sourdéac* (Le Neubourg, 1961).

did not, and thus the poor musician received no further royal com-
missions or appointments after Mazarin's death.[1] Louvois and Colbert
were patriots; it is not surprising, therefore, that while they were
organizing artistic affairs for the king no Italians received any royal
commands. The king himself had his own whims: Molière replaced
Benserade just as easily as Lully slickly ousted Molière from the king's
favour. An unhealthy spirit of competition was inevitable when all
artistic endeavour was centred on one figure.[2] Royal patronage not only
fostered competition between individuals, it brought about a similar
rivalry between the arts. Du Manoir complains about the activities of
dancers, and his exhortations are parodied in *L'Amour médecin* (1665);[3]
poets quarrel with composers (Molière and Lully), and scene designers
with librettists (Sourdéac and Perrin). All this is reflected in the opening
act of *Le Bourgeois Gentilhomme* (1671).

More serious still are the artistic repercussions of such patronage.
Orders were expected to be carried out at once—*Les Fâcheux* (1661) was
perhaps the only work that profited from such speed. Only the scene
designer could hold out for more time. Works were frequently huddled
together awkwardly, with ballets haphazardly knitted into the fabric of
operas merely because the king wished to offer himself and his courtiers
the satisfaction of a dazzling dancing display. Thus the Sun King
dominated even the form of the ballet, which revolved around his image.
His yearning for yet more glory caused prologues of victory to be introduced into operas, and choreographic offerings to be appended to every
act. The need to project his person into every corner of every artistic
work threatened to invade opera further: he would choose the subject
from several suggested by Lully and Quinault, and he saw himself, his
affections and his military prowess, reflected through the allegories.
Fortunately, however, the elaborate allegories freed the poet from the
need to congratulate the monarch more overtly, so the complimentary
verses of Benserade and others could disappear. Without the support
of the French monarch and his ministers French opera could hardly
have come into being. Yet by virtue of that support we feel the all-
abiding presence of the Sun King, limiting the thematic and musical
possibilities of this new genre. It could be said that one of the biggest
obstacles to the birth of French opera was the generosity of the king
himself.

[1] See Prunières in *Année musicale*, ii (1912), p. 222.

[2] The musical demands made by a court like Versailles are discussed, in part, in a series
of articles devoted to Versailles and its music in *XVIIe siècle*, xxxix (1958).

[3] Guillaume du Manoir, *Le Mariage de la musique avec la dance* (Paris, 1664), ed. Jules
Gallay (Paris, 1870).

THE JESUITS

The Jesuits[1] contributed another form of patronage which is frequently ignored in the discussion of the beginnings of opera in France; it seems important to give some brief idea of their dramatic enterprise. In their colleges they encouraged their noble and bourgeois pupils to love the theatre and in particular to become expert dancers and singers. It is to be noted that this encouragement was extended to all their colleges in France; thus in a sense they disseminated a knowledge of plays and operas throughout the provinces. At least once a year, usually in August, their annual distribution of prizes was celebrated by a Latin play with interludes of music and dance: the five tragedies performed at St. Omer between 1623 and 1631 all had choreographic interludes;[2] and *Tartaria Christiana* at the Collège de Clermont in 1657 was accompanied by four ballets, as the loquacious Loret informs us:

> Et pour augmenter la liesse
> Que cauzoit cette Sainte Pièce,
> On y dansa quatre Balets,
> Tant mystérieux, que folets . . .
> Plusieurs illustres s'y trouverent.[3]

Later in the century, as the theatre collections in the Municipal Library at Lyons testify,[4] it also became a habit to produce opera in the month of February. So magnificent, indeed, could these festivities be that the king and his entire court were frequent spectators. Louis XIII was greeted by song and dance—executed by pupils disguised as nymphs, Mercury, Ceres, Pallas, Apollo, and Pan—when he visited the Collège de la Flèche in 1614; and in the same year plays on chivalric and romantic themes, *Godefroy de Bouillon* and *Clorinde*, were performed.[5] A similar honour was paid by Louis XIV to the Collège de Clermont in 1661, when *Le Théâtre de la Justice* was performed with ballets and the most elaborate machines.[6] The Jesuits were very alive to the propagandist advantages of such performances, and some of their displays could

[1] A great deal of work is now being done on the contribution of the Jesuits to the theatre in the sixteenth and seventeenth centuries. Studies so far attempted include François de Dainville, 'Lieux de théâtre et salles des actions dans les collèges des Jésuites de l'ancienne France', *Revue d'Histoire du Théâtre*, iii (1950), p. 185; Robert W. Lowe, 'Les représentations en musique dans les collèges de Paris et de Province 1632–1757', ibid., p. 120; and idem, 'Les représentations en musique au collège Louis le Grand 1650–1688', ibid., xi (1958), p. 21. Most recently there is *Le Théâtre des Jésuites* (*Dramaturgie et Société*, ii, ed. Jean Jacquot, Paris, 1968), and Lowe, *Marc-Antoine Charpentier et l'opéra du collège* (Paris, 1966).

[2] See McGowan, op. cit., p. 212, n. 29.

[3] See Loret, op. cit. (18 August 1657).

[4] These came from the Collège de la Trinité and may well have formed part of the evidence used by Menestrier in his writings.

[5] See McGowan, op. cit., p. 210, n. 22.

[6] See Loret, op. cit. (3 September 1661).

seriously be said to have rivalled the splendour of court occasions. For the royal entry into Lyons in 1622 the Collège de la Trinité composed a *Pastorelle sur les victoires de la Pucelle d'Orléans*—a mixture of ballet and pastoral performed with all the necessary scenic apparatus. Dunkirk in 1640 witnessed a show—half play, half ballet—publishing the glories and world-wide achievements of the Jesuits. And such instances could easily be multiplied.

Music naturally played an important role on all these occasions. Annibal Gantez goes so far as to claim that music in 1643 enjoyed a better fate than previously, precisely because the Jesuits had encouraged that science in their schools,[1] in many of which there was apparently a daily music class.[2] The airs that one Intermet composed on the occasion of the king's visit to Avignon in 1622 were so successful that copies were snatched from the musicians' hands, and the king personally asked for a set. Eminent musicians were frequently called upon to work for the Jesuits in Paris: Thomas Gobert (director of the Ste.-Chapelle in Paris) was summoned by the Collège de Navarre in 1649, for instance; Cambert composed the airs for the Feast of St. Francis on 6 October 1657 and collaborated with Jesuits in 1671;[3] Marc-Antoine Charpentier often gave his services (cf. his work for the Collège de Harcourt, and his *Combat de l'amour divin*, composed as part of the entertainment when Corneille's *Polyeucte*, accompanied by ballets, was performed at that school);[4] and, later in the century, Lully's pupil Pascal Colasse contributed works for 'religious' occasions.

Although much of the musical evidence for these works is still fragmentary, it is nevertheless clear that the Jesuit contribution to music in the seventeenth century was not insignificant. These worthy fathers created the conditions for composite art-forms to flourish; they developed taste and a demand; and in their early presentations they often anticipated later developments, creating mixed dramatic forms before these were seriously considered by more professional theatres. One wonders how far Molière's taste, to take but one example, was developed by his days as a pupil at the Collège de Clermont.

PERRIN AND CAMBERT

Cambert was by no means insensible to the experiments in poetry and music that were being attempted in Paris and elsewhere. In 1658,

---

[1] See Annibal Gantez, *L'Entretien des musiciens* (Auxerre, 1643), ed. Thoinan (Paris, 1878), p. 27.

[2] See Lowe in *Revue d'Histoire du Théâtre*, xi (1958), p. 22.

[3] See Nuitter and Thoinan, op. cit., p. 221.

[4] See Lowe in *Revue d'Histoire du Théâtre*, iii (1950), p. 120. The music for this occasion is preserved in Bibliothèque Nationale, MS. Rés. Vm¹ 259, vol. xvii.

in a short elegy entitled *La Muette ingrate*, he tried his hand for the first time at composing a dramatic musical piece for three voices.[1] The experiment came to the ears of Pierre Perrin who, a well-tried poet in devising texts to be set to music, thought he would like to essay something more ambitious.[2] He and Cambert composed together a *Pastorale* for seven players, which was performed at Issy in April 1659 without dances or machines. Immediately, it seems, spectators felt that there was something new in this performance. There seemed to be a naturalness about the way in which words and music were moulded together. The setting for the play was intimate, the characters were few in number, their simple songs (fourteen of them) were linked together in one continuous musical movement. There was no dramatic cohesion, no plot, merely a set of singers communicating their feelings of love to the audience. The success of this venture was such that in the following month Mazarin had the piece performed at court and commissioned another play.

Perrin did not see either performance. He had been languishing in prison for some months in 1659, and he obviously felt that he could not let pass the opportunity of making public the importance of his contribution to the occasion.[3] In a letter written to the archbishop of Turin he explains why the *Pastorale* was different from anything else so far attempted in France.[4] Given his vulnerable position it is natural that he should overstate his case; but it is interesting to note that both his explanations and positive suggestions are argued through a systematic and conscious attack on the faults of the Italian conception of opera and singing. He, Perrin, has avoided their exaggerated and embellished style of singing, he has reduced their excessive length of play and speech, he has abandoned both the use of castratos ('l'horreur des dames, et la risée des hommes')[5] and the extraordinarily large theatres where nothing can be heard. His aim is a simple one: to communicate feeling in as varied a way as he can. In order to make this possible and attractive, he has composed short, irregular verses better fitted to musical accompaniment than the resounding alexandrine;[6] and, most important, he

[1] See his *Mémoire* in the archives of the Comédie Française, described by Nuitter and Thoinan, op. cit., p. 33. The music is lost.

[2] His poems written to be set to music are printed in his *Œuvres* (Paris, 1661), pp. 215–72.

[3] His trials and tribulations, and his quarrels with Sourdéac, Lully, and others are examined in detail in Nuitter and Thoinan, op. cit., and in Pougin, op. cit.

[4] The letter is published in his *Œuvres*, p. 273.

[5] The power of the singing of castratos is noted by Raguenet, op. cit.; see Strunk, op. cit., p. 483. Carlo Vigarani had mentioned the moral attitude of many Parisians in a letter of 18 March 1667 quoted by Prunières, *L'Opéra italien en France*, p. 318.

[6] Michel de Pure makes the same criticism of the alexandrine: cf. his *Idée des spectacles anciens et nouveaux* (Paris, 1668), pp. 297–8. It did, however, continue to be used for recitatives in particular.

has abandoned the notion of intrigue and those grave themes of Corneille which demanded such deep reasoning. Here he touches on the clash, which St.-Evremond was to diagnose, between sense and sensibility, consciously choosing to support the latter and to use the lyrical qualities of French rather than impose a style that could only be absorbed awkwardly into the language.

The death of Mazarin in March 1661 brought a halt to these experiments, and although the rehearsals of *Ariane et Bacchus* (their second play) were well advanced the project was abandoned. St.-Evremond records the beauty of Ariadne's lament, suggesting that it was as good as anything composed by Lully. We shall never know, for the music is lost.

It would be easy to exaggerate the importance of Perrin and Cambert in a discussion of the origins of French opera were it not for the fact that in June 1669 Perrin officially obtained permission from the king 'to establish in Paris and other towns of France music academies to sing plays in public, as is done in Italy, Germany and England'.[1] So runs the opening sentence of the letters patent. It seems that the need for such an institution,[2] and official recognition of this need were to serve as a kind of catalyst to the ambitious and increasingly successful Lully. Having found a theatre, Perrin and Cambert, together with the Marquis de Sourdéac and Beauchamps, started on their new work *Pomone*, performed for the first time on 3 March 1671.[3] Its success, which lasted eight months, was phenomenal. The theme of the work is trivial: Vertumnus loves Pomona, who rejects him, only to discover suddenly that she loves him. It makes no dramatic demands, but it does provide a simple thread along which can be set a series of songs, dialogues, and dances. An overture—with the now established form of a slow, stately section followed by a faster, livelier one—precedes the Prologue, where a nymph praises Paris and its king. Already the tone that is characteristic of this work as a whole has been set: it is sweet, very melodious and charming. Cambert seems to excel in expressing tender feelings in finely modulated phrases. Pomona's opening song, with its clear rhythms and elegance, is typical of his style:[4]

---

[1] The matter is set out in detail in Pougin, op. cit., pp. 96–9.

[2] See Nuitter and Thoinan, op. cit., p. 93.

[3] Details of the singers are given in Pougin, op. cit., p. 11.

[4] Only the music to Act I survives. There is an edition in vocal score, ed. J. B. Weckerlin (Paris, [1881]), in which the following five examples appear on pp. 13, 18, 45, 27, and 47 respectively.

Ex. 96

(Let us pass our days in the meadows, away from love and shepherds.)

In Venilia's *ariette* which comes shortly afterwards the tone moves gently towards a more marked gaiety, as the vocal line shows:

Ex.97

(The sweet pleasure of love is a fragile, tiny flower, which lasts but a morning.)

and Vertumnus's plaintive notes, full of languor and weariness (scene 7), mirror his character and predicament exactly, while recalling at the same time the long tradition of melancholy French *airs de cour*:

Ex. 98

Hé - las! que me sert – il de chan - ger tous les jours?

(Alas! what good does it do me to change every day?)

Thus Cambert carefully matches his music to the temperament of the characters and their changing fortunes. He extends as much care to the composition of descriptive passages, such as the following, which seems to reflect the energetic movements of the faun, who is the singer (scenes 4 and 5):

Ex. 99

C'est bien à toi, dieu mi - sé - ra - ble, De pré - tendre à tes

maux quel - que sou - la - ge - ment!

(It is just like you, miserable god, to expect some comfort for your woes!)

And the final example shows his skill in writing a livelier, more clear-cut recitative when Volumnus summons up the elves:

Ex. 100

Vous, que le ciel sou - met à mon o - bé - is-

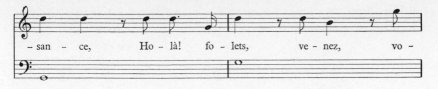

(You, whom the heavens have subjected to my obedience, you spirits, come, fly, follow my steps.)

The same qualities of melody, sweet and perhaps a little subdued, recur in his second opera, *Les Peines et les plaisirs de l'Amour* (1672),[1] which was based on a libretto by Gabriel Gilbert. In spite of its dedication to the powerful minister Colbert the life of this work was abruptly cut off. By order of the king the theatre was closed. The ever rapacious Lully, who since 1653 had extended his activities over every field of dramatic endeavour, realized the importance not only of the success of *Pomone* but more especially of the official privileges that Perrin had been given over musical and dramatic performances in France. Feeling that his years of apprenticeship were over, he had from 1670 exerted pressure upon the court and upon Perrin until he finally constrained the latter to sell him Louis's official royal favour. The Paris *Parlement* finally ratified new letters patent in June 1672, and Lully founded the Académie Royale de Musique. His only serious rival, Molière, died in February 1673, and the way was open for the effervescent Italian to receive accolades of the type recorded by Menestrier: 'since M. Lully has taken upon himself the organization of these musical productions, we have seen that perfection which can be achieved only by art, knowledge, genius, and a long experience'.[2] This comment appropriately points to the wide range of Lully's artistic experience. By 1673 he had collaborated with every major dramatic poet in France; he had perfected his trade not only from observation of the works of others but through close participation as dancer, singer, actor, poet, and composer. He had worked very hard to earn for himself the unassailable position he now held; and although one might question the methods he used to attain his exalted state, he was eminently capable of maintaining it with distinction.

[1] Of this work too there is a vocal score of Act I only, ed. Weckerlin (Paris, [1881]).
[2] Menestrier, op. cit., p. 150.

IV

FRENCH OPERA FROM LULLY TO RAMEAU

By Paul-Marie Masson

THE NATURE OF LULLIAN OPERA

OPERA, as conceived by Jean-Baptiste Lully (1632–87), with the help of Philippe Quinault, was a form of tragedy, sung from beginning to end, with an instrumental accompaniment. Its impact was further heightened by lavish scenery and stage effects and by having the action interspersed with dancing and mime. There can be no doubt that French opera at this period was really thought of in these terms. The phrase 'tragédie en musique' constantly recurs in the titles of Lully's operas and in contemporary writings. French opera, which came into being in the golden age of French classical tragedy when Racine was producing his masterpieces, can itself stake a claim to a place in the ranks of literature and can, like the earliest Florentine operas, be linked with the dramatic art of the ancient Greeks. For the librettos are poetic creations and may be judged as such, independently of the music.

The typical libretto of an opera by Lully takes a very special form. The poem is short, although the overall structure retains the five acts of the contemporary French drama, and there is a prologue in addition. The scenes may well appear short to the reader, and they are often written in short lines. This brevity is, of course, dictated by the relative slowness of the musical action, by repetitions in the musical setting and by the time taken up by passages for the orchestra alone. It is the poet's task tersely to explain and to indicate emotional processes rather than to describe. Furthermore, operatic poetry contains an element peculiar to itself: the element of the supernatural. It can people the stage with gods, goddesses, demigods, and sorcerers, who interfere in the affairs of men: it fuses cardinal elements of tragedy and epic. Greek and Roman mythology provide most of the material for the plots of French operas at this time, with the rare exceptions of subjects borrowed from Italian epic poetry or Spanish romances. This use of the pagan supernatural originates in the mythological masques, masquerades, and processions of the Renaissance, and French opera inherits it from early Italian opera; an even more important influence here is that of the court ballet, whose popularity was so enormous throughout the first half of the seventeenth century.[1] Whereas the Italians quickly discarded mythological subject-matter in favour of historical material and purely human stories, the French clung for a long time to the tradition of mythological opera.

A conception such as this has far-reaching consequences for the scheme of the operatic poem. If the gods or other supernatural characters take part in the action, their appearance (or 'descent', as it was then described) involves, on the one hand, extravagant stage sets generally out of place in tragedy and, on the other, many vicissitudes in the action, or unexpected dénouements which are no longer, as with Corneille and Racine, motivated solely by conflicting tragic passions. Opera relies on a *deus ex machina* to unravel the plot and move the action forward. The dramatic psychology, already lessened because of the necessary brevity of the literary text, is further weakened by these supernatural interventions, which all too often replace voluntary acts on the part of the characters. Human psychology is not entirely lacking, but a kind of artificial, unnatural psychology—it might be described as 'divine'—was a more important element in French opera for almost a century. Finally, the famous set of rules governing the three unities was no longer obeyed; there was no unity of time or place, and little unity of action.

However, leaving aside these literary peculiarities, what made opera an entirely original creation in French art was the fact that it achieved a union between literature and the other arts: with music, in its vocal parts and symphonies; with the plastic arts, in the various aspects of stage production; and with the dance, which is, in a sense, music in movement. The great innovation was the continuity of the music. All the elements of these condensed tragedies are translated into music, intimate dialogues as well as passages of high drama. This change, which decisively marks the birth of French opera several decades after similar continuity was achieved in Italian opera, was accomplished by Lully thanks to recitative, which as much as anything invests his work with its great emotive power. Audiences wept during sad scenes in opera as they wept at moments of pathos in literary tragedies: emotion in the French theatre received a powerful stimulus from opera.

Since opera was designed to be seen, the costumes, scenery, and stage effects were not the least of its attractions. French stage designers followed in the footsteps of their Italian counterparts, and Jean Bérain

---

[1] See the preceding chapter. Recent standard works include Margaret M. McGowan, *L'Art du ballet de cour en France, 1581–1643* (Paris, 1963) and Marie-Françoise Christout, *Le Ballet de cour de Louis XIV, 1643–1672* (Paris, 1967).

and Charles Errard learned their craft from Francesco Galli Bibiena, Giovanni Burnacini, Giacomo Torelli, and the Vigarani family. Their contributions were as vital as those of the poet and composer. The weaving together of poetry, ballet, and the plastic arts created a problem which succeeding generations have grappled with in various ways without achieving any definitive solution. It is essentially a problem of balance and harmony. La Fontaine went into this whole question very thoroughly—even then it corresponded almost exactly to the problem of the Wagnerian music drama—and decided that it was insoluble, since even the principle of a music drama is debatable. Nevertheless, if we take into account the techniques of his age, Lully's operas offer a notably successful artistic solution to the question.

THE BIRTH OF LULLY'S OPERATIC STYLE

What is this powerful, vigorous art form that so obsessed French dramatic composers up to and beyond the time of Rameau? It is the old French conception, revitalized by the Italian Lully.[1] Dramatic art according to Lully is a synthesis and a renewal. Up to the time of his first attempt at lyric tragedy Lully was still an Italian. Despite Jean-Baptiste Boësset's example and Michel Lambert's teaching, his vocal music in his early ballets was limited to Italian songs. For the *Ballet des Bienvenus* in 1655 he wrote an 'air grotesque italien', and in the *Ballet de l'Amour malade* (1657)[2] there are several more in this strain, the most famous being 'Ecche scibbe amor senza cochette'. While Lully specialized in this style of writing, Boësset wrote French *airs* for many of the same ballets. It seems therefore that initially the young Lully would not—or could not—write French tunes. Reports refer to him as 'the Italian composer', and at this stage of his career he drew his stylistic inspiration from the cantatas of Carlo Caproli and Luigi Rossi. The two styles clash for the first time in the *Ballet de l'Impatience* (1661). From that date Lully renounced his allegiance to the Italian style. His collaboration with Molière in the composition of *comédie-ballets* imposed a new discipline, for music was not to be introduced into these pieces except

---

[1] For biographical information about Lully these are some works that may be consulted: Lionel de La Laurencie, *Lully* (Paris, 1911); Henry Prunières, *Lully* (Paris, [1919]); idem. *La Vie illustre et libertine de Jean-Baptiste Lully* (Paris, 1929); and Eugène Borrel, *Jean-Baptiste Lully* (Paris, 1949).

[2] This is one of the few works discussed in the present chapter to appear in the incomplete collected edition of Lully's works, *Œuvres complètes*, general editor Prunières, 10 vols. (Paris, 1930-9); it is in *Les Ballets*, i. The only operas in the 'complete' edition are *Alceste*, *Amadis*, and *Cadmus et Hermione*. Nine others—*Armide*, *Atys*, *Bellérophon*, *Isis*, *Persée*, *Phaéton*, *Proserpine*, *Psyché*, and *Thésée* (along with *Alceste* and *Cadmus et Hermione*)—appear in late nineteenth-century vocal scores, ed. Théodore de Lajarte, in the series *Chefs-d'œuvre classiques de l'opéra français* (Paris, various dates).

at such times as it would be appropriate in everyday life. The co-authors set out to demonstrate this in *Les Fâcheux* (1661). In *La Princesse d'Élide* (1664) the whippers-in, awakened by Dawn, sing a fanfare which rouses the sleeping Lysicas. *Le Sicilien* (1667) contains serenades; and *Le Bourgeois Gentilhomme* (1670)[1] has music in the Turkish ceremony, for which the comedy has paved the way. Lully's style had now been stripped of all Italian embellishments. In *Psyché* (1671) this tendency is even more apparent. In other respects, too, this work represents an entirely new genre. It is no longer a comedy-ballet, but a tragedy-ballet, basically made up of mythology and stage effects. The numerous *airs* at the end of its third act are purely operatic in character. It is interesting to note that in Psyche's lament 'Deh, piangete al pianto mio', notwithstanding the Italian text, the musical setting is 'in the French style', though it does bear a few traces of the rich musical heritage of Monteverdi.

LULLY'S RECITATIVE

Influenced by the exaggerated eulogies of Le Cerf de la Viéville,[2] there has been a tendency to overrate the originality of construction in Lully's dramas. The innovation that unquestionably stemmed from Lully was the creation of a particular type of recitative, with or without orchestral accompaniment, in an operatic style: without this there could be no real dramatic development. The whole question of lyrical declamation hinges on it. Everything depends on the marriage of the music to the words; this created a special problem with French, which is not a resonant language. Lully faced this difficulty squarely, although it had already proved too much for any number of talented musicians, including Pierre Guédron, Jean-Baptiste Boësset, and Michel Lambert. Even Robert Cambert had not ventured to grapple with it. Recitative gives musical expression to the action as it unfolds. From time to time this action opens out in the form of *airs*, coinciding with moments of dramatic climax, as the characters assume the wings of passion or become sunk in the slough of despond. Recitative is the 'natural', stabilizing element in the drama. Its ingredients are rhythm and melody, with harmony as an added resource. In French opera, as in Italian, it is accompanied for the most part by a simple *basso continuo*; but this is by no means an invariable practice for (as we shall see) Lully wrote several notable recitatives with orchestral accompaniment, while many

---

[1] These two works are in *Œuvres complètes: Les Comédies-ballets*, ii and iii respectively.
[2] See his *Comparaison de la musique italienne et de la musique française* (originally printed in three parts, 1704–6), translated in part in Oliver Strunk, *Source Readings in Music History* (London, 1952), pp. 489–507; much of this extract is devoted to praise of Lully.

of his *airs* are supported only by the continuo. The narrative of the nymph of Fontainebleau in the *Ballet des Saisons* (1661) represents Lully's first use of this particular form. As early as 1665, in the *Ballet de la Naissance de Vénus*, Ariadne's lament is a perfect example of expressive recitative.[1] Both these *récits* are comparatively melodious— another important, continuing feature of French recitative in relation, for example, to Italian.

Despite the earlier attempts already mentioned, Lully deserves to be considered the true creator of French recitative. He drew his inspiration from the oratorical style of various French actors and in particular from La Champmeslé, Racine's leading actress.[2] The character of this style, emphatic, histrionic, and vibrant, endowed Lully's recitative with an acute inner intensity that moved its hearers. Though it may have been discarded by Pierre Perrin for *airs*,[3] the alexandrine was considered a suitable verse-form for recitative, since short lines and frequent rhymes would disrupt the line too much: the essence of recitative is that it should be smooth, evenly flowing and majestic. Sometimes Lully employed recitative very extensively: it may be noted in passing that the entire name part of *Amadis* is written in recitative.[4]

In his *Dictionnaire philosophique*,[5] Voltaire compares the recitative of Lully and Carissimi, drawing a parallel between Carissimi's motet 'Sunt rosae mundi breves' and Act IV of *Roland* (1685). Lully must surely have studied Carissimi's oratorios and other church music: it is clear that in his own motets he combined the French genius and the Italian more conspicuously than in his operas, which were no doubt more consciously French in style. There can be no question but that the musical basis of recitative in his operas lies in the Italian music that was native to him and that he transferred it from the church to the theatre, at the same time taking into account the characteristics of the French language (one or two subtleties of which seem, however, to have escaped him).

The melodic curve of the recitative, to which the words are set, is moulded to fit them in its rhythm and pitch. Expressive passing notes occur here and there, and there are some standard progressions, as shown in the following examples selected almost at random:[6]

---

[1] On these two ballets see Christout, op. cit., pp. 105–6 and 112–13 respectively.
[2] See p. 185, n. 2, for references to Mme. de Sévigné's enthusiasm for La Champmeslé.
[3] See pp. 201–2.
[4] *Œuvres complètes: Les Opéras*, iii.
[5] First published in 1764; see the section 'Opéra: du Récitatif de Lulli'.
[6] Lajarte eds., pp. 307; and 132 and 191, respectively.

Ex. 101

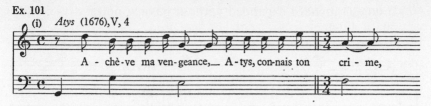

(i) *Atys* (1676), V, 4

A - chè - ve ma ven - geance,— A - tys, con-nais ton cri - me,

(Complete my vengeance, Atys, know your crime.)

(ii) *Bellérophon* (1679), II, 6

l'A - ché - ron, Le Co - cy - te, le Phlé-gé - ton,

(iii) *Bellérophon*, III, 5

Vous l'a - vez en - ten - du, Je n'ai rien à vous

di - re; Je plains vos dé-plai - sirs, Comme vous j'en sou - pi - re,

(You have heard, I have nothing to say to you; I regret your displeasure, like you I sigh over it.)

Broken harmonies or chord expansions are frequent in *Bellérophon* and in subsequent works.[1] The following examples show:

(*a*) distribution of a common chord by means of the descending minor sixth:[2]

Ex. 102

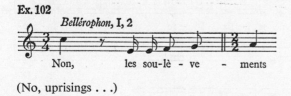

Bellérophon, I, 2

Non, les sou-lè - ve - ments

(No, uprisings . . .)

[1] E.g. *Alceste* (1674), I, 8 (edition in *Œuvres complètes: Les Opéras*, ii, p. 95); *Psyché* (1678), III, 2 (Lajarte ed., p. 115); *Proserpine* (1680), Prologue, 2 (Lajarte ed., p. 33).

[2] References in Lajarte eds.: (*a*), p. 42, (*b*), p. 65, (*c*), p. 55, (*d*), p. 54, (*e*), p. 203, (*f*) p. 252, and (*g*), p. 158.

(*b*) a common chord expanded without passing notes:

Ex. 103

(Having ordered two peoples under my laws . . .)

(*c*) a common chord extended with passing notes:

Ex. 104

(To the Athenians, to the opposite party . . .)

(*d*) a minor common chord spread to express rage and terror:

Ex. 105

(It is done! The crime is too great.)

(*e*) the chord of the diminished fifth distributed over two harmonies:

Ex. 106

(and to satisfy myself against a son I do not know, I love his own father.)

(*f*) the range of a minor seventh distributed over two harmonies, dominant and tonic in this instance:

Ex. 107

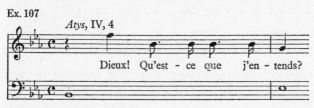

Atys, IV, 4

Dieux! Qu'est - ce que   j'en - tends?

(O gods! what do I hear?)

(*g*) spreading out of the chord of the dominant seventh (cf. Cavalli's recitative):

Ex. 108

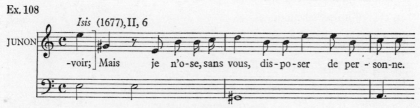

Isis (1677), II, 6

JUNON

-voir; Mais   je n'o-se, sans vous, dis-po-ser   de per - son-ne.

(But I dare not without you dispose of anyone.)

Lully used many old formulas, such as cadences on the third of the tonic chord, but also made some innovations, such as (*a*) melodic formulas found in Italian folk music:[1]

Ex. 109

Atys, Prologue

Quel Dieu   les fait   re - naî - tre?

(What god causes them to be reborn?)

There are also (*b*) stepwise melodic rise and fall diatonically, or, in moments of emphasis, chromatically as well:

Ex. 110

(i)

Thésée, I, 4

U - ne grê - le de traits ne l'a point re - te - nu.

(i) (A hail of arrows has not deterred him.)

---

[1] References in Lajarte eds.; (*a*), p. 10, (*b*), pp. 63 and 225, and (*c*), pp. 89, 168, and 124.

(ii) (What I have done, prompted by glory . . .)

and (*c*) brief chromatic upward movements and novel downward melodic leaps, as here:

Ex. 111

(i) (. . . of a new splendour.)

(ii) (And it is through him that I return to life.)

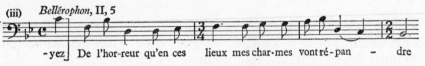

(iii) (. . . The horror that my charms will spread through these places.)

Often he punctuates phrases with expressive silences:[1]

Ex. 112

(i) (You have seen me, it is done, you will lose me, farewell!)

(ii) (Come! hate, vengeance . . .)

[1] Lajarte eds., pp. 122–3 and 55 respectively.

He also alters the time-signature in order to follow the natural rhythm of the words[1] and makes use of dotted notes for specific purposes, as he does in *Atys* to create a mood of solemnity.[2] He also uses striking syncopations to highlight interjections and important monosyllables,[3] giving a feeling of urgency and vivacity.

The harmony of Lully's recitatives is simple and not very varied; but he does his best to enliven the monotony by adding more lyrical passages, in an attempt to heighten still further the melodic line of the recitative, as in *Thésée* or *Armide* (1686). This led to his adoption of the recitative with orchestral accompaniment (*récitatif obligé*), which tends to be similar to *airs*, but is distinguishable from them by its greater freedom of construction and by the absence of repetition. Lully uses this type of recitative in moments of pathos or of passion, such as invocations and laments. It is rarely found in his early works, but in a late work such as *Armide* it is splendidly in evidence, above all in Act V, scene 5, at 'Le perfide Renaud me fuit', where the expressive power and wholly appropriate declamation are superb:[4]

Ex. 113

[1] See *Bellérophon*, I, 2, at the words 'Si pour chercher à vaincre il court dans les hasards' (Lajarte ed., p. 51) and some of the foregoing examples.

[2] At Cybele's narrative 'Malgré le Destin implacable qui rend de ton trépas l'arrêt irrévocable' in V, 6: Lajarte ed., p. 321.

[3] See *Thésée*, IV, 5, for example: Lajarte ed., p. 180.

[4] Lajarte ed., p. 313. There are several further examples, not only of recitative but from other forms besides in Lully's operas, in the by no means entirely accurate Norman Demuth, *French opera: its development to the Revolution* ([Horsham], Sussex, 1963), especially in chap. ix.

(Faithless Rinaldo pursues me! Faithless though he is, my faint heart follows him. He leaves me dying, he wants me to die! I see the light shining, the horror of eternal night yields to that of my pain . . .)

LULLY'S *AIRS*

In his *airs*, Lully is much more conservative. Unlike the recitatives, they are not peculiar to theatre music. They are the operatic counterpart of the old *chansons* and the later, more aristocratic *airs de cour*. Whereas the recitative describes the development of the action, *airs* indicate a pause, a moment of reflection or a point of climax. Lully is fond of two types of *air*, one more important than the other. The less important might be called the 'maxim' *air*, since it normally treats a general idea, a psychological maxim, either poetic or amorous. As a rule this type is sung by one of the minor characters (a practice frequently adopted later by Metastasio in his librettos) and tends to be inessential to the drama as a whole. In style it resembles the court *airs* of Guédron and Antoine Boësset and their contemporaries. The more important kind of *air* is the large-scale expressive *air*, occurring at a moment in the action when a principal character, finding himself in a tense situation, gives free rein to his feelings. This type is longer than the 'maxim' *air*, since its text analyses the singer's emotional state and the music is developed at greater length, with a more elaborate harmonic structure. It may be in binary, ternary, or *rondeau* form. These two different genres, so extensively used by Lully, remained in use throughout the period of French classical opera. Lully's *airs* lack the high degree of purely musical elaboration typical of the corresponding arias in Italian opera at this time. They are simply lyrical translations of the texts, more 'musical' than the recitatives, but still in the same spirit; as in so much French vocal music the words remain an important element in the general conception.

Lully is at his best in *airs* of a pastoral nature. Here he is the ardent follower of his father-in-law, Lambert (as in *Thésée*, Act IV). Often such *airs* take the form of sung dances: there are several attractive examples in *Bellérophon*, in Act V of *Alceste*, and in the prologues to *Psyché* and *Proserpine*. Through their simple charm they very quickly became street songs and ballads. Lully applied himself to developing the popular side of these songs: there is a story that he would sometimes stop his carriage on the Pont-Neuf to give the note to the singer and the fiddler who were performing his music.[1] Thus he both drew his inspiration from popular songs (*brunettes*) and added to their repertoire, for his *airs* themselves emerged as *brunettes*, as for instance 'Sommes-nous pas trop heureux?' from the *Ballet de l'Impatience*, in which, as has been pointed out above, he first found himself as a French composer. Popular music is indeed a far from negligible aspect of Lully's art.

---

[1] See Strunk, op. cit., pp. 498 ff., for Le Cerf de la Viéville's remarks on this subject.

His works are by no means lacking in dramatic *airs*, either. Io's fine F minor *air* from *Isis*, 'Terminez mes tourments', as well as the great impassioned *airs* in *Roland* and *Atys*, are masterpieces of vocal writing:[1]

Ex. 114

[1] Lajarte ed., p. 330.

(End my torments, powerful master of the universe; without you, without your love, alas! I should not suffer, reduced to despair; dying, wandering, I have taken my pain to a thousand terrible lands; a dreadful fury, dogging my steps, has followed me across the vast bosom of the sea . . .)

By contrast with Italian composers—and herein lies Lully's claim to originality—his *airs*, both large and small, are, as has already been suggested above, closely linked in style with the recitatives. The two types of writing are not set off sharply from each other as are elaborate, almost concerto-like arias and *secco* recitative in Italian operas: this is an important contribution to the unity of classical French opera.

The accompaniment to *airs* sometimes consists of a simple *basso continuo*; but some are provided with quite full support from the orchestra. In most cases, such an accompaniment follows the vocal line step by step, though from time to time Lully also wrote independent, thoroughly instrumental accompaniments expressing or implying the main ideas contained in the words. Thus in *Alceste*, IV, 1, the moving bass which from beginning to end accompanies Charon's *air* suggests the movement of the river or of his boat:[1]

Ex. 115

(Sooner or later you must pass over in my boat!)

Numerous other examples may be found: for instance, in Act V, scene 2, of the same opera, at the end of the duet, the accompaniment reproduces in the bass the phrase to which the word 'enchaîné' is set.

---

[1] *Œuvres complètes: Les Opéras*, ii, p. 235. Recorded in *The History of Music in Sound*, v.

Lully's few vocal ensembles—duets, trios, quartets—display equal mastery. The writing is mainly homophonic, with brief excursions into polyphony. They are so closely involved in the action that it is even possible to find recitative duets, as in *Alceste*, Act V, scene 4,[1] and *Atys*, Act III, scene 2.[2] Ensembles bring scenes to a satisfying close, or else they form the middle part of a chorus in *rondeau* form. They are also in some cases written to dance tunes, especially the duets, and it is not unusual to find them containing expressive interludes. A whole range of combinations is possible, the guiding principle, as with the expressive *airs*, always being to avoid disrupting the dramatic action. Lully has few trios; but one notable example is that sung by the Fates in *Isis*, anticipating the trio of Fates in Rameau's *Hippolyte et Aricie*:[3]

Ex. 116   LES TROIS PARQUES

----

[1] Where Alcestis and Admetus sing 'Pardonnez aux derniers soupirs' just before their *rondeau* duet: op. cit., p. 296.

[2] Here three phrases of recitative duet, for Doris and Idas, alternate with Atys's replies; typically they recount new developments in the plot. Then comes a duet proper for the same two characters, to be followed by yet another recitative duet. This is in the Lajarte ed., pp. 174 ff.

[3] Lajarte ed., p. 321.

mains. Le fil de la vi - e De tous les hu - mains

mains. Le fil de la vi - e De tous les hu - mains

mains. Tour - - - - - - ne dans

(The thread of life in all human beings, following our desire, rests in our hands . . .)

LULLY'S OPERATIC CHORUSES

Although it has sometimes been suggested that the choruses in Lully's operas are not entirely his own work and that only the top parts are his, he was nevertheless responsible for their re-introduction into opera. They had gradually disappeared from Venetian opera and by the early 1640s were largely a thing of the past, their place being taken by trios and quartets that threw the principal characters into greater relief.

This use of choruses (in binary, ternary, or *rondeau* form) is a unique characteristic of classical French opera, 'representing one of its finest features'.[1] Although it was usual to place them at the end of each act, their distribution is somewhat irregular: *Proserpine* has twenty-seven, *Psyché* only three. The function of the chorus is especially important in underworld scenes, or scenes involving magic incantations; but they are also useful for creating specific dramatic effects, and Lully does not hesitate to disrupt a chorus for a few bars if this suits his dramatic scheme. In the final divertissements, the chorus takes its place in the 'grand spectacle', alternating with the dances. It is not uncommon for the chorus to participate in the action, as in the sacrificial scene from *Bellérophon* (III, 5), the combat scene from *Thésée* (I, 1–3), and the underworld scenes from *Armide* (III, 4 ff.). Though the writing is simple, the chorus in *Persée* is treated with admirable skill, as Le Cerf de la Viéville recognized when singling out 'Descendons sous les ondes' (IV, 6) for special praise;[2] and those from *Armide* may well have influenced the choral writing of both Purcell and Handel. Lully's choruses are occasionally polyphonic—there are examples in *Alceste* and *Psyché* —but more often are so homophonic that some of his critics have mistakenly found them rather dull. To appreciate the guiding principles of Lully's work, we have to realize first and foremost that their clear-cut

---

[1] See Le Cerf de la Viéville, op. cit., ii, p. 74.   [2] See ibid., i, pp. 72–3.

harmony is better suited to the clear-cut syllabic rhythm that is so vital for the comprehension of the text.

It should be remembered that in seventeenth-century France people went to the opera not so much to hear the music as to follow the words through which the plot was worked out and eventually resolved. Music was the servant of the text. The music is there to create the proper atmosphere; Lully the mainly harmonic composer becomes Lully the more assertive contrapuntist as the action demands. These rare moments are, generally speaking, the tender passages in the small choruses, as for instance in the slumber scene from *Atys* (III, 4), or a comparable passage in Act IV, scene 4, of *Roland*. At times Lully momentarily uses choruses completely unaccompanied, as in the nymphs' chorus from Act III, scene 4, of *Isis*.[1] Elsewhere, for reasons of expression, he may score for double chorus (e.g. the shepherds' chorus in *Alceste*, V, 5), but it should be noted that such choruses are all alternating, not simultaneous ones, with the single exception of one in *Bellérophon* (I, 5).[2]

THE FRENCH OVERTURE

The exquisite artistry that charms the ear in Lully's vocal music is also found in his purely instrumental writing, particularly in the overtures and *airs de danse*. Lully was responsible for establishing the prototype of the French overture, drawing his inspiration principally from the *ballet de cour*; his first distinctive overture is that to the *Ballet d'Alcidiane* (1658).[3] This 'symphony' that preceded the opera and was resumed after the prologue soon lent itself to independent performance and was for long a major ornament of French music.[4] Lully's contemporaries and successors appreciated it greatly:

> Quand la toile se lève et que les sons charmants
> D'un innombrable amas de divers instruments
> Forment cette éclatante et grave symphonie
> Et par qui le moins tendre en ce premier moment
> Sent tout son corps ému d'un doux frémissement . . .[5]

---

[1] Lajarte ed., p. 204.

[2] Lajarte ed., p. 70.

[3] See *supra*, pp. 176–80, and Ex. 91.

[4] See Prunières, 'Notes sur les origines de l'ouverture française', *Sammelbände der internationalen Musikgesellschaft*, xii (1910–11), p. 565; also Nils Schiørring, *Allemande og fransk ouverture* (Copenhagen, 1957), and C. L. Cudworth, 'Baptist's vein: French orchestral music and its influence', *Proceedings of the Royal Musical Association*, lxxxiii (1956–7), p. 29, which also considers Lully's other orchestral music and its influence; also more generally see J. Eppelsheim, *Das Orchester in den Werken J.-B. Lullys* (Tutzing, 1961).

[5] Charles Perrault, *Le Siècle de Louis le Grand* (Paris, 1687), p. 20. 'The curtain rises and the enticing sounds of innumerable and divers instruments strike up that brilliant, solemn symphony, which from the first sets even the most unresponsive listener tingling with anticipation...'

Foreigners as well as Frenchmen succumbed to the fascination of these overtures and made their splendours known in their own countries: the French overture soon passed into the mainstream of European instrumental music, its influence surviving into the classical period.

The French overture consists of two, sometimes three movements. The first, slow and stately, has a dotted rhythm, the second is quick and fugal; the third, when it occurs, is again slow, but its material is always different from that of the opening slow section. Until the time of Rameau no composer made even the slightest attempt to alter this established form. It is obvious that the Lullian overture is no mere formal lucubration designed to give the audience time to settle down at their leisure. It is an introduction of solemn brilliance, designed to capture and hold the attention of the spectator and prepare him for the magnificence of the performance that is about to take place before his eyes. It must condition the spectator to tragic emotion and in this respect has an expressive role, albeit in the abstract, for it is unrelated to the drama. Not until later, in *Le Carnaval et la Folie* (1703) by André Destouches and in Rameau's *Zoroastre* (1749),[1] do certain themes in the overture recur in the course of the opera itself.

LULLY'S ORCHESTRAL MOVEMENTS AND BALLET MUSIC

Lully developed the composition of descriptive symphonies accompanying the action. They were already known and appreciated by the French, who delighted in relating sounds to images or to specific ideas: throughout its history, of course, French music has produced an abundance of descriptive music. Court ballet, where the music provides a commentary on the mime, contains in embryo most of the symphonies characteristic of opera. Lully, who was schooled in the disciplines of the actor-dancer, derived at least as much profit from the *ballet de cour* in writing his lyrical tragedies as he did from the *sinfonie* of Venetian opera. These descriptive passages, notwithstanding the slender orchestral resources available, were enthusiastically received by opera-goers and were used as models by other composers. Every composer did his best to 'paint' or 'describe', often at some length, as in the symphonies of a martial, pastoral, or funereal nature. Other passages might be shorter, as with the brief preludes prefacing arias, or the instrumental sections incorporated into vocal movements. Often their impact is strengthened by the addition of dancing, to underline a change, describe a stage effect, mark a step forward in the action, draw attention to a striking gesture or reinforce some mournful concept expressed by the singer. All these features help preserve the dramatic unity.

[1] See *infra*, p. 257.

The same desire motivates Lully's careful attention to his *symphonies de danse*.[1] He regarded pantomime as a major art-form calling for the strongest possible musical support. The divertissement in each act was a legacy from the old court ballet and in the minds of the librettist and the composer constituted an integral part of the action. This explains the inclusion—apart from traditional dances such as minuet, jig, canaries, passepied, bourrée, chaconne, and passacaglia—of purely descriptive dances, which he strips of all ritual associations. They reflect the action, or the emotions stemming from the action, or may even define some character or other, and be given a specific title, as for instance 'Airs pour les Nymphes', 'Air pour Jupiter', or 'Entrée des Forgerons'. To increase the expressive potential of the dance, Lully may vary its construction or speed up the movement. Treated thus, the dance becomes dramatic, a 'personality dance' in the most modern sense of the word. It varied according to a whole range of emotions and situations, to which it was perfectly related. Thus the slumber scene in *Atys* (III, 4), with its wonderful breadth and musicality, can even establish an ethereal quality comparable, in its own way, with that of the Good Friday music from Wagner's *Parsifal*:[2]

Ex. 117

[1] See Meredith Ellis, 'Inventory of the dances of Jean-Baptiste Lully', *Recherches*, ix (1969), p. 21.
[2] Lajarte ed., p. 135.

Related to the dance movements are the marches and processions, whose pomp was perfectly in keeping with the sumptuous way of life at the court of Louis XIV. Their effect on the French (and European) public was similar to that of Corneille's poetry, and they scored a resounding success not only with French armies but with those of foreign powers.

THE UNITY OF LULLIAN OPERA

Despite the wide variety of expressive means at his disposal, Lully's work presents, as we have seen, an aspect of perfect unity. The elements that his work contains grow from one another, and all blend together. This stems from the fact that perfect understanding existed between the composer and his regular librettist, Quinault. Quinault was purely and simply a tool in the composer's hands, with the result that classical French opera is, from one point of view, an early instance of the type of music drama represented by the work of Wagner or Debussy. The concept, the feeling, the adaptation of the situations, come not from the poet, but from the composer; it is of small consequence that some writer, however talented, puts all this into words.

LULLY'S INFLUENCE

The extent of Lully's influence inside and outside France is vouched for by the comments of his contemporaries. During this period two main styles of dramatic music co-existed in Europe—Italian and French.[1] Lully's great achievement was the crystallization of the French style. His music had universal appeal. The man in the street sang it on the Pont-Neuf, the aristocracy brought up their children on it, and until the end of the eighteenth century the students of St. Cyr performed it. As an old man Rameau was still paying him homage. His popularity stretched far beyond the frontiers of his adopted country. In Italy, his dances and overtures to some extent inspired the instrumental music of Corelli. In Germany, Muffat, Fischer, Kusser (who even Frenchified his name to Cousser), Telemann, Mattheson, and Bach all owed something to him, notably through his overtures. As for London, according to Roger North, 'all the compositions of the town were strained to imitate Baptist's vein'.[2] Lully achieved this success because he struck a mean by being neither over-simple nor over-pompous. His contact with the French helped him to acquire the classical virtues of moderation and 'honnêteté'—a sense of the fitness of things. Grandeur, magnificence, and dignity are distributed in just measure throughout his works. Everything is in proportion; the beauty of Nature is displayed and human character never idealized. There is not the heroism of Corneille, but rather the humanity of Racine.

THE OPERATIC SCENE AFTER LULLY

Lully continued to cast a long shadow over French dramatic music for a hundred years, and his works were still being performed on the

[1] See Lloyd Hibberd, 'Madame de Sévigné and the operas of Lully', *Essays in Musicology: a birthday offering for Willi Apel*, ed. Hans Tischler (Bloomington, Indiana, 1968), p. 153.
[2] *Memoirs of Music*, in John Wilson (ed.), *Roger North on Music* (London, 1959), p. 350.

eve of the Revolution. For French musicians he remained the great initiator and model, and the framework of opera as he had created it remained unchanged up to and beyond the time of Gluck.

After Lully's death, in Louis XIV's declining years, court entertainments were decentralized. Musical entertainments were transferred to the great houses of noblemen, whose libertarian spirit was in marked contrast to the formal piety of Versailles. These patrons of the arts took special delight in the *fêtes galantes*, whose shorter, airier pieces of music had an immediate appeal.

It was the freedom now abroad in Paris that set the tone at this time, not the decrees of Versailles. Just as artists abandoned history paintings, so composers wrote music that was more appealing and more accessible. Watteau succeeded Lebrun, and the Regency spirit was born. Rustic charm held a high place in the new style; the happy tranquillity of the countryside was dedicated to the pleasures of love. The *pastorale*, a literary genre neglected since 1630, found a new home in opera: Cambert's *Pomone* (1671)[1] and Lully's *Acis et Galatée* are harbingers of this new style. Gradually public interest in the purely literary aspect of opera waned, giving way to a keen musical curiosity. Recitative, the cornerstone of the whole operatic edifice, aroused a great deal of comment. Destouches, wedded to the ideal of dramatic expression, was almost the only composer in the interval separating Lully and Rameau who was to achieve absolute perfection in the traditional form. The metamorphosis of the popular forms was facilitated by Italian influence, which helped to develop musical skill and technique. In addition the tremendous popularity of ballet led to a pronounced development of ballet music. The imbalance between music, poetry, and ballet resulted in a new art form, which was more in tune with the prevailing fashion and challenged the popularity of lyrical tragedy. This new genre was opera-ballet.

OPERA-BALLET[2]

Opera-ballet is a type of opera in which songs and dances predominate and where, under a single title, we find as many different themes as there are acts, in place of the single action of lyric tragedy. This succession of varied intrigues is held together by only a tenuous overall theme, expressed by the title. Thus we have the Seasons, the Ages, the Elements, each act a little opera on its own, with limited action, the sophisticated subject being merely an excuse for a succession of dances. The whole

---

[1] See *supra*, pp. 202–5.

[2] See James R. Anthony, 'The French opera-ballet in the early 18th century: problems of definition and classification', *Journal of the American Musicological Society*, xviii (1965), p. 197; and idem, 'Some uses of the dance in the French opera-ballet', *Recherches*, ix (1969), p. 75.

work is orientated towards the dance, although it is cast in a sham operatic mould. Accordingly people soon fell into the habit of describing it as ballet, although in this case the description was naturally somewhat ambiguous. It can be seen that in construction opera-ballet is diametrically opposed to lyric tragedy. In the former the plot arises from the divertissement and serves as its basis, whereas in the latter the divertissement arises from the plot. The admirable unity of the *tragédie en musique* was disrupted, and poetry was now merely the servant of the ballet and of the instrumental music.

The first example of this new genre is *L'Europe galante* (1697),[1] with a text by Antoine Houdar de la Motte and music by André Campra (1660–1744). It cannot strictly be called an innovation, since the older court ballet was conceived in the same vein: for example Lully had written *Le Triomphe de l'Amour* in 1681 and Pascal Colasse his *Ballet des Saisons* in 1695. But throughout the eighteenth century *L'Europe galante* was referred to as the point of departure of this new lyrical art form. 'In the year 1697,' wrote Louis de Cahusac, 'Rameau's librettist Lamotte [*sic*], by creating an entirely new type of work, achieved the advantage of being copied in his turn. *L'Europe galante* is the first lyrical work that bears no resemblance to the operas of Quinault.'[2] In character the new form was thoroughly French and owed nothing to Italy. Although opera-ballet did not actually dethrone Lully's operas, it shared their popularity and occupied an important place in the public's affections. Among Lully's successors, there was not one composer who did not sacrifice on the altar of opera-ballet. Between 1697 and 1735, the date of Rameau's *Les Indes galantes*, some forty opera-ballets were given at the Académie Royale de Musique out of 130 works staged there.

Apart from *L'Europe galante*, the most celebrated works of this type are *Les Fêtes vénitiennes*, by Campra (1710), *Les Fêtes grecques et romaines*, by François Colin de Blamont (1723), *Les Eléments*, by Michel-Richard de Lalande and Destouches (1725), *Les Stratagèmes de l'Amour*, by Destouches (1726), and *Les Amours des Dieux*, by Jean-Joseph Mouret (1727). The diversity of the genre called for lavish costumes, scenery and production, especially when the subjects were exotic or necessitated local colour. Efforts were made to enrich the plot in order to lend it a more operatic air, by introducing a kind of over-simplified psychology to sustain the dramatic interest. This resulted in the 'heroic opera-ballet', a description coined to fit *Les Fêtes grecques et ˜omaines*. The popularity of episodic works is further shown in various

---

[1] See idem, 'Printed editions of André Campra's *L'Europe galante*', *Musical Quarterly*, lvi (1970), p. 54.

[2] See Cahusac, *La Danse ancienne et moderne* (The Hague, 1754), p. 108.

arrangements, or 'fragments', by one or more composers, put together by a younger composer. These are composite works, created by juxtaposing excerpts from a number of different sources which may also be linked to each other by newly composed recitatives and *airs*. Thus we have *Les Fragments de M. de Lully* and *Télémaque, fragments des modernes*, both by Campra, with the librettist Antoine Danchet. Furthermore, the autonomy of the various acts in opera-ballet meant that material could be added or replaced; at the end of the eighteenth century, for example, *Les Fêtes vénitiennes* was subjected to this treatment. Abandoning the division into five acts and a prologue, as specified by Lully, composers now reduced opera-ballet to three-, two-, or even one-act form, which is the logical culmination of the genre. In this abbreviated form it was all the rage at the court and in Paris and was the perfect musical expression of the ages of Louis XV and Louis XVI. It was also highly vulnerable to infiltration by foreign elements, especially those of Italian origin.

RESURGENCE OF ITALIAN INFLUENCE

It is true to say that in France the influence of Italian music made itself felt, in greater or less degree, from the end of the sixteenth century until the middle of the nineteenth. Lully's reforms, however, checked this influence abruptly: partisans of Italian music were regarded as heretics, and their devotion to it set them beyond the pale as far as court music was concerned. They met privately, in small groups, went to great lengths to secure copies of Italian scores and turned to church music. For a time they found an unexpected ally in Paolo Lorenzani, a Roman musician brought to France in 1678 by the Duc de Vivonne. But he was quickly eliminated by Lully, who, however, did not disdain to profit from the music of his native country nor to keep abreast of latest developments there. Some of his later works reveal that he was familiar with the idioms and techniques of the newest Italian music.

When Lully died, the Italians and their French disciples were able to breathe more freely. In 1688 Lorenzani arranged a performance at Chantilly of his opera *Oronthée* (with libretto by Michel Leclerc adapted from Giacinto Andrea Cicognini's libretto for Cesti's *Orontea* of 1649); but except for a few *airs de ballet* the score of this work has been lost.[1] In 1693 Marc-Antoine Charpentier, whose works had been more or less suppressed by Lully's influence, presented his opera *Médée*, showing his marked interest in Italian music. Political events in their turn conspired to ease the situation, for in 1696 the signing of the Treaty of

[1] See André Tessier, 'L'Oronthée de Lorenzani et l'Orontea de Cesti', *Revue musicale*, viii (1928), p. 169, and Prunières, 'Paolo Lorenzani à la cour de France', *Revue musicale*, ii (1922), p. 97; on *Orontea* also see *supra*, pp. 22–3.

Pignerol restored peace to France and Savoy and encouraged relations between them. The discriminating public now became increasingly enthusiastic over Italian music. The sonatas of Corelli and the cantatas of Giovanni Maria Bononcini were the staple fare of connoisseurs, and even Rameau did not escape their influence. French opera was affected by this new wave of Italian influence, though indirectly, and certainly much less than opera elsewhere in Europe. The general conception of lyric tragedy as formulated by Lully remained totally unchanged; but Italy left her mark on the music itself. Playing and listening to more intellectual types of music had a refining effect on composers, and through the cantatas—both Italian ones and Italian-influenced ones such as those of Rameau—audiences became more demanding when it came to theatre music.

At this time the cantata was a kind of miniature opera, in which recitatives alternated with arias. It provided a useful testing ground for stylistic and formal innovations, some of which—for example, the *da capo* aria, echoes, moving bass parts, chromatic harmony—very soon found their way into operas. Italian influence was not, however, wholly salutary, for the fashionable bravura aria, quite divorced from the surrounding action, gradually forced its way into French music; extraneous elements of this nature occur more frequently in opera than in ballet, where the plot is looser. Campra's *Les Fêtes vénitiennes* has three cantatas, and Destouches spiced his *Le Carnaval et la Folie* with a number of Italian arias. Thus the atmosphere of the concert-hall invaded the theatre, and dramatic interest gave way to sheer musical enjoyment. With this growing taste for pure music, the attention of audiences was diverted from the spectacle and concentrated more and more on the actual singing; thus the cantata helped to destroy the balance of lyrical tragedy and appreciably changed its character.

The best opera composers of the early eighteenth century readily incorporated the new trends into their works, but none had the originality to give opera a new impetus. They are not men of the stature of Lully and Rameau; yet it would be unjust to ignore them, for two figures, Campra and Destouches, do stand out to some extent among the rest.

CAMPRA

Campra (1660–1744),[1] who came from Provence, was the ablest of the dramatic composers who came after Lully; his long career made him

---

[1] On Campra see La Laurencie, 'Notes sur la jeunesse d'André Campra', *Sammelbände der internationalen Musikgesellschaft*, x (1908–9), p. 159; idem, 'André Campra, musicien profane', *Année musicale*, iii (1913), p. 153; and Maurice Barthélemy, *André Campra, sa vie et son œuvre (1660–1774)* (Paris, 1957). See also *André Campra: Operatic Airs*, ed. Graham Sadler (*The Baroque Operatic Arias*, ii) (London, 1973).

both the younger contemporary of Lully and the older contemporary of Rameau. His good education, enriched by his experience in the field of church music, together with his Italian ancestry, set him apart from his most popular rivals, Destouches and Mouret. He was the first composer to translate the conception of opera-ballet successfully into music, and his *Les Fêtes vénitiennes*[1] was a real triumph. His achievements in this genre have often detracted attention from his ten genuine operas, among which *Hésione* (1700) and *Tancrède* (1702),[2] at least, deserve recognition as first-rate works. Rameau himself thought *Tancrède* a masterpiece.

Campra's musical credo is set out in the preface to his first book of cantatas (1708): 'to the best of my abilities', he writes, 'I have endeavoured to temper the delicacy of French music with the liveliness of Italian music'. He was one of the first French composers to exploit the newly-imported Italianate form of the cantata, and the more personal and animated melodic lines and the feeling for development that we find in his cantatas, owing a good deal to Italian example, appear also in his stage works. At times his use of wide intervals creates a pathos in the melody hitherto rarely achieved: we find a falling minor sixth at dramatic moments, or a penultimate downward-leaping diminished seventh (*L'Europe galante*, 1697, II, 1):[3]

Ex. 118

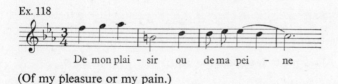

De mon plai - sir   ou   de ma pei - ne

(Of my pleasure or my pain.)

Here the melody drops a seventh in two stages (*L'Europe galante*, IV, 2):

Ex. 119

Et me   fait dé - vo-rer mes sou - pirs et mes lar - mes.

(And makes me feed on my sighs and my tears.)

Elsewhere a falling minor seventh comes to rest on the tonic, sometimes through octave displacement (*Tancrède*, IV, 5):[4]

---

[1] Vocal score ed. Alexandre Guilmant (Paris, [1883]).

[2] Vocal score ed. Guilmant (Paris, [1882]).

[3] Vocal score ed. Lajarte (Paris, [1880]); this and the next example are on pp. 83–4 and 150, respectively.

[4] Guilmant ed., p. 268.

Ex. 120

Pré - fé - rer l'a - mour à la gloi - re.

(To prefer love to glory.)

There are evocative progressions, some thematic repetition,[1] and modulations on key words; and now and then Campra creates a simple and relatively modern impression of folk music, as in the opera act of *Les Fêtes vénitiennes*. This same work also contains a *villanelle*, inspired by folk music but ingeniously constructed, followed by a duet and a chorus in the same rhythm (Prologue, 2).[2]

Campra's expressive melodic lines follow rhythms entirely dictated by the words. He has a preference for certain rhythms, for instance dotted rhythm in 6/8 or 6/4. Like Lully, he uses striking syncopations at exclamations, punctuation by means of rests, or systematic, not to say thematic, silences recurring during the entire length of a piece, as in the gigue in *Les Fêtes vénitiennes* (Prologue, 2): a rest totalling one 6/8 bar occurs regularly all through this piece.[3] Some of his rests have a descriptive function, as when in *Les Fêtes vénitiennes* the singing teacher arrives angry and out of breath (III, 3):[4]

Ex. 121

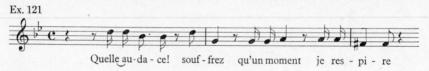

Quelle au - da - ce! souf - frez qu'un moment je res - pi - re

(What audacity! Allow me to breathe a moment.)

or as in this excerpt from the recitative of the dying Clorinda in *Tancrède* (V, 3):[5]

Ex. 122

Cher a - mant, a - vec mes a - dieux Re -

-çois dans ce sou - pir une â - me qui t'a - do - re...

(Dear love, with my farewells receive in this sigh a soul that adores you . . .)

[1] See Anthony, 'Thematic repetition in the opera-ballets of André Campra', *Musical Quarterly*, lii (1966), p. 209.

[2] Guilmant ed., p. 21.

[3] Ibid., p. 15.

[4] Ibid., p. 158.

[5] Guilmant ed., appendix 1, p. 320.

Although church music naturally gave greater scope for the development of contrapuntal writing, Campra uses it in his operas in the symphonies and choruses and even refuses to abandon it in the arias.[1] As a representative example of his contrapuntal writing here is part of the second section of the overture to *Les Fêtes vénitiennes*:[2]

Ex. 123

Campra uses rare keys such as E major,[3] which was not used by Lully; and there are fleeting references to keys such as F sharp minor and C sharp minor. He likes striking modulations—in contrast to Lully, who is very sparing of them—and uses them to express the gradations of feeling he wishes to convey. His quest for descriptive effects is also reflected in his judicious use of certain chords and intervals: for

---

[1] See *Tancrède*, Guilmant ed., p. 237, for a good example.
[2] Guilmant ed., p. 2.
[3] E.g. in Roxana's jealousy recitative in *L'Europe galante*, Lajarte ed., p. 156, and in the duet in *Les Fêtes vénitiennes*, Guilmant ed., p. 274.

example, the interval of the diminished third at the end of the symphony introducing Discord in *L'Europe galante* (Prologue, 2),[1] which, incidentally, is his first major work:

Ex. 124

Although full scores of Campra's works are something of a rarity—what few there are are in the Bibliothèque de l'Opéra, Paris—it is possible from those we do possess to form some impression of his instrumentation.[2] As with Lully, a violin line often follows the vocal line at the third or in short imitations. Like Lalande and Destouches, however, he often writes a dialogue for voice and instruments, either flutes and strings or two different wind instruments; sometimes he alternates groups of woodwind and strings in the dances, and he incorporates trumpets in martial passages. His use of the orchestra shows as great a degree of expressive colour as his harmony, and it often functions independently, making its own contribution to the dramatic impact of the work, a feature further developed by Destouches.

DESTOUCHES

Campra's pupil Destouches (1672–1749)[3] immediately reacted against the Italian elements in his teacher's music: he incorporated them purely for parody and pastiche, as in the Italian airs from *Le Carnaval et la Folie* (1704). He is much more consciously a French composer. His adventurous youth—he made the journey to Siam at the age of seventeen and was a musketeer—had left him with an easy manner which is reflected in his music. His success in the field of opera was due to his gifts as a writer of charming melodies, already revealed in his short *airs*. His pastoral *Issé*, written in 1697 (the same year as *L'Europe galante*)

---

[1] Lajarte ed., p. 22. The original 1697 edition gives only the outer parts, with figured bass, but the MS. full score of 1724, in the Bibliothèque de l'Opéra, Paris, gives all the parts, including the B flat in the second bar of the example.

[2] See Barthélemy, 'L'orchestre et l'orchestration des œuvres de Campra', *Revue musicale*, numéro spécial 226 (1955), p. 97.

[3] On Destouches see L.-J. Pelissier, 'Famille, fortune et succession d'André Cardinal Destouches', *Mémoires de la Société de l'Histoire de Paris et l'Île-de-France*, xxvi (1899), p. 25; Kurt Dulle, *André Cardinal Destouches, 1672–1749* (Leipzig, 1909); and Renée P.-M. Masson, 'André Cardinal Destouches, surintendant de la musique du Roi, directeur de l'opéra, 1672–1749', *Revue de Musicologie*, xliii (1959), p. 81.

for the marriage of the Duc de Bourgogne and Princess Adelaide of Savoy, was given a tumultuous reception by the court and then by the citizens of Paris. Louis XIV told the young composer that not since Lully had any music given him greater pleasure than his. Not all his works achieved the same popularity; but a few really brilliant triumphs greatly increased his fame and fortune—*Amadis de Grèce* (1699), *Omphale* (1701), which later provoked a violent controversy, and in particular *Callirhoé* (1712), his best work. *Le Carnaval et la Folie*, one of the few lyric comedies of the age, and *Les Eléments* (1725),[1] written in collaboration with Lalande, both contain passages of real beauty. From 1718 he was one of the masters of the king's music. An important element in the success of stage works by Destouches and his contemporaries should not be overlooked: the continuing tradition of sumptuous presentation, and particularly the work of Bérain.[2]

Destouches's music is always spontaneous, and elegant to a degree. It is true that he is primarily a melodist, but his melodies are enhanced by the studied elegance of his harmony, his lively rhythms, and his sonorous ensemble writing and rich instrumentation. He greatly admired Lully and regarded *Armide* as the perfect opera. His melodies are well-balanced, clearly defined and elegant, and he makes use of the expressive intervals we have already seen handled by Lully and Campra. The outwardly spontaneous melodies are in fact very carefully organized.[3] It is clear too from his recitatives that Destouches's speech melody is worked out with the utmost attention to accuracy and dramatic intensity. To an even greater extent than in the *airs*, he explores the expressive possibilities of intervals and of tonality. His feeling for literature and his knowledge of the humanities possibly helped to make him the best French composer of classical recitative, surpassing even Lully and Rameau. He had an advantage over Lully in that Lully was not French and, despite all Quinault could do, did not always grasp subtle nuances in the French language. *Issé* abounds in tuneful recitatives, always adapted to suit a particular set of circumstances: by contrast there are in *Omphale, Callirhoé*, and *Télémaque* (1714) passages of stark, dramatic simplicity.

Destouches's harmony is often bold and interesting. He liberally introduces dominant sevenths, diminished sevenths, and unprepared ninths, as in the sailors' chorus in *Les Eléments* (II, 1) or in the very

---

[1] There are vocal scores of *Issé* and *Omphale*, ed. Hector Salomon, and of *Les Eléments*, ed. Vincent d'Indy (all Paris, [1883]).

[2] See Roger-Armand Weigert, *Jean Bérain, dessinateur de la Chambre et du Cabinet du roi, 1640–1711*, 2 vols. (Paris, 1937).

[3] On Destouches's formal melodic patterns see the article in *Die Musik in Geschichte und Gegenwart*, iii (1954), col. 242.

17

striking opening of an *air* in the same scene.[1] He took great pains with the basses, which include chaconnes.

Accompaniments to recitatives afford Destouches another vehicle for expressive writing. He uses accompanied recitative more than Lully, for he tends in his own works to emphasize those elements he most admired in *Armide*. He and Campra were two of the first composers to use the orchestra with psychological intent, as Rameau was later to do. His preoccupation with the expressive role of the orchestra suggests, quite justifiably, that he was a highly skilled composer for the orchestra.

His overtures are notable. He rethinks the form in *Omphale* by turning it into a binary piece without contrast of tempo between the two sections and by introducing thematic links between them,[2] and the 1743 overture to *Callirhoé* (the 1712 version is less successful) is on a par with Rameau's overtures. In the descriptive symphonies, the psychological undercurrent recurs, as when the prophetic trembling of the foliage of Dodona's oak trees in *Issé* deepens the atmosphere of mystery.[3] The *airs de danse* are less successful: except for the sarabande from *Issé*,[4] which soon became extremely popular, it must be acknowledged that this aspect of opera did not greatly inspire him.

Destouches's constant corrections, designed to achieve greater expressiveness, are symptomatic of his whole approach to his art: he seems to have looked more closely at the problem of musical expression than any of his French contemporaries. His preoccupation with emotion is confirmed by the extreme preciseness of his directions, printed, or added in his own hand to his operatic scores: for example, 'lightly', 'very detached and very gay', 'even more sorrowfully', 'with tender reproach'. It is possible that he pursued his ends empirically, that what his ear found attractive must be right and would therefore stand the test of time. The perennial charm of Destouches's art springs from the simple fact that his music comes from the heart, to go to the heart: it was no doubt this quality that caused his music to be performed so widely in his own day, not just in France but in other European countries.

MOURET

Mouret (1682–1738)[5] who, like Campra, hailed from Provence, was a silk-merchant's son from Avignon who migrated to Paris at the age of twenty-five on the strength of his reputation as a regional composer.

[1] d'Indy ed., pp. 110 and 102, respectively.
[2] Salomon ed., pp. 1–3.
[3] Salomon ed., p. 162.
[4] Ibid., p. 191.
[5] On Mouret see Renée Viollier, *Jean-Joseph Mouret, le musicien des Grâces* (Paris, 1950).

Soon afterwards he was appointed musician to the Duchesse du Maine and composed the celebrated divertissements for her brilliant entertainments known as the Grandes Nuits de Sceaux, and also for the Théâtre Italien. He made his début at the Opéra in 1714 with the ballet *Les Fêtes, ou le Triomphe de Thalie*, which scored a great success, and he wrote motets and cantatas for the Concert Spirituel, in which he became one of the partners, as well as artistic director. The strain of coping with administration, coupled with several unhappy love affairs, completely unbalanced him, and he was committed to an institution.

Despite his relatively short career, his output was considerable. He had no real bent for tragedy, though he made two not unimportant contributions to this genre—*Ariane* (1717) and *Pirithoüs* (1723). He was more at home in the new medium of opera-ballet, which, for all its dramatic emotion, was better suited to his light, graceful style. Following *Les Fêtes de Thalie*, works such as *Les Amours des Dieux* (1727) and *Les Sens* (1732) enjoyed a wide and lasting popularity among audiences recovering from Rameau's daring innovations. Mouret's great strength lay in his treatment of the divertissements, and he was given ample opportunity to keep up a steady flow of them, not only for the galas at Sceaux but also for opera-ballets and for comic operas at the Comédie Italienne. Though Italian ariettas are by no means uncommon in his works, he is for the most part faithful to typically French tunes, with their flowing lines, and their rhythms possibly deriving from folk music. They provide the basis of his charming dances which, though relatively straightforward in construction, are even more varied and sometimes more artfully composed than those of Rameau. It is worth noting that, with the exception of Destouches (*Le Carnaval et la Folie*) and Rameau (*Platée*, 1745), Mouret was at this time the only composer in France of lyric comedies sung from beginning to end. *Les Amours de Ragonde*, originally written in 1714 for the Nuits de Sceaux and subsequently revived at the Opéra after his death, is one of the few examples of eighteenth-century lyric comedy, less musically interesting but more realistic than *Platée*. Mouret, with his gifts as a writer of light music, is in fact the typical French Regency composer.

CHARPENTIER, LALANDE, AND MINOR CONTEMPORARIES

Campra, Destouches, and Mouret are usually mentioned in the same breath as standing for what was best in French secular music between Lully and Rameau. But there were others besides these three, musicians of varying degrees of importance, who also contributed to the progressive transformation of French opera. Two of them, Charpentier and

Lalande, are especially distinguished figures, who were most famous for their splendid church music[1] and wrote little for the stage.

Charpentier (1634–1704)[2] appears to have been the victim of his Italian sympathies and of Lully's domination. For a long time his dramatic output was confined to the music he wrote for Latin tragedies performed by the Jesuits and for the Comédie Française. In 1672 and 1673 he collaborated with Molière, after the latter had broken with Lully, in works such as *Le Malade imaginaire* (1673)[3] and retained connections with the same theatre until 1685. Only once did a work of his grace the stage of the Opéra; but it was an important event, for the piece in question, *Médée* (1693), was written in a new style owing, as was mentioned above, a good deal to Italian music—a not surprising influence in a composer who had studied in Italy with Carissimi. Charpentier was the first French composer to try and shake off the influence of Lully.

Lalande (1657–1726)[4] is a dominant figure of his age by virtue of the breadth, variety, and expressive power of his splendid motets, in which Italian craftsmanship is allied to originality and a dramatic temperament. After Lully's death Lalande became the favourite composer of both Louis XIV and the court. Versailles, where he spent his entire working life, formed the perfect framework for his music. His stage music is largely confined to a number of ballets and divertissements dating from 1682 onwards, though, as has been indicated above, he also contributed to Destouches's opera-ballet *Les Eléments*.

Other composers who were more faithful to Lully's precepts produced stage works of uneven quality, though they include a number of attractive passages. Colasse (1649–1709), Lully's secretary and protégé, who was also keeper of his manuscripts, followed more closely than any other composer in his master's footsteps. In 1687 he completed the opera *Achille et Polixène*, begun by Lully, and thereafter he staged some ten works, of which *Thétis et Pélée*,[5] with libretto by Bernard de Fontenelle, is the most original; we have already seen too that the

---

[1] See *infra*, pp. 453–71.

[2] On Charpentier see Claude Crussard, *Un Musicien français oublié, Marc-Antoine Charpentier* (Paris, 1945), and Robert W. Lowe, *Marc-Antoine Charpentier et l'opéra de collège* (Paris, 1966).

[3] Vocal score ed. Camille Saint-Saëns and Gabriel-Marie (Paris, [1894]).

[4] On Lalande see Norbert Dufourcq (and others), *Notes et références pour servir à une histoire de Michel-Richard Delalande* (Paris, 1957), and Dufourcq, 'Quelque réflexions sur les ballets et divertissements de Michel Delalande', *Les Divertissements de cour au XVIIe siècle* (*Cahiers de l'Association Internationale des Etudes Françaises*, ix, 1957), p. 9. There is no agreement on the spelling of the composer's name: the traditional form 'Lalande' is used in the present volume despite Dufourcq's advocacy of the form 'Delalande'.

[5] Vocal score ed. Louis Soumis (Paris, [1882]).

Ballet des Saisons (1695) heralded the advent of opera-ballet. Even if Colasse's style is often indistinguishable from that of Lully, it can be said that he at least shows a degree of individuality in his appreciation of the expressive possibilities of orchestration. In this respect the name of Marin Marais (1656–1728) should also be mentioned. Marais, a performer of remarkable virtuosity on the viol, was a *batteur de mesure* (i.e. a director of the orchestra) at the Académie Royale de Musique. Of his four operas,[1] *Alcyone* (1705), once famous for its storm, has in its symphonies and accompaniments certain subtle instrumental effects which were not lost on Rameau.

Henry Desmarest (1661–1741)[2] appears to have been one of the most gifted of all the composers schooled in the Lully tradition. Even in his first opera, *Didon* (1693), he reveals qualities of expressive vigour which might well have singled him out as Lully's true successor had he not been exiled in 1700 for contracting a secret marriage. The favourable impression of his talent is confirmed by a study of his main work, *Iphigénie en Tauride* (1704)—completed by Campra—the more eloquent passages of which were quoted during the eighteenth century as being among the most notable things in musical tragedy.[3]

Shortly before Rameau made his bow in the theatre, Michel de Montéclair (1667–1737) presented his biblical opera *Jephté* (1732),[4] which made a profound and lasting impression on the public. This vigorous work, original in inspiration and solid in construction, is particularly significant in that it seems to have had a decisive effect on Rameau's career as a dramatic composer.[5]

Finally, we come to a group of composers who, although younger than Rameau, made their début with him and produced works which in some instances served as his examples and models. Three of these men are worthy of note. The first is Colin de Blamont (1690–1760), a pupil of Lalande and a master of the king's music at the same time as Destouches; his *Fêtes grecques et romaines* (1723) is one of the most important opera-ballets of the time. There remain the two inseparables,

[1] See Barthélemy, 'Les Opéras de Marin Marais', *Revue Belge de Musicologie*, vii (1953), p. 136.

[2] On Desmarest see Michel Antoine, *Henry Desmarest (1661–1741): biographie critique* (Paris, 1965).

[3] By, for instance, Titon du Tillet, *Le Parnasse français*, supplement (Paris, 1743), pp. 753 ff.

[4] See Borrel, 'Notes sur l'orchestration de l'opéra *Jephté* de Montéclair (1733) et de la symphonie *Les Elémens* de J.-F. Rebel (1737)', *Revue musicale*, numéro spécial 226 (1955), p. 105, and Viollier, 'Trois Jephté, trois styles' (abstract), *Revue de Musicologie*, xliii (1959), p. 125.

[5] See *Mercure de France*, March 1761, p. 153.

François Rebel (1701–1775) and François Francœur (1698–1787),[1] who are like a single composer split into two and who, before Rameau came on the operatic scene in 1733, had produced their lyric tragedy *Pyrame et Thisbé* (1726), a brilliant and moving work much admired by opera-goers; they followed it up with two others, but nearly all their later works are in the lighter forms of the opera-ballet, ballet, divertissement, and *pastorale*.

To sum up, the period of almost half a century from the death of Lully to the emergence of Rameau has, contrary to general belief, a wealth of interesting works well worth rescuing from oblivion. Instrumental and church music are represented by the famous names of Couperin and Lalande; but dramatic music can be justly proud of those of Campra and Destouches. These years are more than what is conveniently described as a period of transition: they are years of striking innovations as well as gradual transformations, produced not by any one composer of genius but more generally by men of lesser stature, sometimes in collaboration. Not until Rameau do we have the feeling that operatic music has entered a new phase, an impression which, even after his very first dramatic venture, was shared by all his contemporaries. After the Regency, Rameau's dramatic music assumed the proportions of a musical revolution.

RAMEAU: INTRODUCTION

Jean-Philippe Rameau (1683–1764)[2] embarked on his theatrical career in 1733, at the age of fifty, with the opera *Hippolyte et Aricie*. Between 1733 and 1739 he produced in all five dramatic works, which rank among his best: *Hippolyte et Aricie, Les Indes galantes* (1735), *Castor et Pollux* (1737), *Les Fêtes d'Hébé* (1739), and *Dardanus* (1739). Then followed five years of silence, during which he cut himself off from the theatre, doubtless as a result of differences of opinion with the management of the Opéra. However, he continued to write for the stage, and a second version of *Dardanus*, revealed when that opera was revived in 1744, contains two entirely new acts, perhaps the finest he ever wrote. The following year, 1745, four of his works were staged. Between then and 1752 (when the 'Guerre des Bouffons' began[3]) Rameau, now officially recognized as a court musician, composed some dozen pieces of

[1] See La Laurencie, 'Une dynastie de musiciens français: les Rebel', *Sammelbände der internationalen Musikgesellschaft*, vii (1905–6), p. 253.

[2] There are two standard works on Rameau's dramatic music, which are all that need be mentioned here: Paul-Marie Masson, *L'Opéra de Rameau* (Paris, 1930), and Cuthbert Girdlestone, *Jean-Philippe Rameau: his life and work* (London, 1957). There is a 2nd ed. of Masson (Paris, 1943) and of Girdlestone (Paris, 1962); references in this chapter are to the first editions. Girdlestone gives copious examples in full score.

[3] See *infra*, pp. 241–2.

varying length. These were *La Princesse de Navarre* (1745) (revised and revived the same year as *Les Fêtes de Ramire*), *Platée* (1745), *Les Fêtes de Polymnie* (1745), *Le Temple de la Gloire* (1745), *Les Fêtes de l'Hymen et de l'Amour* (1747), *Zaïs* (1748), *Pygmalion* (1748), *Les Surprises de l'Amour* (1748), *Naïs* (1749), *Zoroastre* (1749), *Linus* (1751) (unperformed and lost), *La Guirlande* (1751), and *Acanthe et Céphise* (1751). In his last period, from 1753 until his death in 1764, Rameau, having taken an active part in the 'Guerre des Bouffons', kept up his output of theatrical works with several lesser compositions, including *Daphnis et Eglé* (1753), *Lysis et Délie* (1753) (unperformed and lost), *Les Sybarites* (1753), *La Naissance d'Osiris* (1754), *Anacréon* (1754), another *Anacréon* (1757), *Les Paladins* (1760), and lastly, in the year of his death, *Abaris, ou Les Boréades*. There are also a few other works, such as *Nélée et Myrthis* and *Zéphyre*, which were not performed in Rameau's day and cannot be dated exactly.[1]

The changes that took place in Rameau's work during his thirty years as a composer for the theatre are not obvious enough to allow us to distinguish the various stages of any real development. The total conception of a work varies little from what it was when he wrote *Hippolyte et Aricie*. As for his style, it shows traces of the successive influences on French music at this period, and clear signs that tastes were changing. Certain instrumental pieces are written with greater austerity and less artifice—a feature already evident in the overture to *Les Fêtes d'Hébé*— and some of the ariettas have a mellow, softly curving vocal line reminiscent of the flowing melodies of Rameau's Neapolitan contemporaries such as Leonardo Leo and Leonardo Vinci. We know, too, that Rameau admired the new French comic operas, inspired by the *intermezzi* of the *bouffons*.

THE 'GUERRE DES BOUFFONS'

Rameau's partiality for lighter music, reflected also in such a work as *Platée* and in much of his later music in particular, did not save him from attack by the champions of comic opera in the so-called 'Guerre des Bouffons', to which reference has already been made. This was basically a quarrel between the devotees of French and Italian music: French music was equated with the stiff, serious, over-complex treatment of old-fashioned and remote subjects, Italian with the simple,

---

[1] All the surviving works mentioned here, except eight, appear in the interrupted complete edition of Rameau's works, *Œuvres complètes*, general editor Saint-Saëns, 18 vols. (Paris, 1895–1924), vi-xviii, more or less in chronological order. The exceptions are *Zoroastre*, of which, however, a full score has been published ed. Françoise Gervais (Paris, 1964), *La Guirlande, Acanthe et Céphise, Daphnis et Eglé, La Naissance d'Osiris*, the first *Anacréon, Les Paladins*, and *Les Boréades* (as *Abaris* is normally known). All the major works appear in vocal scores ed. various editors (Paris, [1880] ff.).

lively, up-to-date treatment of stories involving real, contemporary people. As far as national characteristics are concerned, this was a simplified view of the situation, for there were, of course, innumerable Italian *opere serie* open to the same objections as the serious operas of Rameau: the false distinction arose because the work that sparked off the quarrel happened to be Italian—the revival in Paris in 1752 of Pergolesi's *intermezzo La serva padrona*, which had already been given six years earlier without causing a stir at all among opera-goers still occupied with arguments about the relative merits of Lully and Rameau. Rousseau was a passionate partisan of the new Italian *opera buffa*: he set out his views in 1753 in his *Lettre sur la musique française*[1] and in 1752 went so far as to compose his own opera according to the principles of *opera buffa*, *Le Devin du village*, which was important in establishing the French tradition of *opéra comique*.[2] Rousseau's championship of *opera buffa* naturally led him to attack French opera, a remarkable and not very convincing *volte-face* in the light of his defence of French opera against Italian as recently as 1750.[3] Rameau now became one of his principal targets: for example, he praises the much more impressive effect of an aria by Galuppi compared with that of the passage beginning 'Temple sacré, séjour tranquille' in *Hippolyte et Aricie* (I, 1).[4]

THE LIBRETTOS AND STAGING OF RAMEAU'S OPERAS

Rameau has been criticized for his poor choice of librettists, and with good reason, for they are all men of the second rank with the exception of Voltaire, who collaborated with him in writing *La Princesse de Navarre* and *Le Temple de la Gloire*. It is a great pity that their first joint work, the lyric tragedy *Samson* (*c.* 1733), never reached the stage and is lost. Rameau's most regular librettist from 1741 onwards was Cahusac; three of his works of the early 1750s are to texts by Jean François Marmontel, but all his other collaborators are lesser figures. Production and scenery were in the hands of a number of talented men, the best known of whom are Giovanni Girolamo Servandoni and François Boucher. Costumes had scarcely changed since Lully's time; sketches

---

[1] Substantial extracts in Strunk, op. cit., pp. 636–54, together (pp. 619–35) with much of another pro-Italian document, Friedrich Melchior von Grimm's *Le Petit Prophète de Boehmisch-Broda* (1753).

[2] Discussed in its context in Vol. VII, pp. 202–4.

[3] Cf. his letter to Grimm reprinted in Albert Jansen, *Jean-Jacques Rousseau als Musiker* (Berlin, 1884), pp. 455–63.

[4] *Œuvres complètes*, vi, p. 53; see Strunk, op. cit., p. 640. Further on the 'Guerre des Bouffons' and related matters see Paul-Marie Masson, 'Lullistes et Ramistes', *Année musicale*, i (1911), p. 187; idem, 'La "Lettre sur Omphale"', *Revue de Musicologie*, xxvii (1945), p. 1; Noël Boyer, *La Guerre des Bouffons et la musique française* (Paris, 1945); and Barthélemy, 'Les deux interventions de Jacques Cazotte dans la Querelle des Bouffons', *Recherches*, viii (1968), p. 191. See also Vol. VII, p. 201.

preserved in the library of the Paris Opéra give some idea of their style. All the characters from antiquity wore costumes from the reign of Louis XV, which were given a touch of local colour by means of some stylized symbol or other. With such costumes it was difficult to convey that impression of reality which was necessary if any profound dramatic emotion were to be evoked. However, the illusion was strengthened by the continual presence of the music, which served to minimize all the improbabilities of the imaginary stage-world and transposed the whole production to the realm of make-believe. It is in this light that the music must be examined and judged.

RAMEAU'S RECITATIVE

That part of Rameau's work which the public found hardest to accept was his treatment of recitative. Contemporary critics, too, usually judged it very harshly. When *Les Indes galantes* appeared feelings ran so high that he decided to publish his score without all but one of the recitatives, as for concert performance. Even after he had overcome the opposition, he never quite succeeded in having his recitatives generally accepted.[1]

Rameau uses three types of recitative: simple, accompanied, and 'measured'. The simple variety had already fulfilled two clearly defined purposes in Lully's operas: (a) it served to further and explain the action, while preserving the musical continuity, and (b) it gave expressive musical utterance to human emotions. Rameau's chief concern is to express the poetry while remaining faithful to the prosody, which may produce constant changes of time-signature and, more generally, may mean adapting the notation to the syllables, since this guides the singer to a much greater extent than does the time-signature. In marking his divisions Rameau uses Lully's method, a simple one involving the breaking up of the alexandrine into anapaests of equal value, or expressive variations of tempo. On the contrary he may divide the line unevenly, the divisions being slightly varied by rests and dotted notes. Everywhere we see evidence of his desire to determine the value of each syllable in the text either to accord with the natural rhythm of the words or for the purpose of creating special expressive effects. He would seem to have gone further than Lully in this direction: we find him using semiquavers on weak beats, unexpected caesuras, syncopations, cross-accents (especially in dialogues), and augmentation or diminution of the melodic intervals to add more life and spirit.

While he follows Lully in using the same close melodic intervals he

---

[1] See, for example, obituaries of him such as the one in the *Mercure de France*, October 1764, p. 197.

makes greater use of wider intervals such as the sixth, major and minor.
The originality of his recitatives is based to a great extent on the falling
seventh. Diminished, its mood is one of pathos; when major, it is more
violent. Intervals of an octave or more are infrequent, although at one
point in *Platée* he uses a tenth:

Ex. 125

Dans   un ma-rais   pro – fond

(In a deep marsh)

and there is an eleventh in *Les Indes galantes*:[1]

Ex. 126

Tom-bez sur   moi,   ro – chers   brû-lants!

(Fall on me, burning rocks!)

—both examples of word-painting.

The same care is given to the grouping of intervals, which sometimes
indeed leads to formulas. More than in Lully there is a spreading-out
of common chords, interspersed with chords of the seventh, in particular
the dominant seventh, which is more commonly used by Rameau than
by his predecessors. Take, for instance, this lovely phrase in *Hippolyte
et Aricie*:[2]

Ex. 127

A   quel a – veu   l'ar – deur____   qui me dé –

- vo - re,   Au mé-pris de ma   gloi – re, en – fin   va me for - cer!

(To what confession will my consuming passion finally force me, to the lessening
of my glory!)

Rameau's conception of recitative is based on the principle of a
purely musical melody and not on the intonation of the words. This
may involve the use of embellishments, short or longer, on specific

[1] *Œuvres complètes*, xii, p. 104, and vii, p. 237, respectively.   [2] Ibid., vi, p. 200.

words; and grace-notes, which after all are shorthand versions of embellishments, are of importance both melodically and harmonically. These are two of the features that do most to bring out the truly musical character of the recitatives, and Rameau himself confirms this conception of recitative when he says 'Lully can have his actors; but I need singers'.[1]

As one would expect of a composer who had studied harmony exhaustively and scientifically, Rameau regulates his harmonies so that they give the most effective possible support to the melodic lines of his recitatives. Starting from an intensive study of Lully's practice, he for instance imparts new meaning to the tonal function of the subdominant and makes systematic use of the chord of the added sixth, which gives his music a flavour that was almost unknown in Lully's time and was invaluable for suggesting different shades of expression and for the articulation of the words. Note, for instance, the stress that the added sixth gives to the word 'foi', and the emotive force of the tonal aspects of this excerpt from *Castor et Pollux*:[2]

Ex. 128

(He knows that you have my faith, that I love . . . No, cruel one, you have not loved me.)

Discords, which are always effective, are scattered through Rameau's music with unusual freedom, their use always justified by the nature of the melody or the meaning of the words. His application of the various chords of the seventh, with occasional ninths, gives the harmony of his recitatives an entirely original appearance.

Modulation is an essential adjunct to harmonic declamation, and in Rameau's recitatives it is used with superlative ease and with a subtlety

---

[1] See Paul-Marie Masson, *L'Opéra de Rameau*, p. 161.
[2] *Œuvres complètes*, viii, p. 286.

that has often been ignored. He sometimes moves to very distant keys
and even uses enharmonic changes; allowing for differences in style,
some of these modulations in the most subtly varied passages recall the
delicate harmonies of a Fauré song. To give some idea of the gulf
separating Rameau's recitatives from those of his predecessors in this
respect, here is a phrase from Act V, scene 3, of the 1744 version of
Dardanus:[1]

Ex. 129

(My daughter, it is too much, in the end one must surrender)

Castor et Pollux and *Dardanus* contain Rameau's finest recitative scenes,
those that have most in common with the great dialogues of Corneille
and Racine: there are fine examples in *Castor et Pollux*, IV, 2, and V, 2,
while the following example is from *Dardanus* (II, 5):[2]

Ex. 130   Lent

---

[1] Ibid., x, appendix, p. 50.
[2] Ibid., p. 218. See *infra*, pp. 264–5, for more on Rameau's harmony, from a theoretical
point of view.

I. -reur, Et vous fré-mi-rez de m'en-ten - dre.

D. Où tend, de ce dis-

B.C. 6 6/5 7

I. Il faut donc ré-vé-ler ce se - cret o-di-

D. -cours, le sens 'mys - té-ri - eux?

B.C. 6 7 #6 6 #6/5 4 #

Gravement

Str. Vn. 1 *fort* Vn. 2 +Va. *fort* (Va.) *doux*

I. eux. Par l'ef-

B.C.

Str.

I. -fort de votre art ter - ri - - - - - ble Vous ou - vrez les tom-

B.C. Vc. + harpsichord *doux* 9 6 #6

(I: Alas! D: You are sighing? I: What have I just learned of you? Ah! if I open my heart to you, you will see me with horror and will tremble to hear me. D: Where is the strange sense of this conversation leading? I: This hateful secret must be revealed. Through the strength of your terrible art you open tombs, you arm the underworld, you are able, in a word, to shake the world.)

That example serves also to introduce the second type of recitative, that with orchestral accompaniment, which Rameau normally uses to represent either solemnity or pathos. His 'solemn' recitative has little figuration and is supported by simple string chords; he generally reserves this kind for invocations and prophecies. 'Pathetic' recitative—the term was used in Rameau's day—occurs at moments of dramatic crisis, rather as accompanied recitative is used in Italian operas. Even during the Regency, composers had quite frequently introduced pathetic recitative into their operas, but Rameau made it much more potent and expressive and through it achieved some of his finest effects. It occurs mostly in monologues: *Hippolyte et Aricie* (V, 2)[1] offers a magnificent example when Theseus calls on Neptune to rid him of Hippolytus, and with the utmost simplicity, using only a string orchestra, Rameau underlines his alternating weakness and resolution.

[1] *Œuvres complètes*, vi, p. 333.

Rameau also took the unprecedented step of using accompanied recitative in the dialogue proper, for example in two successive scenes (II, 6 and 7) of *Les Indes galantes*. The originality of this form of recitative depends largely on the descriptive and expressive nature of the orchestral accompaniment, which provides, as it were, a series of commentaries; it is this that makes it essentially different from 'solemn' accompanied recitative. Without entirely abandoning traditional practices, Rameau clearly used the orchestra in his recitatives to the extent that he felt the dramatic situation, rather than tradition, warranted, and, setting his face, too, against tendencies apparent in Italian music, forestalled Gluck in abolishing the distinction between simple and accompanied recitative.

'Measured' recitative differs from the other types only in that its rhythm is more marked and its melody more clearly delineated, and it may contain symmetrical elements. *Récitatif mesuré* is in effect a series of short melodic fragments, for which the term 'arioso' has usually been adopted. But at the time when Rameau was writing, Italian arioso had an extended form which lent it quite a different character. *Récitatif mesuré* was used in classical French opera when, in the course of a simple recitative, the composer decided to emphasize an important passage or intensify a moment of passion. Used thus, it gives the voice part a more strongly rhythmic character, sometimes extended through a modulating repeat. It may also be a momentary elaboration of melodic declamation.

Subsequent operatic developments have endorsed Rameau's view of recitative. It crops up again as one of Gluck's essential reforms when he recommends that in the use of the orchestra there should be no 'sharp contrast between the aria and the recitative';[1] eventually, of course, Wagner was to carry this principle even further, and Debussy focused attention exclusively on sung declamation. Rameau's recitative is one of the most fertile and 'modern' conceptions in eighteenth-century dramatic music.

RAMEAU'S *AIRS*

Rameau's *airs* conform to the pattern laid down in traditional French opera, though they strive towards a more musical formula, whose novelty was resented by the composer's contemporaries. Their character varies according to whether they are included in the main scenes or in *divertissements*.

The former type may be divided into dialogue and monologue *airs*.

---

[1] Dedication to *Alceste* (1768), quoted from Strunk, op. cit., p. 674.

In the eighteenth century dialogue *airs* were described as *airs de mouve-ment*. They are closely related to *récitatif mesuré*, though in some cases they hark back to the old court *airs*, *brunettes*, and tender little songs fashionable at that time; indeed the words '*air tendre*' frequently appear in Rameau's scores to denote dialogue airs. They may or may not contribute to the actual dramatic progress of the scene. Some are indispensable, others express more general ideas less vital to the action. Rameau uses them less often than Lully.

The monologues, apart from their usual meaning, have a special significance with which we are today unfamiliar. Such pieces generally take the form of a single *air* without addition of a recitative and forming a whole scene on its own. They are very different from Italian arias. They are not square-cut, have no incisive rhythm, no striking motive developed in an instrumental style. In construction they are regular and clear; most are written in binary form, or *rondeau* form with one or two couplets. Their melodies do not follow a rigid pulse but are a kind of stylized declamation intimately related to the inflections of the words. The situations in which French monologues have been used have some-times caused them to be thought rather rhythmically amorphous and irritatingly languid: they normally appear at points in the action which preclude the use of sharply defined rhythms or vigorous movement. When they do express strong emotions, movement and rhythm come into their own, as in certain fast-moving dialogue arias. A good example can be found in *Castor et Pollux*, V, 1.[1] This opera, in fact, has an unusually large number of monologues. But it is in *Dardanus* that the monologue reaches its greatest heights of dramatic power and musical beauty. The finest of all occurs in the 1744 version—the monologue in Act IV sung by Dardanus in prison:[2]

---

[1] *Œuvres complètes*, viii, p. 272.

[2] Ibid., x, appendix, p. 26. Iphise's *air* 'O jour affreux', which opens the third act of *Dardanus*, is recorded in *The History of Music in Sound*, v.

Ex. 131

hon - te et la douleur, Du dé-sespoir, som - bre et cru - el em -

- pi - re, L'hor-reur que votre aspect m'ins - pi - re Est le moin-dre des

maux qui dé - chi - rent mon cœur. L'hor-reur

que votre as-pect m'ins - pi - re Est le moin-dre des maux qui dé -

(Melancholy regions, where shame and grief dwell, the cruel, sombre empire of despair, the horror that you inspire in me is the least of the evils tearing at my heart.)

Another fine one is Iphise's monologue at the start of Act V (1744).[1]

The airs of the divertissements—or sung dances—are used by Rameau as by his predecessors; the words are superimposed on the music, as distinct from being set to music. Sometimes the vocal line reproduces the instrumental melody, sometimes not; variants make the adaptation of the words much easier, but Rameau develops this procedure to such an extent that his transformations sometimes amount to paraphrase, and occasionally—without, however, quite losing sight of its instrumental model—the variation has the effect of being a new piece. For example, comparing the air 'Permettez, astre du jour' from *Les Indes galantes* with the *rondeau*-form loure on which it is based,[2] we find that the instrumental theme is preserved in the bass of the refrain but that the music as a whole is almost entirely new, though from beginning to end of the *air* the rhythm of the loure persists. The scene with the 'ombres heureuses' in *Castor et Pollux* (IV, 2) contains a remarkable sung gavotte treated so elaborately that it takes on the form of a true *air*.[3]

Ariettes have a very strictly defined role in Rameau's operas. They are not, as one might assume, 'little arias'. On the contrary they correspond to what are conveniently known in Italian opera as bravura arias, and their function is for the most part purely decorative, so that they are incidental to the progress of the action. They have the customary roulades on key words such as 'cours' and 'fuis', following the pattern set by the Italian arias. Rameau's admirers have been loud in their praise of those ariettas which emphasize most obviously, if not most

---

[1] *Œuvres complètes*, x, appendix, p. 46.
[2] Ibid., vii, pp. 199 and 197 respectively.
[3] Ibid., viii, p. 242.

profoundly, the stylistic differences between him and Lully. Examples of these are the ariettas 'Règne, Amour' in *Pygmalion*, 'Rossignols amoureux' in *Hippolyte et Aricie*, and 'Brillez, astres nouveaux' in *Castor et Pollux*.[1] In the course of his long career Rameau made changes in their style; at the outset this was more polyphonic but towards the end of his life became more flowing and more purely melodic. Of two ariettas in Act I, scene 6, of *Les Indes galantes*, 'Hâtez-vous de vous embarquer' and 'Régnez, Amour',[2] the first is in the style of Alessandro Scarlatti, the second is in the style of Pergolesi.

Most of Rameau's *airs* are in the usual binary (AB) or *rondeau* (ABA) forms.[3] In binary *airs* the second part is invariably more developed and interesting than the first. In *rondeau* airs A is extensively developed, with orchestra, B less fully developed, with harpsichord, and there is a return to A. Rameau varies this form in an infinite number of ways. His *rondeaux* with modulating refrains are even more at variance with the traditional form: the first section, A, ends with a modulation and has to be restored to the original key by the repeat. The tripartite aria form ABC is very rare in Rameau's operas.

With Rameau the accompaniment is a major factor, whether it is played by the continuo or by the orchestra. He makes discreet use of figurations in the *basso continuo*, producing a supple counterpoint or an expressive line, according to the meaning of the text. But it is the orchestral accompaniments that provide the greatest interest. These may be homophonic or concertante, the latter kind being the more characteristic of his style: indeed his contemporaries, Rousseau among them, credit him with its invention. It had, however, already been used to a limited extent by Campra and Destouches and even by Lully; but Rameau developed it enthusiastically, and in his hands it became that harmonious polyphony which seemed to him the most perfect form of music. Concertante accompaniments weave a close web around the voice part and often rise above the vocal line. Apart from being thus intimately linked to the voice, the accompaniment is suitably geared to the meaning of the text. Thus in the *air* 'Tristes apprêts' in *Castor et Pollux* (I, 3)[4] the slow, heavy accompaniment, with its long chords and frequent rests, creates an atmosphere of sorrow and oppression. Often the principal line of the accompaniment becomes a theme in itself with a well-defined melodic personality inspired by the main idea implicit in the words being sung; it may even derive from a single key word in the *air*, as for instance in the arietta 'Accourez, riante jeunesse' in the

[1] Ibid., xvii:1, p. 91, vi, p. 395, and viii, p. 330, respectively.
[2] Ibid., vii, pp. 131 and 134, respectively.
[3] See Paul-Marie Masson, op. cit., pp. 238 ff.
[4] *Œuvres complètes*, viii, p. 73.

Prologue to *Les Fêtes d'Hébé*, where the three-note theme is linked with the idea and the rhythm of the word 'accourez'.[1]

RAMEAU'S ENSEMBLES AND CHORUSES

Vocal ensembles are the most stylized ingredient of stage music. By Rameau's day, pieces for two or more voices had almost disappeared from Italian *opere serie*, but in French opera ensembles and choruses were widespread.

Duets are by far the commonest form of ensemble. Rameau uses them in various ways but contributes nothing very new to the genre. For main scenes the 'fragmentary' duet, occurring in the middle of other types of vocal writing, was the only form to find favour in the eyes of the supporters of reason; these snatches of duet vary in length from one to eight bars and sometimes take the place of full-scale duets. These latter were used in the same way as *airs*, in main scenes or in divertissements.

While the two characters involved may be motivated by the same sentiments, it can also happen that they are in emotional conflict. This second type of duet, in which the musical unity must be reconciled to the diversity of the expression, is used by Rameau in rather a novel way, and his treatment of it is his only claim to originality in this particular field. One notable example is the duet between Theseus and the fury Tisiphone in Act II, scene 1, of *Hippolyte et Aricie*;[2] here the lively counterpoint endows each part with a different personality. Of all Rameau's operas, *Zoroastre* contains the largest number of duets, and one of these is an even more striking example of the 'conflict' type, for in the first half the two voices sing entirely different words. This is the duet in Act V, scene 4, between Zoroaster and Abramanus, where each is pitting his magic powers against those of the other.[3]

The use of duets was universally sanctioned for divertissements, where they contribute greatly to the musical interest. They were adapted to the forms currently included in divertissements—sometimes appearing as sung dances (*Dardanus*, III, 3; 'Paix favorable', sung to the tune of the preceding dance),[4] sometimes as autonomous *airs*.

Duets may be homophonic or polyphonic or a mixture of both. Homophonic writing, generally in thirds and sixths, is clearly better suited to the fragmentary duets, since these have only a simple dramatic function and ought to have the same clarity as recitative, and there is no time for the development of contrapuntal writing. But since Campra, French composers were much more drawn to polyphonic writing, which they learned from Italian composers such as Steffani (who is most

---

[1] Ibid., ix, p. 41.   [2] Ibid., vi, p. 120.   [3] Gervais ed., p. 546.
[4] *Œuvres complètes*, x, pp. 261 and 258 respectively.

famous for his chamber duets) and which they maintained even when the Italians were abandoning it. We have just seen, in the case of the duet between Theseus and Tisiphone in *Hippolyte et Aricie*, the strong dramatic force of continuous polyphony, which also vividly creates an atmosphere of tenseness and struggle. Nor is polyphony confined to duets of conflict: so universal a technique has it become that it is sometimes used when two characters share the same sentiment (*Castor et Pollux*, I, 4: 'Éclatez, fières trompettes').[1] An example of a duet containing both homophonic and polyphonic writing—a type going back to Lully—is 'Mânes plaintifs' in *Dardanus*.[2]

Trios are less common than duets, and there is only one genuine quartet in his works (in *Les Indes galantes*, III, 7).[3] Textures and their functions in trios are similar to those of duets. The trio of the Fates in *Hippolyte et Aricie* (II, 2),[4] an extremely beautiful and expressive piece, is an outstanding example of a trio in which the singers express a single sentiment—indeed the Fates are not three characters but rather a single collective character, a feature well brought out in the music. A later trio in this act, incidentally, includes some of Rameau's boldest and most difficult enharmonic writing.[5] Other trios in Rameau sum up the dramatic situation in a lively, convincing way: an example is 'Pour jamais l'amour nous engage' in *Les Indes galantes* (II, 7).[6]

Choral writing is unquestionably one of the glories of French opera in general and of Rameau's works in particular. He willingly conformed to the established custom of choral writing, since it was an excellent medium for illustrating the results of his long theoretical meditations: in his choruses he was free to test the validity of his harmonic discoveries and his expressive devices. His formidable technique, coupled with the originality of his themes, gives most of his choruses an entirely personal flavour, greatly admired by his contemporaries: we read, for instance, in the *Mercure de France*[7] that 'even the most astonishing things one is told concerning the choruses of ancient times cease to amaze when one considers those of M. Rameau'. His choruses are normally in four parts, the alto parts being sung by men. A distinction was drawn between the 'big' chorus (in four or more parts) and the 'lesser' chorus (for fewer than four voices). The small-scale chorus, especially in its three-part form, frequently appears episodically in the course of a big chorus. Sometimes Rameau employs a double chorus, alternating the two or superimposing one on the other (e.g. *Zaïs*, I, 7, and *Les Fêtes de l'Hymen et de l'Amour*, I, 7).[8] There is an even finer example in Entrée II,

[1] Ibid., viii, p. 102.   [2] Ibid., x, p. 105.   [3] Ibid., vii, p. 263.
[4] Ibid., vi, p. 162.   [5] Ibid., vi, p. 178.   [6] Ibid., vii, p. 229.
[7] October 1764, p. 46.   [8] *Œuvres complètes*, xvi, p. 156, and xv, p. 110, respectively.

scene 5, of the latter work.[1] The double chorus 'Impétueux torrents' forms the central part of the scene where the Nile overflows its banks. The two choruses are superimposed one on the other, and to these are added the solos sung by Canopus and the high priest, giving altogether ten vocal strands, all of which are skilfully and dramatically interwoven with the orchestra. The two choruses form a kind of great 'conflict' duet in which the contrasting sentiments stand out extremely clearly. This chorus is one of Rameau's finest achievements.

ORCHESTRAL MUSIC IN RAMEAU'S OPERAS

The purely orchestral passages, which alternate with the vocal sections of the operas, show Rameau at his best. As was customary in those days, these symphonies fall into two major categories: dramatic symphonies and dance symphonies. The dramatic symphonies appear in various forms—overtures, descriptive symphonies, preludes, interludes, and postludes.

When Rameau made his début in the theatre the Lullian overture, completely divorced from the action, still held sway. He at once set about creating a liaison between overture and action, and we are constantly aware of his preoccupation with this question. The overture to his first opera, *Hippolyte et Aricie*, contains thematic reference to the first part of the Prologue, the chorus of the nymphs of Diana.[2] Links are especially clear in *Zaïs* and *Naïs*. The suppression of the prologue in *Zoroastre* leads naturally to emotional links between the overture and the action of the drama. Thus the overture assumes a new significance, since it replaces the prologue, or, as we read at the beginning of the libretto, 'the overture serves as a prologue'. Rameau envisaged it as a synopsis of the whole drama, a piece of symphonic programme music evoking the essence of the subject. The use of the term 'programme music' is by no means inappropriate, for the overture to *Zoroastre* is analysed as follows in all the librettos of the opera. 'The first part paints a most moving picture of Abramanus's barbaric might and the lamentations of the nations he oppresses. A gentle stillness ensues, and hope is reborn. The second part is a lively, cheerful description of the magnanimity of Zoroaster and the happiness of the nations he has delivered from bondage.' This reads like a programme by Lesueur or Berlioz. Each aspect of it is illustrated, and the central andante separating the two fast sections of the symphony has the effect of a real dramatic episode, its simple, supple melody recalling certain lyrical passages in the overtures of Berlioz:[3]

[1] Ibid., xv, p. 169.
[2] See ibid., vi, pp. 1 and 7 respectively.
[3] Full score in Gervais ed., pp. 6 ff.

Ex. 132

Acanthe et Céphise, Les Paladins, and *Les Boréades* all have programme overtures too. Opera-ballet presents a greater problem in that there is no connected plot, and here Rameau reverts to Lully's use of the purely decorative overture.

Rameau asserted the right to vary the form of the overture as he thought fit, and consequently it became adaptable to all types of expression: his contemporaries were first of all amazed, then indignant, and finally enthusiastic. It was in 1739 with the overture to *Les Fêtes d'Hébé*[1] that he made the first definite break with the traditional French overture (though, as we have seen, Destouches experimented in *Omphale* with a binary structure). The two sections are very different from the two- or three-part structure evolved by Lully; the second part is

[1] *Œuvres complètes,* ix, p. 1.

conceived as a kind of sonata movement with two subjects. Taken as a whole, it may give the impression of being perhaps a little facile, but its novelty created a tremendous stir. Rameau continued his experiments elsewhere, and they had a lasting effect on the history of French music, independently of Italian and German influences. His fresh approach to the overture made it one of the most important forms of orchestral music before the classical symphony. When the new German symphonies were introduced into France around 1755, his overtures were almost the only works that bore comparison with them in imaginative vigour and breadth of construction.

Descriptive symphonies, written to accompany various conspicuous events in the action, were of course used by Rameau's predecessors, and he continued to scatter them freely throughout his operas: in particular he painted with more vivid orchestral colour the terrors of natural phenomena—thunder (*Zoroastre*, V, 4), storm at sea (*Les Indes galantes*, I, 2), and the motion of the sea (*Hippolyte et Aricie*, III, 9).[1] By contrast, the gentler side of nature is also conveyed: sunrise (*Zoroastre*, II, 1) and birdsong (*Hippolyte et Aricie*, V, 8), and in *Le Temple de la Gloire* (III, 5) there is a whole symphony devoted to birds, entitled 'Ramage d'oiseaux'.[2] But it is above all in evoking the unleashed fury of nature that Rameau shows his superiority to Lully.

The different steps in the action, when there is no singing involved, are accompanied by symphonies which suggest what is going on; this type of symphony is shorter than those already mentioned. They have several functions; for example, to make marvels more marvellous, highlight sudden changes of scene, emphasize the emotional turmoil of the characters, or herald the approach of battle.

As an entr'acte the usual procedure in Rameau's day was for the orchestra to play either an *air de danse*, borrowed from the previous act, or the overture. However, from the second version of *Dardanus* onwards Rameau introduced an entr'acte symphony continuing the drama, an idea anticipated only once previously, in Mouret's *Pirithoüs*.

The preludes and interludes surrounding the actual singing take up a considerable amount of space in Rameau's operas and fulfil a highly significant dramatic function. Generally speaking, they are related to the psychological content of the action, evoking the singer's emotional state and sustaining the emotion during the intervals in the singing, their expressiveness intensified by their proximity to the words themselves.

[1] See respectively Gervais ed., p. 540, and *Œuvres complètes*, vii, p. 82, and vi, p. 255.
[2] See respectively Gervais ed., p. 115, and *Œuvres complètes*, vi, pp. 389 ff., and xiv, p. 333.

The preludes (or ritornellos) are short symphonies preceding arias and nearly always closely related to them, through structure or through analogies with, or references to the vocal lines or accompaniments of the *airs*. A prelude may be entirely borrowed from the ensuing *air*, or it may be in two parts, one borrowed from the *air* and the other quite original; this second part may constitute a small emotive symphony in its own right, inspired by the psychological content of the situation and the emotional state of the particular character involved. For instance, the prelude to the *air* 'Ah! faut-il en un jour perdre tout ce que j'aime' (*Hippolyte et Aricie*, IV, 1) is thirteen bars long; of these the first four set out the melody of the first line of the *air,* while the last nine continue the mood of the beginning but use a new melody, made up of two phrases, the second of which is a moving evocation of Hippolytus's despair.[1]

When only the accompaniment of an *air* is anticipated in a prelude, we may find too that essential elements in it are inspired by some striking idea suggested by the words. Sometimes an instrumental theme of this kind is so important that it seems to represent the essential melodic element and to be the basis of the whole musical structure. It may be said, therefore, that the prelude and the accompaniment stem from a single theme not represented in the voice part and expressing directly in instrumental form the essential meaning of the words. The combination of prelude and accompaniment gives birth to some of Rameau's finest dramatic symphonies: for instance, Pollux's wonderful monologue 'Nature, amour, qui partagez mon cœur' (*Castor et Pollux*, II, 1)[2] opens with a prelude that is continued in the accompaniment, where the long sinuous line expresses the idea of melancholy uncertainty underlying the whole piece. The most wonderful of all Rameau's preludes is certainly that in Act III, scene 9, of *Hippolyte et Aricie*, preceding Theseus's appeal to Neptune; from beginning to end its lofty style is reminiscent of Bach:[3]

Ex. 133

Strs.
+ B.C.

[1] *Œuvres complètes*, vi, p. 262.   [2] Ibid., viii, p. 116.   [3] Ibid., vi, p. 251.

Examples of the wholly independent prelude are much less common, although *Zoroastre* has one in Act IV, scene 1, introducing Abramanus's monologue 'Cruels tyrans qui régnez sur mon cœur'.[1]

The interludes and postludes bear the same stamp as the preludes. Rameau uses orchestral interludes very freely, guided always by the needs of the dramatic expression and by certain considerations of balance within the musical structure. Their musical content either derives from the recitatives or *airs* to which they are attached or may be independent, though this is somewhat unusual and occurs primarily in association with accompanied recitative. The postlude is always based either on the prelude or the interlude.

Preludes, interludes, and postludes, despite the musical role assigned to them within the architecture of a work as a whole, are none the less always treated by Rameau as symphonies, full of meaning and closely linked with the action. With Lully and his successors the orchestra is still somewhat subservient to the drama; with Rameau, however, its interventions are much more frequent and of much greater significance.

It is indeed true to say that Rameau's operas pave the way for the modern conception of the continuous dramatic symphony Wagner later claimed to have invented.[2] The same concept obtains in the dance symphonies, which are almost as important in Rameau's operas as the truly dramatic symphonies. The divertissement dance, far from losing ground since Lully, went from strength to strength in step with the development of manners and social customs and through the general popularity of dancing in the eighteenth century. Even during the most moving tragedies dancing was always greeted with applause, the only proviso made by the audience being that the dances should have some connection with the dramatic action.

In fact dances are an integral part of the drama, incorporated into every act—not necessarily at the end—instead of being relegated to an

[1] Gervais ed., p. 369.
[2] See Paul-Marie Masson, 'Rameau et Wagner', *Musical Quarterly*, xxv (1939), p. 466.

entr'acte or treated as extraneous matter, as was done by the Italians. Lully, we have seen, included dances freely; Rameau's equally frequent dances gain from an important advance in ideas concerning ballet, as well as a considerable transformation in the actual technique of the art, which had gone some way towards turning pantomime into a kind of dramatic dumbshow. The composer is the natural mediator between the librettist's ideas and their execution by the dancers. Jean Georges Noverre pinpoints exactly this affinity between music and dance.[1] Rameau's music was the very mainspring of contemporary ballet, infusing it with new life and providing choreographers with possibilities for expression which even now have not been exhausted. It seems probable that he intervened personally to explain his ideas to the dancers, just as Lully had done before him, and the story goes that in rehearsing the chaconne of the 'sauvages' in Les Indes galantes he himself sketched out the choreography for the dancer Dupré.[2]

Rameau's dances stand out in that they are meticulously adapted to fit the changing circumstances of the drama, the personalities of the characters involved and the particular mime called for. The prime consideration is clearly to describe or characterize. There is nothing new in this, but what is new is the quality of the musical realization—the individuality of the themes, the incisive articulation of the melodic line, and the bold, yet exquisitely precise treatment of the rhythm, which seems to draw the dancer on. As with Lully, we find Rameau using the dances currently popular in fashionable society: the gavotte, bourrée, rigaudon, tambourin, contredanse, loure, forlane, gigue, saraband, chaconne, minuet, passepied, musette and so on. He is at his best in 'character dances' (danses caractérisées), which might be described as psychological dances, with their descriptive titles such as the one 'for the lovers who follow Bellona' in Les Indes galantes (Prologue, 3).[3] Dances of this kind do not constitute a fixed form: on the contrary, their form is quite free to adapt itself to all types of expression. There is a dance to fit every possible emotional eventuality in the drama, and no other form has greater freedom in its musical development. Furthermore, there has rarely been a more harmonious union of the expressive and the purely formal elements of music. In this sense Rameau's airs de danse are in themselves an important milestone in the history of instrumental music, on a par with the sonata and the concerto in Italy and Germany.

[1] See Noverre, Lettres sur la danse et les ballets (1760), trans. Cyril W. Beaumont as Letters on Dancing and Ballets (London, 1930), p. 144.
[2] See Nicolas Bricaire de la Dixmérie, Les Deux Âges du goût et du génie français (The Hague and Paris, 1769), p. 523.
[3] Œuvres complètes, vii, p. 45.

RAMEAU'S HARMONY

To make the most of all this musical material, Rameau, whose melodies have often been criticized as being poorer than those of his predecessors, clothes his melodic lines with harmonies so rich and original that his music takes on a new lease of life. Harmonic intervals are used in much the same way as in Lully's music, and there is no point in covering this ground again: Rameau's harmonic principles are the same as those of his predecessors. Nevertheless, his preoccupation with harmony was lifelong and fundamental. In his music, especially his dramatic works, he made good use of his scientific observations and discoveries. It was not that he was motivated by any desire to parade his learning in his music; but he was able to put a new and scholarly interpretation on chordal structure. By the discreet application of his findings he brought about certain innovations and showed considerable originality in his handling of modulations. Devotees of new harmonies will find Rameau's less exciting than those of either Couperin or Destouches: his object at all times was 'to conceal art with art'.

For Rameau in his operas the purpose of harmony is above all to support the given vocal line, and expressiveness is the main principle governing the choice of harmonies. As he himself says,[1] melody is for him the first concrete manifestation of musical thought. But the expressive content of this melody springs from the harmony that it implies, and it is the harmony that has the power to stimulate the passions and bring the melody to life. It is therefore the most potent means of expression. Rameau employs a logical range of procedures which he applies in all the various circumstances of dramatic expression. He co-ordinates all the old procedures under the physical phenomena of resonance, superior resonance and inferior resonance,[2] and takes the view that there are two sides to harmony—the dominant, full of joy, light, and strength, and the subdominant, melancholy, dark and feeble. This duality contains almost the whole secret of Rameau's expressive palette, as we soon realize when we study his handling of harmony from a scientific as well as a practical point of view.

In his Traité de l'harmonie Rameau clearly defines the use of consonance and dissonance.[3] Lully made a point of using dissonances to suggest despair or fear; but the spread of Italian works opened French eyes to a still more discordant style, which Le Cerf de la Viéville and other followers of Lully found somewhat disconcerting. Rameau, like

[1] See Rameau, Nouveau Système de musique théorique (Paris, 1726), p. 43.
[2] See Paul-Marie Masson, L'Opéra de Rameau, pp. 466-8.
[3] See Rameau, Traité de l'harmonie (Paris, 1722), p. 141. Also see Hans Pischner, Die Harmonielehre Jean-Philippe Rameaus (Leipzig, 1963).

Bach, took his cue from this new style, thereby incurring the displeasure
of his adversaries. Not content with using discordant intervals, he
neglected to prepare them in the time-honoured way. Chord inversions,
which Rameau was the first to codify, were applied with conscious effect
as a new emotive factor.

All chords are distinguished by the intervals of which they are compounded; seconds, thirds, fourths, and fifths are used no differently by
Rameau than by earlier composers. But with the sixth something new
creeps in. The sixth readily determines the mode; but Rameau broadens
its scope by introducing it into a straightforward chord as an *added*
sixth, a term used to describe every major sixth added to a common
chord. Its most frequent appearance is on the subdominant of the key
to anticipate a final cadence. Thus in the language of music it has overtones of expectation and preparation arising from its tonal function and
from its characteristic intervals. Rameau felt that this chord was basic
and direct, although within it the sixth forms a discord with the fifth;
he classified it as the first inversion of the chord of the seventh, made up
of the same notes. It was not normally used by either the Italians or the
Germans. On the subdominant in the minor mode it has a very striking
effect because of the augmented fourth that appears between the third
and the sixth; a fine example occurs in the sailors' chorus from *Les Indes
galantes*, on the penultimate syllable of the last statement of the phrase
'Serons-nous embrasés par les feux du tonnerre'.[1] Occasionally he makes
use of the augmented sixth between the flattened supertonic and the
leading note, resolving respectively on to the tonic and its octave. This
interval apparently originated in Italy and was of course widely used
later on in the Viennese classics. Rameau also made occasional use of
chords of the eleventh, a word that he introduced into harmonic
terminology (initially without success).

RAMEAU'S SCORING

Rameau's orchestra contained at least some fifty players. Strings were
the basis of this ensemble. The wind instruments included flutes (recorders or transverse flutes), oboes, bassoons, musettes, clarinets (making
a very early appearance in *Zoroastre*), trumpets, and hunting horns. The
percussion section included kettledrum, drum, tambourine, and tabor.
One curious addition was the cannon used in the fireworks scene of
Acanthe et Céphise.

Rameau handled these forces with marked originality: the subtlety
and new timbres of his orchestration are unique in European music of
that time. While he remained faithful to certain instrumental groupings

[1] *Œuvres complètes*, vii, p. 101.

in the Lully tradition his own strong personality left its imprint on the orchestration, as did his preoccupation with dramatic expression. His ingenuity is particularly evident in what might be called the 'counterpoint of timbres', that is to say the art of superimposing or interweaving the different strands allotted to the various instrumental timbres. Sometimes the writing is harmonic, each part having a different type of sonority. Again, one or more parts may be immobilized on held notes, while another part, either accompanied or on its own, outlines the principal melody (see the March in Act V, scene 8, of *Hippolyte et Aricie*).[1] Elsewhere the string ensemble may play a chordal accompaniment to a woodwind melody, as in the gavotte in *Acanthe et Céphise* (II, 4), or the different timbres may mingle freely in an often delicate counterpoint, flutes and violins with oboes or trumpets, for example, or bassoons with lower strings. Finally, this counterpoint of timbres sometimes appears in a more open form, as dialogue, where the different sonorities are juxtaposed without being superimposed on one another, each answering the other. This type of writing was doubtless familiar to composers before Rameau; but he undeniably took a great step towards the independence of the various tone colours. After 1750 the evolution of style and the increasing use of the newer wind instruments are reflected in Rameau's music in passages of orchestration that already bear the stamp of another era. The score of *Acanthe et Céphise* is most interesting in this respect: certain characteristics generally associated with Gluck are already present here.

CONCLUSION

Melody, harmony, movement, instrumental tone quality: these features are constantly at work in Rameau's operas at the behest of the situation created by the text and dramatic content. The composer seeks these situations out, and even induces them, constantly seeking in the unfolding plot the generating force for his inspiration, whether it be an object to paint or a sentiment to describe. If one looks closely at his music, it can be seen to be strong, graceful, and tender; and it is this variety of expression that makes him a great dramatic composer. One can do no better than end with the comment of a contemporary writer:

Sometimes, with a vigorous, masculine touch, he conjured up dread and dismay; or again, with the most dulcet and caressing sounds, moved one to tears. At other times, flirting with the graces or toying with Momus's cap-and-bells, he filled the stage with tableaux of the most pleasing and agreeable sort. Rameau could by turn cause Melpomene to grieve and spread joy and laughter in the train of Terpsichore and Thalia.[2]

[1] Ibid., vi, p. 368.
[2] Hughes Maret, *Éloge historique de Mr Rameau* (Dijon and Paris, 1766), pp. 31–2.

V

OPERA IN ENGLAND AND GERMANY

By J. A. WESTRUP

THE PROSPECTS FOR OPERA IN ENGLAND

THE impact of Italian opera on other European countries was relatively slow. In England there were three main reasons for this: first, the strong tradition of spoken drama in a form acceptable to all classes; secondly, the closing of the theatres during the Civil War and the Commonwealth; thirdly, the apparent lack of funds to meet the considerable expense that opera entails. No one of these reasons was sufficient in itself to prevent the establishment of opera in England. Music was already an indispensable element in Elizabethan and Jacobean drama, and it played an even larger part in the court masque.[1] The closing of the theatres, originally ordered by Parliament in 1642 on the ground that 'publike Stage-playes' did not agree 'with the Seasons of Humiliation', and confirmed by further ordinances of 1647 and 1648, did nothing to prevent private performances, with or without music. That the economy of England was shaken by the Civil War is without question; but the wanton extravagance of Charles II's court showed that money was available for opera, if there had been a serious demand for it. The truth would appear to be that even enlightened men had no experience of opera and therefore no desire to hear it. Visitors to Italy might come back with glowing accounts of the new form of entertainment, as Evelyn did, who wrote in his diary that the opera which he saw in Venice in 1645 held the audience 'by the Eyes and Eares til two in the Morning'; it was 'doubtlesse one of the most magnificent & expensfull diversions the Wit of Men can invent'. But such visitors were few and far between; and even Evelyn, when he went to see 'a new *Opera* after the *Italian* way in *Recitative Music & Sceanes*' in London,[2] was distressed that such vanity should be allowed 'in a time of such a publique Consternation'—the moral objection to opera, which persisted for many years afterwards, was strong. No doubt some at least of the musicians in Charles II's employment would have been glad of an opportunity to try their hand at opera; but their influence was small, and much of

---

[1] See Vol. IV, pp. 813–20.   [2] 5 May 1659.

their energy had to be devoted to extracting arrears of salary from the Exchequer. Projects for the performance of Italian opera in London were made, but they came to nothing.[1]

CUPID AND DEATH

The fact that private performances were possible under the Commonwealth, however, offered composers some opportunity to introduce the idioms of Italian opera into English drama; and music could even be made the excuse for a public presentation. James Shirley's masque *Cupid and Death*[2] was performed in London in honour of the Portuguese ambassador on 26 March 1653; but the preface to the libretto printed in that year mentions that it 'was born without ambition of more than to make good a private entertainment'. This would suggest that it was originally written, like other works of the period, for performance in a school. It was revived at the Military Ground in Leicester Fields (north of Leicester Square) in 1659. The term 'Military Ground' might suggest an open-air performance, but in fact it took place in the meeting house of the Military Company. Nor was the performance public: it was described in the new edition of the text as 'a Private Entertainment'. The music was by Matthew Locke, with some additions by Christopher Gibbons. Locke's autograph score[3] describes the 1659 performance as a 'Morall Representation', which means no more than that the subject was allegorical; certainly there is nothing in the piece which could be said to be 'edifying', in the strict sense of the word.

Shirley seems to have taken the story from John Ogilby's *The Fables of Aesop paraphras'd in verse*, published in 1651. The gist is simple. The arrows proper to Cupid and Death are changed by a dishonest chamberlain at the inn where both of them have stayed. As a result Cupid's shafts spell death to lovers, while Death has the power to awaken amorous desires in aged folk. At the end Mercury appears as a *deus ex machina* and sits in judgement on the two culprits. The lovers who have been killed cannot be restored to life, but they are shown 'in glorious Seats and Habits' in Elysium. It was traditional that the masque should include dialogue, songs, and dances. It is very probable that this was the original form of *Cupid and Death*. The music is known to us only in the 1659 version, and here it has a much more extensive part to play. The dialogue remains but is almost entirely restricted to the opening part of the work. Once the dramatic effect of the exchange of arrows has begun the music takes command, so that much of it suggests a miniature

[1] *Calendar of State Papers, Domestic*, 22 October 1660; Pepys, *Diary*, 2 August 1664, 12 February 1667.
[2] Complete edition with music in *Musica Britannica*, ii (2nd ed., London, 1965).
[3] Brit. Mus. Add. MS. 17799.

opera, particularly those sections which might variously be described as monody, recitative or declamatory song. This may very well be due to the success of Davenant's operatic productions in 1656 (see p. 273).

Monody on the Italian model can be traced back as far as Dowland,[1] but not all his contemporaries and immediate successors were as skilful as he was in adapting Italian idioms to English words. Of the two forms of monody—declamatory song and recitative—the former, akin to Caccini's strophic aria, was not entirely successful in its English dress, perhaps because the genius of the language is more suited to symmetrical lyricism than to a kind of arioso. Recitative, on the other hand, will work well in any language except French, since its shape is entirely determined by the accents of the text.[2] Both types appear in *Cupid and Death*, as well as simple lyrical forms. Where Locke or Gibbons combine declamation and lyricism in the same song, the advantage lies with the purely metrical treatment of the text. This is clear from Gibbons's setting of the second song, 'Victorious men on earth', which begins:

Ex. 134

---

[1] See Vol. IV, pp. 211–15.
[2] For a detailed discussion of these two forms see Vol. VI, chap. II.

Here the attempt to do justice to the text results in a setting which defeats the purpose of the poetry and has no well-defined musical structure. The concluding section of the song (which is repeated by the chorus) not only respects the poet's basic rhythm but is also more convincing as music:

Ex. 135

Where the text was in blank verse (which may have been spoken at the first performance) Locke had the opportunity of writing recitative, which could follow as closely as possible the natural accent of the words and at the same time create dramatic effect by the use of significant turns of melody and harmony. An excellent example is the scene in which Nature, appearing in 'a green mantle fringed with gold, her hair loose', expresses her horror at the consequences of the exchange of arrows. The following excerpt occurs after a lover, shot by Cupid, has died:

Ex. 136

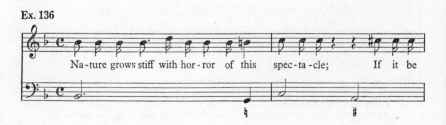

death to love, what will it be When death it-self shall act his cru - el -

Enter DEATH

- ty? And here he comes: what tra - ge -dies are next?

The chromaticisms in this passage, and in particular the abrupt change of harmony at the entry of Death, show how thoroughly Locke had studied his Italian models. Though there is no evidence that he ever visited Italy, he is known to have been in Flanders in 1648,[1] and both there and in England he would have had plenty of opportunity of familiarizing himself with Italian vocal music. Abrupt changes of harmony, which originated as a simple method of harmonizing a chromatic progression in a melody, were used as an emotional means of expression by the later Italian madrigalists and were borrowed from them, for a similar purpose, by the earliest opera composers. The progression in bar 6 of the previous example has its antecedents in the messenger's narrative in Peri's *Euridice* (1600) and also in Monteverdi's *Orfeo* (1607).

It was traditional to introduce grotesque elements into the masque. They appear in *Cupid and Death* in the persons of two old men and women, the chamberlain and a satyr. The old men and women, struck by Death's arrows, drop their crutches, embrace and 'dance with antic postures, expressing rural courtship':

Ex. 137

---

[1] Brit. Mus. Add. MS. 31437 (autograph), fo. 29v: 'A Collection of Songs when I was in the Low-Countrys, 1648'. The 'songs' are Latin motets, some in three parts, some in two, and others for solo voice.

Later the chamberlain, who has abandoned his employment in the inn and makes a living by exhibiting a pair of apes at fairs, is also a victim. He immediately makes amorous advances to his apes, but a satyr appears and takes them from him. A fantastic dance for the satyr and the apes follows. Its jerky movements and changes of time suggest that the actors are striking curious attitudes. This is one of many examples in the music of masques which cannot be properly appreciated without some understanding of the action which was meant to accompany them. A parallel can be seen in the dance for the sailors and witches in Purcell's *Dido and Aeneas* (1689).

REVIVAL OF THE MASQUE

The court masque was revived in the reign of Charles II. We have detailed accounts of John Crowne's *Calisto*, with music by Nicholas Staggins, which was performed at Whitehall in the winter of 1674–5;[1] the music has not survived. But this type of entertainment did not retain the popularity which it had enjoyed under the first two Stuart kings. John Blow's *Venus and Adonis* (*c.* 1682) is set to music throughout and is in effect, like Purcell's *Dido and Aeneas*, a miniature opera. The masque, however, continued to be used as an interlude in spoken drama, as it had been, for instance, in Shakespeare's *Tempest*. The practice was ridiculed in the Duke of Buckingham's comedy *The Rehearsal* (written in 1663–5 but not performed till 1671), where Bayes observes: 'You must ever interlard your Plays with Songs, Ghosts and Dances'. Sir Robert Stapylton's tragi-comedy *The Step-mother* (1663), with music by Locke, includes two masques. In Elkanah Settle's *The Empress of Morocco* (1671) there is a masque representing the descent of Orpheus into Hades

---

[1] Allardyce Nicoll, *A History of English Drama, 1660–1700*, 4th ed., i (Cambridge, 1952), pp. 357–60.

to rescue Eurydice; the music, again by Locke, has been preserved[1] and offers further evidence of a capacity for dramatic representation in music which was frustrated by circumstances. According to Roger North it was 'scandalously performed'.[2] Later examples of the incorporation of masques in drama are to be found in Purcell's *Dioclesian* (1690), *The Fairy Queen* (1692), and *The Tempest* (1695).

DAVENANT

It is ironical that the first attempts at opera in England were made with ulterior motives. In 1656 Sir William Davenant, a Royalist playwright who had spent two years in the Tower of London (1650–2), presented what he called 'The First Dayes Entertainment . . . by Declamations and Musick' at Rutland House, Aldersgate, in the City of London. In spite of the Commonwealth ban on theatres this was a stage performance, including arguments for and against 'Moral Representations', with vocal and instrumental interludes. It was followed in the same year by *The Siege of Rhodes. Made a Representation by the Art of Prospective in Scene, And the Story sung in* Recitative *Musick*, which was performed in the same building. *The Cruelty of the Spaniards in Peru* and *The History of Sir Francis Drake* were presented in 1658 and 1659 respectively. John Aubrey (1626–97) has the following account of this enterprise:

Being freed from imprisonment, (because playes, scil. Tragedies and Comoedies, were in those Presbyterian times scandalous) [Davenant] contrives to set-up an Opera *stylo recitativo*, wherein serjeant Maynard and severall citizens were engagers. It began at Rutland-house, in Charter-house-yard; next, (scil.anno . . .) at the Cock-pitt in Drury-lane, where were acted very well *stylo recitativo, Sir Francis Drake's* . . . , and *the Siege of Rhodes* (1st and 2d part). It did affect the eie and eare extremely. This first brought scenes in fashion in England: before, at playes, was only a hanging.[3]

The particular interest of this rather muddled passage lies in the mention of Sir John Maynard (1602–90), a prominent lawyer under several governments, and in the reference to the novelty of scenery.

The idea of using painted flats was not, in fact, entirely new, since John Webb (a pupil of Inigo Jones), who designed the sets for *The Siege of Rhodes*, had used the same method in Davenant's masque *Salmacida Spolia* in 1640.[4] But Aubrey would have been too young to have seen that performance, and since it was given at Whitehall the new technique is unlikely to have been familiar to the general public. Aubrey's reference

[1] Oxford, Christ Church, MS. 692.
[2] John Wilson, *Roger North on Music* (London, 1959), p. 306.
[3] John Aubrey, *Brief Lives*, ed. Andrew Clark (Oxford, 1898), i, p. 208.
[4] Montague Summers, *The Playhouse of Pepys* (London, 1935), p. 27.

to the Cockpit in Drury Lane is significant. The move from Rutland House was bold, since the Cockpit was a theatre and performances there were technically illegal. For that reason *The Cruelty of the Spaniards in Peru* was not an opera but a mixed entertainment. But when Davenant put on *The History of Sir Francis Drake* and actually revived *The Siege of Rhodes* at the Cockpit the authorities were forced to take notice, and the theatre was closed for a time.[1]

The prologue to *The First Dayes Entertainment* includes the lines:

> Think this your passage, and the narrow way
> To our Elisian field, the Opera.

The progress to the 'Elisian field' was rapid. It is certain that *The Siege of Rhodes* was sung throughout. Quite apart from the title, which specifically refers to '*Recitative* Musick', we know that the cast[2]—a double one, apart from Solyman and Ianthe—consisted entirely of singers, including Locke, who not only played the part of the Admiral but also composed some of the vocal music. In his preface Davenant apologized for the very small stage (11ft. high and 15ft. deep), referred to the five composers and the performers as 'the most transcendent of *England* in that Art, and perhaps not unequal to the best Masters abroad', and justified the variation in the length of the lines by explaining that this was necessary in recitative. He also described recitative as 'unpractis'd here', which was not strictly true, though it is quite possible that most of the people who attended the performances were unfamiliar with it.

Although the music of *The Siege of Rhodes* is lost, the work might still have been hailed as a landmark in English opera if Davenant himself had been willing or energetic enough to continue his experiment after the Restoration. Instead, as Dryden put it, 'he review'd his *Siege of Rhodes*, and caus'd it to be acted as a just *Drama*'.[3] Davenant's object had clearly been to revive dramatic performances during the closing years of the Commonwealth, and the only way to do this was to present a musical entertainment. After the Restoration this subterfuge was no longer necessary. Pepys might record that he 'went forth to Sir William Davenant's Opera'[4] in 1661; and in the same year Elizabeth Bodville, with more respect for phonetics than for orthography, might write that she had been 'at the new aprer'.[5] But in fact *The Siege of Rhodes* was no longer an opera in the Italian sense; it was a play with music, and this

---

[1] Ibid., p. 54.
[2] Printed at the end of the libretto.
[3] Preface to *The Conquest of Granada* (1672).
[4] 2 July 1661.
[5] E. M. Thompson, *Correspondence of the Family of Hatton* (London, 1878), i, p. 21.

was to remain the standard form of theatrical entertainment until the early years of the eighteenth century. The music might consist of nothing more than a series of 'act tunes' (or entr'actes) and a handful of songs, or it might be elaborated to fill an entire scene, particularly one that involved ceremonial or magic. Works of the latter kind were commonly described as 'operas' but Roger North, who had little use for them, nicknamed them 'semi-operas' or 'ambigue enterteinements'. 'They break unity,' he wrote, 'and distract the audience. Some come for the play and hate the musick, others come onely for the musick, and the drama is pennance to them, and scarce any are well reconciled to both.'[1]

LOCKE'S LATER STAGE MUSIC

There was a parallel to the semi-operas in France in the *tragédies de machines*, which made substantial use of music, and in the hybrid form of the *comédie-ballet*, invented by Molière in 1661.[2] Molière's *Psyché*, produced in 1671 with additional verses set to music by Lully, seems to have been the model for an 'opera' with the same title written by Thomas Shadwell. The English *Psyche*, first performed in February 1675,[3] was provided with music by Locke, who wrote the songs and choruses and incidental 'symphonies', and Giovanni Battista Draghi, an Italian domiciled in England, who was responsible for the rest of the instrumental music. Locke published his share of the work under the title *The English Opera, or The Vocal Musick in Psyche, with the Instrumental Therein Intermix'd.*[4] In a characteristically acid preface he justifies the title 'opera', explaining what the Italians understand by the term and emphasizing the wide range of his own contribution, 'from Ballad to single Air, Counterpoint, Recitative, Fuge, Canon, and Chromatick Musick'. In view of this his work 'may justly wear the Title, though all the Tragedy be not in Musick: for the Author [i.e. Shadwell] prudently consider'd, that though *Italy* was, and is the great Academy of the World for that Science and way of Entertainment, *England* is not: and therefore mixt it with interlocutions, as more proper to our *Genius*'.

The music of *Psyche* shows a good deal less imagination than that of *Cupid and Death*. The recitative is mainly humdrum, and too many of the songs are in a perfunctory triple time. One of the reasons for this decline may very well be that Shirley was a poet of some distinction and Shadwell was not: a more inventive genius than Locke's was necessary to turn this fustian into music. But it is also significant that whereas

[1] Wilson, op. cit., p. 307.
[2] See pp. 182–6.
[3] Nicoll, op. cit., p. 348.
[4] London, 1675. The work is dedicated to the Duke of Monmouth, who seems to have attended rehearsals and encouraged the performers.

Cupid and Death was designed for a private entertainment, *Psyche* was written for the public theatre. Locke may have felt disinclined to take trouble over music which most of his audience would consider to be less important than scenery and costumes, and for that reason carelessly adopted a style which he imagined would be popular. The one place where his imagination was stirred was in the scene for 'Two despairing Men, and Two despairing Women' in 'a Rocky Desart full of dreadful Caves and Cliffs'. The following passage, with its expressive intervals and exact accentuation, might have been written by Purcell:

Ex. 138

It is significant that Shadwell, in his preface to the libretto, mentioned this as one of the scenes which were unlikely to appeal to 'the unskilful in Musick'. It is arguable that Locke's true genius was for instrumental music. Certainly the 'Curtain Tune' in his music for Shadwell's version of *The Tempest* (1674) shows unusual imagination in its treatment of the string orchestra. It also illustrates a dramatic approach to instrumental writing which was rare at the time and only gradually became a staple element in opera—and then mainly in the form of interjections in accompanied recitative. A growth in intensity is indicated not only by the dynamic markings—'soft', 'lowder by degrees', 'violent', etc.—but also by the increasingly elaborate figuration, e.g. bars 18–26:

Ex. 139

The attempt to woo English audiences to accept a complete opera
can hardly have been advanced by the activities of Louis Grabu, Master
of the King's Music from 1666 to 1674. His setting of a revised text of
Perrin's libretto *Ariane, ou le Mariage de Bacchus* (previously composed
by Cambert) was performed in 1674 in honour of the Duke of York's
marriage to Mary of Modena. Since it was designed for a special
occasion and was sung in French it is unlikely to have made a permanent
impression. It may be, however, that Dryden remembered it when he
was planning a patriotic play with a prologue in honour of Charles II
and his brother. The prologue grew into a three-act opera, entitled
Albion and Albanius, and Grabu was invited to set it to music, although
he no longer had any official position in London. The performance,
postponed on account of Charles II's death, took place in June 1685.
The outbreak of Monmouth's rebellion cut short any success that might
have been won for it by Dryden's reputation; but the poverty of Grabu's
invention and his ignorance of English declamation were still more
serious obstacles. *Albion and Albanius* remained the only full-length
opera in English to be performed between 1660 and 1700. A French
company which brought Lully's *Cadmus et Hermione* to London in
1686 does not appear to have been any more successful. The music was
admired by connoisseurs, but there was adverse comment on the costumes.[1] Englishmen went to the theatre either to be amused or to see a
spectacle, not to listen to recitative.

BLOW'S *VENUS AND ADONIS*

Private performance was the only outlet for composers who believed
that English opera was possible. Productions of this kind were of
necessity on a smaller scale than the 'semi-operas' presented in the
public theatres. John Blow's *Venus and Adonis*,[2] described as a masque
but in all essentials an opera, has a prologue and three acts; but it is no

---

[1] J. A. Westrup, *Purcell* (5th ed., London, 1965), p. 110.
[2] Ed. Anthony Lewis (Paris, 1939).

longer than a normal one-act opera. In the earliest manuscript,[1] dated
1682, it is entitled 'A Masque for yᵉ entertainment of the King', which
clearly points to a performance at court, and two amateur members
of the cast are mentioned: Lady Mary Tudor, an illegitimate daughter
of Charles II, and 'Mrs. Davys', presumably her mother, an actress and
dancer familiarly known as Moll Davies. Unlike Lully's grandiose
operas, where the prologue pays fulsome tribute to the monarch, *Venus
and Adonis* makes no specific reference to the royal family. Instead the
prologue pokes innocent fun at the morals of the court. Cupid, no
doubt addressing the assembled company, sings:

> Courtiers, there is no faith in you,
> You change as often as you can:
> Your women they continue true
> But till they see another man.

To a shepherd who asks if he has found any instances of fidelity he
replies:

> At court I find constant and true
> Only an aged lord or two.

Until the final tragedy is reached in Act III this is a light-hearted work,
marked by the humour of Cupid's lesson to the little Cupids[2] and
Venus's cascading laughter and by the rough vigour of Adonis's
huntsmen:

Ex. 140

Strings

---

[1] Brit.Mus., Add. 22100, fo. 123.
[2] Recorded in *The History of Music in Sound*, v.

The tradition of the masque is maintained in a number of dances, culminating in an impressive chaconne on a chromatic ground at the end of Act II, which looks as if it served as a model for an instrumental air (on a different bass) printed among Purcell's *Fairy Queen* music in *A Collection of Ayres, Compos'd for the Theatre* (1697).[1]

The style of Blow's vocal writing, which does not exclude *fioriture*, is nearer to Lully's arioso than to Italian recitative or English declamatory song. The character of most of the opera does not call for dramatic emphasis or for any strong expression of emotion. But in the final scene, where Adonis, mortally wounded, returns to Venus, the composer shows that he is capable of something warmer than the agreeably lukewarm temperature of what has hitherto been a pastoral comedy:

Ex. 141

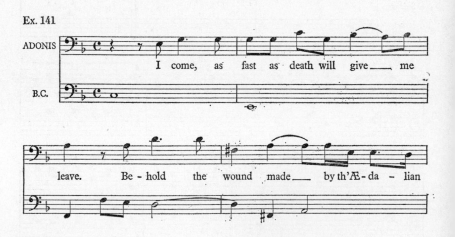

[1] See Lewis, 'Purcell and Blow's "Venus and Adonis" ', *Music and Letters*, xliv (1963), p. 266.

boar, Faith-ful A-do-nis, faith-ful A-do-nis now   must be no more.

The work ends with a chorus of mourners, in which the music rises above the mundane level of the text.

PURCELL

Like *Venus and Adonis*, Henry Purcell's *Dido and Aeneas* (1689) retains an association with the masque, particularly in its fantastic dances for furies, witches, and sailors: it is not without significance that it was written for a girls' school in Chelsea directed by a dancing master, Josias Priest. But its subject-matter is far more dramatic than the story of Blow's opera: there is room for charm and fantasy, but not for mere frivolity. Nahum Tate's libretto[1] opens with a prologue for Phoebus, Venus, Tritons, Nereids, Spring, nymphs, shepherds, and shepherdesses, which would have been appropriate to a pastoral but makes an entirely incongruous introduction to a tragic story. There is no evidence that Purcell ever set it to music. The opera as we have it opens immediately with the presentation of Dido's anguish in love. The tragic note is maintained throughout the work. The witches who plot the fatal end are not comic but sinister; and the joviality of the sailors in Act III only serves to emphasize the suffering involved in their cheerful preparations for departure from Carthage. One further passage from the libretto is missing in Purcell's setting as it has come down to us. After Aeneas's impassioned and reluctant submission to the gods' decree at the end of Act II there is a chorus of witches demanding a dance from the nymphs of Carthage. The argument that music is needed for this passage in order to complete the composer's key scheme is less powerful than the conviction that any setting of this text would be utterly inappropriate at this point in the drama.

[1] The only known copy is in the library of the Royal College of Music. A facsimile edition has been published by Boosey & Hawkes (London, n.d.). The music, like that of other works by Purcell referred to in this chapter, has been published in the *Purcell Society Edition*, and there are several other editions of *Dido and Aeneas*.

Purcell's genius was undoubtedly hampered by the small scale of the work. It is a positive advantage that the recitative proceeds briskly—or would do if singers were to imitate the rhythms of speech. But the quick succession of short movements in different styles is apt to create a breathless effect. The tragedy of Dido's love for Aeneas is too deep and too universal to be passed by in such a narrow room. Only in the dark solemnity of the sorceress's cave:

Ex. 142

and in the two majestic arias on a ground bass for the heroine is the intensity of the subject fully translated into music; and the second of these arias, 'When I am laid in earth', owes something of its power to the two choruses that frame it—'Great minds against themselves conspire' and the final lament 'With drooping wings'. Here at the end of his work Purcell achieved a dramatic unity of the kind that one finds later in the operas of Rameau and Gluck.

Paradoxically he had more scope for extending himself in the semi-operas, since here, though music was largely incidental, the demand for spectacular presentation created an opportunity for scenes which called for a generous amount of music. Examples are to be found in the masque in *Dioclesian* (1690) and in much of *King Arthur* (1691) and *The Fairy Queen* (1692), the latter a much elaborated version of Shakespeare's *A Midsummer Night's Dream*. Even in plays which depended less on music, room was often found for extended treatment, particularly in scenes of sacrifice, dedication, or incantation. The Druids' litany in *Bonduca* (1695) would not be out of place in an Anglican service, provided the words were changed:

Ex. 143

The incantation scene in *Oedipus* (1692), including the hypnotic aria 'Music for a while', might be cited as a further example of atmosphere created on the stage by an imaginative use of music. And the shuddering emergence of the Cold Genius in *King Arthur*, with a cadential passage as remarkable as anything in contemporary opera:

Ex. 144

is more than a skilful tone painting: the Cold Genius is not merely a creature of fantasy on a painted stage—he could, in his tortured plea for release, be a human being.

Elsewhere Purcell was largely concerned with songs, dances, and entr'acte music, all of which he produced with unfailing versatility and a fund of invention. But none of this can be described as a serious contribution to dramatic music, and it certainly did nothing to hasten the production of English opera, a task for which Purcell's gifts made him ideally suited. One can guess what a full-length work by him might have been like by considering his setting of the masque in *The Tempest* (1695), a further Restoration revival of Shakespeare's play. The Italianate *da capo* arias in this work reveal a new development both of style and of scale. One must suppose that audiences were by now sufficiently familiar with the idioms of Italian opera to be able to tolerate pieces whose interest was more purely musical than dramatic. The change of style evinced here has puzzled some modern commentators,[1] who have argued that Purcell cannot have been the composer of this music. The argument would be more convincing if it were supported by any solid circumstantial evidence, or if any of Purcell's contemporaries could be shown to have been capable of work of this quality.

INCREASE OF OPERATIC ACTIVITY IN ENGLAND

By the beginning of the eighteenth century there was a growing interest in opera, stimulated no doubt by the experience of visitors to the Continent. *Arsinoe, Queen of Cyprus*, performed at Drury Lane Theatre in January 1705, was described as 'An opera, after the Italian manner: All sung'—a warning to intending spectators that they must not expect the traditional English form. The music was attributed to Thomas Clayton, who had been a member of William III's orchestra, but there seems to have been a strong suspicion that some at least of the arias were adapted from Italian sources. Hawkins remarks acidly that on his return from Italy

Clayton had brought with him a collection of Italian airs, which he set a high value on; these he mangled and sophisticated, and adapting them to the words of an English drama, [written for the purpose by Motteux, and] entitled Arsinoe, Queen of Cyprus, called it an opera, composed by himself.[2]

The first complete edition of *Songs in the Opera Call'd Arsinoe Queen of Cyprus* (1706) does not bear Clayton's name on the title-page, though the majority of the individual songs are attributed to him.[3]

Two years later Clayton came before the public again with a setting of Addison's *Rosamond*. It was not a success: Addison, who made satirical comments on Italian opera in the pages of *The Spectator*, is discreetly silent about his own libretto. In the meantime a new theatre in the Haymarket had been opened in 1705 with Jakob Greber's *Gli amori d'Ergasto*, and Italian opera was launched on the town. Its progress at first was slow, and for a few years a compromise was tried to obviate the difficulty of listening to a foreign language: some of the

---

[1] See, for example, Margaret Laurie, 'Did Purcell set *The Tempest*?', *Proceedings of the Royal Musical Association*, xc (1963–4), p. 43.

[2] *A General History of the Science and Practice of Music* (London, 1776), v, p. 136. The words in square brackets were added by the author in his own copy after publication. The expression 'mangled and sophisticated' is borrowed from the anonymous *A Critical Discourse upon Operas in England*, a supplement to the English version (1709) of Raguenet's *Parallèle des Italiens et des François*.

[3] See William C. Smith, *A Bibliography of the Musical Works published by John Walsh during the years 1695–1720* (London, 1948), p. 69.

PLATE III

THOMAS CLAYTON'S *ARSINOE, QUEEN OF CYPRUS*

Sir James Thornhill's design for the first scene, for the first production at Drury Lane, London, on 16 January 1705.

singers sang in Italian, others in English. Addison made merry at the expense of these productions:

The King or Hero of the Play generally spoke in *Italian*, and his Slaves answered him in *English*: The Lover frequently made his Court, and gained the Heart of his Princess, in a Language which she did not understand. One would have thought it very difficult to have carried on Dialogues after this manner, without an Interpreter between the Persons that convers'd together; but this was the State of the *English* Stage for about three Years.

At length the Audience grew tired of understanding Half the Opera, and therefore to ease themselves intirely of the Fatigue of Thinking, have so ordered it at present, that the whole Opera is performed in an unknown Tongue.[1]

It is probable that the reason for abandoning English was not so much the absurdity of bilingual performances, which are not entirely unknown in the twentieth century, as the obvious superiority of the Italian singers in dealing with a familiar idiom. It is doubtful whether Italian opera would have maintained its hold on London if it had not been for Handel's successful production of *Rinaldo* in 1711; and even he was forced to realize thirty years later that this 'exotick and irrational entertainment'[2] had ceased to be a sound commercial proposition.

The possibility of establishing a purely English opera was thus frustrated by the feebleness of Clayton's experiments and by the vogue, if only temporary, for the Italian form. Ironically enough, the one English work of the early eighteenth century which might have contributed towards the creation of a national opera was never performed. In December 1707 an announcement was published that

The Opera of Semele for which we are indebted to Mr. C——e, is set by Mr. Eccles, and ready to be practic'd, and from the excellence of those two Masters, in their several kinds, the Town may well expect to be Charm'd as much as Poetry and Music can charm them.[3]

William Congreve had been joint manager of the Haymarket Theatre when it first opened in 1705, and it is not impossible that he originally wrote *Semele* with a view to its performance there. But increasing blindness forced him to sever his connection with the theatre, and the failure of Clayton's *Rosamond* in March 1707 may well have made any management suspicious of the chances of a purely English opera. If this was so, their judgement was at fault.

John Eccles (1668–1735), the composer of *Semele*, had had a wide experience of music for the stage and had written several masques,

---

[1] *The Spectator*, No. 18, 21 March 1711.
[2] Samuel Johnson. *Lives of the English Poets*, ed. G. B. Hill (1905), ii, p. 160.
[3] See Stoddard Lincoln, 'The First Setting of Congreve's "Semele"', *Music and Letters*, xliv (1963), p. 105.

including a setting of Congreve's *The Judgment of Paris* which won
second prize in a competition instituted by members of the nobility in
1700.[1] His music for *Semele*—a full-length opera[2]—is occasionally
naïve; but for the most part it shows a strong feeling for dramatic effect,
particularly in the use of the orchestra, and an unusual capacity for
translating the idioms of Italian aria and recitative into English terms,
e.g., in Semele's recitative in Act I:

Ex. 145

Play softly swelling and sinking by degrees

[Violin solo]

SEMELE

Oh——— Jove, in pi-ty, in pi-ty teach me which to

B.C.

chuse, in-cline me to com-ply, in-cline me to com-

-ply or help me to—— re-fuse, in-cline me to———com-

---

[1] The first prize went to John Weldon, the third to Daniel Purcell, and the fourth to Gottfried Finger. For an account of the competition, including Congreve's description of the trial performances, see Wilson, op. cit., pp. 312 and 354.

[2] Royal College of Music, MS. 183.

- ply, in - cline me to _____ com - ply or help me,

help me, help me to _____ re - fuse.

or in the equally moving arioso in Act II, which Handel later set as an aria:

Ex. 146

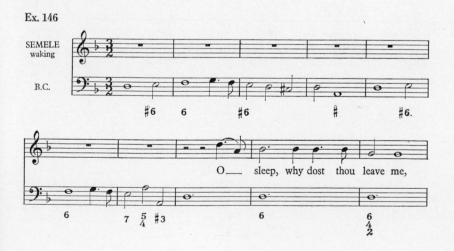

O _____ sleep, why dost thou leave me,

why thy vi-sion-a-ry joys re-move? O sleep, a-gain de-

-ceive me, to my arms re-store my wan-d'ring love.

The rhythm of the *siciliano* is also happily exploited in Cupid's air in the same act:

Ex. 147

See, see, see, see, af-ter the toyls of an a-mo-rous

fight, see, see, see, see, af-ter the toyls of an a-mo-rous

fight, where wea-ry, where wea-ry, where wea-ry, wea-ry and

pleas'd____ still pan - ting, pan - ting, pan - ting, pan - ting she

lyes,____ still pan - ting, pan-ting she lyes.____

Side by side with Italianate forms, including elaborate *da capo* arias, there are also short airs which owe more to a native tradition. The setting of 'Endless pleasure, endless love' employs a rhythm which seems to be French in origin but became so domesticated in England that Purcell's 'Fear no danger' (*Dido and Aeneas*) and 'Fairest isle' (*King Arthur*) sound wholly English in conception. Handel was not impervious to the influence of this engaging rhythm—witness the chorus 'Queen of summer, queen of love' in the oratorio *Theodora*. It appears also in the song 'Cease your funning'[1] in *The Beggar's Opera* (1728), which is quoted here for comparison with Eccles's air:

Ex. 148 (i)

1st AUGUR [alto]

B.C.

---

[1] The tune appears to be an adaptation of a morris dance known as 'Constant Billy'. There is no evidence that Gay was responsible for the corruption of a 'peasant song', as assumed by Cecil Sharp in *English Folk Song: Some Conclusions* (4th ed., London, 1965). The natural explanation is that he was using a version of a tune current at the time. The allegedly Welsh 'The Ash Grove' seems to be a later adaptation of the same melody.

The success of Handel's *Rinaldo* did not entirely extinguish opera in English. A leading partisan was the poet John Hughes, who argued, in the preface to his libretto *Calypso and Telemachus*, that opera 'shou'd be perform'd in a Language understood by the Audience' and added: 'One wou'd think there shou'd be no need to prove this'.[1] *Calypso and Telemachus*, performed at the Haymarket Theatre in May 1712, was set to music by John Ernest Galliard (d. 1749), a German oboeist who had come to England in the service of Prince George of Denmark, Queen Anne's consort, and seems rapidly to have mastered the English

[1] See Malcolm Boyd, 'John Hughes on Opera', *Music and Letters,* lii (1971), p. 383.

PLATE IV

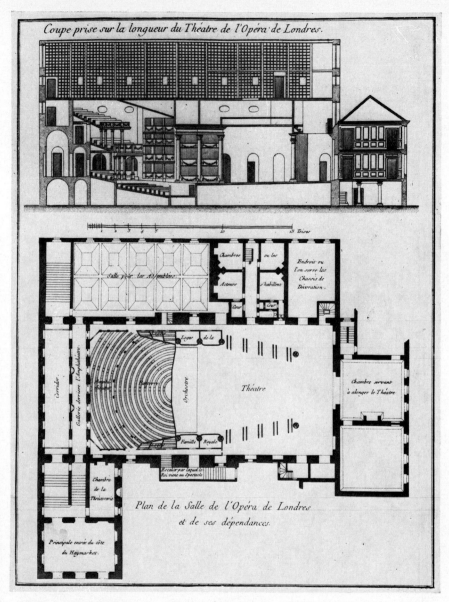

Coupe prise sur la longueur du Théâtre de l'Opéra de Londres.

Plan de la Salle de l'Opéra de Londres
et de ses dépendances.

THE QUEEN'S (LATER KING'S) THEATRE IN THE HAYMARKET: ELEVATION AND GROUND PLAN, AFTER THE ALTERATIONS OF 1707–8

It was here that Handel's operas from *Rinaldo* (1711) to *Arianna* (1734) were produced.

From G. M. Dumont, *Suite de projets détaillés de salles de spectacles particulières* (Paris, ?1775).

language. He had studied with Steffani in Hanover and no doubt was familiar with the music of Handel, in whose orchestra he subsequently played. The *da capo* arias in *Calypso and Telemachus* leave no doubt that he had fully mastered the current Italian style but offer nothing to persuade one to dissent from Burney's judgement:

> With respect to his compositions in general, I must say, that I never saw more correctness or less originality in any author that I have examined, of the present century, Dr. Pepusch always excepted.[1]

Calypso and Telemachus was revived at Lincoln's Inn Fields in 1717, but by that time the attempt to produce full-length operas in English had been abandoned. Galliard's *Pan and Syrinx*,[2] performed at the same theatre in the same year, was in one act. Librettists and composers, including Galliard, Pepusch, and Eccles, turned their attention to masques, which, though in effect one-act operas, could be performed as interludes in spoken plays. There was precedent for this in the incorporation of Purcell's *Dido and Aeneas* into a performance of Shakespeare's *Measure for Measure* in 1700, and in 1704 into *The Anatomist* and *The Man of Mode*.[3]

THE INTERVENTION OF HANDEL

This preoccupation with the masque, which is particularly noticeable during the years 1715–18, obviously interested Handel, whose *Acis and Galatea* was performed about June 1718 at the Duke of Chandos's residence at Cannons, near Edgware.[4] Here there was an excellent group of singers, the nucleus of those for whom Handel wrote the Chandos anthems. This explains the unusual elaboration of the choral writing in the opening pastoral 'O the pleasure of the plains' and even more in 'Wretched lovers', where the combination of sombre polyphony with the dramatic representation of Polyphemus brings to mind the equally dramatic choruses that occur so often in the oratorios. Handel was no more a native Italian than Galliard; but his instinct for development enabled him to transform an Italianate aria into something beyond either the ability or the imagination of his contemporaries in England. A characteristic touch is the sequential treatment of a phrase in Galatea's song 'Heart, the seat of soft delight', where a two-bar figure, first heard in the instrumental introduction:

[1] *A General History of Music*, iv (London, 1789), p. 640.
[2] Brit. Mus., Add. MS. 31588, fos. 13–90.
[3] See Eric Walter White, 'New Light on "Dido and Aeneas" ', *Henry Purcell, 1659–1695: Essays on his Music*, ed. Imogen Holst (London, 1959), p. 14.
[4] Patrick Rogers, 'Dating "Acis and Galatea" ', *Musical Times*, cxiv (1973), p. 792. For the music (like that of other works by Handel mentioned in this chapter) see *The Works of G. F. Handel*, ed. Friedrich Chrysander.

Ex. 149

grows, like the effortless flow of a tranquil stream, into this larger version on the final page:

Ex. 150

If it had occurred to Handel immediately to give performances of *Acis and Galatea* in London, he would not only have triumphed effectively over his English rivals but might well have won the affections of the English public much earlier in his career. But on his return from the Continent at the end of 1719 he was preoccupied with the affairs of the newly formed Royal Academy of Music, whose first season opened with the production of Porta's *Numitore* on 2 April 1720; and for the next twelve years he was fully occupied with establishing his position as an opera composer. *Acis and Galatea*, however, was not unknown in London, since Walsh published *The favourite Songs in the Opera call'd Acis and Galatea* in the autumn of 1722,[1] though without the composer's name, and in March 1731 it was staged at Lincoln's Inn Fields, with the announcement that it was 'Compos'd by Mr.

---

[1] William C. Smith, *Concerning Handel* (London, 1948), pp. 204 ff. The work is described as a 'Mask' inside the volume.

Handel'.[1] This performance, for which Handel does not appear to have been personally responsible, may have suggested to others that the time was ripe for a renewed attempt to present English operas.[2] The new venture was promoted by Thomas Arne, father of the composer, who opened a new season at the New Theatre (also known as the Little Theatre) in the Haymarket in March 1732 with a production of Johann Friedrich Lampe's *Amelia*, the libretto of which was by Henry Carey. By what may or may not have been a coincidence the first announcement of this production was published on 25 February, two days after Bernard Gates, Master of the Children of the Chapel Royal, had revived Handel's religious drama *Esther* (originally performed at Cannons in 1720) for the Philharmonic Society at the Crown and Anchor Tavern in the Strand.[3] It is clear from Viscount Percival's diary[4] that the work was acted: he also describes it as an 'oratoria or religious opera'. There seems to be no evidence for Chrysander's assertion that it was originally called *The Masque of Haman and Mordecai*.[5]

It is evident that Gates's three performances, though technically private, represented a dangerous incursion of Handel's music into the field of English opera. This is probably the reason why a public performance, not apparently authorized by Handel, was given at York Buildings on 20 April 1732. By the time Handel was ready to present it himself at the Haymarket Theatre on 2 May, with considerable additions, the Bishop of London had intervened and the work was given without action.[6] Several successful performances followed, and the foundations of English oratorio were firmly laid.[7] In the meantime a further attempt had been made to make capital out of Handel's name in the shape of a performance of *Acis and Galatea*, described as 'a Pastoral Opera', at the New Theatre on 17 May: the singers were members of the new English opera company. Handel, whether from a desire to stake his own claim to the work or because he wanted to make use of both Italian and English singers, adopted the curious expedient of producing at the Haymarket Theatre on 10 June a so-called 'serenata', consisting of a mixture of movements from the English *Acis and Galatea*

[1] Ibid., pp. 209 ff.

[2] See Phillip Lord, 'The English-Italian Opera Companies, 1732–3', *Music and Letters*, xlv (1964), p. 239.

[3] Otto Erich Deutsch, *Handel: a Documentary Biography* (London, 1955), p. 285.

[4] Ibid., p. 286.

[5] Dean, op. cit., p. 192.

[6] The authority for the bishop's intervention is Burney, *An Account of the Musical Performances . . . in Commemoration of Handel* (London, 1785), pp. 100–1. His information came from two of the singers in Gates's performances.

[7] See Vol. VI, chap. 1.

and the Italian *Aci, Galatea e Polifemo*, originally produced at Naples in 1708. The activities of Arne's company had clearly not persuaded him that there was a future for English opera. In December 1732 the impresario Aaron Hill wrote to him, urging him

to deliver us from our *Italian bondage*; and demonstrate, that *English* is soft enough for Opera, when compos'd by poets, who know how to distinguish the *sweetness* of our tongue, from the *strength* of it, where the last is less necessary.[1]

His advocacy had no effect. Twelve years later Handel wrote to the *Daily Advertiser*:

As I perceived, that joining good Sense and significant Words to Musick, was the best Method of recommending *this* to an English Audience; I have directed my Studies that way, and endeavour'd to shew, that the English Language, which is so expressive of the sublimest Sentiments is the best adapted of any to the full and solemn Kind of Musick.[2]

But by that time he had abandoned opera, and though he continued to write dramatic oratorios he showed no inclination to present them on the stage. In 1749 he wrote incidental music for Smollett's play *Alceste*; but the work was never performed. He incorporated most of the music in *The Choice of Hercules*, the subject of which—the contention of Pleasure and Virtue for the youthful hero—appears also in Bach's birthday cantata for Prince Friedrich Christian of Saxony, *Lasst uns sorgen* (BWV 213). Though the new work is in all essentials a masque it was never staged and was merely introduced as an additional item at a performance of *Alexander's Feast* in March 1751.

RIVAL ENGLISH OPERATIC VENTURES

The partnership between Arne and Lampe which began with the production of the latter's *Amelia* did not survive. Before the year 1732 was out there were two companies presenting English opera, either at Lincoln's Inn Fields or at the New Theatre. Since in 1733 a second Italian opera company was set up in rivalry to Handel's, there were for a short time four opera companies performing opera in London. All this can hardly have been to Handel's advantage and may have persuaded him to pursue the possibilities of oratorio. An anonymous writer in 1732 reports: 'I left the *Italian* Opera [possibly Handel's *Alessandro* at the Haymarket], the House was so thin, and cross'd over the way to the *English* one [at the New Theatre], which was so full I was forc'd to croud in upon the Stage'.[3] It is unlikely, however, that Handel bore

---

[1] Deutsch, op. cit., p. 299.
[2] 17 January 1745; Deutsch, op. cit., p. 602.
[3] Deutsch, op. cit., p. 300; cf. p. 298.

any grudge against his English competitors, since his devoted secretary, John Christopher Smith, was associated with them, and Smith's son, also John Christopher, was one of the composers. The operas performed during these two years included Lampe's *Britannia*, 'Set to Musick after the Italian Manner' (16 November 1732), *Teraminta* by the younger J. C. Smith, aged 20 (20 November 1732),[1] a new setting of Addison's *Rosamond*, by the younger Arne, aged 22 (7 March 1733), and J. C. Smith's *Ulysses*, which had a single performance on 16 April 1733.

Of these composers Smith is the most interesting, on account of his close association with Handel, who had given him some instruction when he was a boy. The fruits of this association are evident enough in *Ulysses*.[2] The music successfully copies the superficial characteristics of Handel's style and dutifully includes both trumpets and horns in the final chorus. What it lacks is Handel's capacity for purposeful development. Perhaps Smith was happiest when he could combine a traditional English style with an Italian accent, as in Antinous's unison aria in Act I:

Ex. 151

---

[1] The score of *Teraminta* in the Royal College of Music (MS. 1020) appears to be a later setting of Carey's libretto by John Stanley: see Mollie Sands, 'The Problem of "Teraminta"', *Music and Letters*, xxxiii (1952), p. 217, and Andrew D. McCredie, 'John Christopher Smith as a Dramatic Composer', ibid., xlv (1964), p. 22.

[2] The autograph score is in the Hamburg Staats- und Universitäts-Bibliothek, MA/279.

spite of each ri-val's re-sis-tance The char-mer for me shall de-

-clare, the char-mer for me shall de-clare,

In

spite of each ri-val's re-sis - tance The char-mer for me shall de-clare,

Elsewhere the Italian manner can prove less adaptable to an English text. In Act II, Antiope, Penelope's confidante, has an aria to the following words:

> O the transports you'll discover
> When the fates your lord and lover
> To your panting breast restore,

where the first syllable of 'panting' is set to a melisma lasting five bars of 9/8 time. It is fair to say that Smith was hampered by his librettist,

21

Samuel Humphreys, the least inspired of the authors who provided texts for Handel's oratorios. Penelope's decision to solve her problems by committing suicide prompts Antiope to reply in recitative:

> I'll still be faithful to my latest breath,
> Nor shall you want society in death.

Even more serious than verbal infelicities is the lack of any attempt at a serious dramatic construction. The rivalry between the suitors, which is an essential part of the Homeric story and is so effectively presented in Monteverdi's *Il ritorno d' Ulisse*, is entirely absent. Instead we merely have a single suitor who is unsuccessful, Antinous, and a husband who triumphs. For a young man Smith's opera is a creditable achievement, but something stronger was needed to put English opera on a sure foundation.

THE BEGGAR'S OPERA

The movement launched by Arne and Lampe in 1732 was short-lived. Occasional productions were given in later years, but there was no consistent attempt to follow the path which they abandoned in 1733. There are three possible reasons for this: first, the fact that two companies were formed; secondly, the lack of any composer of sufficient stature; thirdly, and not least important, the popularity of *The Beggar's Opera*, first produced in February 1728, and its successors. *The Beggar's Opera* had two elements designed to appeal to a wider audience: it was satirical, and it employed popular tunes, including some by Purcell and Handel. In the prologue to Gay's text the Beggar explains that the work 'was originally writ for the celebrating the marriage of *James Chanter* and *Moll Lay*, two most excellent ballad-singers': hence the term 'ballad opera' which came to be applied to all works of this kind, even when the music was no longer restricted to borrowed melodies. Parody of serious plays, with or without music, was a long-standing English tradition. Shakespeare's *Pyramus and Thisbe*, for instance, in *A Midsummer Night's Dream*, is a parody of the choirboy plays of the period. Thomas Duffett's *Epilogue in the manner of Macbeth*, added to his burlesque of Settle's *The Empress of Morocco* (1673), includes songs sung to popular tunes of the day.[1] Italian opera performed in London in the early eighteenth century did not escape. Mancini's *L'Idaspe fedele* (1710) was parodied nine years later in *Harlequin-Hydaspes; or, The Greshamite*, with songs taken not only from Mancini's work but from other operas of the period, including Handel's *Rinaldo* (1711) and *Amadigi* (1715).

[1] See Summers, op. cit., pp. 162–3.

In Gay's introduction the Beggar declares:

I have introduc'd the Similes that are in all your celebrated *Operas*: The *Swallow*, the *Moth*, the *Bee*, the *Ship*, the *Flower*, &c. Besides, I have a prison Scene, which the ladies always reckon charmingly pathetick. As to the parts, I have observ'd such a nice impartiality to our two ladies, that it is impossible for either of them to take offence. I hope I may be forgiven, that I have not made my Opera throughout unnatural, like those in vogue; for I have no Recitative: excepting this, as I have consented to have neither Prologue nor Epilogue, it must be allow'd an Opera in all its forms.

The reference to the rivalries of opera singers is obvious enough; and Gay does from time to time mimic the conventional similes of Italian arias, even to the extent of setting a tasteless text to the melody of 'What shall I do to show how much I love her' from Purcell's *Dioclesian*:

Ex. 152

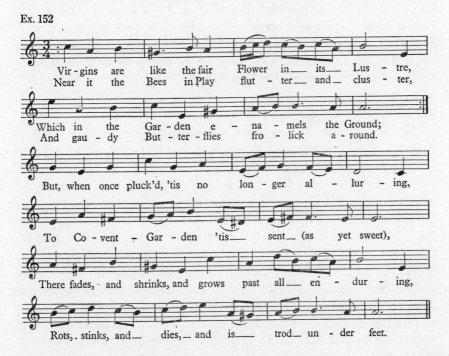

But his satire was not directed primarily against Italian opera. After Macheath has been reprieved the Beggar observes:

Had the Play remain'd, as I at first intended, it would have carried a most excellent moral. 'Twould have shown that the lower sort of people have their vices in a degree as well as the rich: And that they are punish'd for them.

The target was also the Whig government under Sir Robert Walpole. The tune to which Lucy sings 'I'm like a skiff on the Ocean tost', identified in the text as 'One evening having lost my way', was popularly known as 'Walpole, or The Happy Clown'. It can hardly be an accident that this was the tune that Pepusch selected for the second section of the overture which he wrote for the production.

As with satire in the theatre or on television at the present day, *The Beggar's Opera* was roundly condemned by those who saw in it an encouragement to vice and violence. Johnson commented: 'There is in it such a *labefactation* of all principles, as may be injurious to morality'.[1] Hawkins was even more severe.[2] In spite of this the work was enormously successful, and not only in London. It was performed in Dublin in March 1728, in Glasgow later in the same year and in Jamaica in 1733, and it reached New York in 1750. It created an immediate vogue for entertainments of the same kind. One of these—Charles Coffey's *The Devil to Pay; or, The Wives Metamorphos'd* (1731)—was translated into German and performed in Berlin in 1743. A new version—*Der Teufel ist los, oder Die verwandelten Weiber*—with music by J. C. Standfuss, of whom virtually nothing is known, was produced at Leipzig in the autumn of 1752 and led in due course to an extensive cultivation of the *Singspiel* in Germany.[3]

BALLAD OPERA AND KINDRED FORMS: ARNE

The heyday of the ballad opera was roughly from 1728 to 1736; but although after that it lost its initial character and came more and more to include music specially written for it, it created a tradition of comic opera which was successfully revived by Gilbert and Sullivan in the late nineteenth century, though on a rather more ambitious scale. No doubt it was the success of the ballad operas that persuaded the composers of the English opera companies to turn their attention to works in lighter vein. One of the most successful of these was Lampe's *The Dragon of Wantley*, first performed at Covent Garden in November 1737. Carey's libretto was a parody of Handel's *Giustino*, which had been given in the same theatre earlier in the year. Handel himself seems to have taken no offence: according to Lord Wentworth, 'th' it is a burlesque on the operas yet Mr. Handel owns he thinks the tunes very well composed'.[4] If this is true, it must be regarded merely as a tribute to Handel's generosity, since the music, though better than the libretto, is negligible. The younger Arne, perhaps because he was a native Englishman and certainly because he was a better musician, was more successful in this

---

[1] *Boswell's Life of Johnson*, ed. G. B. Hill, rev. ed. by L. F. Powell (2nd ed., Oxford, 1964), ii, p. 367.

[2] Op. cit., v, pp. 315–17.

[3] Haydn's *Der krumme Teufel*, the music of which is now lost, was performed in Vienna earlier in the same year.

[4] Deutsch, op. cit., p. 449.

field. His songs in an adaptation of Milton's *Comus* (1738)[1] and in *The Masque of Alfred* (performed at the Prince of Wales's residence at Cliveden, Buckinghamshire, 1740) show a talent for graceful lyricism and occasionally vigour. The patriotic song 'Rule, Britannia' from the latter work won a reputation far outside its native country.

OPERA IN SEVENTEENTH-CENTURY GERMANY

The story of German opera is on the whole simpler and less fragmented. In view of the very large number of independent states it might very easily be complex. But both the Emperor at Vienna and the great majority of rulers had too keen an eye for fashion to be willing to countenance performances in a language which, though their own, was not considered proper in polite society; and this attitude continued throughout a great part of the eighteenth century. Hence Bach presented the Brandenburg concertos to his patron in French.[2] Frederick the Great wrote the libretto of *Montezuma* in the same language: it was then translated into Italian for setting by Carl Heinrich Graun (1755).[3] Less exalted persons also used French for private correspondence: Handel even wrote in French to his own brother-in-law.[4] Since for the greater part of the seventeenth century there was no French opera, the way was left clear for the introduction of works by Italian composers and the composition of similar works by Germans who were familiar with the Italian style. The only known German opera before 1671 was Schütz's *Dafne*, to a libretto by Martin Opitz, performed at Torgau in 1627. The text is a translation of Rinuccini's libretto set by Peri in 1597: the music, now lost, may be presumed to have expressed Schütz's admiration for the Italian style of the period. There is no evidence, however, that there was any intention to start a movement for opera in the vernacular: the German *Dafne*, like Peri's *Euridice*, was written for a special occasion— the wedding of the daughter of the Elector of Saxony.

Historians of opera are accustomed to include a reference to the school dramas with music published in the first half of the century. A composer active in this field was Sigmund Theophil Staden, whose *Seelewig* (1644),[5] to a libretto by Philipp Harsdörffer, is unusual in being set to music throughout, though none of it is of any great consequence. But didactic works of this kind have little in common with opera as the term is generally understood: they were intended merely

---

[1] Complete edition with music in *Musica Britannica*, iii (London, 1951).
[2] *Bach-Dokumente*, i (Kassel, 1963), pp. 216–17.
[3] *Denkmäler deutscher Tonkunst*, xv (Leipzig, 1904).
[4] Deutsch, op. cit., pp. 84, 86, etc.
[5] Reprinted by Robert Eitner, 'Das älteste bekannte deutsche Singspiel, *Seelewig*, von S. G. Staden, 1644', *Monatshefte für Musikgeschichte*, xiii (1881), pp. 53–147.

for amateurs, perhaps in some cases for purely domestic recreation. The first German opera to deserve the name was a second *Dafne*, performed at Dresden on 3 September 1671.[1] There is a connection here with Schütz's work with the same title: the text was an adaptation and enlargement of Opitz's libretto of 1627. It may also be significant that the performance took place in Saxony. The music was the joint work of Giovanni Andrea Bontempi and Marco Gioseppe Peranda, both of whom were for a short time associated with Schütz, in his old age, as directors of the Saxon *Kapelle*. Bontempi, who in addition to being a composer was a historian and an expert on stage machinery, had been a singer at St. Mark's, Venice, from *c.* 1643 to 1650. Whether or not he knew Monteverdi personally, he must have been familiar with his music and with the new style of the Venetian opera. It is hardly surprising that the music of *Dafne* should be in the main a successful adaptation of that style to a German text, particularly in the frequent use of the fashionable *coranto* rhythm in triple time. The same idiom, when applied to the rustic characters in the story, results in a type of popular song which may easily deceive the ear into supposing it to be characteristically German because of the language in which it is sung. *Dafne* was followed in 1673 by *Jupiter und Jo* by the same composers: this work is known only by the libretto. The collaboration was ended by the death of Peranda in 1675. Bontempi survived him by thirty years, but seems to have taken no further interest in composition. He returned to Italy after the death of the Elector Johann Georg II in 1680 and devoted himself to his historical studies.

OPERA IN HAMBURG

In the event it was not any princely or electoral court that first established German opera on a permanent basis but the free city of Hamburg. The first opera house was erected in 1677 in the Gänsemarkt, not far from where the present Staats-Oper now stands. By all accounts it was not a particularly attractive building, either inside or outside, but it had the merit of possessing a large stage, adequate for the scenic elaboration and the machinery that were indispensable for baroque opera.[2] The theatre opened on 2 January[3] 1678 with an opera on the subject of Adam and Eve, entitled *Der erschaffene, gefallene und auffgerichtete Mensch*. The choice of a Biblical story was perhaps not unnatural in a Protestant city and may very well reflect the popularity

[1] See Richard Engländer, 'Zur Frage der *Dafne* (1671) von G. A. Bontempi und M. G. Peranda', *Acta Musicologica*, xiii (1941), p. 59.
[2] See Hellmuth Christian Wolff, *Die Barockoper in Hamburg (1678–1738)* (Wolfenbüttel, 1957), i, pp. 351 ff.
[3] 12 January according to the Gregorian calendar.

of the earlier school drama. A number of operas on similar subjects were produced in subsequent years,[1] but not to the exclusion of works on historical themes similar to those employed in Italian opera. The composer of *Der erschaffene, gefallene und auffgerichtete Mensch* was Johann Theile, who from 1673 to 1675 had been *Kapellmeister* to Duke Christian Albrecht of Holstein at Gottorf. To judge from the libretto (the score is lost) it is likely that the music was not dissimilar from that of the school dramas. It is also worth noting that the choice of a Biblical subject did not exclude comic relief, which in this case was supplied by the Devil.

Der erschaffene, gefallene und auffgerichtete Mensch was followed by *Orontes*, which on Mattheson's authority must also be attributed to Theile, though Michael Richey[2] mentions Nicolaus Adam Strungk as the composer.[3] The few arias that survive[4] are extremely simple in style and once again suggest a comparison with the school drama: it is evident that Theile lacked either the incentive or the ability to imitate Italian opera. His immediate successors, Strungk and Johann Wolfgang Franck, who later settled in London,[5] were more enterprising. Strungk's *Esther* (1680), another Biblical opera, includes an aria for Haman on an *ostinato* bass,[6] which, though retaining some of the stiffness of the North German school of composers, does at any rate include some of the melodic freedom of the Italian aria:

Ex. 153

[1] For a list see G. F. Schmidt, *Die frühdeutsche Oper* (Regensburg, 1934), ii, p. 67, n. 115.
[2] *Idioticon Hamburgense* (Hamburg, 1755).
[3] Wolff, op. cit., i, p. 200.
[4] Ibid., ii, pp. 3–6.
[5] See W. Barclay Squire, 'J. W. Franck in England', *Musical Antiquary*, iii (1911–12), p. 181.
[6] Wolff, op. cit., ii, p. 16.

(The point breaks easily in ardent heat.)

Similar elements appear in Franck's operas. We are faced here with a transitional form, in which composers, though aware of the seductive charm of Italian melody, were reluctant to abandon entirely the simple songs which were traditional in German drama. Franck is probably seen at his best in pathetic arias, where a natural instinct for sentiment allowed his invention to flow. Aglaure's aria 'Ich kann und mag' in Act IV of *Die drey Töchter des Cecrops*[1] (originally produced at Ansbach in 1679 but revived at Hamburg in the following year) exploits to the full the beauty of the soprano voice:

Ex. 154

[1] Modern edition by Schmidt, *Das Erbe deutscher Musik*, ii, *Landschaftsdenkmale: Bayern*, 2 (Brunswick, 1938).

län - ger, mich län - ger nun— nicht— lei · - den,

(I can now suffer no longer.)

and also allows the string orchestra to add its own contribution in the
shape of a postlude which, while obscuring the key, intensifies the
singer's anguish:

·Ex. 155

The Italian influence percolated slowly, but it came more and more
to dominate the Hamburg opera. It becomes clearly marked in the
work of Johann Sigismund Kusser, who had produced several operas
at Brunswick before his *Erindo, oder die unsträfliche Liebe*,[1] on a
pastoral theme, was performed in Hamburg in 1694. As a young man
Kusser had spent several years in Paris and recorded his admiration for
Lully's instrumental music in a set of six *ouvertures* or suites, described
as *Composition de Musique, Suivant la Méthode Françoise* (1682). Since
the instrumental movements of *Erindo* are lost it is difficult to say how
far his experience of French orchestral playing contributed to his

---

[1] Modern edition of surviving arias, duets, and choruses by Helmuth Osthoff, *Das Erbe
deutscher Musik*, ii, *Landschaftsdenkmale: Schleswig-Holstein*, 3 (Brunswick, 1938).

operas; but it is perhaps significant that one of the arias—'Mich heisst ihr gehorsam beginnen' (Act I)—is accompanied by a trio of two oboes and bassoon. Most of all, however, it is the adoption of an Italian style of vocal writing that impresses one, particularly in slow arias where the voice is able to linger and to expand the melody into a voluptuous cantilena. The triple time in Cloris's aria 'Ich klage mein Leiden' (Act II) is conventional and might be regarded as a slow version of the *coranto* rhythm; but the wandering modulations give it a pathetic insistence which has no parallel in the similar arias of his immediate predecessors:

Ex. 156

(I bewail my sufferings to the fleeting winds and in my love have nothing but vexation.)

For little more than a year—till the end of 1695—Kusser was director of the Hamburg opera. During that time he seems to have done much to raise the standard of orchestral playing; but he seems also to have had difficulties with his colleagues—a certain restlessness is evident in his career. From 1700 to 1704 he directed the opera at Stuttgart; but here again difficulties arose, and he migrated to London and from there to Dublin, where he held a state appointment as composer but had no opportunity, or no inclination, to produce any more operas. He died in 1727. When he left Brunswick in 1694 he was succeeded by Reinhard Keiser, a gifted young man of twenty, who was only four years old when the Hamburg opera opened in 1678. Keiser had been a pupil at the Thomasschule in Leipzig, which probably accounts for his readiness to write Passion music and oratorios from 1704 onwards. But the opportunities created by Kusser at Brunswick and his own position as the new director encouraged him at this stage to try his hand at opera. The experience gained there turned his eyes further afield. He first came before the Hamburg public with his opera *Mahumet II* (1696). From that time he decided to make Hamburg his home and from 1703 was comfortably installed as director of the opera. Though his period of office elapsed in 1707 he continued to write operas for Hamburg for the next twenty-one years.

KEISER

Scheibe[1] declared that Keiser was the greatest original genius that Germany had ever produced: Hasse expressed himself in similar terms to Burney, though he had reservations about his setting of Italian words.[2] These opinions now seem extravagant; but many composers whom we now regard as second-rate were esteemed as highly by their contemporaries. The validity of such judgements can be determined only by considering the point of view adopted. It seems clear that Keiser's popularity was due mainly to two things: his capacity for writing simple tunes in a traditional style and his ability to transfer the idioms of Italian opera to German texts. There was also a third element—the inclusion of ballet music in the French style, which he may have learned from Kusser, though by the time he was an adult there was a widespread familiarity with this kind of music in German-speaking countries. The fact that Keiser sometimes demanded considerable feats of virtuosity should not necessarily be regarded as a conscious effort to emulate the Italians. The singer of the title-role in *Fredegunda* (1715) had to negotiate passages like the following:[3]

---

[1] *Über die musikalische Composition* (Hamburg, 1773).
[2] Burney, *The Present State of Music in Germany, etc.* (London, 1773), i, p. 346.
[3] Wolff, op. cit., ii, p. 113.

Ex. 157

Las - se den Erd-kreÿss mit kra-chen er - be - ben,   mit kra - -

chen

(Let the globe quake with thunderous sound.)

but Bach made equally severe demands on his adolescent soloists at Leipzig. Elaboration of this kind seems almost to create difficulties for their own sake, whereas in the florid Italian aria the *fioriture* grow naturally out of the melody.

Keiser was enormously prolific—he is reputed to have written at least a hundred operas—but that need not be set to his discredit: many of his Italian contemporaries were equally ready to satisfy the demand for something new. What is serious in his work is the lack of any consistent level of achievement. That he had genius is hardly to be disputed; but he was prodigal of his gifts and careless in using them. There is a typical example in *Der hochmüthige, gestürtzte und wieder erhabene Croesus*, first performed in 1710 and substantially revised in 1730.[1] The aria sung by Croesus when he appears in chains before Cyrus in Act II begins superbly, with a tragic intensity which could hardly fail to make an impression in the theatre; but before long the initial impulse has been lost and the music slackens:

Ex. 158

[1] Modern edition by Max Schneider, *Denkmäler deutscher Tonkunst*, xxxvii–xxxviii (Leipzig, 1912); revised edition by Hans Joachim Moser (1958).

(None but heaven can rescue forsaken Croesus from these fetters.)

At his best, however, he was capable not only of creating but also of sustaining a tragic mood, not least in accompanied recitative. There is a magnificent example in *Die Römische Unruhe, oder Die edelmüthige Octavia* (1705),[1] where Nero discovers that he has been abandoned by his friends. The scene is closely modelled on Suetonius's account of Nero's death and is treated with such imagination that one is hardly prepared to discover that the librettist has provided a happy ending to the tragedy. The opening might very well find a place in Bach's St. Matthew Passion without any suggestion of incongruity:

Ex. 159

(Ah! Nero is Nero no longer!)

Keiser's invention remains at this level throughout the scene, which includes a short aria with unison strings, until he ends with the last despairing appearance of a tragic refrain:

[1] Ed. Max Seiffert, *Händel-Gesamtausgabe* (ed. Chrysander), supplement, vi (Leipzig, 1902). The scene referred to is recorded in *The History of Music in Sound*, v.

Ex. 160

(My eye glazes, my lips grow pale, my heart pounds, my veins throb!)

Music of this quality almost persuades one to overlook the inequality that one finds elsewhere, and certainly compensates for the trivialities of the comic opera *Der lächerliche Printz Jodelet* (1726).[1]

One of Keiser's innovations when he took charge of the Hamburg opera was the inclusion of arias with Italian texts, which appear for the first time in his *Die verdammte Staat-Sucht, oder Der verführte Claudius* (1703). Audiences cannot have been unfamiliar with arias in Italian, since Italian operas had already been performed occasionally in Hamburg, as well as original German works and works with texts translated from the Italian. The purpose of the innovation, which recalls a similar expedient in England about the same time (see p. 287), may have been to provide the fullest opportunity for fine singing and also, by using recitative in the vernacular, to enable everyone to follow the story. The result would probably be less incongruous in performance, where the words of an aria are not always clearly heard, than it appears on paper. The use of Italian in arias did not in any case exclude the use of German in similar pieces; and it may very well be that the experience of setting a language so admirably suited for singing fertilized the invention of composers when they turned to their own language. Orsanes's aria 'Lieben, Leiden' in Act I of Keiser's *Croesus* makes effective use of the feminine endings which are almost as common in German as they are in Italian:

[1] Ed. Friedrich Zelle, *Publikation älterer praktischer und theoretischer Musikwerke*, xviii (Berlin, 1892).

Ex. 161

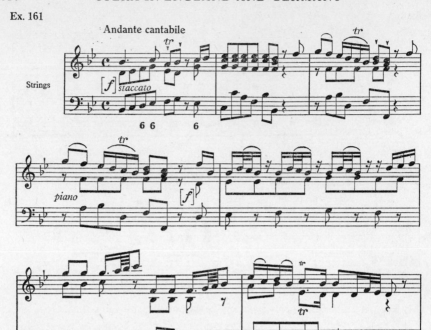

The result is a piece which if translated into Italian could easily be imagined to be the work of an Italian composer.

MATTHESON AND HANDEL

The Hamburg opera came to an end in 1738, by which time Keiser had given up writing works for the stage. He had no lasting influence on German opera, in spite of the fact that his reputation survived him; but he did make a strong impact on two young men who were members of his company when he was director: Johann Mattheson, who was a singer, and Handel, who played the violin in the orchestra. Mattheson's first opera, *Die Pleiades, oder Das Sieben-Gestirne*, was performed at Hamburg in 1699, when he was only eighteen years old: his last, *Die geheimen Begebenheiten Henrico IV, Königs von Castilien und Leon, oder Die getheilte Liebe*, appeared in 1711. That Mattheson had a profound admiration for Keiser is evident from his reference to him as 'le premier homme du monde'.[1] It is probably fair to say that his technique was superior to Keiser's—he even included a four-part canon in his opera *Boris Goudenow, oder Der durch Verschlagenheit erlangte Trohn* (1710)—but he lacked the flashes of inspiration which illuminate

---

[1] *Grundlage einer Ehren-Pforte* (Hamburg, 1740), p. 129.

Keiser's work, and the fact that he abandoned opera after 1711, when he was thirty, suggests that his interest in the stage, in spite of his experience as a singer and a producer, was not deeply engaged. His reputation rests on his critical and theoretical works rather than on his compositions.

Of the three operas[1] which Handel wrote at Hamburg only the first survives: *Der in Krohnen erlangte Glückswechsel, oder Almira, Königin von Castilien*, first performed in January 1705. Like Keiser's *Claudius* this includes a number of Italian arias, one of which, 'Geloso tormento', strikes a more passionate note than is evident elsewhere in the work and also shows considerable freedom in harmonic treatment. The work was so successful that Keiser proceeded to make his own setting of the libretto, which inevitably shows an ease and freedom which contrasts with Handel's rather stiff declamation of the text.[2] That Handel was not unaffected by Keiser's music is evident from the fact that he borrowed freely from *Octavia* in several works written during his residence in Italy (1706–10). For instance, Lucifer's aria 'O voi dell'Erebo' in the oratorio *La Resurrezione* (1708):[3]

Ex. 162

[1] Four, if one counts *Florindo und Daphne*, which was performed in two parts, as two operas.

[2] A number of excerpts from the two works are printed for comparison in Wolff, op. cit., ii, pp. 72–83.

[3] Later transferred, with modifications, to *Agrippina*.

22

(You horrid powers of Erebus, come, arm yourselves with anger and strength!)

is clearly based on the introduction to 'Costante ognor' in *Octavia*:[1]

Ex. 163

TELEMANN AND HIS CONTEMPORARIES

Among the other opera composers active in Hamburg were Christoph
Graupner, who left for Darmstadt in 1709, and Georg Philipp Telemann.
Graupner's works show no outstanding originality. Telemann's, on the
other hand, are marked by the technical assurance which distinguishes
all his music and enabled him, with no apparent effort, to cover an
enormously wide field. Side by side with simple songs of the traditional
German type and arias which imitate the Italian style even more
effectively than Keiser's, there are pieces which employ contrapuntal
elaboration in a way which often suggests a comparison with Bach's
church cantatas. The practice of earlier Hamburg composers hardly
prepares us for the relative severity of the following, from Act II of
Emma und Eginhard (1728)[2]—the extract begins at the first entry of
the voice:

---

[1] For other examples see Sedley Taylor, *The Indebtedness of Handel to Works by other
Composers* (Cambridge, 1906), pp. 168–71, and Dean, 'Handel and Keiser: further borrowings', *Current Musicology*, ix (1969), p. 73.

[2] Wolff, op. cit., ii, p. 181.

Ex.164

(My tears become waves, my sighs a hurricane.)

It is true that the counterpoint is soon relaxed in a way that Bach would hardly have admitted, but the song as a whole is far more than a vehicle for virtuoso singing. One finds a similar subtlety in the opening of the duet quoted below as Ex. 169. Less significant is the comic *intermezzo Pimpinone, oder Die ungleiche Heirat* (1725),[1] on the theme which was later treated by Pergolesi in *La serva padrona.* Here all is froth and gaiety, but there is no great substance. A better example of Telemann's flair for comedy is *Der geduldige Socrates* (1721),[2] described as a *musicalisches Lustspiel,* in which Socrates has to cope with the problem of having two wives. It includes some charming Italian arias and one in German for

[1] Ed. T. W. Werner, *Das Erbe deutscher Musik,* i, *Reichsdenkmale,* 6 (Leipzig, 1936).
[2] Modern edition by Bernd Baselt (Kassel, 1967).

Melito, 'Auf! erscheinet', which would not be out of place in a Bach cantata.

After Keiser had left Brunswick in 1696 the opera there was entrusted in the following year to the twenty-seven-year-old Georg Caspar Schürmann, who had been a singer at Hamburg under Kusser. His direction falls into two periods, separated by visits to other centres: the first from 1697 to 1701, the second, and the more important, from 1707 till his death in 1751. His first opera, *Endimione* (1700), was an Italian pastoral; but after that he devoted practically all his attention to German opera, though he performed Italian works by other composers and was responsible for a certain number of pasticcios. Schürmann was an experienced and sincere artist. His recitatives are far from perfunctory, and his arias, whether passionate or vivacious, show a range of imagination and invention which mark him out as one of the most important opera composers of his time. Three excerpts from *Ludovicus Pius, oder Ludewig der Fromme* (1726)[1] will serve to illustrate his mature work. The first is a slow aria, the bass marked '*senza cembalo*', which is equally not unworthy of Bach:

Ex. 165

---

[1] Ed. (incomplete) by Hans Sommer, *Publikation älterer praktischer und theoretischer Musikwerke*, xvii (Berlin, 1890).

(Kind cupids, weep; my need is all too great.)

The second, a bravura aria for bass, illustrates the active participation of the violins:

Ex. 166

The third is a graceful and sensuous treatment of the *siciliano* rhythm accompanied only by violins and violas:

Ex. 167

(Faithfulness clothes me in purest silk; constancy adorns my longing breast.)

Schürmann impresses not only by his writing for voices but also by his vivid and purposeful treatment of the orchestra. Claudius's aria 'Soll ich hoffen', in Act I of *Ludovicus Pius*, again *senza cembalo*, has an expressive obbligato for oboe d'amore. Cassandra's aria 'Kühle Göttin' in *Das verstöhrte Troja* (1706) is introduced by two *chalumeaux* and pizzicato strings:[1]

Ex. 168

Telemann, in Act III of *Emma und Eginhard*, uses pizzicato strings as a delicate background to an imitative duet:[2]

[1] Schmidt, op. cit., ii, p. 381.
[2] Wolff, op. cit., ii, p. 195.

Ex. 169

(Good night! dear friend, parting pains me: your sympathy . . .)

Indeed throughout this period there is constant evidence that the German opera composers were far more resourceful in their handling of the orchestra than their Italian contemporaries. This is particularly true of their use of wind instruments. Kusser, for example, in *Erindo*, has an aria with obbligato parts for two bassoons. Keiser's *Octavia* even has an aria accompanied only by five bassoons and continuo. Writing of this kind demanded not only technique but also artistry from the players. Few composers, however, wrote anything so elaborate for the horn as the obbligato in Emma's aria 'Jemehr dass ich mich widersetze' in Telemann's *Emma und Eginhard*:[1]

---

[1] Ibid., p. 173.

Ex. 170

If the institution of German opera meant that singers had to learn a new technique, as Mattheson pointed out,[1] composers could at any rate draw on a long-standing tradition of expert wind-playing.

[1] *Der Musicalische Patriot* (Hamburg, 1728), p. 181: 'Die neue Sing-Art wurde zu dieser Zeit eingeführet, und musten die ältesten Sänger Schüler werden'.

VI

CHURCH MUSIC AND ORATORIO IN ITALY AND CENTRAL AND EASTERN EUROPE

(a) ITALIAN ORATORIO AND PASSION

By HELLMUTH CHRISTIAN WOLFF

INFLUENCE OF THE COUNTER-REFORMATION

THE art of oratorio in Italy must be considered in conjunction with the Counter-Reformation, which aimed at disseminating Roman Catholic doctrine in vivid and arresting ways. The Spanish *autos sacramentales*, religious plays performed each year on Corpus Christi Day, provided a direct stimulus, as did the seventeenth-century Jesuit dramas. The resources of symbolism, allegory, and mysticism were drawn together to portray effectively Christian thought and ideas, personalities and saints. In Calderón's *autos sacramentales* the symbol of the cross itself formed part of the stage scenery, where it dominated the play's final scene; and Metastasio's oratorio *Santa Elena* is centred on the search for the sepulchre of Christ and the three crosses. The ecstasy and hyper-emotionalism of the baroque era joined forces with the new musical ideal of depicting the emotions: oratorio therefore merged imperceptibly into opera, although originally it had been much more akin to Renaissance drama. By the second half of the seventeenth century there was often scarcely any difference between opera and oratorio so far as the outline of the librettos and the musical forms were concerned.

LATIN ORATORIO IN THE SEVENTEENTH CENTURY: CARISSIMI

In the first half of the seventeenth century, two separate categories of oratorio developed in Italy, one in Latin and the other in Italian.[1] The Latin oratorios grew out of the older liturgical dialogues representing biblical scenes such as the three women at Christ's tomb, or the shepherds and angels celebrating the Nativity. Latin was, and always

---

[1] Two general histories may be mentioned at this stage: Arnold Schering, *Geschichte des Oratoriums* (Leipzig, 1911), and Domenico Alaleona, *Storia dell'oratorio musicale in Italia* (2nd ed., Milan, 1945); see the relevant sections in both. The origins of oratorio are briefly discussed in Vol. IV, pp. 835–7.

remained, the language of cultured men, clerics and scholars alike, so that any appeal to a wide public was impossible. Despite this, a succession of distinguished Latin oratorios emerged in the seventeenth century, developing the new, intensely emotional style of declamation and providing a strong stimulus to composers of opera. Some of the most notable of these are the oratorios of Giacomo Carissimi (1605–74),[1] who took as his subjects famous characters from the Old Testament in works such as *Jonas*, *Jephte*, *Ezechia*, *Balthazar*, *Job*, and *Abramo e Isacco*.[2] The Latin texts are partly taken from the Vulgate, and arias and independent episodes are added to them. A narrator (*historicus*) explains the action, supported by choruses and two-part ensembles.

Performances of these oratorios or biblical scenes generally took place in the oratory (*oratorio*) of San Marcello in Rome; Carissimi was choir-master at the Jesuit Church of San Apollinare. The object of the performances, presented in concert form, was to provoke a violently emotional religious response, achieved by dramatic recitation of the text and the conjuring up of colourful, arresting pictures. One such example is Jonah's shipwreck, dramatically described by an eight-part double chorus.[3] The rapid and unexpected alternation of short arias, recitatives, and choral passages continually captured the audience's interest anew. The arias are mostly in the form of strophic songs, very similar to the arias in the early Venetian operas; the frequent use of evocative dactylic and anapaestic rhythms is another feature common to both.

The impassioned delivery of Carissimi's recitatives has often aroused particular attention, and earned him his one-time reputation as the outstanding seventeenth-century composer. Mattheson hailed him as 'the father of modern recitative', and other extravagant tributes were paid to him: nowadays, for all his fine achievements, we value him lower than Monteverdi, Schütz, or Purcell. Rhetoric, the old art of oratory, had developed a great many rigid devices and rules, which in the sixteenth century were applied to the polyphony of motets and madrigals, as in the works of Lassus. In the seventeenth century these figures were used even more frequently, especially by Carissimi. Since

[1] See, among other literature, Günther Massenkeil, 'Die Wiederholungsfiguren in den Oratorien Giacomo Carissimis', *Archiv für Musikwissenschaft*, xiii (1956), p. 42, and Wendelin Müller-Blattau, 'Untersuchungen zur Kompositionstechnik in den Oratorien Giacomo Carissimis', *Die Musikforschung*, xvi (1963), p. 209.

[2] Four of Carissimi's oratorios, *Jephte*, *Judicium Salomonis*, *Balthazar*, and *Jonas*, ed. Friedrich Chrysander as *Carissimi's Werke*, i: *Oratorien*, *Denkmäler der Tonkunst*, ii (Bergedorf, 1869). A modern edition is in progress, *Istituto Italiano per la Storia della Musica: Monumenti*, iii (Rome, 1951 ff.): i, ed. Carlo dall'Argine, Federico Ghisi and Lino Bianchi, subsequent vols. ed. Bianchi alone. There are several modern editions of *Jephte*, the most recent ed. Gottfried Wolters (Wolfenbüttel and Zürich, 1969).

[3] Chrysander ed., pp. 86–101.

the music was closely connected to the text and its declamation, it followed that the refinements of rhetoric could be transferred to music.[1] He used a wide range of recurring devices—intervals, harmonies, rests— to the same end. The following example from a recitative of Jephtha's in *Jephte* shows the application and distribution of such figures:[2]

(Woe is me! my daughter, alas you have deceived me, my only daughter.)

Suspiratio is a sigh, expressed by means of a rest; *saltus duriusculus* is a harsh, dissonant leap; *heterolepsis* is a leap ending in a discord; *prolongatio* represents a discord which lasts longer than the preceding concordant note; and *multiplicatio* is the division of a note into two or more parts. It is clear, then, that the figures were applied to the harmony as well as to the rules of part-writing. It would, however, be a mistake to exaggerate the conscious use of such figures: composers such as Lassus and Carissimi wrote spontaneously, and their art was certainly not dictated by ingenious text-book rules, as some modern critics would have us think. It is nevertheless true that these figures of speech were widely known and were more or less consciously taken into account. Dramatic and emotional expression in delivery of the text was of primary importance for Carissimi, exactly as it had been for Monteverdi; thus Carissimi often repeats short motives, as in the recitative 'Justus es, Domine' in *Jonas*.[3]

---

[1] See in particular Massenkeil, op. cit.
[2] Wolters ed., p. 24.
[3] Recorded in *The History of Music in Sound*, v. In Chrysander ed., pp. 110–13; part of it is included in an extract from *Jonas* in Archibald T. Davison and Willi Apel, *Historical Anthology of Music*, ii (London, 1950), pp. 45–7.

The swift succession of varying musical forms—recitatives, ariettas, duets, and choruses—follows the plan of Stefano Landi's Roman operas. The chorus have very varied functions: narrative, active, and reflective— a practice continued in oratorios written in Italian. The plangent final chorus of *Jephte* is as fine as anything composed in Italy at that time, a moving lament with dissonant appoggiaturas in the Monteverdi tradition.[1] Carissimi sometimes combines arias with little echoes from the chorus, as in the daughter's lament from *Jephte*. When she begins to sing in praise of God, her themes, with their vigorous leaps of fourths and fifths, already look forward to Handel:[2]

Ex. 172

(Sing with me unto the Lord, sing all ye people, praise the prince of war, who has given us glory and victory to Israel.)

The use of Latin in oratorios and dialogues continued until the end of the seventeenth century and into the eighteenth, in works by Bonifazio Graziani, Alessandro Stradella, Alessandro Scarlatti,[3] Antonio Vivaldi (*Juditha triumphans*, 1715—his only oratorio),[4] and Baldassare Galuppi.

ORATORIOS IN THE VERNACULAR

Italian-language oratorio (*oratorio volgare*) reached a much wider public, and this determined the history of the genre for more than a century. Originally the subjects were taken from the Old Testament or

[1] Wolters ed., p. 35.
[2] Ibid., p. 19.
[3] An edition of Scarlatti's oratorios is in progress, ed. Bianchi (Rome, 1964–).
[4] Facsimile of autograph (Siena, 1948); vocal score, ed. Vito Frazzi (Rome, 1949).

from the lives of the saints. The first performances had taken place in the Oratorio della Vallicella in Rome, in 1632, under the direction of the singer Girolamo Rosini. Only the librettos of these early works have survived: *La purificazione*, by Pietro della Valle; *Il trionfo* and *La fede*, both by Francesco Balducci;[1] and, in 1666, a version of *Abele e Caino* by Cesare Mazzei.[2] Composers such as Agostino Diruta, Teodoro Massucci, and Marco Marazzoli wrote the music for these oratorios and also for dialogues harking back to the older tradition referred to above.

After 1650 oratorio was already moving towards opera in that, in structure and diction, the texts are similar to opera librettos. The *historicus* and, for a time, the choruses disappear, leaving a work sustained by soloists alone. Exciting plots were created from the lives of famous biblical characters such as Samson, David, Bathsheba, Esther, and Judith. The conversion of a sinner was a favourite subject, for instance that of Saul (already a popular subject in sixteenth-century painting); the final scene always shows the return of the converted sinner. The miracles and conversions that abound in the histories of saints made them ideal subjects for oratorio. But now love stories, exorcisms, and invocations, and even battles, hunting scenes, and dance interludes were added, all of them deriving from opera, just as angels also appeared in opera at that time. In addition to dramatic subjects of this type, one frequently finds allegories in which the characters personify moral attributes—Chastity, Obedience, Humility, Innocence, Hope, Grace—but also worldly conceptions such as Beauty and Ambition. The influence of *autos sacramentales* and Renaissance dramas was clearly taking effect here, just as in the operatic prologues of the time.

Arcangelo Spagna became the most famous of the librettists: *Deborah* (Rome, 1656) was the first of no fewer than thirty-one oratorio texts by him. In 1663 he wrote an oratorio, *Pellegrino nella patria*, around the story of St. Alexis, which in 1632 had been used by Cardinal Rospigliosi for the libretto of Landi's opera *Il Sant' Alessio*.

ORATORIO AND OPERA

In his 'Discorso dogmatico' printed in the first volume of his *Oratorii overo Melodrammi sacri* (Rome, 1706)[3] Spagna traces the aims and the history of Latin and Italian oratorio up to that time. '*Melodramma*' was the general term used at that time for opera, so that Spagna was inviting

---

[1] Reprinted in Alaleona, op. cit., pp. 289–303.

[2] Reprinted in ibid., pp. 303–12.

[3] Reprinted in ibid., op. cit., pp. 313–21, together (pp. 321–3) with the complementary prefatory note to the second volume.

direct comparison between oratorio texts and opera librettos. Apart from the subject matter, the main difference between opera and oratorio was that oratorios were performed without scenery. Spagna took as his models Seneca's tragedies and Rospigliosi's religious dramas. He limited the number of characters, just as Zeno was doing in his opera librettos. Spagna also preserved the unities of time and place and gave expression to universal truths in the form of aphorisms (Metastasio certainly learned a great deal from him). He laid considerable stress on the swift progress of the dramatic action; this was in his view a cogent reason for avoiding long choral interludes, which in any case savoured too much of the church and of old-fashioned polyphonic music—and this was something he wanted at all costs to avoid. The arias, therefore, took pride of place, and in the hands of his composers they were extended by means of repetitions, coloratura passages, and instrumental ritornellos, all elements of the operas of the day. Even the characters were stylized as they were in opera: the virtuous saint was contrasted with the heathen tyrant, while the faithful wife and the loyal friend kept their virtue intact, following the example set by so many operatic heroes and heroines.

Italian oratorio in the vernacular was practised in three main areas: Rome; cities in northern and central Italy (notably Bologna, Modena, and Florence); and Vienna. Whereas the presentation of Latin oratorio in Italy was the privilege of the Oratorian monks,[1] Italian oratorio was performed by many other monastic orders. During Lent, when opera-houses were forbidden to open, the gap was filled by concert performances of oratorios. But oratorios were also performed on other occasions, such as dedications or receptions. In Holy Week it sometimes happened that a different oratorio was given on each successive day. Some of these performances also took place in the open air, as happened at Bologna on a hill outside the city, and in Naples in the courtyard of the monastery of Sant'Agnello Maggiore. It is still uncertain whether or not these oratorios were performed with scenery and, if so, how; but it is quite conceivable that they were. After all, operas could be written on purely religious subjects, as Landi's *Il Sant'Alessio* for one had already shown.

Again it is unfortunate that in most cases only the librettos have survived, as with Maurizio Cazzati's *Caino condannato* (1664) and *Il zelante difeso* (1665), composed for Bologna and based on the same material as Mendelssohn's *Elijah*. Giovanni Antonio Manara was the librettist of a *Conversione di Sant'Agostino* (Bologna, 1672), a subject

---

[1] See Guido Pannain, *L'Oratorio dei Filippini e la Scuola Musicale di Napoli* (Milan, 1934), and Carlo Gasbarri, *L'Oratorio Filippino, 1552–1952* (Rome, 1957).

which Metastasio and Hasse were to make world-famous in the eighteenth century.[1]

Many well-known composers of opera turned to oratorio, among them Giovanni Legrenzi, Giacomo Antonio Perti, Domenico Gabrielli, Carlo Francesco Pollaroli, Giovanni Battista Bassani, Giovanni Bononcini, Francesco Gasparini, and Alessandro Scarlatti.[2] The oratorios of Alessandro Stradella in particular could compete with even the most compelling operas: they include *Ester, liberatrice del popolo ebreo* (date and place unknown), *San Giovanni Battista* (Rome, 1675),[3] with the characters of Herod and Salome, and *Susanna* (Modena, 1681), which contains frivolous and burlesque scenes. The celebrated Venetian opera composer Carlo Pallavicino set a dramatized version of the story of Genevieve in *Trionfo della castità* (1688). These composers would frequently send their scores to one of the aforementioned centres of oratorio if they were themselves unable to travel there. In all of their oratorios the musical style broadly conforms to that of the operas of the time, although polyphonic choral passages occasionally reappear, as in the settings of *Giona* by Bassani and Vitali (both 1689).

ITALIAN ORATORIO IN VIENNA BEFORE 1700

In Vienna the encouragement of oratorio was closely connected with events at the Austrian imperial court. Obsequies, receptions, meetings of the Imperial Diet, solemn occasions of every description: all were enhanced by oratorios. Consequently the oratorios were always written with a certain element of dignity and tradition in mind, and this is reflected in the polyphonic style of the music, which is similar to that derived from the church music of the Netherlanders.

One type of oratorio that was particularly fostered in Vienna was the so-called *santo sepolcro*, staged every year on Good Friday in the imperial family chapels; the Emperor Leopold I (1640–1705) wrote some of them. This genre stemmed from the scenes at Christ's tomb and the lamentations of Mary and Mary Magdalene that had been familiar to churchgoers since the Middle Ages and were now enacted among the festive decorations of the church oratorios. Different settings were chosen each year—portraying a crypt, for instance, or the Last Supper— and the performances were operatic in character. A large curtain con-

---

[1] See Schering, op. cit., pp. 104–7, for detailed accounts of the librettos for *Sansone* by Benedetto Ferrari (*c.* 1660) and *Giona* (1689) by Giovanni Battista Vitali. See also Francesco Vatielli, *L'oratorio a Bologna* (Rome, 1938), *passim.*

[2] The operas of most of these composers are discussed in chaps. I and II.

[3] See Raffaele Casimiri, 'Oratorii del Masini, Bernabei, Melani, Di Pio, Pasquini e Stradella, in Roma, nell'Anno Santo 1675', *Note d'Archivio*, xiii (1936), p. 157, and Gino Roncaglia, 'Le composizioni vocali di Alessandro Stradella', *Rivista musicale italiana*, xlvi (1942), p. 1.

cealed the scenery at first and was then drawn aside as in a theatre. Besides characters such as Peter and John, Mary and Mary Magdalene, allegorical figures appeared: Pity, Justice, and the like. Sometimes these Passion-scenes were given concert performances without scenery.

It was mainly after 1700 that the 'Oratorii per il santo sepolcro' developed out of them, to be closely followed by the 'pure' oratorio form of Zeno and Metastasio. But even in the seventeenth century large-scale oratorios were familiar in Vienna. From about 1623 Antonio Bertali (1605–69) was active in Vienna and for nearly half a century provided the music for many great festal occasions at the Habsburg court, including the oratorios *Maria Maddalena* (1663), and *La strage degl'innocenti* (1665); he also wrote a vast amount of other music, including masses, motets, wind sonatas, church sonatas, and operas. Bertali widened the scope of the old polyphony by using modern harmonies; for example, a choral lament from *La strage degl'innocenti* has continual dissonant suspensions enhancing the emotional impact of the music:[1]

Ex. 173

[1] Taken from Egon Wellesz, 'Die Opern und Oratorien in Wien von 1660–1708', *Studien zur Musikwissenschaft*, vi (1919), p. 132.

(Weep, eyes.)

Antonio Draghi (*c.* 1635–1700), with more than forty oratorios to his credit,[1] in addition to a host of operas, dominated the musical scene in Vienna during the second half of the seventeenth century. The texts he set were for the most part the work of Nicolò Minato, who was also responsible for nearly all of Draghi's opera librettos. The music in these oratorios is similar to that of his operas, characterized by simple, skilfully wrought strophic songs and short *da capo* arias. Whereas oratorios in Italy were scored for a modern string orchestra, in Vienna the instrumentation was sometimes much more colourful (on occasion because it was more old fashioned). Draghi's *Il terremoto* (1682) contains a five-part sonata for violin, quartet of viols, and *basso continuo*. He used viols again in *Il libro con sette sigilli scritto dentro e fuori* (1694) to conjure up the storm winds of the Last Judgement. This oratorio is based on the vision of the book with seven seals, as described in the Apocalypse. The scene is the Island of Patmos, with John and the Holy Sepulchre, together with an angel who opens the book. The work includes further remarkable scoring in an 'Infernal symphony' for three trombones and bassoon, followed by an aria for Hate with accompaniment for one trombone and bassoon continuo, in which the instruments clearly combine descriptive and concertante functions[2] (see Ex. 174). Strict, time-honoured techniques also have a place in Draghi's oratorios —see, for instance, the double fugue in *Il crocifisso per gratia* (1692); as one would expect, the ensembles and choruses in particular draw heavily on such established forms and textures.

---

[1] They are listed in the article on him in *Die Musik in Geschichte und Gegenwart*, iii (1954), cols. 737–8. See Max Neuhaus, 'Antonio Draghi', *Studien zur Musikwissenschaft*, i (1913), p. 104.

[2] From Wellesz, op. cit., p. 45.

Ex. 174

(The earth cracks and a frightful gulf opens!)

Draghi was only one of many Italian composers who wrote oratorios for Vienna; among the others were Bernardo Pasquini, Alessandro Melani, Carlo Francesco Pollaroli, Giovanni Bononcini, Giovanni Battista Pederzuoli, Giovanni Legrenzi, and, after 1700, Carlo Agostino Badia, Marc'Antonio Ziani, and Attilio Ariosti. This list alone gives some indication of the large number of performances that must have taken place. The very titles of Badia's *Santa Orsola* (1694), *Il ritorno di Tobia* (1698), *Il martirio di Santa Susanna* (1704), and *Santa Teresa* (1717) suggest the extent of his commitment to baroque subjects and of his efforts to provoke intense emotion and religious ecstasy. The Emperor Leopold I too, whom we have met as a composer of *santi sepolcri*, deserves a place in any history of oratorio, for he was a composer of considerable standing, who wrote eight oratorios, as well as a great deal of other music.[1] The growth of music in Vienna owed much to his personal example, encouragement, and appreciation, and he was responsible for the expansion of the court musical establishment to a strength of some hundred performers.

ALESSANDRO SCARLATTI

As Rome had been the birthplace of oratorio in Italy, so it remained the chief centre of its growth. Works were performed in Rome, generally in the church of San Marcello, which served as models for all Italy. Some composers, among them Bernardo Pasquini and Alessandro Scarlatti, received support from private patrons, such as Prince Ruspoli. At the end of the seventeenth century the Passion of Christ also came to be used as a subject for oratorios, which were later called 'Passion oratorios' or quite simply 'Passions', though they had no connection with the sixteenth-century liturgical passions. Important early examples are Ariosti's *La Passione del Cristo* (1693; repeated in Vienna in 1709) and Scarlatti's *Passio D.N. Jesu Christi secundum Joannem* (Rome, 1708),[2] though these had been anticipated by isolated works such as the *Oratorio per la Settimana Santa* (c. 1643) of Luigi Rossi. Scarlatti's work is typical in its swift succession of passages for narrator (*testo*) and soloists such as Pilate and St. Peter, and dramatic crowd (*turba*) choruses. Metastasio's text for *La Passione di Jesu Cristo*, performed in Vienna in 1730 to the music of Antonio Caldara, contributed more than anything else to the general recognition of the Passion as a separate genre in Italian music.

[1] See ibid., pp. 25–6, and H. V. F. Somerset, 'The Habsburg emperors as musicians', *Music and Letters*, xxx (1949), p. 204; extracts from six oratorios by Leopold I in Guido Adler (ed.), *Musikalische Werke der Kaiser Ferdinand III., Leopold I., und Joseph I.*, ii (Vienna, 1893), pp. 27–92. Cf. *infra*, pp. 618–19.

[2] Ed. Edwin Hanley (New Haven, Conn., 1955). Also see idem on this work in 'Current Chronicle', *Musical Quarterly*, xxxix (1953), pp. 241–7.

The development of Italian oratorio from the later seventeenth century into the new era of the eighteenth century may be traced particularly in the works of Alessandro Scarlatti (1660–1725), who wrote fifteen oratorios.[1] An early example, *Il trionfo della grazia ovvero, La conversione di Maddalena* (Rome, 1685)—revived in Vienna in 1693 as *La Maddalena pentita*—is written for only three characters: Mary Magdalene, Penitence, and Youth. Here Scarlatti portrays Mary Magdalene's transformation from sinner to saint; the actual conversion is depicted musically by means of a slow, tremolando string symphony, *senza cembalo*: this 'trembling' was a favourite seventeenth-century device for denoting death, terror and fear, as well as more programmatic scenes such as the appearance of the Frost Genius in Purcell's *King Arthur*. Scarlatti first suggests Mary Magdalene's character by his use of gay dance rhythms:[2]

Ex. 175

(I feel new life in my soul, with your movements eternally . . .)

Besides artless little songs such as this, Scarlatti provides arias and duets in imitative style, as for instance this aria for Penitence:

[1] See Edward J. Dent, *Alessandro Scarlatti: his life and works* (new impr. ed. Frank Walker, London 1960), *passim*.
[2] This and the next two examples are from manuscripts at Dresden, Landesbibl.

Ex. 176

(You spirits, who rule the heavens with everlasting and beautiful labour . . .)

The development from a single main motive is very clear in this case: the descending C major triad is alternately inverted and extended.

In *Il Sedecia, rè di Gerusalemme* (1706) Scarlatti treats the story of Nebuchadnezzar, already familiar from Legrenzi's oratorio (Venice, 1667). Scarlatti's use of concertante trumpets and oboes, two solo violins, and two solo cellos lent greater colour and variety to his score than had been apparent in the earlier work. Parallel with developments in opera, oboe and violin have their own solo motives in this aria of Nebuchadnezzar:

Ex. 177

(Go to the petty kings of Egypt, away! . . .)

Among Scarlatti's remaining oratorios is *San Filippo Neri* (1713), which records the life of the founder of the Roman Congregation of the Oratory. In *La SS. Trinità* (1715)[1] the focal point is a discussion of the Trinity, after the style of the older allegorical oratorios.

LIBRETTOS IN THE EARLY EIGHTEENTH CENTURY

We have seen that Arcangelo Spagna brought oratorio closer to opera; after the narrator and the chorus had been dispensed with or reduced in importance, the centre of the stage was free for the three to five soloists. Whereas Spagna had chosen a wide variety of historical subjects and had been a champion of 'saintly' oratorio, Apostolo Zeno advocated that the subject matter of oratorio should be taken only from the Old Testament. In this way he carried out a reform in oratorio comparable with that which he had already achieved in the field of the opera libretto. Oratorios were usually divided into two parts, operas into three acts: the absence of staging in oratorios seemed to demand a certain brevity. Zeno's first oratorio, *Sisara*, dates from 1719 and was

[1] Ed. Giuseppe Piccioli (Bologna, 1953).

performed in Vienna with music by Giuseppe Porsile. The story (taken from the Book of Judges) concerns the victory of the Prophetess Deborah over the blasphemous Sisera; there is practically no action, although a dramatic chorus provides an effective contrast to the soloists.

Gioaz is generally accepted as the best of Zeno's oratorio texts. Both he and Metastasio, who wrote a text of the same name, modelled these works on Racine's *Athalie*, and through them one of the most frequently performed of Racine's plays was introduced into Italian-speaking countries. Metastasio's dramatization (to be mentioned in a moment) is an altogether more elegant piece of writing, and it contains more 'musical' verses, as is shown by a comparison with other librettos by Zeno, for example, *Il Battista* (1727), *Sedecia* (1732), or *Gerusalemme convertita* (1733), all of which were first performed in Vienna, with music by Caldara or Francesco Conti.

Metastasio used many ideas inspired by Zeno, but his poetry is even more melodious and elegant. His were the most frequently set to music of eighteenth-century oratorio librettos. In his essay referred to earlier in this volume in connection with Metastasio's opera texts, Raniero de' Calzabigi also discusses Metastasio's oratorio texts, defending them against the charge of being too dependent on the work of other writers. More specifically he argues that in *Gioas, rè di Giuda* Metastasio borrowed only the bare bones of the story from Racine: the dramatic characterization, the details of the action and the disposition of the scenes are entirely original. He even suggests that on occasion Metastasio's characterization surpasses that of his model, as in Athalia's temple scene.[1]

The eighteenth century hailed the oratorio text *Giuseppe riconosciuto* as Metastasio's crowning achievement. The theme is Joseph's exposure of his brothers' treachery. The suspicion, fear, and guilty conscience of the brothers are most powerfully described; the variety of linguistic resources, the terse precision of the poetry, are as characteristic of Metastasio's oratorio texts as they are of his opera librettos. In contrast to Zeno, Metastasio set greater store by the portrayal of inner experiences and emotional reactions, though he did not allow this to inhibit dramatic considerations; even so, while Zeno was always alive to the possibility of stage presentation, Metastasio was less preoccupied with theatrical impact. His dialogues thus assumed the greatest importance, as in *Sant'Elena al Calvario* (1731), where the discovery of the True Cross and its consequences are described in detail and with impressive urgency. The problems of Christianity are examined in dialogues, and

---

[1] See Calzabigi, 'Dissertazione su le poesie drammatiche del Sig. Abate Pietro Metastasio', in Metastasio, *Poesie* (Turin, 1757), i, *passim*, and *supra*, p. 338.

dramatic and idyllic scenes provide strong contrast, as in *Isacco* (1740). *La morte d'Abele* is a work of strictly lyrical character, referred to in detail below in connection with Leonardo Leo's setting of it. In general the recitatives are just as significant as the arias. Metastasio showed his exceptional gifts in the language and expression of both: small wonder that up to the end of the eighteenth century his oratorio librettos were universally admired and frequently set to music and translated.

VIENNA IN THE EARLY EIGHTEENTH CENTURY

Compared with opera, oratorio continued to play a much smaller role in Vienna's musical life, since performances were for the most part restricted to Holy Week. But the appointment of Zeno, and later of Metastasio, as court poet, meant that henceforth the decisive stimulus for Italian oratorio emanated from Vienna; their works were written, set to music and given their first performances in the Austrian capital, and they very quickly found their way to Italy. The printed editions of their texts did still more to bring them before a wider public, especially after their respective complete editions first appeared, Zeno's in 1744, Metastasio's in 1755.

The outstanding composers of oratorio in Vienna were Caldara, Porsile, Conti, and Georg Reutter the younger—all of whom set librettos by Zeno and Metastasio—and Johann Joseph Fux (1660–1741), whose chief librettist was the popular Pietro Pariati, who occasionally collaborated with Zeno. Fux wrote ten oratorios, notable for their contrapuntal choruses and instrumental passages, as well as for their colourful orchestration:[1] his use of chalumeaux and theorboes was made possible by the resources of the Vienna court orchestra.

Between 1717 and 1735 Caldara (1670–1736)[2] was the most important composer to set texts by Zeno and Metastasio. Of his twenty-five oratorios for Vienna, the following (to texts by Zeno) are of special interest: *Gioaz* (1727), *Il Battista* (1727), and *Gerusalemme convertita* (1733). Conti (1681–1731) was an important colleague of Caldara's; like Fux, he wrote ten oratorios, of which *David* (1724, with libretto by Zeno) must be acknowledged as a masterpiece of its kind. Powerful emotional climaxes, such as Saul's madness, give scope for striking accompanied recitatives, in which Conti also employs rapid variations in tempo:[3]

[1] See Wellesz, *Fux* (London, 1965), pp. 31 ff. A complete edition of Fux is in progress, ed. Hellmut Federhofer (Kassel and Graz, 1959–); the oratorios are in ser. iv.

[2] See Ursula Kirkendale, *Antonio Caldara: sein Leben und seine venezianisch-römischen Oratorien* (Graz and Cologne, 1966); as the title implies, this touches only very briefly on Caldara's Viennese oratorios.

[3] The complete recitative is in Schering, op. cit., pp. xxxvi-xxxix, from which this example is taken.

Ex. 178

(Leave me alone, furies of hell! I have enough, and maybe worse. Alas! what burning consumes my bones and marrow? If you enjoy some peace, damned souls . . .)

Marc'Antonio Ziani, Giovanni Bononcini, Luca Antonio Predieri, and Giuseppe Bonno were also active in Vienna in this period.

ITALY AFTER 1700

In Italy, too, oratorio continued as a Lenten substitute for opera. The various conservatoires in Venice organized performances of oratorios so as to afford their female pupils the opportunity of appearing in public. Many fine oratorios were written for them, by Ariosti, Lotti, and Benedetto Marcello, and later by Hasse and Galuppi. Marcello wrote both the music and the text of his *Giuditta* (1710), set Zeno's *Gioaz* in 1726 and composed two secular oratorios, *Il pianto e il riso delle quattro stagioni dell'anno* (1731) and *Il trionfo della Poesia e della Musica* (1733). Marcello here provided passages of pure descriptive music for the orchestra, as when in the former an aria of Winter's is highlighted by the raging of winter storms in the orchestral accompaniment.[1] Vivaldi's *Quattro stagioni* violin concertos were the prototype for such music. Depictions of nature, especially in troubled mood, were very popular at that time in opera and instrumental music, with clouds, winds, and waves as the favourite themes. By contrast, the seventeenth century had preferred the more tranquil aspects of nature, as reflected in the gently rocking waves of some aria ritornellos in Lully's and Legrenzi's operas; but, as has been mentioned above, Carissimi had already in *Jonas* written a chorus evoking a storm at sea. This awareness of nature in music and the fine arts anticipated the enthusiastic cult of nature in the later eighteenth century.

Several of Scarlatti's oratorios, as we have seen, were written for performance in Rome, and here, too, the young Handel's first two oratorios were given. Easter 1708 saw Scarlatti's *Oratorio della Santissima Annunziata* presented in Prince Ruspoli's palace, and this was soon followed by Handel's brilliant *La resurrezione*[2] in the Palazzo Bonelli under Corelli's direction. Later in the same year, 1708, another of Handel's oratorios was given in Rome, at the sumptuous palace of Cardinal Ottoboni, who organized many performances of operas and oratorios there: the new work was *Il trionfo del tempo e del disinganno*, with libretto by another Cardinal, Benedetto Pamfili. This was the first version of the oratorio recast for London in 1737 and finally in 1757 translated into English and more drastically rewritten as *The Triumph of Time and Truth*. The precept of the work, that time and truth are worth more than the transience of beauty and youth, had flowered from the fertile soil of Italian baroque poetry. For his first setting, Handel, in writing for concertante instruments and a concerto grosso ensemble, could look for inspiration to Scarlatti, Corelli, and

---

[1] This aria and the preceding *sinfonia* and recitative are recorded in *The History of Music in Sound*, v.

[2] The works by Handel are in his *Werke*, ed. Chrysander, xxxiv, xxiv, and xx.

also Perti, who composed a large number of oratorios for Bologna between 1679 and 1723.

New concepts of style and texture arose in Italy with the oratorios of Leonardo Vinci, Leonardo Leo, and Giovanni Battista Pergolesi. As in contemporary opera, the solo voices of the singers now became the dominant feature, displayed to advantage by the structural refinements of the *da capo* aria. The accompaniment became a mere background of sound, dominated by the strings. This new style had been developed largely by Vivaldi in Venice, whence it spread to Naples. There, oratorios were performed in a number of monasteries or their court-yards, in the royal palace and in the conservatoires. Oratorio had been part of Neapolitan musical life as far back as the middle of the seventeenth century, with works like *La battaglia spirituale* (1681) by Cristoforo Caresana. Alessandro Scarlatti wrote some of his oratorios for Naples, and in the eighteenth century Leonardo Vinci came to prominence there with his *Gionata* (1729), *Il sacrificio di Jephte*, and *Maria addolorata* (both 1731). Broad triadic themes and a dramatic vocal style characterize Vinci's arias, and also those of Pergolesi's *La morte di San Giuseppe* (*c*. 1731), which was performed in the Chapel of the Oratorians in Naples. Pergolesi's *Li prodigi della divina grazia nella conversione di San Guglielmo d'Aquitania*[1] (performed in the courtyard of the monastery of Sant'Agnello in 1731) gives a dramatic account of William of Aquitaine's conversion; it is in three parts instead of the more usual two. Tension mounts with the intervention of an angel and a demon, who struggle for possession of William's soul after the hero, blinded in combat, asks for divine grace. One of the characters in this oratorio is a comic Captain Cuesemo, and the demon also displays comic traits; such features show how close oratorio could be to opera and even to *opera buffa*. The inclusion of comic episodes was of course a feature of the old Mystery plays, where comic roles were generally allotted to devils, and there is conceivably some historical connection between the two genres. However, it must be stressed that this mixture of comic and tragic elements was not usual in Italian oratorio, and it may be significant that in subsequent performances of the *Conversione de San Guglielmo* the comic scenes were omitted.[2]

The most important Italian oratorios of this period are by Leonardo Leo (1694–1744);[3] his first nine were performed in Naples, while the

---

[1] Both works are in the complete Pergolesi edition, *Opera omnia*, ed. Filippo Caffarelli, i and iv, respectively (Rome, 1939).

[2] See Giuseppe Radiciotti, *Giovanni Battista Pergolesi* (2nd ed., Milan, 1945), rev. and enl., trans. into German and ed. Antoine-E. Cherbuliez as *Giovanni Battista Pergolesi: Leben und Werk* (Zürich and Stuttgart, 1954), pp. 283–90.

[3] See Giuseppe A. Pastore, *Leonardo Leo* (Galatina, 1957).

most famous of his later oratorios—*Sant'Elena al Calvario* (1734) and
La morte d'Abele (1738)—were first presented in Bologna; the librettos
of both are by Metastasio. They are the last great masterpieces of Italian
oratorio. *La morte d'Abele* in particular remained well known, and it is
not unknown in Italy even today.

The drama and unconventionality of Leo's vocal writing is obvious in
the theme of the aria in which Cain repents of his brother Abel's death;
Leo conveys Cain's horror at the murder in wide, disconnected staccato
leaps:[1]

Ex. 179

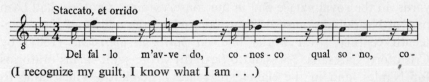

(I recognize my guilt, I know what I am . . .)

The strict polyphonic technique that Leo sometimes employed in contrast to the prevailing neutral accompaniments is shown in the following
aria for Adam, in which the strings play as a string quartet without the
harpsichord; even so, powerful octave passages (bars 5 and 6) and
passages of pure accompaniment (bars 9 and 10) alternate with the
imitations:

Ex. 180

[1] This and the next three examples are taken from the manuscript at Dresden, Landesbibl.

(Thus a heart burdened with cares overflows in tears, and the very tears explain . . .)

Leo perfected a musical language, not only for the voices, but for the instruments too, that enabled them to express rapid changes of mood. An example of this is the instrumental introduction to Eve's aria 'Non sà che sia pietà':

Ex. 181

Eve's agitation is suggested by the demisemiquavers, and the syncopated 'Lombard' rhythms of the second phrase express lamenting: thus two contrasting emotions are harmoniously set side by side.

Leo adheres throughout to the expressive declamation of Metastasio's verses, in recitatives and arias alike, and achieves an ideal fusion of textual declamation and vocal melody. Abel's arias are mainly based on dance and march rhythms, to portray the optimism of his character. After the murder an angel curses Cain, opening his eyes to the horror of war in Metastasio's telling words: 'Vivrai, ma sempre in guerra'; the very varied treatment of the word 'Vivrai' is an excellent illustration of Leo's methods. Both parts of the oratorio end with a full-scale chorus. The first is a tirade against envy, written in powerful homophony. The second finale warns against the ways of the ungodly: here the style is polyphonic, with frequent dissonances to create an impression of urgency:

(All men hate the ways of the wicked; yet they follow them . . .)

HASSE

From 1731 the fortunes of Italian oratorio in Dresden took a strong upward turn, following the appointment of an outstanding composer of opera, Johann Adolf Hasse (1699–1783). He had previously written one or two oratorios for the Conservatorio degl'Incurabili in Venice. His output continued in Dresden with some eight works suited to the solemn ceremonials of the Saxon court, which were held in the Catholic court chapel, whose very resonant acoustics possibly helped to determine their predominantly homophonic textures; these works were also performed in Protestant churches in the second half of the eighteenth century. They include historical, allegorical, and Passion oratorios.[1]

As with Leo and Vinci, it is above all Hasse's vocal writing which stands out, with the orchestral accompaniment reduced to a mere background. Lyrical narratives and sentimental meditations occupy a central place, as in *Sant'Elena al Calvario* (1746): the typical nature of an oratorio by Hasse can be grasped very readily if his setting of this libretto by Metastasio is compared with the much more dramatic and polyphonic style adopted by Caldara in his setting of fifteen years earlier. Hasse appears to have been so impressed by the intense spiritual drama unfolded in this fine libretto that he set it again in 1772, this time for Vienna.

Hasse's *I pellegrini al sepolcro di Nostro Redentore* (1742) is a notable example of the new type of lyrical oratorio. Four pilgrims journey to Jerusalem to visit the Holy Sepulchre, where a guide shows them the details of the tomb and explains them. The pilgrims thereby relive the sufferings of Christ, showing the utmost sympathy with Him. Hasse mingles soft, gentle sounds with powerful accents giving expression to the staunchness of the pilgrims' faith, as in the aria 'Scaccia l'orror', sung by the pilgrim Teotimo. Vigorous trills, leaps, and syncopations give a similar effect in this aria for Albino:[2]

Ex. 183

Allegretto

Non co - sì cer-vo af-fet - ta - to___ .a - ne - lan - do a -
- spi - ra al fon - te, co - me noi_giun-ge - re al mon-te,

(The wounded, panting stag is not more eager to reach the spring then we were eager to reach the mountain.)

[1] See Lucian Kamieński, *Die Oratorien von J. A. Hasse* (Leipzig, 1912).
[2] This and the next example come from Leipzig, Städt. Mus. Bibl., MS. III. 2/85.

The final quartet gives a good idea of Hasse's style on the rare occasions when it is fugal in character:

Ex. 184

(Man is a pilgrim through the world.)

The accompanied recitatives provide some of the dramatic highlights of Hasse's oratorios, as when in *I pellegrini* Teotimo tells the story of the Crucifixion in such a piece. There are several examples in *La conversione di Sant'Agostino* (1750),[1] which were widely admired in the eighteenth century: for instance, Johann Friedrich Agricola singles them out in his *Anleitung zur Singkunst* (Berlin, 1757).[2] This oratorio is a setting of a libretto by the gifted young Saxon Electress, Maria Antonia Walpurga, who had taken as her model the *Theatrum asceticum* of the Jesuit Franciscus Neumayr. Augustine's conversion is shown in five stages, which are clearly depicted through Hasse's music. Many of the arias show strong operatic influence, especially the laments, the descriptive arias and those involving some kind of conflict, such as Alipio's aria 'Piange',[3] which is accompanied by two flutes and strings. Hasse had the gift of using the slenderest means to achieve powerful effects, as in this aria for Simpliciano:[4]

Ex. 185

(Never abandon faith in God: just and clement, the soul that fervently implores His favour . . .)

This firm and simple beginning is followed by florid passages equally strong in contour. The meaning of *La conversione* might be summed

[1] Ed. Schering, *Denkmäler deutscher Tonkunst*, xx (Leipzig, 1905); see, for example, pp. 9–10 and 69–70.

[2] On pp. 95 and 151 ff. His work is basically a translation of Pier Francesco Tosi's *Opinioni de' cantori antichi e moderni* (1723), better known under its English title of 1742, *Observations on the Florid Song*.

[3] Schering ed., p. 77.

[4] Ibid., p. 31.

up in a phrase from the final chorus[1] that could well be seen as the objective and watchword of most Italian oratorios of the period: 'Avvalori l'esempio ogni timido cor' (Let this example strengthen all faint hearts).

(b) LITURGICAL MUSIC IN ITALY, 1610[2]–60

By JEROME ROCHE

THE CONCERTATO MOTET

The publication of Viadana's *Cento concerti ecclesiastici* in 1602 had an impact on the style of Italian church music out of all proportion to the intrinsic worth of its contents.[3] It had proved the viability of a small-scale medium and, in introducing the *basso continuo*, had broken the dominance of a conventional four- to six-part texture. Not that the latter could yet be said to be moribund (like the madrigal after 1600): the concertato principle infused new life into music for the more traditional choral texture of four to six voices, for it did not preclude the use of counterpoint, and encouraged a new awareness of contrasts of texture and sonority. Thus sacred music in any number from two to six parts with organ flooded the Venetian publishers in the early decades of the seventeenth century: now that the pomp of the Counter-Reformation was on the wane, the need for a small-scale, practical music in many provincial churches urged scores of new composers into print, many with considerable talent. Their style combined a freshness of melody with polyphonic and rhythmic interest, and mood-expression.

The most notable writers of concertato motets in the second decade of the century were Alessandro Grandi (*c.* 1575–1630) and Ignazio Donati (*c.* 1575–1638). Grandi, who worked at Ferrara and later became Monteverdi's assistant at St. Mark's, Venice, published five volumes of motets within ten years, all of them running into several editions. By his Fourth Book (1616) he showed himself a sure master of melody, as we can see from the dialogue 'Surge propera':[4]

---

[1] Ibid., p. 115.

[2] In order to treat this subject satisfactorily it is necessary to begin by discussing in more detail music already treated briefly in Vol. IV, pp. 536–43.

[3] See ibid., pp. 533–6.

[4] Other motets from the Fourth Book reprinted by Friedrich Blume, *Das Chorwerk*, xl (Wolfenbüttel, 1936); two duets reprinted in *Proceedings of the Royal Musical Association*, xciii (1966–7), pp. 44–50; and two motets, 'Exaudi Deus' and 'Veniat dilectus meus', ed. Jerome Roche (London, 1968).

Ex. 186

(The flowers appear on the earth. The voice of my beloved calling me. Behold, he standeth behind our wall, he looketh in at the windows.)

Viadana and Adriano Banchieri had pioneered the dialogue motet, which became popular with composers of Christmas motets, where different groups of voices represent angels and shepherds, or of motets based on the Song of Songs, where two voices represent the two lovers, as in Ex. 186.[1] Donati, whose career took him to many Italian cities, produced many excellent examples of the five-part concertato motet,[2] as well as melodious duets and trios. The opening of 'Ecce confundentur' (1618) presents several noteworthy ideas ripe for mutual development and contrast:

Ex. 187

[1] See also 'Veniat dilectus meus', referred to in the previous footnote. More on Grandi in Denis Arnold, 'Alessandro Grandi, a disciple of Monteverdi', *Musical Quarterly*, xliii (1957), p. 171, and on duet motets in Roche, 'The Duet in early seventeenth-century Italian church music', *Proceedings of the Royal Musical Association*, xciii, p. 33.

[2] See the opening of his 'Languet anima mea' in Hugo Leichtentritt, *Geschichte der Motette* (Leipzig, 1908), p. 255.

(Lo, let them be confounded who fight against thee and let them all blush with shame.)

In general, where motets in the more orthodox five parts do not have dialogue elements or refrain forms (with solos or duets offset by a repeated tutti—composers were becoming more conscious of the need for structural unity), they are divided into sections of text each having a characteristic theme or motive that is developed contrapuntally, often with a textural build-up to a climax.

As the century progressed, the duet and trio motet tended towards a more expressive, declamatory idiom of which emotional expression, ornaments in moderation, and above all melody are the main features. Composers who added to Grandi's and Donati's achievements include Giovanni Rovetta at Venice and Orazio Tarditi, Alberto Lazari, and Giovanni Battista Aloisi in the provinces. Typical of this manner is Aloisi's trio 'Quid mihi est' (1637):

Monteverdi, too, made a belated contribution to the repertory, of which
the second 'Salve Regina' from the *Selva morale* (1640)[1] is a towering
masterpiece, with its static pedal harmonies and impassioned climaxes
of supplication. By the 1650s, middle baroque tendencies could be seen
in the wider range of keys and dissonances in the small motet.

As well as duets and trios, the 1620s produced many good motets for
the four- to six-part medium. Grandi had now turned to writing small
motets with obbligato violins,[2] and other composers, such as Giovanni
Battista Crivelli at Ferrara and Tarquinio Merula at Cremona, made
their mark.[3] Merula is better known for his development of the early
church sonata; his vocal writing is capricious, as in the four-part 'In
dedicatione templi', where the tenor leaps a major ninth:

[1] In Monteverdi, *Tutte le opere*, ed. Gian Francesco Malipiero, xv.2 (Asolo, 1940),
p. 736.
[2] See *infra*, pp. 364–6.
[3] See Crivelli's 'O Maria mater gratiae', ed. Roche (London, 1968).

Ex. 189

This motet is in the form AABBC, with two repeated sections and an Alleluia coda. The use of the word 'Alleluia' for a refrain—stemming from Giovanni Gabrieli—can be seen in Donati's 'Alleluia haec dies' (1629),[1] to name but one of countless pieces. As with Gabrieli, the refrain is in triple time.

After 1630, composers of motets abandoned these more traditional textures, preferring to write duets or trios or to include instruments: the more intimate medium of two or three voices and organ, with its potential for delicate expression of the text, proved more attractive. Such a development was paralleled in the decline both of the conventional five-part madrigal and of the importance of the chorus in opera.

PSALM-SETTING IN THE GRAND CONCERTATO MANNER

The setting of complete psalms or the *Magnificat*, associated with Vespers and other liturgical offices, presented the composer with quite different problems. He had no choice of text, since certain psalms were prescribed for each feast, and the texts themselves were long, amorphous, and lacking in possibilities for word-painting. Thus he either adopted the *stile antico* or, if he were associated with a more opulent establishment, the grand concertato manner. This took its starting-point from the polychoral style of Venice, which was by now almost a century old, and had generally been associated with psalm settings. Though this straightforward antiphonal singing persisted in many cities well into the seventeenth century, it is more interesting to follow its transformation into a thoroughly baroque concept that foreshadows the concerto grosso. The change can already be seen in a psalm collection of 1609 by Girolamo Giacobbi, the first of a line of illustrious *maestri* at San Petronio, Bologna. Here the two choirs are unequal (choir II is of lower tessitura), and both choirs provide solo voices from time to time, while

[1] Ed. Roche (London, 1968).

the low choir includes trombone parts as well. A few bars of the
Magnificat will show the colourful possibilities:

Ex. 190

It was always possible, as composers tell us, to add other choirs in
various parts of the church and to use stringed continuo instruments as
well as organs, so what looked on paper like little more than a double-
choir psalm could easily be transformed into a feast of impressive
music.[1]

Although several large-scale psalm publications continued this idea
of two balanced choirs both providing solo singers in contrast to tuttis,
the trend was towards investing the main body of the music in choir I,
which became a group of concerted soloists, while choir II formed a
ripieno which occasionally sang antiphonally but often only reinforced
the soloists by doubling them in tuttis. Monteverdi's first 'Confitebor'

---

[1] See Gaetano Gaspari, *Catalogo della Biblioteca Musicale G. B. Martini di Bologna*
(repr. Bologna, 1961), ii, pp. 46 and 420; A. W. Ambros, *Geschichte der Musik*, iv, 3rd ed.,
rev. Leichtentritt (Leipzig, 1909), p. 239; and Banchieri, *Conclusioni nel suono dell'organo*
(repr. Milan, 1934), appendix, for various composers' prefaces and remarks.

from the *Selva morale*[1] exemplifies this approach: three solo voices have long arioso passages in triple time, and there is a repeated tutti in which five *ripieno* parts join. This sectional treatment of a psalm text, with short tutti refrains and solo movements alternating, can also be seen in Grandi's psalms of 1630; it points towards the baroque cantata.

The other, more experimental, approach to the large-scale psalm is found in the 'mixed concertato' style, where textures and groupings change freely throughout, and obbligato instruments are liberally mixed with voices. Gabrieli's later motets had a profound influence here. The first provincial composer to write psalms of this type was Amadio Freddi at Treviso.

Ex. 191

Ex. 191 shows the spirited music near the end of his 'Nisi Dominus' (1616); the similarity to the opening of Monteverdi's Vespers, with instrumental scales over repeated chords, will be noticed. His scoring, for medium-sized choir and two obbligato instruments, was to become normal in large-scale music, although the more grandiose type required a full church orchestra of violins and trombones. Freddi was followed in

[1] Monteverdi, op. cit., xv.1, p. 297.

1623 by Donati, whose *Salmi boscarecci* offer a vast choice of alternative methods of performance; Donati explains how the part-books can be made to provide anything from a simple six-part piece to one for five choirs, including up to twelve soloists, *ripieno*, violins, trombones, and so on.

During his period as *maestro* at St. Mark's, Venice, Monteverdi's principal contribution to sacred music lay in the mixed concertato psalm. Some of the *Selva morale* works, such as the first settings of 'Beatus Vir' and 'Laudate Dominum',[1] are justly becoming better known: they exemplify Monteverdi's craftsman-like treatment of structure, introducing rondo elements and ostinato bass figures from the strophic aria and canzonet of the time to provide unity in a long psalm. The most daring, and brilliant, instance of chaconne technique occurs in the posthumous 'Laetatus sum',[2] in which a wonderful variety of activity goes on above the endlessly repeating four-note bass. These are the works of Monteverdi's maturity, far more thoroughly modern than those in the Vespers; if they are less flamboyant, the ornamentation here is always subjugated to melodic beauty and never becomes mere display. Monteverdi's influence was strong around Venice, especially in the psalms of Rovetta, his assistant (and successor after his death in 1643), and of Giovanni Antonio Rigatti, whose publication of

Ex. 192

[1] The *Selva morale* works are all in op. cit., xv, and there are modern editions of 'Beatus vir', ed. John Steele (London, 1965), and 'Laudate Dominum', ed. Arnold as an Eulenburg score (London, 1966).

[2] Monteverdi, op. cit., xvi, p. 231.

1640 closely resembles the *Selva morale* in content. Rigatti's fascinating *Magnificat*, for seven-part choir and orchestra of violins and viols, contains a *toccata da guerra* (see Ex. 192) in Monteverdi's *stile concitato*, recalling, too, Andrea Gabrieli's battle pieces of half a century earlier. Such grand music as this was now becoming less common, however, and it was only in connection with the great Venetian basilica itself that Francesco Cavalli's Vesper psalms of 1656 would have been performed. The more typical scoring of medium-sized choir with strings was more normal in the provinces: such a combination is used in the early psalms of Maurizio Cazzati (later to achieve fame at Bologna). Here the triple-time sections have a more varied rhythm, and the 4/4 ones have semiquaver figurations, both pointing to mid-baroque practices.

Ex. 193

THE EARLIEST ORCHESTRAL MASSES

Large-scale publications of psalms often included a ceremonial Mass as well, and it is from these that we can trace the evolution of the new form. Its broad, solemn style has roots in Giovanni Gabrieli's Mass movements published posthumously in 1615.[1] Many Masses had no *Sanctus* or *Agnus Dei*, since in Venice it was felt that these movements detracted from the liturgical actions they accompanied. Perhaps the earliest Mass to include a full five-part orchestra of violins and trombones is the one by Ercole Porta (1620), who worked in a small town near Bologna. The careful distinction of idiom between vocal and instrumental parts is most evident in the *Sanctus*, the unadorned writing being especially appropriate for trombones (see Ex. 193).

[1] Giovanni Gabrieli, *Opera omnia*, ed. Arnold, iv (Rome, 1965), pp. 97 and 116.

Typical of ceremonial Mass style is the interruption of the *Credo* of this Mass by a 28-bar *sinfonia* for orchestra.

Both Grandi and Monteverdi made notable contributions to the early orchestral Mass: Grandi's Mass of 1630 is basically for four soloists, who have splendidly melodious parts, and optional but extremely effective *ripieno* parts for choir and mixed orchestra. The latter have ceremonial interludes to play before the *Gloria*, but perhaps the outstanding moment is the ravishing 'Crucifixus' for *solo* tenor:

Ex. 194

(And was crucified for us under Pontius Pilate, suffered and was buried.)

Although the styles are different, there are many similarities of structure between the *Gloria* of this Mass and Monteverdi's seven-part *Gloria* in the *Selva morale*,[1] thought to have been part of a solemn Mass to celebrate the end of a disastrous plague in 1630–1. Both composers use a variety of repeated material to unify the whole, in Grandi's case chord-sequences, in Monteverdi's a ritornello for strings. Monteverdi, writing for Venice, naturally adopts a more brilliant, showy style; Grandi was writing for the celebration of the name-day of his church at Bergamo, where he died of the plague in 1630. The effects of this plague on north Italian music were profound, for many musicians lost their lives, choirs re-emerged in an emaciated state, and music printing was at a standstill for several years. Thus it is not surprising that a moneyed city like Venice should be one of the few continuing centres of the orchestral Mass, as of the big psalm. Rovetta's Mass of 1639 is very Monteverdian in manner:

---

[1] Monteverdi, op. cit., xv.1, p. 117.

Ex. 195

(We praise thee, we worship thee, we glorify thee.)

It also shows some stylistic advance with its many 7–6 suspensions, more flowing triple time and less angular bass line. Monteverdi's orchestral Mass music, had more of it survived, might have proved to be very like this. The big Masses of Cazzati, Tarditi, and Cavalli, dating from the 1640s and 1650s, show a tendency towards 'orderliness' and predictability, with their long triple-time episodes in cantata style, and the exciting chordal tuttis reminiscent of the far-off days of the Gabrielis are fewer and further between. Cavalli's melodic gift is less apparent than in his operas: the extended solo sections in his Mass[1] consist largely of graceful padding, making the work incredibly long compared with the more concise Masses of earlier composers.

[1] Ed. Raymond Leppard (London, 1966).

SMALL-SCALE PSALMS AND MASSES: THE 'TWO PRACTICES'

Orchestral Masses and psalms were generally intended for special feast days or ceremonial occasions, when outside musicians would be hired to swell the regular size of a choir; for ordinary Sundays (and weekdays in Venice, where there was a tradition of daily music) a simpler kind of liturgical *Gebrauchsmusik* had to suffice for the Mass and prescribed psalm texts. For this purpose the *stile antico*, or 'first practice'—as Monteverdi named it—survived well into the seventeenth century even though the concertato style, which incorporated the principles of the 'second practice', was fast developing beside it. This was because psalm texts and much of the Mass (certainly the *Gloria* and *Credo*) presented little opportunity for word-painting or musical organization. The old style was considered quite adequate. Monteverdi's three surviving Masses are all written in it, though they are quite distinct in language, as they are based on different models.[1] The last (posthumous) Mass of 1651 is the finest, containing elements of Monteverdi's own early madrigal style mixed with sequences, modality, and restrained chromaticism. Its thematic unity is astonishing in a work of this date. Other composers acknowledged the existence of both old and new styles by publishing, in the same collection, Masses in each of them, a practice inaugurated in Monteverdi's 1610 publication, featuring 'old' Mass and 'new' Vespers. The old-style pieces were written in an updated, post-Palestrina idiom. Donati's 'Missa sine nomine' (1622) exemplifies this well:[2]

Ex. 196

[1] All three are reprinted as Eulenburg scores, ed. Hans F. Redlich, Arnold, and Redlich respectively (London, 1962, 1962, 1952).

[2] More on the old style in Roche, 'Monteverdi and the *Prima Prattica*', in *The Monteverdi Companion*, ed. Arnold and Nigel Fortune (London, 1968), p. 167.

The concertato style was thus slow to catch on with composers of such rough-and-ready liturgical music. Grandi's four-part Mass of 1610 is a particularly fine early example, showing a strong influence of Giovanni Gabrieli (who may have been his teacher), while Donati's and Rovetta's psalm settings of slightly later date have fine extended melodies and exciting counterpoint.[1] There were very few psalms or Masses for fewer than four parts, since the more intimate duet and trio medium was less suited to large musical structures, though it is interesting that a collection of duet and trio psalms by Carlo Milanuzzi (Venice, 1628) hints at the chaconne forms of some of Monteverdi's Venetian psalms. Chaconne or *ostinato* techniques provided some answer to the structural problems in long psalm or Mass movements and became increasingly common in the 1640s and 1650s. Such a device appears thus in Biagio Gherardi's 'Ecce, nunc' (1650):

Ex. 197

---

[1] See Rovetta's 'Laudate Dominum' (1626), ed. Steele (London, 1966).

25

(Who made heaven and earth.)

Towards the middle of the baroque period the purely choral psalm or Mass setting survived only in the *stile antico*: modern-style settings tended to include strings, affording greater variety of colour. If they lack strings they normally show (like Ex. 197) the four-part layout that has become conventional to this day.

SOLO VOICES AND INSTRUMENTS: 'FOR CHURCH OR CHAMBER'

There was some discussion of early ecclesiastical monody in the previous volume;[1] an interesting outgrowth of this is the motet for one or more solo voices with obbligato instruments. The novel sonorities of this medium had been anticipated in parts of Monteverdi's large *Magnificat* of the 1610 Vespers, and the idea of having a repeated violin *sinfonia* in a small motet occurred to Severo Bonini, a Florentine, as early as 1615. It was Grandi who, as Monteverdi's assistant at Venice, developed the medium in three publications of the 1620s. The fact that at St. Mark's instrumental playing was taken almost as seriously as singing (as is shown by Giovanni Gabrieli's innovations in this field) enabled Grandi to introduce idiomatic violin writing into the solo motet. The violins not only play ritornellos but sometimes answer the voice or voices in dialogue or partake in contrapuntal interplay, and Grandi's melodic gift is always evident. One or two pieces use chaconne devices, while others exhibit strophic-variation technique, where a melody is progressively ornamented at each return. This is taken furthest in 'Amo Christum' (1629), in which both the violin *sinfonia* and the vocal tune are varied and yet preserve their own distinct idioms:

[1] See Vol. IV, pp. 532 ff.

Ex. 198

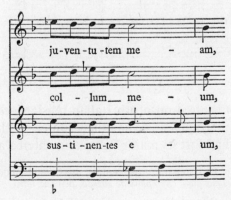

(I love Christ who renews my youth, who encircles my neck with jewels.)

There is clearly a resemblance too between this and the keyboard variations of northern countries. Grandi's style is also closely reflected in Schütz's *Symphoniae sacrae* of 1629, 1647, and 1650—Schütz would almost certainly have met Grandi on his second visit to Venice in 1628, since he learned more from him than from Monteverdi.[1]

Although much of this music was as apt for 'princely apartments' as for church use—amorous texts from the Song of Songs were often set— the medium also came to be used for liturgical psalm and hymn music, as instanced in Monteverdi's *Selva morale* and 1651 publications. The latter includes a 'Confitebor' for two voices and violins which is a perfect gem; it has both an *ostinato* bass and a violin ritornello.[2] Motets with violins remained in vogue too, leading naturally to the baroque cantata and ultimately to the arias of Bach. The style in the 1650s can be seen from Tarditi's 'Ave maris stella', where the violins join the voice for the final verse after playing a *sinfonia* in alternation with the vocal verses:

Ex. 199

CHURCH MUSIC IN ROME

The discussion has so far been centred on north Italian music since it was here that the styles of early baroque music had their source. With Palestrina's death in 1594 Rome had lost its major figure and entered a

---

[1] Grandi's motet 'Lilia convallium' for two sopranos, two tenors, two violins, and continuo was the model for Schütz's 'O Jesu süss' (*Symphoniae sacrae*, iii): see *infra*, p. 718.

[2] Monteverdi, op. cit., xvi, p. 144.

period of subservience to influence from the north. Despite the per-
petuation of the Palestrina ideal in the polyphony of his immediate
successors it would be quite incorrect to claim that all Roman church
music was impervious to the advance of the concertato style, for a great
many younger composers (e.g. Agazzari, Landi, and Giovanni Francesco Anerio) wrote duet and trio motets in a post-Viadana idiom.
Luigi Rossi (1598–1653), well known as a composer of operas and
cantatas, also wrote motets for a varying number of voices, often with
string accompaniment. 'O sequis daret concentum' for three sopranos
and continuo has, exceptionally, a part for harp as well as one for violin.
But in general Rome lagged behind the north, and there was no evidence
of interest in the novel sonorities of solo voices mixed with instruments
either in large- or small-scale music, and there were no outstanding
talents to develop such a style. The *stile antico* was more prevalent,
certainly for strictly liturgical music such as psalms and hymns, and
especially at the Sistine Chapel, which had no organ. An excellent
example of the kind of music Pope Urban VIII would have heard on a
Sunday is furnished by Gregorio Allegri in his six-part Mass 'Vidi
turbam magnam':

Ex. 200

This music, based on the late style of Palestrina, is much preferable to the ornamental note-spinning and empty virtuosity of some of the solo motets being written (by Johann Kapsberger, for example) in Rome at this time.

Another vogue in Rome was for what has been called the 'colossal baroque',[1] an outcrop of the old *cori spezzati* style, which was by now becoming a comparative anachronism like any other form of *stile antico* composition. Large-scale music flourished in the form of huge Masses by Orazio Benevoli, Carissimi and others, in which the 'Amen' chorus at the end of the *Credo* might last as long as a whole *Sanctus*. Large choral church music was not displaced, as in the north, by the rise of opera or instrumental music, and it had connections with oratorio, which, as we have seen earlier in this chapter, flowered in Rome in this period; yet it seems that economy of means and respect for the text had here become obscured by grandness for its own sake. Benevoli's famous 54-part Mass of 1628,[2] written for the consecration of Salzburg cathedral, is a monumental work for two choirs and four independent instrumental groups, which are, however, handled in a quite unimaginative way.

The development of oratorio, Rome's counterpart to opera in Venice, infused a new lease of life into liturgical music there in the 1640s, and several anthologies of motets appeared towards the end of the decade. At last Roman church music had found a modern idiom not based on outmoded ideas. Instrumental *sinfonie*, a *bel canto* style of triple-time writing with hemiolas and cross-accents providing plenty of rhythmic variety, and the use of a wider range of keys and key-signatures indicating the further progress of tonality, all feature here. The motet 'Miserator Dominus' by Alessandro Leardini even has a 32-bar fugue complete with a set of middle entries in the relative major and its dominant, opening thus:

Ex. 201

[1] See Vol. IV, pp. 531–2.
[2] Ed. Adler, *Denkmäler der Tonkunst in Österreich*, xx (Jg. 10 (1)) (Vienna, 1903).

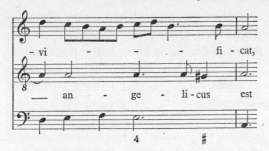

MID-BAROQUE TENDENCIES

Whereas in the early years of the seventeenth century Italy had been the cradle of early baroque style in sacred music, a teacher of countless composers of other nationalities, and its music a yardstick against which to measure their achievements, by the mid-century it boasted very few important sacred composers except Carissimi. Middle and late baroque church music seems dominated by the Lutheran tradition, and the continuation of Catholic music in Italy is obscure. It is true that the end of the Thirty Years' War in 1648 resulted in an upsurge of the Protestant spirit in Germany which manifested itself in the more austere late works of Schütz. The end of Italian dominance is symbolized by this abandonment of earlier influences.

In Italy two factors were responsible for the decline of liturgical composition: the rise of opera and of instrumental music. Opera was no longer restricted to the courts, it was a commercial activity. It competed with the churches in offering employment to singers and instrumentalists. *Maestri di cappella* began to find the writing of opera a profitable proposition, especially in Venice, and to treat their church positions merely as a means to a stable income. By the 1650s only churches in cities with public opera-houses tended to attract talented composers. The media of church music came to resemble those in opera—mixed bodies of voices and strings, with the emphasis on solo singing of a high standard. Gone were the days of Viadana and the unambitious small choir.

With the development of stringed instruments the instrumental sonata and concerto displaced the motet as a form of extra-liturgical music at Mass, becoming in particular the glory of church music at San Petronio, Bologna, where trumpets also were favourite instruments.[1] The string body in vocal music took over the function of the full choir so that the contrast was now between solo voices and instruments instead of

---

[1] See *infra*, pp. 374–5, and Peter Smith, 'The Bolognese school', *Musical Times*, cix (1968), p. 28; also, on somewhat later music, Jean Berger, 'Notes on some 17th-century compositions for trumpets and strings at Bologna', *Musical Quarterly*, xxxvii (1951), p. 354.

soloists and *ripieno* voices, and with the greater interest in idiomatic string writing composers concentrated less on word setting to sustain musical inspiration. The Counter-Reformation spirit had indeed waned, and church music had lost some of the 'passionate' feeling of earlier years and gained in charm, poise, and gracefully florid ornament, characteristics of much mid-baroque art.

(c) LITURGICAL MUSIC IN ITALY, 1660–1750

By PETER SMITH

INTRODUCTION

In the middle and later years of the baroque period, Italian composers, both at home and abroad, continued to write actively for the church in the familiar categories already established a generation or two earlier and described in the previous section. The quantity of music produced in the main creative centres, not to mention the smaller provincial towns, was very great (at least in the later seventeenth century), and much of it remains unexplored. However, it is possible to notice a general falling-off, in quantity and quality, both in Rome and Bologna after the turn of the eighteenth century, even though Venice and Naples continued to produce lively church music for several further decades. During these years, which witnessed the supremacy of the opera-house and the astonishingly fertile growth of instrumental forms, Catholic church music inevitably mirrored the changing fashions which took place in these secular fields. On the other hand the *stile concertato* in the sacred music of the north Italians, which became especially important in Bologna after the 1660s, played a significant part in the formation of the concertos of Corelli and later composers.

Venice continued to exert a powerful influence, not only over Bologna but also over Rome, Naples, and Vienna (where Caldara worked in the early eighteenth century). The polychoral style which had assumed massive proportions in Rome in the 1620s remained fashionable, if lighter in weight, in the Italian cities which could afford elaborate musical establishments; Naples went on enjoying it at least until the 1750s. The concertato techniques in Monteverdi's *Selva morale* (1640), referred to in the previous section, awoke strong echoes in Bologna, and Cavalli's *Musiche sacre* (1656) and *Vespri* (1675) must have made a similar impact. New contrapuntal techniques in vocal composition, based on modern harmonic procedures, were closely linked with the experience gained in writing for keyboard and stringed instruments.

Here Bologna took the lead in the seventeenth century, and Naples, which specialized in fugue, was a close rival in the eighteenth. Although the older *prima prattica* of the sixteenth century was slowly fading, it either persisted in a wholly artificial and 'academic' manner or, in the hands of some of the more creative composers, became a vehicle for personal expression and sentiment. The Venetians and Neapolitans, especially in the eighteenth century, were often moved to set emotional texts, such as the 'Crucifixus' from the Mass, and the *Miserere*, to rich and startling harmonies, delighting in sensuousness rather as the mannerist painters used colour as a chiaroscuro effect on their canvases.

ROME: CARISSIMI AND OTHERS

The Roman fondness for heavy polychoral writing, seen in the Masses of Benevoli[1] and his pupil Ercole Bernabei, is also found, though in a less 'colossal' manner, in most of the thirteen surviving Mass settings of Carissimi.[2] Only one, for four voices, is composed according to the *prima prattica*, in a style similar to Monteverdi's Mass for four voices in his collection of 1640. Most of the others are written for from eight to sixteen voices, with *basso continuo*, in a blend of imitative and homophonic textures, showing both conservative and modern traits. Four of Carissimi's Masses bear titles. 'L'homme armé', one of the last compositions on this ancient theme, is in the imitative style of the sixteenth century. In 'Ut queant laxis', however, the hexa-chordal motive is handled in a more up-to-date variation technique. The Mass in C minor, 'Sciolto havean dell'alte sponde', for five voices (also existing in a version for nine voices and two violins), is a late example of a parody mass, based on Carissimi's own cantata of that name. The material in the impressive opening *Kyrie* forms the basis of the other sections of the Mass, which is thus tightly knit in a cyclic manner. In at least six of his other masses Carissimi also strives for unity by opening each movement with the same melodic material. The *Missa a quinque et a novem* in C was the only one printed in his lifetime (in 1666); unlike the others it is in the concertato style. Here, structural unity in the *Gloria* and other movements is aided by using different forms of the same descending *ostinato* figure in the bass, which also appears in the instrumental ritornellos and at times in the vocal lines. This Mass must have achieved a certain popularity, as it also exists in English sources in a simpler form for two tenors, bass, and two violins, without the reinforcing four-part choir.

[1] See *supra*, p. 368.
[2] See Massenkeil, 'Über die Messen Giacomo Carissimis', *Analecta Musicologica*, i (1963).

The concertato style was also practised by Carissimi in some of his settings of the psalms for Vespers. His *Magnificat* for double four-part choir in A minor, and his five-part 'Dixit Dominus' in B flat,[1] are both spacious works with lively homophonic choruses alternating with brilliant florid passages for soloists. The *Magnificat* uses plainsong themes—a practice which persists into the eighteenth century in many large choral works. A later work in the same tradition is the setting of 'Dixit Dominus' that is the finest of the sacred works that Handel composed during his early years in Italy;[2] it dates from 1707. It includes sections, such as the opening and closing choruses, which are worthy of the mature Handel in their harnessing of German solidity to Italian fire and energy. Giuseppe Ottavio Pitoni (1657–1743), a composer of enormous fertility, continued the grand Roman tradition and passed it on, in some measure, to the Neapolitans Durante, Leo, and Feo, who studied with him (some of his music is mentioned below). His 'Dixit' in F for four choirs[3] was still sung regularly at St. Peter's during Holy Week at the beginning of the present century.

Rome played a leading role in the cultivation of the Latin motet for solo voice or small vocal ensemble. This flourished beside the chamber cantata, which it at first closely resembled and which had grown in importance and sophistication as the Roman opera declined in the 1630s. The pattern of motet composition set by Luigi Rossi and others was carried on by Carissimi and Bonifazio Graziani (1605–64), who was *maestro di cappella* at the church of the Gesù and produced six books of *Motetti a voce sola* for soprano and continuo. His decorated vocal writing demanded the highly accomplished bravura singing associated with the *bel canto* style, as in 'Dominus illuminatio mea':[4]

Ex. 202

[1] Respectively in Brit. Mus. Add. MS. 31478, fo. 30ᵛ, and Oxford, Christ Church, MS. 55.
[2] In Chrysander's complete edition of Handel's works, xxxviii, p. 53.
[3] Brit. Mus. MS. Egerton 2459, fo. 202.
[4] Oxford, Christ Church, MS. 7.

me prae - - - - - - li - um.

7   6

Semiquaver patterns like these indicate the extent to which by the mid-seventeenth century violin and keyboard virtuosity was affecting vocal technique—an influence which was in fact mutual. These motets were usually constructed in a series of fairly short, rhythmically contrasting sections. Although solo motets were the most numerous to begin with, the proportion of those for two, three, and more voices quickly increased as the century went on. A favourite combination was the vocal trio for two sopranos and bass—a direct translation of the trio-sonata into vocal terms. A pair of violins was commonly included in the ensemble, reflecting the concertato practice in the larger choral pieces. Meticulous imitative counterpoint over the continuo bass is typical of this style, in which small rhythmic cells are repeated to form larger units, as in Carissimi's motet 'Laudemus virum gloriosum':[1]

Ex. 203

Sop. 1

Lau - de - mus, lau - de - -

Sop. 2

Lau - de - mus, lau -

B.C.

- mus, lau - de - mus vi - rum glo - ri - o - sum, et___

- de - mus, lau - de - mus vi - rum glo - ri - o - sum,

[1] Brit. Mus. Add. MSS. 17835, fo. 5ᵛ, and 31472, fo. 22ᵛ, and Oxford, Christ Church MSS. 13 and 53.

Some of Carissimi's motets contain a narrative, which nearly places them with oratorios. The lengthy 'Filiae Jerusalem'[1] of Marc'Antonio Cesti (1623–69) also falls into this category: it is scored for three sopranos and a bass, who takes the part of narrator. However, the recitative found in the oratorio proper is replaced by a more melodious arioso in this type of motet. Other seventeenth-century composers who wrote in the motet style of Carissimi and Graziani included Orazio Tarditi, Stradella, and Cazzati, and in the eighteenth century this technique was still carried on in, for example, the psalms of Benedetto Marcello and the sacred duets of Caldara and Steffani.

BOLOGNA

The flowering of musical activity in Bologna in the second half of the seventeenth century can be partly explained by the rising prestige of the professional guilds—in particular the Accademia Filarmonica— against the background of the lively intellectual and artistic life which centred on the ancient university and the various monastic orders. An impressive number of skilled composers and highly trained performers were members of the Accademia, which demanded high standards for admission to its exclusive circle. The basilica of San Petronio was the largest and most important of a number of Bolognese churches where music was regularly performed; it was here that

---

[1] Oxford, Christ Church, MS. 83.

the string and trumpet music, which was actively encouraged by the enlightened church authorities, came to play such a vital part in the history of the instrumental sonata and concerto. It is not surprising that the Bolognese composers made liberal use of these instrumental techniques in their elaborate concertato works for chorus and soloists.[1]

The arrival in 1657 of Maurizio Cazzati (*c.* 1620–1677) as *maestro di cappella* at San Petronio marked the beginning of this era of great activity; in 1674 he was replaced by Giovanni Paolo Colonna (1637–95) after a professional quarrel with the critic and composer Giulio Cesare Arresti. Colonna was succeeded after his death by Giacomo Antonio Perti (1661–1756), who remained in this post for sixty years, until his own death. Other composers associated with the Bologna school included Giovanni Battista Vitali, Giovanni Battista Bassani, Giovanni Maria Bononcini and his son Giovanni, Francesco Antonio Urio, Carlo Maria Clari, and, later in the eighteenth century, Giovanni Battista (Padre) Martini. Some of these worked in neighbouring towns: Bassani, for example, worked in Ferrara and Clari in Pisa.

Cazzati, whose output was enormous (nearly fifty collections of his sacred vocal music alone were published between 1641 and 1678),[2] composed in all the current styles but seemed more at ease in the *stile antico*. In a *Messa a cappella* published in 1670 his technique is smooth and assured even if the musical result is not especially memorable. The 'old' practice was modernized, to some extent, by the young Giovanni Bononcini, who, in 1688 at the age of eighteen, produced four settings of the *Missa brevis* for double choir, with two organ continuo parts. His teacher, Colonna, reverted to a consciously modal manner in the set of Vesper psalms that he dedicated to Pope Innocent XII in 1694. These are also set for double choir and two organs. Colonna's many works for two choirs must have been the result of his study under Benevoli and Carissimi in Rome, and two organ parts are frequently included in Bolognese church music, since San Petronio had been furnished with a second organ in 1596.

The sectional thinking which still dominated musical composition in the 1660s and 1670s posed formal problems for Cazzati in his concertato works for choir and soloists. In a *Magnificat a 4* (1670) florid duets for soloists, in the manner of Monteverdi, are separated by verses for chorus in the style of the *prima prattica*, with little sense of continuity between the sections. A happier example of formal unity is found, however, in his smaller-scale setting of 'Laudate Dominum' (1666), where the music in

[1] See *supra*, p. 369, n. 1.
[2] The sources of all works by Bolognese composers referred to in this section are found in Bologna, in the Civico Museo Bibliografico Musicale or the archives of San Petronio.

the first section is repeated towards the end at 'Sicut erat', thus rounding-off the design. The homophonic outburst of the choir in the tenth bar contrasts effectively with the lightweight and pointed imitative opening by the soloists, which begins as follows:[1]

Ex. 204

[1] Bologna, Civico Museo, MS. Y32; San Petronio, MS. 49.

(Praise the Lord, praise him all ye nations, all ye people.)

The treatment of the soloists and chorus here directly corresponds to the *concertino* and *ripieno* in the later concerto grosso. This piece shows several other standard features also found in the concertato writing of Vitali, Bassani, and Colonna. The easy-going *bel canto* duet in triple time, with strong hemiola rhythms near cadences, continued to be employed. Blocks of monumental sound from the chorus, *grave* and *fortissimo*, found here on the word 'Gloria' and followed by swift homophonic declamation, had already been a favourite device of Monteverdi and Cavalli. A final fugato section for chorus also became standard practice in Bologna, which enjoyed the fluent and effective counterpoint of its composers, who, however, seldom extended these finales into full-scale fugues, as the Neapolitans did, until the eighteenth century.

In Vitali's only published collection of sacred vocal music, *Salmi concertati* (1677), the sections have expanded and, taken together, form a more unified whole. A contributing factor in some of these psalm settings is the way the string passages—ritornellos and shorter interjections—recur and are related to the vocal parts. Some of the choruses are written in a weighty and solemn style, mixing chordal and polyphonic textures and incorporating many suspensions. An example of this is found in the opening chorus of the *Magnificat*, which is probably the best work in this set:[1]

Ex. 205

[with 5-part Strings and B.C.]

[1] Bologna, Civico Museo, MS. CC131 (also in Busi MS. 52); San Petronio, MS. 229.

- gni - fi-cat a - nima me - a, a - nima me - a Do - - -

- mi - num, anima mea Do - - - mi - num.

Colonna frequently makes use of this heavy texture to allow a few bars of contrast in, for example, an otherwise quick and brilliant choral movement. In the 'Offertorium' from a Requiem he employs it with stirring effect throughout the length of the piece, which is scored for five-part choir, soloists, and strings. It is a sign of the times that Colonna shows a more highly developed sense of tonality than his predecessors. A more 'grammatical' feeling for harmonic direction, which was obviously of benefit to his structural designs, was brought to a still more sophisticated level by Corelli (who was trained in Bologna) in his sonatas and concertos a few years later. Bassani's constructions, on the other hand, sometimes continue longer than is warranted by the basic material. In a setting of 'Beatus vir' he proceeds at an alert pace, in a series of imitative entries, through sixty-four pages of score. However, the more successful concertato movements of Bassani and (especially) Colonna are often convincingly pulled together by a free but judicious mixture of homophonic and fugal textures within the same rhythmic framework and by the composers' ability to expand phrases by side-stepping expected cadences. An attractive feature also frequently found here (and similarly in the concertos of Torelli and Corelli) is the repetition, marked *piano*, of a short vocal phrase, often near the end of a movement. Colonna's finest sacred music is probably found in the *Messa e salmi concertati* of 1691. An extract from the *Kyrie* of this Mass, for five-part choir and strings, well illustrates the brisk contrapuntal style which is typical of concerted church music in Bologna at the end of the seventeenth century:[1]

[1] Bologna, Civico Museo, MS. Y164 (also in Busi MS. 63); San Petronio, MS. 68; also in London, Royal College of Music, MS. 801.

Ex. 206

In these works the string accompaniment (which in the above example is basically a rearrangement of the vocal parts) was gradually being emancipated from the vocal lines. In the time of Cazzati and Vitali the violin and viola parts, for example, merely tended to invert the soprano and alto lines. Although this was still the basic method of Colonna and Bassani, more independent and idiomatic figures began to appear in the string parts. Repeated patterns, sometimes intricately interlocking between two violins, were borrowed from the concerto. This is even more noticeable later on in the church music of Vivaldi and Durante. Perti frequently includes trumpets in pairs, and oboes, with the strings in his orchestra. A brilliant *Messa concertata* written by Perti after the turn of the eighteenth century is scored for four trumpets, two horns, and strings, with double four-part choir and soloists. Here the arias and ensemble movements for soloists, near-relations of their counterparts in the opera-house, are brief and well integrated into the whole design.

Much of this Bolognese music was obviously intended for the vast, reverberant space of San Petronio, which did not allow much subtlety of detail to be heard nor encourage it to be written. The strict technical standards upheld by the Accademia Filarmonica were admirable in one sense, but by their conventional attitudes this society must have had the effect of discouraging individuality of expression. This could partly account for the fact that the Bolognese school, instead of producing occasional masterpieces, assumed a more collective importance with their accumulation of technical experience during this phase in the development of Italian church music.

VENICE

Giovanni Legrenzi (1626–90), besides his activities as a composer of operas and sonatas, was also a key figure in Venetian church music. Near the end of his life, in 1685, he was appointed *maestro di cappella* at St. Mark's, and at various times he had taught Lotti, Vivaldi, Caldara, and Francesco Gasparini. These composers, however, scarcely constitute a school: their approaches to church composition varied widely and reflected the different spheres in which they worked. Gasparini, for example, having taught Benedetto Marcello in Venice in the early eighteenth century, later became *maestro di cappella* at St. John Lateran in Rome, where he wrote *a cappella* music in an archaic style and engaged in a professional feud with Alessandro Scarlatti.

In 1667 Legrenzi published his *Messa e salmi a due chori con stromenti a beneplacito*, a conservative collection in which he maintained the grand manner of Cavalli. Massive homophonic blocks of choral sound compete with each other and with a third, optional, 'choir' of stringed instruments. Harmonies are still used for broad, sonorous effect rather than formal direction; the frequent changes of time-signature are a legacy from Monteverdi and Cavalli. A more up-to-date work is his admirable *Missa brevis* in C[1] for five-part choir and strings. He obviously became keenly interested in the question of overall design: the *Kyrie* and *Christe* sections are separated by related string ritornellos, which together form larger, balancing units. This formal approach finds a parallel in his instrumental sonata 'La Buscha'.[2] Irregular phrase-lengths and subtle rhythmic organization compensate for the narrow harmonic range, which is still the rule at this time.

The progress in tonal thinking had, as indicated earlier, a direct bearing on the time-scale of the orchestral and concerted type of Mass composition. As individual parts of the Mass became longer and more complex, composers often set only the *Kyrie* and *Gloria* for ordinary practical purposes. For special occasions (which must often have resembled a concert rather than an act of worship) separate and elaborate settings, in many movements, of the *Kyrie*, *Gloria*, and *Credo* were often composed in Venice and Naples in the eighteenth century. In Vivaldi's large corpus of church music (of which less than a quarter has yet been published) there is, as far as we know, no single setting of the complete Mass. His *Kyrie in due cori*, *Credo* in E minor, and well-known *Gloria* are all large-scale works of this 'concert' variety.[3] The *Credo* in G minor for double choir and strings by Antonio Lotti (*c*. 1667–1740)[4] is a work of considerable weight in nine movements, of which the 'Crucifixus' in six parts is probably the finest.

The *Missa brevis*, for everyday use, was simpler and shorter than this: each of the main liturgical sections was generally set as a single move-ment, with little or no subdivision of the text and without extended solos. The eight shorter *a cappella* settings of the Mass, *à la* Palestrina, with which Lotti's name has more often been associated, were also intended for everyday use. Lotti is conditioned by modern tonality, and the rhythmic flow of the parts seems constrained by the bar-lines, as seen in the following:[5]

---

[1] Oxford, Christ Church, MS. 1000.

[2] Davison and Apel, op. cit., p. 70.

[3] Vivaldi's vocal church music, comprising about sixty works, is housed in the Biblioteca Nazionale, Turin. It is in course of publication, ed. Renato Fasano, as *Musica sacra di Antonio Vivaldi* (Vienna, 1969). Recent vocal scores of the *Gloria* include those ed. Mason Martens (North Hollywood, 1961) and Cor Backers (Hilversum, n.d.).

[4] London, Royal College of Music, MS. 1088.

[5] This, together with Lotti's other *a cappella* Masses, is ed. Hermann Müller, *Denkmäler deutscher Tonkunst*, lx (Leipzig, 1930).

Ex. 207

In this music Lotti displays great technical fluency; despite its mellifluous qualities, however, it fails to make a lasting impression. If this
might be justly considered a dead style, it does, nevertheless, form the
basis of a type of deeply felt vocal music, referred to earlier in this
section, which is usually associated with poignant texts. In this vein
Lotti is at his best. In his famous *a cappella* setting of the *Miserere*,
composed about 1735 and performed at St. Mark's every Maundy
Thursday for many years, he is carried away by the emotional nature of
the words. The opening gives some idea of the general style:[1]

Ex. 208

[1] Brit. Mus., Add. MS. 14177, fo. 36.

(Jommelli borrowed the first eighteen bars of this work in 1751 to begin his own *Miserere*, a work of equal beauty.)

Lotti's expressive settings of the 'Crucifixus' in six, eight, and ten parts probably inspired Caldara's even finer version for sixteen voices,[1] a work of great technical mastery and finesse, with a striking chain of dominant-seventh harmonies towards its close. Both Lotti and Caldara control their emotional chromaticisms within a 'grammatical' framework; Vivaldi, however, sometimes indulges in purple passages, luxuriating in the purely sensual impact of harmonies for their own sake. The surprising orchestral passage which opens his G minor *Kyrie* is also found in the *Magnificat*, in the first chorus:[2]

Ex. 209

---

[1] Published along with several other church compositions by Caldara, ed. Eusebius Mandyczewski, *Denkmäler der Tonkunst in Österreich*, xxvi (Jg. 13(1)) (Vienna, 1906).
[2] Ed. Malipiero (Milan, 1961).

This anguished aspect of Italian baroque expression is frequently found too in the pulsating slow movements of Corelli's concertos; its emotional ancestors might well be the chromatic word-painting and daring harmonies in some of the madrigals of Gesualdo and Monteverdi.

Vivaldi was evidently as well known to his contemporaries for his sacred music as for his secular. Some of it must have been intended for St. Mark's (the *Mercure de France* records in 1727 a performance there of his *Te Deum*), but most of it was probably performed in the Ospedale della Pietà, for female orphans, where he was choirmaster from 1703 to 1735.[1] It is therefore not surprising that soprano and alto voices are prominent in so much of his church music. He frequently accompanies simple homophonic choruses with the incisive, bare and muscular string-writing of his concertos. The opening chorus of the *Gloria* and the first movement of the less known but equally attractive 'Nisi Dominus' are good examples. His 'Beatus vir' for chorus, soloists (two sopranos and an alto), and strings is an extended single movement with the ground plan and general musical style of a concerto grosso. The double choir of the older Venetian tradition survives in his G minor *Kyrie*, also scored for double orchestra. The first 'Kyrie' section, in which the sensuous harmonic passage referred to above is combined with a vigorous quaver rhythm, is followed by a light, *galant* 'Christe' for soprano and alto soloists from each choir. The final 'Kyrie' is a well integrated fugue with a chromatic theme. However, the *galant* arias and duets, elegant and operatic, are more characteristic of Vivaldi. Passages in bare octaves (as at 'Deposuit' in the *Magnificat*), throbbing bass-note patterns under richly intertwining vocal lines (as in the opening movement of the 'Stabat Mater'), and repeated short snatches of melody all belong to the *galant* style and are also an important element in the lightweight, operatic church style of Pergolesi, Leo, and Durante.

The setting of the first fifty psalms by Benedetto Marcello (1686-1739) enjoyed enormous popularity in the eighteenth century. The eight volumes, which appeared between 1724 and 1726, were entitled *Estro poetico-armonico: parafrasi sopra i primi 50 psalmi, poesia di Girolamo Arcanio Giustiniani*.[2] Eulogies by Mattheson, Telemann, Charles Avison, and others were somewhat tempered by Burney's opinion that they were 'overpraised'. Eighteenth-century listeners were undoubtedly attracted to Marcello's ingratiating melodies and facile vocal part-writing. The *Miserere* is a long and elaborate setting in many movements, for three

[1] See Arnold, 'Orphans and ladies: the Venetian conservatoires (1680-1790)', *Proceedings of the Royal Musical Association*, lxxxix (1962-3), p. 31.
[2] There have been several editions since.

voices and two *violette*, displaying many beautiful and original effects of harmony and scoring. Marcello's independent thinking could well be explained by his position as a noble musical 'amateur'. A remarkable Requiem Mass[1] in many movements reveals a lively and somewhat bizarre mind at work. Current styles, old and new, sit together in uncomfortable proximity: sixteenth-century polyphony and touches of plainsong, the grand concertato, expressive fugal passages and *buffo* solos, not to mention the modern string patterns from Vivaldi's and his own concertos.

VIENNA: CALDARA

Antonio Caldara spent most of his creative life in Vienna, where the greater part of his vast output of sacred music still exists in manuscript. At the invitation of Charles VI he took the post of deputy conductor at the Imperial Court in 1716 and worked under Fux. Most of the Catholic courts in south Germany and Austria had long been accustomed to the presence of Italian composers; Vienna, especially, had always felt the attraction of Venice. In his Masses (which are discussed in chapter IX) Fux pays homage to the Italian concertato style, but his own position as a learned contrapuntist placed him at the head of what could be regarded as a Viennese school of church music. Its discipline had a marked effect on Caldara's work, shown in his contrapuntal precision and solid harmonic direction, which are sometimes more Teutonic than Italian. A predecessor of Caldara was the prolific Antonio Draghi, musical director of the Imperial Chapel from 1682, who also displayed certain Germanic traits. Besides his innumerable operas and oratorios he wrote some large concertato settings of the Mass, remarkable not only for their use of brass (there are, for instance, two cornetti and four trombones in the 'Missa assumptionis' of 1684)[2] but also for their heavy-handed, conservative manner. But while Draghi's Masses usefully remind us of the kind of church music turned out by average composers in the middle years of the baroque period, the church compositions of Caldara provide, on the whole, music by a much greater artistic personality. Perhaps his most refined and spontaneous work is found in the motets (published in Rome in 1714 and in Bologna in 1715)[3] for two and three solo voices with continuo, in which at times one finds an almost Mozartian chromaticism. This chamber combination, gracefully fluent and at the same time

---

[1] Brit. Mus. Royal Music MS. 24.c.1.
[2] Draghi, *Kirchenwerke*, ed. Adler, *Denkmäler der Tonkunst in Österreich*, xlvi (Jg. 23(1)) Vienna, 1916), p. 43; the volume contains four other works.
[3] *Denkmäler der Tonkunst in Österreich*, xxvi (Jg. 13 (1)), *passim*.

strictly controlled, forms an important ingredient in his numerous large choral works, in which are found all the prevailing forms of the day.

One of the grandest concertato Masses of the early eighteenth century was written by Caldara for the canonization of John of Nepomuk in 1726. The 'Missa Sanctificationis Sancti Joannis Nepomuceni' presents an array of powerful double choruses, solid fugues, and elegant duets. However, Caldara experiences a difficulty (shared by Francesco Durante, Leo, and others) inherent in long works of this kind: how to obviate the tendency of the many different movements to fall apart. His 'Stabat Mater', on a rather smaller scale, is more successfully designed. The pathetic and beautiful opening chorus features a theme with a drooping diminished fourth which again appears in a fugal section towards the end:[1]

Ex. 210

[with Strings, 2 Trombones, Organ and B.C.]

[1] *Denkmäler der Tonkunst in Österreich*, xxvi (Jg. 13(1)), p. 34.

THE 'STABAT MATER': STEFFANI

A great number of remarkable settings of the 'Stabat Mater' by Italian composers have survived from this period. Besides Caldara's there are settings by, among others, Lotti, Vivaldi, Steffani, Antonio Bononcini, Clari, d'Astorga, and Alessandro and Domenico Scarlatti, not to mention the celebrated work by Pergolesi. One of the finest is that by Agostino Steffani,[1] whose skilful and expressive six-part writing for chorus reveals a strong musical personality with complete control over his structure. The 'Stabat Mater' ascribed to Antonio Bononcini,[2] Giovanni's young brother, is another work of individuality, showing a musical style related to Caldara's in the expressive and singable vocal lines. Alternating four-part choruses and solo arias, with string orchestra, reveal careful workmanship and sometimes surprising harmonic twists.

The other church music of the much-travelled Steffani (1654–1728), though well executed, seems to be somewhat more conventional. For example, his setting of 'Laudate Dominum', from his collection *Psalmodia vespertina* for two four-part choirs published in Rome in 1674, follows the *stile concertato* practice of the other Italians to the south, in which double choruses alternate with florid, imitative duets in a narrow harmonic range, analogous to his secular chamber duets, which were regarded in his days as models of their kind. His motets for one, two, and three voices display the same neat craftsmanship that was especially dear to the Germans, among whom he worked. These motets are closely related to those of Carissimi and Bassani, but Steffani's German environment is betrayed by a contrapuntal technique even more integrated and tidy, often delighting in canonic imitation and carefully balanced phrases. The motet 'Reginam nostram' shows a typical passage of this kind:[3]

Ex. 211

[1] Ed. C. Kennedy Scott (London, 1938) and Heinrich Sievers (Wolfenbüttel, 1956).
[2] Bologna, Civico Museo, MS. DD187; ed. Peter Smith (London, 1974).
[3] *Ausgewählte Werke von Agostino Steffani*, i, ed. Alfred Einstein and Adolf Sandberger, *Denkmäler der Tonkunst in Bayern*, vi, 2 (Leipzig, 1905), p. 150.

NAPLES

Two distinct types of church composition were characteristic of Naples in the eighteenth century, a phenomenon which serves to emphasize the curious dichotomy underlying the whole of Italian baroque sacred music. The decorated, even frivolous, style of the opera-house has moved many critics to wonder at the lax indulgence of the church authorities. The severe, but 'modern', contrapuntal style that flourished alongside it was largely the product of the famous conservatories. At the turn of the century Naples supported four of these. The Conservatorio de'Poveri di Gesù Cristo was then probably the most distinguished; here Alessandro Scarlatti taught Durante, who in turn taught Vinci and Pergolesi. The latter three had pupils at Santo Onofrio a Capuana, which produced Jommelli, Sammartini, Paisiello, and Piccinni. The Conservatorio di Santa Maria di Loreto was the celebrated 'Scuola di canto italiano': most of the great singers were trained here. It was led by Porpora (a pupil of Scarlatti), who taught Farinelli and was said to be the greatest singing-teacher of his time. In composition, however, the Conservatorio della Pietà dei Turchini came to the fore through the personality of Leo, who specialized in counterpoint and fugue. The polyphonic 'church style' of the later eighteenth century, with its modern view of harmony, owed much to his influence, through his pupils.

At first the Roman tradition to the north was powerfully felt in Naples. The Roman composer Pitoni, who has already been mentioned, was a keen student of Palestrina's music and also composed works for multiple choirs. Francesco Durante (1684–1755), who studied under him, wrote a Mass in the Palestrina style, which, however, resembles the earlier master only in its outward and visible aspect; the spirit is thoroughly eighteenth century in its D minor tonality and the square regularity of its sequences. Alessandro Scarlatti (1660–1725), who spent at least two periods in Rome, had already written eight out of his ten Masses in the *stile antico*; the severe style of his earlier Masses is softened in some of the others. In the attractive Mass in E minor written in 1706 for Cardinal Ottoboni, the sentiment, and the handling of harmony, including dissonance, are more attuned to his own time. Leo's eight-part *Miserere* of 1739 may have been inspired by the famous setting by Gregorio Allegri, which was annually performed in the Sistine Chapel from the 1620s. In Leo's work, also famous in its time, the 'old' style has taken on a melodic attractiveness and charm and a certain spirit of personal prayerfulness. Some of the cadences are prepared with a long pedal point, as in this example, which also gives an idea of the general character of the work:[1]

[1] Brit. Mus. Add. MS. 31616.

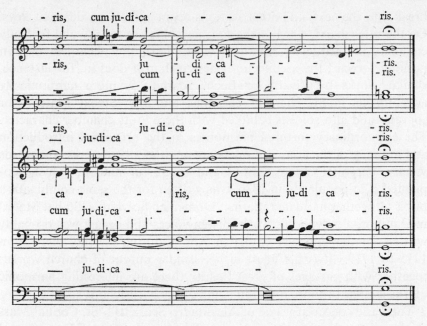

Writing for two choirs or more was nearly as common in Naples as it had been in Rome, but usually there was less massive competition between the choirs, and a larger element of fugue. These features are seen in Durante's eight-part Requiem[1] and in Pergolesi's two Masses, in D and F respectively; the F major Mass, written in 1732 for two five-part choirs and two orchestras, was arranged for Rome (1734) in a version for four choirs. A high proportion of Neapolitan choral works contain fugal sections in Leo's thorough but somewhat stolid manner. Plainsong continued to be used as an archaic effect by Durante, Leo, and Porpora. In a 'Dixit' in D by Durante,[2] probably composed in the 1740s, a plainsong theme is sung at the opening by the sopranos in unison, to a rhythmic orchestral accompaniment. (This work is quoted in Ex. 213.)

Alessandro Scarlatti wrote his two 'orchestral' Masses in 1707 and 1720 respectively. The latter, the A major 'St. Cecilia' Mass, and the Gradual 'Audi, filia',[3] its companion, display an experienced technique in the brilliant and incisive textures for voices and strings. There is much in common here with the large concertato works of the Bolognese, both in the taut dialogue between soloists and tutti and in the sectional overall planning of the whole. Sometimes one section leads without a

---

[1] Brit. Mus. Add. MSS. 14103, 14111, and 31611.

[2] Brit. Mus. Add. MS. 14101, fo. 75; this is the second of two settings in D of this text by Durante.

[3] Both ed. John Steele (London, 1968).

break into the next, and other sections begin and end in different keys. On the other hand, some of the solo numbers are tonally and formally complete in themselves. In these works harmony plays less part in pushing forward the architectural design than it does in, for instance, similar works by Vivaldi or Bach. Scarlatti is more harmonically adventurous in his chamber cantatas, and the 'Stabat Mater'[1] for soprano and alto soloists is linked with these in its chamber character. The extraordinary tortured harmonies in the orchestral introduction and in many of the arias and duets are an attempt to express the words vividly. Pergolesi's more famous and successful version,[2] which supplanted it in popularity in 1736, was written for the same combination but is altogether more ingratiating. Domenico Scarlatti's 'Stabat Mater' in C minor, a polyphonic work for ten voices and organ, was probably written for the Cappella Giulia in Rome, during his stay there from 1715 to 1719.[3] It is the finest in his slender output of church works; together with passages of great beauty there are interesting harmonic quirks similar to those found in some of his harpsichord sonatas.

The tense concertato style of Alessandro Scarlatti's 'St. Cecilia' Mass slackened considerably in the longer choral movements of Durante and Leo, written in the 1740s and 1750s. The chorus parts became a simpler foil to the florid parts of the soloists. An unorthodox arrangement of the vocal lines is found in many of Durante's scores, emphasizing the high priority the Neapolitans gave to their opera singers. For instance, in his eight-part Requiem, already referred to, the two soprano staves are written out together over the other six parts, which are divided into two three-part choirs. The sopranos, in a duet above, often sing independently of the others in a flamboyant but easy-going style, largely consisting of thirds and sixths. Graceful curves and flourishes typical of the *galant* style inform Durante's arias, which require a high standard of vocal bravura; a soprano aria from his second D major 'Dixit', also mentioned above, affords an example:

Ex. 213

[1] Ed. Felice Boghen (Milan, 1928).

[2] *Opera omnia*, xxvi (Rome, 1942), p. 1; recent editions include the Eulenburg miniature score ed. Einstein (London, 1949) and that of Philipp Mohler (Mainz, 1954).

[3] Ed. Alfredo Casella (Rome, 1941).

27

The long Mass and psalm movements of Nicola Porpora (1686–1768) are similar in scale and content to those of Durante and Leo, but the great singing-master demands even more vocal agility. He spent some years in Venice and wrote motets in the 1740s for the female pupils of the Ospedale della Pietà and the Ospedaletto, where Vivaldi also worked. It seems to be no accident, therefore, that in his 'Laetatus sum' for two choirs and orchestra (1742)[1] the structural plan and brilliant violin figurations are directly reminiscent of Vivaldi's concertos, such as that in A minor, Op. 3, no. 8, for two violins and strings.

The change from late baroque to *galant* style in this type of church music has already been noted. The influence of *opera buffa* is unmistakable: the same thin textures, pulsating basses and brief, repeated melodic motives are found in the sacred arias. A 'Laudate pueri' for four voices and strings composed by Durante in the 1730s[2] would make a hilarious *buffo* finale if transferred to the opera-house. Another interesting sidelight here is the link with Domenico Scarlatti's keyboard sonatas: many turns of phrase and harmonic and rhythmic effects in Neapolitan church music are clearly echoed in them, and the two genres have the *opera buffa* style as their common denominator.

The early symphonies by Viennese composers in the 1740s emphasize another connection with Neapolitan church music, in the use of the orchestra. Durante, Leo, and Porpora often include two horns, and sometimes flutes, with strings and oboes in their scores, and also make use of Bolognese trumpet techniques. The orchestral writing has generally become weightier. *Forte* and *piano* indications are common. An anticipation of the 'Mannheim crescendo' is seen at the beginning of Pergolesi's Mass in F: an impressive vocal crescendo is effected by piling up the notes of the prolonged opening chord by entries alternating between the two choirs.

Pergolesi (1710–36) has had many more compositions attributed to him than he could possibly have found time to write during his short life. Many of the instrumental and secular vocal works have been proved to be spurious,[3] and only a fraction of the church music that has been published under his name seems to be authentic. The two Masses[4] are both 'short', with *Kyrie* and *Gloria* only. They have much in common in their basic ground-plan and material (no. 5, the duet 'Domine

[1] Brit. Mus. Add. MS. 14128, fo. 40.

[2] Brit. Mus. Add. MS. 14107, fo. 159.

[3] See Frank Walker, 'Two centuries of Pergolesi forgeries and misattributions', *Music and Letters*, xxx (1949), p. 297, mainly on the secular music.

[4] They are in *Opera omnia*, xv.2 and xviii (Rome, 1941), respectively. See Francesco Degrada, 'Le messe di G. B. Pergolesi: problemi di cronologia e d'attribuzione', *Analecta Musicologica*, iii (1966).

Deus', is common to both), but the second, F major one is the finer.
Leo, who was lukewarm in his feelings about the first, publicly praised
the second, which seems to have been written in honour of S. Emidio
after the deliverance of Naples from a serious earthquake, and performed annually thereafter. The 'Gloria in excelsis' from the Mass in D
enjoyed a great vogue in England during the nineteenth century, in all
manner of arrangements.

One of Pergolesi's happiest characteristics, contributing to the grace
and elegance of his arias and duets, is his fondness for phrases of
irregular lengths—a subtlety that his imitators often missed. Perhaps
the most expressive and moving of his sacred pieces are the two settings
of the 'Salve Regina', respectively in A minor and C minor. The small-
scale church works of the Neapolitan composers generally seem to be
the most successful, especially when an emotional text fired their
imagination. For example, Durante's motet 'Misericordias Domini' for
double choir and 'Nunc Dimittis' (1749) for five voices with strings[1] are
pieces of considerable beauty. Leo, however, emerges as a man of
greater stature than Durante. His four-part *Credo* with two violins[2] and
'short' Mass in F[3] are both works of larger dimensions, which
successfully combine personal sentiment with considerable architectural
strength.

(d) CHURCH MUSIC IN CENTRAL AND
EASTERN EUROPE

By GERALD ABRAHAM

POLAND

The firm establishment of an Italian tradition of church music in
Poland under the Vasa kings, Sigismund III and Ladislas IV, has been
described in the preceding volume.[4] The accession of John Casimir in
1648 brought to an end the line of Italian masters of the royal chapel—
Asprilio Pacelli, Giovanni Francesco Anerio, Marco Scacchi—who
had held sway for half a century, but their Polish successors in the office,

---

[1] Brit. Mus. Add. MS. 14107, fos. 89 and 46 respectively.
[2] Brit. Mus. MS. Egerton 2453.
[3] Brit. Mus. Royal Music MS. 24.b.3.
[4] Vol. IV, pp. 304 ff.

Bartłomiej Pękiel (d. *c.* 1670) and Jacek Różycki (*c.* 1630–*c.* 1707)—continued the twofold tradition of *a cappella* and concertante church music. They were troubled times; John Casimir was driven into exile by a Swedish invasion in 1655, and Pękiel left Warsaw at the same time, but when the king returned in 1657 Pękiel soon went to the cathedral at Cracow, and Różycki succeeded him as master of the royal chapel. He was the last of the line, for when Augustus II, Elector of Saxony, was elected to the throne of Poland in 1697 the Polish royal chapel was amalgamated with the electoral court chapel in Dresden, where Różycki had to share the directorship with Johann Christoph Schmidt.

A great deal of Pękiel's church music is *a cappella*;[1] one of his Masses is actually inscribed, though not in his own hand, 'in the manner of Palestrina' (this is the *Missa pulcherrima ad instar Praenestini* of 1669).[2] But now and again he writes a continuo part, as in the five-part 'Dulcis amor',[3] and in two of his Masses he introduces instruments. The *Missa concertata La Lombardesca a 13*[4] is a magnificent ceremonial composition for two four-part choirs, two violins, three trombones, and organ, obviously written for some royal occasion, almost certainly for the arrival in Poland, or the coronation, of Ladislas IV's second wife, Maria Gonzaga, in 1646. Pękiel's music is not without Polish traits. It was natural that his *Missa paschalis* of 1662[5] should be based on the Easter hymn 'Christus Pan zmartwychwstał' (Christ the Lord is risen); others, including Marcin Leopolita,[6] had used such tunes before him, but two delightful short works, independent settings of the *Credo* on *rotuły* (Christmas songs) (1661–4),[7] have no known precedents. In the first a number of Latin and Polish Christmas melodies are strung together to form a tenor *canto fermo*; in the second, fragments from a similar collection, some of them the same, are used more freely. Thus the melody 'Nuż my, dziatki, zaśpiewajmy' (Here, children, let us sing) appears in both:

---

[1] See the motets published in the volume *Muzyka staropolska*, ed. Hieronim Feicht (Cracow, 1966), pp. 134, 138, 141, and 146, and in the series *Wydawnictwo dawnej muzyki polskiej*, ed. Feicht and Zygmunt Szweykowski, nos. 19 and 52, all probably written for the Roranists at Cracow during the last decade of his life, and the four Masses in the same series, nos. 17, 58, 62, and 69.

[2] *Wydawnictwo*, no. 17.

[3] Printed in the volume *Muzyka w dawnym Krakowie*, ed. Szweykowski (Cracow, 1964).

[4] *Kyrie*, ibid., p. 157. Another manuscript, Gdańsk, Bibl. Państ. Akad., Joh. 406, has different instrumental parts: two violins, viola bassa, two cornettini, bombardo and bassoon, the work of a later hand.

[5] *Wydawnictwo*, no. 58.

[6] See Vol. IV, p. 301.

[7] *Wydawnictwo*, no. 52.

Ex. 214

Pękiel's most interesting work and also one of his finest is the *dialogus* 'Audite mortales' for six soloists, three viols, and continuo, the earliest Polish example of the form known.[1] It successfully integrates dramatic,

[1] See Feicht, '"Audite mortales" Bartłomieja Pękiela', *Kwartalnik muzyczny*, i (1929), p. 366, though this study is based solely on Berlin, Deutsche Bibl., MS. 16900. Szweykowski's edition, *Wydawnictwo*, no. 4, is based on Upsala, Univ., MS. 83; the differences are discussed in his introduction; e.g. the bass A in bars 7–8 of Ex. 215 is A flat in the Berlin version, and the continuo is fully figured throughout.

polyphonic, and concertante techniques, and pictorial coloratura (for instance, a three-bar passage for the first alto illustrating 'Ecce tuba canit') is contrasted with poignant expression of emotion:

Ex. 215

Heu me mi - se - rum! Quid di - cam co - ram te ve - re

Viols

(+ B.C.)

Ju — di - ce?   Cla - ma - bo, cla - ma -

- bo, qua - re ja - cens con - su - mor.

The work of Różycki and the Piarist Father Damian Stachowicz (1658–99) represents a rather later style. Różycki wrote a number of four-part *a cappella* hymns[1] but generally preferred a more lively and florid concertante idiom, as in the two *Concerti de Sanctis a 3* (1674)[2] for three voices with continuo; his 'Confitebor'[3] introduces two violins,

---

[1] Nine in *Wydawnictwo*, no. 3.   [2] Ibid., nos. 16 and 44.   [3] Ibid., no. 60.

and the *Concerto de Martyribus*, 'Iste sanctus' (1676)[1] has three-part strings—violins and gamba—alternating with three-part voices—alto, tenor, bass. The 'Alleluia' of 'Iste sanctus' is typical of his cheerfully quasi-secular vein:

Ex. 216

[1] *Muzyka staropolska*, p. 216.

which is paralleled in Stachowicz's 'Veni, Consolator' for solo voice and trumpet:[1]

Ex. 217

[1] *Wydawnictwo*, no. 13.

The Italianate concertante style also characterizes the work of the Cistercian father Stanisław Szarzyński, the copies of whose compositions date from the period 1692–1713. Most of them are 'concertos' for one or two voices and instruments;[1] the motet 'Ad hymnos, ad cantus'[2] is similar in style but on a larger scale. He also left a *Missa septem dolorum Beatae Mariae Virginis* and a Completorium (the psalms, hymn, and canticle for Compline on Sunday).

The removal of the royal chapel to Dresden was naturally a blow to Polish church music, but Cracow, with its cathedral of the Wawel and the great Chapel of the Jesuits, resumed the place it had held up to 1596 as the cultural capital of the country. The master of the cathedral choir from 1698 until his death was Grzegorz Gorczycki (*c.* 1667–1734), the outstanding Polish composer of the late baroque period. Although a younger man than Różycki, Stachowicz, and Szarzyński, he was much more liable to revert to severe *a cappella* writing, as did his Italian and Austrian contemporaries, Fux, Lotti, and Leo.[3] The *Benedictus* of his *Missa paschalis* is actually based on a long-note *canto fermo*—though the *canto fermo* is Polish, the traditional 'Christus Pan zmartwychwstał'. Sometimes he mildly colours the music by the addition of a pair of violins, as in his introits 'Justus et palma' and 'Os justi' (plainsong *canti fermi* in the bass)[4] and hymns[5] (which borrow more freely from plainsong). But on the rare occasions when he adopts the concertante style, as in his Completorium[6] and the 'concerto' 'Laetatus sum"[7], he does so with festive brilliance enhanced by a pair of trumpets. The same may be said of Wincenty Maxylewicz (1685–1745),[8] who directed the cathedral choir from 1739 until his death, Staromieyski (d. *c.* 1737),[9] the leading Jesuit composer, and the more fully scored Masses and other works of the Paulite Brother Marcin Żebrowski (1702–70).[10]

TALO-POLISH INFLUENCE IN RUSSIA

During the last quarter of the seventeenth century Italo-Polish influence even reached Russia, which had only recently begun to use staff-notation and, in consequence of the Patriarch Nikon's ecclesiastical

[1] Examples in ibid., nos. 5, 10, 25, and 50.
[2] Ibid., no. 26.
[3] Cf. his *Missa paschalis*, *Wydawnictwo*, no. 7, and 'Judica me', *Muzyka w dawnym Krakowie*, p. 242.
[4] Both in *Wydawnictwo*, no. 63.
[5] 'Crudelis Herodes' in *Muzyka staropolska*, p. 239.
[6] Ed. Jan Węcowski, *Zródła do historii muzyki polskiej*, vii (Cracow, 1963).
[7] *Wydawnictwo*, no. 37, and *Muzyka w dawnym Krakowie*, p. 225.
[8] 'Gloria Tibi Trinitas', in *Muzyka w dawnym Krakowie*, p. 246.
[9] Excerpts from his *Vesperae de Sanctis*, ibid., p. 260, and in *Florilegium Musicae Antiquae*, ed. Tadeusz Ochlewski, xvi.
[10] *Magnificat*, *Wydawnictwo*, no. 64, and 'Salve regina', ibid., no. 68.

reforms, to practise 'Kiev part-singing' in church, in the manner of the Ukrainians and Poles. The Treaty of Andrusovo in 1667 inaugurated a period of relatively friendly contact between Poland and Russia, and about 1680 there appeared in Moscow an Ukrainian musician, Nikolay Diletsky, who had studied in Poland with Marcin Mielczewski[1] and now took with him to Russia a knowledge of the Venetian and Polish poly-choral music of an earlier period and a somewhat imperfect under-standing of Zarlino's *Istitutioni harmoniche*. Diletsky had already tried to convey the latter in Polish in his *Gramatyka muzyczna* (Vilna, 1675), of which the first Russian version appeared two years later (Smolensk, 1677); when he settled in Moscow as director of Count Stroganov's private choir he brought out a revised version,[2] a work which, with all its limitations, had an enormous effect on the course of Russian church music. Diletsky himself was a composer of no great distinction,[3] but he conveyed the concepts of canonic imitation, polychoral effects, and the contrasting of solos with *ripieni* to a considerable number of pupils, the most important of whom were Vasily Titov (*fl. c.* 1680–1710) and Nikolay Kalashnikov. These and other composers poured forth a profusion of services, vespers, hymns, and *dukhovnïe kontsertï* (sacred concertos), mostly in twelve parts and sometimes in twenty-four. The voices were usually divided into four-part choirs singing antiphonally (a condition which has been obscured by the erroneous scoring of nearly all modern transcriptions), though sometimes they sing continuously together or the antiphony is between choirs of different pitch. All these compositions are unbarred, though it is very easy to bar them sym-metrically, and a much more serious difference from Western 'concertos' was the lack not only of concertante instruments but also of continuo support. This excerpt from a twenty-four-part concerto by Kalashnikov[4] is characteristic (see Ex. 218). The technical crudities would have been unperceived and if perceived would have meant nothing, but such effects of mass and contrast must have been overpoweringly impressive to ears accustomed to monophonic *znamenny* chant[5] and the simple note-against-note counterpoints to it that had come into use a century or so earlier.

---

[1] See Vol. IV, pp. 307–8.

[2] Modern edition, ed. Stepan V. Smolensky (St. Petersburg, 1910).

[3] See Yury Keldïsh, *Russkaya muzïka XVIII veka* (Moscow, 1965), pp. 54, 55, and 64, for specimens of his work.

[4] Rescored from Tamara Livanova, *Ocherki i materialï po istorii russkoy muzïkalnoy kulturï* (Moscow, 1938), p. 120; the treble part of the second choir is lost. Livanova gives no text, but the piece seems to be a 'Kheruvimskaya' ('Cherubim . . . singing to the Trinity their thrice-holy song') with a possible underlay on the lines suggested.

[5] See Vol. II, pp. 52–7.

Ex. 218

I - zhe kheru - vi-mï ta - y-no o - bra - zu - yu - shche, I - zhe kheru -

BOHEMIA

The political and cultural position of Poland after the election of a Saxon king had been anticipated seventy years earlier in Bohemia. But the situation there was much worse. It was not merely that a monarch foreign to a large proportion of the people, a Habsburg, made a foreign city, Vienna, the cultural capital of his dominions and reduced Prague to the status of a provincial town; a great number of Czechs were persecuted or driven into exile for political and religious reasons, and the German-Bohemians became hardly distinguishable from Austrians; even the Czech nobility turned towards Vienna. Nevertheless, there were Czech composers of Latin church music who at the same time remained always mindful of their national traditions. By far the most important of these was Adam Václav Michna (*c.* 1600–76), who continued the tradition of simple vernacular religious songs in his *Czeská Maryánska muzyka* (Prague, 1647),[1] *Lautna čzeska* (Prague, 1653), and *Swato-Ročnij Muzyka* (Prague, 1661), and also produced a collection of *Officium vespertinum sive Psalmi vespertini, cantica B. Virginis, Antiphonae, Litaniae . . . vocibus aliis et instrumentis intercinentibus* (Prague, 1648), of which only the soprano part has survived, *Sacra et litaniae a 5.6.7.8. vocum cum instrumentis* (Prague, 1654), containing five Masses and a Requiem,[2] *Litaniae de BMV* and *de ss. nomine Jesu*, and a *Te Deum* for double chorus. Michna was not the pioneer of the concertante style in Bohemia—he had been preceded by Jakub Kryštof Rybnický (*c.* 1600–1639), of whose eight-part *Missa concertata super Exaltabo Domine* only the cantus and continuo parts survive—but he was its most gifted exponent. The third of the Masses in *Sacra et litaniae* is a giant passacaglia on an eight-bar *ostinato* which is repeated fifty times, while the second is based on a Czech Christmas song, 'Již slunce z hvězdy vyšlo' (Already the sun has risen out of the star). These, however, are overshadowed by the Mass 'Sancti Wenceslai',[3] probably composed in 1661 for the cathedral at Olomouc but never published in his lifetime. This is a Mass for some festive occasion, for six-part soloists and choir, two trumpets, two violins (or cornetts), four-part viols, and organ. There is a great deal of doubling of voices by strings, with trumpets used antiphonally. Quotation of the opening gives a good idea of Michna's method of working with concise themes:

---

[1] One example in Jaroslav Pohanka, *Dějiny české hudby v příkladech* (Prague, 1958), p. 76.

[2] 'Lacrimosa', ibid., p. 77.

[3] Ed. Jiří Sehnal in *Musica Antiqua Bohemica*, ser. ii, 1 (Prague, 1966).

Ex. 219

Michna devoted himself entirely to religious music, liturgical or domestic, but the leading composers of the later part of the century— Pavel Josef Vejvanovský (c. 1640–93), Václav Holan Rovenský (1644–1718), Jan Křtitel Tolar (fl. 1669–73)—cast their nets wider; indeed Vejvanovský and the Jesuit Tolar are more important as instrumental than as religious composers, and even Tolar's two Masses, 'sopra la Bergamasca' and Missa vilana, have a markedly popular, if not secular, flavour. Holan Rovenský published two a cappella Passions, according to Matthew and John (Prague, 1690 and 1692), a form generally neglected by Czech musicians. Except that these composers sometimes set Czech as well as Latin texts, there is little to distinguish them from their contemporaries, such as Biber and Antonio Draghi. As for such men as Nikolas Wentzely (Vencelius) (c. 1643–1722),[1] who held various posts in Prague, including that of Kapellmeister of the cathedral from 1688 to 1705, it is impossible to determine whether they were Czech or German; indeed Wentzely himself declared that he composed 'in stylo bohemico germanico';[2] the fact that he introduced the melody of the Christmas song 'Narodil se Kristus Pan' (Christ the Lord was born) into his Litania de ss. nomine Jesu proves nothing. Conversely Jan Dismas Zelenka (1679–1745), pupil of Fux, from 1729 Saxon-Polish court composer at Dresden (where he was held in high esteem by Bach), composer of Italian oratorios and numerous Masses, is typical of the emigrant Czechs who never lost touch with their homeland, while Josef Plánický (1691–1732) must be considered a Bavarian by adoption and a Neapolitan in style.[3]

More firmly rooted in his native soil, despite four visits to Italy, was Bohuslav Černohorský (1684–1742). He and his so-called 'school'[4]— Jan Zach (1699–1733?), František Tůma (1704–74), Josef Seger (1716–1782), and others—are generally, and rightly, considered as first and foremost instrumental and particularly organ composers. Yet all contributed a great deal to the music of the Roman rite, mainly in the florid, almost operatic idiom of the contemporary Viennese school. The 'Regina coeli' for solo voice, solo violoncello, and continuo by Černohorský[5] is typical:

[1] 'Salve Regina' from his Flores verni (Prague, 1699), which also contains five Masses and a Requiem, reprinted in Prager deutsche Meister, ed. Theodor Veidl, Das Erbe deutscher Musik, ii, Landschaftsdenkmale: Sudetenland, Böhmen und Mähren, 4 (Reichenberg, 1943).
[2] Preface to Flores verni.
[3] On his collection of solo motets in aria form, Opella ecclesiastica (Augsburg, 1723), see Camillo Schoenbaum, 'Die Opella ecclesiastica des Joseph Anton Planicky (1691?–1732): eine Studie zur Geschichte der katholischen Solomotette im Mittel- und Hochbarock', Acta Musicologica, xxv (1953), p. 39. Pohanka prints no. 2, op. cit., p. 88.
[4] See Otto Schmid, 'Die musikgeschichtliche Bedeutung der altböhmischen Schule Czernohorsky's', Sammelbände der internationalen Musikgesellschaft, ii (1900–01), p. 133.
[5] Pohanka, op. cit., p. 108.

28

Ex. 220

Re - gi - na coe - li lae - ta - - - re,

B.C.

6 6

Vc.

Re - gi - na coe - li lae -

unis.

- ta - - - re, lae - ta - - - - - -

6   ♮   6

- - - - - - re, Al - le - lu - ia,

5   6

♮6 ♮5

Zach, Tůma, and Seger wrote great numbers of Masses—Zach and Tůma more than thirty each—as well as church music in other forms. Tůma's 'Stabat mater'[1] manifests both expressive power and technical mastery, and Zach has been put forward[2] as the possible composer of the 'Tantum ergo' which Ludwig von Köchel numbered 142 in his original *Verzeichniss sämmtlicher Tonwerke W. A. Mozarts* (Leipzig, 1862).

HUNGARY

It is easily understandable why the other Habsburg kingdom, freed from the Turks and united only in 1699, contributed little or nothing to the music of the Roman Church—apart from the fact that a large part of the population were Protestant, Orthodox, or Uniat. The Masses and other pieces collected in tablature by the Transylvanian Franciscan Joannes Kajoni in his *Organo-Missale* of 1667[3] are very naïve and primitive, and the generally much more sophisticated collection of concertante church music, *Harmonia Caelestis*, published by Prince Paul Esterházy some forty years later (Vienna, 1711)[4] seems to consist largely of 'arrangements of vocal and instrumental compositions of the most heterogeneous origins',[5] by no means all Hungarian.

---

[1] Ed. Josef Plavec (Prague, 1959).

[2] By Robert Münster, 'Das Tantum ergo KV 142—eine Bearbeitung nach Johann Zach?', *Acta Mozartiana*, xii (1965), p. 9.

[3] See Bence Szabolcsi, *A magyar zenetörténet kézikönyve* (revised edition, Budapest, 1955), p. 25, English ed., trans. Sára Karig and Florence Knepler, *A Concise History of Hungarian Music* (Budapest, 1964), p. 41. Four examples in musical appendix, pp. 55–7, only two of these are given in the English edition, p. 129. The *Organo-Missale* is not to be confused with the so-called Kajoni Codex (lost since 1945), a collection of secular music.

[4] See Szabolcsi, op. cit., p. 26 (examples in appendix, pp. 50, 58, and 61); English ed., p. 42, examples pp. 126, 130, and 133; and idem, 'Probleme der alten ungarischen Musikgeschichte', *Zeitschrift für Musikwissenschaft*, viii (1926), p. 485.

[5] Schoenbaum in *Acta Musicologica* xxv, pp. 58–9.

VII

CHURCH MUSIC IN FRANCE

(a) 1630–60

By DENISE LAUNAY

HISTORICAL INTRODUCTION

IN the course of this troubled period in the history of France, church music takes on different, even contradictory, aspects which reflect the complexity of religious history. These must be set against a general outline of the situation, the chief features of which were the question of the relation of Catholics to the Reformed churches, the relationship of the Gallican Church to the Holy See, and the development of the Counter-Reformation in the monastic orders and among the clergy.

Armed conflicts between the Catholics and the Reformed churches ceased for the time being with the capture of La Rochelle in 1628. They were succeeded by an era of accommodation and of controversy before the stiffening of attitude which culminated in 1685 in the revocation of the Edict of Nantes.

This state of affairs had some effect on church music: among the Reformed churches, the Psalter in the vernacular, completed in the sixteenth century, was still used without notable change, and psalm singing was forbidden outside the act of worship. Among Catholics, sacred songs in the French language continued in fashion outside the liturgy.

Relations between the Gallican Church and the Holy See were still strained—less, however, than they had been under Henry IV. The religious question was reinforced by a political question: to the Roman (Ultramontane) party, supported by the Jesuits and by a small proportion of the higher clergy, was constantly opposed the Gallican party, which was upheld by Parliament and others and which feared the intrusion of Rome into the internal affairs of the state. It is for these reasons that the Council of Trent has never been officially accepted in France; the Assembly of the Clergy in 1615 alone and on its own responsibility decided to apply the findings of the Council.

These contrary tendencies showed themselves in music—in plainsong, for instance. During the half-century following the closing of the Council of Trent, the texts of the Roman Missal and Breviary underwent transformations that brought about the reform of the books with music (Graduals, Antiphonaries, Pontificals, Processionals, etc.). At the end of the sixteenth century, in imitation of what was going on at Rome, the French clergy decided to commission the printing of new books, including the collections with music, 'following the Roman use'. For many reasons, deriving from the Gallican opposition, the work of reform was carried on in some disorder: edition, whether officially sponsored or not, followed edition, revision followed revision, throughout the seventeenth century and even beyond. Few copies of the editions of this period survive. There are enough, however, for us to see the Roman influence behind the work that was done: the alteration of Gregorian melodies and of psalmodic rhythm, according to the taste of the humanists, advocates of a return to 'quantity' in liturgical Latin.

The effects of the Council of Trent were also felt on polyphonic church music, in two different directions: that of austerity, or of stripping down, which gives primacy to words over music (the Masses are the best example, since they are usually short and written in homophonic, syllabic style); and that of brilliance for everything concerning the glorification of the Eucharist (which is dominant in the motets and in settings of the *Te Deum*—a song of glory—and is expressed in the use of a concerto style and in double choruses).

From the point of view of the Counter-Reformation, the first period of activity was over. It had been dominated by two essential and great preoccupations: the sanctification of souls and the missionary apostolate (in France and abroad, even as far as Canada). These two themes animated reform alike among the monastic orders, the secular clergy, and the laity, a reform which continued until the middle of the seventeenth century. The spirit of penitence and abnegation which guided the reformers did not favour music at all. In the majority of the monasteries that were reformed it was forbidden to sing 'with notes', and to use instruments, even, sometimes, the organ. The reform of the secular clergy did not prove favourable to music either. Under the impetus of St. Vincent de Paul and others, priests were given a solid training: singing came last, after Latin, theology, liturgy, and doctrine, and could not, at this level, go beyond the rudiments.

Nevertheless, at this same period the cathedrals and the big urban parishes regularly maintained choir schools, which continued to ensure, as in preceding centuries, a rich employment of music in religious services. On occasions, use was made of musicians from outside: the Chapel Royal when it was on its travels, and groups of singers and instrumentalists for exceptional ceremonies such as the *Te Deum*, the consecration of bishops and the installation of abbots and of abbesses (even in the reformed convents), which were crowded with select audiences.

It must be said that the spirit of austerity which is at the root of the Counter-Reformation tended to relax progressively during this period. Although maintained even to the point of paradox in the circle of Port-Royal (until the signing of the Formulaire in 1656), elsewhere it softened little by little: the Benedictines of Montmartre asked Antoine Boësset to instruct them in singing; those of Faremoutiers had the organs repaired; the Fathers of the Oratory introduced polyphony into their services, which were regularly attended by the court; those of the Order of Mercy, the Carmelites of the Old Observance, and other orders, opened their churches to sacred concerts.

The difficult years of the Fronde, 1648–52, reduced musical activity, both sacred and secular. With the return of peace, the young king, Louis XIV, crowned in 1654, was soon a centre of attraction for all artists: around him, in the last years of Mazarin's ministry, was prepared the flowering of religious music which came about after 1661, when the king personally assumed supreme power.

LATIN MUSIC: INTRODUCTION

To avoid confusion in discussing the music, it seems preferable to distinguish between sacred music sung in Latin, intended for the celebration of Catholic services, and sacred music in French.

It is worth recalling that in the years 1630–60 the Catholic liturgy was made up, in large part, of the pieces sung in the course of the Canonical Hours. To these were added, especially after the Council of Trent, the motets sung at Benediction. Music intervened, besides, in the course of the additional liturgies so frequent at this period: *Te Deum*, processions, etc. Polyphony never had an official function in these ceremonies, since the church's song was monodic; depending on the circumstances, it was introduced into them by a more or less benevolent tolerance. It was substituted for plainsong, using the same words and based on the same melodies as themes. For this reason the true import of polyphonic church music can be grasped only through its relation to plainsong.

PLAINSONG

It has already been noted that in France plainsong had suffered the consequences of the great Roman reform which followed upon the Council of Trent. When in 1631–2 the Assembly of Clergy entrusted an association of booksellers with the task of publishing liturgical books (including the collections with notes) 'reformed by N.S.P.',[1] it was continuing work started in the last quarter of the sixteenth century: the unification of song in the church 'according to Roman use'. For sixty years financial advances were made to the association of booksellers. Copies of the Gradual, Antiphoner, and Psalter were on sale in 1636.

In terms of technique, it is possible to define the reformation of plainsong as concerning two points: the length of melismas, which were considered too long and which were now abbreviated; and the Latin prosody, which was judged defective and which was reformed for the better observation of quantity and for separating the syllables in accordance with its rules. It was in the name of erudition, in fact, that serious harm was done to plainsong, even to the point of giving it far more the appearance of mensural chant than of traditional Gregorian chant.[2] Melismas were abbreviated principally in the Alleluia verses and in many clausulae, which were often reduced to a single note. In spite of tradition, syllables were regrouped and neumes displaced, to avoid prolonging the breves to the detriment of the longs[3]:

Ex. 221

Ve - ni   Cre - a - tor   Spi - ri - tus   (1542)

becomes[4]

Ex. 222

Ve - ni   Cre - a - tor   Spi - ri - tus   (1615)

In accordance with this principle, as well, the values used for mensural music were introduced, in notated recitation in psalmody and even in melismatic chant:[5]

Ex. 223

Di   -   ri - ge   Do - mi - ne   (1574)

---

[1] See *Collection des Procès-verbaux des Assemblées générales du clergé de France depuis 1560* (Paris, 1767–78).

[2] For the history of the reform of plainchant in Rome see Raphael Molitor, *Die Nach-Tridentinische Choral-Reform zu Rom*, 2 vols. (Leipzig, 1901–2), and Karl Weinmann, *Das Konzil von Trient und die Kirchenmusik* (Leipzig, 1919). For the influence of this reform in France see Charles Dejob, *De l'influence du Concile de Trente sur la littérature et les beaux-arts chez les peuples catholiques* (Paris, 1884), and Amédée Gastoué, *Le Graduel et l'Antiphonaire romains* (Paris, 1913).

[3] *Pontificale secundum ritum S.S. Romanae Ecclesiae* (Loudun, 1542).

[4] *Pontificale romanum* (Paris, 1615).

[5] *Manuale sacerdotum* (Paris, 1574).

becomes[1]

Ex. 224

Di - ri - ge Do - mi - ne   (1646)

Some, like the Oratorians, went so far as to propose for the notation
of plainsong a choice of four long values: 'very [long], less, still less,
scarcely at all'.[2] Others suggested values 'of incommensurable inequality'.[3]

Thus disfigured, and assimilated to theatrical recitative, plainsong
became a mere caricature of itself.

FAUXBOURDON

Monodic plainsong seemed to the public of the day the 'poor relation'
of church music; it was reserved for times of penitence and for liturgies
of the dead. In cathedrals and in parish churches with choir schools,
services were made more solemn by the introduction of polyphonic
vocal music, ornamented to a greater or less degree according to the
solemnity of the occasion: between plainsong and 'music', fauxbourdon
constituted an intermediate rung. It can be defined as note-against-note
counterpoint clothing the Gregorian *canto fermo*. This style of chanting,
practised in Italy after the Council of Trent, was much in favour in
France in the seventeenth century: music in this way gave its brilliance
to the words without harming their comprehension, thus following the
wish of the Council. In 1636 Mersenne wrote that 'fauxbourdon commonly pleases more in churches and has more power over its hearers,
than figural counterpoint'.[4]

Now, everything so far said about the spoken rhythm introduced into
psalmody applies to fauxbourdon, which composers noted down with
the values of mensural music. This rhythm is no different from that
which was adopted at the time in secular songs—the *mesure d'air*—and
which was governed by the enunciation of the words. What was sung in
fauxbourdon? The psalms, the *Magnificat*, hymns, and certain sequences;
in general all strophic pieces and not those of the Proper, nor antiphons,
whose texts are continuous. In mid-seventeenth-century France the
fauxbourdons in use were those of Lassus, the *Octo cantica* of Jean de

[1] *Rituale parisiense* (Paris, 1646).

[2] François Bourgoing, *Brevis psalmodi ratio* (Paris, 1634), and *Le David françois* (Paris,
1641).

[3] J. Le Clerc, *Méthode courte et facile pour apprendre le chant de l'Église*, etc. (Paris,
Bibliothèque Nationale, Dep. de MSS., MSS. fr. 19103 and 20001–2).

[4] Marin Mersenne, *Harmonie universelle* (Paris, 1636–7) (facsimile, ed. François Lesure,
Paris, 1963, ii, p. 272).

Bournonville (1612 and 1625), and the harmonizations at the end of the *Airs sur les hymnes sacrez* (1623–55), whose music is probably by the Jesuit Charles d'Ambleville. Here is an example from a *Magnificat* by the latter published in his *Harmonia sacra, seu Vesperae* (1636):[1]

Ex. 225

(The Tenor part in Choir 1 and the Bass of Choir 2 are missing and have been supplied by the author.)

It is probable that many manuscript fauxbourdons used in parish churches have been lost.

POLYPHONIC MUSIC: INTRODUCTORY

At the summit of the hierarchy of services we find music composed in figural counterpoint, as opposed to the simple counterpoint of fauxbourdon. In the statutes and rules of the choir schools it was stipulated that on major feast days the Ordinary of the Mass should be sung 'in music' (either in alternation with the organ or plainsong, or composed throughout), and also the antiphons of Vespers, the *Magnificat* in its entirety, the antiphon to the Virgin, and the hymns. To these must be added numerous motets sung at the close of Vespers, in processions, at Benediction, in the course of Low Mass, or even on the occasion of unusual liturgies. At this time, the most diverse styles were practised; but this diversity, far from being accidental, was related directly to the liturgical function of the texts set to music. For this reason the Masses were very different from the motets.

[1] Cf. *infra*, pp. 421–2 and 426, for more on this publication.

MASSES

Which Masses made up the current repertoire of the choir schools in the middle years of the seventeenth century? We have information from various sources on this point. In spite of losses, the collection of printed Masses is still quite large; only slightly fewer Masses have survived in manuscript. A very useful source of information is provided by the sale catalogues of the publishing firm of Ballard, and especially by the lists published at the end of the period: up to the beginning of the eighteenth century they offered their clientèle of choirmasters a large quantity of Masses which dated from the previous century and had been reprinted to satisfy demand. The lists of purchases by the choir schools are also extremely instructive. We can fill out our information by consulting the manuscript catalogue of the collection of Sébastien de Brossard, as well as the chapter in the *Harmonie universelle* in which Mersenne enumerates religious music by his contemporaries.[1]

For long, under Louis XIII, performers remained faithful to composers of the preceding generations. Foreign composers such as Andreas Pevernage, Philippe de Monte, and Francisco Guerrero loomed large, but above all Lassus, whom all church musicians of the time took as their master: his Masses 'Ad placitum' and 'Domine Deus noster' were still being sung around 1630; and as late as 1707 the Ballards stocked ten of his Masses—proof that they were still in the repertoire. The latter was gradually enriched, however, with new Masses by young French composers—choirmasters or organists composing out of professional necessity. Few among them occupied the highest posts in the kingdom; and one may rightly be surprised that the masters of the royal chapel left so little printed music. For instance, four of the five Masses— three for four voices and 'Quam bonus Israël est' (number of voices not known)—of the most celebrated of them, Eustache Du Caurroy, choirmaster to Henry IV, are lost today; the only one surviving is his five-part Mass 'Pro defunctis', which remained in the repertoire until the eighteenth century for royal obsequies.[2] Mersenne could also write of Du Caurroy that 'all French composers see him as their master'. Of the works of Nicolas Formé (1567–1638), Du Caurroy's successor in office and a man greatly favoured by Louis XIII, Ballard printed only two Masses: one, 'in simple counterpoint for four voices', is lost; only the Mass for double chorus remains. This was published in 1638, just

---

[1] See *Catalogue des livres de musique théorique et pratique, vocale et instrumentale, tant imprimée que manuscripte, qui sont dans le cabinet du Sr. Sébastien de Brossard* (Paris, Bibliothèque Nationale, Dép. de la Musique, Rés. MS. Vm. 20); and Mersenne, op. cit., iii, bk. vii, pp. 61 ff. (also trans. Roger E. Chapman as *Harmonie universelle: the books on instruments*, The Hague, 1957, pp. 560 ff.); also see i, préface générale (unpaginated).

[2] Ed. É. Martin and J. Burald (Paris, 1951); see also Vol. IV, p. 253.

before the death of its composer, who was very proud of it and prided himself on being the first in France to compose in this polychoral style—in which, however, Du Caurroy had anticipated him.[1] No other director of the Chapelle Royale had any Masses printed.

It was other choirmasters who provided the Ballard presses with their harvest of polyphonic Masses—those who received financial aid from some powerful protector or those who wished to offer a collection of printed Masses to some important chapter to support an application for a vacant choirmastership. Thus in 1626 Jean Titelouze, the organist of Rouen cathedral, offered the chapter a collection of his Masses (now lost). Besides the Mass 'In ecclesia', which was printed by Ballard, there was performed in 1632 another Mass by Titelouze, 'with two choruses with symphony', under the vaulted roof of Notre-Dame, Rouen, 'where four large stages had been constructed'; this Mass is also lost. Jean de Bournonville published in 1619 his *Missae tredecim*, which were sung right to the end of the century. His Masses, written in four or five parts with a very simplified figural counterpoint, usually syllabic, are characteristic of the religious style peculiar to the genre and to the period. He still used parody techniques after the end of the Council of Trent, which had condemned them so roundly; they appear in the Masses 'Le Rossignol', 'Dessus le marché d'Arras', 'J'ay senti les doux maux', 'La bataille française' (after Janequin), 'Par un matin d'été', and 'Narcisse'.

Pierre Lauverjat and Hugues de Fontenay were two more choirmasters who published Masses. The eight in four and five parts of the former, printed by Ballard between 1613 and 1623, were still on sale in 1707. Their success is justified because they are written in excellent (scarcely imitative) counterpoint and are very melodic, in the tradition of Lassus. Nothing survives of the three Masses of Fontenay, published between 1622 and 1625, although they remained in the repertoire almost as long as those of Lauverjat.

Almost all the Masses of Louis XIII's time resemble each other, like products of the same workshop: they show the same adoption of syllabic writing, the same lightly imitative counterpoint, the same feeling for tonality. There are, however, exceptions, such as the five-part Mass 'Pro defunctis' of Étienne Moulinié, published in 1636;[2] from his pen, practised in writing court *airs*, flowed fugal counterpoint worthy of Claude Le Jeune or Du Caurroy. Such also are the two Masses of d'Ambleville, one in four parts, the other in six, included in his already

---

[1] The *Sanctus* and *Agnus Dei* have been ed. Gastoué (Paris, n.d.). See Denise Launay, 'Les Motets à double chœur en France dans la première moitié du XVIIème siècle', *Revue de musicologie*, xxxix-xl (1957), p. 173.

[2] Ed. Launay (Paris, 1953).

mentioned *Harmonia sacra* of 1636: the counterpoint has beautiful melodic outlines.

One name in this period rises above those of his contemporaries for all sacred music, including Masses: that of Guillaume Bouzignac. The work of this southerner, which remained in manuscript,[1] comprises three Masses, one in five parts in traditional counterpoint, another in seven parts in the Italian concerto style, the third for two female voices with an obbligato organ part. Particularly remarkable is the seven-part Mass, which, by introducing some solos in dialogue with the tutti, produces a double-chorus effect, as in this extract from the *Gloria*:

Ex. 226

---

[1] Bouzignac's works survive in two manuscripts: Tours, Bibliothèque Municipale, MS. 168; and Paris, Bibliothèque Nationale, Dép. de la Musique, Rés. MS. Vma. 571. See the

In the two-part Mass the syllabic writing that predominated to excess in sacred music gives way to luxuriantly embellished lines wholly exceptional in France at that time.

Shortly after the publication in 1638 of the double-chorus Mass of Formé, music publishing seemed to pick up again, and Ballard's presses produced a large number of Masses by contemporary composers, choirmasters like their predecessors: Annibal Gantez of Marseilles, who was always seeking new posts; Artus Aux-Cousteaux, under the protection of President Molé; and Henri Frémart, languishing in Rouen and ambitious to direct the music at Notre-Dame, Paris.

With the four- and six-part Masses of Gantez (1641) and the eight Masses of Frémart (1643–5) there is still no escape from syllabic, tonal counterpoint. With Aux-Cousteaux and his *Huit Messes sur les huit tons* (1643–54) the style sometimes assumes a forthright manner that gives his *Kyries* and *Glorias* the feeling of drinking songs, as in this excerpt from his *Missa quinti toni*:

Ex. 227

---

article on him in *Die Musik in Geschichte und Gegenwart*, ii (1952), cols. 170–3, which is complemented by the introduction to Launay, *Anthologie du motet latin polyphonique en France (1609–1661)* (Paris, 1963).

In spite of the troubles of the Fronde the years of the regency of Anne of Austria were fairly favourable for the publication of religious music and especially of Masses. Although the royal choirmasters Thomas Gobert, Eustache Picot, and Jean Veillot continued to refrain from publication, their less highly placed colleagues made up for them. These were masters of the Paris cathedral choir school such as Pierre Cheneveuillet (whose three four-part Masses are lost) and François Cosset, composer of eight Masses in from four to six parts in excellent, solid, harmonious counterpoint (published between 1649 and 1682); or Paris musicians, like the organist Nicolas Métru (one of Lully's teachers), whose four-part Mass 'Brevis oratio', published in 1663, is lost; or provincials, such as Charles d'Helfer, author of eight Masses in from four to six parts, published between 1653 and 1669, and republished down to 1729, whose Mass 'Pro defunctis', published for the first time in 1656, was sung as late as 1774 in the basilica of St. Denys on the occasion of the funeral service to the memory of Louis XV, who had died four months earlier. The opening of this Mass gives a good idea of its general style:[1]

Ex. 228

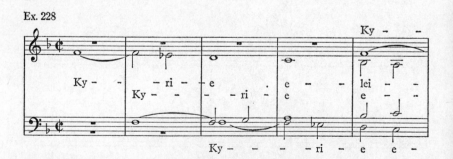

[1] Louis XV's courtiers apparently found the counterpoint of this Mass too strict, since it was given an instrumental accompaniment that effectively blotted it out. There are two different versions of this arrangement at the Bibliothèque du Conservatoire, Paris. See Launay, 'A propos d'une Messe de Charles d'Helfer', *Les Colloques de Wégimont*, iv: *Le Baroque musical* (1963), p. 177.

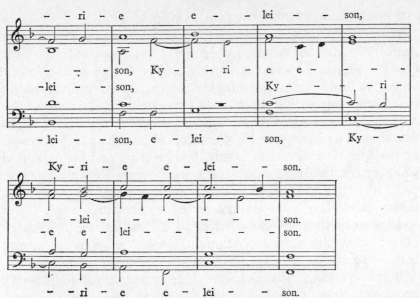

To the same period probably belong three undated manuscript Masses,[1] copied in score with the name 'Boësset' at their head. The question of the likelier first name has been much discussed: can it be Antoine (*c.* 1585–1643), superintendent of the King's Music; or his son Jean-Baptiste (1614–85), who succeeded his father in that office? Brossard was inclined towards the attribution to Jean-Baptiste, which is probably the right one.[2] Of these Masses, two are in lightly imitative counterpoint (*Messe à 4 voix du 4ᵉ mode*; *Messe du tiers*, in four parts alternating with plainsong). The third, in five parts, introduces a solo soprano in dialogue with the chorus, with lively rhythms; such music looks forward to works such as Marc-Antoine Charpentier's *Messe de Minuit pour Noël* much more than it recalls the graceful melancholy of the *airs de cour* of Antoine Boësset.

While at this time in France the severe style, more or less impregnated with tonality and consonant harmony, was becoming established, the young Charpentier was studying under Carissimi in Rome. There he copied out Masses for four choirs, and he learned the art of pitting soloists against tutti, of producing dramatic effects and of mingling orchestra and voices. Everything that Bouzignac had already sketched out was to be introduced into France by Charpentier towards the end of the century, even into that most liturgical of forms, the Mass.

[1] Paris, Bibliothèque Nationale, Dép. de la Musique, Rés. MS. Vma. 571.
[2] For a discussion by Launay of the question of the attribution of these Masses and of the accompanying motets, see Norbert Dufourcq, *Jean-Baptiste de Boësset, 1614–1685* (Paris, 1962), pp. 57–63.

POLYPHONIC SETTINGS OF THE PSALMS

There were many polyphonic settings of the psalms at this time. This genre differed from fauxbourdon, which presented formulas which could be adapted to verses of varying lengths; it differed also from the motet, for it was part of the liturgical service, and its text had therefore to be completely audible. Such psalms were authorized for most solemn Vespers and were given different music for each verse. The composer was allowed a certain amount of freedom to introduce such procedures as the repetition of certain words, fugal entries, and highly imitative counterpoint. In his *Harmonia sacra, seu Vesperae*,[1] d'Ambleville compares directly one series of psalms, 'musicae simplicis, quam vocant falsum burdonum' with another series, 'musicae figuratae': the two series were written for two alternating choirs, but the first series is homophonic, the second contrapuntal, with verses independent of each other.

In this style Formé wrote excellent four-part verses for the *Magnificat*, on all eight tones; here is an extract from those on the second tone:[2]

Ex. 229

---

[1] Also cf. *supra*, pp. 419 and 421–2.
[2] Formé, *Le Cantique de la Vierge Marie selon les tons, ou modes usitez en l'Église, mis à 4 parties* (Paris, Bibliothèque Nationale, MS. fr. 1870).

D'Ambleville's sequence of verses in five parts, also for the *Magnificat* (*Octonarium sacrum*, 1634), are much richer than those in his *Harmonia sacra*; Aux-Cousteaux's *Psalmi aliquot* (1631) also contains polyphonic psalms for from four to six voices. The composers of the following period seem not to have been tempted by this genre; they were more attracted by the freedom that the motet and the motet-psalm offered them.

MOTETS

The motet has no fixed function in the liturgy. In the sixteenth and seventeenth centuries its presence in the course of solemn Mass was tolerated during moments of silence—after the Epistle, during the Offertory, after the Consecration.[1] A motet was sung at the end of Vespers and Compline; it was very suitable for filling in gaps in special ceremonies. But its chosen place, especially after the Council of Trent, was during Benediction. When they were by skilful composers, motets were even to be heard outside the liturgy: those of Moulinié and of Henry Du Mont were undoubtedly sung at private concerts in the homes of noblemen or the composers themselves. In motets the composer enjoyed greater freedom of invention than in the Mass or in psalms, and his piety could be expressed in a more subjective manner.

The small quantity of printed motets surviving from this period can be explained not by a lack of interest in this form—hardly likely at the time of St. Vincent de Paul and Port-Royal—but rather by the very high cost of music-printing. From what remains, both printed and in manuscript, we may conclude that several types of motets were in use at this time.[2] The majority of choirmasters continued to compose in the traditional style in figural counterpoint with or without a *canto fermo*. They wrote motets in this style for the musical prize festivals, the 'Puys', much in favour at Evreux, Le Mans, and other places, where the prize went to the most able and not to the most daring. Among the composers

---

[1] From the accounts of contemporary gazette-writers it would seem that even before Louis XIV motets were sometimes sung during Low Mass.

[2] For a selection see Launay, *Anthologie du motet latin*.

29

who excelled in this genre, several names survive: André Péchon, Bourgault, Pierre Tabart, Jean-Baptiste Boësset; but the majority of motets in this style, preserved in manuscript, are anonymous.

The concerted motet appeared first towards the middle of the reign of Louis XIII, about 1625. The motet for double chorus, with or without instruments, was no doubt known already and had been for some time, but not in this particular style, which was imported from Italy and which, in a dramatic and expressive style, set solos against the choruses. Once again it is Bouzignac who appears as the innovator. Coming from the south of France he certainly had some acquaintance with the work of the Italian madrigalists and also, perhaps, with the church music of Catalonia. He left in manuscript some hundred motets of great originality and real dramatic force, written with an expressive intensity unequalled at the time; Ex. 230 is an extract from 'O flamma divini amoris':

Ex. 230

The solo parts are not yet independent *airs*, as they were to be under Louis XIV; but by his liking for dialogue and contrasts, the plan of Bouzignac's motets looks forward to those of the great motets at the end of the century. Among the most characteristic are: 'Ex ore infantium', 'Cantate Domino', 'Gaudeamus omnes', 'Tu quis es?', 'Ave Maria', and 'Unus ex vobis'.[1]

Other composers attempted this concerted style, though with less originality than Bouzignac: Formé printed at the end of his Mass for double chorus, the motet to the Virgin, 'Ecce tu pulchra es',[2] also for choirs in dialogue, in which the brisk and lively style (Ex. 231) contrasts notably with the severity of the counterpoint of Péchon:

Ex. 231

[1] For modern editions of the first four of these pieces see ibid., pp. 85, 69, 94, and 100, respectively; also items in the series *Collection d'œuvres . . . du temps de Richelieu* (Paris, various dates).

[2] Idem, *Anthologie*, p. 106.

At the Chapelle Royale, Gobert wrote in 1646, complaining of his burden of work, to his friend Huygens and added that he was composing with two choirs, and four or five voices, opposing solos and tutti[1]. Unfortunately no motet by Gobert survives. His colleague Veillot (who is thought to have made use of the unpublished works of his predecessor, Formé) also wrote in the concerted style. Three of his motets have come down to us: one, copied on vellum in 1644, gives the *grand chœur* of an antiphon for All Saints, 'Angeli, archangeli'[2]; the *petit chœur* is unfortunately lost. The syllabic writing and dotted rhythm, in a lively tempo, make it typical of its time. The other two motets, preserved in a late copy (1697),[3] were probably composed and performed in 1659 and 1660: the hymn 'O sacris solemniis' and the prose 'Alleluia, O filii et filiae', motets for double chorus with solos, with a symphony providing interludes, already display the plan of the great motets of Versailles; the verses, independent of each other, are sung alternately by the chorus and the soloists. The melodic outline is a simple imitation of that of plainsong, with the rhythm modified. While close to the large-scale motet, Veillot's style still lacks the melodic development and melismatic writing found in that form.

Fettered by the excessive use of syllabic writing, church music had forgotten the long melisma on a single syllable which gives singers the

[1] See W. J. A. Jonckbloet and J. P. N. Land, *Musique et musiciens au XVIIe siècle: correspondance et œuvres musicales de Constantin Huygens* (Leyden, 1882), p. ccxvii.

[2] Paris, Bibliothèque Nationale, Dép. de la Musique, Rés. MS. Vm. 256.

[3] Paris, Bibliothèque du Conservatoire, Rés. MS. F. 542.

opportunity to display their talents. When Moulinié announced in the preface to his *Meslanges de sujets chrestiens* ... (published in 1658 under a privilege dated 1651) that the public would find in them bold innovations, he made no idle boast; for he introduced into the motet the secular charm of the melismas of court *airs*. In the five-part motets 'Domine, salvum fac regem', 'Amavit eum Dominus', and 'Veni, sponsa mea',[1] and in antiphons such as 'Dum esset rex' or 'Speciosa facta es', the melismas, though timid, borrow something from those in the airs of Michel Lambert; the following is a typical example from 'Cantemus Domino':

Ex. 232

We may suppose that the fashion was changing rapidly at this time because in 1652 the young Du Mont, from Liège, published in his *Cantica sacra* and in 1657 in his *Meslanges* motets which include excellent attempts at melodic solos;[2] in him can be detected Italian

---

[1] Launay, *Anthologie*, p. 191.
[2] Four of these motets are in ibid., pp. 128 ff. Cf. *infra*, pp. 446–9.

influence which had come to him in Belgium from German collections of religious music. From now on most of the elements that later make up the fabric of the grand, large-scale motet are brought together. Their co-ordination had to await the time when Louis XIV decided to encourage church music, to select his composers, and to impose his personal taste for the sumptuous and the brilliant.

SETTINGS OF FRENCH TEXTS

It remains to consider religious music in the French language which in this period, as in the preceding one, was an important branch of composition. No notable change had come about since the beginning of the century in the singing of the psalms by the Protestants. In spite of the official authorization, the service was conducted without pomp, without the solemn music in favour in the Reformed churches in England and Germany. 'The reign of Louis XIII is one of the periods during which the psalms were least often published in France; the Geneva editions issued after the Edict of Nantes (1605, 1606, 1618, etc.) were no doubt sufficient to meet current demand . . .'[1] This is sufficient to explain why the music of the psalms of the Reformed church was not renewed at this time.

On the contrary, it was on the Catholic side that various experiments were attempted. To understand what took place, we must look at the origins of the movement and recall that in the reign of Henry II Clément Marot's French verse translations of the psalms had an unprecedented literary and popular success. This version, together with the music that had been adapted for it, subsequently became the property of the Reformed church and was forbidden to Catholics. The latter, however, in a spirit of emulation also undertook to translate the Psalter. Jean-Antoine de Baïf was the first to undertake the task and gradually completed the translation of all the psalms, either in rhymed verse or in *vers mesurés*.[2] Of the poets who followed him, by far the most successful, because of his popularity with musicians, was Philippe Desportes: his psalms, two of which are in *vers mesurés*, were set to music until as late as 1650.[3] The following example is from a setting by Signac of Psalm 94, published in 1630 in *Cinquante psaumes . . . mis en vers français par Philippe Desportes*:

---

[1] Jacques Pannier, *L'Église réformée de Paris sous Louis XIII (1610–1621)* (Paris, 1922), p. 229.

[2] Cf. Vol. IV, p. 447.

[3] See André Verchaly, 'Desportes et la musique', *Annales musicologiques*, ii (1954), p. 271.

Ex. 233

Ve - nez, et nous ré - jou - is - sons Au Sei-

-gneur a - vec ré - vé - ren - ce;

(Come, let us rejoice in the Lord with reverence.)

PARAPHRASES

By the 1630s the new literary genre of the paraphrase tended to replace the literal translation of the psalms: among musicians the series of paraphrases by Antoine Godeau was welcomed the more warmly because Louis XIII himself had set several of them to music (which is lost). However, the way in which composers worked on these poems immediately gave rise to controversy.[1] Godeau, once a familiar of the Hôtel de Rambouillet, now Bishop of Grasse, wished to bring about the missionary ideal of the Counter-Reformation, to which he had been converted. When in 1648 he published the complete series of 150 paraphrases, the fruit of fifteen years' work, he indicated to musicians what he expected of them: on the one hand to substitute for the more or less bawdy songs of the public repertoire a choice of edifying words enhanced by beautiful tunes; and on the other hand to propagate the Christian doctrine and the psalms of David in the most distant lands by means of music. The musicians, thus invited to set to work, interpreted his advice in different ways: some who worked for the worldly public, for those who loved *airs de cour* and drinking songs, composed *airs* in the taste of the day in several parts; others, aiming at the lower classes, composed syllabic melodies for a single voice, imitated from Protestant psalms, which could be hummed at work.

[1] See Launay, '*La Paraphrase des Pseaumes* de Godeau et ses musiciens', *Revue de musicologie*, 1 (1964), p. 30.

The first to start work was Jacques de Gouy, canon of Embrun, a friend of Lambert, Moulinié, and La Barre; the *Cinquante airs à 4 parties sur la paraphrase des pseaumes de Godeau*, which he published in 1650, had no sequel, in spite of their musical qualities—which can be gauged from the opening of Psalm 15:

(Lord, since my hope lies in your help...)

since the publishers (and probably Godeau himself) thought the music adapted to the psalms too studied. On the other hand, during the following years, several series of paraphrases for solo voice, written syllabically, appeared one after the other: those of Antoine Lardenois in 1655 and 1658, those of Aux-Cousteaux in 1656, those of Gobert in 1659 (with a bass added in 1661). It is most surprising that the choirmaster of the Chapelle Royale, trained in polyphonic writing for double chorus, should have opted for the barest, most austere interpretation of Godeau's intentions:

Ex. 235
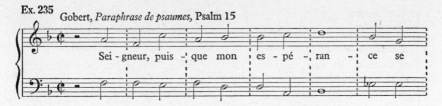
Gobert, *Paraphrase de psaumes*, Psalm 15

Sei - gneur, puis - que mon es - pé - ran - ce se

fonde en   ta seule   as - sis - tan - ce,

While de Gouy's *airs* remained without successor, Gobert's monodies were reprinted several times down to the time of the Revocation of the Edict of Nantes (1685): this is because these songs were used both by missionaries in their campaigns of reconversion and by the Protestants themselves, to whom the psalms of Marot and Théodore de Bèze were forbidden outside church.

There were, however, some attempts at a polyphonic interpretation of Godeau's *Paraphrase*. In 1658 Moulinié included in his *Meslanges* a vocal trio on Godeau's translation of the Canticle of Moses.[1] In 1663 Du Mont published a selection from the *Paraphrase* in his extremely beautiful *Airs . . . en forme de Motets*, with violin and *basso continuo*; Ex. 236 shows the opening of Psalm 32:

Ex. 236

Vn.

Sops.
1 & 2

Bass

A   pei - ne de nos   jours la   trame est -

B.C.

[1] Modern edition in the series *Collection d'œuvres . . .*

(Hardly is the course of our days ordained ...)

In these, as in Moulinié, the melismatic writing is remarkably developed.

OTHER FORMS

Any account of French sacred music at this period would be incomplete without some mention of two types of piece which seem to have had some vogue at the time: 'spiritual canticles' and parodies. By 'spiritual canticles' is meant, on the one hand, the *Quatrains moraux* of Pierre Matthieu (set to music by Jean de Bournonville in 1622 and by Aux-Cousteaux in 1643 and 1652), the *Noëls et cantiques spirituels* for two voices (1655) by Aux-Cousteaux, and the *Cantiques spirituels* of Denys Lefebvre, also in two parts (1660); and on the other hand, the French translations of Latin hymns such as those that the Jesuit Michel Coyssard had published in 1592, with music by Virgile Le Blanc, and which were revised and reprinted down to 1655. In these collections the canticles of the Old Testament mingle with rhymed translations of the 'Veni creator', the *Te Deum*, and the chief Latin hymns of the liturgy.

The four-part songs were reworked (by d'Ambleville?) in homophonic, syllabic style. It goes without saying that these *Airs sur les hymnes sacrez, odes et noëls ... pour chanter aux catéchisme* could also be performed by singing only the top part. The principal responsibility for missions rested with the Capuchins; and a Capuchin father, Irénée d'Eu, wrote for his brothers some 'spiritual canticles' which Denis Macé set to music (published in 1639 and reprinted in 1648).

The practice of re-using secular tunes with religious words had, of course, had a long history. Following many successful collections earlier in the century, the genre continued to flourish. François Berthod appears to have been a specialist in it, for between 1656 and 1662 he published three books of *Airs de dévotion à 2 parties*, in which airs by Lambert and other fashionable musicians were adapted.

If, from the musical point of view, there is a conclusion to be drawn from this study, it can be stated as follows. In this period preceding the personal reign of Louis XIV, sacred music in the concerto style encountered many kinds of obstacle that impeded its progress: a difficult political and religious situation, racked with serious crises; a decline in patronage; and above all the spirit of austerity that dominated the Counter-Reformation. But the deepest cause of this state of affairs seems to have been aesthetic: under the delayed influence of the Humanists, French music, secular as well as sacred, was for long subordinated to words. To avoid distorting enunciation it permitted the dominance of syllabic writing, which in turn paralysed the growth of melody. The perfect balance between melodic writing, reserved for soloists, and syllabic writing, characteristic of recitative, had to await the influence of Italian music.

(b) 1661–1750

By JAMES R. ANTHONY and NORBERT DUFOURCQ

INTRODUCTION

In the ninety years from Louis XIV's assumption of the throne in 1661 to the mid-eighteenth century, the art of religious music underwent a complicated process of development in France. Some essential features can be noted: the importance of certain centres of music in Paris (Notre Dame, the Sainte-Chapelle), in Versailles (the Chapelle Royale) and in the provincial cities of Aix, Arles, Toulouse, Strasbourg, Tours, Orléans, Meaux, Rouen, Chartres, and Amiens; the influence of the monarchy upon religious art; the drain of talent from the provinces to Paris; the proliferation of collections of religious *Gebrauchsmusik* composed for the many new convents founded in the wake of monastic reforms; and the pride of place accorded the *grand motet*.

Much of the church music composed in France during this period survives in the form of hundreds of printed and manuscript scores, several of which have not yet been thoroughly examined.[1] We are still plagued by losses that obstruct the study of religious music of the mid-seventeenth century. Where, for example, are the motets by Cambert alluded to by Robinet and Loret? Veillot's *Te Deum* is not extant. Performed in April 1660 for the double celebration of the Peace of the Pyrenees and the marriage of Louis XIV, it drew upon the king's *24 violons* as well as 'all the best instrumentalists of Paris'. It is tempting, though fruitless, to conjecture direct influence of this work upon the *Miserere* of 1664, the first of Lully's *grands motets*. Other lost works include the late motets of Étienne Moulinié, mentioned in the preface to his *Airs à 4 parties* of 1668, as well as the religious pieces he presumably composed to texts by the Abbé Perrin. We are fortunate, however, to have available most of the known sacred music by such masters as Henry Du Mont, Jean-Baptiste Lully, Marc-Antoine Charpentier, Michel-Richard de Lalande, François Couperin, André Campra, and Jean-Philippe Rameau and by other less well-known contemporaries.

In the previous section of this chapter we have seen the importance assumed by certain institutions in which church music was cultivated. Let us consider some of them in Paris, Versailles, and the provinces; then let us note general changes in style and turn, finally, to the works of specific composers.

GROUPS AND INSTITUTIONS IN PARIS

The history of the choir at Notre Dame has been partly told by François Chartier,[2] but there is still much to be learned of the part played by its singers. It was a stronghold of musical conservatism, its programme dominated by the 1662 *Ceremoniale parisiense*, in which the stern voice of the Council of Trent is heard again admonishing those who would use any instruments other than the organ in their churches.

Michel Brenet has described the social and musical conditions of the Sainte-Chapelle du Palais.[3] Its director, who was supposed to be celibate

---

[1] They can be found in libraries such as the Bibliothèque Nationale, Bibliothèque du Conservatoire and Bibliothèque Sainte Geneviève in Paris, the municipal library at Versailles and the library of St. Michael's College, Tenbury.

[2] François Chartier, *L'Ancien Chapitre de Notre-Dame de Paris et sa maîtrise, d'après les documents capitulaires, 1326–1790* (Paris, 1897; repr. Geneva, 1971).

[3] See Michel Brenet, *Les Musiciens de la Sainte-Chapelle du Palais* (Paris, 1910).

(as Charpentier was, though some, such as Nicolas Bernier, were not), was master of one of the most famous French choral establishments, which remained generally faithful to the *a cappella* tradition until late in the seventeenth century.

Parish churches in Paris were of two types: those which were attached to the past and had scanty musical resources, and those which looked to the future and, being well endowed, were not afraid of innovation nor of attracting the kind of congregation that demonstrated its advanced taste by showing a partiality for concertante music. Among the more adventurous, Saint Germain-l'Auxerrois is noteworthy as the parish church of the Louvre and thus as a royal parish. Its musical director in 1661 was François Chaperon, who was later appointed to the Sainte-Chapelle. He discovered and guided young Lalande and the no less talented Marin Marais. Bernier, like Jean François Lallouette before him, earned recognition at Saint Germain before promotion to the Sainte-Chapelle. Saints Innocents is another example of a church which, by its performance of music in the Italian style, attracted an audience that was increasingly appreciative both of fine singing and of instrumental *symphonies*. The convent at Longchamp and the conventual chapels of the Augustinians in the Place des Victoires, of the Jesuits in the Faubourg Saint Antoine, of the Feuillants, and of the Théatins, whose famous choir was directed for a time by Paolo Lorenzani, undoubtedly deserved the admonition of the pious Mme. de Maintenon that they had 'made an opera house of their church'. In his *Comparaison de la musique italienne et de la musique française,* Le Cerf de la Viéville paints a vivid picture of performances by popular singers at convents: 'They are paid to perform the most pious and solemn motets! Singers, who are placed behind a curtain which they draw apart from time to time to smile at friends among the listeners, are praised for singing a Good Friday lesson or a solo motet for Easter. . . . In their honour the price that would be charged at the Opera is charged for a seat in the church.'

THE ROYAL CHAPEL

In principle if not in practice, all these religious communities followed the guiding light of the Chapelle Royale, which had first been established in Paris (Louvre, Tuileries, Saint Germain-l'Auxerrois), then in Saint Germain-en-Laye (until 1670) and finally at both Versailles and Fontainebleau. After the first two private chapels at Versailles, about which our musical information is scanty, there were three successive ones. The first of these existed about 1672–82 in the Aile-de-la-reine, a great one-storey *salon*. The second, the official chapel used by Louis XIV for most of his reign, was founded in 1681 or 1682 and was in use until 1710. Designed on two levels, it was located in the Aile-du-roi on the site of the present Salon d'Hercule. In 1698 the king laid the foundation-stone of the Sainte-Chapelle of the palace of Versailles. It was inaugurated in 1710.

The Chapelle Royale was not simply a consecrated building; rather was it an institution, whose origins went back to the early sixteenth century. Around 1650 there were two musical directors, who served six-month terms, together with eight boys, a cornett-player, an organist, a lutenist to instruct the boys, and fourteen choristers, some of whom were clerics. In 1663 Louis XIV appointed four musical directors (Gobert, Robert, Expilly, and Du Mont), each to serve for one quarter of the year. They were known as *sous-maîtres*, the position of *maître* being a titular honour reserved for an archbishop or other church dignitary. In 1678 the king appointed four organists (Nivers, Lebègue, J.-D. Thomelin and J.-B. Buterne) each of whom held the post for a quarter. In 1683, after the retirement of Du Mont and Robert (Expilly had retired in 1668, Gobert in 1669), the king, eager to dramatize his personal interest in the music of his chapel, ordered a solemn competition to be held for the position of four *sous-maîtres*. Thirty-five musicians from all over the realm competed. Among them were Jean Mignon, Guillaume Minoret, Jacques Lesueur, Nicolas Goupillet, Paolo Lorenzani, Guillaume-Gabriel Nivers, Jean Rebel, Pascal Collasse, Henry Desmarest, Charpentier, and Lalande. Four *sous-maîtres* were chosen: Goupillet,[1] Collasse, Minoret, and Lalande. A 'consolation prize' in the form of a generous pension was awarded to Charpentier, who, the *Mercure galant* informs us, was 'extremely ill' at the time and could not participate in the final competition.

By 1712, according to Félix Raugel,[2] the Chapelle Royale boasted 88 singers (ten sopranos, twenty-four countertenors, twenty tenors, twenty-three baritones and eleven basses). In addition to strings, a harpsichord and the fine Clicquot organ completed in 1711, the instrumental complement now included three oboes, two transverse flutes, 'un gros basson à la quarte', and two serpents, as well as viole da gamba, perhaps the earliest violoncellos in France, *violini*, archlutes, crumhorns, and theorboes, which constituted an unparalleled 'batterie de basses' illustrating the French predilection for heavy doubling of the outer voices of the five-part texture. By the middle of the eighteenth century

---

[1] Goupillet (or Coupillet) was a mediocre musician from Senlis whose subsequent *grands motets* were ghost-written by Desmarest; when discovered, this ruse cost him his job in 1693.

[2] Félix Raugel, 'La Musique à la Chapelle de Versailles sous Louis XIV', *XVIIᵉ Siècle: Bulletin de la Société d'étude du XVIIᵉ siècle*, xxiv (1957), p. 25.

the country's economy was so reduced that in 1761 the musical resources of the royal chamber and chapel were pooled and the number of performers drastically pruned.

THE *CONCERT SPIRITUEL*

The *Concert Spirituel*, founded in 1725 by Anne Danican-Philidor, was the first permanent concert organization to give a series of subscription concerts on a commercial basis. The concerts, about twenty-four a year, took place on religious holidays when the Paris Opera was closed. The inaugural concert was held on 18 March (Passion Sunday) 1725 in the Salle des Suisses of the Tuileries Palace. This room was a gift from Louis XV and remained the home of the *Concert Spirituel* until 1784. Invariably the concerts included two *grands motets* by Lalande, which must have brought pleasure to the old master, on whom Louis XV had bestowed the title of 'Chevalier de Saint Michel' in 1722.

The vocal soloists at the *Concert Spirituel* came from the Opera, while the chorus was recruited from the best singers of the Chapelle Royale and the principal Parisian churches. Under the direction of Jean-Joseph Mouret, Jean-Ferry Rebel, Pancrace Royer, and Jean-Joseph Mondonville, the main significance of the *Concert Spirituel* lay more and more in the domain of instrumental music. It existed for sixty-six years and opened up the concert hall to religious music. Offering an outlet for new music of every kind, it exerted an important influence on French composers, performers, and audiences in the eighteenth century.

RELIGIOUS MUSIC IN THE PROVINCES

From what we know of the music performed in the parish churches of Paris and may infer from the organization of the Chapelle Royale, it seems that religious music was diffused throughout France chiefly through the medium of the great *maîtrises* of the cathedrals. Certainly we know that large numbers of choristers were employed at cathedrals such as those at Cambrai, Rheims, Rouen, Metz, Strasbourg, Dijon, Meaux, Nantes, Orléans, Tours, Angers, Bordeaux, Toulouse, Aix-en-Provence, and Avignon. Many details, however, are lacking: we are uncertain about the precise composition of the choir (whether men, women, or boys were used), the role of the choirmaster, and the number and function of the instrumentalists. Instrumental music may often have been represented solely by the organ, the serpent, or the double-bass, supplemented, perhaps, by temporary violinists. Where there was an academy of music, the metropolitan *maîtrise* took advantage of the presence of visiting dramatic singers and instrumentalists.

Contrary to the widespread belief that centralization was the order of the day and that the authority of Paris was recognized throughout France, many provinces retained their musical individuality along with their financial, administrative, and political autonomy. In spite of a natural conservatism reflected by attachment to *a cappella* polyphony, a number of the more distant *maîtrises* viewed the new, more personal art with favour. From the seventeenth century onwards, the whole of Provence was intoxicated, as was Paris, with the new and heady wine of Italian music. *Grands motets concertants* were sung in Aix, Narbonne, Montpellier, and Toulouse, as in Paris. But it was only at the end of the seventeenth century that Campra was allowed to introduce violins into the cathedral of Notre Dame in Paris—although they had been used at Saint Étienne, Toulouse, for twenty years. In Normandy, musical experimentation went on as it had in the days of Jean Titelouze.[1] Shortly after 1626 the *maîtrise* at Rouen bought three bass viols, a serpent, bassoon, cornett, sackbut, and violins for the accompaniment of the Lamentations. At Rheims, on the other hand, Henri Hardouin, *maître de musique* from 1748 to 1791, wrote twenty-four Masses which evidently were always performed *a cappella*.

CHANGE OF MUSICAL STYLE

Belated acceptance of the *basso continuo* brought about a more homophonic style. The decline of traditional polyphony was paralleled after 1650 by the decreasing importance of the polyphonic setting of the Ordinary of the Mass, for Louis XIV favoured the *grand motet*. Yet Masses continued to be composed. Most of them (always excepting those by Charpentier) remained conservative, even archaic in style. Such were the Masses by François Cosset (d. 1673) and Charles d'Helfer, *maître de chapelle* at Soissons in the 1650s. From the last years of the seventeenth century, instrumental parts were grafted on to such Masses to make them more palatable to the contemporary listener. Brossard, who blamed the conservative Ballard publishing monopoly for their reluctance to add continuo parts in subsequent editions of *a cappella* works, himself added a *symphonie* to Cosset's *Missa Gaudeamus te* for a performance at the Chapelle Royale in 1688. Somewhat less conservative are the six Masses (published between 1678 and 1706) which are all that survive of the output of Jean Mignon (1640–1710), who spent his entire working life at Notre Dame. The traditional polyphony of these works co-exists with Lullian homophony and even a madrigalian spirit, so that Mignon stands between Cosset and Charpentier; certain bolder passages even anticipate Lalande.

[1] See Vol. IV, pp. 672–5.

For high Mass Louis XIV went to a royal *paroisse* in Paris, to Saint Germain-en-Laye and, after 1690, to Notre Dame, Versailles. But in his chapel he enjoyed the form of the low Mass which enabled him to hear a *grand motet* and perhaps two *petits motets*. Pierre Perrin described the arrangement of motets in the service in his *Cantica pro Capella Regis* (Paris, 1665): '. . . There are ordinarily three [motets], one *grand*, one *petit*, for the Elevation and a "Domine, salvum fac regem".[1] I have made the *grands* of such a length that they take up a quarter of an hour . . . and they may be worked in from the beginning of the Mass to the Elevation.' Perrin, author of the texts for Lully's *petit motet* 'Ave coeli manus supernum' and his *grands motets* 'Plaude laetare' and 'O lachrymae fidelis', gives one of the earliest definitions of the seventeenth-century motet in France: 'the motet', he wrote, 'is a piece varied by having different musical sections strung together'.

The title-pages of the collections of fifty *grands motets* composed by Du Mont, Pierre Robert, and Lully and printed by Ballard between 1684 and 1686, inform us that they were 'Printed by the express order of His Majesty'. They glorify the King of France as well as the King of Heaven, and they became the models for the *grands motets* used in the Chapelle Royale, the *Concert Spirituel*, and provincial music academies right down to the Revolution. Because of its function as the chief decorative element in the king's Mass, the *grand motet* in France from its inception took on the features of a sacred concert. Its composers favoured settings of non- or paraliturgical texts and seemed to make no effort to co-ordinate their motets with the liturgical year.

The fate of Gregorian chant during the earlier part of the seventeenth century has been mentioned in the previous section. Plainsong lost ground with each passing decade, yet some still wished to resuscitate it. One such was Nivers, whose *Méthode certaine pour apprendre le plain chant* was published in 1667 and who wrote a *Dissertation sur le chant grégorien* in 1683. Others, such as Robert, Lully, Lalande, and Campra distorted the flexible rhythm of Gregorian melody to fit it into a metrical scheme. Only the musical integrity of an antiphon to the Virgin or a *Leçon de ténèbres* by Couperin or Charpentier allows us to accept chant melodies overladen with *tremblements* and *ports de voix*. An emasculated Gregorian style was doubtless used in Paris by cathedral and parish singers, and in certain provincial centres too, for unison performance of unsubtle, lifeless, Jansenist verses; but the most powerful

---

[1] Psalm 19:10, 'Domine, salvum fac regem: Et exaudi nos in die qua, invocaverimus te' ('Save the king, O Lord, and answer this day our appeal'). The 'Domine, salvum', a salutation to the king, was traditionally used as a closing motet for both high and low Mass from the days of Louis XIII.

30

enemy of Gregorian chant was François Bourgoing, the Oratorian whose previously mentioned versions of the chant were published from 1634 onwards.[1] The modern, simple, more metrical style was eventually enshrined in the *Cinq messes en plain-chant* (Paris, 1669) by Du Mont.[2] The improvisatory nature of Gregorian melisma succumbed before the rigid declamation of so-called *plain-chant musical*; and the eighteenth century witnessed the total eclipse, even in monasteries, of the earlier forms of plainsong.

Are we to conclude that plainsong was replaced by vernacular canticles or chants? This was certainly true in part, as had been shown by Gastoué.[3] We should particularly bear in mind those delightful *noëls*, sung throughout France since the Middle Ages, which inspired so many sacred and secular songs. After the Edict of Nantes was revoked in 1685, however, there was a decrease in the composition of paraliturgical music for secular words,[4] although Du Mont, Nivers, and Lebègue wrote new melodies for the Latin hymns of their contemporary Jean de Santeul. This decline was equally true of both Protestant chorales, canticles, and psalms and Catholic music of this type, which in imitation of the Protestants and on the initiative of Godeau had enjoyed thirty successful years.

DU MONT AND ROBERT

In turning to the religious music of the composers who were active between 1643 (when Louis XIII died) and 1715 (when Louis XIV died), we must single out five names for separate discussion: Du Mont, Robert, Lully, Charpentier, and Lalande. In a single line of development these men and their contemporaries expanded and refined existing forms and created a type of religious music that best exemplifies the spirit of the *grand siècle*.

Henry Du Mont (1610–84)[5] was born near Liège, where he studied.

---

[1] See *supra*, p. 418, n. 2.

[2] See Amédée Gastoué, *Les Messes royales de Henry Du Mont* (Paris, 1909), including transcriptions of three of the Masses. The Masses were edited by Alexandre Guilmant (Paris, 1896); there are several other editions of single Masses, mostly unreliable.

[3] Gastoué, *Le Cantique populaire en France* (Paris, 1926), pp. 191ff.

[4] However, many translations of the psalms into French verse or prose were available to musicians in the seventeenth century, from the collections of Philippe Desportes (1603), Jean Métezeau (1610) and Jean Desplanel (1612) to those of Pierre Nicole (1676) and Dralincourt (1694). In his translation (1648 and reprinted as late as 1686) Godeau expressed the hope that musicians might provide for these psalms 'simple and pleasant tunes, so that they may become popular and replace those many vain or dangerous words hitherto embellished with music'. See *supra*, p. 433.

[5] See Henri Quittard, *Un Musicien en France au XVIIe siècle: Henry Du Mont* (Paris, 1906.) See also Denise Launay, *Anthologie du motet polyphonique en France* (Paris, 1963), introduction, and the article in *Die Musik in Geschichte und Gegenwart*, iii (1954), cols. 930–40.

He appeared on the Parisian scene as organist at Saint Paul (from 1640 to 1684) and as harpsichordist, first to the Duke of Anjou and later (1660) to the young queen, Marie-Thérèse. As we have seen, he became one of four *sous-maîtres* at the Chapelle Royale in 1663. In 1668–9 Gobert and Expilly retired, leaving Du Mont and Robert as the only *sous-maîtres* until both left the service of the king in 1683, thus precipitating Louis XIV's great *concours*.

Du Mont's *Cantica Sacra* (1652) and *Meslanges* (1657) have been mentioned above.[1] The Brossard collection at the Bibliothèque Nationale includes a *Dialogus de anima* (1668) which is a dialogue between God, a sinner, and an angel. Brossard describes this work as a 'type of oratorio', fairly, since it is organized into three scenes, each preceded by a *symphonie*, and uses a *petit chœur* and *grand chœur* as well as solo *récits*. The *Motets à deux voix avec la basse continue* (1668) include thirty motets of which five are in dialogue form. This collection illustrates the extent to which Du Mont was influenced by Carissimi, especially in the use of repeated text fragments and dramatically placed rests, 'affective' intervals and a discreet chromaticism (see, for example, 'O fidelis miseremini'). In the *Motets à II, III et IV parties* (1671) Italian and French elements co-exist. 'Doleo super te' (Ex. 237 (i)), with its chains of suspensions, and 'In lectulo' (Ex. 237 (ii)), with its use of echo effects, derive from such composers as Alessandro Grandi and Antonio Cifra, whose motets Du Mont may have heard in Flemish churches. In contrast, such a motet as 'Unde tibi' (Ex. 237 (iii)) is clearly based on French dance rhythms and even uses a type of rhythmic counterpoint (see the dotted rhythms in the bass and melody of bars 1 and 3) which became commonplace in the religious music of such later composers as André Campra.[2]

Ex. 237 (i)

---

[1] See *supra*, p. 431.
[2] From MSS. 713 and 899 at St. Michael's College, Tenbury. Where no sources are cited in footnotes, examples in this section are taken from contemporary printed versions.

The twenty *grands motets* by Du Mont, published posthumously in 1686, were probably written during the twenty years he served in the Chapelle Royale. He developed the approach of Formé and Veillot in creating a continuous chain of episodes—solo *récits* and ensembles alternating with instrumental *ritournelles* and music for the *grand* and *petit chœurs*—which may be virtually self-contained but more often succeed each other without interruption. Du Mont's *grands motets* became a model for the distribution of parts which was followed throughout the century. In Brossard's words:[1]

To perform [Du Mont's motets] one must have five solo voices that constitute the *petit chœur*, including C.A.T.T.B.;[2] five parts of the same distribution for the *grand chœur*; and five instrumental parts including violins I and II, violas (*haute contre* and *taille*), *basse de violon*, and *basse continue*. Thus one should have a rather large group of performers . . . however, five solo voices, two violins, *basse de violon*, and a *basse continue* would suffice.

The *symphonies* which introduce Du Mont's *grands motets* vary considerably. 'Confitebimur tibi Deus' (no. 4) begins with a *symphonie* of thirty-five bars, 'Domine in virtute tuo' (no. 6) with a tutti chorus. The *symphonies* of 'Quemadmodum desiderata' (no. 19) and 'O dulcissima' (no. 16) are closed binary forms that resemble allemandes and have little to do with what follows. In the short motto-beginning to the *Magnificat* (no. 13), independent part-writing for the orchestra reminds one rather of the composer's Flemish background than of French music of the day. In such expansive works Du Mont was not always inspired, for he was essentially a miniaturist. Some of the large syllabic choruses of the *grands motets* are dull, lacking the propulsive drive of Lully in similar compositions. On the other hand, the five-part polyphony of the 'Gloria patri' from the *Magnificat* is worthy of Lalande. In the instrumental accompaniments to his *grands motets* Du Mont often succeeded in freeing the instruments from the role of doubling the vocal lines. The second violin in particular is involved in independent counterpoint, and in the opening chorus of 'Benedictus' (no. 2) a first-violin countermelody is clearly heard against the five-part chorus. Of particular interest are the accompaniments to the *petit chœur*, in which the orchestra on occasion will introduce an independent motive to be developed later by chorus and orchestra, as in Ex. 238, from 'Confitebimur tibi Deus'. Du Mont's *grands motets* were impressive models for the next

---

[1] *Catalogue des livres de musique théorique et pratique* (Paris, Bibliothèque Nationale, MS. 1724).
[2] That is, soprano, alto (actually countertenor), tenor, tenor (*basse taille* or baritone), and bass.

Ex. 238

generation, notably for Lalande, whose first motets were certainly contemporary with the last of Du Mont's.

Pierre Robert (*c.* 1618–99)[1] was a product of the *maîtrise* of Notre Dame, which he directed from 1653 to 1663. His career at the Chapelle Royale paralleled that of Du Mont. No secular music by Robert survives, although he spent seventeen years attached to the king's chamber. His major contribution is the collection of *Motets pour la chapelle du Roy* (1684). These twenty-four *grands motets* closely resemble

[1] See Hélène Charnassé's articles dealing with Robert's *grands motets* in *Recherches*, i (1960), pp. 61–7; ii (1961–2), pp. 61–70; iii (1963), pp. 49–54; and iv (1964), pp. 105–20. She has also edited two *grands motets* ('Deus noster refugium' and 'Quare fremuerunt gentes') for the series *Le Pupitre* (Paris, 1969).

those of Du Mont and Lully. It is only in the *petit chœur* with its *ensembles de récits* that the composer's individuality is expressed. Choosing from eight possible solo voices (two each of sopranos,

countertenors, and tenors and one each of baritone and bass), Robert contrasts sonorities by a rapid and occasionally quite arbitrary juxtaposition of voices. In Ex. 239, chosen from the final verset of Psalm 2, 'Quare fremuerunt gentes', he makes a distinction between the dominating voice of the *ensemble de récits* (labelled 'Récit') and the accompanying voices (labelled 'R').

In his *petits motets*, ten of which are in a Philidor copy at the Bibliothèque Nationale (Vm^b. MS. 6), Robert was more sensitive to the expressive power of dissonance and modulation. For example, the Italianate dialogue which closes 'O flamma' with textual repetition, melodic sequences, and chromaticism is far removed from the frequently stiff *récits* of the *grands motets*.

LULLY

The importance of the operas of Jean-Baptiste Lully (1632–87)[1] should not obscure the merits of his religious music, which exerted considerable influence over half a century—a notable achievement on the part of one who never directly participated in the musical life of the Chapelle Royale. Lully composed at least twenty-five motets between 1664 and his death. Eleven are *grands motets* of which six were printed by Ballard in 1684 'by express order of His Majesty'.[2] The remaining *grands motets*, all in manuscript,[3] are found today in the Berlin Staatsbibliothek, the Bibliothèque Nationale, the Bibliothèque Royale, Brussels, and St. Michael's College, Tenbury.

In its expansiveness and depth of feeling, the *Miserere* of 1664 surpasses earlier essays in the genre by Veillot and Formé and undoubtedly antedates most of the *grands motets* composed by Du Mont, who had been appointed only one year earlier to the Chapelle Royale. At a performance in 1672 for the funeral of Chancellor Séguier, Mme. de Sévigné was moved to write that during the 'Libera me' 'all eyes were filled with tears. I do not believe any other music to exist even in heaven' (letter of 2 May). The sensuous melodies of several of the *récits* of the *Miserere* remind us that 1664 was also the year of the *comédies-ballets Le Mariage forcé*, *Les Amours déguisés*, and *La Princesse d'Élide*. The crossing of voices and the chains of parallel thirds in the dialogue of Climène and Philis in the fifth *intermède* of *La Princesse d'Élide* (Ex. 240 (i)) are echoed in the *récit* 'Redde mihi' for

Ex. 240 (i)

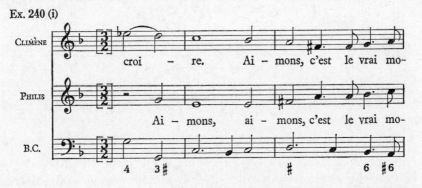

[1] For literature on Lully, see p. 208, n. 1. For a complete listing of his religious music see Jacques Chailley's article in *La Musica*, iii (1966), p. 213. In the still incomplete *Œuvres complètes*, general editor Henry Prunières, the *Miserere* has been published as *Les Motets*, i (Paris, 1931); the *Te Deum* and 'Dies irae' are in *Les Motets*, ii (Paris, 1935), pp. 41 and 211 respectively. There is a vocal score of the *Te Deum*, ed. W. K. Stanton (London, 1955).

[2] *Miserere*, 1664; 'Plaude laetare', 1668; *Te Deum*, 1677; 'Dies irae', date unknown; 'De profundis', 1683; 'Benedictus Dominus', date unknown.

[3] 'Domine salvum', date unknown; 'Exaudiat', 1685; 'Notus in Judaea', after 1689; 'O lachrymae', date unknown; 'Quare fremuerunt', 1686.

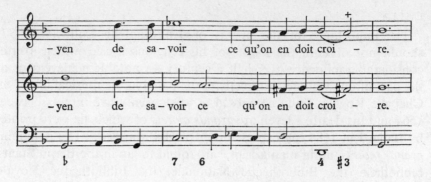

two sopranos (Ex. 240 (ii)).[1] Although much of the *Miserere* was conceived for vertical sonorities, it does contain passages of closely-knit polyphony, often centring on one key word such as 'impii' ('sinners') (see Ex. 241).

The *Te Deum* was composed for the baptism of Lully's eldest son (then aged 13) at Fontainebleau on 8 September 1677. It was heard

---

[1] Exx. 240 and 241 are from Lully, op. cit., *Les Comédies-ballets*, ii (Paris, 1933), p. 61, and *Les Motets*, i, pp. 45 and 50 respectively.

Ex. 241

again at Versailles in October 1679 when 'at least 120 persons sang or played instruments' (*Mercure galant*, October 1679). It was this work, performed on 8 January 1687 at the Paris chapel of the Feuillants, that contributed inadvertently to the death of Lully. The composer 'in the heat of the moment' (Le Cerf de la Viéville) hit his toe with the point of the long stick with which he was beating time to control the more than 150 musicians. Gangrene resulted and by March Lully was dead.

It may well have been this work with its trumpets and drums and its spectacular, warlike choruses that gave Louis XIV the idea of utilizing such large-scale compositions to form the core of the music for his Chapelle Royale. In common with most of Lully's *grands motets*, the *Te Deum* is clearly divided into sections—a structural device that apparently pleased the king ('What was particularly admired was that each couplet was composed of different music. The king found it so beautiful that he wished to hear it again': *Mercure galant*, September 1677). The larger sections are set apart by *symphonies*. Shorter divisions, seldom truly self-contained, are created by dividing the text into *récits*, recitatives, and choruses.

The use of recurring choral fragments separated by *récits* or *symphonies* is borrowed from the *tragédie lyrique*. Such is the treatment of 'In gloria numerari' illustrated in Ex. 242.[1]

The sheer length of the *Te Deum* (over 1,200 bars) and its many pages of quite similar heavy homophonic choruses result in monotony, which is compensated for in part by the hypnotic effect of exciting speech rhythms sometimes combined with rapid tempo changes (see, for example, the 'Sanctus' of the opening section). The homophonic

[1] Lully, op. cit., *Les Motets*, ii, p. 68.

Ex. 242

character of Lully's *grands motets* produces a rather simple, static harmony. Yet there is a certain harmonic interest in the borrowing of chords from the opposite mode to produce a type of 'bi-modality' common in French baroque music. This may combine with a dramatic tempo change to emphasize the text. Such a passage is the four-bar 'Sanctus' in G minor in the *Te Deum* which is set within a larger harmonic frame of C and G major.

Lully's *petits motets* are probably mostly late works.[1] He knew that the king liked Paolo Lorenzani's church music, and the style of these works suggests that he deliberately adopted an Italian idiom.

CHARPENTIER AND LALANDE: A COMPARISON

Marc-Antoine Charpentier (1634–1704)[2] and Michel-Richard de Lalande (1657–1726)[3] between them produced more than 150 *grands motets*. Their careers were very different. Lalande held most of the court appointments open to musicians; and his motets comprised the basic repertory of the Chapelle Royale and later the *Concert Spirituel*. Charpentier never held a direct court appointment; his motets were mostly written for the Jesuit church of Saint Louis (the Dauphin's chapel) and the Sainte-Chapelle, where he was *maître de musique des enfants* during the last five years of his life. However, even without actual court appointments he enjoyed the king's favour. He was employed as teacher of the king's nephew Philippe of Orléans and his eldest son, the Dauphin; and he was 'composer in residence' for the king's cousin Mlle. de Guise. The 500-odd works in the twenty-eight volumes of manuscript *Meslanges*[4] do not suggest a lack of occasions for composition.

The music of both composers was popular during their lifetimes and later. Le Cerf de la Viéville's judgement—'I do not understand by what miracle Charpentier could be considered an expressive composer of Latin music'—was not widely shared. Brossard praised Charpentier's music, and the Parfaicts approved 'a harmony and science hitherto unknown in France'. Rousseau described Lalande's motets as 'masterpieces of the genre', and as late as 1769 Nougaret wrote in his *De l'Art*

---

[1] Ten of them are found in Philidor's manuscript *Petits motets et élévations* of 1688.

[2] See Claude Crussard, *Un Musicien français oublié: Marc-Antoine Charpentier* (Paris, 1945). For Charpentier's Masses, see Günther Massenkeil, 'Marc-Antoine Charpentier als Messenkomponist', *Colloquium Amicorum: Joseph Schmidt-Görg zum 70. Geburtstag*, ed. Siegfried Kross and Hans Schmidt (Bonn, 1967). For his Masses and motets, see Clarence Barber, *The Liturgical Music of Marc-Antoine Charpentier* (Diss., unpub., Harvard, 1955). For his oratorios, see idem, 'Les Oratorios de Marc-Antoine Charpentier', *Recherches*, iii (1963), pp. 90–130; H. Wiley Hitchcock, *The Latin Oratorios of Marc-Antoine Charpentier* (Diss., unpub., University of Michigan, 1954); and idem, 'The Latin Oratorios of Marc-Antoine Charpentier', *Musical Quarterly*, xli (1955), pp. 41–65. Several works are available in recent editions, some of which are referred to in subsequent notes.

[3] See Norbert Dufourcq (and others), *Notes et références pour servir à une histoire de Michel-Richard Delalande* (Paris, 1957). As explained on p. 238, n. 4, *supra*, the form 'Lalande' is used in the present volume. For a study of Lalande's motets, see James E. Richards, *The 'Grand Motet' of the Late Baroque in France as Exemplified by Michel-Richard de Lalande* (Diss., unpub., University of Southern California, 1950); and idem, 'Structural principles in the *grands motets* of de Lalande', *Journal of the American Musicological Society*, xi (1958), pp. 119–27. Also see Dufourcq, 'Retour à Michel-Richard Delalande', *Recherches*, i (1960), p. 69.

[4] Now preserved on microfilm in the Bibliothèque Nationale.

du théâtre: 'Delalande still enjoys a reputation of which nothing dims the lustre. . . . They even perform many of his motets in Italy.' Although Charpentier and Lalande remained firmly rooted in the French tradition, both composers, in their use of bold dissonance, long suspensions, dramatic rests, and *ostinato* basses, brought to it something of Italian freedom. Charpentier acquired this Italian influence at first hand, the result of three years in Rome under the tutelage of Carissimi; in the case of Lalande it stemmed from his being introduced (possibly by Charpentier) to the Italianate coterie surrounding the Abbé Mathieu of Saint André-des-Arts and from his inheriting the Italian cantatas and motets that were prized possessions of the *curé*.

CHARPENTIER'S MOTETS

Charpentier's *grands motets* bridge the gap between those of Du Mont, Robert, and Lully and those of Lalande. Some, in traditional fashion, create large sectional units out of unbroken episodes of motto-preludes, solo *récits*, ensembles, and choruses; others, resembling the late motets of Lalande, include sections which are themselves made up of several self-contained, unlinked episodes. Charpentier's occasional use of rondo structure, as found in 'Epithalamio' (*Meslanges*, vol. VII) and 'Lauda Jerusalem' (vol. XXXVII), is unusual in French religious music. A large, tripartite structure unifies his longest motet (1,383 bars), 'In obitum' (vol. XX), composed to lament the death of Marie-Thérèse (1683). The symmetrical plan of the *Magnificat* in D (vol. XI) for double chorus and two orchestras is worthy of Bach; a double chorus serves as a centre-piece flanked by trios and solos, the whole being balanced by introductory and concluding double choruses.[1]

In number and quality, the *petits motets* of Charpentier surpass those of his contemporaries. Almost half (66) are set as trio textures with the countertenor, tenor, and bass combination particularly favoured.[2] Most are either Elevations (motets for the Holy Sacrament) or Marian motets. Five of the Passion *petits motets* are classified by Hitchcock as oratorios because of their use of dialogue techniques.

In his short treatise (*Règles de Composition*) written for Philippe of Orléans, Charpentier justified the use of such harmonic devices as parallel fifths, augmented sixths (characterized in the treatise as a 'very plaintive chord'), augmented octaves, and cross-relations. Charpentier, in common with Lalande, Couperin, and others, also used the strikingly dissonant sonority of a mediant ninth chord having a major

[1] See Dufourcq, 'Le Disque et l'histoire de la musique', *Recherches*, iii (1963), p. 214.
[2] See Barber, *The Liturgical Music of Marc-Antoine Charpentier*, p. 168.

seventh and augmented fifth among its components.[1] However, like most French composers of the time, Charpentier was essentially conservative with regard to harmony. Practices as described above were carefully restricted to those moments when the text dictated particularly dramatic musical expression. Ex. 243 (i) is extracted from *Règles de Composition* and gives a theoretical basis for some of the dissonances that follow in Ex. 243 (ii–iv). In Ex. 243 (ii and iii), both drawn from the six-part *Miserere* (vol. VII), are two different harmonic settings for the important word 'peccatis' ('sins'). In Ex. 243 (ii) a carefully placed melisma generates an augmented octave between the outer voices (bar 3) at this word; in Ex. 243 (iii) the mediant $\frac{9}{7}$ chord in powerful six-part homophony appears only at this key word in bar 2. Ex. 243 (iv), taken from a *Salve Regina* (vol. III) for triple chorus and orchestra, is one of the most compelling of all examples of word-painting in French baroque music. To depict 'in hac lacrymarum valle' ('in this vale of tears'), Charpentier chose descending augmented triads which terminate in an augmented sixth chord resolved by an A major triad.

Ex. 243 (i)

(ii)

---

[1] See James R. Anthony, *French Baroque Music* (London, 1973), p. 187.

31

(iii)

a pec - ca - tis me - is.

a pec - ca - tis me - is.

(iv) Grand motet

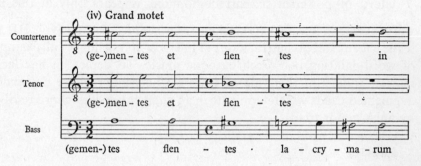

Countertenor: (ge-)men – tes   et   flen – tes   in

Tenor: (ge-)men – tes   et   flen – tes

Bass: (gemen-)tes   flen – tes · la – cry – ma – rum

hac   la – cry – ma – rum   val – le.

in   hac   la – cry – ma – rum   val – le.

val – le,   la – cry – ma – rum   val · – le.

CHARPENTIER'S MASSES

Charpentier was one of the few French composers of his time to contribute significantly to the repertoire of the polyphonic Mass. His twelve Masses[1] exemplify every type of seventeenth-century Mass, including some for which there was no precedent in France. They

---

[1] *Messe à quatre chœurs* (vol. XXII), *Messe pour le Port Royal* (vol. XXII), *Messe pour le Samedy de Pasques* (vol. V), *Messe pour M. Mauroy* (vol. X), *Messe des Morts à 4 voix* (vol. XXIV), *Messe des Morts à 4 voix et simphonie* (vol. XXVI), *Messe pour les Trespasses* (vol. I), *Messe à 8 voix et 8 violons et flûtes* (vol. XV), *Messe à 4 voix et instruments* (vol. XIV), *Messe de Minuit pour Noël* (vol. XXV), *Messe pour plusieurs instruments au lieu des orgues* (vol. I), and *Missa Assumpta est Maria* (vol. XXVII).

range from a simple setting for solo voice and unison chorus, written for the nuns of Port-Royal, to a large concertato Mass for choirs, which is perhaps the only work of its kind in seventeenth-century France and may be an early work influenced by the Roman polychoral tradition.[1] It is not known whether it was ever actually performed. Another possibly unique Mass is the *Messe pour plusieurs instruments au lieu des orgues*. In this substitution for the traditional organ Mass, Charpentier attempted to imitate the registration of the French classical organ by specifying four recorders, three transverse flutes, one crumhorn, two oboes (and a bassoon), four *basses de flûtes* (probably bass recorders), and four-part strings. The *Kyrie* complex given below illustrates his method of mixing and separating instrumental colours (the numbering is his original, the even-numbered 'Kyries' being marked 'pour les prestres'):

Kyrie I: 'tous les instruments'
Kyrie III: 'pour les hautbois'
Kyrie V: 'pour les viollons du petit chœur'
Kyrie VII: 'flûtes' [for a recorder choir]
Kyrie IX: 'pour tous les instruments'

Sections of the *Kyrie* and *Gloria* are based on the Gregorian plainchant *Cunctipotens Genitor Deus*, which he treated as a *canto fermo* in long notes in the bass (see Ex. 244). As in the organ Masses, there is no *Credo* and the *Agnus Dei* is incomplete. The musical style is simple. It contains elements of the dance and of *airs sérieux*; a French overture appears as the Offertory.

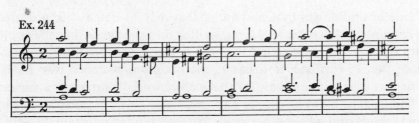

Ex. 244

Besides this Mass, there is a substantial amount of purely instrumental religious music in the Charpentier *Meslanges*. It includes preludes or overtures to motets, *symphonies* for consecrations and street processionals and for alternating Mass movements, and versets of hymns and ensemble settings of *noëls*.[2] Although popular as

[1] Barber, op. cit., p. 83.
[2] See Hitchcock, 'The Instrumental Music of Marc-Antoine Charpentier', *Musical Quarterly*, xlvii (1961), pp. 58–72.

a basis for organ and ensemble pieces, French *noëls* did not often supply material for Masses or motets. Charpentier's *Messe de Minuit pour Noël* appears to be the earliest example of such a Mass.[1] It is effectively scored for solo voices, a four-part chorus, flutes, strings, and organ. Charpentier was able through the simplest means to shape the original tunes appropriately for their new settings without violating their popular and naïve quality. Ex. 245 shows how this was accomplished by the introduction of discreet melismas and typically French vocal ornamentation:

Ex. 245 (i)

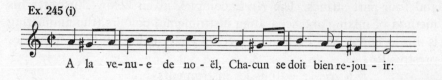

A la ve - nu - e de no - ël, Cha-cun se doit bien re-jou - ir:

(ii)

Soprano 1 (Solo)

Et in Spi - ri - tum sanc - tum, Do-mi-num et____

____ vi - vi - fi - can - - tem,

One of the Masses by Charpentier that may be dated with a degree of certainty is *Assumpta est Maria*, written for the Sainte-Chapelle at the turn of the century. A six-part chorus is used (two sopranos, counter-tenor, tenor, baritone, and bass); the orchestra includes two flutes, four-part strings, and organ. In this mature work Charpentier achieved a fine balance between chorus and orchestra, between polyphony and homophony and between prayerful introspection and a dramatic sense of musical characterization. Ex. 246 shows two extracts from it which will give some idea of Charpentier's remarkable range of musical expression and diversity of style. The 'non' from 'Cujus regni non erit finis' of the *Credo* is repeated and treated, almost in the manner of Bouzignac, as an emphatic dialogue between the upper three and lower

[1] See Hitchcock's edition (St. Louis, c.1962) for the *noël* melodies and texts. For his *Missa quinti toni pro nocte ad die festi natalis Domini* of 1700 Brossard may have used Charpentier's work as a model. Boismortier's *grand motet* 'Fugit nox' (1741) and the much later *Messe-Oratorio de Noël* (1786) by Jean-François Lesueur also use *noël* tunes.

three voices of the chorus (Ex. 246 (i)), and 'Dominus Deus' from the *Sanctus* is organized as a short minuet—even retaining the **four-bar** phrases of that popular dance (Ex. 246 (ii)):

Ex. 246 (i)

CHARPENTIER'S ORATORIOS

It was Charpentier who introduced oratorios, or, as he called them, *historiae*, into France about 1685, no doubt inspired by his stay in Italy and his studies with Carissimi. But his compositions, though impressive, were without musical issue in France, perhaps because, as Schering suggested,[1] the French 'could not accept the inherent contradiction of oratorio: dramatic plot without stage and action. The predilection for the visible, for the stage, for representation, dancing, and scenery, was too deeply rooted in the spirit of the French nation for the lack of these accessories to be explained away by aesthetic reflection.' It is true that Marmontel, in his article 'Concert Spirituel' in Diderot's *Encyclopédie*, observed that 'some weak essays in this genre [oratorio] have been performed at the *Concert Spirituel* in Paris'. This must refer to the two

[1] Arnold Schering, *Geschichte des Oratoriums* (Leipzig, 1911, repr. 1966), p. 514.

sacred oratorios by Mondonville, *Les Israélites à la montagne d'Horeb* (performed in 1758) and *Les Fureurs de Saul* (performed in 1759). In the libretto of *Les Israélites* we read that 'Monsieur Mondonville has enriched our music with *a new genre* . . .' (the present writer's italics). In his *Present State of Music in France and Italy* Burney wrote: 'the French have never yet had . . . a regular oratorio of any sort performed in their country'. And in the 1781 edition of his *Dictionnaire* Rousseau states that the practice of performing oratorios during Lent was unknown in France. Charpentier's oratorios were brought to light (by Michel Brenet) only at the end of the nineteenth century.

Charpentier himself classified his thirty-four Latin oratorios into *historiae*, *cantica*, and *dialogi*. The fourteen *historiae* are large-scale works in the manner of Carissimi's *Jephte* or *Judicium extremum*, with solo *récits*, ensembles, chorus, and orchestra. The *cantica* and *dialogi* are shorter works that demand fewer performers.

Charpentier's oratorios display both French and Italian traits.[1] The choral writing embodies both the concertato principle of the *grands motets* of Lully and Lalande and the Roman polychoral style. Although the style is basically homophonic, some choruses have polyphonic textures reminiscent of Lalande, for example 'Flevit amare', which closes *Le Reniement de Saint Pierre*.[2] Choruses from some of the nativity *cantica* (e.g. 'Pastores undique' from *In nativitate Domini canticum*) are however called 'chansons' and resemble popular *noëls*. The solo vocal music is mostly recitative, simple or accompanied, or arioso. The *airs* are few and relatively unimportant. Some use French dance measures, and some resemble the Italian *da capo* aria, with extended roulades and ritornellos.[3]

Charpentier habitually employed a larger instrumental ensemble than Carissimi—this is indeed the most noticeable difference between their oratorio styles. *Caecilia virgo et martyr* employs two four-part string orchestras, and the final section has a concertante organ part. *Judicium Salomonis* uses flutes, oboes, and bassoons as well as strings. The *tragédies lyriques* of Lully surely influenced the dramatic *symphonies* of Charpentier's oratorios. For instance, the prelude to the second part of *Judicium Salomonis* resembles the 'sommeil' from Lully's *Atys* (Act III, scene 4):

[1] See Hitchcock, *The Latin Oratorios of Marc-Antoine Charpentier*, Diss., unpub., p. 384.
[2] A dialogue from *Le Reniement de Saint Pierre* is in Archibald T. Davison and Willi Apel, *Historical Anthology of Music*, ii (Cambridge, 1950), pp. 86–9; and a scene from the same work is in Carl Parrish, *A Treasury of Early Music* (New York, 1958), pp. 244–52.
[3] See Solomon's *air* 'Benedictus es' from *Judicium Salomonis*. *Judicium Salomonis* has been edited by Hitchcock, *Recent Researches in Baroque Music*, i (New Haven, Conn., 1964).

Ex 247 (i)

Charpentier developed musical characterization in his oratorios as much as in his operas. Witness the scene from *Le Reniement de Saint Pierre*[1] in which the relentless questioning of Peter by the maids and doorkeeper alternate with his persistent denials. It is doubtful whether either French or Italian opera taught Charpentier how to generate the dramatic excitement found in his three duets between the True and False Mothers in *Judicium Salomonis*. The final duet recalls the touching scene from Carissimi's oratorio of the same name; both composers used a naïve madrigalism on the word 'dividatur'. In Charpentier's version, however, the intensity is heightened by the presentation of two opposing ideas at the same time:

Ex. 248

(True mother: Give her the child alive and do not kill him. False mother: Let him be divided.)

LALANDE

The known motets of Lalande, 71 in number, bridge the time

[1] Parrish, loc. cit.

span between the *grands motets* of Du Mont and the 'motets à grands chœurs' by Rameau. Although of modest origins (he was the fifteenth child of a Parisian tailor), Lalande became an accomplished organist and violinist who wrote mainly secular music early in his career. After assuming the responsibility for much of the music of the Chapelle Royale, he turned increasingly to the composition of sacred music. He wrote no polyphonic Masses and few canticles or lessons for the Tenebrae. Instead, knowing the king's partiality for motets, he used them to 'preach' every Sunday at the 'Messe basse solennelle'. Their eloquent message affected all classes: the king and Mme. de Maintenon (whom the king had secretly married in 1683), the favoured few who attended the king's Mass, and, after 1725, the crowds who applauded them at the *Concert Spirituel*. It is not true that they represent the 'most conservative spirit of the period'.[1] Lalande aimed for balance between old and new. Weighty homophonic choruses with driving speech rhythms stem from the motets (and operatic choruses) of Lully (see, for example, 'Conturbatae sunt gentes' in 'Deus noster refugium'). At the same time Lalande 'thought' polyphonically more than any French contemporary. The 'Requiem aeternam' in 'De profundis', for instance, is a five-part fugue in which chorus and orchestra combine in linear tension worthy of Bach.

In 1729 a former pupil, Colin de Blamont, characterized Lalande as a 'Latin Lully', that is, as a composer who succeeded in humanizing the *grand motet*. The description of his style is a model of clarity and accurate observation:[2]

His [Lalande's] great merit . . . consisted in a wonderful choice of melody, a judicious choice of harmony and a nobility of expression. . . . Profound and learned on the one hand, simple and natural on the other . . . the mind is refreshed . . . by the ingenious disparities with which he ornaments his works and by the graceful melodies that serve as contrasting episodes to the most complex choral sections.

An example of 'ingenious disparity' is the soprano *récit* 'Anima nostra' in 'Nisi quia Dominus' (1703) for which Lalande borrowed from the opera of his day the texture and colour of flute and soprano 'accompanied' by violin. The text 'et nos liberati sumus' ('and we were freed') suggested a long melisma on 'liberati' in which flute, voice, and violin

---

[1] Manfred F. Bukofzer, *Music in the Baroque Era* (London, 1948), p. 259. The neglect of Lalande in English-language sources of the twentieth century is surprising. Over thirty years ago, Paul Henry Lang hailed him as 'one of France's greatest musicians' (*Music in Western Civilization*, New York, 1941, p. 540), yet he receives but four lines in Bukofzer and one sentence in Edith Borroff, *The Music of the Baroque* (Dubuque, 1970) and is totally ignored in Claude V. Palisca, *Baroque Music* (Englewood Cliffs, 1968).

[2] Preface to the posthumously printed edition of forty motets (1729).

engage in a gentle dialogue that resembles more the *style galant* than
the Versailles *grand motet*:

Ex. 249

Most of Lalande's motets are organized formally in self-contained
movements—*récits* and ensembles—placed between choral sections.
They resemble the German cantata of the same period. Some show a
preference for symmetrical structures. 'Usque quo', for example, which
dates from 1712, is framed by two large choruses; two other choruses
are placed at its centre, with solo pieces symmetrically disposed around
them. The words given to soloists in this setting of Psalm 144 are the
more intimate and personal ones, whereas the text in the big choruses

suggests collective fervour and universal homage—emotions to which the music responds magnificently.

Lalande often presented two independent motives consecutively in both the opening *symphonie* and solo *récit*; he then offered them simultaneously in the chorus that followed. In the fifth verset, 'Hostem repellas longius, Pacemque dones protinus' ('Repel afar our earthly foes. Let us dwell henceforth in peace'), from 'Veni creator spiritus', the paired ideas in the opening tenor *récit* receive totally different music, which is subsequently combined in a ten-part double chorus. Each half of this chorus retains its own text and musical individuality.[1] In the *Miserere* (1687) two motives marked 'a' and 'b' in Ex. 250 (i) occur in succession in the introductory *symphonie*. In the chorus that follows, motive 'b' is employed as a counter-subject to motive 'a', with the first entry of 'b' given to the violins (Ex. 250 (ii)).

Lalande's harmonic vocabulary was undoubtedly enriched by exposure both to the motets of Charpentier (with whom he came into

[1] See Anthony, op. cit., p. 191.

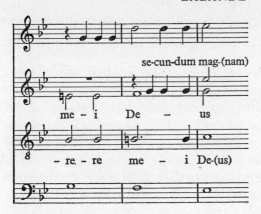

contact while organist at the Jesuit church of Saint Louis) and to the Italian motets which he inherited from the Abbé Mathieu. Ex. 251, from 'Pange lingua', will show how carefully he selected the most expressive devices to dramatize the meaning of the psalm verset. An overwhelming sense of mystical veneration of the Sacrament must

Ex. 251

have suggested to him the use of diminished seventh chords and the mediant $\frac{9}{7}$ chord in such close proximity; the text repetition, coupled
$$\#5$$
with the dramatic use of silence, deepens the mystery. In no other French composer before Rameau do we find such frequent commitment to the diminished seventh chord as an expressive harmonic tool.

Most of Lalande's motets are found in three sources: (1) the manuscript copy of twenty-seven motets made by Philidor 'l'aîné' in 1689 and 1690, now in the Bibliothèque Municipale, Versailles (MSS. 8–17); (2) an edition of forty motets printed posthumously under the direction of Colin de Blamont in 1729; and (3) the manuscript copies of forty-one motets and some shorter pieces made for (or by?) one Gaspard Alexis Cauvin and now, except for the last volume, in the Bibliothèque Municipale, Versailles (MSS. 216–35).[1] The Cauvin manuscript is evidently a later eighteenth-century copy of the 1729 printed edition, with the order of motets changed and one motet, 'Exaudi Deus', added. However, it includes the instrumental 'parties de remplissage', whereas the printed edition reduces Lalande's large orchestra to two violins and continuo. Eight motets[2] in the Philidor copy also appear in the Cauvin manuscript and in the printed edition.

It is instructive to compare the versions of motets in different sources. These seem to reflect in part changes in fashionable taste, in part maturer compositional skill. Ex. 252 (i) illustrates the opening bars of 'De profundis' in the Cauvin manuscript; Ex. 252 (ii) is that of the Philidor version. The *symphonie* in the Philidor copy is 26 bars long; in the Cauvin it has been reduced to 17 bars. The texture in the Cauvin is in four parts, giving added support to a later date for this manuscript. The part-writing itself is more interesting and less note-against-note, although the drive to a climax on the diminished seventh chord (bar 6 of (ii)) has been eliminated. Ex. 252 (iii and iv) show how a simple bass *récit* (iii) was converted into a fashionable soprano *air* (iv). It can be seen that, though ornamentation is added, the basic melodic shape remains the same but that the repetition of the second phrase gives more amplitude to the melody. The motet is the *Miserere* (Psalm 50); the

---

[1] The last volume is at the Bibliothèque Nationale (Rés. Vm^b. MS. 16). There are also eleven *grands motets* of Lalande in the important Toulouse-Philidor collection at St. Michael's College, Tenbury. Certain of these works (e.g. 'Super flumina') differ slightly from the Philidor manuscript. Three hitherto missing motets and an early version of 'Veni, creator spiritus' are in a private collection owned by M. R. Lutz of Strasbourg: the motets are 'Cantate Domino', 'Eructavit cor meum', and 'Dies irae'. See Laurence Boulay, 'Notes sur quatre motets inédits de Michel-Richard Delalande', *Recherches*, i (1960), p. 77; also see Dufourcq, ibid., p. 69.

[2] *Te Deum*, 'Dixit Dominus', 'Miserere mei', 'Exaudi Deus', 'De profundis', 'Domine in virtute tua', 'In convertendo', and 'Lauda Jerusalem'. 'Exaudi Deus' is not in the printed edition.

récit is 'Amplius lava me ab iniquitate mea' ('Wash me yet more from my iniquity').

Ex. 252 (i)

am-pli-us— la-va me   ab in-i-qui-ta-te me-a,

(iv)

am-pli-us___ la - va me   ab in - i - qui - ta - te me -

- a,   ab in - i - qui -ta -te   me.   - a.

SOME CONTEMPORARIES OF CHARPENTIER AND LALANDE

The *petits motets* of Guillaume-Gabriel Nivers (1632–1714) and Louis-Nicolas Clérambault (1676–1749) remain in the French tradition and contain no virtuoso elements from Italian cantatas or operas. Nearly a hundred are extant—all composed for the young women of the Maison Royale de Saint Louis at Saint Cyr, where both composers served as *maîtres de chapelle*. The motets were written for one or two solo voices alternating with a unison or two-part chorus. Most lack a *basso continuo*.[1] French vocal *agréments* decorate what are basically simple diatonic melodies moving in conjunct motion, as may be seen in Ex. 253, from Nivers' *Motets à voix seule avec la basse continue* (1689). Jean-Baptiste Moreau (1656–1733), Lalande, Pascal Colasse (1649–1709), and Louis Marchand (1669–1732) in their settings of Racine's *cantiques spirituels* supplied the young women of Saint Cyr with a similar type of functional music.[2]

Ex. 253

plan —   — ge qua —   — si vir - go.

Daniel Danielis (1635–96),[3] like Du Mont a Walloon born near Liège, was from 1684 *maître de chapelle* at St. Pierre, Vannes. Le Cerf, among others, thought him to be an Italian, and certainly his

[1] For a discussion of religious music at Saint Cyr see Marie Bert, 'La musique à la maison royale Saint-Louis de Saint-Cyr', *Recherches*, iii (1963), pp. 55–71; iv (1964), pp. 127–31; and v (1965), pp. 91–127.

[2] See Boulay, 'Les cantiques spirituels de Racine mis en musique au XVIIᵉ siècle', *XVIIᵉ Siècle: Bulletin de la Société d'Étude du XVIIᵉ Siècle*, xxxiv (1957), pp. 79–92.

[3] On Danielis see Elisabeth Lebeau, 'Daniel Danielis', *Revue Belge de Musicologie*, xii (1958), pp. 70–4, and Guy Bourligueux, 'Le mystérieux Daniel Daniélis', *Recherches*, iv (1964), pp. 146–78.

motets, with their textual repetitions, vocalises, rapid and frequent modulations, chromaticism, and word-painting, are closer in spirit to the religious music of Carissimi than to that of Lully. There are 72 extant motets by Danielis for one to four voices (with continuo and in some instances with obbligato instruments), manuscript copies of which may be found in the Bibliothèque Nationale (Fonds du Conservatoire) and the University Library at Uppsala (Düben Collection). Four motets were printed by Ballard in his *Meslanges de musique latine, françoise et italienne* for the years 1725–7.

Trained by Robert, Du Mont, and Lully, Henry Desmarest (1661–1741)[1] was one of the fifteen finalists in the great *concours* of 1683 to choose four *sous-maîtres* for the Chapelle Royale. As a test piece all candidates were required to compose a motet to the text of Psalm 31, 'Beati quorum remissae sunt'. Desmarest's setting (which is lost) was 'one of the most beautiful . . ., but the king thought him too young to hold one of the appointments' (Titon du Tillet). He was never to realize his ambition of becoming a *sous-maître*. He was exiled from France in 1699 for the abduction of the daughter of the director of taxation for the Senlis district.[2] Nonetheless, his style remained close to that of his great contemporary Lalande. He had the same preference for large choral masses with voice parts carefully scored to emphasize expressive dissonance (see Ex. 254). The density of his polyphonic writing does

Ex. 254

[1] See Michel Antoine, *Henry Desmarest (1661–1741): biographie critique* (Paris, 1965).

[2] After his expulsion, he served Maximilian Emmanuel in Brussels (1699–1701); Philip V of Spain in Madrid as director of his *musique de chambre* (1701–7); and Leopold, Duke of Lorraine, in Lunéville as *surintendant de la musique* (1707–37).

not compromise the inner tension and direction of the moving parts (see, for example, 'Laboravi in gemitu meo' in 'Domine ne in furore'). Desmarest's setting of 'De profundis',[1] composed before 1704, was closely modelled on the motet of the same name by Lalande, using the same key and sharing similar melodic material. An extract from the 'Requiem aeternam' is given in Ex. 254.

For thirty-five years Guillaume Poitevin (1646–1706), from Arles, served the *maîtrise* of Saint Sauveur at Aix-en-Provence.[2] Although himself a composer of Masses and motets, he is best known as an inspired teacher of such composers as Campra, Jean Gilles, Jacques Cabassol, Claude-Mathieu Pellegrin, Laurent Belissen, and Esprit Blanchard.

Jean Gilles (1668–1705)[3] directed successively the choir schools at Aix-en-Provence, Montpellier, Agde, Avignon, and Saint Étienne at Toulouse. Eleven *grands motets*, a *Te Deum*, three Lamentations, two Masses (including the famous *Messe des morts*) and several *petits motets* survive in manuscript.[4] His geographical remoteness softened the influence of the 'official' style of Paris, so that his motets seem more personal in style. The *récits* in their melodic lines reflect the irregular phrase lengths of Provençal melody, albeit much ornamented. In the 1760s, long after Gilles' death, his *Messe des morts* caught the fancy of the *Concert Spirituel* audiences and gained a popularity which it has never entirely lost. It was published in Paris, Rouen, and Lyons and was performed at the obsequies of Rameau and Louis XV. Its

Ex. 255

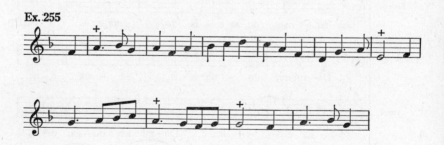

[1] The Toulouse-Philidor Collection at St. Michael's College, Tenbury, includes eleven *grands motets* and one double-chorus Mass by Desmarest. Four psalm settings, each averaging over 100 pages, are located in the Fonds du Conservatoire, now in the Bibliothèque Nationale; single motets are also found in the Bibliothèque Nationale, the Bibliothèque Municipale, Versailles, and the Bibliothèque Municipale, Lyons.

[2] See Raugel, 'La Maîtrise de la cathédrale d'Aix-en-Provence', *XVIIe Siècle: Bulletin de la Société d'Etude du XVIIe Siècle*, xxi (1954), pp. 422–32.

[3] On Gilles see John H. Hajdu, *The Life and Works of Jean Gilles* (Diss., Colorado, 1973, unpub.).

[4] Manuscript copies of Gilles' motets and Masses are in the Bibliothèque Nationale and the Bibliothèque Méjanes at Aix-en-Provence.

popularity is understandable. It has melodic freshness and dance-like melodies in triple metre, asymmetrically phrased, alternating with choral homophony and string *symphonies* reminiscent of Du Mont. Ex. 255 shows part of a characteristic melody in the 'Et tibi'.[1]

Although there is little of the real polyphony of Lalande or Desmarest, the chant-like subject of the final chorus is organized in imitative entries (see Ex. 256). Part of its effectiveness stems from the typically French use of expressive ornamentation. The written out *port de voix* in the third bar of the subject inevitably creates dissonance when combined with other voices, as in bars 8 and 14.

Ex. 256

[1] This and the following example are taken from Paris, Bibliothèque Nationale, MS. Vm¹. 1375.

32

RELIGIOUS MUSIC FROM 1700 TO 1750

As we have seen, the change of style that brought about the 'ingenious disparities' in the later motets of Lalande and converted the simple *récit* into a concert aria took place in the eighteenth century well before the death of Louis XIV in 1715. Religious music, like stage music and instrumental and vocal chamber music, fell increasingly under the spell of Italy. By 1699 Ballard had published his first *Recueil des meilleurs airs italiens*; in 1699 Campra composed a short, self-contained Italian opera, *L'Orfeo dell'inferni*, as part of his ballet *Le Carnaval de Venise*; in 1701 Corelli's violin sonatas, Op. 5, were first printed in Paris and were an instant success; and in 1706 the first book of *Cantates françoises* by Jean-Baptiste Morin initiated the vogue for French adaptations of the Italian cantata.

As early as 1701 Ballard wrote of the motets by Jacques-François Lochon: 'the composer by his genius has found the secret of uniting Italian form and expressiveness with French delicacy and gentleness'. Lochon's motets are in fact mediocre, working a profusion of repeated text fragments into long vocal melismas, but they do indicate a trend that was to continue as the century progressed. Similarly, religious music became increasingly secularized as the *grand siècle* gave way to the Regency. The *petit motet* and the *cantate françoise* tend to differ only in subject-matter and language. They share melodic formulas, characterized by French ornamentation and Italian melisma. Both use recitatives and *da capo* arias; and in both the driving rhythms of the Italian concerto and the gentle homophony of the French 'sommeil' co-exist.

The *grand motet* could not isolate itself from the aggressive state religion it served. Indeed, lacking a firm liturgical base, grounded purely on style, it should never have survived the *grand siècle*. Yet survive it did, permanently stabilized as part of the repertory of the Chapelle Royale and the *Concert Spirituel*. Its composers were such nonentities as Philippe Courbois, François Pétouille, Guignard, and Gomay. Gifted French composers such as Rameau and Leclair were committed to stage and instrumental music from the 1730s on, no doubt realizing that the frivolity and anticlericalism of the times were not propitious to religious music. Nevertheless, the composers whose religious music must concern us in the remainder of this chapter include, in addition to many minor masters, three of the most important names in French eighteenth-century music: André Campra, François Couperin, and Jean-Philippe Rameau.

CAMPRA

André Campra (1660–1744)[1] was born in Aix-en-Provence, where he began his musical studies under Poitevin at Saint Sauveur in 1674. He served as *maître de chapelle* at Saint Trophîme in Arles (1681) and at Saint Etienne in Toulouse (1683). From June 1694 to October 1700 he was *maître de musique* at Notre Dame cathedral, replacing Jean Mignon. During the same period he was appointed a canon at Saint Jean-le-Rond.

Given the repressive climate of the court at Versailles under the puritanical aegis of Mme. de Maintenon, and the opposition to opera on moral grounds expressed by Boileau,[2] the conservative clergy, and the Sorbonne, it was inevitable that the lure of the stage should draw Campra into conflict with the ecclesiastical authorities. Three years after his popular *opéra-ballet L'Europe galante* was first performed (October 1697), Campra terminated his official church functions to become 'conducteur' at the Académie Royale de Musique. He did not return to an active role in the service of religion until 1723, when, at the age of sixty-three, he accepted responsibility for one of the quarters of the year at the Chapelle Royale—a position he kept until 1735.

His five books of *Motets à I, II ou III voix avec la basse continue*

---

[1] For literature on Campra, see p. 230, n. 2, *supra*. Campra's motets are discussed by Lionel de la Laurencie, 'Notes sur la jeunesse d'André Campra', *Sammelbände der internationalen Musikgesellschaft*, x (1908–9), pp. 159–258; see also Maurice Barthélemy, *André Campra* (Paris, 1957), pp. 28–41. The motet 'Cantate Domino' is in Davison and Apel, op. cit., p. 147. Many others are available in modern editions.

[2] Boileau's famous *Satire X*, with its attack on the operas of Lully—'Et tous ces lieux communs de Morale lubrique,/Que Lully rechauffa des sons de sa musique?'—first appeared in 1694.

(1695, 1700, 1703, 1706, and 1720), his *Missa 4 vocibus Ad majorem Dei gloriam* (1699), his Requiem, his two books of psalm settings (1737 and 1738), and his many motets for the Chapelle Royale (most of which remain in manuscript)[1] are evidence of a fertile mind flexible enough to produce a harmonious union of French and Italian styles and imaginative enough to endow his sacred music with something of the drama and pathos of his best stage music.

In the *Avertissement* to his first book of *Cantates françoises* (1708), Campra wrote that he had attempted to 'mix the liveliness of Italian music with the delicacy of French music'. It will be noted that his first four books of motets predate the cantata collections and are preliminary essays in *goûts réunis*. In Books I and II there are many examples of a particularly French type of popular melody in triple metre with a syllabic treatment of the text even of those words that normally invite a more melismatic setting (see Ex. 257 (i) from 'O sacrum convivium'). French vocal ornamentation, especially the *port de voix* (see Ex. 257 (ii) from 'In te Domine spes'), combines with rapid modulations, chains of suspensions and chaconne basses (see, for example, 'Tota pulchra es' in Book I and 'Cum invocarem' in Book II) to begin to move the motets closer to Italian models.

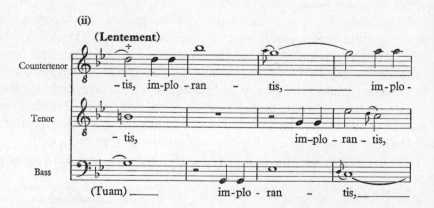

---

[1] These motets, some of which are autographs, are at the Bibliothèque Nationale (Fonds du Conservatoire) and the Bibliothèque Méjanes at Aix-en-Provence. There are also manuscript copies at St. Michael's College, Tenbury, and the University of California at Berkeley.

- ran — — — tis.

im – plo – ran — tis.

im – plo – ran — tis.

In Book III short binary dialogue *airs* and *airs gracieux* similar to those found in contemporary French stage works (see, for example, 'In supremae nocte' from 'Pange lingua') co-exist with virtuoso arias often with elaborate instrumental obbligatos (see, for example, 'Eleva-verunt flumina' in 'Dominus regnavit'). 'Quis ego Domine' is singled out in the title of the collection as a 'motet à la manière italienne'. It is clear that for Campra in 1703 the Italian manner consisted basically of the use of mechanical rhythmic pulsations, fughetta passages and a 'vivace' tempo all borrowed from the Italian sonata and concerto (see Ex. 258). Book IV includes more *da capo* arias which make use of both triadic

Ex. 258

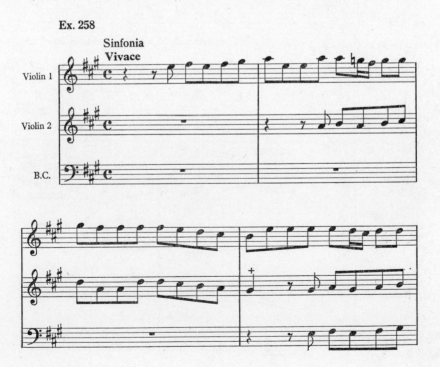

melodies in concerto style and long, sequential vocal melismas. 'Salvum me fac Deum' is prefaced by a *symphonie* which, with its sequence of sevenths, could be from a Corelli trio sonata. Campra did not return to the motet until 1720 with his Book V. In 1735 Ballard printed all five volumes together. The title-page is eloquent testimony to the variety achieved by Campra in this medium: *Recueil de Soixante Motets melez de Symphonies; savoir, 35 à Voix seule, dont 6 Basses ou Bas-Dessus, 18 à deux Voix, la plupart Duos de Voix égales, 6 à trois Voix, 1 à Grand-Chœur.*

The two books of psalms and the bulk of the manuscript motets are *grands motets* composed for the Chapelle Royale. Campra viewed certain psalm versets as dictating a musical vocabulary derived more from the operatic stage than from the sanctuary. In 'Omnes gentes' (1725) a

Ex. 259

soprano voice is linked with trumpet fanfares in acclamation, bringing to mind Alessandro Scarlatti or Handel. The same work also includes some fine polyphonic writing for three basses that rivals the 'trio des basses' from the composer's *tragédie lyrique Tancrède*. In the best operatic fashion 'Notus in Judaea Deus' (1729) includes a 'sommeil'. In 'Lauda Jerusalem' (1727), to depict 'velociter currit sermo eius' ('His word runneth swiftly') (Ex. 259), Campra allowed his orchestra, with its rapid violin figurations, to penetrate the chorus much in the manner of the large choral frescoes in his *Idomenée* (see, for example, 'Laissez nous sortir d'esclavage' in the prologue).

All is not theatrical display, however. 'De profundis' establishes a mood of solemn grandeur, and in the double-fugue setting of 'Et lux perpetua' we have further evidence of Campra's skill in holding together large-scale movements constructed over *ostinato* basses.

COUPERIN

François Couperin (1668–1733),[1] organist (but never musical director or composer) for the Chapelle Royale, wrote motets only for soloists. Some were performed on the occasion of the removal of the court to Fontainebleau; others he wrote for the delicate voice of his daughter Marie-Magdeleine, a nun at the Abbey of Maubuisson, or for his cousin Marguerite-Louise, a well-known singer.

In the preface to his *Les Goûts réunis* (1724) Couperin reminded his readers with typical bluntness that 'Italian and French tastes had shared the republic of music in France for a long time' and that as far as he was concerned he had always 'held in esteem whatever merited it without reference to composer or nation'. The 'sharing' of French and Italian tastes is particularly evident in his religious music and may be the basis for Le Cerf's judgement that he was a 'serviteur passionné de l'Italie'. Couperin accepted from Italy elements of an 'affective' declamatory style whose roots stretch back to Monteverdi (see the 'lament' 'Plorans ploravit in nocte' in the first *Leçon de Ténèbres*). From Italy also came the elaborate vocal melismas that only rarely in Couperin are subverted to mere display purposes, as, for example, in the *Motet pour le jour de Pâques*. More often they are used in the manner of Handel or Vivaldi and generate small contrapuntal cells that serve as unifying devices throughout the texture (see, for example, 'Veni, veni, sponsa Christi' in the *Motet de Sainte Suzanne*). Italianate vocal

Ex. 260

[1] The standard work on Couperin is Wilfrid Mellers, *François Couperin and the French Classical Tradition* (London, 1950); the church music is discussed in chap. VIII. Also see 'Bibliographie chronologique des Couperin', *Mélanges François Couperin* (Paris, 1968). In the *Œuvres complètes* the church music appears, ed. Paul Brunold, in vols. xi–xii (Paris, 1932–3). An edition of the three *Leçons de Ténèbres*, ed. D. Vidal, is included in the series *Le Pupitre* (Paris, 1968). For information regarding a recently discovered collection of motets probably by Couperin at St. Michael's College, Tenbury, see Philippe Oboussier, 'Couperin Motets at Tenbury', *Proceedings of the Royal Musical Association*, xcvii (1971–2), p. 17; nine of these motets have been ed. idem, *Le Pupitre* (Paris, 1972).

melismas are on occasion modified by Couperin's highly developed
sense of variation and his sensitivity to the expressive potential of
French vocal ornamentation. Ex. 260 shows how he constantly varied
the shape of the melisma on the words 'in aeternum' in the final duo of
'Mirabilia testimonia tua'.

In addition to ornamentation French elements in Couperin's religious
music include the use of short phrases with many cadence points and
melodic patterns whose origins may be traced to French dance music
and the *air sérieux*. In his treatment of dissonance he also combined
French and Italian practices. Of special interest is the careful and
deliberate use of the chord of the mediant $\frac{9}{7}$ to portray a feeling of total
desolation in the *Leçons de Ténèbres*. It occurs in the first lesson on the
words 'Ex omnibus charis ejus' ('Of all who cherish her, she [Jerusalem]
hath none to comfort her'). Its most poignant use is reserved for the
words 'posuit me desolatam' ('He hath made me desolate') in the final
lesson, where it is found in conjunction with a melodic diminished octave
(see Ex. 261). The editor of the *Œuvres complètes*[1], although ack-
nowledging the use of this interval in the 'édition originale', apparently
found it too harsh to include in the edition.

Ex. 261

---

[1] See *Œuvres complètes*, 'Musique vocale', ii, p. 236. Ex. 261 is taken from the edition
by Daniel Vidal, *Le Pupitre* (Paris, *c.* 1968).

As a miniaturist, Couperin, unlike Lalande, wisely restricted his settings to the more intimate verses of the psalms. His descriptive instincts, seen to such advantage in the *Pièces de clavecin*, were brought to bear on his psalm settings as well. Nature scenes borrowed from contemporary opera abound in the selected versets of Psalm 80, 'Qui regis Israel, intende', which constitute the *Sept Versets du motet* of 1705.[1] The high tessitura of two sopranos and the sound of recorders 'accompanied' by a violin characterizes the *Quatre Versets d'un motet* (1703) chosen from Psalm 118, 'Mirabilia testimonia tua'.[2] The two soloists, one of whom, the score informs us, was Marguerite-Louise Couperin, establish the characteristic sound of this psalm setting at the very beginning in a duo scored for two sopranos 'sans Basse Continue ny aucun Instrument':

Ex. 262

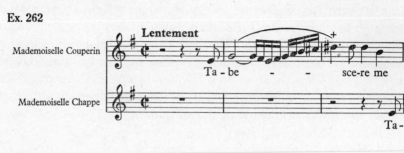

In contrast, the sound of tenors and basses accompanied by the more brilliant transverse flutes and oboes dominates the *Sept Versets du motet* of 1704 based on Psalm 84, 'Benedixisti, Domine, terram tuam'.[3]

In his last and greatest religious composition, the *Leçons de Ténèbres* composed between 1713 and 1717 for the nuns of the Abbey of Longchamp, Couperin stripped the music of any exterior descriptive elements. What remains is a stark simplicity in which every nuance of textual meaning is mirrored in the music (see Ex. 261 above).

CONTEMPORARIES OF CAMPRA AND COUPERIN

We need not linger over the two books of motets and a four-part

---

[1] *Œuvres complètes*, 'Musique vocale', i, pp. 149–84.
[2] Ibid., pp. 87–113.
[3] Ibid., pp. 115–48.

Mass by Jean-François Lallouette (1651–1728). The veneer of Italianisms does little to compensate for the overall mediocrity of this music. Lallouette's colleague, the great bibliophile Sébastien de Brossard (1655–1730), directed successively the choir schools at Strasbourg (from 1687) and Meaux (from 1698). For these he composed three volumes of *Élévations et motets* (printed by Ballard in 1695, 1698, and 1703) as well as numerous manuscript motets now in the Bibliothèque Nationale. Although he was happy to acknowledge that 'never has there been more taste and passion for Italian music than exists now in France', his own music with its conventional harmony and short phrases is generally devoid of Italian influence. Original touches are provided occasionally by the use of sudden contrasts in dynamics and rapid tempo changes. The motet 'Domine quid multiplicati' (1703 collection), for example, changes from Adagio to Prestissimo within seven bars. Brossard's motets are made up of several short sections, many of which have their own 'Alleluia' or 'Amen' finales. These were designed as possible termination points should the motets (in the words of the preface) 'appear to be a little long'.

Nicolas Bernier (1664–1734)[1] studied in Rome with Antonio Caldara. He then directed the choir schools of Chartres and Saint Germain-l'Auxerrois—stepping-stones in a career which led him to the Sainte-Chapelle in 1704 as successor to Charpentier. In 1723 he joined Campra and Gervais at the Chapelle Royale. Forty-five *petits motets* (in printed editions of 1703, 1713, and 1741) and eleven *grands motets* (in manuscript copies at the Bibliothèque Nationale and the Bibliothèque de la Ville, Lyons) constitute his extant religious music. The *petits motets* are mostly for solo voice with occasional violin or flute obbligatos. The *grands motets* reveal Bernier to be totally within the tradition of the Versailles motet, with the five-part chorus doubled by the orchestra. Harmonically they are more conservative than the motets of Charpentier and Lalande.

The two books of *petits motets* by Jean-Baptiste Morin (1677–1745) show a strong Italian bias. They include some *da capo* arias as well as some self-contained 'Alleluia' finales in the style of Brossard. The twelve *Motets à I, II et III voix* (1711) by Edme Foliot (dates unknown) were engraved in a *de luxe* edition at the composer's expense and dedicated to Lalande. Foliot's motets, like those of Nivers and Clérambault, were composed with the limitations of the 'dames religieuses' in mind. Harmonically they are less static than the motets of Brossard or Bernier. Like the *petits motets* of Brossard they may be

---

[1] On Bernier's motets see Philip Nelson, 'Nicolas Bernier: a résumé of his work', *Recherches*, i (1960), p. 93.

abridged 'in order not to prolong the Divine Office', and they too include brilliant 'Alleluia' and 'Amen' finales which often resemble vocal gigues.

Jean-Joseph Mouret (1682–1738)[1] composed his *petits motets*, as he did his cantatas, for performance at the *Concert Spirituel*, which he headed as artistic director from 1728 to 1734. These motets, which were printed posthumously in Paris (the privilege is dated 1742), exhibit a superficial elegance and revel in vocal display. Several have the by now familiar 'Alleluia' finales and one ('O sacrum convivium') even includes a soprano cadenza. In contrast, the *Te Deum* by Colin de Blamont, from his only extant book of motets (Paris, 1732), is closely modelled on the *grands motets* of his teacher Lalande. He even makes use of the device of presenting two contrasting motives first consecutively and then simultaneously, as may be seen in Ex. 263 (i and ii):

Ex. 263 (i)

[1] See Renée Viollier, *J. J. Mouret, le musicien des grâces* (Paris, 1950).

RAMEAU

The reputation of Jean-Philippe Rameau (1683–1764)[1] is rightly that of a composer of opera. His motets, however, though uneven in quality, contain some fine music and deserve to be more widely performed than at present. There are four *grands motets* which can reasonably be identified as his:[2] 'Deus noster refugium' (before 1716), 'In convertendo' (*c.* 1718), 'Quam dilecta' (*c.* 1720), and 'Laboravi' (before 1722). Of these, 'Laboravi' is a setting for five-part chorus of the fifth verse of Psalm 69 (reproduced as an illustration of fugue in Book IV of Rameau's *Traité de l'harmonie*). 'Deus noster refugium', a setting of Psalm 46, is a more typical *grand motet*. The setting is divided into nine self-contained parts, four *airs*, a duet, a trio, a quartet, and two choruses. The third verse, 'Sonuerunt et turbatae sunt aquae corum', organized as a concerto grosso, is a 'storm scene'. The trio 'Propterea non timemus' similarly employs string tremolos to represent mountains being carried down to the sea in an earthquake. In this way Rameau transferred to the *grand motet* something of the scene-painting familiar in opera, though not on the scale of the *tonnerres* and *orages* in his cantata *Thétis* of about the same date.

'In convertendo', although uneven, is Rameau's best religious work. The opening solo for countertenor is an elegiac monologue, operatic in character and employing the varying metre of French recitative, which is rarely found with Latin texts. The ornaments aid rather than hinder

[1] The standard work on Rameau is Cuthbert Girdlestone, *Jean-Philippe Rameau* (London, 1957); the motets are discussed on pp. 73–105. In the *Œuvres complètes*, ed. Camille Saint-Saëns, they are in vols. iv–v (Paris, 1898–9).

[2] A fifth motet, 'Diligam te', is attributed to Rameau and included in the *Œuvres complètes* but is thought to be spurious. 'Laboravi', 'In convertendo', and 'Quam dilecta' are available in modern editions (Paris, n.d.). The chorus 'Cor meum et caro mea' from 'Quam dilecta' is recorded in *The History of Music in Sound*, v.

expressiveness, and though it seems declamatory in style, it is in fact a
rondeau air with *ritournelles* before and after. The bass solo 'Converte,
Domine' is somewhat mechanical, though the orchestra effectively
imitates the sound of the 'streams in the south' until the entry of the
famous dialogue between soprano and choir to the words 'Laudate
nomen Dei'. (The theme of this dialogue, with its harmonization, was
later used by Charles-Hubert Gervais and Esprit Blanchard in their
settings of the *Te Deum*.) Rameau's 'Laudate' successfully integrates the
solo voice, embellished in the Italian manner, with a simple, folk-like
four-part chorus.

The concluding chorus of the motet, 'Euntes ibant et flebant', is
probably the 'greatest piece in all Rameau's church music'.[1] A setting
of the seventh verse, 'Euntes ibant et flebant, mittentes semina sua.
Venientes autem venient cum exultatione, portantes manipulos suos'
('He that goeth forth and weepeth, bearing precious seed, shall doubtless come again with rejoicing, bringing his sheaves with him'), the
chorus is based on two contrasting motives. The first, expressing
sorrow, is a descending chromatic motive; the second, denoting joy,
is a paroxysm of ascending scales and sudden leaps. After the initial
statement of the first motive the large orchestra (flutes, oboes, bassoons,
and strings) intervenes to state the second motive. These motives are
later expanded, contracted, and combined with great skill:[2]

---

[1] Girdlestone, op. cit., p. 98.
[2] *Œuvres complètes*, iv, p. 70.

in spite of Mondonville's fashionable Italianate airs and his keen sense of orchestral sonorities, his *grands motets* today seem tired exercises in an outmoded style. They serve only to emphasize the superiority of Lalande, the one composer of religious music in France whose *grands motets* did not become outdated.

VIII

ENGLISH CHURCH MUSIC[1]

By ANTHONY LEWIS

INTRODUCTION

DURING the period of the Commonwealth (1649–60) the tradition of English church music suffered an interruption more severe than at any other time in its long history. The large choral establishments of the great cathedrals, in which the composers of the Tudor epoch had found their training and inspiration, were summarily disbanded, and the organs and other instruments which were gradually coming to be associated with the voices were as decisively silenced. Such a forcible and drastic severance of the main arteries, material and creative, of the system might have been expected to have had fatal results, or at least to have led to a seriously crippling paralysis. The remarkable fact is that within twenty years church music in England had regained its former vitality and was pressing on towards new achievements that bade fair to rival the most impressive triumphs of the Elizabethans.

To this outcome the harshly suppressive methods of the Puritans may themselves have contributed. For although the Puritans strongly objected to music in church, they were by no means averse to it elsewhere, and the record of their régime is one of active encouragement in the secular field. Consequently for a time the attention of composers was directed away from the choral and liturgical aspects of music and focused more on its instrumental and dramatic functions. They began to concern themselves seriously with the problems of opera and of music for the theatre generally and set about developing a chamber-music and orchestral style suited to the special characteristics of the now rapidly predominating violin family. This led to a broadening of vision on the part of those who had been in some danger of becoming limited by too narrow an outlook. An ecclesiastical atmosphere, as we have since learned to our cost, can smother, as well as quicken, the creative flame, and the judicious admission of a current of air from outside has

---

[1] The best anthology of this music is *A Treasury of English Church Music, iii: 1650–1760,* ed. Christopher Dearnley (London, 1965). Sources for individual composers are referred to in subsequent footnotes.

often a stimulating effect. In practice, events proved that this enforced banishment of many musicians from their customary milieu was not so protracted as to obliterate the deeply ingrained traditions they had acquired, but was sufficiently long for them to be able to gain wider experience before making a fresh approach to their former task.

THE RESTORATION AND FRENCH INFLUENCE

If the suspension of the monarchy thus radically affected musical activities, its restoration also had certain artistic consequences. In a society where music was still mainly dependent on patronage, especially royal patronage, the tastes of the king whose restoration brought the Commonwealth to an end would be expected to exert a material influence on the response of those in his service. During his exile Charles II had been deeply impressed by the type of music in favour at the French court and had determined that his own future royal establishment should be planned on lines similar to those of Louis XIV. So he caused a private band to be formed after the model of Louis's 'vingt-quatre violons du roi' and required that it should take part in church services as well as entertain at court functions. Charles had also grown to prefer the style of the French music of this period, with its more direct melodic line and clearer rhythmic definition as compared with the relatively elusive texture of the English polyphonic composers. He therefore decided to found a new school that should be in greater sympathy with his inclinations and as a first step sent one of the most brilliant of the Chapel Royal choirboys—Pelham Humfrey—over to France to be grounded in the technique of Lully. This appears to have had at least the correct superficial effect, since Pepys tells us that Humfrey returned 'an absolute Monsieur', while his music confirms that the French influence was not confined to his appearance and affectation. At the same time a considerable number of French musicians of uneven capacity were encouraged to visit this country to teach the English the secrets of their art. Such expressions of the royal attitude towards music made their impact on church composers, who sought to adapt their methods in accordance with the king's wishes, with results that were sometimes incongruous in those to whom the idiom was uncongenial, and often lacking in dignity when the application of the style was perfunctory or insincere.

But important as was the king's preference in this respect, it should not be over-estimated. To a large degree Charles II merely accentuated what was already a marked tendency in music in general and hastened the emergence of methods that were almost bound to predominate eventually. Certainly to accuse him of the 'secularization' of English church music is unduly flattering to the extent of his control and mainly unjust to the manner of its operation. It may seem surprising that he sent Humfrey to study church music with Lully, a voluminous composer for the stage, but this was not so foolish as might appear at first sight. For Lully, as well as producing many operas and ballets, was one of the leading church composers of the day, to which his great *Miserere* stands material witness. Furthermore, if Humfrey's anthems are studied closely, their most significant feature is seen to be the character of the declamation rather than any indecorous rhythmic quality. Expressive verbal accentuation of this type springs not from French operatic recitative, to which it is unsuited from the nature of the language, but from the Latin church music of the period, in which Lully's motets hold a distinguished place. As for the increasing definition of the rhythm and the unconcealed frankness of the melodic line in many places, these are peculiar neither to Humfrey nor to Lully, nor indeed to contemporary secular music as a whole. A natural evolutionary process was taking place of which these were symptoms common to every manifestation of the art, whatever its function. In fact as far as Restoration church music is concerned the emphasis has been misplaced. What is remarkable is not the adoption of methods hitherto associated with secular entertainments but the survival, when it had been mainly discarded by the rest of Europe, of the polyphonic technique of the sixteenth century in many of the full anthems and elsewhere. The entry of the string orchestra into the church has also been directly ascribed to the English king's desire to fashion himself after the manner of 'le Roi Soleil', but in reality this was quite a normal development, which merely brought England into line with Continental practice and would most likely have taken place in any case without royal initiative. Those who objected to the employment of violins in ecclesiastical surroundings were taking rather a narrow and insular view of a practice that had already been put into noble effect abroad by Monteverdi, Schütz, and others.

THE DECLAMATORY STYLE

Nor was the French style, associated with Charles II, the only, or even the chief influence on English church music. Italian methods, and especially Italian dramatic methods, were equally, if not more, pervasive. Ever since the pioneer days of Italian opera earlier in the century the setting of words had undergone a gradual change, even in those departments of music farthest removed from the theatre. The ideals of the Florentine dilettanti in regard to the musical presentation of a text had spread beyond the limited and particular scope of their original conception to a much more general field. The genius of Monteverdi established verbal declamation, moving in free rhythm over an instrumental bass and transmitted by means of subtle and expressive melodic inflections, as an accepted technique in the opera-house, and his contemporaries and successors, such as Carissimi, soon applied the same principle to dramatic oratorios. English composers had early employed the style of 'recitative musick', as they called it, in solo song, and its palpable advantages in conveying the rhythm and meaning of the words faithfully and clearly to the hearer made it also seem well suited to religious usage. There had been a perceptible tendency in this direction in the first half of the seventeenth century, but strongly ingrained cathedral traditions had restricted the extent of the movement away from polyphony. The break caused by the Commonwealth eventually cleared the way for composers, and declamation by a solo voice, or group of solo voices, is a regular feature of Restoration church music.

Such methods represented a fundamentally altered view of the relationship between a religious text and its musical setting. In a preponderantly polyphonic style a short verbal phrase will be allied to an appropriate melodic strain that forms the basis of imitation between the voices. In the course of such imitation the contrapuntal lines will tend to cross and merge to an extent that makes it difficult in performance to follow the text at any particular point. Nor is it the composer's intention to place each individual word in its correct perspective immediately but rather to convey the general implication of the whole phrase from the character of the section based on its associated musical theme. There may be a limited amount of word-painting, but the main object will be to communicate the prevailing mood of the religious context without undue preoccupation with detailed verbal expression. The Restoration church composer, on the other hand, is concerned to present the text in such a way that it can be immediately apprehended by the congregation, with every word receiving its fitting emotional emphasis and making a direct impact on the mind of the hearer. Consequently he is inclined to reduce the number of conflicting melodic lines in the interests of clarity, a procedure which, in extreme cases, results in a relatively small proportion of choral passages, in block harmony, while the bulk of the text is delivered by solo voices over a bass that gives support but never interferes or distracts.

CHORAL RESOURCES

The practical conditions of the time gave stimulus to these technical developments, since the disbandment of the choirs by the Puritans had produced a dearth of trained choristers which could not be quickly remedied. It seems that most establishments had to rely on a nucleus of singing-men to carry the main burden, the boys being entrusted only with the simplest tasks in the tutti. Under exceptional circumstances and for special occasions a complete ensemble, balanced in skill and sonority, could be provided, but, in the early days of the Restoration at least, it was in the adult voices that composers were accustomed to place their chief confidence. Choral resources being thus limited, it was natural to increase the scope of the solo element, and the verse anthem, in which a varying number of solo voices declaimed the text singly or in combination, found much favour.

To compensate for the lack of a dependable soprano line, the male alto or counter-tenor voice was much cultivated in the English church music of this period. The counter-tenor voice had always been more popular in England than elsewhere and was constantly to be found in the choral music of the Elizabethan era. In the present circumstances it was clearly of great value in extending the compass of the ensemble of men's voices and in adding a new and brighter tone quality to those of the tenors and basses. Its special characteristics and potentialities were fully recognized by Purcell and his contemporaries, who wrote counter-tenor parts that have never been surpassed in brilliance or expressiveness.

The emergence of the virtuoso singer in general was an external factor undoubtedly taken into account by the choral composer in shaping his style. The congregation at which the composer's music was directed would have expected it to be couched in a current idiom, and in such a case the solo singer was bound to be prominent, since so much of the vocal music of the day was designed to exhibit his powers. Thus the artistic tendencies of the time, the composers' own inclination, and popular taste combined to make inevitable the separation of the individual from the choral group. If church music lost thereby some of its intimacy it also gained much in declamatory power. The great solos which Purcell wrote for the famous bass John Gostling are superbly evocative and majestic, and much of the composer's inspiration in such music surely derived from this splendid instrument at his service. The English school was reaching the height of its achievement in the art of declamation, and the treatment of religious texts for solo voices is notably sensitive and plastic.

THE ENGLISH IDIOM

If English composers had learned something from Italy in this respect they had certainly also added a great deal of their own. The Italian *recitativo secco* had never been popular in England, even for dramatic purposes, and there is always a perceptible melodic intention in English 'recitative musick', which is, therefore, closer to arioso. The more astringent nature of the language, compared with Italian, enabled greater emphasis to be derived from the sounding of the consonants and made it easier to articulate sharply dotted rhythms; of both of these facts Purcell and his contemporaries took full advantage. The English declamation had a firm metrical basis that not only kept it under control but also enhanced the effect of any rhythmical freedom that might be employed. Added to these qualities was a remarkable strength and vitality, which might sometimes lead to exaggeration and distortion but normally preserved the line from the limp and nerveless character of much continental writing. At its best it had an irresistible impulse that carried the force of the words onward until their import was decisively pressed home:[1]

Ex. 266

[1] Purcell, anthem 'Why do the heathen?', *Purcell Society Edition*, xvii (rev. ed., London, 1964), pp. 3–4.

If one is seeking French influence it is more in the instrumental ritornellos than in the declamation that it is to be found. In graceful measures such as these there is certainly a flavour of the ballet music of the French court, though there is a noticeable extra harmonic pungency and rhythmic tautness that is foreign to the Lullian manner:[1]

Ex. 267

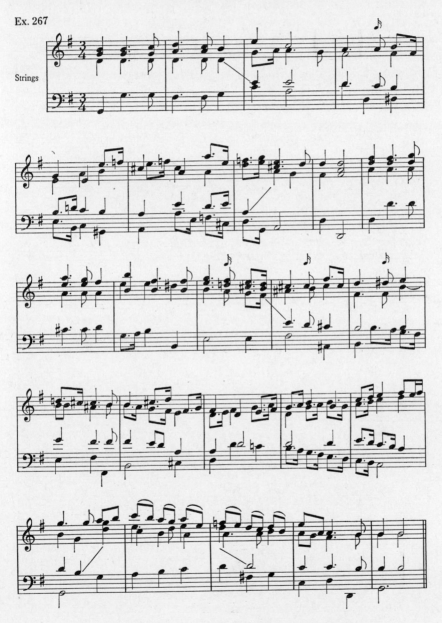

[1] Idem, anthem 'I will give thanks unto thee, O Lord', ibid., p. 48.

But before making too far-reaching deductions from the style of this passage one should not neglect to examine the section that immediately precedes it in the same anthem. For therein is revealed a progression which for intricacy, complexity and intensity of expression has few rivals anywhere in the music of its time, and still less in that of France:[1]

Ex. 268

The problem of obtaining variety and, at the same time, continuity in an extended choral work built up out of a sequence of self-contained sections was one common to all seventeenth-century composers, and English church musicians sought guidance in this respect from their colleagues abroad, who had a rather longer and wider experience on which to draw. The internal construction of the more elaborate services and anthems of the Restoration owed much to French and Italian models. The subtleties of phrasing in the former and the dramatic instinct of the latter were absorbed into the technique of the English composers, without detracting from the independence of their material. Though the main outline of the design might have an underlying foreign origin the melody retained a specifically English quality:[1]

Ex. 269

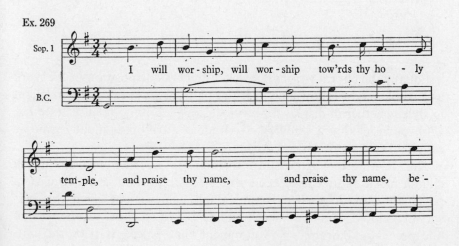

[1] Ibid., pp. 51–2.

Equally the choral writing, however much its disposition in the work as a whole might follow a continental pattern, was perfectly self-reliant in style, whether in displaying a lavish contrapuntal opulence[1] (see Ex. 270), or in making a ceremonial parade of richly individual harmonic resource[2] (see Ex. 271).

That in a period of artistic transition and social upheaval English church music should have been able to establish and assert so clear a personality was in itself a commendable achievement. That this personality should gain such depth and power in so short a time was an unexpected and dramatic development that placed it with the outstanding creative manifestations of the century.

[1] Anthem 'My heart is inditing', ibid., pp. 73–5.   [2] Ibid., pp. 93–4.

Ex. 270

Ex. 271

- to the king's pa - lace.

- to the king's ___ pa - lace.

- to the king's pa - lace.

- to the king's pa - lace.

LOCKE

Prominent among the founders of the English Restoration school was Henry Cooke (*c.* 1616–72), though he was assuredly more important as Master of the Children in the Chapel Royal than as a composer: his anthems are not of high quality. A far more distinguished composer was Matthew Locke (1622–77). Locke was a chorister of Exeter Cathedral and a pupil of Christopher Gibbons, and he later became 'composer in ordinary' to Charles II. He was in many ways a rugged individualist: whatever he touched—and he was a composer of great versatility—bore his imprint. His is not always a mature and fully formed style—that could hardly reasonably be supposed, given the background of his formative years—but it has a remarkably virile cast. His master, Christopher Gibbons, and the other older men, such as William Child, had largely avoided the challenge of the new continental methods, but Locke recognized that it was no use any longer living in the past and that a fresh approach must be made. What form that approach should take was by no means clear, but a visit to the Low Countries in 1648, during which he made copies of current Italian motets, served to give him some indication. Not that there was much in the music he encountered to stir his imagination—it consisted mainly of the mechanical products of second-rate minds—but the routine of its construction provided at least a starting-point for more genuinely creative developments.

In any case he had a sufficiently fertile invention not to be in need of any prompting in that respect from other sources.

Locke by no means accepted the Italian style entirely as he found it. He followed the same principles of declamation, but construed them in terms of his own robust vitality. Refinement of manner pursued contrary to the spirit of the text he rejected brusquely, with the result that his line may sometimes be rough and awkward, but it is rarely tame or insipid. In order to extract the full emotional content of a word or phrase he will employ some unusual appoggiatura, some striking device of rhythm or recondite harmonic progression that might seem crude to the Burneys of the next century, but which, observed in its true perspective, is seen to have a greater force than the more polished idiom of most of his contemporaries. Locke's problem lay not in the means of obtaining effective verbal accentuation, for which he was well equipped, but in securing that emphasis while preserving the music's natural momentum. This is a fundamental difficulty, and one that was particularly troublesome to the English school, since the more powerful and dramatic the point of stress, the greater the need for adjustment in resuming the normal flow. This applies not only in detail, but also in the larger view. The Restoration anthem consisted usually of a sequence of short sections, and the more contrasted and distinctive these were, the less amenable they became to being linked together to form a continuous whole.

In his verse anthems Locke was constantly being faced with technical questions of this sort. A typical example is 'Blessed is the man',[1] a verse anthem for two tenors and bass, where passages of telling declamation alternate with points where the vocal line seems stiff and halting. This is in some respects due to a lack of appreciation of the true relationship between the melody and the bass, a matter in which composers firmly grounded in a polyphonic tradition, as Locke was, did not always see clearly. In a contrapuntal texture any single voice is rarely isolated for long and consequently does not need to be self-reliant for its rhythmic impulses.

'Arise, O Lord' (ATB)[2] is more successful in its organization. From the solo entries of the opening to the alternating counterpoint and homophony of the trio-writing later, there is a sense of control as well as imagination—an unusual and welcome combination in Locke's church music. He manages here to obtain plenty of variety of mood without allowing the general impression to become fussy or spasmodic. He is

---

[1] Autograph in Brit. Mus. Add. MS. 31437, fo. 1^v; this is a collection of autograph anthems and motets by Locke.

[2] Ibid., fo. 14^v.

34

equally adroit in that attractive miniature, 'Let God arise' (ATB),[1] in which he displays his power of vivid illustration within a very narrow frame and, despite the sharpness of the contrasts, produces a result that has an unexpected degree of unity. In 'O give thanks unto the Lord' (ATB)[2] he uses the recurring refrain in the text to good purpose, making its setting for the two upper voices a standard point of departure and return for the varying excursions of the bass and consequently enhancing the effect of the moment when all three parts join in a final chorus of jubilation.

There are several instances where one becomes especially conscious of Italian influence: the use of elaborate coloratura in 'Sing unto the Lord a new song' (ATB) and the long declamatory solos in 'A hymn, O God, becometh thee in Sion'[3] are cases in point. The former is also interesting in having an 'Alleluia' which shows the seventeenth-century development of the successive duple and triple measures of which the Elizabethans were so fond. One notes, too, the emergence of those clearly defined rhythms which have been condemned by some as unsuited to sacred choral music.

As would be expected, there is strong evidence of Italian methods in Locke's settings of Latin words. These comprise some of his most finished work in the present field. Particularly fluent and genial are the motets which he contributed to John Playford's *Cantica sacra* in 1674. These are in two parts with a bass for organ and were probably intended for domestic use. 'Omnes gentes' is frank and unselfconscious, with a naïve but pleasing echo effect for the last repeat of 'plaudite manibus'. 'O Domine Jesu Christe' is in quite another vein. Here is a quiet tenderness and sincerity of appeal that is most touching (see Ex. 272).

'Cantate Domino' returns to a more objective mood, with a fine rising sequence at the beginning of the middle section, and a concluding 'Alleluia' full of character and sinew (see Ex. 273).

Ex. 272

---

[1] Ibid., fo. 4ᵛ.
[2] Ed. J. E. West (London, 1908).
[3] The former ed. West (London, 1905), the latter in Brit. Mus. Add. MS. 31437, fo. 16ᵛ (autograph).

Ex. 273

Of the motets outside this collection 'Domini est terra'[1] is noteworthy as an example of Locke's use of strings in company with voices. The instrumental introduction shows the compression of his style, still based inherently on the contrapuntal approach of his predecessors:

Ex. 274

[1] Ibid., fo. 24ᵛ.

As a result of the practical conditions as well as the artistic tendencies
of his time, most of Locke's church music is of the 'verse' type, with rare
'full' sections in which he often seems to have in mind a solo ensemble
rather than a large chorus. An exception to this general rule is his set
of responses to the Ten Commandments.[1] These are simple, four-part
homophonic pieces and reveal his considerable skill in working on such
a restricted plane. Each response is subtly varied in rhythmic pattern
and harmonic direction and is so shaped as to fit neatly into a well-
balanced sequence—a minor, but not inconsiderable, achievement.

There is rather more emphasis also on the choral writing in the
expressive 'Lord, let me know mine end',[2] although much of it is only
an echo of the solo ensemble. But it is here that Locke gets nearest to
that spaciousness in presenting his material which marks the more
mature art of Purcell. The poignancy of the declamation has time to tell
and rises to a moving climax of intensity in the final bars (see Ex. 275).

Yet with all the passionate conviction and dynamic vigour that Locke
managed to infuse into his church music one is still left with the
impression that he is not entirely at home in this medium, that he feels
cramped by its few remaining restrictions and that its atmosphere is
not suited to his expansive nature. He does not touch the same emotional depths as in his chamber music, nor display the brilliant
resourcefulness of his compositions for the theatre. But, as in those
other fields, by his courageous pioneer work he laid an admirable
foundation on which others could build.

Ex. 275

[1] They appear in his pamphlet *Modern Church-Musick Pre-accus'd, Censur'd and*

Obstructed . . . (1666); a good copy of this is MS. Mus. 24.H.19 in the Fitzwilliam Museum, Cambridge.

² In Brit. Mus. MS. Harl. 7340, fo. 189ᵛ, among other sources.

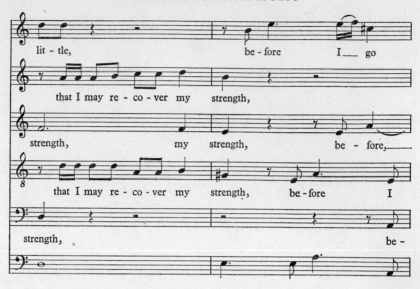

PELHAM HUMFREY

One of the first to benefit from Locke's initiative was Pelham Humfrey (1647–74),[1] a musician connected with the Chapel Royal intermittently throughout his short life. He left England in 1664 to study in France and Italy and was away some three years. The visit was sponsored by the king, and funds were drawn for the purpose from the Secret Service. Paris was by no means an unsuitable place for a young composer to gain insight into the most productive Continental trends in church music; it is known that Lully's *Miserere* was performed in Paris in Holy Week 1666, when Humfrey could well have heard it. He learned hard, and for the most part learned wisely, since he returned having absorbed the methods, while retaining few of the mannerisms of the foreign idiom (at any rate so far as his music was concerned). Indeed it says much for the strength of his creative personality that he was able to withstand the impact of a well-established European tradition at a most impressionable point in his career. For it would be a great mistake to assume that his music is a mere pale reflection of French originals. He is a rather uneven composer, but he is not lacking in invention and can produce a striking progression or turn of phrase of a kind that he would certainly not have acquired at the court of Louis XIV. Unfortunately such felicities are all too often surrounded by much that is indifferent or even inept. At times his declamation seems cogent and well-planned, rising occasionally to real nobility, at others it is flabby and amorphous, bereft of motive power and abounding in faulty accentuation. The bass solo at the beginning of his anthem 'O Lord my God' is representative of the virtues and weaknesses of his style:[2]

Ex. 276

---

[1] See Peter Dennison, *The Life and Work of Pelham Humfrey* (Diss., Oxford, 1970, unpub.), *passim*.

[2] Taken from Brit. Mus. Add. MS. 33235, fo. 21ᵛ. It is in *Humfrey: Complete Church Music*, ii, ed. Dennison, *Musica Britannica*, xxxv (London, 1972), p. 20.

Especially characteristic are such rhetorical devices as the use of the hiatus and of repetition to produce emphasis or pathos. Their employment notably contributes to the fine solo writing in 'Like as the hart' and 'By the waters of Babylon'.[1] Humfrey also contrives to distribute such effects over a number of voices in a verse, as in his setting of the words 'Where is now thy God?' in 'Like as the hart', or in the following passage from 'By the waters of Babylon', in which the emotional force of the successive entries is intensified by the boldly unorthodox suspensions:

Ex. 277

[1] These works appear in *Humfrey: Complete Church Music*, i, ed. Dennison, *Musica Britannica*, xxxiv (London, 1972), pp. 107 and 6 respectively.

The sensitive manner in which the short coda for strings takes up the mood of the voices is typical of Humfrey's treatment of instrumental sections in general. Whenever he introduces violins into his church music the result is, with a few exceptions, markedly felicitous and entirely appropriate in style. He has been censured for aiding the king in establishing the 'vingt-quatre violons du roi' in the Chapel Royal. But if the king's intention seemed to some unworthy, its artistic execution by the composers in his service was not only decorous from the religious standpoint but brought rich musical advantages too. Humfrey's use of strings is felt to be a valuable extension of the expressive power of the voices and in no sense a mere exotic irrelevance. In general it can be said that his vocal writing shows the influence of earlier experiments by English composers of the seventeenth century in a style emanating from Italy, while the string sections are decidedly after the French manner.

Even from his relatively small output it is clear that Humfrey was a sincere and talented composer of distinct individuality. His influence was greater than his achievement, though that achievement would no doubt have been more firmly defined had he lived longer. On the other hand there are no strong grounds for lamenting in him a potential genius of the calibre of Purcell: Humfrey's art has a limited range, beyond which he shows little inclination to venture.

BLOW

One of Humfrey's fellow-choristers at the Chapel Royal was John Blow, who was born in 1649 and died in 1708 and was thus destined to survive Humfrey, and even also to encompass the life of Henry Purcell, his junior by ten years. Thus while Locke may be considered to link the end of the polyphonic era in England to the rise of the Restoration school, Blow's career started at this latter point and continued until the early manifestations of the eighteenth-century style. Yet although he reached into the eighteenth century Blow was far less a part of it than Haydn was of the nineteenth. Blow was a typical Restoration composer and remained true to that conviction: the works that he wrote towards the end of his life show little sign of the change of outlook that came over English music generally at that time.

In keeping with his greater life-span Blow left a correspondingly larger quantity of church music than either Humfrey or Locke. But his work was not only more extensive than theirs, it also marked a distinct advance in scope and technique. This progress was to a great degree made possible by the pioneer achievements of Locke, to whom, in common with most other composers of his generation, Blow was strongly indebted. Of Humfrey's influence there is less trace: it would seem that Blow found his rhetorical methods uncongenial.

The kinship of Blow with Locke is most apparent in their declamation. Here Locke's pursuit of detailed verbal accentuation is carried on by Blow and extended in new directions. One finds an even wider range of expressive ornaments and inflexions, while the contours of the melodic line can be just as jagged and irregular where appropriate to the text. The cadences often have a decisiveness and force above those of Locke, who did not always recognize their structural importance in a long stretch of recitative. But Blow's most valuable contribution in this domain was undoubtedly the strength of his basses. These are seldom hesitant or equivocal, like those of many of his predecessors, but are firm and full of impulse and motive power. They are rich in harmonic implication and sometimes even have a spasmodic contrapuntal interest, but they are never allowed to evade their essential function of providing a steady support to the melody. In many respects Blow still had strong ties with sixteenth-century tradition, but in composing his basses he rightly cast off any lingering adherence to polyphonic principles, which could only serve to distract and confuse under a different system.

The type of declamation favoured by Locke and Blow was especially well suited to the portrayal of spiritual conflict or stress of emotion. It is in such moods that they attain their loftiest heights of eloquence in their verse anthems. A fine instance in Blow is the alto solo 'Behold, O Lord' in the anthem 'How doth the city sit solitary'.[1] There is great subtlety here in the use of chromaticism, in the distribution of emphasis and the control of rhythm. The skilful adjustment of phrase-lengths and the judicious timing of pauses contribute much to the deeply moving effect of this passage. 'I said in the cutting off of my days' and 'As on Euphrates' shady bank'[2] also show this composer's sensitive response to a poignant text; in the latter (a solo anthem for two sopranos and bass) the vocal line is dynamic to the point of disintegration. In his anxiety to underline every detail of the text Blow is in danger of defeating his own ends by failing to persuade us of his sincerity. One is inclined to feel that the music 'doth protest too much'. The following extract represents a point of relative repose and yet contains in the leap of a diminished octave in the fifth bar a hint of restless stringency. Less sensational but more significant musically is the imitation between the bass and the voice and the characteristic shift to a duple rhythm in the melody at the point indicated:

---

[1] A good source is Brit. Mus. Add. MS. 33235, fo. 125ᵛ.
[2] The former ed. Harold Watkins Shaw in *Musica Britannica*, vii (2nd rev. ed., London, 1970), p. 78; the example from the latter is taken from Brit. Mus. Add. MS. 22100, fo. 73ᵛ.

Ex. 278

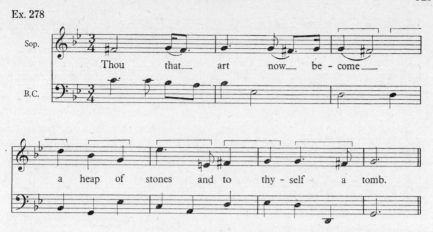

More restrained, and consequently more convincing, is the mood of supplication in 'Turn thee unto me'.[1] The impressiveness of the appeal is gained from the mounting fervour of each repeated clause rather than from a series of dramatic expostulations. The little gesture of pathos made by carrying a harmony note up to a dissonance before a falling interval, as in bars 9–11, is typical of the period and of Blow in particular:

Ex. 279

[1] The source used was Brit. Mus. Add. MS. 33234, fo. 72ᵛ.

soul and de - li - ver__ me,   O let me not be con-found-ed,

let me not be con - found - ed,   for I have put my

trust in thee, I have put my trust,   I have put my trust_____ in____thee.

That Blow could also command a more exuberant vein is agreeably demonstrated by such anthems as 'I beheld and lo' and 'And I heard a great voice'.[1] These have justly won their popularity by the bracing freshness of their melodic strain and by their firm and spirited measure. He would be churlish indeed who pretended to look askance at such qualities in church music; it would be as reasonable to object to Haydn's *Creation*. In being frankly tuneful Blow by no means descends to the crude or the trivial; he pursues a different artistic criterion with the same energy and integrity that he applies elsewhere. He is not in the least apologetic and thereby earns our respect. In fact these seemingly ingenuous pieces contain many adroitly felicitous touches, such as the cross-rhythms at the words 'Fell down before the lamb' in 'I beheld and lo'. Whether or no the royal foot was constrained to beat time during these anthems they are never unworthy of their function, and their enduring zest and vitality cannot be denied.

It is, however, in passing to his full anthems that one appreciates the extra range of Blow's achievement. For he is here working in territory barely touched by Locke and Humfrey. Naturally he has his guides, and these are mostly found among Jacobeans such as Orlando Gibbons.

[1] The former ed. Shaw (London, 1953); the latter ed. idem in *Musica Britannica*, vii, p. 62.

But he also has new controlling factors to deal with in respect of which they can give him little assistance—principally the clear definition of tonality and the changed role of the bass. To a great extent he manages to evolve a technique that combines elements of both styles, and if there is some loss of individuality he serves at least to maintain the continuity of the English choral tradition. It may be possible to regard 'O God, my heart is ready', 'Praise the Lord, ye servants', and even 'Bow down thine ear, O Lord'[1] as mere antiquarian exercises, but the value of such researches is triumphantly displayed in the sturdy independence of the contrapuntal writing in 'Praise the Lord, O my soul' and 'I will praise the name of God' and in the spacious design of 'God is our hope and strength'.[2] Blow was an able craftsman, and his part-writing is invariably sonorous and eventful.

In his more extended works for full choir, such as the services, he is not always successful in creating a sense of continuity. The hard task of welding together a long series of separate clauses, as in the *Creed*, sometimes proves beyond his powers, though he secures a laudable variety by the alternation of homophonic and contrapuntal sections and in subtle differences of phrasing. But if they thus fail to link up into a coherent pattern, many of the individual episodes are none the less attractive. Such a passage as 'He remembering his mercy' from the *Magnificat* of the G major Service is truly delicate and sensitive, while the 'Gloria' of the *Jubilate*[3]—a canon four-in-one—is much more than just technically efficient.

When an orchestra is added to his resources there is a perceptible gain in spaciousness, and the outline is broader and more flowing. The architectural importance of the orchestral element in Restoration church music has often been underestimated. In Blow's case the instrumental symphonies provide a desirable expansion of his choral material and lend a more impressive proportion to the whole. In 'O give thanks unto the Lord',[4] for instance, the opening symphony is based on a ground which is prolonged to accompany the initial entries of the voices. Conversely the concluding phrases of the choral sections are often echoed by instrumental ritornellos, thus further strengthening the bond between them. Furthermore the treatment of choir and orchestra is by no means always antiphonal; Blow makes liberal use of strings in conjunction with voices, either playing obbligato in the solos or lending brilliance

[1] All appear in *Blow: Fourteen Full Anthems*, ed. Heathcote D. Statham (London, 1925), nos. 12, 10, and 8 respectively (the last reprinted, London, 1964).

[2] The first two ed. Statham, op. cit., nos. 1 and 5 respectively (the latter reprinted, London, 1964), the third ed. Statham (London, 1931).

[3] The Service has been ed. Shaw (transposed into A) (London, 1941).

[4] This appears in Brit. Mus. Add. MS. 31444, fo. 152ᵛ, and other sources.

35

to the tutti. 'The Lord is my shepherd' and 'When Israel came out of Egypt'[1] have many judicious examples of this intermingling; in the latter the first violins linger on effectively after the introduction to supply a descant to the chorus. One of his most ambitious anthems with strings is the imposing 'God spake sometime in visions',[2] which was composed for the coronation of James II. Here the monumental character of the initial eight-part chorus is undoubtedly enhanced by the dignified French-style overture that has preceded it, while the low tessitura of the voice parts, which is inclined to make the texture rather thick, is substantially relieved by the brighter tone of the violins playing above them. Like many occasional pieces, in this anthem Blow displays an impressive structural control; it is an unusually large-scale conception and contains many noble pages.

It is a noteworthy fact that English composers of church music have put some of their richest and most personal creative thought into settings of Latin texts. It was so with Byrd and, as has been recorded earlier in this chapter, also with Locke. In the case of Blow his two-part Latin motets are of unusual melodic interest and show considerable resourcefulness in handling an original type of ground bass, though in this respect they cannot survive the inevitable comparison with Purcell. As the number of parts increases so does the degree of harmonic complexity, and Blow's innate adventurousness leads him down some strange paths. In 'Gloria patri',[3] he becomes fascinated by the emotional effect produced by the deliberate reiteration of very close intervals and obviously enjoys keeping the listener in suspense as to the exact nature and direction of their eventual resolution (see Ex. 280).

This is perhaps more to be praised for its enterprise than for its artistic result, but the same comment cannot be applied to the even bolder strokes in the great 'Salvator mundi'.[4] In this short motet every harmonic clash, and there are many, seems entirely spontaneous and appropriate, every unorthodox progression and independent device of scoring is not merely justified but profoundly convincing. At this truly sublime level even Blow's most doubtful experiments appear to have found a profitable culmination, and one can see behind his pungent style a rare spirit—passionate, sensitive, and courageous.

---

[1] The former ed. Shaw in *Musica Britannica*, vii, p. 93; the latter is in Brit. Mus. Add. MS. 30931, fo. 109, and other sources.

[2] Ed. Anthony Lewis in *Musica Britannica*, vii, p. 1; also published separately (London, 1953).

[3] Ed. Shaw (London, 1958).

[4] Ed. Shaw (London, 1949); also in Dearnley, op. cit., p. 58.

PURCELL

The emergence of a dominating figure in the music of any period is apt to have such an adverse effect on the repute of his neighbours that it begins to seem as if those who came before him merely existed to suggest lines of approach that he alone could follow productively. To such a degree does the church music of Henry Purcell (1659–95) transcend the general level of his time that one has to be careful not to belittle the previous achievement on which it is based nor the individuality of those who contributed much to its character. Composers of such distinctive personality as Locke, Humfrey, and Blow might appear to be in no danger in this regard, yet with such ease are various elements of their respective styles exploited by Purcell that one is inclined to overlook their origin and to ascribe to the younger man qualities that belong more properly to his forerunners. But while thus pleading the integrity of Purcell's masters and colleagues, one cannot fail to recognize that he was in many cases able to find a solution to artistic problems at which they had often only succeeded in making a bold, but imperfect, hazard.

There are frequent moments in Locke and Blow when one feels that their harmonic daring is spectacular rather than musical, that it sounds uncomfortable and self-conscious, and that the violence of its effect is ill-matched to the nature of the context. Purcell is scarcely less adventurous, yet he rarely seems anxious to draw attention to recondite appoggiaturas and accented discords, nor, on the other hand, does he fail to convince us that they are logical and appropriate when he has need of them. A judicious use of dissonance is indeed the life-blood of his harmonic style, but he uses it for dynamic, not disruptive, purposes. In the introductory symphony to his anthem 'Why do the heathen?' the boldness of the clashes finds its justification in the validity of the part-writing by which they are engendered. Far from being halted the movement is impelled irresistibly onward by each harmonic stress[1] (see Ex. 281).

The dramatic opening of the metrical psalm-setting 'Plung'd in the confines of despair' is also typical of his firm control over a highly individual texture. This is an instance where the jagged contour of the melodic line, with its final descent of a diminished fifth, might well have occurred to the more imaginative of his predecessors, but it is unlikely that they would have been able to contain it within such a satisfactory harmonic framework. Whereas others might have been forceful but uncouth, Purcell manages to convey the same depth of sentiment without appearing extravagant or hysterical. The successive

[1] *Purcell Society Edition*, xvii, pp. 2–3.

Ex. 281

entries have an air of entire spontaneity, while their effect in conjunction and modulation seems technically quite effortless:[1]

Ex. 282

[1] Ibid., xxx (London, 1965), pp. 180–1.

The ease with which Purcell thus ranged among varied tonalities and was able to give his harmony sudden turns of direction without distorting the even flow of his line enabled him to overcome most of the difficulties of construction that had so beset his older contemporaries. The restricted key scheme which had been such a handicap to the early Restoration anthem, tending to make it monotonous and emphasizing its sectional character by the similarity of the cadences, was now superseded by a much wider and more resourceful disposition. Not only was there more contrast and relief, but there were many opportunities for dramatic transitions, and the general outline of the structure could be made clearer.

If the main plan of the anthem was in this way given a sounder basis, so also did Purcell strengthen the details of the construction. Previously much of the arioso writing—the standard medium of the Restoration church composer—had been inclined to drift along aimlessly when not directed to some strongly defined illustrative or emotional purpose. There is a good deal of vague meandering in the weaker solo passages of Locke and Blow which is not merely tedious in itself but, in its loosening of the fabric, imperils the whole architecture of the composition of which it forms part. Purcell seldom rambles ahead without some underlying design; if his declamation occasionally fails to grip the attention the fault lies rather in the subject-matter itself than in the method of presentation. Yet though his arioso is shapely it avoids the sense of rigid sequence and antithesis to which the eighteenth century was prone. The phrase-lengths are kept elastic, and the internal stresses are constantly redistributed to secure new rhythmic life and rhetorical power. The following extract from his verse anthem 'It is a good thing to give thanks' shows also his fine judgement in the use of coloratura and its contrast with a simpler, quasi-*parlando* style:[1]

[1] Ibid., xiv (rev. ed., London, 1973), p. 12.

Ex. 283

It can be seen therefore that Purcell was particularly well equipped for the special technique required by the verse anthem, a form in which the circumstances and outlook of his time demanded that he should be unusually active. Indeed, of the seventy-odd anthems[1] of his that are extant, only a small percentage can be described as full, and of these practically all have verse sections. It would be idle to pretend that the whole of this considerable output is of equally high value, but few indeed are the pages that do not reveal some point of interest. For Purcell does not allow himself to fall into a routine; his lively invention is continually seeking fresh methods of approach and striving to increase its expressive vocabulary. It is fascinating to study his varied treatment of the solo voices that form the conventional group in the verse anthem or hymn. Every device of entry, of dialogue, and of ensemble is incorporated at some stage, and it is never safe to predict what his response will be to any given text, even in the Alleluias and Glorias. Very often it is in a quiet contrapuntal opening, such as that of 'Ah! few and full of sorrows',[2] that he is at his most impressive. Each individual voice loses nothing of its personality in combination, yet the result is homogeneous and deeply moving.

He will often make use of the opportunities for cumulative emphasis offered by a solo ensemble and will absorb for the purpose some rhetorical figure into a polyphonic texture. Thus in 'Lord, I can suffer thy rebukes', another metrical psalm, he adopts a phrase, which by its reiteration suggests Humfrey, and develops it imitatively so that the mounting cries of appeal reach a climax of stringency in the final bars. It is noticeable that whenever Purcell seems to share in the idiom of another he does not let its principal features degenerate into mannerisms. This is equally true of foreign influence as of that of his own countrymen; he can be Italian without ceasing to be English. He can also, as this passage reveals, be contrapuntal without being in any way anachronistic[3] (see Ex. 284).

To a Restoration composer a group of solo voices would imply a measure of dramatization, and this is apparent in Purcell's sacred music in every degree, from the slight, but effective, suggestion of dialogue in 'Out of the deep' to the tremendous histrionic power of the magnificent scena 'In guilty night'.[4] It is interesting in this respect to compare Purcell's methods with those of Schütz, whose long life just overlapped

---

[1] There are in addition a dozen pieces for three or four voices, most of them settings of metrical psalms.

[2] Ibid., xxx, p. 109. This is an ensemble setting of a paraphrase by George Sandys from the book of Job.

[3] Ibid., pp. 138–9.

[4] Ibid., xxxii (rev. ed., London, 1967), pp. 8 and 128 respectively.

Ex. 284

his. So inclined was Schütz to the dramatic approach that he would create a pretext for characterization if it were not already explicit; but Purcell, in his beautiful and sensitive 'My beloved spake',[1] is content with lively and graphic illustration where Schütz, in similar settings of the Song of Solomon, might have made his singers actually represent characters.

It was not only the prevalence of certain types of voices (and the absence of others) that affected Purcell's style of solo writing, but even more the existence of one particular voice—that of the Rev. John Gostling, Gentleman of the Chapel Royal. This phenomenal voice, of tremendous range and reputedly of great power, dominates a great number of Purcell's anthems. Some of the more famous instances are 'I will give thanks unto thee, O Lord', which makes splendid use of the illustrative capacity of a wide compass, and 'They that go down to the sea in ships',[2] written specially for Gostling and at his request. In the course of musical history one becomes constantly aware of the intimate relationship between the music of a composer and his available performers, who are often the most important factors in his artistic calculations. To say that Gostling was to Purcell what Joachim was to Brahms would probably be to rate too low the influence of the singer.

Gostling was clearly in Purcell's mind when he wrote the verse anthem 'Behold I bring you glad tidings', a work of considerable interest from several points of view, which includes a characteristically elaborate bass solo. The comparison with Handel's treatment of the same words in *Messiah* naturally presents itself, and indeed in many ways the two settings might be taken as representative of the difference in outlook between their respective epochs. For example, Purcell anticipates Handel's massive brilliance in 'Glory to God on high', but the corollary 'And on earth peace, goodwill towards men' evokes a much more personal and subjective response. The use of the string orchestra in this anthem is also significant. The opening symphony is admirably linked to the first recitative by the use of material from the former to serve as accompaniment to the latter. This was a favourite and effective device with Purcell and can be seen to good advantage also in 'O sing unto the Lord' and 'Awake, put on thy strength',[3] where a further bond is established by the transfer of instrumental motives from the symphony to the voices at a later point in the work. The repetition of choral phrases by the orchestra is almost a cliché of the period, but Purcell is rarely content with exact imitation, and the orchestral answer is usually an expansion of the choral statement:[4]

[1] Ibid., xiii (London, 1921), p. 24.
[2] Ibid., xvii, p. 47, and xxxii, p. 71, respectively.
[3] Ibid., xvii, p. 119, and xiv, p. 41, respectively.
[4] Ibid., xxviii (rev. ed., London, 1967), pp. 15–16.

Ex. 285

The relationship between choir and strings is very close throughout this anthem and demonstrates clearly how impossible it is to regard Purcell's instrumental symphonies as mere extraneous interpolations. If further proof were needed to dispel this lingering illusion the study of a number of his large-scale anthems from this point of view should be conclusive. In many of them there are obbligato violin parts in the solos and verses, a notable example being 'O praise God in his holiness',[1] at the end of which two independent string parts and a double chorus are

[1] Ibid., xiv, p. 21.

combined in a veritable *tour-de-force* of counterpoint. A similar degree of virtuosity is to be found in 'Behold now, praise the Lord',[1] where in the antiphonal 'Gloria' the orchestral phrases overlap those of the solo trio and the chorus, thus making the texture very firmly interwoven. Even when the voices and instruments are kept separate the strings are never superficial to the design but have a vital, organic role. How essential the orchestral passages are to the composer's architectural and expressive purpose is impressively revealed in 'Praise the Lord, O my soul, and all that is within me', 'In thee, O Lord',[2] 'I will give thanks unto thee, O Lord', and above all the magnificent 'My heart is inditing'.[3] It is clear that the string orchestra is no casual adjunct but an integral and highly significant feature of Purcell's total conception.

In his full anthems Purcell shows that the legacy of the past can be an asset and not a handicap. He certainly makes use of the matchless technique handed down from the sixteenth century, but so highly individual is his choice of polyphonic subjects and so distinctive his employment of harmonic resource that his style is free of archaism and truly characteristic of the spirit of his age. It might seem hard for a Restoration composer to deprive himself of the emotional power of declamation, but when it is here renounced Purcell convincingly replaces it by the expressive character of his contrapuntal line. No solo singers could rival the poignant effect of the chromatic inflection to the words 'And let my crying come unto thee' in 'Hear my prayer, O Lord',[4] as it passes in continual imitation through eight parts. Nor could a single voice develop so revealingly a simple three-note figure as in the section 'O deliver us' in 'Lord, how long wilt thou be angry?',[5] nor yet exploit to the full the superbly illustrative impression given by the disjunct motive of 'scatter'd us abroad' in 'O God, thou hast cast us out'.[6] The personal flavour of the harmony is very apparent in the funeral sentences, whose touching sincerity also pervades the appealing 'Remember not, Lord, our offences'.[7] This special harmonic quality emerges strongly in the central section of 'O Lord God of hosts',[8] which strikingly exemplifies the exclusive nature of the English idiom of this time. Such pages would not have come from a contemporary hand in any other country in Europe.

These full anthems are mostly short and based on comparatively brief texts, as befits their species. The genre could not easily be adapted to the setting of lengthy canticles, as Purcell's B flat Service[9] shows, but

[1] Ibid., xiii, p. 14.
[2] Ibid., xiv, pp. 131 and 53 respectively.
[3] Ibid., xvii, p. 69.
[4] Ibid., xxviii, pp. 135–8.
[5] Ibid., xxix (rev. ed., London, 1965), pp. 23–5.
[6] Ibid., pp. 120–2.
[7] Ibid., xxxii, p. 19.
[8] Ibid., xxix, pp. 135–7.
[9] Ibid., xxiii (London, 1923), p. 1.

required the relief of short solo passages, which could be introduced without affecting the fundamentally concerted style. A judicious mixture of this kind provides the basis for the great Latin motet 'Jehova, quam multi sunt hostes'[1] which is Purcell's most triumphant metamorphosis of the Italian manner. The derivation is as patent as in the trio sonatas— and the originality no less so. This profoundly beautiful and majestic composition touches the sublime at the words 'Ego cubui et dormivi', justly famed as a moment of outstanding inspiration.

'Jehova, quam multi', 'My heart is inditing', 'Bow down thine ear',[2] 'In guilty night'—to take only four outstanding works—show by their difference in approach the great range and scope of Purcell's church music. But they share in common one characteristic in particular—that complete adjustment of style to content which is one of the signs of artistic maturity in any age. In a remarkably short period the English Restoration School had succeeded in creating and establishing an independent language fit to serve a creative genius of the stature of Purcell. Without attempting to disguise its indebtedness to a number of sources (not the least distinguished of them being the native choral tradition) Purcell made this pungent and expressive vocabulary his own. He used it without self-consciousness or affectation, but with the natural confidence of one speaking his mother tongue. With this rich and vital idiom to draw upon he was able to develop the full force of his originality and to extract from his ideas their utmost significance. For his anthems are not only strongly personal in style, they are vigorously productive in thought and contain some of the most enduring conceptions of their genre. In Purcell the Elizabethan cathedral composers found a successor fully worthy of their calibre, and seventeenth-century sacred music, already superbly enriched by Monteverdi and Schütz, found yet another brilliant interpreter of its special needs.

PURCELL'S MINOR CONTEMPORARIES: CROFT

Purcell was the centre of a very active, if not always highly distinguished, circle. Of the older generation, apart from those already mentioned, were Michael Wise (*c.* 1648–1687), whose anthem 'The ways of Zion do mourn' contains some sensitive declamation, Thomas Tudway (*c.* 1650–1726), a professed reactionary who nevertheless did not disdain the new methods when they suited his purpose, and William Turner (1651–1740). Mention should also be made of an older composer, George Jeffreys (d. 1685), who had no connections with music in London and was in effect an amateur, living in the country.

---

[1] Ibid., xxxii, p. 147.   [2] Ibid., xiii, p. 103.

Yet in his English and Latin sacred music, whether liturgical or for domestic devotions, he shows himself, especially in his Latin songs and dialogues of the 1650s and 1660s, perhaps the most original and enthusiastic follower of declamatory Italianate music in England, as

Ex. 286

well as a composer of considerable harmonic daring and dramatic power.[1] Among the younger men in London one notes the presence of Jeremiah Clarke (1673/4–1707) in this field, though he produced little to suggest that he was not better suited to the secular vein, while John Goldwin (c. 1670–1719), a pupil of William Child, emulated with some distinction the contrapuntal style of his master in his anthems 'Hear me, O God' and 'O Lord God of hosts'.

But of those who were born during Purcell's lifetime the most considerable figure was undoubtedly William Croft (1678–1727).[2] It would not be unfair to say that all that was best in Croft came from Purcell— indeed Croft made no secret of his indebtedness. His setting of the Burial Service,[3] admirable in its quietly restrained sincerity, contains a double tribute to his great predecessor—a short literary acknowledgement couched in engagingly unequivocal terms, and a touching act of musical homage, by refusing to attempt to supersede Purcell's setting of certain lines. Croft achieves his greatest warmth of expression in his full anthems in contrapuntal style, and it is here that the influence of Purcell is most apparent. The opening subject of Croft's 'Hear my prayer, O Lord' is so close to Purcell's phrase to the same words as to suggest deliberate quotation, while the whole of the ensuing texture woven round it clearly draws its inspiration from the same source. Nevertheless this fine anthem has an incontestable claim to recognition in its own right for its excellent workmanship (Croft was often dull but never shoddy) and its depth of sincere feeling. 'Hear my prayer'[4] shows that this normally phlegmatic composer could achieve real emotional conviction (see Ex. 286).

Of similar calibre is the appealing 'O Lord, rebuke me not',[5] though Croft hardly succeeds here in maintaining so high a level of intensity. His response to the text seems to come less from the heart; and there is an unwelcome hint of artifice in the reintroduction of the initial theme at the end to words to which it is indifferently suited. The verse anthems are in general not so interesting, and here also the more expressive passages are those of which the artistic lineage is clearly recognizable:[6]

---

[1] See Peter Aston, 'George Jeffreys', *Musical Times*, cx (1969), p. 772. A few sacred pieces of Jeffreys have been published, ed. Aston (London, 1969 ff.).

[2] See Adrian Carpenter, 'William Croft's church music', *Musical Times*, cxii (1971), p. 275.

[3] Ed. G. C. Martin (London, 1894). It was printed, together with much of Croft's other church music, in his *Musica Sacra: or, Select anthems in score*, 2 vols. (London, 1724– c. 1725).

[4] Ed. C. Hylton Stewart (London, 1925).

[5] Ed. Stewart (London, 1925), and in Dearnley, op. cit., p. 124.

[6] 'Teach me, O Lord', taken from Brit. Mus. Add. MS. 17847, fo. 85 (an imperfect autograph copy).

Ex. 287

Agreeable moments of this kind are unfortunately rather rare, but there are occasional good things in 'Praise the Lord, O my soul' (which has a somewhat unusual solo, 'He layeth the beams of his chambers in the waters'), in 'I will magnify thee, O Lord', and in 'Offer the sacrifice of righteousness', with its effective four-part verse 'There be many that say, Who will show us any good'.[1] Elsewhere Croft is inclined to relapse into a respectable monotony, for which a certain rhythmic stodginess is largely responsible. He is in any case not at his best in solo writing, since his declamation lacks both power and continuity, and there is often a perceptible rise in quality in the choral sections. Thus much of 'O Lord, thou hast searched me out'[2] verges on the pedestrian, but the final chorus, 'Look well if there be any way of wickedness', is a sensitive reflection of the psalmist's mood, imparted with a rare intimacy of style.

Croft could not for long remain facing the past, however congenial that prospect might be for him. The artistic trend of his day was in the direction of balance and refinement, dignity and elegance, and away from anything that savoured of violence or 'enthusiasm'. To the early eighteenth century the bold and vigorous harmonic methods of the Restoration school merely seemed crude, and the forcefulness of its

[1] The first two of these works appear in ibid., fos. 22^v and 65^v respectively, the last in a later collection of Croft's anthems, Brit. Mus. Add. MS 17844, fo. 33.
[2] Ed. Stewart (London, 1925).

declamation extravagant and uncouth. Nevertheless in shunning these imputed vices, minor composers had difficulty in finding positive virtues to take their place. The result with Croft, and with many lesser than he, was a marked loss of individuality and a corresponding increase in decorous platitudinizing. Never a very resilient character, under the pressure of eighteenth-century convention Croft stiffens into a formal rigidity beneath which few signs of vitality can be detected. Unimaginatively employed, the monumental style could be as impassive as a block of concrete. There is a certain amount of bluff cheerfulness about 'Sing praises to the Lord' and 'God is gone up'[1] (despite its unflinching metrical regularity); but in this mood Croft is probably best represented by his hymns, which remain unsurpassed of their kind. In the noble grandeur of their harmonies and the broad majestic sweep of their rhythm, these hymns epitomize the more estimable characteristics of their epoch. For if Purcell was the child of the Restoration, Croft was no less symbolic of the age of Anne.

HANDEL

Croft supplies a link, however insubstantial, between Purcell and the great cosmopolitan who was to exercise marked influence over English church music for much of the eighteenth century—Handel. Handel first arrived in England in 1710, and at once asserted his predominance in the field of opera. It was not, however, until early in his second visit that he was given an opportunity of proving his worth as a church composer. The occasion was the Peace of Utrecht (1713), for the celebration of which Handel was asked to compose a festival *Te Deum and Jubilate*.[2] Adaptable as he was, he drew variously from his earlier experience to accomplish this task. A solid basis was provided by his training under Zachow in the German ecclesiastical style, and over this—often completely obscuring it—he disposed the whole apparatus of Italian technique (mainly secular), which he had acquired since. The solo cantatas he wrote for princely entertainments in Rome,[3] the diverse types of operatic ensemble, the chamber duets he wrote in imitation of Steffani—all these were to serve him in meeting the demands of sacred music. Nor had his brief acquaintance with the English tradition been unproductive. That he had been quick to note the brilliance and sonority of Purcell's choral writing and the rhythmic energy of his orchestral accompaniments is clear from the very first pages of the *Utrecht Te Deum*:

---

[1] Respectively ed. John Stainer (London, n.d.) and anon. (London, 1898).
[2] *The Works of G. F. Handel*, ed. Friedrich Chrysander, xxxi.
[3] On Handel's Italian church music, see p. 372.

Ex. 288

Viewed in perspective against the background of Handel's later achievements this *Te Deum and Jubilate* seems rather immature and conventional, overworking certain harmonic formulas and indulging a little too readily in mechanical sequences. But Handel gauged with unerring precision what the contemporary English public required, and the impact at the time was profound. He caught exactly the right spirit of dignified acclamation and festive splendour that would be congenial to his hearers and animated his music by an inexorable impetus that made its measured progress wellnigh irresistible. Such dazzling assurance was unknown to a generation that fell instantly under his spell.

Handel soon had a chance of developing this promising initiative on more extensive lines. Under the patronage of the Duke of Chandos he wrote during 1718 and the years following a series of anthems for voices and orchestra in which he further exploited his command of the Italian style. In six of these anthems the choir is in three parts only (soprano, tenor, and bass), and much of the choral technique may be regarded as an extension of methods used in the Italian chamber duets: thus by rather a devious path it has some relationship with the earlier English verse anthem, which made use of similar sources. Otherwise there is not much in common between the Purcellian and Handelian types. The Chandos anthems deal with successive clauses of the text in separate short movements which are virtually independent of each other, and any unifying principle there may be resides in the consistency of style and subject. There is little sign of the kind of structural organization and continuity that characterizes the more successful Restoration verse anthems. While there is some affinity between the plan of the verse anthem and that of the *sonata da chiesa*, the 'cantata' anthem of the Chandos species seems to spring rather from the *sonata da camera*, with its loosely strung chain of contrasted movements.

True to his constant maxim of 'ploughing back his profits' Handel makes use of the *Utrecht Jubilate*, suitably modified, for the first of the Chandos anthems, 'O be joyful in the Lord'.[1] It is very informative to observe his methods in compressing four voice parts into three, and later, in the two versions of 'As pants the hart',[2] expanding three voice parts into six. As one notes here the presence also of discreet levies on earlier vocal and instrumental chamber music, it truly seems that Handel was one of the most economical (as well as one of the most profuse) of the great composers. He certainly appears to have wasted nothing.

If the amount of actual fresh material used is thus variable in quantity, the resulting product in these anthems does not thereby suffer in quality. There are many delightfully fresh and lyrical pages, with much firm and energetic choral writing, while the orchestration for strings and wood-wind has the resourcefulness and enterprise of Handel's Italian period. 'O praise the Lord with one consent',[3] in particular, has some fine ringing choruses (even if the verbal accentuation occasionally goes a little astray), and a tender vein of poetry runs through 'As pants the hart'. The soprano solo from this latter, 'Tears are my daily food', has quite a Purcellian flavour. Of exceptional interest are those anthems in which the text gives scope for vivid descriptive movements of the kind that were to occupy such an important place in Handel's dramatic oratorios. In 'The Lord is my light' and 'Let God arise'[4] may be found

[1] *Works*, xxxiv, p. 1.
[2] Ibid., pp. 207 and 239.
[3] Ibid., xxxv, p. 98.
[4] Ibid., pp. 151 and 211 respectively.

Ex. 289

the obvious prototypes of the great illustrative scenes in the choral works of twenty years later. Indeed the first of these contains an aria, 'It is the Lord that ruleth the sea', that was taken as a basis for 'But the waters overwhelmed them' in *Israel in Egypt*, and a graphic chorus, 'The earth trembled and quak'd', of which the substance reappears in *Joshua*. Not all of these essays carry the force which Handel was to display at the height of his powers, but there are moments that can stand comparison with anything that came after. It would be hard to find amongst his works a subject more telling or a development more cogent and expressive than in the fugue 'They are brought down and fall'n' from 'The Lord is my light' (see Ex. 289).

The four Coronation anthems[1] he wrote for George II in 1727 drew forth the full panoply of Handel's ceremonial manner. And what a superb master of ceremonies he was! For sheer stage management there is nothing to surpass the famous opening of 'Zadok the priest', with its gathering surge of strings slowly and majestically rising to meet at its crest a mighty wave of choral sound. Even at this distance in time the splendour of the scene survives in the music. Nor is any break allowed in the imposing spectacle. As soon as one brilliant cavalcade has halted, to the sound of drums and trumpets, another procession gets under way, to equally aspiring strains. Handel holds his audience so fascinated by the uninterrupted magnificence of his effects that none would pause to consider the slender means by which they are produced. Yet all this tremendous glittering fabric is conjured up out of very little—except a genius for musical pageantry. Where even this falters (as it does frequently in the *Dettingen Te Deum*)[2] the result is empty and grandiose, but there is sufficient musical substance in the Coronation anthems to avoid mere pretentious magniloquence, while it needs often only an extra touch of invention to bring forth superlative abundance. Nevertheless when it comes to 'My heart is inditing' Handel, for all his unrivalled instinct and self-assurance, cannot surpass in musical quality Purcell's setting of the same words some forty years before. In this instance the confident man of the world has to acknowledge the imaginative superiority of his more self-effacing predecessor. There is far more genuine feeling in the Funeral Anthem for Queen Caroline, 'The ways of Zion do mourn',[3] which stands apart from the rest of these occasional works by reason of its thoughtful, elegiac character.

GREENE AND OTHERS

So universal was Handel's prestige that it is scarcely to be wondered at if his native-born colleagues seem to have found its weight rather oppressive. On the whole they were most successful when they did not try to compete with the colossus on his own ground. The most enduring work of Thomas Augustine Arne (1710–78) is that in which he cultivates a slender but individual vein of delicate, fanciful melody, and when that is present his short 'Libera me'[4] possesses a certain tender charm.

---

[1] Ibid., xiv.   [2] Ibid., xxv.   [3] Ibid., xi.   [4] Ed. Lewis (London, 1950).

William Boyce (1710–79) is, in his church music, rather unimaginative: 'O where shall wisdom be found' and 'By the waters of Babylon' have solid virtues, but not much personality.[1] One important thing that Boyce did do, however, was to publish in his *Cathedral Music* (3 vols., 1760) the first printed collection of English church music of the past. From the rest of the minor figures of the first half of the eighteenth century little emerges above the level expanse of respectable mediocrity.

It was the young man who first sat with Handel in the organ loft at St. Paul's that was to approach him most nearly in this field: Maurice Greene (1695–1755) did not seek to avoid comparison with Handel's ceremonial style (and from time to time he showed himself by no means incapable of holding his own there), but his most valuable contribution was in *a cappella* writing, for which Handel showed little inclination. The wholly or partly unaccompanied anthem lay at the heart of the English tradition, and therein Greene excelled. In these full anthems Greene, like Purcell before him, was not content to rely on inherited lustre from the past, but with an alert and constructive mind took a fresh view of the problems and potentialities involved. In this he was greatly assisted by a fine contrapuntal technique and, when he chose to use it, a keen sense of balance. The *Forty Select Anthems*,[2] upon which his reputation mainly rests, show abundant evidence of the work of an accomplished and fastidious stylist, who often seems to make a more sensitive approach to church music than his great contemporary. The Chandos anthems represent the formal devotions of a great nobleman; Greene's 'Lord, how long wilt thou be angry?' is the earnest, affecting cry of a humble community in distress. With all his careful, and sometimes rather studied, phraseology Greene attains here a degree of simple, intimate sincerity rarely to be found in Handel's more ambitious designs.

Greene has a strong instinct for the use of the chorus collectively in expressing personal sentiments; he will sometimes break down a verbal phrase and distribute it between a number of voices, thus securing, by a series of apt and well-timed entries, a much enhanced rhetorical force. In the gravely beautiful opening of 'How long wilt thou forget me, O Lord?', he is not over-punctilious that each part should express a complete idea by itself—the overriding aim is to obtain greater emphasis in combination:

---

[1] Boyce's services and anthems were ed. Vincent Novello, 4 vols. (London, 1858).

[2] 2 vols. (London, 1743). All the anthems mentioned below appear in this collection. There are modern editions of 'Lord, how long?', 'How long wilt thou', and 'Arise, shine' (all ed. Stewart, London, 1925) and of 'Lord, let me know' (ed. Ernest Bullock, London, 1938). 'Arise, shine' also appears in Dearnley, op. cit., p. 152.

Ex. 290

The relative disposition of homophonic and contrapuntal passages, upon which the inner vitality of the full anthem of this period so largely depends, clearly engaged Greene's attention very closely, and his skill in alternating the two types of presentation was an important factor in his success in covering a fairly wide canvas. An underlying common element was obviously a further advantage from the point of view of unity, and Greene makes striking use of a device of this sort in 'Lord, let me know mine end', where the solemn tread of the bass continues uninterrupted throughout. While it moves on with steady, deliberate pace, the voices discourse above in quiet meditation, as if contemplating some passing cortège:

Ex. 291

In more exultant mood Greene is no less resourceful. The chorus 'I will greatly rejoice in the Lord' from 'Arise, shine, O Zion' is a kind of fugal rondo, and the recurrent refrain and final peroration emerge triumphantly from the intervening episodes. On a smaller scale, but equally distinctive, is the choral ending of the solo anthem 'The Lord, ev'n the most mighty God hath spoken'. Here Greene takes three different constituents—a melodic figure in short detached notes, a slow sustained phrase and a fragment of coloratura—and works them together in skilful conjunction to produce a most buoyant and spirited result. Again, in the splendid 'O clap your hands'[1] we are treated to no mere conventional parade of jubilation. The striding, muscular counterpoint of the opening carries unmistakable conviction, and the strength of the block harmonies used later is genuinely monumental in character. But Greene reserves his most imaginative stroke for the concluding pæan. There the theme of praise is gradually elaborated in a rhythmic crescendo of excitement until it reaches its culmination in a brilliant and decisive stretto:

[1] Recorded in *The History of Music in Sound*, v.

Ex. 292

sing ye prais — — es,

prais — — — es, sing ye

prais — es, sing ye

— es, sing ye prais — — es, sing

prais — es, sing ye prais —

sing ye prais — — es, sing ye prais — —

prais — es, sing ye prais — — —

prais — — es, sing ye

prais — es, _____ sing ye

— es with un — der — stand — ing, with

Greene has distinct limitations, which become increasingly apparent when he is without the choral ensemble, but inside these bounds (imposed, one feels, more by his inclination than his capacity) he is a composer of some consequence. His achievement is all the more important from his historical position. At a moment when the intense creative activity of the Restoration was spent, and native musical talent was wellnigh submerged by the mighty tide of Handel's genius, one gratefully acknowledges Greene's indispensable part in upholding the essential continuity of English church music.

IX

GERMAN CHURCH MUSIC

By PAUL STEINITZ

(*a*) INTRODUCTION

RELIGIOUS AND SOCIAL BACKGROUND

AN enormous quantity of sacred vocal music was written in Germany
between 1630 and 1750, some of it by some of the most prolific composers in the history of music; much of it will have to be omitted from
the survey which follows. This music was composed by *Kapellmeister*
and organists employed by the rulers of the numerous German states, as
well as by musicians employed in towns both large and small throughout
the country. Nearly all of it was produced out of routine duty and for
immediate performance. Music for a court chapel had generally to please
the reigning prince or duke, but other church music might or might not
satisfy a congregation, since it was primarily designed to please God;
however, such music did on the whole successfully fulfil both temporal
and spiritual functions.

There are three main reasons for so vast a production. Firstly, the
Lutheran faith held music to be an absolutely essential part of worship,
and Lutheranism was firmly established in north and central Germany,
despite the almost continuous religious wars of the seventeenth century
and the growth of Calvinism and Pietism, both of which opposed
elaborate church music; moreover, Lutheran music was by tradition
elaborate and from the early seventeenth century involved instruments
as well as voices. Secondly, people turned more and more for solace to
religion and its music, a fact that offset a temporary reduction in the
elaboration of music through economies demanded by wars. Finally,
towards the end of the seventeenth century, court establishments tended
to increase in size and number in emulation of Louis XIV's court at
Versailles.[1]

The Thirty Years' War (1618–48) was the most terrible of the century.
Through it Protestantism lost its rich abbeys and bishoprics in the south,
but the effects of the war were most severe in central Germany, which

[1] See Chap. VII, *passim*.

produced many of the finest composers, including the great Bach family. Not only were musical establishments weakened or broken up, but the very nature of the music itself was affected—for example, many of the texts chosen for setting at this time look forward to escape from the sorrows of this world to the joys of the next.

The Peace of Westphalia in 1648 entrenched Catholicism in the hereditary Habsburg lands, including Bohemia. In the rest of the Empire the general principle of *cujus regio, ejus religio* still applied, except that a ruler who changed his religion was obliged to leave the established faith of his subjects untouched (as happened in Saxony in 1697 when the Elector turned Catholic in order to become King of Poland); but Calvinist rulers were now given equal rights with Lutheran and Catholic ones, and various provisions were made to permit considerable toleration, a concept which developed slowly though surely during the next hundred years. It was this period that, especially after *c.* 1675, saw the spread of the movement known as Pietism, which emphasized the need for bible-study and deeper devotional life, for tolerance rather than strict orthodoxy. As a curious but important by-product, it gave rise to much mystical and emotional verse, but it was fostered by the growing intellectualism of the Lutheran church, and its main centre was the University of Halle.[1] Musically, it was unfortunate in that its adherents disliked the elaborate church music of the 'state religions', Lutheran as much as Catholic, and preferred the simplest hymns and songs, the texts for which were often to be found in the many books of religious verse published at this time.

Other types of music began to flourish again after the end of the war, and by the end of the century, when conditions were more stable, the beginnings of another movement, the German 'enlightenment', not unrelated to intellectual Pietism, were already foreshadowed, particularly in the works of Telemann, Reinhard Keiser, and Johann Kuhnau, and in the music and writings of Johann Mattheson.

MUSIC AND THE CHURCH

Not only were Lutheran services the sole reason for the composition of Masses, Passions, motets, and cantatas in Protestant Germany, but the musical and poetical heritage of Lutheranism provided a large amount of the basic material for them in its hymns and hymn tunes. Books of chorales—hymns, some of them original, some adapted from

---

[1] A good recent account of Pietism in Germany at this time is to be found in F. Ernest Stoeffler, *The Rise of evangelical Pietism* (*Studies in the History of Religions*, ix) (Leiden, 1965), pp. 180-246.

older melodies—had appeared at frequent intervals from 1524 onwards;[1] Johann Walther and Johann Crüger are two of the best-known composers in this field, and Paul Gerhardt and Johann Rist among the most inspired of the verse-writers after Luther. Hymns provided the basis of thousands of compositions, as also did verses on the borderline between hymns used in public worship and pious songs intended for domestic use. They might be used in simple, unadorned form, with or without an independent accompaniment, or as a basis for elaborate fantasias; sometimes, when they appeared in an instrumental part only, they would naturally call the words to mind. Parallel with chorale compositions in the seventeenth century there now developed the more dramatic concertato type of work in which, although chorale texts were sometimes used, their melodies seldom appeared.

MUSICAL RESOURCES

All musicians, including composers, were employed either by noblemen for their court and chapel music or by municipal authorities in the secular field or for music in churches, where composers might be cantors or organists; civic employers were considered to offer greater security, though the status of court composers was higher. Thus all music was written for a specific and immediate purpose, and nearly everything performed, therefore, was new.

Unlike the kings of England and France, the Emperor had little artistic domination over his nobility, who could thus develop their establishments, including musical ones, much as they wished. Since the fifteenth century the Imperial Diet had consisted of three chambers: the Colleges of Electors, of Princes, Barons, and Counts, and of Imperial Free Cities. The power of the last, strong in the Middle Ages, had considerably waned by the seventeenth century, and in 1653 their voting rights were curtailed. But though they had no political power there were still some fifty of them in 1715. Many, however, had lost their independence too: Leipzig, for instance, was subject to the Elector of Saxony, and Bremen to Sweden. By the beginning of the eighteenth century there were no fewer than 365 states and cities in Germany. During the latter part of Louis XIV's reign, more and more of them tried to establish themselves as miniature Versailles, and pamphleteers such as Chemnitz and Leibniz saw salvation for Germany in increased power for the princes. A musical establishment had always been regarded as an important part of the household of any nobleman worthy of the name, and often as evidence of his power; as has already been mentioned, returning prosperity after the ravages of war saw a big

[1] On chorales see Vol. IV, pp. 420 ff.

increase in the number of musicians, and the size of a court band became an even more important indication of status. As well as performing in chapel and at court, musicians in the employ of ruling nobles had frequently to discharge non-musical duties, too. As we have noted, those who worked for city councils supplied music for both sacred and secular occasions; in cities such as Leipzig the professional *Stadtpfeifer* combined with amateurs to form church orchestras.

The varying size, composition, and skill of these choirs and orchestras can to some extent be assessed from the scoring of the music written for them, and a good deal of documentary evidence is available too.[1] Choirs and orchestras balanced each other, the orchestras being if anything slightly the larger. It is very difficult to form an accurate opinion of standards, which evidently varied enormously with the size and status of the court or town. However, the intonation of woodwind instruments must have been very poor by our standards. Burney, writing of Germany in 1773, continually complains about it, and singing seems to have been scarcely better: in Leipzig he found that singers produced 'just the same pert snap in taking the high notes as in our common singing in England . . . which they do with a kind of beat and very loud instead of a mezza di voce or swell'.[2] It is not to be supposed that things were any better in earlier decades. However, against Burney's impressions may be set the undoubtedly high standard of certain instrumentalists. Among these were many trumpeters and kettle-drum-players, who since the Middle Ages had enjoyed special rights and privileges; they certainly played in court orchestras, as well as carrying out their main duties in military and ceremonial music, and must have influenced the standards of the other players. Trombones had been used for many generations in vocal polyphony to support the voices by doubling them, and as their intonation depended solely on the player's lip and ear, and not on mechanical devices, one may safely assume that the standard of playing was fairly good.

Larger resources were called for by choral music written for the church than for any other music. The instruments commonly required were those of the viol and violin families, two kinds of flute, three kinds of oboe, and a large assortment of brass and partly brass instruments; of the latter, cornetti were perhaps the commonest. The orchestra was treated contrapuntally in nearly all the works to be considered in this chapter.

[1] Adam Carse, *The Orchestra in the XVIIIth Century* (repr., Cambridge, 1940), gives, pp. 18–27, a list including some two dozen relevant German court orchestras, and, *passim*, a great deal of information about standards, personnel, and status.

[2] See Charles Burney, *The Present State of Music in Germany, the Netherlands and United Provinces* (London, 1773), pt. ii, p. 78, and *passim*.

PLATE V

INSTRUMENTAL MUSIC IN A CHURCH

From an engraving by J. C. Deliné of Nuremberg in J. G. Walther's
Musikalisches Lexicon (Leipzig, 1732).

ITALIAN AND FRENCH INFLUENCE

The spread of Italian influence to German church music in the work of composers such as Hans Leo Hassler and Michael Praetorius has already been discussed in Vol. IV.[1] But it was through Schütz, who studied in Italy with Giovanni Gabrieli and possibly later with Monteverdi, that the concertato and polychoral styles became more widely known in Germany. More important, it is to him that we must mainly attribute the introduction into the north of the passionate declamatory style of early seventeenth-century Italian music. Two other factors influenced standards of performance and the style of composition: the more frequent employment of Italian musicians in positions of importance, and the introduction of Italian opera. That centres such as Stuttgart and Dresden, where Italian musicians were strongest, apparently had the highest standards is probably not a coincidence, nor need it have been simply because such places were large, for in another large centre, Leipzig, Italian musicians were few and standards amateurish. It was in Vienna that Italian opera[2] first and most strongly affected church music through the introduction of solo and concertato writing into Mass settings; in any case the proximity of the Catholic south to Italy and the fact that the head of the Catholic church was an Italian kept Vienna closely in touch with Italian music.

The Italian style, which was simpler and less contrapuntal than German 'cantor's music', was in the following century associated by writers such as Mattheson and Rousseau with 'enlightenment', thus increasing the Italians' grip over German music. Protests were made against this domination and its abuses, and more particularly against the gullibility of Germans under it; an entertaining example is Kuhnau's novel *Der musikalische Quacksalber* (1700).[3]

French influence was felt most in north and central Germany, chiefly through the adoption of the French overture and French dance rhythms and through vocal and instrumental ornamentation; one specially French court, said to have been even more French than Versailles itself, was that at Celle. The integration of aspects of French style into the Lutheran choral tradition can be seen in the works of Bach and many other composers. Later on, Frederick the Great, who came to his throne in 1740, thought and spoke in French, yet wished to create a more thoroughly German style of music in Berlin.

[1] See pp. 452–4 there.

[2] Cf. *supra*, pp. 47 ff and 131 ff., for some discussion of Italian opera in Vienna.

[3] Repr., ed. Kurt Benndorf (Berlin, 1900); see also Romain Rolland, *Voyage musical au pays du passé* (Paris, 1919), p. 12; Eng. trans., London, 1922.

We are now in a position to embark on a detailed study of the evolution of the principal forms of German church music: Mass, oratorio, Passion, motet, and cantata. The period is bounded by the two giants Schütz and Bach, and this fact has caused much worthwhile music by other distinguished men to be overlooked. It will be a function of this chapter to do justice to the best of this music as well as to place in their contexts the works of the two great masters.

(b) THE NORTH GERMAN (PROTESTANT) MASS

INTRODUCTION

Forms of service in the Lutheran church were established in the 1520s by Luther himself. These included the order for the Communion service set out in his *Formula Missae*[1] of 1523 and, most relevant to our present purpose, the form of the German Mass set out in his *Deudsche Messe und Ordnung Gottesdiensts*, which has been discussed in Vol. IV.[2] There were some notable differences in services between one part of Germany and another, and Luther's wishes were increasingly forgotten as time went on, but they continued to form a recognizable basis for services in all Lutheran churches. As far as the Mass is concerned, it is clear that the *Kyrie* and *Gloria* were the only parts regularly set to music; other sections were occasionally set for use at festivals, but the majority of Masses to be discussed below belong to the *Missa brevis* type consisting of *Kyrie* and *Gloria* only. Furthermore, Masses form only a tiny proportion of the output of German baroque composers, and this proportion gradually dwindled as the number of *geistliche Konzerte*, or sacred concertos, increased. This reflects the emphasis laid upon the Gospel and its teaching, presented by means of sermons and sacred concertos; it was also natural with the advent of the Age of Enlightenment that these two parts of the service, which were the longest and were in the vernacular, should gain ascendancy over the more formal ritual parts.

Almost to the end of the seventeenth century German composers favoured *a cappella* Mass settings, but the austerity of such music was gradually modified by the use of a chorale melody as the basis of a work, analogous to the use of a *canto fermo* by composers of Catholic polyphony. Masses using chorales were known as *Lied* Masses. All these

---

[1] See B. J. Kidd, *Documents illustrative of the continental Reformation* (Oxford, 1911), p. 127.
[2] Cf. pp. 425–7 in that volume.

a cappella Masses had continuo support (often omitted in modern editions) doubling the lowest vocal line; and contemporary pictures leave us in little doubt that the vocal parts would normally have been doubled by whatever instruments were suitable and available. Later, orchestral accompaniments became more independent and idiomatic, and Masses eventually incorporated operatic elements and began outwardly to resemble oratorios.

A CAPPELLA MASSES

A Mass for six voices and continuo (1668) by Johann Rudolph Ahle[1] (1625–73), organist at his native Mühlhausen from 1656, is a representative work of the mid-century. The severity of the *a cappella* writing is tempered by the influence of instrumental music, and there is a happy balance between this type of texture and homophonic passages in which the parts are still individual and shapely. This variety of texture, as well as of themes and cadences, offsets the rather limited range of harmony and modulations. The expressive and dignified opening of the *Kyrie* (Ex. 293(i)) and the vigorous, if slightly empty, setting of 'In gloria dei Patris' (Ex. 293(ii)) give a good idea of this work at its best:

[1] Published in *Johann Rudolph Ahles ausgewählte Gesangswerke*, ed. Johannes Wolf, *Denkmäler deutscher Tonkunst*, v (Leipzig, 1901), p. 51. See also Wolf, 'Johann Rudolph Ahle: eine bio-bibliographische Skizze', *Sammelbände der internationalen Musikgesellschaft*, ii (1900–1), p. 393.

A five-part Mass (1680) by Johann Theile (1646–1724),[1] a pupil of Schütz who wrote twenty-three Masses, is at once more severe than Ahle's Mass and yet shows a more pronounced influence of instrumental music, as in this 'Amen' fugato theme from the *Gloria*:

Ex. 294

[1] Published in *Johann Theile und Christoph Bernhard: Zwei Kurzmessen*, ed. Rudolf Gerber, *Das Chorwerk*, xvi (Wolfenbüttel and Berlin, 1932), p. 1. On Theile's Masses, see André Pirro, *Dietrich Buxtehude* (Paris, 1913), pp. 129–33.

Ex. 295, from the end of the *Kyrie*, shows another feature setting off this work from Ahle's—the use of expressive dissonance:

Ex. 295

Harmonic resource, typified by the following extract from the *Gloria*, is also a notable feature of the five-part *Missa brevis*, probably of the early 1670s, by Dietrich Buxtehude (1637–1707):[1]

Ex. 296

---

[1] Published in *Dietrich Buxtehudes Werke*, iv, ed. Hilmar Trede (Hamburg, 1931), p. 12. The Mass is discussed in Pirro, op. cit., pp. 137–40.

This Mass, too, shows, even more clearly than Theile's, how florid instrumental idioms were undermining the old *a cappella* ideal; the change is well seen in the very varied themes of the *Gloria*, where the composer's technique is at its most skilful. He also lends unity to his opening movement by reworking in triple time as the basis of his second *Kyrie* the common-time theme of the first one. A four-part Mass in D minor (though actually in the Dorian mode) by Johann Rosenmüller (*c.* 1619–1684),[1] who worked in Italy as well as in Germany, is a full-scale Catholic Mass, possibly composed in Venice, but is so firmly rooted in the North German Protestant style as to demand inclusion in this section. The fusion of the *a cappella* tradition with expressive harmonic writing and the use of short florid figures yields music more distinguished than that of most German Masses of this period. Ex. 297 shows how Rosenmüller uses these ingredients to build up an expressive climax towards the end of his *Kyrie* before relaxing in the last two bars:

Ex. 297

[1] In Franz Commer (ed.), *Musica sacra*, xxiv (Berlin, 1883), p. 19.

And this passage from the *Credo* illustrates the no less appealing expressiveness of his more purely harmonic writing:

Ex. 298

More prolific composers of Masses, such as Andreas Hammerschmidt (1612–75) in the mid-seventeenth century and Johann Philipp Krieger (1649–1725) two generations after him, hardly rise to these heights; Krieger was especially prolific, and the catalogue (partly thematic) of the works that he composed and performed at Weissenfels between 1684 and his death includes as many as ninety-one Latin *a cappella* Masses and four German ones.[1] Johann Pachelbel's (1653–1706) *Missa brevis* in D[2] singularly lacks the qualities that lend distinction to some of his other music; his more interesting Catholic Mass in C is mentioned *infra*, p. 590. More stimulating in the present field are the three Masses of Johann Christoph Schmidt (1664–1728), who worked at Dresden. In a Mass for five voices[3] the common ways of achieving variety of texture—crossing of parts, syncopation, scale passages and the like—are used with more resource than was usual at the time; the following excerpt from the *Kyrie* will support this claim:

Ex. 299

[1] See Johann Philipp Krieger, *21 ausgewählte Kirchenkompositionen*, ed. Max Seiffert, *Denkmäler deutscher Tonkunst*, liii-liv (Leipzig, 1916), pp. xxiv-lii.
[2] Ed. Dietrich Krüger (Hilversum, 1962).
[3] Berlin State Library MS. 30.172.

An independent *Sanctus* by Georg Böhm (1661–1733)[1] is one of the earliest pieces to show French influence, which causes the composer to shed almost every trace of Teutonic heaviness. Ex. 300, with its long semiquaver runs and syllabic writing, gives an idea of the style of this work:

Ex. 300

[1] *Sämtliche Werke*, ed. Johannes Wolgast, ii: *Vokalwerke* (Leipzig, 1932), p. 115.

Masses by two lesser-known composers use larger forces than those we have so far encountered. Sebastian Knüpfer (1633–76), Thomas-cantor at Leipzig for nineteen years until his death, composed five *a cappella* Masses, one of which is in twenty-four parts, including two choirs and trumpets, another in twenty, and a third in fourteen, half vocal, half instrumental. A short Mass by Thomas Selle (1599–1663),[1] who worked in Hamburg, shows strong Venetian influence in its layout for two four-part choirs and is a work of some harmonic imagination.

In the eighteenth century the Protestant Mass grew less and less important and, apart from Bach (whose Masses are discussed in a later section), only two composers whose work falls wholly within the century need be mentioned, Gottfried Heinrich Stölzel (1690–1749) and Carl Heinrich Graun (1704–59). Vocal polyphony was now largely instrumental in character, yet the tradition of composing Masses in the *stile antico* died hard in north and central Germany. Independent instrumental parts became increasingly frequent, too, as in the *Gloria* of Stölzel's Mass in C illustrated in the following example:[2]

---

[1] In *Thomas Selle: zwei Kurzmessen*, ed. Joachim Birke, *Das Chorwerk*, xc (Wolfenbüttel, 1963), p. 1.
[2] Taken from the copy in Brit. Mus. Add. MS. 31307, fo. 62.

Ex. 301

But it was still usual for instruments simply to double the voices in the *Kyrie* and the closing section of the *Gloria*. And the final triumph of tonality over modal writing was particularly evident in homophonic passages.

Stölzel wrote several other Masses, of which the *Missa canonica* shows him at his best;[1] it is scored for two four-part choirs and five-part string orchestra and employs a wide range of techniques. In the *Kyrie*, which is in the *stile antico*, he uses short phrases, starting with the highest voice of the first choir and working down to the lowest of the second in such a way that never more than five parts sing at once; eight-part writing is on the whole reserved for cadences. The *Gloria* is in concertato style, and a common procedure, shown in Ex. 302, is for short canonic passages to be punctuated by cadences:

Ex. 302

<hr>

[1] Ed. Georg Poelchau (Vienna, *c.* 1820).

A more extended concertato canon is illustrated in the following example:

With Graun we reach the *galant* style in the shape of many of the themes and cadences, but the formal fugal sections are more conservative. Ex. 304 shows how the spirit of a new age suffuses the music in the opening movement of his Mass in B flat:[1]

Ex. 304

*Viola has D in MS.

[1]Taken from the copy in Brit. Mus. Add. MS. 32394, fo. 24.

LIED MASSES

A notable Mass of this type is the so-called *Deutsche Messe*[1] of Heinrich Schütz (1585–1672), which probably dates from the 1650s; the text is German. The *Kyrie* is based on a troped *Kyrie*, 'Fons Bonitatis' (in the version of the Dresden *Gesangbuch* of 1622–25), and the *Gloria* on 'All Lob und Ehr soll Gottes sein' (from the same source); the *Credo* is freely composed; the *Sanctus* is missing, but the setting includes music for the Institution and Distribution of Communion. There are a number of imaginative touches, notably in the *Credo*, where the imitative writing has an animation lacking in most of the works discussed above, and also in the Communion movement at such a moment as the impassioned repetition of the words 'Nehmet hin und trinket':

Ex. 305

[1] See Hans Joachim Moser, *Heinrich Schütz: sein Leben und Werk* (2nd ed., Kassel and Basle, 1954, pp. 539–49; Eng. trans. by Carl F. Pfatteicher, St. Louis, 1959, pp. 635–41). The Mass itself consists of the first five items in Schütz's *Zwölf geistliche Gesänge* (Dresden, 1657), which appear in his *Sämmtliche Werke*, ed. Friedrich Chrysander and Philipp Spitta, xii (Leipzig, 1892), and also in an edition by Günter Graulich (Stuttgart, 1971).

(Take and drink ye all of it.)

Schütz wrote no other Masses, but his pupil Christoph Bernhard (1627–92) was a notably successful composer of them. He wrote five: one an early work in ten parts, the others all probably later works. One of these is a five-part setting based on the chorale 'Christ unser Heiland zum Jordan kam'.[1] It is a concise and homogeneous work, and the polyphonic web derived from the chorale is both imaginative and skilfully laid out; the following brief extract from the *Gloria* shows one way in which the melody is used:

Ex. 306 (i)

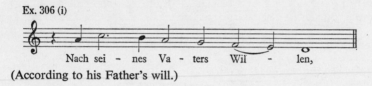

(According to his Father's will.)

Another work worthy of mention is the four-part Mass that Friedrich Wilhelm Zachow (1663–1712), of Halle, based on the chorale 'Christ lag in Todesbanden'.[2] His treatment of the *canto fermo* is on the whole more obvious and restricted than Bernhard's, but the work shows plenty of tonal variety and an imaginative use of suspensions, as in this extract from the *Gloria*:

---

[1] In *Johann Theile und Christoph Bernhard: Zwei Kurzmessen*, p. 23.

[2] In *Gesammelte Werke von Friedr. Wilh. Zachow*, ed. Seiffert, *Denkmäler deutscher Tonkunst*, xxi-xxii (Leipzig, 1905), p. 304. On Zachow generally, see Günter Thomas, *Friedrich Wilhelm Zachow* (Regensburg, 1966).

Ex. 307 (i)

There are also two attractive *Lied* Masses by Knüpfer, using the melodies 'Herr Jesu Christ ich weiss gar wohl' and 'Herr Jesu Christ wahr Mensch', and three by Johann Philipp Krieger, on 'Allein zu dir', 'Ein feste Burg', and 'Erbarm dich mein' respectively—far fewer than his total of *a cappella* Masses. Finally, as it is based on the chorale melody, one must draw attention here to Ahle's splendid setting of the German Creed 'Wir glauben all' an einen Gott',[1] a piece full of rhythmic and harmonic variety, and livelier than his *a cappella* Mass mentioned in the previous section.

THE MASSES OF J. S. BACH

Bach's four short Masses[2] consist almost entirely of music from church cantatas adapted to the new text. There is nothing inherently wrong with this sort of transference of music, from either the aesthetic or the stylistic point of view, especially if the same basic mood or

---

[1] In *Johann Rudolph Ahles ausgewählte Gesangswerke*, p. 121.

[2] Edited in *Johann Sebastian Bach's Werke* (Leipzig, various dates), viii. On their origin, see Arnold Schering, 'Die Hohe Messe in h-moll', *Bach-Jahrbuch*, xxxiii (1936), pp. 26–30, and Paul Steinitz, 'Bach's Lutheran Masses', *Musical Times*, cix (1968), p. 231.

emotion is found in both works. These Masses are, however, the least happy of Bach's self-borrowings. The Mass in F, BWV 233,[1] is by far the most successful of the four. For the *Kyrie*, *Gloria*, and 'Domine Deus' no 'originals' have been discovered, except for an earlier version without orchestra of the *Kyrie* (BWV 233a);[2] indeed these movements give the impression of having been composed with care rather than transcribed in haste. Unusual coherence obtains throughout the *Kyrie* by means of the unifying influence of *canti fermi*: the Litany chorale 'Christe, du Lamm Gottes' appears on instruments (in the earlier *Kyrie* it is given to an extra soprano voice), and the thematically related final *Kyrie* melody of the Lutheran Litany[3] is sung by the basses; the chorale also influences the thematic material of all three sections. It is written in the *stile antico* with doubling instruments (apart from the *canto fermo*). The *Gloria in excelsis*, which incorporates the 'Gratias agimus'— not altogether successfully—develops its material with much exuberance for 171 bars of quick 6/8 time. 'Domine Deus' (bass solo and strings) has a boldly declaimed vocal line with cheerful obbligato figures in the first violin. 'Qui tollis' is a careful arrangement of 'Weh! der Seele' from Cantata 102. 'Cum sancto spiritu' is a splendid adaptation of the opening chorus of Cantata 40; the application to '. . . in gloria Dei Patris, Amen' of passages originally set to '. . . that he may destroy the works of the devil' illustrates extremely well the folly of attempting to tie music down to one set of words.

The other Masses are unequal. In the A major setting, BWV 234, *Kyries* I and II have the uneasy charm of some contemporary settings by operatic composers, while the recitative fugato setting of the 'Christe' seems curiously out of place. In borrowing the *Gloria* of this Mass from the bass aria with chorus of Cantata 67 ('Peace be unto you'), Bach preserved the same mood by allocating at least part of it to 'et in terra pax', but his judgement seems to have been at fault in foisting the text 'Gloria in excelsis' on to the bustling angular music of the orchestral ritornellos of the original movement. Perhaps the most insensitive borrowing in these Masses is the adaptation to 'Christe eleison' in the Mass in G minor, BWV 235, of the jerky, staccato fugal theme for 'Du schlägest sie!' ('Thou smitest them!') from the chorus of Cantata 102. This Mass provides a number of examples of bad declamation and doubtful affinities of mood with the originals. The fourth Mass, in G, BWV 236, is generally successful, and the adaptations are illuminating; for instance, the chorus of Cantata 179 serves admirably for the *Kyrie*,

---

[1] The *Kyrie* is recorded in *The History of Music in Sound*, v.
[2] *Werke*, xli, p. 187.
[3] See Albert Schweitzer, *J. S. Bach* (4th ed., Leipzig, 1922), pp. 697–8; Eng. trans., London, 1911, ii, p. 327), for a comparison of the two melodies.

the chromaticisms, originally on 'false heart', being perfectly apposite to the new words.

There remains the Mass in B minor.[1] Bach presented the *Kyrie* and *Gloria* to Dresden in 1733, as evidence of his skill as a composer and with an earnest plea for a court title; this was granted, though not until three years later. He had already composed the *Sanctus* in Leipzig for Christmas, 1724, and he completed the remaining movements during the last year or two of his life. The following discussion of some aspects of the work is intended as a supplement to existing fuller accounts.[2]

In this Mass is found the culmination of several styles of composition of the period. For instance, the concertato style is perfected and polished, and its fugal writing achieves a relationship between voices and instruments freer than hitherto; the ritornello form, often in conjunction with fugato, is used on a bigger scale than previously, and in the motet movements in the *stile antico* the doubling instruments sometimes develop independent lines at climactic points. From the fact that Bach composed so much of the Mass towards the end of his life it is possible to draw various conclusions. The most logical and satisfactory view would seem to be that, in spite of the increasing number of borrowings from his earlier compositions that he made when thus completing the work as a Catholic Mass, it was not in fact a compilation put together in thoughtless haste, as some have suggested; rather was it intended as an example of the best that he could offer in this highest and most challenging field of composition, a monument of his skill, worthy to stand with the other masterpieces of his last years, *Die Kunst der Fuge*, *Das musikalische Opfer*, and the Goldberg Variations. If he wished to offer the finest music of which he was capable, it was perfectly natural for him to turn to some of his best work of the past for movements where the same mood prevailed and where the earlier music seemed ideal, provided that it was possible to adapt it satisfactorily to the new words. No fewer than seven movements (eight with 'Dona nobis', whose music is the same as that of 'Gratias agimus tibi') are adaptations of music originally composed to German texts, as in the short Masses, and it is noteworthy that the distinctive features which it shares with the other big original Latin work, the *Magnificat*, are seen most strongly in the movements of the Mass that are not borrowed. The most important are the five-part choral texture (very rare in the cantatas), the 'suave

[1] The best edition is in the *Neue Ausgabe sämtliche Werke*, ii, 1, ed. Friedrich Smend (Kassel and Basle, 1954); a miniature score was published in 1955 and the *Kritische Bericht* in 1956. For an authoritative critical view, see Georg von Dadelsen, 'Friedrich Smends Ausgabe der h-moll-Messe von J. S. Bach', *Die Musikforschung*, xii (1959), p. 315.

[2] See the copious bibliography in Wolfgang Schmieder, *Thematisch-systematisches Verzeichnis der Werke J. S. Bachs* (Leipzig, 1950), pp. 315–16, to which should be added those in the *Bach-Jahrbuch*, xl (1953), p. 141, xlv (1958), p. 135, and liii (1967), p. 138.

and mellow duets in the vein of Steffani', the coloratura arias with obbligato instruments 'in the Venetian-Neapolitan manner',[1] and the absence of extravagant, even morbid, 'symbolic' harmonies and melodic lines such as one finds from time to time in the cantatas.

Structurally the most important aspect of the Mass is the use of ritornellos. These are usually long (e.g. twenty-five bars in *Kyrie* I, twelve bars in 'Laudamus te') but are so rich in material that their constant recurrence either whole or in part or in some form of development throughout a movement produces variety within a unified structure. The subtle alterations to which these ritornellos are subjected, for example in 'et resurrexit', is truly astonishing.

(c) THE SOUTH GERMAN (CATHOLIC) MASS

INTRODUCTION

At first the music of the Gabrielis was the strongest Italian influence on seventeenth-century composers of Catholic Masses in southern Germany, and it continued for many years to lie behind the development of effects prompted by space and resonance, with increasingly simple harmonies. Later in the century opera became more and more influential. The resources available after the Thirty Years' War were substantial, and the concertato style was universally adopted.[2] The Habsburg Emperors actively encouraged music, and Leopold I, no mean composer himself, had about a hundred singers and players in his court chapel: there were eight trombonists, five trumpeters, four oboists, three cellists, two gamba-players, five organists, and other performers in proportion. By the time of Charles VI the numbers had risen to 140. In the present field, even more strikingly than in Protestant Masses in the north, we see the principles of Renaissance polyphony supplanted by the use of imitative themes generated more from short instrumental figures conceived harmonically rather than from those capable of creating an intricate contrapuntal texture. In short, part-writing, when it appears, is conditioned now by the harmonic ground-plan instead of itself determining the harmony. Characteristic styles for solo and choral writing were developed, as well as idiomatic instrumental writing.

---

[1] Both quotations are from Paul Henry Lang, *Music in Western Civilization* (London, 1942), p. 498.

[2] See Guido Adler, 'Zur Geschichte der Wiener Messkomposition in der zweiten Hälfte des XVII. Jahrhunderts', *Studien zur Musikwissenschaft*, iv (1916), p. 5.

SOME REPRESENTATIVE MASSES

Interesting evidence of the transition from Renaissance counterpoint to the concertato manner can be seen in the Venetian-style compositions of the Viennese Christoph Strauss (*c.* 1575–1631), who composed sixteen Masses for from eight to twenty vocal and instrumental parts, with continuo (his Requiem is discussed *infra*, p. 598), and also in the numerous Masses of another composer who worked mostly at Innsbruck, Johann Stadlmayr (d. 1648), several of which again are for large forces. Later in the century a work such as the *Missa nuptialis*,[1] one of the two Masses of another prominent Viennese composer, Johann Heinrich Schmelzer (*c.* 1623–1680), still shows in its antiphonal effects the influence of Venetian music and in its contrapuntal textures the survival of an earlier Renaissance ideal. There are independent parts at times for the four trombones that are conspicuous among the instruments supporting the six-part chorus, and solo passages are contrasted with sections for full choir. The work is also unusually concise: the *Gloria*, for instance, is only fifty-seven bars long. Ex. 308, from the end of the first 'Kyrie', illustrates the 'open' concertato textures characteristic of the age:

Ex. 308

[1] Ed. Adler in *Denkmäler der Tonkunst in Österreich*, xlix (Jg. xxv (1)) (Vienna, 1918), p. 48,

Ex. 309, from the corresponding place in the *Missa cujus toni* (1687) of Johann Caspar Kerll (1627–93),[1] a German who worked alternately in Munich and Vienna, shows the more solid textures also still commonly found:

Ex. 309

[1] Ibid., p. 74.

Ex.310

Even so, Kerll, who composed some ten Masses, used his mixed vocal and instrumental forces, which are similar to Schmelzer's, in a similar way to him too. It can be said that Kerll was more at home when writing even larger-scale polychoral music, such as his *Missa a tre cori*.[1] Here there are seven separate groups—the three choirs, each in four parts, two clarini, two cornetti, three trombones, and two violins, plus continuo; that they cannot have been widely spaced in performance is suggested by the concerted imitative and florid counterpoint for solo parts for the different groups found in, for example, the 'Christe eleison', 'Qui tollis', and 'Et iterum venturus est'. There is some striking scoring for solo groups, e.g. three solo sopranos for 'Ex Maria virgine' and three solo basses and three trombones in the 'Crucifixus'. Although his harmonic writing is suitably direct for such a spaciously conceived work, Kerll does not disdain more affective, chromatic writing for such appropriate places as in the 'Qui tollis' (see Ex. 310).

Another spaciously conceived Mass is the *Missa Sti. Henrici* (1701), one of the few sacred works of Heinrich Ignaz Franz von Biber (1644–1704),[2] high steward and *Kapellmeister* to the Archbishop of Salzburg. The instrumental writing—for two clarini, three trumpets, and timpani, three trombones doubling voices, two violins, three violas, and continuo —is, as one might expect from such a practised composer of instrumental music, exceptionally resourceful and idiomatic; a fine moment is the fanfare before 'Et resurrexit':

Ex. 311

This is an idea which is treated antiphonally with good effect throughout this section of the *Credo* and in the setting of 'Et incarnatus' for solo soprano and two violins. As with Kerll, the harmonic writing is on the

[1] Ibid., p. 106.   [2] Ibid., p. 1.

whole conventional, and Venetian characteristics can still be found, especially in the *Kyrie* and *Agnus Dei*.

There is a marked tendency towards spectacular display in the music under discussion. Even so, more restrained Catholic Masses were still composed, among them the two by Leopold I (1640–1705)[1] and the Mass in C by Pachelbel, his only Mass apart from the *Missa brevis* referred to above. Pachelbel certainly builds up structurally satisfying edifices, which in the fugal movements are often capped with telling entries at high pitch on the clarini; the 'Osanna' is a movement in which the themes (Ex. 312(i) and (ii)) are treated in a particularly lively way, and chromaticism beyond the conventional level can be seen in the final poignant 'Miserere' in the *Gloria* (iii):[2]

[1] The *Missa angeli custodis* is in Adler (ed.), *Musikalische Werke der Kaiser Ferdinand III., Leopold I. und Joseph I.*, i (Vienna, 1892), p. 55. See H. V. F. Somerset, 'The Habsburg emperors as musicians', *Music and Letters*, xxx (1949), p. 204.

[2] Autograph copy in Tenbury, St. Michael's College, MS. 1209, fo. 188.

But the work is still not on the high level of some of his other music, such as his *Magnificats* discussed below.

By the eighteenth century the tendency towards display increased, though not to the extent to which it did in Neapolitan church music.[1] In fact, the Neapolitan style was considerably modified when it was taken over by north Italian and south German composers, who continued to rely to some extent on long-standing contrapuntal traditions and on the now hallowed concertato style. None did more so than Johann Joseph Fux (1660–1741),[2] director of music at the Imperial court in Vienna from 1715, and the most prolific, celebrated, and influential composer of Masses in the city from the turn of the century.

---

[1] See *supra*, pp. 391 ff.

[2] See Egon Wellesz, *Fux* (London, 1965), pp. 11–17 and 22–5. A complete edition of Fux, *Gesammelte Werke*, is in progress, ed. Hellmut Federhofer (Kassel and Graz, 1959—); the Masses are in ser. i.

His Masses fall into two classes sharing an essentially contrapuntal texture: the old-fashioned *a cappella* style and the modern concertato type. The former are on the whole the more satisfying works—despite the intrinsic unreality of the style at that date—for the pseudo-Renaissance themes, textures and harmonic style show a genuinely sensitive approach to the words. The *Missa canonica*,[1] in which all kinds of canon occur, is a notable *tour de force*, whose high quality can be gauged from this extract from the 'Christe eleison':

Ex. 313

<hr />

[1] Ed. Johann E. Habert and G. A. Glossner in *Denkmäler der Tonkunst in Österreich*, i (Jg. i (1)) (Vienna, 1894), p. 67.

Even so, the freely composed works, such as the *Missa quadragesimalis*,[1] whose 'Dona nobis' is quoted here, are of greater artistic worth.

Ex. 314

[1] Ibid., p. 89. There is also a modern edition of the *Missa Sancti Joannis*, ed. J. H. van der Meer (Regensburg, 1956).

Of Fux's concertato Masses those for large forces are the most successful, especially when he exploits the antiphonal splendour of two choruses. But in those for more modest resources he seems unable to think in terms of the melodies of the *galant* style, which he to some extent adopts, and produces instead solid contrapuntal textures conventionally deployed. Fux's Venetian-born chief assistant, Antonio Caldara (1670–1736), was more successful at reconciling Neapolitan tunefulness with 'northern' counterpoint; his sacred music is discussed elsewhere in this volume.[1]

In the Masses of composers whose work falls wholly within the eighteenth century—men such as Georg Matthias Monn (1717–50), Georg Reutter the younger (1708–72), and Johann Adolf Hasse (1699–1783)—the *galant* style is far more in evidence, and current operatic manners are accepted without question. This development is found, too, in the work of the elder Georg Reutter (1656–1738), who, like his son, worked in Vienna. His Mass in C shows, notably in its thematic material, the standard he could reach; the following example from the opening of the 'Domine Deus' will suggest something of this quality:[2]

Ex. 315

[1] See pp. 339–41 and 388–9.   [2] Vienna, Nat. Bibl. MS. 10432.

Monn composed four Masses and can be well represented by his Mass in C,[1] which is exceptionally concise for a Catholic Mass of this period and is actually less operatic than the elder Reutter's C major Mass; but the eighty Masses of the younger Reutter, as represented by his *Missa S. Caroli*, also in C,[2] are as operatic in spirit as any Masses of the time. The somewhat more solid Masses—there are eleven of them—of the Italianized Hasse, who worked principally in Dresden, provide a link between this early *galant* style and the Viennese Masses of the end of the century. Within its elegant formality his Mass in D minor (1751?)[3] can boast both graceful melodic lines and vigorous rhythms and is not without agreeable harmonic surprises: the work is seen at its best in the chromatic fugue of the second 'Kyrie' and in the attractive 'Qui tollis'.

[1] Vienna, Nat. Bibl., MS. 5532.

[2] Georg Reutter the Younger, *Kirchenwerke*, ed. Norbert Hofer, *Denkmäler der Tonkunst in Österreich*, lxxxviii (Vienna, 1952), p. 1.

[3] Brit. Mus. Add. MS. 32393, fo. 15. Further on Hasse's church music see Vol. VII, pp. 291–3.

(*d*) REQUIEM MASSES

SCHÜTZ

The greatest German funerary work of the seventeenth century is Schütz's *Musikalische Exequien* (1636).[1] The text consists of verses from the Bible and from church hymns, and the whole is divided into three main parts:

(i) German Funeral Mass, for soloists and six-part chorus, which itself divides into sections corresponding to the *Kyrie* and *Gloria*. In the former the chorus three times punctuate the funeral sentences sung by the solo voices with the cry 'Have mercy', addressed once each to the three persons of the Trinity. The quasi-*Gloria* ('Also hat Gott die Welt geliebt') is constructed on similar principles.

(ii) Funeral Motet for double chorus, treated antiphonally: 'Herr, wenn ich dich nur habe' ('Lord, if only I have thee').

(iii) Concerto for a large five-part chorus (singing the *Nunc dimittis*, 'Herr, nun lässest du') and a small solo group of three, two soprano seraphim and a baritone *beata anima*, placed at a distance, singing 'Selig sind die Toten' ('Blessed are the dead'). Schütz states that in some churches it may be effective to double the solo group in two different parts of the building. (Schütz's preface gives other suggestions about performance and also throws interesting light on the reasons for the choice of texts.)

This work, which does not belong completely either to Schütz's experimental period or to his *a cappella* style, displays his mastery of form through the use of keys and varying textures and well repays detailed analysis. Its word-engendered phrases are smooth and flowing yet full of rhythmic subtleties and surprises. Realistic pictures are rare, but 'wool' is depicted by the somewhat flippant gambolling of sheep:

Ex. 316

¹ Schütz, *Sämmtliche Werke*, xii, ed. Spitta (Leipzig, 1892–3), and *Neue Ausgabe sämmtlicher Werke*, iv, ed. Friedrich Schöneich (Kassel and Basle, 1956), also ed. Arthur Mendel, as *A German Requiem* (New York, 1957); see Moser, op. cit., pp. 418 ff.; Eng. ed., pp. 485 ff.

(Ye shall be like wool.)

And Schütz's interpretation of the spiritual meaning of the text generally shows the greatest insight, as can be seen in these simple yet poignant phrases:

Ex. 317

(Though your sins be as scarlet, they shall be as white as snow.)

The third part is a moving example of the use of space and of the inspired juxtaposition and combination of different texts.

AUSTRIA

The Requiem Masses of Austrian composers show the same general characteristics as their other Masses, discussed in the preceding section. Christoph Strauss in his Requiem,[1] published in 1631, displays a fine sense of colour in handling two choirs of voices and instruments, one high, one low. His melodic and harmonic writing shows him straddling older and newer means of expression. On the one hand, for example, the 'Christe eleison' begins with a subject containing two diminished intervals accompanied by its own inversion in diatonic form, and quick repeated notes illustrating the words 'tremor est' show further that Strauss was familiar with the more emotive Italian music; on the other hand, the textural continuity is a more traditional feature. Later in the century there is a Requiem by Kerll,[2] written for modest resources, which reinforces the view expressed above in connection with his Masses that he was at his best when handling larger forces; the *Agnus Dei*, however, is a more rewarding movement.

With its frequent subtle and sensitive touches Biber's Requiem[3] is, in its more withdrawn way, a match for his more spectacular *Missa Sti. Henrici* discussed above. Biber set the *Dies irae* in the multi-sectional way usually found in the seventeenth century; a memorably effective passage is the setting of 'Quantus tremor' for two sopranos with a chain of close dissonances introduced and accompanied by throbbing quavers on the strings (see Ex. 318).

An equally simple yet convincing section is the 'Recordare', with its thrice-repeated four-note figure; and in the 'Lacrimosa' Biber manages most beautifully to temper the severity of a five-part vocal fugato with sensitively curving contrapuntal lines and the addition of an obbligato violin. An impressive Requiem in C minor by the younger Reutter[4] may be mentioned here as a fitting companion to Biber's work.

---

[1] Ed. Adler in *Denkmäler der Tonkunst in Österreich*, lix (Jg. xxx (1)) (Vienna, 1923), p. 1.
[2] Ibid., p. 73.   [3] Ibid., p. 41.   [4] Reutter the younger, op. cit., p. 58.

Ex. 318

(e) SOME SMALLER FORMS

SETTINGS OF THE *MAGNIFICAT*

Catholic composers adopted for their settings of texts such as the *Magnificat* and *Stabat Mater* the same elaborate, sumptuous style that they employed for their Masses. With the composers of north and central Germany, on the other hand, a distinction can be drawn between their Masses and their other sacred music, for which they drew upon the more modern concertato style instead of the *a cappella* style that characterizes their Masses.

The most substantial group of works to be dealt with here are the settings of the *Magnificat*.[1] That by Ahle dating from 1657[2] well illustrates the early development of the concertato style. Although the four instrumental lines have achieved independence of the voices, they have not yet acquired any individuality of style but are used for sober contrapuntal ritornellos between choral sections, as an antiphonal choir to the vocal chorus or for fanfares at appropriate moments; in *forte* choral passages they still double the voices. Structurally the work is multi-sectional, with many cadential punctuations giving considerable variety of key. Each verbal phrase gives birth to a fresh musical idea, but this is the only visible survival of Renaissance methods. For the essence of the new style is its lack of homogeneity; the ideas are varied according to the nature of the text, and while many are treated imitatively none is developed at any length or to a strong climactic point. Thus the music for the 'Dispersit' phrase lasts for only four bars, even though its theme is imitated in all voices in the manner of Bach (who incidentally is very likely to have seen the work when he was at Mühlhausen); the three descriptive figures for 'Deposuit . . . humiles' occupy only nine bars; there are no fugato movements; and the longest section (the *Gloria*) is homophonic.

The six *Magnificat* settings of Schütz, five of them to German words, belong mainly to his middle and last years. The single Latin setting[3] is

---

[1] An interesting *Magnificat* by Samuel Scheidt, published in 1635, is described *infra*, pp. 693–5, in the section devoted to sacred concertatos based on chorales, since nearly half the text is from a chorale, and another chorale-like melody is introduced too. Settings of the German text by Zachow and J. S. Bach (BWV 10) are also dealt with below as cantatas, since the texts include such a high proportion of inserted paraphrases: cf. *infra*, pp. 738 and 743–4.

[2] Ahle, op. cit., p. 132.

[3] *Sämmtliche Werke*, xviii, ed. Heinrich Spitta (Leipzig, 1927); also ed. Wilhelm Ehmann (Kassel, 1962).

one of his most impressive essays in the Venetian polychoral style and is worth considering in more detail. It is scored for five 'choirs': a quartet of soloists (S.A.T.B.); two S.A.T.B. choruses ('to reinforce the tone and for magnificence', as the composer writes); and two instrumental groups, one consisting of two violins and violone, the other of three trombones. Schütz illuminates the text by treating every phrase, and often individual words, with extraordinary imagination and by making the most of the effects of space and colour to be derived from his varied resources. As in all his works, the overall design is enhanced by the scheme of modulations and by the placing of the tutti: both features are present in the following passage, which illustrates this work and Schütz's art at their finest:

Ex. 319

In this setting Schütz would seem to have extracted every ounce of meaning that he could from the text. It is thus instructive to contrast this spacious vision of it with the more intimate and no less subtle setting that he made in 1671; this is his last work, and it too harks back to the Venetian style, though with much more modest forces.[1]

---

[1] Ed. Steinitz (London, 1966).

The thirteen settings of the *Magnificat* by Pachelbel[1] are among his finest music. He achieves constant variety by skilfully ringing the changes on his varied choral and orchestral resources, which range from four-part chorus with strings in three parts to a double chorus of voices and instruments totalling twenty-four parts and always written for idiomatically. All the settings are in a fully mature concertato style and no trace of modal writing remains—indeed, the influence of Italian opera is at times quite marked. Contrapuntal movements are worked out as genuine, usually double, fugues frequently including independent instrumental parts. The following excerpt from a C major *Magnificat*[2] gives an idea of the skill that Pachelbel displays in opening a reflective fugato movement:

Ex. 320

---

[1] Eleven are contained in four autograph manuscripts at Tenbury, St. Michael's College, MSS. 1208–9, 1311, and 1356. Three of Pachelbel's settings are available in modern vocal scores, one ed. Henry Woodward (Evanston, 1952), another, for double four-part chorus, ed. Hans T. David (New York, 1959), the third, a four-part setting, ed. Hans Heinrich Eggebrecht (Basle and St. Louis, 1963) in his series *Johann Pachelbel: Das Vokalwerk*. See Eggebrecht, 'Johann Pachelbel als Vokalkomponist', *Archiv für Musikwissenschaft*, xi (1954), p. 120 (with a catalogue of works).

[2] In Tenbury, St. Michael's College, MS. 1208.

His careful reading of the text always governs the precise nature of the music. For example, in the following passage, taken from another C major setting,[1] it can be seen how the vocal line falls for 'Deposuit' and ascends at 'exaltavit', only to fall abruptly at 'humiles':

Ex. 321

[1] Ibid., MS. 1311.

And Ex. 322, from the same setting, shows a treatment of 'inanes' vividly suggesting emptiness:

Ex. 322

The *Magnificat* settings of Johann Philipp Krieger may exceed Pachelbel's in quantity, but they by no means match them in quality; he listed some forty in the catalogue of his works already referred to, and the setting in C for New Year 1685 may be taken as typical.[1] The quality of the thematic material is vitiated by exasperatingly facile working-out, but against this it has to be said that Krieger handles his numerous forces with some brilliance and that felicitous touches appear here and there. But just as this work is less interesting than Pachelbel's and also than a setting attributed to Buxtehude,[2] so does it pale, of course, beside the greatest setting of the words in the early eighteenth century—J. S. Bach's. This exists in two versions:[3] (*i*) in E flat, BWV 243a, 1723, with four Christmas interludes—a plan anticipated, as we have seen, by Zachow; and (*ii*) a revised version in D, BWV 243, *c*. 1730, without the interludes. Of the interludes two are settings of German, two of Latin verses. Part of the last is lost but can be completed from its other version as the duet 'Ehre sei Gott' in Cantata 110, composed for Christmas 1725. The first, 'Vom Himmel hoch', is a particularly fine example of the type of chorale prelude associated with Pachelbel. Except for the key and a few small details, chiefly of orchestration, the two versions of the *Magnificat* proper are identical. They are admirably concise, and there is scarcely a weak bar. Ritornello form is used in most of the movements, fugal writing in the others, and the last twenty-three bars of the last movement are based on the material of the first. One or two especially fine features may be singled out: the way in which the twenty-seven-bar five-part fugato on 'Omnes generationes' breaks in suddenly on the final cadence of the soprano's tranquil 'Quia respexit' to complete her sentence with striking dramatic force; and the splendid combination of fugue with powerful homophonic hammer-strokes that forms the setting of 'Fecit potentiam'.

SETTINGS OF OTHER TEXTS

A number of other texts were set many times over, but only a handful of works may be mentioned here.[4] Two emperors, Ferdinand III (1608–1657) and Leopold I, composed *Misereres*. Ferdinand's[5] is a competent and not unimaginative work, but it is eclipsed by Leopold's G minor

---

[1] Krieger, op. cit., p. 1; the catalogue is on pp. xxiv-lii of that volume.

[2] Ed. Bruno Grusnick (Kassel and Basle, *c*. 1950).

[3] Bach, *Neue Ausgabe*, ii, 3, ed. Alfred Dürr (Kassel and Basle, 1955). For a good account of the work see Donald Francis Tovey, *Essays in Musical Analysis*, v (London, 1937), pp. 50–60. See also Dürr, 'Bach's Magnificat', *Music Review*, xv (1954), p. 182; and Stanley Godman, 'Die Erstfassung von Bachs Magnificat', *Musik und Kirche*, xxiv (1954), p. 119.

[4] A setting by Erasmus Kindermann of the German *Te Deum* using a chorale melody is referred to below in the section on sacred concertatos based on chorales: cf. pp. 695–6.

[5] Adler (ed.), *Musikalische Werke der Kaiser*, i, p. 1. Again see Somerset, op. cit.

setting,[1] which is a work of considerable beauty and superior to his other Latin church music. It is scored for much more modest forces than those that he provided for his subjects: soloists, a four-part chorus, and a few strings, which he uses expressively and economically. The declamation is sometimes almost Purcellian in its power:

Ex. 323

and the sorrowing, resigned mood of the opening of the following passage makes all the more effective the impassioned sequences that follow (see Ex. 324).

Another *Miserere* by Leopold, in C minor,[2] is more ambitious, both in scale and in the forces it demands. But again, though it is a lesser work than the G minor setting, words of penitence and sorrow inspired Leopold to rise above conventional figures and formulas. His setting

---

[1] Vienna, Nat. Bibl., MS. 16263.   [2] Adler (ed.), op. cit., i, p. 257.

Ex. 324

of the *Stabat Mater*[1] disappointingly falls into routine blandness and obvious rhythms, and he does not penetrate, as he does with the *Miserere* text, to the heart of the words. Also in Austria there is a fine setting by Fux of the *Te Deum*[2] (1706), the only one of his six settings to survive in full score; in it luxuriant counterpoint characteristic of Austrian baroque church music is fused with clearly tonal harmonies typical of the new century. These can also be heard to advantage in a fine setting of the *Miserere* by Hasse.[3]

It remains to mention a deeply felt setting by Rosenmüller of the *Lamentationes Jeremiae*;[4] this work contains passages of great emotional force, characteristic of this uneven composer at his best, and the finely curving monody of Ex. 325 provides one of them:

Ex. 325

(She weepeth sore in the night, her tears are on her cheeks. Among all her lovers she hath none to comfort her.)

[1] Vienna, Nat. Bibl., MS. 15731.
[2] Ed. I. Kecskeméti, *J. J. Fux: Gesammelte Werke*, ii, 1 (Kassel and Graz, 1963). See Wellesz, op. cit., pp. 25–9.
[3] Vocal score, ed. R. M. Thackray (London, 1968).
[4] Ed. Fred Hamel (Hanover, 1929); excerpt ('Aleph. Ego vir') in Archibald T. Davison and Willi Apel, *Historical Anthology of Music*, ii (London, 1950), p. 65.

(f) ORATORIOS[1]

THE EARLIEST GERMAN ORATORIOS

The origins of oratorio in Italy have been described in an earlier chapter;[2] the earliest German examples date from the second decade of the seventeenth century. Schütz's *Historia der Auferstehung Jesu Christi* of 1623[3] is only to a limited extent a 'modern' oratorio and still owes a good deal to the traditions of sixteenth-century Passion music; it is, in fact, closely modelled on the *Auferstehungshistorie* by Antonio Scandello (1517–80), an Italian predecessor of Schütz's at the Dresden court. The Evangelist's declamation is old fashioned in that it is closer to psalm-tone recitation than to recitative. Another traditional feature, strongly setting off the work from overtly dramatic oratorios, is the scoring of a number of 'solo' parts for more than one singer: for instance, the words of Mary Magdalene are set in a closely worked duet texture, both homophonic and imitative, for alto and bass soloists, though it is true that other characters are represented more realistically, for example the Three Marys by three solo sopranos. In addition to the chorus there are modest instrumental forces. Some of the textures, especially in the duets and trios, are in an up-to-date Italianate concertato style, and the harmonic writing also shows the influence of recent Italian music: the following setting of Mary Magdalene's opening sentence shows, in addition to the textures already mentioned, the juxtaposition at the crucial word 'Herren' of chords whose roots are a third apart—a progression often found at emotional moments in the music of Monteverdi and his Italian contemporaries (see Ex. 326).

Nearer to the true oratorio and also dating probably from the 1620s is the Italianate *Repraesentatio harmonica conceptionis et nativitatis S. Joannis Baptistae . . . composita modo pathetico sive recitativo* of Daniel Bollius (*c.* 1590–*c.* 1642), dedicated to an Elector of Mainz who died in 1626.[4] The narrator, first Isaiah and then St. Luke, is a soloist, as are all the 'acting' personages; in the third scene John himself sings a highly ornamented aria. There is even a foreshadowing of naturalism in the treatment of the chorus. And a small orchestra of two violins, viola bastarda, flautino, flutes, cornetti, bassoon, and organ plays in

---

[1] Excluding Passion oratorios, which are discussed in section (*g*) *infra*.

[2] See chap. VI, pp. 324 ff.

[3] Ed. Walter Simon Huber, *Neue Ausgabe*, iii (2nd ed., Kassel and Basle, 1956); there is a miniature score, ed. Fritz Stein (Leipzig, 1935). See Moser, op. cit., pp. 317 ff.; Eng. ed., pp. 365 ff.

[4] Described at length in Carl von Winterfeld, *Johannes Gabrieli und sein Zeitalter* (Berlin, 1834), ii, pp. 206–7.

Ex. 326

(They have taken the Lord from the grave.)

five *symphoniae* which open, articulate, and close the work.[1] The Nuremberg *Freuden- und Trauerspiele* of the mid-century[2] were didactic sacred
dramas with music (now lost), including solos, choruses and occasionally
chorales, by Sigmund Theophil Staden (1607–55), but the narrative was
spoken. The next true oratorio which we know after Bollius's *Repraesentatio* is an *Actus Musicus de Divite et Lazaro*, performed in 1649, by
the Stettin cantor Andreas Fromm (1621–83).[3] This is essentially a
dramatic work influenced by Italian oratorios. It consists of eighteen
sections—solos, choruses, and *sinfonie*—including four chorales, which
represent the single most significant way in which an Italian Catholic
form was adapted to a German Protestant environment. This work also
treats a subject frequently set by earlier German composers, though not
always in dramatic form. Perhaps the most relevant setting is that by
Schütz, probably dating from the 1620s, 'Vater Abraham, erbarme dich
mein';[4] but that work lacks linking narrative and therefore really
belongs to the type of dramatic dialogue discussed below.

Very few other large-scale oratorios apart from Passion oratorios
survive from mid-seventeenth-century Germany; for example, all the
music of the four oratorios composed by Buxtehude is lost. However,
there remains to be discussed another masterpiece by Schütz, utterly

[1] The opening of the autograph score of the *secunda symphonia* is reproduced in facsimile
in *Die Musik in Geschichte und Gegenwart*, ii (1952), col. 83.
[2] See Arnold Schering, *Geschichte des Oratoriums* (Leipzig, 1911, repr. 1966), p. 140.
[3] Ed. Hans Engel, *Denkmäler der Tonkunst in Pommern*, v (Kassel, 1936). See Schering,
op. cit., pp. 154–5.
[4] *Sämmtliche Werke*, xviii, ed. Heinrich Spitta (Leipzig, 1927), p. 37; also ed. Seiffert
(Leipzig, 1924). See Moser, op. cit., pp. 421 ff.; Eng. ed., pp. 489 ff.

different from his *Auferstehungshistorie*. This is the *Christmas Oratorio*, or, to give it its cumbersome German title, *Historia der freuden- und gnadenreichen Geburth Gottes und Marien Sohnes, Jesu Christi*;[1] it was published at Dresden in 1664 in an incomplete form, and most modern editions include completions of varying merit. The narration is written in modern recitative very similar to that found in Italian operas of the time, and Schütz justifiably claimed in his preface that he was presenting this manner of writing for the first time in print in Germany; there is no trace of the Gregorian overtones of the narratives in the *Aufer-stehungshistorie* and indeed in the Passions[2] that he composed in the same period as the 'Christmas Oratorio'. This recitative is divided into nine sections by eight vocal and instrumental ensembles with continuo, called *intermedii*. The variety of scoring for the voices and melody instruments does indeed link these movements with Italian *intermedii* and to such a work as Monteverdi's *Orfeo* influenced by them. They consist (not in the following order) of:

Angel's Chorus: six voices, two violins
Trio of shepherds: three altos, two recorders
Trio of Wise Men: three tenors, two violins
Quartet of High Priests and Scribes: four basses, two trombones
Three solos for the Angel: soprano, two viols or *violette*
Solo for Herod: bass, two clarini.

The actual choice of instruments, for example trombones for the priests and recorders for the shepherds, also falls within the well-established traditions of instrumental characterization in *intermedii*. The ensembles interpret the words in a vivid manner and are largely contrapuntal, a feature which in addition to the scoring sets them off from the recitatives; the following extract from the trio of the Wise Men is representative:

Ex. 327

---

[1] *Neue Ausgabe*, i, ed. Schöneich (Kassel and Basle, 1955). There is also a good vocal score, ed. Mendel as *The Christmas Story* (London, 1960), and a miniature score, ed. Fritz Stein (Leipzig, 1935). See Moser, op. cit., pp. 550 ff.; Eng. ed., pp. 649 ff.

[2] See *infra*, pp. 625–8.

(Where is the newborn King of the Jews?)

This alternating structure of recitative and ensembles is framed by choruses in four parts. These, like the *intermedii*, are centred firmly on F major. Thus Schütz employs tonality as well as symmetry of texture to further the unity of the work; by doing so he enhances the high quality of the invention throughout and produces one of his happiest masterpieces.

There are also two short oratorios by Selle, both of them interesting examples of the form: a Christmas oratorio ('Es begab sich aber zu der Zeit') and one for Easter ('Und als der Sabbath vergangen war').[1] The former is the more sumptuously scored and includes a double chorus and a large array of brass, wind and stringed instruments; Selle takes full advantage of his forces, as when the appearance of the Angel to the shepherds is heralded by a *sinfonia* for three flutes (or cornetti) and four trombones, each group with its own continuo.

DRAMATIC DIALOGUES

The scale of Selle's Easter oratorio in particular is hardly larger than that normally found in a type of composition analogous to oratorios: the dramatic dialogue, which could take the place of the motet in the service. There exists an extensive literature of these small-scale sacred dialogues (sometimes for more than two voices, and with chorus) cultivated by several leading composers in the seventeenth century. Some dialogues, notably those of Hammerschmidt and Pfleger, are allegorical pieces involving God and a Believing Soul and other characters, and it is more appropriate to consider them in the discussion of free concertatos.[2] But many are settings of familiar scenes from the Gospels, which were the quarry for oratorios. In them the concertato style predominates, and the only accompaniment is for continuo instruments. There is some characterization, though quite often even obvious characters are not named in the scores. For instance, all are anonymous in three pieces by Ahle—representative of his numerous dialogues— which obviously treat the stories of respectively Mary at the tomb on Easter morning (published in 1648), Doubting Thomas (1666) and the Pharisee and the Publican (1648).[3] Yet in the first one, for example, Thomas maintains his doubts through fifty bars of Jesus's 'Peace be unto you' and then obsessively sings 'My Lord and my God' with new flourishes added and with increasing intensity. There is a similar degree of characterization in a 'Dialogue between Christ and the Sinner' (Nurem-

---

[1] In Selle, *Ausgewählte Kirchenmusik: Die Kantate*, nos. 155–6, ed. Klaus Vetter (Stuttgart, 1963).

[2] Cf. *infra*, pp. 725–6.

[3] Ahle, op. cit., pp. 3, 6, and 9 respectively.

berg, 1643)[1] by Johann Erasmus Kindermann (1616–55), who possibly studied in Italy, and worked in Nuremberg. Christ (tenor) calls urgently for repentance in rapid quaver arpeggio figures approaching the *stile concitato*; and the Sinner (soprano) bemoans her manifold sins in affective rhythms and harmonies. A later reply by the Sinner is for two sopranos, a non-realistic treatment harking back, as we have seen, to sixteenth-century practice. The work ends with a fine chorus in seven parts, five vocal, two instrumental.

Some dialogues are settings of Latin texts. One such is Kindermann's on the Institution of the Eucharist.[2] There are also three notable ones, virtually oratorios, by Kaspar Förster the younger (1616–73),[3] who studied with Carissimi and later worked in North Germany and Denmark. The following excerpts from one of these works, the *Dialogi Davidis cum philisteo* indicate the strength of the Italian influence on Förster:

Ex. 328

(i)

Nunc ub - i pug - na - ces, nunc ub - i fe - ra - ces

---

[1] *Ausgewählte Werke*, ed. Felix Schreiber, *Denkmäler der Tonkunst in Bayern*, xiii (Leipzig, 1913), p. 155.
[2] Ibid., p. 85.
[3] Upsala, Univ. Bibl., MS. 78.

Several of the finest of these miniature oratorios are by Schütz and are to be found among his manuscript pieces and here and there in his important published collections of *Kleine geistliche Konzerte* and *Symphoniae sacrae*, whose principal contents are discussed later. The most important are the Easter dialogue 'Weib, was weinest du?' (1624),[1] an incomplete reworking of themes from the *Auferstehungshistorie*; a setting of uncertain date of the parable of the Pharisee and the Publican, 'Es gingen zweene Menschen hinauf';[2] 'Sei gegrüsset' (from the *Kleine geistliche Konzerte*, 1636-9);[3] and three works from the third and last set of *Symphoniae sacrae* (1650)—'Mein Sohn, warum?' (based on the episode of the twelve-year-old Jesus in the temple), 'Siehe, es erschien der Engel', and 'Meister, wir wissen' (the parable of the tribute money).[4] In all this music Schütz gives free rein to his dramatic genius. Not least is this true of 'Mein Sohn, warum?', yet it is interesting that he abandons the individuality of the solo voices in this work when the main episode has been dealt with and the chorus enters with a new train of thought, referring back to Psalm 84. 'Siehe, es erschien' may be compared with Schütz's later setting of the same words in his 'Christmas Oratorio'; in the latter work the treatment as recitative is much sparer than in the more opulent dialogue. 'Sei gegrüsset' may also be compared with another setting of basically the same text, 'Gegrüsset seist du', by Matthias Weckmann (1619-74),[5] a pupil of Schütz. Schütz maintains distinct characterization of Mary and the Angel throughout the piece (which also boasts an introductory *symphonia* and a chorus), but Weckmann's characterization is even more clear-cut; he allots differing instruments to distinguish Mary (recorders) and the Angel (violins) and differentiates their parts with persistent characteristic figures until they coalesce in a final fugal 'alleluia'.

LATER GERMAN ORATORIOS

Meanwhile, oratorio could be heard in a highly Italianate form in Austria; many works were to Italian texts, continued to be so in the eighteenth century with Fux and Hasse and have thus been discussed already in chapter VI.[6] Among works with German texts may be men-

---

[1] *Sämmtliche Werke*, xiv (Leipzig, 1893), p. 60; also in A. Hänlein (ed.), *Schütz: Drei biblische Szenen* (Leipzig, 1897), p. 9, and ed. Werner Bittinger (Kassel and Basle, 1964).
[2] *Sämmtliche Werke*, xiv, p. 55; also in Hänlein, op. cit., p. 1.
[3] *Neue Ausgabe*, xii, ed. Ehmann (Kassel, 1963), p. 36.
[4] The first two in *Sämmtliche Werke*, x (Leipzig, 1891), pp. 42 and 58 respectively; the third in xi (Leipzig, 1891), p. 86. The first also ed. Steinitz (London, 1962) and the third ed. Holle (Kassel, 1940); the first is also in Hänlein, op. cit., p. 18.
[5] *Matthias Weckmann und Christoph Bernhard: Solocantaten und Chorwerke mit Instrumentalbegleitung*, ed. Seiffert, *Denkmäler deutscher Tonkunst*, vi (Leipzig, 1901), p. 22.
[6] Cf. *supra*, Chap. VI (a), *passim*.

tioned two by Leopold I, *Die Erlösung des menschlichen Geschlechts* (1679) and *Sieg des Leidens Christi über die Sinnlichkeit* (1682).[1] In both, movingly simple or shapely passages alternate with stiffer and more trite material; admirable instances of the former (in addition to the passages printed by Adler) are the final ensemble of the earlier work and Mary's aria 'Grimme Nägel' in the later one.

Except for the so-called oratorios of J. S. Bach there is little in Germany in the eighteenth century to set beside the Italian oratorios of Fux and Hasse. Only a few by Telemann survive, and all are late works outside the scope of this volume.[2] One of the cantatas of Zachow, 'Ruhe, Friede, Freud und Wonne', is dramatic enough to be considered a miniature oratorio.[3] One prolific composer of oratorios was Johann Mattheson (1681–1764) of Hamburg, a highly influential theorist whose music supported his critical advocacy of the Italian style, not least in his oratorios, which are, however, rather over-simple and harmonically predictable.[4] Bach's cantata 'Lobet Gott in seinen Reichen', BWV 11, known as the 'Ascension Oratorio',[5] and the six cantatas forming his *Weihnachts-Oratorium* (the Christmas Oratorio), BWV 248,[6] all belong to the same type: they resemble choral cantatas without chorale fantasias (the fourth of the categories of Bach cantata proposed later in this chapter), the sole difference being that the texts here include a biblical narrative, which is divided between an Evangelist, the chorus, and other characters. The Christmas Oratorio dates from late 1734 and early 1735, the Ascension Oratorio from a few months later.

As in the Passions (discussed *infra*), the soloists in the Christmas Oratorio interpolate non-biblical devotional commentaries, and the words sung by the chorus are also non-scriptural; the main functions of the chorus are to establish the mood of each cantata (except the second) in a big opening movement and to interpolate suitable chorales throughout. The latter can justly be called the most beautiful to be found in any of Bach's major works. He borrowed from his earlier works in the Christmas Oratorio more extensively than in any other work: twelve of the choruses and arias are borrowed thus, the chief sources being two secular cantatas dating from 1733, BWV 213 and

[1] Excerpts from these works in Adler (ed.), op. cit., pp. 60 and 71 respectively.
[2] See Vol. VII, p. 328, for a reference to his *Der Tag des Gerichts*.
[3] See *infra*, pp. 738–9.
[4] See Heinrich Schmidt, *Johann Mattheson, ein Förderer der deutschen Tonkunst, im Lichte seiner Werke* (Leipzig, 1897), including excerpts from *Der reformirende Johannes* (1717); there is an extract from *Die heylsame Geburth und Menschwerdung unsers Herren* (1715) in Schering, *Geschichte der Musik in Beispielen* (Leipzig, 1931; Eng. ed., New York, 1950), p. 393.
[5] *Werke*, ii, p. 1.
[6] *Neue Ausgabe*, ii, 6, ed. Walter Blankenburg and Dürr (Kassel, 1960).

214.[1] The transferences are mostly successful, even when the new context is dissimilar to that of the original work: for example, at the very outset the unaccompanied timpani beats make an effectively rousing, if unusual, start to a festive oratorio even though divorced from the text, 'Tönet, ihr Pauken!' ('Beat, kettledrums!'), that had prompted them in BWV 214. Even so, many of the most sublime moments occur in newly-composed music—the chorales (as already mentioned), the accompanied recitatives, and the 'Pastoral Symphony'. There are some equally fine movements in the Ascension Oratorio, among which two may be singled out: the opening movement, which is one of Bach's most splendid choruses in ritornello form; and the affecting, grief-stricken alto aria 'Ach, bleibe doch', which he later reworked as the *Agnus Dei* of the Mass in B minor.

(g) PASSION MUSIC

TYPES OF PASSION

Up to the beginning of the seventeenth century settings of the Passion had taken two basic forms: the original type, in which the plainsong narrative alternates with short choruses, often homophonic; and the motet Passion, which is a polyphonic composition throughout.[2] The latter flourished throughout the sixteenth century in several countries; many of them have Latin texts, but a number of others are in the vernacular. The finest examples are not necessarily by the most celebrated composers: Lassus and Rore, for example, are eclipsed by Johann Walther and Leonhard Lechner. In Germany Latin settings died out early in the seventeenth century; the last German setting followed twenty years later and is discussed below. Three new forms of Passion— listed at (2)–(4) below—became established in their stead.

The Passions discussed in the following pages are grouped under the following four headings:[3]

(1) Motet Passions. This type died out early in the seventeenth century,

---

[1] See Schmieder, op. cit., p. 365, and J. A. Westrup, *Bach Cantatas* (London, 1966), pp. 21–3, among other Bach literature.

[2] See Vols. III and IV, *passim*.

[3] For general studies of Passion music see Basil Smallman, *The Background of Passion music: J. S. Bach and his predecessors* (2nd. rev. and enl. ed., New York, 1970); Gerald Abraham, 'Passion music in the fifteenth and sixteenth centuries', *Monthly Musical Record*, lxxxiii (1953), pp. 208 and 235, and 'Passion music from Schütz to Bach', ibid., lxxxiv (1954), pp. 115, 152, and 175; Walter Lott, 'Zur Geschichte der Passionskomposition von 1650–1800', *Archiv für Musikwissenschaft*, iii (1921), p. 285; and Werner Braun, *Die mitteldeutsche Choralpassion im 18ten Jahrhundert* (Berlin, 1960). Also see the long article 'Passion' in *Die Musik in Geschichte und Gegenwart*, x (1962), cols. 886–933, including admirable lists of works and editions, and bibliographies.

and only one such work, by Christoph Demantius (1567–1643), remains to be considered in this volume. Motet Passions are *a cappella* works.

(2) Dramatic Passions. These consist of plainsong or pseudo-plainsong, with the various characters taken by different solo voices, interspersed with choruses. Everything is by liturgical custom unaccompanied. To this type belong the St. Luke Passion of Christoph Schultze (1606–83), and the three Passions of Schütz, all from the middle years of the seventeenth century, after which it died out.

(3) Oratorio Passions. In addition to the biblical text, principally allotted to the Evangelist, this type includes non-Gospel interpolations as texts for arias and other movements. All works of this kind are accompanied by continuo and frequently by other instruments as well. The first such work, by Thomas Selle of Hamburg, dates from 1643; eight others followed by the end of the seventeenth century, all by minor composers, and Schütz's *Die sieben Worte* ('The Seven Words on the Cross') also belongs fundamentally with these works, though it lacks non-biblical interpolations. The series was crowned in the 1720s by Bach's two great Passions.

(4) Passion Oratorios. This rather operatic type of Passion was the last to be evolved, in the early eighteenth century; the texts, although based on the Passion story, are not biblical, are written entirely in verse and can properly be thought of as librettos. To this type belong Handel's Brockes Passion and several works by Georg Philipp Telemann and Reinhard Keiser, among others.

Most composers chose to set St. Matthew's version of the Passion story. This may seem strange in view of the much longer and more dramatic crowd scenes in St. John's version, but it is probably explained by the fact that Passions were traditionally performed in two parts, before and after a sermon, and St. John's account does not lend itself to such a division: the break would either have to intrude disastrously into the sharp battle of words between Pilate and the Jews or it would have to come before this scene begins (as in Bach), leaving the first part far too static. St. Matthew's account falls easily into scenes and dwells more than St. John's on the meditative aspects of the story, which are lyrical and therefore suitable for music. On the other hand, the extremely long section from 'Herr, bin ichs?' ('Lord is it I?') to 'Er ist des Todes schuldig' ('He is guilty of death'), without any choruses, can make for monotony when set by composers less inspired than Schütz was in his 1666 setting. No doubt this factor was at least partly responsible for the inclusion of choruses or arias set to free texts at strategic (and unfortunately sometimes at non-strategic) moments in the drama. The first time such insertions were written into a score was in Christian Flor's

St. Matthew Passion in 1667, but Selle had introduced two long passages from the Old Testament, as well as a closing chorus and chorale, into his St. John Passion as early as 1643, and Thomas Mancinus had indicated places for interpolated chorales and symphonies in his St. Matthew Passion of 1620.

St. Luke's Passion story contains an extended account of the disciples' suggestion of defending Jesus by force but omits to mention one or two other dramatic points, such as the earthquake and the account of Peter's weeping. (St. John also omits the latter, which caused Bach to insert St. Matthew's description of it into his St. John setting.) St. Luke was certainly not very popular with composers; St. Mark, perhaps because of his brevity, was even less so.

MOTET PASSIONS AND DRAMATIC PASSIONS

The last motet Passion, which just falls within the scope of the present volume, is the St. John Passion of Demantius, who worked at Freiberg, in Saxony.[1] In this genre a shortened text prevents monotony, though in the present work the excisions include much of Pilate's part in his exchanges with the Jewish mob. Demantius works within the tradition represented by Lechner's Passion published in 1594. He overcomes restrictions in regard to characterization, the exploitation of dramatic elements, and word-painting by associating different groups of voices with different characters, though not rigidly or even consistently. He uses lively declamation to paint a picture or to highlight a dramatic moment:

Ex. 329

[1] Christoph Demantius, *Passion nach dem Evangelisten Johannes und Weissagung des Leidens und Sterbens Jesu Christi*, ed. Friedrich Blume, *Das Chorwerk*, xxvii (Wolfenbüttel and Berlin, 1934).

(Then cried they [all].)

Phrases are occasionally repeated for emphasis:

Ex. 330

(What is truth?)

Six-part writing gives a rich sonority, as can be seen from these two examples; it is all the more effective for being used sparingly. And a certain amount of typically baroque chromaticism added to harmony that is generally Renaissance in spirit combines with the features just mentioned to make of this Passion a work of real substance. A novel feature of it ought to be stressed too—the fact that as an appendix Demantius published a setting of the passage in chapter 53 of Isaiah foretelling the Passion: it is not impossible that the example of this addition helped to prompt the interpolations that, as we shall see, were so common in later Passions.

(Away, away with this man, and give us Barabbas.)

The dramatic Passion was established by the middle of the six-teenth century; just before the period covered by the present volume there are a St. Matthew Passion by Melchior Vulpius (1613) and the

one by Mancinus (1620) already referred to. The next work of importance is Christoph Schultze's St. Luke Passion (Leipzig, 1653),[1] which
contains many features familiar from Schütz's Passions. The recitatives
are not based on the traditional Passion tone, but are set in what has
been called 'unmeasured . . . Teutonized plainsong'.[2] Any descriptive
touches would be out of place in such impersonal music, whose most
noteworthy feature lies in the differing pitches for the various characters;
this tradition is ancient but in the seventeenth century became highly
dramatic, as when, in Mancinus's setting, Peter recites vehemently on
high Fs. Melismas are used in cadence formulae to indicate who sings
next and not, as in later settings, at climactic or emotional points.
Schultze's choruses (four-part early in the work, six-part later on) are
mostly short and homophonic; their harmony is plain, and they are
tonal, though still with modal touches. That Schultze's dramatic sense
inspired him to quite striking effects may be seen in such a passage
as Ex. 331.

With the three Passions of Schütz's old age—St. Luke (1664), St. John
(1665), and St. Matthew (1666)[3]—we are withdrawn even more compellingly into a spiritual world far removed from the material world of
operatic recitative and instrumental accompaniment; they afford a
fitting climax to our study of the dramatic Passion. In his very original
style of recitative[4] Schütz usually adds melismas for colour or pic-
torialism: for instance, the crowing of the cock is melismatic in all three
Passions (and in nearly every subsequent setting too). Only in the St.
Luke Passion does this unaccompanied recitative show much connection
with the old Passion tone, but even here Schütz is really writing the
free 'Teutonized plainsong' we have encountered in Schultze, with
expressive declamation, and melismas on important words:

Ex. 332

(Father, I commend my spirit into thy hands.)

[1] Ed. Peter Epstein (Berlin, 1930).

[2] Abraham, *Monthly Musical Record*, lxxxiv, p. 118.

[3] Ed. Wilhelm Kamlah and Fritz Schmidt, *Neue Ausgabe*, ii (Kassel and Basle, 1957);
there are miniature scores of all three ed. Stein (Leipzig, 1932–4). See Moser, op. cit.,
pp. 560 ff.; Eng. ed., pp. 660 ff.

[4] See Gerber, *Das Passionsrezitativ bei Heinrich Schütz und seine stilgeschichtlichen
Grundlagen* (Gütersloh, 1929).

The choral writing includes some splendidly vivid passages, such as the following:

(Away, away with this man, and give us Barabbas.)

In the St. John Passion the atmosphere of tragedy is heightened by the strong Phrygian flavour. The recitative is entirely free of traditional formulae. In Ex. 334 the melismas marvellously anticipate the frenzied excitement of the crowd in the chorus 'Kreuzige ihn' ('Crucify him'),

which follows immediately and where the melismas on the first syllable
sound literally like the howling of the mob:

Ex. 334

schrie – – en___ sie und___ . sprach- en

(They cried out and said)

Other exceptionally dramatic choruses are: 'Bist du nicht?' ('Art thou
not?'), more concise than Bach's setting; 'Wäre dieser nicht ein übel-
täter' ('If this man were not a malefactor'), with its impatient repeated
quavers at 'wir hätten dir ihn nicht':

Ex. 335

(We had not delivered him to thee.)

and 'Sei gegrüsset' ('We greet thee'), in which the cruelly mocking descending quavers at 'lieber Jüdenkönig' ('dear King of the Jews') paint a vivid picture of false obeisance.

The St. Matthew Passion is one of Schütz's most consistently inspired works and an astonishing achievement for a man of eighty-one. The purposeful and shapely recitatives command attention throughout. Unexpected, subtle, and powerful touches abound, both here and in the choruses, and a few may be cited as evidence of Schütz's sensitive response to the words. There is, for example, the telling repetition of words and phrases at Judas's anxious 'Bin ichs, bin ichs, Rabbi?' ('Is it I, is it I, Master?'), answered by Jesus's calming slurred notes, or Peter's 'so will ich dich, so will ich dich nicht verleugnen' ('but I, but I will not deny thee'). There is, too, the transference of 'Eli, eli' from Jesus's bass to the Evangelist's tenor at the same pitch—to a lower, less effective register in the new voice—so as not to create an anticlimax after the agony that Schütz has put into Jesus's cry; and the characterization of Caiaphas:

Ex. 336

(I adjure thee by the living God, that thou tell us whether thou be the Christ, the Son of God.)

In the choral writing one might mention the hissing of the consonants dominating the antiphonal texture at 'Wer ist es?' ('Who is it?') near the end of the chorus 'Weissage uns'; and the use of low voices for the High Priests and Elders in 'Es taug nicht' ('It is not lawful'), a tremendously powerful chorus, more solemn even than Bach's setting.

ORATORIO PASSIONS IN THE SEVENTEENTH CENTURY

We have already seen that the St. John Passion by Selle[1] is the earliest Passion setting to have independent instrumental accompaniment and non-gospel interpolations, both of which must have seemed startling innovations in the context of Passion music up to that

[1] Selle, *Johannes-Passion mit Intermedien*, ed. Gerber, *Das Chorwerk*, xxvi (Wolfenbüttel and Berlin, 1934). See *supra*, pp. 621–2.

date, but especially the introduction of instruments, which were traditionally silent not only in Passions but in all other services in the most solemn week of the Christian year. The instrumental writing is, moreover, more imaginative than that in any other seventeenth-century Passion. Selle's setting can be considered here with three later works, all St. Matthew Passions, with which it shared many features. They are settings published in 1672 and 1673 respectively, by Johann Sebastiani (1622–83), who worked mainly in Königsberg, and by Johann Theile (1646–1724), a Schütz pupil at Lübeck, and one probably by Friedrich Funcke (1642–99), of Lüneburg, which was published in 1683;[1] they are all works of lesser artistic stature than Selle's.

Let us consider instrumentation first. All four works have continuo support. Selle deploys a large band of other instruments to give individuality to the characters and to create Venetian effects in the big choruses; the additional instrumental forces in the other works are more modest. In Selle's work two bassoons accompany the Evangelist, two violins and one bassoon Jesus, three violins without continuo the Maid, two recorders and bassoon Peter and the Servant, and two cornetti and one trombone Pilate:

Ex. 337

(Art thou the King of the Jews?)

These instruments are rarely used idiomatically, but rather to supply the harmony, and for the most part they duplicate the vocal rhythms. An exception to this is the Evangelist's accompaniment: the bassoons assume complete rhythmic independence, with animated figures in imitation which might even be thought to hamper the free movement of the vocal part. Nevertheless, Selle gives proof of a fine ear for colour and spacing in his scoring.

[1] All these works are in modern editions; the first two are in *Johann Sebastiani und Johann Theile: Passionsmusiken*, ed. Friedrich Zelle, *Denkmäler deutscher Tonkunst*, xvii (Leipzig, 1904), pp. 7 and 111 respectively; and Funcke's is ed. Birke, *Das Chorwerk*, lxxviii–lxxix (Wolfenbüttel, 1961). On Funcke's see Birke, 'Eine unbekannte anonyme Matthäuspassion aus der zweiten Hälfte des 17. Jahrhunderts', *Archiv für Musikwissenschaft*, xv (1958), p. 162.

No attempt at characterization by affective orchestration comparable with that found in Selle's score distinguishes the Passions of either Sebastiani or Theile, but perhaps it is only fair to Theile to mention that he aimed at simplicity in order to please the Protestants and even suggested that instruments could be dispensed with altogether. Funcke relegates his four-part string orchestra to playing *sinfonie* and accompanying the chorus, although in its latter function it has a reasonably independent role. Sebastiani allots two violins to Jesus and three violas to the Evangelist; he uses all these for *sinfonie* and to accompany the chorus. Elsewhere he is somewhat inconsistent: for example, Peter is sometimes accompanied by the two violins, at other times by the three violas. Like Bach, he omits string accompaniment to the words from the Cross, 'Eli, eli . . .'. The string writing in the recitatives fulfils its purpose of supplying the harmony, yet at the same time the individual lines have a certain amount of character; the textures are not very imitational, but there is plenty of air in them:

Ex. 338

(Then went one of the twelve, named Judas Iscariot, to the Chief Priests and said:)

With Theile we find a good deal of imitation of the voice part in the accompaniment by two gambas for the Evangelist and in the two violas that accompany Jesus, yet there is also much monotonously busy movement, merely filling out the harmony, which seriously impedes the natural declamation of the voice part. Theile does write repeated string semiquavers, quasi-tremolando, to depict the earthquake, but this effort of imagination seems to have drained his harmonic resources, for the whole passage employs only a single chord. The omission of obbligato instruments from the music for the lesser characters, however, gives the *dramatis personae* a distinctiveness which is lacking in the otherwise more imaginatively scored work of Sebastiani.

In the matter of recitative, with Selle alone do we hear genuine echoes of the old Passion tones. Theile avoids monotony in a wide variation of reciting notes for the Evangelist, and he gives to Jesus a more shapely melodic line than to the other characters. Ex. 339 shows his recitative at its best:

Ex. 339

auf, lasst uns ge - hen;   sie - he,   der ist da, der mich ver-rät

(Ah! Sleep on now and take your rest. Behold, the hour is at hand, and the Son of Man is betrayed into the hands of sinners. Rise, let us be going; behold, he is at hand that doth betray me.)

Throughout, he evinces imagination in treating important words and phrases, though he is almost the only composer of Passions to set the cock crowing without a melisma. Sebastiani's writing is more lyrical than Theile's, but he manages to emphasize key words such as 'flohen' ('fled') and 'schüttelten' ('trembled') just as effectively. Funcke, though probably writing later than either Theile or Sebastiani, bases his recitatives on the outlines of the Passion tones, with modifications, but the most significant feature here, because the most modern and secular, is the fact that the part of Jesus is written in rhyming verse: the emergence of Passion oratorio followed inevitably within about twenty years.

In the choral writing we again find most imagination in Selle's setting. In the *turba* choruses he is simple and concise, limiting himself to homophony; but the harmony is never sterile. In the eight-bar 'Weg, weg mit dem, kreuzige ihn' modulating harmonic sequences are dramatically used:

Ex. 340

(Away with him, crucify him.)

and even in the short 'Jesum von Nazareth' chorus a telling effect is produced simply by three statements of key words at different pitches, with different cadences and an increase in volume through setting them first for solo voices, then for chorus, and thirdly for all voices together. Sebastiani, too, makes his effects through simplicity and brevity; we find no word repetition in, for example, the choruses 'Er ist des Todes schuldig' ('He is guilty of death') and 'Weissage uns' ('Prophesy to us').

Theile's choruses are slightly longer than either Sebastiani's or Selle's. They usually begin with fugato writing—striking exceptions include 'Barrabam' and 'Lass ihn kreuzigen' ('Let him be crucified')—and conclude with forceful homophony, but the opening themes are declamatory enough for no loss of dramatic impact to be felt; in fact Theile's *turba* choruses are more effective than those of the other three. Except possibly in 'Herr, bin ich's?' ('Lord, is it I?'), Funcke's harmony and textures are as simple as those of the earlier composers of dramatic Passions; he makes no attempt at all to produce histrionic effects, apart from the somewhat absurd reiterations of the dominant and tonic chords *subito* and *presto* at 'So steig herab vom Kreuz' ('Come down from the cross'). The role of the instruments and the rhythmic impetus in his choruses would make many of them come to life were it not for the distressing poverty of the melodic and harmonic invention. In all four of these settings the non-biblical opening and closing choruses show the greatest imagination, and in the case of Selle this can also emphatically be said of the interpolated Venetian-style *intermedia*, settings of Old Testament and chorale texts from one of which Ex. 341 is taken.

The interpolations in Sebastiani, Theile, and Funcke were no doubt prompted by Selle's revolutionary example and are as follows. In Sebastiani there are twenty-six chorale stanzas, half of them in two hymns of eight and five verses respectively, which are sung straight through; the chorales are set to their original melodies, mainly as solos, and inserted at well-chosen places. Theile interpolates, not chorales, but four solo arias, and he concludes with a fifth interpolation, set for five-part chorus and orchestra; the position of the solo arias focuses the attention on such important moments as the Institution of the Eucharist and Peter's denial. (One may here mention the custom going back to the sixteenth century of singing Jacob Handl's setting of 'Ecce quomodo' after the death of Christ; the seventeenth saw a gradual break with this tradition.) Funcke's interpolations are extremely numerous and varied, and they contain his most interesting music.

Ex. 341

(My God, I cry in the daytime, but thou hearest not; and in the night season, I am not silent. But thou art holy, O thou that inhabitest the praises of Israel.)

Many of them are short symphonies, others are for a solo voice with instrumental accompaniment; they make only occasional use of chorale material.

Other works of the same period show how far Passions had developed through interpolations and orchestral accompaniment in the direction of oratorios. The text of a lost St. Matthew Passion of 1664 by Thomas Strutius, of Danzig, shows that it was divided into 'acts' and included eight chorales, four of which were apparently set as solos; and his four-part string ensemble is said to have anticipated Theile's repeated semiquavers at the death of Jesus (see *supra*) by writing a similar effect at the death of Judas.[1] Another St. Matthew Passion, written three years later at Lüneburg by Christian Flor (1626–97),[2] shows how chorales were set as solo arias; Flor interpolated several other arias too, as well as instrumental pieces. There are also several vivid *turbae*, such as the one beginning:

Ex. 342

(Not upon the Feast, lest there be an uproar.)

---

[1] See Abraham in *Monthly Musical Record*, lxxxiv, pp. 153–4.

[2] See Epstein, 'Ein unbekanntes Passions-Oratorium von Christian Flor (1667)', *Bach-Jahrbuch*, xxvii (1930), p. 56, including numerous musical examples, from one of which Ex. 342 is taken.

The set pieces are clearly what interested Flor most, for he did not even bother to compose the narratives at all; he simply took them all over from Vulpius's St. Matthew Passion of 1613 and in doing so took the unique step of transposing the Passion tone (down a third).

Two hybrid works remain to be discussed before we move on to eighteenth-century Passions: *Die sieben Worte Jesu Christi am Kreuz*, set by Schütz[1] in 1645 and by Augustin Pfleger,[2] at Gottorf, in 1670. Schütz's text is entirely from the gospels (making use of all four), apart from the traditional opening and closing choruses, which are separated from the main action by identical instrumental symphonies; but though there are no interpolations the work is certainly not liturgical and is in reality more oratorio than Passion. The words of the Evangelist are allotted to differing solo voices, and another exceptional feature is that Jesus is a tenor instead of the usual bass. The narrative is set in the new dramatic recitative, whose strength and simplicity do much to make the work so extraordinarily moving. Jesus is accompanied by two unnamed melody instruments (probably viols) as well as by continuo, and there is imitation between them and the vocal line. Chromaticism is reserved for emotional moments such as the following:

Ex. 343

(I thirst.)

Pfleger's work shows the dignifying influence of Schütz, especially in the declamation of an introductory dialogue between Christ and the Daughter of Zion (see Ex. 344).

Not only does he add this dialogue to the original text but also seven other lyrical interpolations, where the almost total reliance on chains of Italianate thirds for soprano and alto, with continuo, becomes wearisome; the original text is shortened to accommodate this plentiful

---

[1] Ed. Grusnick, *Neue Ausgabe*, ii, p. 1; there is a miniature score ed. Stein (Leipzig, 1934). An extract is recorded in *The History of Music in Sound*, v. See Moser, op. cit., pp. 424 ff.; Eng. ed., pp. 492 ff.

[2] Ed. Stein, *Das Chorwerk*, lii (Wolfenbüttel, 1938). On Pfleger see Annemarie Nausch, *Augustin Pfleger: Leben und Werke* (Kassel, 1955).

Ex. 344

(Oh! [that] my eyes were springs of tears, that I might weep day and night for Jesus the crucified.)

added material. The use of obbligato instruments (violas) to accompany Jesus is another feature possibly deriving from Schütz's setting, though a tradition was gradually establishing itself whereby his words were heightened by as it were a halo of instrumental sound. There is very little choral writing in Pfleger's Passion.

Two more oratorio Passions date from the period before Passion oratorios first appeared. Both are based on Matthew's Gospel, and both date from 1700; one is by Johann Valentin Meder (1649–1719), who worked at Danzig and Königsberg, among other places, the other is by Johann Kühnhausen (d. 1714),[1] of Celle. Meder's is the more interesting.[2] In it we again find numerous interpolated chorales, treated as arias, duets, and choruses, and both obbligato and continuo instruments. The recitatives of Jesus are, like Bach's, set in quasi-arioso style, but the dictates of metrical rhythm now take precedence over natural

Ex. 345

(The blood of Jesus Christ, the Son of God.)

[1] Ed. Adrio, *Das Chorwerk*, 1 (Wolfenbüttel, 1938). See idem, 'Die Matthäus-Passion von J. G. Kühnhausen', *Festschrift Arnold Schering zum sechzigsten Geburtstag*, ed. Helmuth Osthoff, Walter Serauky, and Adrio (Berlin, 1937), p. 24.

[2] Material on Meder supplied by Basil Smallman from a copy in the possession of Patience Robertson.

declamation; there are a few effective pictorial passages.[1] The expressiveness that Meder on occasion attains can be seen in the extract from one of the interpolated pieces (see Ex. 345).

And the following excerpt is notable for the power generated by a fusion of florid writing and harmonic sequences:[2]

(He is guilty of death.)

Kühnhausen has ten chorale verses interpolated into his gospel narrative, and he sets five as congregational chorales and five as soprano arias; but the only instruments are continuo ones. The four-part chorales and the contrapuntal choruses contain the best music in this rather limited work.

PASSION ORATORIOS: THE LIBRETTOS

It was at this point in the history of Passion music that the Passion oratorio emerged. It did so in Hamburg and was an extension of sacred opera, which was popular there.[3] It is a musico-dramatic form taking

---

[1] One is quoted in Smallman, op. cit., p. 114.

[2] The alto part between the asterisks is a tone lower in the original, which is obviously wrong. The suggested reading produces consecutive fifths at one point between alto and tenor, but there are several other instances of these elsewhere in the same work.

[3] Cf. *supra*, pp. 304–5.

the Passion story as its subject: it has *dramatis personae*, who include symbolical characters, among whom the Believing Soul and the Daughter of Zion are found especially frequently. The entire gospel narrative was paraphrased, versified and rhymed by poets whose taste was poor and who had little genuine sympathy with the subject. The emergence of Passion oratorios coincided with—indeed might be seen as a product of—the increasing emphasis then being placed on the delineation of emotions in music, a development that also prompted the cantata texts of Neumeister and his imitators.[1] The librettists of these oratorios certainly exploited through colourful imagery the more gruesome aspects of the Passion story and in so doing fired the imagination of composers. At first the texts presented the story complete, but by the middle of the century interpolated arias and ariosos that were of a reflective nature and did not further the story had become so long, numerous, and popular that the narrative had to be shortened (as we have already seen happen with Pfleger); for instance, Johann Ernst Eberlin's *Der blutschwitzende Jesus*, composed in 1750, treats only the Institution of the Eucharist and part of the scene in the garden but includes several very long *da capo* arias.[2] The most famous and popular libretto of Passion oratorios was *Der für die Sünde der Welt gemarterte und sterbende Jesus* by Barthold Heinrich Brockes (1680–1747), of Hamburg, who apparently enjoyed a somewhat exaggerated reputation, since in fact he frequently made use of other poets' material.

Side-by-side with the Passion oratorio the now firmly established oratorio Passion continued to develop and culminated in J. S. Bach's masterpieces. These later Passions were certainly influenced by the new oratorios; indeed several composers, such as Keiser and Telemann, composed both kinds, but since these are essentially different it seems best to consider them separately, taking the oratorio Passion first.

ORATORIO PASSIONS IN THE EIGHTEENTH CENTURY

In 1704 a St. John Passion appeared at the same time as the first Passion oratorio, Keiser's *Der blutige und sterbende Jesus*. This St. John Passion was formerly attributed to Handel but is now considered not to be by him.[3] The narrative part is faithful to St. John's gospel; the interpolated verses include no chorales and are all by the opera librettist Christian Postel. These verses are all set as arias or duets—there are

---

[1] Cf. *infra*, p. 738.

[2] Cf. *infra*, pp. 663–4.

[3] As such it was published in the complete edition of Handel's works, ed. Chrysander, ix, where it is misleadingly styled a Passion oratorio; vocal score ed. Harald Heilmann (Berlin, 1957). Recent research suggests that it is by Böhm: information contributed by Harald Kümmerling.

thirteen of them—and in them we find the early appearance of ideas that were to become firmly established in Passion oratorios as well as in oratorio Passions. One of these, the appeal to the elements to intervene at the moment of Jesus's arrest:

*The consecutive fifths are the composer's

(Quake now, with crashing [and roaring].)

was further developed by Brockes and reached a magnificent climax in the second half of no. 33 in Bach's St. Matthew Passion. The librettist and composer seem to have been fond of this type of aria and inserted another, even stronger one—'Bebet, ihr Berge' ('Crack now, ye mountains')—after the words 'Und neiget das Haupt und verschied' ('And he bowed his head and gave up the ghost'). Of the arias and duets, two are full-scale *da capo* arias, and a few others are in ABA form, but most are through-composed and short. They are uneven in quality, but the placing of the earlier ones shows a feeling for dramatic effect.

Dramatic sense is also evident in the distinction drawn between the activity of the longer Part I and the more reflective Part II through the length and construction of the scenes and the fact that all accompanied recitatives in Part II are reserved for Jesus. The other recitatives are surprisingly unconventional (though the cadences are the standard ones): there is rather an extravagant effort to be expressive in setting certain passages, such as 'Es ist vollbracht' ('It is fulfilled'):

Ex. 348

*The consecutive fifths are the composer's.

(It is fulfilled!)

The composer then develops this idea in the last half of the following fine bass aria, 'O grosses werk' ('O work sublime'), rather as Bach was to do at the very outset of *his* ensuing number, no. 58, in the St. John Passion. Of the characters only Pilate (alto) has much individuality;

this is achieved through consistent use of solemn phrases containing many repeated notes, which gives the music a certain appropriate pomposity. The choruses are effectively concise, except for 'Lasset uns den nicht verteilen' ('Let us not divide it'), which is in the *stile antico*, starting with fugato writing and becoming more homophonic. 'Kreuzige' ('Crucify') is set very impressively, adagio, with few repetitions, and the traditional final chorus addressed to the Saviour resting in the grave is also imaginative and worthy of comparison with Bach's two great examples, for which it was perhaps a model.[1] Midway between the style of this work and that of the mature Passions of Telemann discussed below is the *Passio Jesu Christi* (1723) of Johann Friedrich Fasch (1688–1758),[2] who worked in various towns in Germany and Bohemia. He took part of his text from Brockes, though the work is more oratorio Passion than Passion oratorio. There is a short *da capo* introductory chorus, after which the narration begins with the Institution of the Eucharist. There are few solo interpolations, but several harmonized chorales.

The next work demanding discussion is the St. Mark Passion (1717 at the latest) by Reinhard Keiser (1674–1739),[3] director of the opera at

Ex. 349

(for which, though poor and weak, we give thanks.)

[1] See *infra*, pp. 655 and 658.
[2] MS. in Leipzig, Musikbibliothek.
[3] Ed. Hans Grischkat (Stuttgart, n.d.). See Rudolf Petzold, *Die Kirchenkompositionen und weltlichen Kantaten Reinhard Keisers* (Düsseldorf, 1935).

Hamburg. It is somewhat inferior to his Passion oratorios and to many of his cantatas and operas, but Bach performed it and copied some of the parts and seems to have been influenced by it in his St. Matthew Passion: compare, for example, in Bach, the last five bars of no. 24, seven bars from the end of no. 34, and the chorus of no. 67 with the corresponding passages in Keiser's nos. 4 (see Ex. 351), 9, and 34. respectively. The freshest music occurs in the interpolated numbers, which consist of chorales and ten short Italianate arias, all except one of which are in *da capo* form. The chorales are traditional in choice and placing. 'O hilf, Christe' ('Help us, O Christ') has expressive harmonies (with which those in no. 65 in Bach's St. John Passion may be compared) (see Ex. 349).

And 'Was mein Gott will' ('What God ordains') has independent orchestral figuration, which strikingly includes *moto perpetuo* semiquavers in the first violins. One surprising feature, compared with

Ex. 350

(Crucify him!)

Bach's setting in the St. Matthew Passion, is the elaborate continuo part to 'Wann ich einmal soll scheiden' ('When I come to die'); it is a beautiful conception, and the fact that the chorale melody is given to a solo voice gives it a personal character. The texts of the arias are restrained, their music shapely and expressive, if sometimes rather tame and lacking in the tension to be derived from dissonance. In the settings of gospel words, the splendid *turbae* stand out (see Ex. 350).

Their declamation is admirable, and all are concise, except for 'Gegrüsset seist du' ('We greet thee'), an *alla breve* fugue of thirty-six bars whose mock-solemnity creates a subtle effect. The opening chorus, however, is disappointing and so, on the whole, is the recitative, which veers between conventional formulas and some rather more imaginative moments, such as Jesus's 'Meine Seele ist betrübt':

Ex. 351

(My soul is troubled, even unto death.)

Georg Philipp Telemann (1681–1767), who worked in Hamburg from 1721, was, after Bach, probably the finest eighteenth-century composer of Passion music. Certainly he was prolific in this as in other fields: he composed forty-four settings, both oratorio Passions and Passion oratorios, and twenty-three survive.[1] For the interpolations in

Ex. 352 (i)

(He stirreth up the people teaching [throughout all Jewry].)

[1] See Hans Hörner, *G. Ph. Telemanns Passionsmusiken* (Leipzig, 1933), for a detailed study and thematic catalogue.

Ex. 352 (ii)

(Away with this man.)

his oratorio Passions he used texts by Postel and other poets and also
adapted Brockes. Telemann maintains a remarkably high standard
throughout these works, which are characterized by shapely melodies,
including many expressive, even exaggerated, figures, compelling decla‐
mation and vigorous rhythms; on the whole the most inspired music
occurs in the arias, which increase in number in the later Passions as the
number of characters to whom they are assigned also increases.

The first of three oratorio Passions by Telemann to be considered
here is the St. Luke Passion of 1728.[1] It is on a different plan from most
of the others: in five sections, each of which is introduced by an inter‐
polated episode based on some relevant incident in the Old Testament
from which a moral can be drawn. Thus the first part, which begins with
Judas's conspiracy to sell Jesus to the Jews, is introduced by recitatives
and arias referring to the selling of Joseph by his brethren to the
Ishmaelites for twenty pieces of silver. Except for chorales the five
introductions account for all the extra-scriptural numbers. Of the solo
writing, that for Christ is especially dignified and is, incidentally, not

[1] Ed. Hörner and Martin Ruhnke, *Georg Philipp Telemanns Musikalische Werke*, xv
(Kassel, 1964).

consistently accompanied by the texture for full strings that had by now become traditional. But finer than the solo music are the choruses, which are among the most distinguished in Telemann's Passion music. The dramatic excitement that he is capable of generating in them is illustrated in Ex. 352 (i) and (ii).

Telemann's St. Matthew Passion of 1730[1] is on a very large scale. The choral writing is mainly in two parts, with paired voices—sopranos with tenors, altos with basses—singing in octaves, but many of them, such as the one illustrated here, are dramatically effective:

Ex. 353

(He is guilty of death.)

The solo writing reveals the best and the worst of Telemann; Ex. 354 shows one of the most imaginative passages, where the interlocking chromatic lines, contrasted in note-values and articulation, admirably enhance Jesus's final words:

Ex. 354

By 1759, when Telemann composed his St. Mark Passion,[1] the number of insertions had greatly increased: there are sixteen arias, two non-biblical recitatives, and many chorales, out of a total of sixty-one numbers. The characters include allegorical figures such as Religion, Courage, Reason, Zeal, and Devotion. The finest arias are 'Verräterische Frage' ('Treacherous question') for tenor, very personal and dramatic with its rapid string staccato scales and its furious 'fleuch, Kaiphas, fleuch' ('Fly, Caiaphas, fly'), and 'Dich Kuss, der Freundschaft sich'res Zeichen' ('Kiss, the sure sign of friendship'), the climax of which is shown in Ex. 355 (i):

Ex. 355 (i)

[Allegro]

ein Bö - se - wicht, ein Bö - se - wicht, ein Bö - se - wicht,

(A scoundrel)

(ii)

Strings

JESUS

E — — — li,   E — — · li,   la - ma

B.C.

[1] Ed. idem (Liechtenstein, 1963).

a – sab-tha – ni,   la – – – ma_____   a – sab – tha – ni?

The recitative and ariosos (cf. Ex. 355 (ii)) are typical of Telemann's Passions in being the most conventional music in the work. His chorale harmonizations are also typical of him in being plain and diatonic. Of the other choruses the most effective are the short dramatic ones, which are in the majority: 'Weissage uns' ('Now tell us') and 'Pfui dich, wie fein zerbrichst du den Tempel' ('Shame upon thee, thou that destroyest the temple') deserve special mention.

Taste in Leipzig was much more conservative than in Hamburg. Before we turn to Bach's Passions it is worth mentioning a slightly earlier Leipzig setting, the St. Mark Passion (1721) of Johann Kuhnau (1660–1722).[1] The old dramatic Passions were still preferred at this date even to the innovations of Selle and Sebastiani, but taste was slowly changing, and Kuhnau's setting includes twenty chorales as well as eighteen arias, which, however, are simple and hymn-like, with none of the operatic overtones of Hamburg Passions.

THE PASSIONS OF J. S. BACH

Bach's St. John Passion, first performed in 1724, and the St. Matthew Passion, dating from 1729 (but begun seven years earlier), are still oratorio Passions, and they are the last except for a few settings by Telemann (such as the last two works of his discussed in the previous section) and also his own St. Mark Passion, of 1731, the music of which is lost, except for seven numbers found in other works, principally in Cantata 198.[2] Many features of both of the extant Passions were hallowed by tradition: for example, the allotting of the Evangelist to a tenor and Jesus to a bass; the halo of string sound accompanying Jesus'

---

[1] MS. formerly at Königsberg, Universitätsbibliothek.

[2] The Bach Passions appear in the *Werke*, St. John, xii, 1, St. Matthew, iv; and there are miniature scores, St. John, ed. Schering (Leipzig, 1925), and St. Matthew, ed. Georg Schumann (Leipzig, 1929). For bibliographies see Schmieder, op. cit., pp. 353–4 (John) and 342–4 (Matthew), and *Bach-Jahrbuch*, xl (1953), p. 137, xlv (1958), p. 135, and liii (1967), p. 138. On the lost St. Mark Passion of 1731, see Schering, 'Zur Markus-Passion und zur "vierten" Passion', *Bach-Jahrbuch*, xxxvi (1939), p. 1, and Smend, 'Bachs Markus-Passion', ibid., xxxvii (1940–8), p. 1. On Cantata 198 see *infra*, p. 762.

words in the St. Matthew Passion; the quasi-operatic recitative; the interpolations—congregational chorales, choruses other than the *turbae*, contemplative arias for symbolic figures such as the Daughter of Zion; the terseness of the *turbae*; the use of instruments throughout. We have already encountered these features in earlier works, though hardly at all in Leipzig, and they must have seemed quite new, even startling, in that conservative city. But Bach goes further still. He was aware, too, of Hamburg oratorio Passions and Passion oratorios; he almost certainly knew that anonymous St. John Passion of 1704 once thought to be Handel's, and he copied Handel's Brockes Passion (discussed in the next section). In his St. John Passion we find that of the twelve lyrical interpolations Bach adapted the texts of eight from Brockes, and two are from Postel. The entire text of the St. Matthew Passion outside the gospel narration and the chorales is by 'Picander', the pseudonym of Christian Friedrich Henrici (1700–64). It is thus a more unified piece of work than the text of the St. John Passion and is virtually tantamount to a libretto; it is also of high quality. Bach's music almost throughout both works is of such overwhelming beauty and power that we can readily apprehend the synthesis of liturgy and oratorio or even opera that he achieved in them so infinitely more compellingly than did his contemporaries.

Nevertheless, the St. John Passion[1] is not an unflawed masterpiece, as we shall now see in a more detailed study of it. It has already been pointed out that the narrative in St. John's gospel does not divide easily. Bach offsets this to some extent by introducing two scenes from St. Matthew, but on the other hand he makes the first part more static and diminishes what tension there is by interpolating two arias—nos. 11 and 13—during the most dramatic scene, that of the arrest; and only three bars of recitative separate the two arias. In the second half the extremely long tenor aria no 32 immediately follows an interpolated arioso, and as a result the tension sags here too; moreover, the text is one of Brockes's most gruesome conceits. The use of identical music for nos. 34 and 50 can perhaps be defended, but the re-use of no. 38 in no. 42 is more questionable on emotional grounds and also because it leads to unhappy word-setting (e.g. at bar 20, alto, or the final bar, tenor).

The texts of the interpolated arias and ariosos are, except for no. 32, comparatively restrained. Among them we find some of the greatest music in the work. Nos. 11, 31,[2] 58, 60, and 63 stand with the finest

---

[1] Cf. *supra*, p. 653, n. 2.
[2] Recorded in *The History of Music and Sound*, v, together with everything preceding it from bar 5 of the recitative forming no. 26. Bach wrote no. 31 for the second performance, in 1727, when it replaced a tenor aria, 'Ach, windet euch nicht so, geplagte Seelen'.

PLATE VI

THE OPENING OF THE SECOND PART OF BACH'S *ST. MATTHEW PASSION* IN THE ALTNICKOL COPY OF *c.* 1741.

The earliest surviving source for the original version of the Passion is this copy by Bach's pupil Johann Christoph Altnickol. (Cf. Plate VII.)

things in Bach. No. 19, a violently jagged piece, expresses Peter's remorse most movingly, yet the deeper insight that Bach gained during the next five years in setting such poignant texts can immediately be seen if one compares this aria with the sublime no. 47 in the St. Matthew Passion. For all its excessive length there is some notable music too in no. 32, but no. 62 is perhaps diminished by word-painting of a rather naïve order.

The recitatives are for the most part highly expressive, none more so than no. 49, the crucifixion scene, with its marvellously heightened setting of the superscription on the cross. Bach breaks with tradition in not using strings to accompany Jesus's words, but he abides by it in writing vivid roulades to emphasize the words 'weinete' ('wept') in no. 18 and 'geisselte' ('scourged') in no. 30. These are indeed the most prominent instances of word-painting in the score. They are thoroughly operatic in inspiration and must owe something to the example of the Hamburg oratorios; and it is arguable that in their contexts they are too disruptive and self-conscious.

Bach makes the most of the cruelty of his *turba* choruses, but the effect of the rapid interchanges with Pilate is reduced by their excessive length—only nos. 29 and 46 are concise. Several of these choruses are rough, with rather forced chromatic harmonies: such are nos. 23, 25, and 36. Though no. 54 is musically one of the most fascinating numbers, the development of the basic material as a fugato for fifty-five bars with invertible counterpoint and a *moto perpetuo* obbligato lessens the dramatic impact of the movement. The opening chorus and the final one before the closing chorale are both in *da capo* form: the first is texturally complex, with almost continuous two or three-part swaying semiquavers on the strings, partially prompting the mainly independent vocal parts, and with beautiful wailing woodwind parts; the last is a high peak in the series of final Passion choruses dwelling on the idea of the Saviour resting peacefully in the grave.

Into this fabric of recitative and set numbers, solo and choral, the chorales (several of which are heard twice) are placed with superb skill, just as they are chosen with unerring rightness. Moreover, they are harmonized with consummate artistry.[1] Word-painting produces unusual but restrained harmonic colouring in nos. 20, 40, 52, and 56; and the harmonization of the closing chorale, 'Ach, Herr, lass dein' lieb' Engelein' ('Ah, Lord, let thy beloved angel'), provides perhaps the

[1] See Charles Sanford Terry, *Bach's Chorals*, i (Cambridge, 1915), Johannes Zahn, *Die Melodien der deutschen evangelischen Kirchenlieder* (Gütersloh, 1888–93), and Walter E. Buszin, 'The chorale in the baroque era and J. S. Bach's contribution to it', *Studies in Eighteenth-century Music: a tribute to Karl Geiringer on his seventieth birthday*, ed. H. C. Robbins Landon in collaboration with Roger E. Chapman (London, 1970), p. 108.

greatest moment in the whole work: Bach's treatment of this chorale makes the most of the contrast inherent in the twofold idea of resting in the grave and the triumph of the resurrection, and, while to introduce the latter into Passion music for Good Friday may be theologically erroneous, this piece certainly creates an overwhelming climax. There are sections of the work, in particular the trial scene, in which Bach builds up larger forms of rondo-like structure: the use of tonality, the repetition of certain music and the placing of different types of movement all play a part in these 'internal' forms.

The instrumentation of the St. John Passion is somewhat lacking in variety. All the choruses except for no. 5 are scored for the full orchestra of strings, two flutes, two oboes, and continuo, but the woodwind seldom achieve independence. The scoring of the arias is more individual, and nos. 11, 13, 31, 32, 58, 62, and 63 all have their own characteristic colours, which include viole d'amore, viola da gamba, and lute.

Hardly any of the miscalculations of the St. John Passion are to be found in the St. Matthew Passion.[1] The fact that the narrative begins much earlier and includes accounts of Judas's plot and the Institution of the Eucharist creates a satisfactory balance between the two parts and makes the first half more dramatic than that of the St. John Passion. In fact, the accumulation of dramatic and emotional tension in Part I never flags. This is because the nature, length, and placing of the interpolated numbers ensure that they either provide the occasional momentary relaxation that is needed, as in the accompanied recitatives and arias for alto, soprano, and bass (nos. 9, 10, 18, 19, 28, and 29), or else they intensify the drama, as in the accompanied tenor recitative no. 25 and the duet with chorus no. 33. Part I finishes, not with the end of chapter 26 of St. Matthew's gospel, but with the tense moment of the arrest of Jesus and the disciples' flight.

The longer Part II starts slowly with the Daughter of Zion's aria with chorus, 'Ach, nun ist mein Jesus hin' ('Ah, now is my Jesus gone'), and leads through the scene of the false witnesses (who sing, following tradition, in canon) to the first of the *turba* demands for Jesus's death, at 'Er ist des Todes schuldig' ('He is guilty of death') at the end of no. 42. From this point, tragic events follow in quick succession: the physical assaults, Peter's denial and remorse, Judas's repentance and suicide, and the scourging (the last only mentioned in passing by the Evangelist, but described in the accompanied alto recitative no. 60, 'Erbarm' es Gott' ('God, have mercy')). After this there is a lull of considerable length in the unfolding of the story, allowing for the insertion of some long arias

[1] Cf. *supra*, p. 653, n. 2.

PLATE VII

THE OPENING OF THE SECOND PART OF BACH'S
ST. MATTHEW PASSION IN THE AUTOGRAPH SCORE
OF *c.* 1747–8.

The autograph score of the final version shows a number of alterations: e.g.
vn. I, bars 6, 8, 16, 22, 24; vn. II, bars 5, 7, 21, 23, 26, 28; viola, bars 6, 8;
bass, bar 20, etc. (Cf. Plate VI.)

which must be performed with the utmost conviction if the work is not to sag unduly at this point. The scene of the crucifixion (starting with no. 67) is shorter, but more violent, than in the earlier setting. It is interrupted by two numbers for alto, no. 69, 'Ach, Golgotha', and no. 70, 'Sehet, Jesus hat die Hand' ('Behold, Jesus has his hand . . .'). This last movement, incidentally, has choral interjections of 'Wohin?' ('Whither?') which were almost certainly suggested by those in a soprano aria in Handel's Brockes Passion.[1]

At this point, although the drama must continue to unfold, the tempo has become slower; this fact, together with the high emotional content of these last two interpolations, means that no real break in the continuity is felt during this scene. With no. 71, 'Und von der sechsten Stunde' ('And from the sixth hour'), the work moves very rapidly to its climax. The cry of 'Eli' (whereat the upper strings, which have hitherto accompanied Jesus, are silent); the comments of the bystanders; the death, followed by an intensely chromatic setting of the traditional chorale; the rending of the veil; the earthquake and opening of the graves: all these episodes lead swiftly to the words of the centurion and 'them that were with him': 'Wahrlich, dieser ist Gottes Sohn gewesen' ('Truly this was the Son of God'). Here, in no. 73, Bach employs a double choir of voices and instruments, mainly in their highest range, and adds a discord in the continuo part; the preceding bar contains a violent switch from G minor to A flat major harmony on the Evangelist's 'erschraken sie sehr' ('they feared greatly'), and an ominously long note in the continuo. All these contribute something to the creation of perhaps the two most impressive bars of music to be found in all Bach's works; it is surely evident that he intended them to be the climax of this Passion setting, as he deliberately inflated words spoken by a few people into such a tremendous affirmation of faith. After this the tranquil accompanied recitative no. 74 comes as a perfectly timed moment of relief. Although the chorus of priests and Pharisees (no. 76) is, from a dramatic viewpoint, on the long side—indeed none of the closing numbers is short—this section is so well conceived that no question of an anticlimax arises.

Bach employs unusually large forces in this work: a double choir, and double orchestra of four woodwind instruments (including three varieties of oboe), strings, and organ; to these are added a viola da gamba and four solo voices, in addition, of course, to Evangelist and Christus and numerous lesser characters. These forces are used with the utmost skill

---

[1] Cf. Handel, *Works*, ed. Chrysander, xv, p. 115, and *Hallische Händel-Ausgabe*, ser. i.7, ed. Felix Schroeder (Kassel, etc., 1965), p. 119. Also see a comparable example in no. 48 in Bach's St. John Passion.

and economy to produce the greatest possible variety of texture, colour, and dynamic. Each chorus has its own function when deployed separately: the first represents the twelve disciples, the second the wider and more general circle of followers. Together they form the vast congregation of Christians in the chorales and the *turba* in the narrative. They also combine in the great ritornello chorus opening Part I (where an additional part is added in the form of *ripieno* sopranos singing 'O Lamm Gottes unschuldig' ('O guiltless Lamb of God')), in the long chorale fantasia 'O Mensch bewein' that closes Part I, and in the sublime final *da capo* chorus.

A noteworthy feature is the greater conciseness of all the *turba* choruses compared with those in the St. John Passion. Even those employing fugato writing create a dramatic impact through their brevity and by such devices as, for example, the angular chromaticism in 'Lass ihn kreuzigen' ('Let him be crucified'). Antiphonal effects are used in nos. 5, 43, 49, and 67; otherwise these effects are reserved for the opening and closing choruses and for the dramatic 'Sind Blitze und Donner' ('Have lightnings and thunders') in no. 33. The recitatives show Bach deeply sensitive yet disciplined in his reaction to the words describing the poignant events; there are none of the extravagances that appear in the St. John Passion (e.g. in nos. 18 and 30) and in certain cantatas. The texts of the interpolations are not only restrained, they often embody beautiful ideas. The treatment of the chorales is, if anything, even finer than that found in the earlier Passion; one, the memorable 'O Haupt voll Blut und Wunden', is heard five times—another unifying feature of the work. Finally, for all its dramatic moments, the work is more meditative than the earlier Passion, and it is the noblest of all settings of the Passion story.

PASSION ORATORIOS[1]

As has been pointed out, the first Passion oratorio, Keiser's *Der blutige und sterbende Jesus*, appeared in Hamburg in 1704. Here for the first time in the history of Passion music is a work whose text is wholly the work of a poet—in this case Christian Friedrich Hunold (1681–1721), known as 'Menantes'—and thus dispenses with gospel narrative. Menantes's imagery in this text is lurid, his emotions sentimental, and with it he fell foul of even the liberal Hamburg clergy. There is finer music—indeed some of the finest Passion music of the age—in two later oratorios by Keiser, his setting (1712) of Brockes's celebrated text, *Der für die Sünde der Welt gemarterte und sterbende Jesus*, and his *Der zum Tode verurtheilte und gecreutzigte Jesus* (1715), with words by

[1] Cf. *supra*, pp. 621–2.

Postel.[1] Brockes's text (based on all four Evangelists) may be doggerel, his imagery and emotional expression may, in their exaggeration, be akin to Menantes', but this one libretto was particularly successful in catching the imagination of composers and audiences alike: it was the most popular of all Passion oratorio texts and is the most representative. Keiser was the first composer to set it, and we can readily admire here and in the 1715 oratorio the affecting, essentially vocal melodies, strongly influenced by Italian opera, that he found for the vivid words. As can be seen in the typical examples quoted here from his Brockes Passion, he was also a master of arioso and recitative, at his best not unworthy to be placed with Bach:

Ex. 356

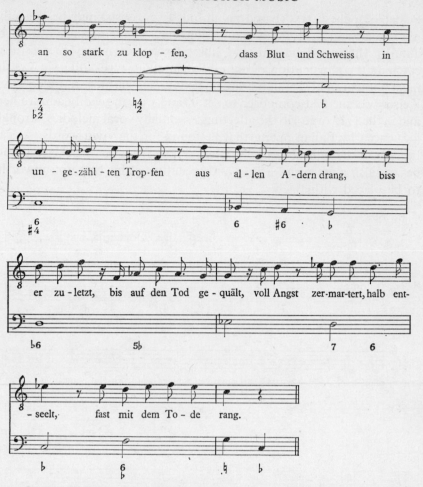

(The agony increased with cruel tremors, so that he could hardly gasp for pain. One saw the weak limbs tremble, his dry mouth could hardly breathe. The frightened heart began to throb so hard that blood and sweat poured from every vein in countless drops, until at last, tormented to the death, racked by anguish, half lifeless, he almost struggled with death.)

Some four years after Keiser, Handel rather surprisingly set Brockes's text;[1] it is not known why he composed a German Passion when he was firmly settled in London, but it was possibly in response to a commission from Hamburg. He does full justice to the more gory and lugubrious passages in the text, but he does tend to lapse into one or two rather routine types of motion—dotted rhythms and gentle triple time. Yet several of the very numerous arias and ariosos are very fine and are recognizably from the hand of the great opera composer that

[1] Editions as in n. 1, p. 657, *supra.*

Handel had become: witness—to mention two utterly contrasted pieces —the fine bravura aria for Peter, 'Gift und Glut' ('Poison and fire') (no. 14), and the exceptionally beautiful *siciliano* for the Daughter of Zion, 'Die Rosen krönen' ('Roses crown') (no. 35). There is also a notable sequence of movements surrounding Jesus's death, which includes a magnificent trio in F minor for three Believers:

Ex. 357

Tod und Höl - le scheu - en

Tod und Höl - le scheu - en

Tod und Höl - le scheu - en

(O awful word! O cry most fearful! Sound from which death and hell shrink)

Thus Handel the born dramatist reacts passionately to a strongly dramatic scene. The recitatives are lively and colourful and rarely fall to a purely conventional level. The choruses rely on sonorous homophony rather than on contrapuntal textures. As has already been mentioned, Bach was possibly influenced by this work: compare, for instance, no. 41, 'Eilt, ihr angefochten Seelen', and no. 53, 'Bei Jesus' Tod und Leiden', respectively with nos. 48 and 62 in Bach's St. John Passion. The year 1718 saw the composition of two more settings of Brockes's text, by Mattheson[1] and Telemann,[2] respectively. The former is rather a superficial work, but expressive recitative is a feature of Telemann's setting:

Ex. 358

Strings

PETER

Welch' un - ge - heu - rer Schmerz be - stür - met mein Ge -

B.C.

[1] Examples in Winterfeld, op. cit., iii, pp. 50–8.
[2] Ed. Helmut Winschermann and Friedrich Bruck (Hamburg, 1964).

- müth, ein kalt-er Schau-er schreckt die See-le

(What overwhelming pain assails my spirit, a cold shudder frightens the soul.)

Later Passion oratorios illustrate the increasing inroads of the *galant* style on this baroque form. The tendency is apparent in Carl Heinrich Graun's *Trostvolle Gedancken über das Leiden und Sterben unsers Herrn und Heilandes Jesu Christi* (1730)[1] and is even clearer in his *Der Tod Jesu* of 1755.[2] This was the most popular Passion music of the age, 'a sentimental tragedy of the Age of Enlightenment',[3] indistinguishable from oratorios on other, less hallowed subjects and completely removed from liturgical music in spirit as in form. It even omits the trial and death of Christ, has no characters and is really a cantata based loosely on sentiments engendered by the Passion story. It contains a good deal of imaginative music. Comparable qualities mark the later Passion music of Stölzel and other lesser composers. Melodies are generally sweet and simple, and harmonizations of chorales have shed all traces of the chromaticism of Bach's versions. The Salzburg composer Eberlin's *Der blutschwitzende Jesus* (1750),[4] referred to above, is typical of mid-eighteenth-century Passion oratorios. The very title and the nature of the text lie well within the Brockes-Menantes tradition; the text is entirely in verse and makes no pretence of telling the complete Passion story— it deals instead, in leisurely fashion, only with the Last Supper and the Agony in the Garden (with the foretelling of Peter's denial). Most of the arias are enormously long and are totally operatic in character, even to the nature of the broken-up roulades illustrating sighs in Christ's aria in the Garden, 'Ach sich, O Vater, meine Not'. There is one oddity in this work: for the Evangelist's narrative Eberlin reverts to a version of the old sixteenth-century Passion tone, but put into a metrical strait-jacket and accompanied by orchestra. The effect is quaintly anachronistic: it is almost as though Eberlin, a church musician writing a totally

[1] There is a copy in Brit. Mus. Add. MS. 31051.

[2] The full score was first published at Leipzig in 1760, a vocal score at Breslau in 1785, and several subsequent editions appeared; the chorus 'Christus hat uns' is in Schering, *Geschichte der Musik in Beispielen* (Leipzig, 1931; Eng. ed., New York, 1950), p. 464.

[3] Abraham in *Monthly Musical Record*, lxxxiv, p. 178.

[4] Ed. Robert Haas, *Denkmäler der Tonkunst in Österreich*, iv (Jg. xxviii (1)) (Vienna, 1921).

unliturgical work, yet wished, a little shamefacedly, to retain some connection, however maladroit, with the austere origins from which even Passion oratorios had distantly sprung.

(h) MOTETS

INTRODUCTION

In the later Renaissance the motet was, broadly speaking, a choral work written according to the principles of polyphonic composition, non-declamatory in style and without obligatory *basso continuo*. There were, however, many such works in which the continuo was indispensable, a feature that naturally became firmly established by the early seventeenth century; yet there were still a few exceptional works, such as Kindermann's *Tenebrae* of 1639 and Schütz's *Geistliche Chormusik* of 1648, in which the continuo was not needed. Instruments other than those playing continuo roles were also used increasingly from the end of the sixteenth century to double the vocal lines, and their introduction sowed the seeds of gradual disintegration in the older type of motet. Although at first voices and *colla parte* instruments might in performance be interchangeable as well as simultaneous, many motets in the seventeenth century include instrumental parts that are largely independent of the vocal parts—a natural development given the improving skill of players, the greater range and flexibility of their instruments, and their increasing role in musical performance. Large-scale motets continuing the Venetian tradition virtually became concertos, small-scale ones such as strophic arias frequently had short *sinfonie* and ritornellos added to them. At the same time there appeared genuinely concerto-type pieces—*geistliche Konzerte* ('sacred concertos') —stemming not from Renaissance counterpoint but from the new Italian continuo style of about 1600 onwards: in these pieces the vocal parts, which were declamatory, and the obbligato and continuo instrumental parts were all independent. For at least a century there prevailed considerable confusion as to nomenclature, involving words such as 'concerto' and 'motet': in north and central Germany many works with independent instrumental lines were still called motets. Even in the Catholic south, where instrumental and declamatory vocal writing, influenced by opera and other secular forms, took root earlier in the seventeenth century, the term 'motet' continued to be applied to non-liturgical music that, like the Masses discussed earlier in this chapter, inevitably belonged to the concertato style and in form and texture proclaimed an ancestry quite different from that of traditional motets.

In the following account the term 'motet' is reserved for works, whether in German or Latin, recognizably belonging to the older motet tradition, while more modern concerted music will be referred to by the appropriate terms.

With the growing participation of instruments and the indirect influence of other aspects of early Italian baroque music, polyphonic motets lost much of the rhythmic flexibility that in the Renaissance was one of their most glorious qualities; although counterpoint remained the driving-force, the themes themselves, as well as the timing of their entries, were influenced more and more by the demands of metrical stress, while the harmonic rhythm was increasingly affected by the metre of dance music. For a time the older style continued alongside the newer concerted music and was enriched by it. An important development in Germany, and not at all a surprising one, was the inclusion in motets of chorale melodies. But even with this transfusion the popularity of motets steadily waned, and by the middle of the century they were regarded as distinctly old fashioned: austere polyphony yielded before an increased desire for direct and realistic interpretation of the texts that found a much more suitable outlet in *geistliche Konzerte*, with their greater freedom in word-setting and their more colourful resources. Among the first generations covered by the present volume the leading composers of motets are Schütz, Hammerschmidt, Selle, Rosenmüller, Ahle, and Kindermann, each of whom displays certain individual characteristics; later on, several early members of the Bach dynasty added something to a dying tradition, which came to its final flowering in the 1720s with the motets of J. S. Bach. Several of the aforementioned composers wrote simpler chorale settings in motet style, and the name of Crüger must be added to them.

THE TRADITIONAL MOTET: SCHÜTZ

Mention must first of all be made of motets by Johannes Schultz (1582–1653) of Lüneburg; some of these significantly appeared in a mainly secular collection, his *Musicalischer Lüstgarte*,[1] in 1622, and they are among the most expressive motets of their time. The motets of Christoph Demantius (1567–1643)[2] combine mainly traditional writing with more forward-looking features such as the repetition of words to stress a dramatic text. The finest traditional motets in these early years of the century are the *Cantiones sacrae* (1625) of Schütz,

---

[1] Ed. Hermann Zenck, *Das Erbe deutscher Musik*, ser. 2, i (Wolfenbüttel, 1937). On the secular pieces see Vol. IV, pp. 118–19 and 597–8.
[2] See Demantius, *Vier deutsche Motetten*, ed. Anna Amalie Abert, *Das Chorwerk*, xxxix (Wolfenbüttel, 1936).

already discussed in the preceding volume.[1] His *Geistliche Chormusik*,[2] a collection of twenty-nine pieces for from five to seven voices, published as the Thirty Years' War ended in 1648 but written over the preceding years, similarly shows the motet at its best in the middle of the century; he dedicated this music to the choir of St. Thomas's, Leipzig, and the Council of that city, then, as in J. S. Bach's time, a relatively conservative musical centre.

The outstanding feature of Schütz's 1648 collection, apart from its demonstration of the virtues of counterpoint, are (1) his vivid interpretation of the words through declamatory writing within a polyphonic texture; (2) the combination of modal writing with more modern principles of structural balance based on cadential key contrasts, of which there is an extraordinary variety; and (3) the colourful contrasts deriving from the juxtaposition of few and many voices and of high and low. Concerning the first of these features, it should be remembered that Schütz's main aim as a composer was to illuminate the Word with music of the utmost expressiveness, and in doing so in these relatively conservative works he breathed new life into the *stile antico*, especially through his plastic rhythms: the fact that he was aware of the danger of monotony arising from the growing subjection of polyphony to regular accent no doubt helped to make him a greater composer of such music than a more complacent man like Hammerschmidt (accomplished though he is). As to the second point, Schütz stressed its importance in the long and important preface, where he states that music lacking both this quality and certain contrapuntal techniques that he specifies was worth no more than 'an empty nut'. It was no doubt his desire to bring the polyphonic style to a new pitch of excellence that led him not to print a continuo part in the purely vocal pieces: his other music shows that he wrote enthusiastically in the continuo style when it was appropriate, but here, where perfection of counterpoint was his aim, it would have been a hindrance. He does not, however, disdain to write independent instrumental parts in nos. 24, 26, 28, and 29, all but the second of which are probably early works. No. 27 is a transcription of Giovanni Gabrieli's 'Angelus ad pastores' (published in 1587);[3] and no. 20, 'Das ist je gewisslich wahr', which between bars 31 and 70 includes some outstandingly expressive harmonic colouring, was composed for the funeral of Johann Hermann Schein and can therefore be ascribed to 1630. Nos. 12, 'Also hat Gott die Welt geliebt', and 17, 'Das

---

[1] See Vol. IV, pp. 463–4.

[2] Schütz, *Neue Ausgabe*, v, ed. Kamlah (Kassel and Basle, 1955). See Moser, op. cit., p. 493, Eng. ed., p. 580.

[3] Giovanni Gabrieli, *Opera omnia*, ed. Denis Arnold, i (American Institute of Musicology, 1956), p. 34.

Wort ward fleisch', are just two pieces showing Schütz's command of plastic rhythm at its subtlest, and a distinctive feature of the seven-part no. 25, 'Ich weiss das mein Erlöser lebt', is the way the powerful ending sets the seal, as it were, on the rollicking triple and hemiola rhythms of its earlier pages. No. 18, 'Die Himmel erzählen die Ehre Gottes', is remarkable for the number and variety of its word-engendered phrases and for its use of repetition and antiphonal devices to produce an especially coherent structure. No. 23 is in marked contrast to these majestically cheerful works. The mood of the opening words, 'Selig sind die Toten' ('Blessed are the dead'), is beautifully caught in the slow, recurring chords of F major separated by chords of D minor and B flat major; the imitative phrases that follow maintain the peaceful mood with equal simplicity by entering at regular intervals and often at the same pitch or at the octave; while the words at 'sie ruhen' inspire perhaps the most moving music in the entire collection:

Ex. 359

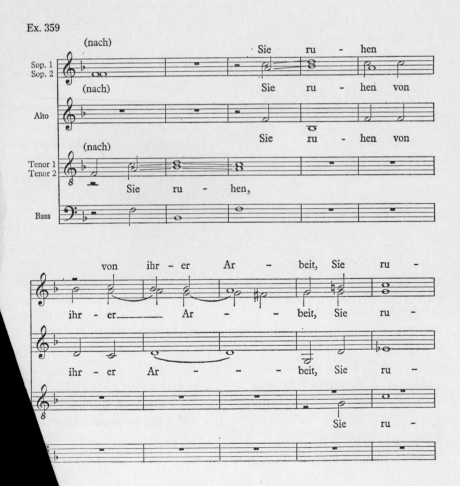

(They rest from their labours, and their works follow after them.)

One cannot perhaps help missing in this collection the excitement that Schütz generated in his more spectacular Italianate music, yet for immensely satisfying sober dignity there is nothing to rival it in German music at the time apart from certain other works by Schütz himself.

THE MOTETS OF HAMMERSCHMIDT, SELLE, AND OTHERS

Hammerschmidt, who worked at Zittau from 1639, was on most prolific composers of motets at this time;[1] he publi collections including motets, under the title *Musicalische* between 1639 and 1646. It has been unkindly said of

---

[1] See Hugo Leichtentritt, *Geschichte der Motette* (Leipzig, 19

'watered down the achievements of Schütz for the multitude',[1] but this is not entirely just. It is true that he wrote a good deal of facile, though craftsmanlike, music, but motets such as 'O barmherziger Vater' and 'Wie lieblich sind deine Wohnungen' (both published in 1641)[2] are beautiful pieces scarcely falling below the general level of Schütz's *Geistliche Chormusik*, as may be suggested by the following few bars from the second of them:

Ex. 360

[1] Manfred F. Bukofzer, *Music in the Baroque Era* (London, 1948), p. 87.

[2] *Ausgewählte Werke von Andreas Hammerschmidt*, ed. Leichtentritt, *Denkmäler deutscher Tonkunst*, xl (Leipzig, 1910), pp. 32 and 51 respectively; this edition includes other motets too. Other sources of motets by Hammerschmidt are Commer (ed.), *Musica sacra*, xxiv–xxvi (Berlin, 1883–5), and Winterfeld, *Der evangelische Kirchengesang*, ii (Leipzig, 1845), pp. 90–129.

(How lovely are thy dwellings, O Lord of hosts.)

These works are free from Hammerschmidt's besetting faults of excessive length and repetitiveness, and another piece of which this can be said is 'Herr, wie lange willst du mein so gar vergessen?', for five-part *favoriti* and *cappella*,[1] from the same collection. This shows that he had a sensitive ear for harmonic colour and vocal scoring, an ability to increase emotional tension in the building-up of contrapuntal points and an instinct for well-balanced forms; we find here, too, surprising anticipatory dissonances recurring in the opening fugue, and a quick homophonic section in triple time used as a rondo theme in a comparatively modern manner.

The large-scale double-choir setting of the Lord's Prayer, for fourpart *favoriti* and five-part *cappella*,[2] published in 1646, contains some rather repetitive passages but also others showing Hammerschmidt at

---

[1] *Ausgewählte Werke*, p. 57. *Favoriti* were a small group of 'favourite' singers, the *cappella* the main chorus.
[2] Ibid., p. 78.

his best: the *favoriti* unfold the first two phrases and are then interrupted by the *cappella*'s emphatic and effective repetitions of 'geheiligt werde dein Name' ('hallowed be thy name'); 'unsere Schuld' ('our trespasses') and 'unsern Schuldigern' ('those that trespass against us') receive pointedly different treatments, the former diatonic, the latter involving poignant augmented triads; and finally, in the doxology, the two groups come together almost for the first time in impressive and

Ex. 361

(Have mercy on me, Lord Jesus.)

sonorous homophony. Several of Hammerschmidt's other motets are based on chorales. But the later *Chormusik . . . auff Madrigal Manier* (Leipzig, 1653) is more Italianate, lighter and more concise, yet also more daring in the use of chromaticism. 'Sei gegrüsset', an unusually short piece with the light texture of a sacred madrigal by Schein, and 'Mein Herr Jesu',[1] the placid opening of which is shown in Ex. 361, are especially noteworthy.

Ex. 362

(Out of the deep.)

[1] Commer (ed.), op. cit., xxiv, pp. 44 and 50 respectively.

Selle was another prolific composer of motets: his manuscript collection *Omnia opera*, dated 1653, contains 282 pieces to German and Latin texts, many of them motets.[1] Most of this music is conservative, especially the Latin works, written in what is still recognizably the *stile antico* of Palestrina, though with much less real counterpoint, rather lax rhythms and almost no dissonance. However, a larger-scale work such as 'Veni Sancte Spiritus',[2] for three contrasting four-part choirs, has a certain splendour deriving from the rich sonorities and some appropriate melodic flourishes. The German settings include writing in which the harmonic rhythm and figuration are more modern and Italianate than the Latin music: the striking beginning of 'Aus der Tiefe'[3] offers evidence of this (see Ex. 362).

Rosenmüller wrote fewer motets than Hammerschmidt and Selle, but they include several pieces distinguished by shapely melody and by chromaticism used in an unconventionally expressive manner. His two books of *Kern-Sprüche*—the first published in 1648, the second (*Andere Kern-Sprüche*) in 1652–3—each contain a number of Latin and German motets and include fine pieces such as 'Ich hielte mich nicht dafür' and 'Die Gnade unseres Herren' (both in the second set).[4] The latter is a setting of the grace and is appropriately simple. There is a delicate balance between chordal and imitative textures and a welcome variety in the organization of both phrases and tonality:

Ex. 363

---

[1] Examples in Selle, *Ausgewählte Kirchenmusik*, ed. Vetter (Stuttgart, 1963).
[2] Ibid.: *Die Motette*, no. 344.
[3] Ibid., no. 339.
[4] Both ed. A. Tunger (Stuttgart, 1963); other pieces from the *Kern-Sprüche*, ed. Krüger (Stuttgart, n.d.).

(The grace of our Lord Jesus Christ, and the love of God . . .)

The motets of Ahle are comparably distinguished.[1] For example, the seven-part funeral motet 'Unser keiner lebet ihm selber' preserves a certain Renaissance grandeur and rhythmic flexibility and yet makes great play with affective figures that are both expressive and unobtrusive. The piece also includes striking antiphonal effects:

Ex. 364

---

[1] Several are published in *Johann Rudolph Ahles ausgewählte Gesangswerke*; the three motets singled out here are at pp. 67, 76, and 48 respectively.

(And no one dies unto himself, so live we and die we unto the Lord.)

Such textures form the basis of his dialogue motet 'Wer ist der, so von Edom kommt', where a S.S.S.T. chorus asks the questions and a lower one, A.T.T.B., answers them: the two groups come together impressively for the triple-time doxology. In the six-part 'Ach, Herr, mich armen Sünder', the famous Passion chorale is imaginatively treated. Kindermann also composed motets that for fluency of technique and imaginative expressiveness are above the average productions of the time; some fine ones, including pieces based on chorales, appear in his *Friedens-Seufftzer* (1642) and *Musica Cathechetica* (1643).[1]

MOTETS BY EARLY MEMBERS OF THE BACH FAMILY

A survey of motets by members of the Bach family must begin with the handful of pieces by Johann Bach (1604–73), of Erfurt, which are generally simpler than many of the motets discussed in the two foregoing sections. Like that of all these Bachs his work is uneven. His finest motet is 'Unser Leben ist ein Schatten',[2] written for a main six-part chorus, with a 'hidden' three-part (A.T.B.) chorus and continuo. The sole function of the 'hidden' chorus is to sing comforting hymn verses, as from another world, in response to the insecurity expressed in both the text and music of the main chorus. Thus the opening words ('Our life is but a shadow') are answered by 'und weiss, dass im finstern

---

[1] Some of Kindermann's motets appear in the first volume, referred to *supra*, devoted to his *Ausgewählte Werke*.

[2] *Altbachisches Archiv aus Johann Sebastian Bachs Sammlung von Werken seiner Vorfahren*, i: *Motetten*, ed. Max Schneider, *Das Erbe deutscher Musik*, i (Leipzig, 1935), p. 9, and Karl Geiringer, *Music of the Bach Family: an anthology* (Cambridge, Mass., 1955), p. 6. On Johann Bach and later members of the family see Geiringer, *The Bach Family* (London, 1954), *passim*, and Percy M. Young, *The Bachs, 1500–1850* (London, 1970), *passim*.

Grabe Jesus ist mein helles Licht' ('and I know that in the dark grave Jesus is my bright light'); the main chorus is sufficiently convinced by this to echo the last phrases, from which point the mood of the whole piece changes to one of optimism, with the larger group proclaiming its faith in the Resurrection. The treatment is mainly homophonic throughout, but 'Schatten' ('shadow') is tellingly depicted in imitative semiquaver runs in thirds, while in setting the closing words '... müssen alle, alle davon' ('all must die'), Bach reduces the number of voices—a favourite realistic device of the time for the very end of a work. The two-dimensional feature of this work had its origins in Venetian music, but through a sobering association with the Lutheran chorale it became one of the commonest ways of preaching through music in Germany during the seventeenth and early eighteenth centuries. It was seldom used with more subtlety than by J. S. Bach's ancestors, while Bach himself brought it to its highest point in his early cantatas (e.g., BWV 106, 131, and 161), where he sometimes (as in BWV 106) even introduced a third dimension.

Another early member of the family to write simple motets was Johann Michael Bach (1648–94), but in his case the simplicity was certainly conditioned by the modest resources of the church at Gehren, near Arnstadt, where he worked. About a dozen of his motets survive,[1] all but two of which combine biblical and chorale texts, a literary union that was by now becoming increasingly common. One of the composer's finest works, 'Nun hab' ich überwunden', in fact has no biblical words at all. It is scored for double chorus, whose antiphonal exchanges are enhanced by dramatic use of rests and repetitions and by sequences using a wide variety of keys and cadences:

Ex. 365

[1] Eleven are printed in *Altbachisches Archiv*.

(Now have I overcome . . . Cross, sorrow, anguish, and need.)

'Herr, ich warte auf dein Heil'[1] is another fine piece, in which the roles of the two choruses are not unlike those of the two groups in Johann Bach's 'Unser Leben ist ein Schatten', just described. The second chorus begin by singing the words of the title to phrases expressively extended by affective melismas on 'warte' ('wait'), while the first chorus replies quietly with the hymn 'Ach wie sehnlich' ('Ah, with what yearning'). The latter is plainly harmonized, and scored at a low pitch, which gives it a certain remoteness from the more passionate declamation of chorus II. After one stanza, however, chorus I, as though unable any longer to restrain itself, takes over the words and music of chorus II; the ensuing antiphonal treatment becomes more and more fervent until the composer introduces slow falling repetitions of the words 'O komm und hole mich' to make a touchingly peaceful conclusion.

The motets of Johann Michael's more famous brother, Johann

---

[1] Also in Geiringer, *Music of the Bach Family*, p. 59.

Christoph (1642–1703), of Eisenach, are of uneven quality, but there are three which are magnificent by any standards and show the seventeenth-century motet at its finest outside the work of Schütz. All are early works: 'Unser Herzens Freude' (1669?),[1] 'Der Gerechte, ob er gleich zu zeitlich stirbt' (1676)[2] and 'Ich lasse dich nicht' (date uncertain).[3] Each is composed on a different plan. In the first section of the first one, two S.A.T.B. choruses answer each other; the phrases overlap and at the end of each line of text the choruses often come together in eight parts:

Ex. 366

---

[1] Commer (ed.), op. cit., xiv (Berlin, 1873), p. 91, and ed. Steinitz (London, 1968).
[2] *Altbachisches Archiv*, p. 101.
[3] This has appeared in many editions. It was at one time attributed to J. S. Bach (who was Johann Christoph's nephew), and it appears in *Johann Sebastian Bachs Werke*, xxxix

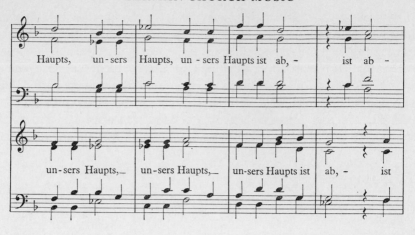

(The crown is fallen from our head.)

The second section is short and entirely in eight parts. In the third the words and musical ideas of the first two sections come together, and for the final section the second is repeated and extended to finish in the tonic with an imperfect cadence, underlining the doubt and insecurity expressed in the words.

The second of these motets is also in four sections but for single five-part chorus. In the first section the anticipatory dissonances which colour the drooping suspensions indicate the composer's acutely sensitive response to his text:

(Leipzig, 1892), p. 157. Of more modern editions, that by Ameln and Gottfried Wolters (Wolfenbüttel, 1950) should be mentioned. Recorded in *The History of Music in Sound*, v,

Ex. 367

(Though he die before his time)

and the rest of the work continues on this imaginative plane. The third
motet is, like the first, a monumental work for antiphonal four-part
choirs. In the first of its two sections repetition of the text is taken to the
utmost limit, but variety of key centres and the mounting tension
generated by the drawing together and eventual combination of the
choirs produce a magnificent effect and a wholly satisfying structure.
In the second section the choirs combine in a chorale fantasia looking
forward to eighteenth-century works of this kind: the sopranos sing

45

Hans Sachs's 'Warum betrübst du dich, mein Herz', while the lower voices, still repeating the words of the first section, weave an accompaniment of 'instrumental' counterpoint, with inversions and strettos. The lines surge forward with such relentless vigour that the moment when movement suddenly ceases and the lower voices three times sing the imploring words 'mein Jesu' to a simple, pleading phrase goes straight to the heart.

CHORALE SETTINGS IN MOTET FORM

Parallel with motets, some of which, as we have seen, incorporate chorales,[1] there flourished a smaller type of composition in which a chorale (either borrowed or original) and its treatment provide the principal interest; most of these pieces can be classified between simple songs with continuo (see Vol. VI) and polyphonic motets. Many composers contributed to this literature, not only those we have encountered in this volume as composers of motets and other forms but also others such as Albert and Crüger.[2] Some of the earliest of these pieces are by Johann Stobäus (1580–1646), pupil of, and collaborator with, Johannes Eccard[3] and from 1626 Kapellmeister to the Margrave of Brandenburg. He set his chosen melodies in such a way that all the lower parts have melodic and rhythmic individuality without affecting the basically simple homophonic character of the texture; he also included in these parts some imitation of the chorale melody, a Renaissance device for which he was noted and which may be seen in the bracketed lines at the start of Ex. 368.

Qualities similar to those of Stobäus mark the chorale settings of Heinrich Albert (1604–51) and Samuel Scheidt (1587–1654); the former, who worked at Königsberg, was a pupil of Stobäus and Schütz and a leading song-writer and poet; the latter, who settled in Halle, was one of the most distinguished German composers of the time, some of whose music has been considered in Vol. IV[4] and whose *geistliche Konzerte* are discussed in (*i*) below. In the present context both are overshadowed by the Berlin composer Johann Crüger (1598–1663), who was an outstanding melodist (some of whose tunes have become well known— though their original lively rhythms are often ironed out—through their use by later composers such as J. S. Bach) and who displayed infinite variety in his settings of his own and other men's tunes.[5]

---

[1] On chorales, see *supra*, p. 655, n. 1.
[2] The biggest single source of this music is Winterfeld, op. cit., ii.
[3] See Vol. IV, p. 452.
[4] On pp. 459–61.
[5] Among modern editions see Crüger, *Neun geistliche Lieder*, ed. Christhard Mahrenholz (Kassel, n.d.).

Ex. 368

(He brought me out of the horrible pit, out of the mire and clay, and set my feet upon the rock and ordered my goings.)

He frequently added two violins to his chorale settings, either to make the texture richer or more brilliant, as in 'Herr, ich habe missgehandelt' (1658), or for introducing symbolic figures, as in 'Lasset uns den Herren preisen'.[1] His setting of 'Ein' feste Burg'[2] is scored for five trombones as well as four voices, and a sober magnificence derives from the interplay of simple choral harmony and more active instrumental textures:

[1] Winterfeld, op. cit., ii, pp. 60 and 61 respectively.
[2] Ibid., p. 68.

Ex. 369

*Underlay of Tenor part not given in source.

(A safe stronghold is our God, a good defence and weapon; he frees us from all distress which has now befallen us.)

There are also many attractive chorale settings by Hammerschmidt, Ahle, Kindermann, and Selle, which should not be overshadowed by the more ambitious works by them already discussed. Many are simple, unpretentious pieces, especially those of Kindermann,[1] which were

---

[1] Examples in Winterfeld, op. cit., and in Kindermann, *Ausgewählte Werke*, ed. Schreiber, *Denkmäler der Tonkunst in Bayern*, xxi-xxiv (Leipzig, 1924), *passim*.

designed to be sung by the choir after the sermon on the various Sundays and festivals of the Church's year. The melody at least of Ahle's 'Es ist genug',[1] a six-part antiphonal setting, has become famous through Bach's amazing harmonization in his Cantata 60, which in turn was incorporated by Berg into his Violin Concerto. Selle and another Hamburg composer, Johann Schop (c. 1590–1667), specialized in setting the verses of the Hamburg poet Johann Rist; Schop's settings particularly are enhanced by lively, plastic rhythms.

LATER MOTETS

By the end of the seventeenth century *a cappella* settings were composed far less frequently than hitherto, and they now showed little trace of their Renaissance ancestry: the place of the motet in the Lutheran service was more and more taken by forms of 'sacred concerto' which developed into the church cantata; but special occasions sometimes gave rise to the composition of *a cappella* motets. A motet such as 'Christus ist des Gesetzes Ende',[2] for two choirs, one high, one low, by Johann Schelle (1648–1701), cantor at St. Thomas's, Leipzig, for twenty-four years until his death, demonstrates that even in conservative Leipzig the concept of post-Renaissance polyphony and the resources of expressive harmony must have been regarded as old fashioned and are replaced in this work by echoes, quick antiphonal interplay and mellifluous writing in thirds and sixths. Now and in the eighteenth century, textures influenced by instrumental music were the rule, and they are generally simple. The small amount of contrapuntal writing is largely confined to short passages of fugato writing, where foursquare themes are imitated at regular intervals. Harmony had become completely tonal, a development frequently emphasized by reiterated 'hammerstrokes' of tonic and dominant chords. Motets with these characteristics make an immediate impact on the listener, and a number of effective ones were composed by Pachelbel, Telemann, and lesser men, mostly in southern and central Germany—men such as Philipp Heinrich Erlebach, Nikolaus Niedt, and Johann Topff.[3]

A number of these works are for double chorus, and several by Pachelbel are conspicuous among those that make splendid use of antiphony ranging from short overlapping phrases to longer self-contained sections. Dual texts—biblical words and a chorale often

---

[1] Ahle, op. cit., p. 47. (There are other chorale settings in this edition, too.)

[2] The edition by Karl Straube, *Ausgewählte Gesänge des Thomanerchores*, ii (Leipzig, 1929), p. 23, is unreliable.

[3] The biggest single modern collection of such music is *Thüringische Motetten der ersten Hälfte des 18. Jahrhunderts*, ed. Seiffert, *Denkmäler deutscher Tonkunst*, xlix-1 (Leipzig, 1915). The *basso continuo* has unfortunately been omitted from these editions, as it also has in several more recent editions of individual works.

with its own tune—are very common and are often deployed in ways identical with, or similar to, the plan of Johann Christoph Bach's 'Ich lasse dich nicht', which has been described above.[1] Notable works by Pachelbel in this style are 'Singet dem Herrn' and 'Troste uns, Gott',[2] and the five-part Passiontide motet 'Tristis est anima mea' by Kuhnau, J. S. Bach's predecessor at St. Thomas's, Leipzig, is of unusual expressive power.[3] The motets of another member of the Bach dynasty, Johann Ludwig (1677–1731),[4] of Meiningen, are mostly for double chorus and worth singling out for the distinction of his scoring and his handling of spatial effects. 'Das ist meine Freude'[5] is a particularly charming work, with its echo effects, happy coloratura passages (in which Ludwig's motets abound), and dancing rhythms (including hemiola).

Textures deriving from the *stile antico* still survive here and there amid the new lighter, homophonic style. For instance, they motivate the motet by Kuhnau just referred to, and the motets of Eberlin, composed about 1740,[6] still show a synthesis of the two styles. But, as with the Mass, it was the motets of Fux[7] in Vienna that most resolutely enshrined the *a cappella* ideal at this time, though they were no doubt performed with continuo and doubling instruments. As in his neo-Renaissance Masses, Fux recreates sixteenth-century techniques with great imagination to produce works that are not, as might be feared, museum pieces but valid works of art. Naturally they vary in quality: the offertory 'Benedixisti, Domine'[8] represents them at their most expressive. Other motets by Fux are more modern in style and include solo recitatives and arias.

THE MOTETS OF J. S. BACH

Seven German motets by J. S. Bach survive—six if 'Lobet den Herrn' is excluded.[9] Only two, 'Der Geist hilft' (BWV 226) and 'O Jesu Christ,

---

[1] Cf. pp. 681–3.

[2] Both in Commer (ed.), op. cit., iii (Berlin, 1841), pp. 72 and 65 respectively; the latter also in *Nürnberger Meister der zweiten Hälfte des 17. Jahrhunderts: Geistliche Konzerte und Kirchenkantaten*, ed. Seiffert, *Denkmäler der Tonkunst in Bayern*, vi, 1 (Leipzig, 1905), p. 93.

[3] Ed. August Langenbeck (Stuttgart, 1953).

[4] An extract from 'Gott sey uns gnädig' is in Geiringer, *Music of the Bach Family*, p. 87.

[5] *Johann Ludwig Bach: Zwei Motetten*, ed. Geiringer, *Das Chorwerk*, xcix (Wolfenbüttel, 1964), p. 8; the other motet in this edition is 'Unsere Trübsal, die zeitlich und leicht ist', p. 1.

[6] Several edited separately by Reinhard Pauly (London/New York, 1960–1).

[7] There are twenty-seven ed. Habert, *Denkmäler der Tonkunst in Österreich*, iii (Jg. ii (1)) (Vienna, 1895). Also see Fux, *Gesammelte Werke*, iii, 1, ed. Federhofer and Renate Federhofer-König (Kassel and Graz, 1961).

[8] Ibid., p. 18.

[9] The best edition is in Bach, *Neue Ausgabe sämtlicher Werke*, iii, 1, ed. Ameln (Kassel, 1965). On the motets in general, see Bernhard Friedrich Richter, 'Über die Motetten Seb. Bachs', *Bach-Jahrbuch*, ix (1912), p. 1, and Ulrich Siegele, 'Bemerkungen zu Bachs Motetten', ibid., xlix (1962), p. 33, and on the authenticity of 'Lobet den Herrn' see *infra*.

mein's Lebens Licht' (BWV 118), can be dated precisely: they were composed for funerals that took place in October 1729 and October 1740 respectively; 'Singet dem Herrn' (BWV 225) dates from some time in 1727;[1] and the remaining four are probably Leipzig works too. In four of them biblical and hymn texts are heard either in succession or together: these are 'Singet dem Herrn', 'Der Geist hilft', 'Jesu, meine Freude' (BWV 227), and 'Fürchte dich nicht' (BWV 228). The texts of 'Komm, Jesu, Komm' (BWV 229) and 'O Jesu Christ' are entirely non-biblical; on the other hand, the dubious 'Lobet den Herrn (BWV 230) is simply a setting of Psalm 117. Four of these works are written for double S.A.T.B. chorus, but, although there is so much antiphony, only in the opening bars of 'Komm, Jesu, komm' does one feel any affinity with the old *cori spezzati* style; this is the only one probably intended for unaccompanied performance.[2] 'Jesu, meine Freude' makes extraordinary demands on the voices owing to its great length and the high tessitura of the divided soprano voices, but internal evidence suggests that certain sections may be performed by soloists.

As with every branch of composition to which he turned, Bach brought the motet to a new high point through the variety of choral techniques that he employed and the wide range of emotions that he depicted. Fugues and fugatos, plain and dramatic chorale settings, chorale variations, rugged, typically Teutonic counterpoint, and graceful, florid 'homophonic' counterpoint—all combine to make these works collectively the most remarkable concentration of choral writing of the early eighteenth century. Only in 'Lobet den Herrn' does the hand of the mature composer seem to be lacking; here, although the opening theme strides powerfully upward through the compass of a twelfth, the rest of the motet consists of a competent rather than original working-out of commonplace material.[3]

On a very different level is the three-movement 'Singet dem Herrn', where overwhelming energy is generated in the opening pages through the building up of modulating sequences and through the homophonic shouts of 'Singet'; the latter also accompany and often dominate the

[1] On the dating of this masterpiece, see Ameln, 'Zur Entstehungsgeschichte der Motette, "Singet dem Herrn ein neues Lied" von J. S. Bach', *Bach-Jahrbuch*, xlviii (1961), p. 25.

[2] See Alfred Heuss, 'Bach's Motetten, begleitet oder unbegleitet?', *Zeitschrift der internationalen Musikgesellschaft*, vi (1904-5), p. 107. The slight evidence for the genuinely unaccompanied performance of the motets in Bach's lifetime had already been presented and largely dismissed by Philipp Spitta, *J. S. Bach*, ii (Leipzig, 1880), pp. 438–42; Eng. ed. by Clara Bell and J. A. Fuller Maitland (London, 1889), ii, pp. 607–11. But see also Roger Bullivant, 'Zum Problem der Begleitung der Bachschen Motetten', *Bach-Jahrbuch*, liii (1966), p. 59.

[3] The present writer shares the doubts that have recently been expressed about the authenticity of this work; see, for example, a review by Bullivant in *Musical Times*, cix (1968), p. 1149.

fugue that brings the first movement to its impressive culmination. The next movement shows Bach treating the combination of chorale text and free commentary beloved of his ancestors in a highly expressive and convincing manner. In the last movement, percussive homophony, dissonance, and imitation are used antiphonally with ever-increasing tension until both choruses unite in a fugue to the final words of praise; the closing bars, from the last entry of the subject onwards, are perhaps the most powerful passage anywhere in Bach's motets:

Ex. 370

(All that has breath praise the Lord. Hallelujah.)

In 'Jesu, meine Freude' the risk of tonal and thematic monotony, always present in chorale variations, is avoided not only by the infinitely varied treatment given to the *canto fermo* but also by the interpolation of movements on biblical texts in differing styles and with contrasted scoring.

(i) SACRED CONCERTATOS, I: CHORALE CONCERTATOS AND VARIATIONS

INTRODUCTION

The monodic style and the concertato treatment of voices and instruments reached Germany by the third decade of the seventeenth century, and many thousands of small-scale sacred works employing them were written there during the remainder of the century. The terms '*geistliches Konzert*' ('sacred concerto') and '*symphonia sacra*' were used—the former more frequently than the latter—to describe them; the term 'cantata' did not come into general use until about 1700. The narrow dividing line and confused nomenclature between '*geistliches Konzert*' and 'motet' have already been mentioned.[1]

The vast corpus of *geistliche Konzerte* falls into two main groups: those that are based on chorales and those that are not. The former, which are discussed in the present section, include both concertatos[2] and variations (some of the latter treating the tunes 'per omnes versus') and are essentially non-dramatic in character and form; there are a number of fine pieces here, but there are also those in which the chorale melody appears to have fettered the composer's imagination because of the inherent difficulty in achieving variety of key and thematic material. The free concertatos will be discussed in the next main section (*j*), together with certain hybrid forms. The music in all but a few later concertatos is continuous.

SCHEIDT AND KINDERMANN

One of the earliest, largest, and most important bodies of this music is the four volumes of *Geistliche Konzerte* published by Scheidt in 1631, 1634, 1635, and 1640[3] (two later volumes have not survived). The occupation of Halle, where Scheidt was Court *Kapellmeister*, by Imperialist troops from 1625 to 1631 closed the Court chapel and drove away most of the singers and all the instrumentalists, so that when the brief liberation by the Swedes encouraged him to publish the first set of *Newe*

[1] Cf. *supra*, pp. 664–5.

[2] We follow modern practice here in distinguishing by use of the word 'concertato' vocal 'concertos' of the early baroque period from instrumental concertos; cf., for instance, Bukofzer, op. cit., p. 21, n. 2.

[3] They are published in *Samuel Scheidts Werke*, viii-xii, ed. Mahrenholz, Adam Adrio and Erika Gessner (Hamburg, 1957–65). Cf. Vol. IV, pp. 460–1, and Gessner, *Samuel Scheidts geistliche Konzerte* (Berlin, 1961).

geistliche Concerten he had to do so in reduced versions for two or three vocal parts and continuo only.[1] In the second set he increased the number of parts to as many as five—six in the later sets—and for a *Miserere* adds parts for four viols and bass viol, explaining to purchasers that the pieces had been originally composed for 'eight to twelve voices, two, three or four choirs, with symphonies and all sorts of instruments and many tablatures for organ' and that 'whoever may wish to print these for the honour of God, may have my authority at any time'. Most are founded on chorales, and those based on the shorter melodies and with fewer verses tend, as always, to be the most successful. Scheidt shows the characteristically German fusion of old and new in which modern declamatory or florid themes are still treated contrapuntally rather than harmonically (as was common in Italy).

In most of his chorale concertatos Scheidt treats each phrase of the melody as a fugato, without presenting it as a *canto fermo* in long notes. With regard to form and texture, such pieces therefore anticipate the organ preludes of Pachelbel, who was a great admirer of Scheidt and was no doubt influenced by these pieces. Scheidt lightens his contrapuntal textures with homophonic passages, and a unifying structural feature (which we have seen Hammerschmidt adopting later)[2] is the repetition of such a passage in the manner of a rondo theme. He is skilful in blending Italianate pictorial figures, stock chromaticisms, and contrapuntal devices into a homogeneous whole. Chromaticism is particularly conspicuous in the 1634 set,[3] since this includes a high proportion of penitential and Passiontide chorales. One exceptional piece,[4] from the first set, is a quodlibet in which three chorales, sung by soprano, tenor, and bass respectively, are cleverly interwoven, though the texture is at times somewhat crabbed. Sometimes, as in no. 9, 'Wenn wir in höchsten Nöten sein', variation treatment of a chorale foreshadows Bach's chorale cantatas.[5]

Scheidt's third volume contains thirty-four pieces, all but two based on the church's calendar. The finest of the short chorale numbers, which may be singled out as pieces showing Scheidt at his best, are 'In dulci jubilo', 'Mit Fried und Freud ich fahr dahin', 'Ich weiss, dass mein Erlöser lebt', and 'Christ unser Herr zum Jordan kam'.[6] But this volume also includes some larger works, including three settings of the Latin

---

[1] Eight-part version of no. 4, 'Wie schön leuchtet der Morgenstern', and original version of no. 10, 'Nun lob mein Seel' ', in *Werke*, viii, appendices i and ii respectively, for former incompletely.

[2] Cf. *supra*, p. 670.

[3] See, for instance, the passage from no. 4 quoted in Vol. IV, pp. 460–1 (Ex. 205).

[4] *Werke*, viii, p. 8.

[5] See Vol. IV, p. 461.

[6] *Werke*, x, pp. 59 and 107, and xi, pp. 7 and 87, respectively.

Magnificat—one for Christmas and New Year, one for Easter, and one for Whitsuntide; each is based on one of the plainsong melodies associated with this canticle and is divided into six sections, each followed by a seasonable German hymn verse.[1] Only in the first setting is the *canto fermo*, Ex. 371(i), allowed not only to dominate the Latin sections but also to invade the territory of the German hymn. This work,[2] which is a fine example of Scheidt's skill, is worth analysing in the following table to demonstrate many of the compositional techniques of the time. The first four hymn verses (2, 4, 6, 8) are all from 'Vom Himmel hoch', and the first three are set to the plainsong melody; the last (12) introduces a new melody, 'Joseph, lieber Joseph mein', in a four-part setting. This is the scheme:

Verse no.	Words	Musical material	Treatment
1	Et exsultavit		Fugato for S.T.B.
2	Vom Himmel hoch		Free imitation for S.S. (Ex. 371(ii))
3	Quia fecit		Close imitation for T.T. (Ex. 371 (iii))
4	Euch ist ein Kindlein		As 2, but for T.T. and with voice parts interchanged
5	Fecit potentiam	*Magnificat* plainsong	*Canto fermo* long notes in T.; free imitation, mainly derivative, in S. and B.
6	Lob, Ehr sei Gott		Like 2 and 4 at start, but combines inversion of melody with itself and later breaks into triple time
7	Esurientes		*Canto fermo* in B. (long notes); S.A.T. lively, mainly derivative (Ex. 371(iv))
8	Das Kindelein	Free	S. T.
9	Sicut locutus est	*Magnificat* plainsong	Mainly homophony for S.A.T.B.; includes two 'reciting notes'
10	Psallite unigenito, Christo	Free	Motet style
11	Sicut erat	*Magnificat* plainsong	Strict, almost canonic; for A.T.B.
12	'Joseph, lieber Joseph mein'	'Joseph, lieber Joseph mein'	Mainly homophony, with echoes and sequences

[1] Cf. the E flat version of J. S. Bach's *Magnificat*, BWV 243a, which is discussed *supra*, p. 608.

[2] *Werke*, x, p. 78.

Ex. 371 (i)

Mag - ni - fi - cat an - i - ma me - a Do - mi - num.

(ii)

(ii) (I come from heaven on high.)

Twelve movements all in the same key indicate a possible weakness of the piece to modern ears, but one should bear in mind that in all the *Magnificat* settings variety would probably have been provided by having the groups of singers separated.

Of chorale pieces by other early seventeenth-century composers those by Kindermann should be mentioned.[1] His setting of 'Wachet auf'[2] is a particularly rousing piece. There are lively contrasts between the verses, the last including two striking features: choral recitative, and bell-like treatment of the words 'Ewig in dulci jubilo' (Ex. 372).

Another interesting piece by Kindermann is his setting of the German *Te Deum*, 'Herr Gott, dich loben wir';[3] after the very opening phrase the Lutheran version of the melody is on the whole referred to only fragmentarily.

Ex. 372

[1] Examples in Kindermann, op. cit., *passim*.
[2] Ibid., p. 12.
[3] Ibid., p. 23.

-lo, in dul - ci ju - bi - lo, e - wig in dul - ci

dul - ci ju - bi - lo, e - wig in dul - ci

e - wig in dul - ci

e - wig in dul - ci

ju - bi - lo.

ju - bi - lo.

ju - bi - lo.

ju - bi - lo.

(for ever in dulci jubilo.)

SCHÜTZ

Schütz used chorales in as many as fifty works, a few of which are concertatos. He explored so thoroughly the possible methods of treating a melody that there were few subsequent developments in this field until near the end of the century. In his earlier settings, such as those published in his two sets of *Kleine geistliche Konzerte* (1636 and 1639 respectively),[1] these methods include *ostinato* and variations. For example, in the *ostinato* treatment of the eighteen-strophe 'Ich hab mein Sach Gott heimgestellt',[2] for S.S.A.T.B. (soloists and chorus) and continuo, he anticipates nineteenth-century methods of variation. The *basso continuo* part, which provides harmonies for the chorale in the first verse,

---

[1] *Neue Ausgabe*, x–xii, ed. Ehmann and Hans Hoffmann (Kassel and Basle, 1963).
[2] Ibid., xii, p. 1.

serves also for the remaining seventeen verses. Thus Schütz is able
completely to bury the *canto fermo* itself in its own basic harmonies,
to develop freely the themes that he invents as counterpoints to the
ostinati or to give only the embellished outlines of the *canto fermo* to
one voice while others are wholly independent. Textures are widely
varied; the *canto fermo* is heard unadorned only in the first and last
verses; and the full forces are rarely used—the chorus (not included in an
earlier version of the piece dating from 1625) sings in only three stanzas.
Less ingenious though more exciting is the four-part 'Nun komm, der
Heiden Heiland',[1] which is faithful to the ancient melody throughout.
At the beginning the first phrase is treated in canon, with a quasi-
ostinato 'rocking' bass added. Schütz then combines in masterly fashion
serious counterpoint and almost flippant Italianate embellishments. The
last line of the melody is much extended: at first a rather lightweight
two-bar phrase is repeated seven times as a counterpoint by the upper
voices, after which the *canto fermo* itself begins slowly to build up
sequentially (Ex. 373(i)) to an intense and fully scored climax (ii):

Ex. 373 (i)

[1] Ibid., xi, p. 91.

(ii)

(God ordained such a birth for him.)

Another fine work is 'Ich ruf zu dir',[1] for three sopranos, bass, and continuo, in which the melody is treated throughout in fugato textures.

[1] Ibid., p. 55.

In Schütz's three sets of *Symphoniae sacrae* (1629, 1647, 1650) there are only very few compositions based on chorales.[1] Whereas the pieces from the *Kleine geistliche Konzerte* have essentially contrapuntal textures deriving from the Renaissance motet, the treatment in the *Symphoniae sacrae* is far more passionate, and the textures and declamation stem entirely from Schütz's response to the words: the difference is that between Monteverdi's *prima* and *seconda prattica*. The pieces in the 1647 set are especially ardent, as befits music whose texts are in part pleas for deliverance from the Thirty Years' War, which still had a year to run. A fine example is the setting of Luther's hymn 'Verleih uns Frieden' ('Grant us peace'),[2] the text of which Schütz set on two other occasions; it is scored for two sopranos (or tenors), two violins, and continuo. It begins with Italianate vocal and instrumental thirds, enhanced by echo effects, and when imitation is used it is clear that it is to build up emotional intensity and that the development of a contrapuntal structure is a secondary consideration. Schütz uses his *canto fermo* as a quarry for several of his word-engendered phrases, and occasionally he abandons it altogether. The two chorale-based pieces in the 1650 set, scored for larger forces, are more monumental, and close in style to the bulk of the contents, which are discussed below.

SOME OTHER SEVENTEENTH-CENTURY COMPOSERS

From the same period as the works by Schütz just discussed date the *Geistliche Konzerte* of the elder Johann Schop (Hamburg, 1644), which were as popular in his day as his settings of Rist mentioned above.[3] They are generally restrained pieces; he dispenses with instruments even in his setting of Psalm 150; and he treats his chorale melodies quite freely. His technique can be seen at its best in his eight variations on 'Vom Himmel hoch'.[4] Knüpfer[5] is another lesser composer of chorale concertatos. His textures are unrelieved by Italian influence, and their general solidity is reinforced by the use of cornetti and trombones. But the contrapuntal writing and the treatment of the *canti fermi* show the hand of a minor master in such pieces as 'Was mein Gott will' and

[1] The first set in *Neue Ausgabe*, xiii–xiv, ed. Gerber and Gerhard Kirchner (Kassel and Basle, 1957–65); the second set, ibid., xv–xvii, ed. Bittinger (Kassel, 1964–8); the third, ibid., xviii–xxi, ed. Bittinger, in progress; older edition in the *Sämmtliche Werke*, ed. Chrysander and Philipp Spitta, x–xi (Leipzig, 1891). In view of the accessibility of most of this music, references are not given in footnotes to the numerous editions of individual pieces.

[2] *Neue Ausgabe*, xvi, p. 12.

[3] Cf. *supra*, p. 687.

[4] Ed. A. Strube (Hanover, 1930).

[5] On Knüpfer, in this connection, see Schering, 'Über die Kirchenkantaten vorbachischer Thomaskantoren', *Bach-Jahrbuch*, ix (1912), particularly pp. 87–93.

'Es spricht der Unweisen Mund wohl',[1] even if there is some tonal monotony.

Though his output was small, Franz Tunder (1614–67),[2] who studied in Rome with Frescobaldi and was from 1641 organist at the Marien-kirche in Lübeck, is a finer composer of chorale settings than Schop. His two best-known pieces, 'Ach Herr, lass deine lieben Engelein' and 'Wachet auf',[3] are in fact lesser works than his bigger choral pieces such as 'Wend' ab deinen Zorn' and 'Ein' feste Burg',[4] which are the true prototypes of early eighteenth-century chorale cantatas such as J. S. Bach's 'Christ lag in Todesbanden' (BWV 4). 'Ein' feste Burg' is excep-tional in Tunder for its extravagant figuration and sudden tempo changes underlining Luther's famous text. A work by Scheidt has already been analysed; here for comparison is a detailed account of Tunder's 'Wend' ab deinen Zorn', showing the varied way in which he, too, treats chorale melodies. It is a work in six verses scored basically for S.S.A.T.B. (soloists and chorus), six strings, and continuo, but there are at times more vocal parts.

(i) chorale in soprano with anticipation of each line in the orchestra;

(ii) two tenors in close imitation and faithful to the chorale; imagina-tive figures and harmonies illuminate the text;

(iii) a big six-part fantasia, in form rather like a chorale variation for organ; the melody is in long notes in the soprano, and the other parts anticipate it in diminution though later move away from it;

(iv) for S.S.A.; the freest in treating the chorale and the most expres-sive (Ex. 374(i));

(v) the chorale is in the bass voice, with four violas above it (Ex. 374(ii)), a fascinating sound offering problems of balance akin to those presented by Bach's 'Christ lag in Todesbanden', which it foreshadows in texture if not in dramatic power;

(vi) extended treatment for full forces; there are effective contrasts between soloists and chorus and high and low voices; the rousing triple-time treatment of the last two phrases often spreads out into eight real parts (Ex. 374(iii)):

---

[1] *Sebastian Knüpfer, Johann Schelle, Johann Kuhnau: Ausgewählte Kirchenkantaten*, ed. Schering, *Denkmäler deutscher Tonkunst*, lviii-lix (Leipzig, 1918), pp. 1 and 30 respectively. Schering also prints verse 4 of 'Es spricht der Unweisen Mund' in the appendix to 'Über die Kirchenkantaten vorbachischer Thomaskantoren'.

[2] Examples in *Franz Tunders Gesangswerke*, ed. Seiffert, *Denkmäler deutscher Tonkunst*, iii (Leipzig, 1900).

[3] Ibid., pp. 101 and 107 respectively; the former also ed. Seiffert (Leipzig, n.d.) and ed. G. Göhler (Leipzig, 1924), the latter in Davison and Apel, op. cit., p. 59, ed. Seiffert (Leipzig, n.d.), ed. H. Meyer (2nd ed., Kassel and Basle, 1956, and ed. Felix Günther (New York, 1949).

[4] *Franz Tunders Gesangswerke*, pp. 124 and 142 respectively; the latter also ed. Seiffert (Leipzig, n.d.).

Ex. 374 (i)

(Are we not yet poor worms, dust, ashes, and earth?)

(Ah, father, let us not perish.)

mit   dir   zu   le – – ben,

mit dir zu   le – ben, mit   dir   zu   le – – ben,

le – ben, zu   le – – ben,   zu   le – ben,

zu   le – – ben,   zu   le – ben,   mit

mit dir zu   le – ben, zu   le – ben,   mit

dir   zu   le – ben,   mit   dir   zu   le – – ben,

*Original ⅜ with note-values of twice the length.

(To live with thee)

Ahle earns a high place among the composers of chorale concertatos with his two very fine works 'Merk auf, mein Herz' and 'Zwingt die Saiten in Cithara', published in 1657 and 1665 respectively.[1] The former employs six verses of 'Vom Himmel hoch', and the tune is varied freely and imaginatively in a structure looking back to Michael Praetorius's 'Wie schön leuchtet der Morgenstern';[2] the diverse textures range from canon in the introductory *sinfonia* and elsewhere to unadorned homophony in the final section. The melody and the words of the sixth verse of 'Wie schön leuchtet' are in fact the basis of 'Zwingt die Saiten'; Ahle develops the melody for 166 bars, throwing up a wealth of figuration expressing the fervour of the text and contrasting these with soberer contrapuntal sections. Ex. 375 is a characteristic passage in which many notes in the florid scales show outlines of the chorale.

The chorale compositions of Pachelbel[3] are on the whole similar in form to Tunder's. A series of contrasting textures as in the latter's 'Wend' ab deinen Zorn' also inform characteristic works of Pachelbel's

[1] Ahle, op. cit., pp. 147 and 160 respectively.
[2] Cf. Vol. IV, p. 549.
[3] See Eggebrecht, op. cit., and Friedhelm Krummacher, 'Kantate und Konzert im Werk Johann Pachelbels', *Die Musikforschung*, xx (1967), p. 365.

Ex. 375

(Strike the strings of the lyre)

such as 'Was Gott tut, das ist wohlgetan' and 'Christ lag in Todesbanden'.[1] Other composers who should be mentioned here are Nicolaus
Bruhns (1665–97), who worked in Schleswig-Holstein, Bernhard,
Zachow,[2] and Schelle. We have already seen Schelle to be a transitional
composer of motets straddling essentially seventeenth- and eighteenth-
century procedures, and his fine set of chorale variations 'per omnes

---

[1] The first in *Nürnberger Meister*, p. 100, and ed. H. A. Metzger (Berlin, 1957); the second
ed. Eggebrecht (Kassel, Basle and St. Louis, 1954) in his series *Johann Pachelbel: Das
Vokalwerk*. Another cantata, 'Jauchzet den Herrn', ed. Krüger (Stuttgart, n.d.).
[2] See Thomas, op. cit.

versus', 'Vom Himmel kam der Engel Schar',[1] can boast a simple splendour whose technical apparatus is largely characteristic of later baroque music, just as the large forces are typical of so much of his own music. Ex. 376 shows the brilliance generated in this piece.

BUXTEHUDE

It is, however, in the chorale concertatos and variations of Buxtehude that (as in his other works) the styles and textures of previous decades are most noticeably simplified and refined to produce music more direct in expression and concise in form. They still belong to the tradition discussed in the preceding sections, so that, strictly speaking, the modern term 'cantata' usually applied to them is misleading; and the same is true of the free concertatos. The most impressive features of Buxtehude's chorale-based works are the sculptured shapeliness of the vocal lines, the idiomatic and usually thematically derived instrumental writing, and the simple brilliance of the scoring. There is a marked contrast between the declamatory homophony of the choral sections and the generally more imitative writing of the intervening passages for solo voices and instruments, which is heightened by subtle embellishments.

About half of Buxtehude's numerous concertatos are based, wholly or partly, on chorales,[2] sometimes so freely decorated that the pieces seem scarcely different melodically from his free pieces. They include settings that are virtually strophic, so slight are the variants from verse to verse. Of the more extended variations 'per omnes versus' the well-known 'Jesu, meine Freude'[3] and the profound 'Nimm von uns'[4] (based on the chorale 'Vater unser') are fine examples. But the second setting of 'Wachet auf', in D,[5] is finer still and a work whose vigour and clarity make many similar works by earlier composers sound stiff and heavy-footed; an earlier setting, in C,[6] is more uneven. In other works a strophic aria based on a chorale is flanked by completely free material: 'Drei schöne Dinge sind'[7] is an example. There are others, such as 'Gen Himmel zu dem Vater mein',[8] in which the chorale is immediately

---

[1] *Knüpfer, Schelle, Kuhnau: Ausgewählte Kirchenkantaten*, p. 167. See also Schering, 'Über die Kirchenkantaten vorbachischer Thomaskantoren'.

[2] Many appear in *Dietrich Buxtehudes Werke*, i–iii and v–vii, ed. Wilibald Gurlitt, Harms, and Trede (Klecken and Hamburg, 1925–37). Another good source is *Dietrich Buxtehude: Abendmusiken und Kirchenkantaten*, ed. Seiffert, *Denkmäler deutscher Tonkunst*, xiv (Leipzig, 1903). See Pirro, op. cit., particularly pp. 400 ff., and Blume, 'Die Kantatenwerke Dietrich Buxtehudes', *Jahrbuch der Musikbibliothek Peters*, xlvii (1940), p. 10.

[3] *Werke*, v, p. 87; also ed. Grusnick (Kassel, 1931).

[4] Ed. idem (Kassel, 1934).

[5] *Werke*, vi, p. 60; also ed. Traugott Fedtke (Stuttgart, 1963).

[6] *Werke*, vii, p. 100.

[7] Ibid., iii, p. 10.

[8] Ibid., i, p. 23.

Ex. 376

(From heaven came the angel host.)

broken up and embellished at the dictates of the words, while 'Jesu, komm, mein Trost und Lachen', in which Buxtehude treats as an *ostinato* the bass of his opening harmonization of the chorale, harks back to Schütz's 'Ich hab mein Sach Gott heimgestellt'.[1] Of works in which church melodies and words alternate with biblical texts—a type of composition that reaches its apogee in Bach's 'Wachet auf', BWV 140 —some beautiful examples are 'Erbarm dich mein', 'Alles, was ihr tut', the non-dramatic dialogue 'Wo soll ich fliehen', and 'Ihr lieben Christen freut' euch'.[2] And finally mention must be made of 'In dulci jubilo',[3] one of Buxtehude's finest and most popular works; Ex. 377 shows the opening bars, with the attractive extension on the last syllable, which Pirro[4] fancifully suggests 'imite les cornemuses au souffle inégal':

Ex. 377

---

[1] Buxtehude's work in ibid., vii, p. 81; on Schütz's cf. *supra*, pp. 696–7.
[2] The first ed. Grusnick (Kassel, 1937), the last three in *Buxtehude: Abendmusiken und Kirchenkantaten*, pp. 39, 85, and 107 respectively.
[3] *Werke*, v, p. 69; also ed. Grusnick (Kassel, 1932).
[4] Op. cit., p. 253.

(j) SACRED CONCERTATOS, II: FREE CONCERTATOS

SCHEIDT AND KINDERMANN

When they made no use of chorales in their sacred concertatos, composers interpreted their texts dramatically. Those who employed chorales all seem to have composed in this free style, though the reverse is not true. Free concertatos include biblical scenes, mainly by Schütz and Hammerschmidt, and semi-dramatic, allegorical scenes of which Scheidt and Pfleger were skilled exponents; these and countless other men also interpreted biblical words, sometimes in conjunction with verses by popular poets such as Rist, through various forms determined by the words, which in turn also governed rhythms and textures.

Scheidt's four volumes of *Geistliche Konzerte* (1631–40) have already been discussed in some detail,[1] and it remains here to characterize a few of the free pieces among them. One structural principle that Scheidt is fond of here is that employing a rondo refrain that we have seen in certain chorale-based works. Here the fourteen verses of his setting of Psalm 149, 'Lobet, ihr Himmel, den Herrn', are held together by a lively homophonic 'Alleluia', and 'Herr, unser Herrscher' and 'Jauchzet Gott'[2] are other pieces in which a similar form obtains. Thematic repetition of a subtler order informs 'Ist nicht Ephraim',[3] whose harmonic tension and vocal scoring help to make it one of Scheidt's most expressive works. 'Kommt her, ihr Gesegneten'[4] is a dialogue for five voices and continuo worth outlining in more detail as a counterpart to the chorale-based *Magnificat* analysed above.[5] The form is enhanced by thematic repetition and a convincing tonal scheme. Soprano and first tenor represent 'Redeemed souls on the right', alto and second tenor 'Condemned souls on the left', and the bass is Christ. Christ first addresses the Redeemed in declamatory style ranging over a wide melodic compass (A): at 'for I was hungry and ye gave me food' the music is chanted on a monotone in a pseudo-plainsong style, the reciting notes becoming lower and lower (B). The Redeemed answer 'Lord, when saw we thee hungry? . . .', at first in a cheerfully irresponsible mood but becoming more serious and intense with a modulation to the dominant (C). Christ's reply (D), in the tonic, is made emphatic by word repetition. Immediately after, he turns to the Damned with 'Depart from me' set with symbolic drops of a fourth and fifth on 'cursed' and 'fire' respectively (E). Then the music of B is repeated, only slightly adapted, to the

[1] See *supra*, pp. 691–5.
[2] These three pieces are in Scheidt, op. cit., ix, pp. 37, 7, and 107 respectively.
[3] Ibid., p. 127.
[4] Ibid., p. 20; also ed. Steinitz (London, 1974).
[5] Cf. pp. 693–5.

words 'I was hungry and ye fed me not . . .'. The reply of the Damned is
full of dramatic pathos (*F*). Christ's condemnatory reply uses *D*
extended and developed to a cadence in the dominant on a low E and D
for 'cast' ('into everlasting torment'); this is followed by three cruelly
cheerful bars in triple time for '. . . but the righteous into everlasting
life'. The last section, back in the tonic, though including a dominant
modulation, consists of a combination and alternation of *F* and a
derivative (with new material) of *C*, sung by Redeemed and Damned
respectively.[1]

Whether Kindermann studied in Italy or not, his free concertatos
certainly show Italian influence. It is apparent in much of the harmony
and declamation, and in textures such as two equal voices singing in
passionate thirds over a relatively static bass, in such pieces as the trios
'Tenebrae factae sunt', 'O vos omnes', and 'O amantissime Jesu'.[2] He
can rival Schütz in passionate expressiveness in such a passage as the
wonderful chain of suspensions for two sopranos with continuo at the
words 'in die heiligen fünf Wunden dein' in his 'Benedictio matutina et
vesperina'.[3] Some of Kindermann's slighter pieces are simple dramatic
dialogues.[4]

SCHÜTZ: *KLEINE GEISTLICHE KONZERTE*

The bulk of Schütz's two sets of *Kleine geistliche Konzerte* (1636–9)[5]
are freely composed. Most of the fifty-six pieces are German, the others
Latin; the number of voices ranges from one to five; the total absence of
obbligato instruments was due to wartime conditions, but this lack and
the relatively simple part-writing hardly diminish the ecstatic fervour
that habitually permeates Schütz's works in concerto style. Many of
these pieces show in how masterly a fashion Schütz transferred to
German music the Italian monodic and concertato styles that he
absorbed during his two periods of study in Italy, especially the second,
in 1628–9, when he may have met Monteverdi.[6] Like Monteverdi, he
shows a predilection for vocal writing less declamatory than that often
found in the Italian monodists of the earlier seventeenth century and
more characteristic of the suave, rounded arias of Venetian composers.
Much of this kind of music is in a dancing triple time and, together with

[1] See Vol. IV, Ex. 205 (pp. 460–1).
[2] Kindermann, op. cit., xiii, pp. 91, 96, and 102 respectively.
[3] Ibid., xxi–xxiv, p. 149.
[4] See Schering, *Geschichte des Oratoriums*, pp. 150–1.
[5] Cf. *supra*, p. 696, including details of editions in n. 1; one piece, 'Sei gegrüsset', also
discussed under 'Dramatic dialogues', *supra*, p. 618. See Moser, op. cit., pp. 434–52; Eng.
ed., pp. 505–28.
[6] See Walter Kreidler, *Heinrich Schütz und der Stile concitato von Claudio Monteverdi*
(Stuttgart, 1934).

bell-like 'Alleluias' (such as the one used as a refrain in 'Ich will den Herren'),[1] this accounts in large measure for its freshness and immediate appeal. Sometimes this newer Italianate style appears side-by-side with motet-like themes and textures, but, however different the individual sections, there is always to be found the overriding structural coherence found in all Schütz's music; moreover, superficially dissimilar ideas can often be shown to spring from a single melodic germ. The scoring, as always in Schütz, is masterly: in the three-part pieces he favours resonant close harmony (no doubt fundamentally Italian in inspiration), whereas in those for four and five voices he devised the more varied textures that can be conjured from larger forces. Here, as in his other music, his inspiration only rarely flags.

A few specific pieces may be mentioned to illustrate some notable features. Of the solo works, 'O süsser, O freundlicher',[2] for tenor, displays the greatest mastery of expressive declamation, balanced form and variety of resource. It is tonally and harmonically adventurous—starting in E flat it has reached A minor and C by the tenth bar. And the emotional and melodic climax is finely handled through heightened repetition and disjunct, rising melismatic phrases contrasting with smoother, conjunct falling ones:

Ex. 378

(O how my soul longeth after thee.)

[1] *Neue Ausgabe*, x, p. 4.   [2] Ibid., p. 83.

Even more abrupt juxtapositions of contrasting note-values distinguish the dramatic Christmas duet 'Hodie Christus natus est', for soprano and tenor, the inspiration for which seems to lie in movements such as 'Pulchra es' and 'Audi coelum' in Monteverdi's *Vespro*.[1] On the other hand, a remarkable unity of mood sustains 'Wann unsre Augen schlafen ein',[2] a duet for soprano and bass, whose seventy-six bars stem from just three simple ideas. The quartet 'Siehe mein Fürsprecher'[3] is notable not only for its inventively varied textures and rhythms but also for the plangent dissonance of the closing bars:

Ex. 379

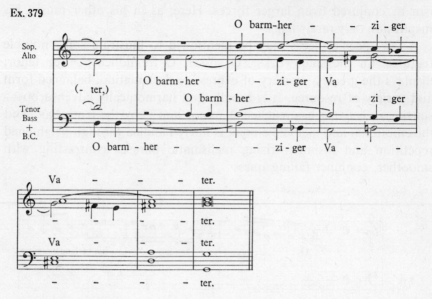

(O merciful Father.)

SCHÜTZ: *SYMPHONIAE SACRAE*[4]

Schütz's *Symphoniae sacrae* also proclaim his debt to Italy. The title was inspired by the *Sacrae symphoniae* of Giovanni Gabrieli, with whom he had studied from 1609 to 1612, and he published the first set in Venice in 1629 when he was back there, sufficiently humble in his middle forties to be studying again in Italy. The twenty pieces in

---

[1] Schütz: ibid., xi, p. 5; Monteverdi: *Tutte le opere*, ed. G. Francesco Malipiero, xiv (Bologna, 1932), pp. 170 and 227 respectively.

[2] *Neue Ausgabe*, xi, p. 15.

[3] Ibid., p. 104.

[4] Cf. *supra*, p. 699, for consideration of the pieces based on chorales, and details of editions in n. 1. Cf. Moser, op. cit., pp. 400–11, 462–86, and 511–34; Eng. ed., pp. 464–77, 542–71, and 602–29. Schütz's dedications of all three sets and the forewords he provided for the last two are translated in Oliver Strunk, *Source Readings in Music History* (London, 1952), pp. 432–41.

this set are solos, duets, or trios, with from one to four obbligato instruments, which are always exactly specified and include a wide range from violins and recorders to bassoons and trombones. As many as seven of the texts are from the Song of Songs, another twelve from psalms and other Old Testament sources. These works show Schütz's early mastery of concertato music for small forces through a fusion of happy melodic invention, airy textures, colourful scoring, and satisfying, rounded forms. Among them is one of his finest works, 'Fili mi, Absalon', a setting of David's lament for Absalom.[1] The interrelation of a solo bass voice and a quartet of trombones produced an elegy of quite unusual power. The vocal line in particular is a miracle of economy and meaningful order, dominated by a small number of motives, important among which is the dotted figure sung to 'Absalon' in Ex. 380; this example, the opening vocal music of the work, shows at the very outset the daringly simple and original ideas of interlocking tonic and dominant triads, incidentally producing from the fourth to the sixth notes, to the complete phrase 'Fili mi', an augmented triad graphically expressing David's anguish (see the bracketed notes):

Ex. 380

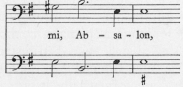

Most of the contents of this set are lighter than this, and the settings from the Song of Songs are among Schütz's most sensuously Italianate music: perhaps the one of which this can most assuredly be said is 'O quam tu pulchra es' (with its second part, 'Veni de Libano'),[2] for tenor, baritone, two violins, and continuo; the setting of the opening words, establishing a mood of ecstatic wonderment, permeates the entire piece

---

[1] *Neue Ausgabe*, xiv, p. 30; ed. Gerber (Kassel, 1949).
[2] *Neue Ausgabe*, xiii, p. 80. See the excellent analysis by Claude V. Palisca, *Baroque Music* (Englewood Cliffs, New Jersey, 1968), pp. 94–8.

47

through its use as a vocal refrain or instrumental ritornello recurring six times.

The music of Schütz's second set of *Symphoniae sacrae* (1647) is, if anything, more Italianate than that of the first set and even more passionate and pictorial with the adoption of the *concitato* style, about which he no doubt learned from that enthusiastic exponent of it, Monteverdi.[1] There are twenty-seven pieces altogether (including the two based on chorales): twelve solos, ten duets, and five trios, the great majority to Old Testament words. In addition to continuo, all have parts for two obbligato instruments imitating the voices, but, except in a German *Magnificat* setting, where various pairs of instruments play successively, no indications as to scoring are given after the very first piece, 'Mein Herz ist bereit', where two violins are called for; such sparse directions are in marked contrast to the explicit instrumentation of the 1629 volume. However, in 'Lobet den Herrn'[2] the organ part is specially written out at the words 'Lobet ihn mit Psalter und Harfe'. A progressive feature of this publication is the inclusion of tempo directions such as '*tarde*' and '*presto*', demonstrating how important Schütz considered freedom of pulse and a flexibility of performance amounting almost to *rubato*. The *Magnificat* (omitting the 'Gloria' and verse 3) is for solo soprano and differs from the other solo pieces by virtue of its affective instrumentation. Schütz here removed all the robust turns of phrase that one might expect but which would be unsuited to the character of the Blessed Virgin (with the single but effective exception of 'Er übet Gewalt') and replaced them by delicate curves in the melodic line and an extremely sensitive use of harmony.

Apart from the *Magnificat*, outstandingly fine solo numbers include, in sharply contrasting moods, the cheerful 'Mein Herz ist bereit' and the powerful 'Hütet euch',[3] which is in a forbidding vein throughout, with 'Lobet den Herrn', a virtuoso piece for tenor, as perhaps the most satisfying of all. Three duets may be singled out: 'Was betrübst du dich', 'Es steh Gott auf', and 'Herr, neige deine Himmel'.[4] In the first, for two sopranos, the instrumental parts are thematically integrated with the vocal lines to a greater degree than in any of the solos, and Schütz uses changes of time and tempo to make the most of the sharp contrasts within the text (which is from Psalm 42); and the last of these

[1] See Kreidler, op. cit., pp. 87 ff.

[2] The three pieces named here are in *Neue Ausgabe*, xv, pp. 1 and 32, and xvii, p. 1, respectively. Schütz's *Magnificat* settings are discussed *supra*, pp. 600–4. The most recent editions are ed. Bittinger (Kassel and Basle, 1963–4).

[3] *Neue Ausgabe*, xv, p. 102; ed. Bittinger (Kassel and Basle, 1964).

[4] Ibid., xvi, pp. 1, 27, and 83 respectively; an earlier version of the last-named is in ibid., p. 107; the first also ed. E. Klause (Berlin, 1956).

three duets is a particularly exuberant virtuoso piece for two basses.
But 'Es steh Gott auf' is the most fascinating of the three, since it is a
reworking for two sopranos (with two obbligato instruments) of Monteverdi's tenor duets 'Zefiro torna' and 'Armato il cor',[1] first published in
his *Scherzi musicali* of 1632. At the outset Schütz takes over the *stile
concitato* of 'Armato il cor': the affections of the two texts are not
unalike. After this, when he turns to 'Zefiro torna', Schütz uses it as a
springboard. He takes over the *ciaccona* bass unaltered, but whereas
Monteverdi states it at the same pitch sixty-one times in all (with two
breaks for recitative) Schütz states it only thirty-four times, the last
ten a minor third lower. On this bass he builds a solid, virile hymn of
praise, German in feeling yet making full use of Italianate resonance of
scoring; and it is extremely instructive to see how Italianate features
have been modified in German hands. The pick of the trios is 'Drei
schöne Dinge sind',[2] for two tenors and bass, in which Schütz exploits
every possible facet of close homophonic writing:

Ex. 381

*G in source.

(Behold how good and lovely it is that brethren should live together in unity.)

[1] Monteverdi, op. cit., ix (Bologna, 1929), pp. 9 and 27 respectively. On the former, cf.
Vol. IV, p. 182.
[2] *Neue Ausgabe*, xvii, p. 29.

Passages such as this are thrown splendidly into relief by being juxta-posed with elaborate solos, and the extended return of the opening at the end bestows on this long work a satisfying ternary form.

In his third volume of *Symphoniae sacrae* (1650) Schütz returned to the polychoral techniques of his *Psalmen Davids* of 1619.[1] This possibly indicates that more performers were available now that the Thirty Years' War had been over for two years, though, against this, it should be said that some of the contents were probably composed several years earlier. The number of solo voices ranges from three to six, and, with frequent writing for chorus and instruments, there is music in up to eight parts, giving a magnificence superior to all but the biggest numbers in the 1619 collection. The chorus and 'orchestra' are used in varying ways: for example, to introduce a new text dramatically, to achieve a convincing ending, to obtain spatial effects, for emphasis on a text or dramatic situation, and to present a rondo theme. Three of the numbers are dramatic dialogues and have been considered above,[2] leaving sixteen other works not based on chorales. Six of these are singled out here. 'Wo der Herr nicht das Haus bauet'[3] has several entertaining features, including the syncopated watchman's call on cornettino or second violin and the unmistakably satirical melismas on 'lange sitzet', followed by mocking interjections for the bass soloist between passages of smooth thirds for the two sopranos (Ex. 382). The 'Kinder' ('children') and the 'Pfeile' ('arrows') are likewise happily illustrated.

'O Jesu süss'[4] is analogous with the reworking of Monteverdi in the second set in being an embellished version of a motet, 'Lilia convallium', by Alessandro Grandi, whom Schütz must have known in Venice. The chorus are an especially powerful structural feature of the setting of the Parable of the Sower, 'Es ging ein Sämann aus':[5] they interject four times with the refrain 'Wer Ohren hat zu hören' in power-ful homophony and high register, each time closing a section of the long work. The intervening narrative for four soloists is more motet-like in texture than is usual in the *Symphoniae sacrae*. 'Seid barmherzig',[6] another setting of a Parable—that of the Mote and the Beam—is also noteworthy for the dramatic interventions of the chorus, as at the quite fierce treatment of the words 'du Heuchler, zeuch zuvor den Balken' ('you hypocrite, first remove the beam').

[1] Cf. Vol. IV, p. 462.
[2] Cf. *supra*, p. 618.
[3] *Sämmtliche Werke*, x, p. 27.
[4] Ibid., p. 89; ed. Arnold Mendelssohn (Gütersloh, n.d.). Moser prints parallel passages of Grandi and Schütz in op. cit., pp. 520–1; Eng. ed., pp. 613–14.
[5] *Sämmtliche Werke*, xi, p. 3; ed. H. Hoffmann (Kassel, 1934).
[6] *Sämmtliche Werke*, xi, p. 25; ed. Bittinger (Kassel and Basle, 1956).

Ex. 382

(and sit up so late, it is in vain [that ye rise so early and sit up so late].)

The setting of the Lord's Prayer, 'Vater unser, der du bist in Himmel',[1] is a more concise piece, greatly enhanced by the constant repetition of 'Vater' before each phrase of text and even between the last two 'Amens'. 'Saul, Saul, was verfolgst du mich?'[2] is one of Schütz's most famous works and certainly among his finest, a most imaginative recreation of St. Paul's vision on the road to Damascus uniting the double-choir technique of Giovanni Gabrieli and the *stile concitato* of Monteverdi. The beginning in particular is unforgettable, with the voice of God rising from the depths to the heights with more and more voices joining in with dramatic suddenness; near the end there comes a no less impressive passage where the second tenor reiterates the name 'Saul' in long note-values against more agitated writing for the other soloists and the instruments, while the combined choirs cut in with their demand 'Was verfolgst du mich?' Echoes contribute much to the almost terrifying effect of this piece.

THE SCHÜTZ TRADITION

An immense number of free concertatos were composed during the sixty years separating these masterpieces by Schütz from the earliest cantatas of J. S. Bach. Although differences of style are not very marked, the most important contributions to this wealth of music can conveniently be summarized—the most that can be attempted in these pages—under four headings: (1) music in the Schütz tradition, through either direct or indirect contact with him or similarly influenced by Italian baroque music (e.g. works by Weckmann, Hammerschmidt, Bernhard); (2) that by men who had no contacts with Schütz and most of whom were scarcely or not at all affected by Italian music (e.g. Selle, Ahle, and the more Italian-influenced Buxtehude); (3) later works including hybrid forms, leading into the eighteenth century (represented by, e.g., Bruhns, Johann Philipp Krieger, and the earliest works of J. S. Bach); and, very briefly, (4) works from south Germany and Austria, where operatic influence was strongest.

Weckmann spent his earlier years in Dresden (where, as was mentioned above, he was a pupil of Schütz) and his later years in Hamburg. In the best of his concertatos he developed his master's style, though at a lower level. Ex. 383, from 'Wie liegt die Stadt so wüste'[3] (1669), shows some remarkably affective solo writing influenced by Schütz, and the roles of the two solo voices (soprano and bass) and a good deal of the harmonic language also owe much to Schütz's example.

[1] *Sämmtliche Werke*, xi, p. 51; ed. Bittinger (Kassel and Basle, 1964).
[2] *Sämmtliche Werke*, xi, p. 99. Also in Davison and Apel, op. cit., p. 36, and ed. B. Beyerle (Frankfurt am Main, 1961). Recorded in *The History of Music in Sound*, v.
[3] Ed. Seiffert (Leipzig, n.d.).

Ex. 383

(Jerusalem hath sinned; she has become as an unclean woman.)

In 'Kommet her zu mir'[1] Weckmann uses similar techniques. He works on a broader canvas in 'Es erhub sich ein Streit',[2] whose text describes the battle in heaven between the Archangel Michael and the Dragon, of which there are also fine settings by Johann Christoph Bach[3] and J. S. Bach. His opening chorus, fifty-three bars long, develops great power from rising arpeggios over repeated notes hammered out in the bass, and the feeling of spaciousness is enhanced by the very small number of chords employed (even so, more than Johann Christoph Bach uses). In the other two choruses we find hemiolic cadences, and imitations among the vocal and instrumental groups in the manner of Schütz. Bernhard was another composer who studied with Schütz and worked in Dresden and Hamburg. His concertatos are generally less skilful than Weckmann's, though in 'Wahrlich ich sage euch' the homophonic choruses have buoyant rhythms and the contrapuntal ones are

[1] *Matthias Weckmann und Christoph Bernhard: Solocantaten und Chorwerke*, p. 7. The volume includes several concertatos by both composers. 'Gegrüsset seist du, Holdselige' in Richard Jakoby, *The Cantata* (*Anthology of Music*, xxxii) (Cologne and London, 1968), p. 109. The chorus 'Die mit Tränen säen' from the cantata 'Wenn der Herr die Gefangenen zu Zion' in Schering, *Geschichte der Musik in Beispielen*, p. 271.

[2] *Weckmann und Bernhard: Solocantaten und Chorwerke*, p. 29.

[3] Cf. *infra*, pp. 729–30.

adroit, and the four verses for the S.A.T.B. soloists in the extended funeral concertato 'Ich sahe an alles Thun'[1] are constructed as strophic variations.

The free concertatos of Tunder[2] are even more interesting than his chorale concertatos. The affective recitatives and the rounded arias of his solo pieces repeatedly show the influence of his Italian training, and the text, as in all the best Italian music of the early baroque period, absolutely determines the form and content. 'O Jesu dulcissime' is a fine example.[3] In the choral pieces the most arresting feature is the incisive homophonic writing, which is illustrated in the following extract from 'Nisi Dominus aedificaverit':[4]

Ex. 384

[1] These two works are in ibid., pp. 111 and 128 respectively.
[2] Examples in *Franz Tunders Gesangswerke*.   [3] Ibid., p. 4.   [4] Ibid., p. 57.

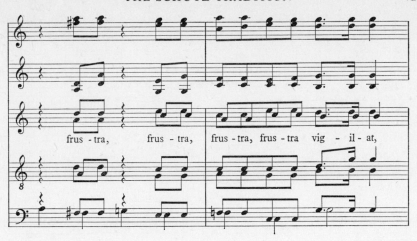

Rosenmüller is another composer who went as a young man to Italy, and the light textures and tunefulness of many of the free concertatos in his *Kern-Sprüche* (1648) and *Andere Kern-Sprüche* (1652) seem to owe something to his visit. He frequently unifies a work by repeating material —in such a piece as 'Ich bin das Brot'[1] from the 1652 set, the closing bars of which are worth quoting to show how he can move purposefully towards a cadence with well-sustained momentum:

[1] This and several others ed. Tunger (Stuttgart, various dates).

Ex. 385

(and whosoever believeth on me shall never thirst.)

The qualities of the motets of Hammerschmidt, outlined above,[1] are also in general terms those of his concertatos in the same sets of *Musicalischer Andachten* (1639–46). The earlier concertatos are on the whole the finest—such a one, for example, as 'Kommet zu mir' (1639),[2] with its convincing rondo form, affective harmonies, and plastic rhythms. His *Fest-, Buss- und Danklieder* (1658–9) are avowedly lighter music, often strophic, with little counterpoint and a good deal of pattering homophony: 'Meinen Jesum lass ich nicht'[3] is a typical example. What really cause Hammerschmidt to stand out in this field are his two sets of dialogues, published in 1645, and his *Musikalische Gespräche über die Evangelia* (Dresden, 1655).[4] These, and pieces like them by other composers, are not unlike dramatic oratorios in miniature, but most of the 'characters' are allegorical or symbolic, and the emphasis lies in the pointing of a moral rather than in presenting a drama: although there is some degree of characterization, these dialogues, unlike works such as Schütz's gospel scenes, would not lend themselves to staging. The commonest 'characters' are Christ and the Soul, but personifications of Fear, Hope, and the Seven Deadly Sins can be found, as well as 'real' biblical characters. Not only were these dialogues, as a musical form, important in fostering interest in oratorio, but the mixture of allegory and mysticism informing their texts, though often naïve, became

---

[1] Cf. *supra*, pp. 668–72.
[2] *Ausgewählte Werke von Andreas Hammerschmidt*, p. 3; this edition includes other concertatos.
[3] Ed. Heilmann (Stuttgart, 1960).
[4] *Andreas Hammerschmidt: Dialogi oder Gespräche einer gläubigen Seele mit Gott*, i, ed. A.W. Schmidt, *Denkmäler der Tonkunst in Österreich*, xvi (Jg. viii (1)) (Vienna, 1901); 'Wende dich, Herr' in Davison and Apel, op. cit., p. 55, and Jakoby, op. cit., p. 104. See also Schering, *Geschichte des Oratoriums*, pp. 151–2.

a cornerstone of German religious thought from the mid-seventeenth century onwards through several generations, as Bach's Passions and church cantatas demonstrate. Many dialogues by Hammerschmidt and other composers are in three parts, a few in four, the almost ubiquitous Soul being sung by a pair of voices sharply contrasting in pitch with the voice allotted to the other character: such 'unrealistic' presentation is another factor militating against dramatic presentation. Several are prefaced by instrumental *sinfonie* and include parts for obbligato instruments. Hammerschmidt's finest music is contained in his dialogues; Ex. 386 is a representative extract from 'Ich bin die Wurzel'.[1]

Pfleger, who worked in various small towns, is another composer who wrote some fine allegorical dialogues.[2] 'Ach, wenn Christus sich liess finden' is one of the most notable and 'Kommt her, ihr Christenleut' an especially joyful one, while 'Hilf, Herr Jesu, lass gelingen',[3] also containing impressive passages, is one of those showing the quaintness that can result from the juxtaposition of biblical text and free verses of a pious character (in this case by Rist).

Although his main output comes slightly later than the other composers discussed in this section, Schelle, the last to be considered, was, like the first two, Weckmann and Bernhard, in personal contact with Schütz as a boy. We have seen his penchant for large-scale works, clear-cut in form and harmony,[4] which he may have inherited from Schütz and which he also exercised in the best of his free concertatos. In 'Lobe den Herrn',[5] for instance, the forces are five-part *favoriti* and main chorus, five-part strings, two cornetti, bassoon, four concertante clarini, three trombones, and timpani. The opening chorus, a triple-time *presto*, looks forward to Handel in its homophonic tutti hammerstrokes and its upward-thrusting scale figures, gestures that gain impetus from the lively movement of the bass line. Schelle deploys his forces spectacularly in this vigorous movement (which he repeats before his final fugal 'Alleluia'): there is in fact a marked lack of solo writing in the work, almost as though he felt that nothing less than massed forces was compatible with this large-scale hymn of praise. 'Ehre sei Gott in der Höhe' and 'Alleluia, man singet mit Freuden vom Sieg' are similar works, while 'Ach, mein herzliebes Jesulein'[6] is one of the most attractive of Schelle's small-scale pieces.

---

[1] *Andreas Hammerschmidt: Dialogi oder Gespräche*, i, p. 5.
[2] Ed. Stein, *Das Erbe deutscher Musik*, 1 (Leipzig, 1961). See Nausch, op. cit.
[3] These three pieces are in *Das Erbe deutscher Musik*, 1, pp. 34, 89, and 102 respectively.
[4] Cf. *supra*, p. 687.
[5] *Knüpfer, Schelle, Kuhnau*, p. 122.
[6] Ibid., p. 219; the previous two pieces named here are ed. Krüger (Stuttgart, 1960).

Ex. 386

★The composer does not specify it.

(. . . a bright morningstar. Come Lord Jesu, yea come and be with us all. Yea, I come quickly.)

COMPOSERS OUTSIDE THE SCHÜTZ TRADITION

There are a number of concertatos by, among others, Knüpfer, Selle, Ahle, and Pachelbel, but only a few are of great interest. One is Knüpfer's 'Ach Herr, strafe mich nicht',[1] in which he not only uses large forces imaginatively but shows himself sensitive to the mood and rhythms of the words, as here:

Ex. 387

(I am weary with sighing.)

[1] *Knüpfer, Schelle, Kuhnau,* p. 60. See also Schering, 'Über die Kirchenkantaten vor-bachischer Thomaskantoren', with an example of Knüpfer's dramatic recitative (from 'Wer

Selle's concertatos are generally more imaginative than his motets, as can be seen in his 'Ich taufe mit Wasser' and 'Ecce quam bonum'.[1] He is liable to lapse into squareness of phrase and metre, a feature refreshingly absent from most of the free concertatos of Ahle, which include 'Misericordias Domini', a resourceful set of thirty variations on a five-bar ground bass always in the tonic, and a short Easter duet, 'Bleib' bei uns, Herr'.[2] The second of these is especially notable for the variety of its phrasing: the voices enter with two three-bar phrases, answered by three bars for strings, upon the last half bar of which the voices intrude with the first of two two-bar phrases, sharply contrasted rhythmically with the previous phrases, and these are again followed by two longer phrases. Pachelbel's concertato psalm-settings[3] are most notable for their energetic counterpoint. Other composers include Wolfgang Carl Briegel[4] (1626–1712), Sebastiani, Christoph Schultze (1606–83), and three members of the Bach family.

The large-scale 'Ich danke dir, Gott' is the only extant composition of Heinrich Bach (1615–92), of Arnstadt,[5] and is most notable for the way in which the large form, expounded through large forces, is held together by tutti recurring in the manner of ritornellos, though without strong thematic relationships. Johann Michael Bach is best represented in this field by 'Ach, bleib' bei uns, Herr Jesu Christ', though the solo concertato 'Es ist ein grosser Gewinn'[6] is interesting for its idiomatic writing for three types of violin. Ex. 388 shows the quietly effective portrayal of the approach of evening in the first of these works, a setting of much the same text as Ahle's 'Bleib' bei uns' just referred to.

In this field, as with motets, Johann Christoph is the most interesting of the Bachs of this period. His large-scale setting of 'Es erhub sich ein Streit' has more in common with Weckmann's setting than with J. S. Bach's.[7] He was more daring even than Weckmann in his opening movement in writing nearly sixty bars on the tonic chord of C for a crescendo of trumpet fanfares with timpani and blocks of exuberant choral antiphony announcing the war in heaven between Michael and

[1] Both ed. Vetter (Stuttgart, n.d.); on the motets cf. *supra*, p. 673.

[2] Ahle, op. cit., pp. 29 and 62 respectively.

[3] In Eggebrecht, 'Johann Pachelbel als Vokalkomponist', these works are listed as motets.

[4] Several pieces ed. Krüger (Stuttgart, 1957–).

[5] *Altbachisches Archiv aus Johann Sebastian Bachs Sammlung von Werken seiner Vorfahren*, ii: *Kantaten*, ed. Schneider, *Das Erbe deutscher Musik*, ii (Leipzig, 1935), p. 3. The other references given in n. 2 on p. 677, *supra*, again apply to the Bachs whose works are referred to in the present section.

[6] Ibid., pp. 61 and 39, respectively.

[7] Geiringer, *Music of the Bach Family*, p. 36; on Weckmann's setting cf. *supra*, p. 721.

ist, der so aus Edom kommt') and a strophic aria by Schelle (from 'Die Liebe Gottes ist ausgegossen') in the appendix.

Ex. 388

(for it is now evening.)

his angels and the dragon, and the noisy reverberation of the Georg-kirche in Eisenach would have made this truly awe-inspiring; it is a moving moment when, at the words 'und siegeten nicht' ('and [the dragon] conquered not'), the music at last moves to a dominant cadence. A curiosity, though a lively one, by the same composer is the wedding 'cantata' 'Meine Freundin, du bist schön',[1] which seems to have been a particular favourite in the Bach family. Words from the Song of Songs are deliberately ridiculed, and this interpretation is emphasized in the music. For example, when the girl takes a big stick, or 'chackan', Johann Christoph punningly writes a chaconne (with sixty-six variations), and his rough humour can also be seen in the following representation of drunkenness:

[1] *Altbachisches Archiv*, ii, p. 91.

Ex. 389

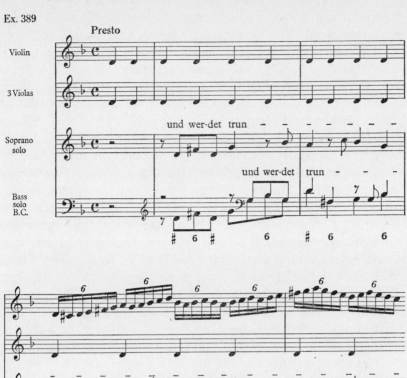

(and become drunk.)

Buxtehude was the most consistently accomplished composer of free concertatos in the later seventeenth century.[1] Most are settings of rhymed verses. His output of them falls broadly into three categories: (1) short, mainly homophonic pieces; (2) those founded on ground basses; and (3) longer, often more introspective works, among them a few dialogues. Most of the first kind are scored for three voices and continuo, and several have parts for two violins as well. 'Cantate Domino', 'Kommst du, Licht der Heiden', and 'Aperite mihi portas justitiae'[2] are especially fine ones. In the second type the ground bass can almost be seen as a counterpart to the chorale in Buxtehude's chorale concertatos. The bass is often treated in a subtle manner, as in 'Illustra faciem tuam',[3] the last of a set of seven cantatas on poems from St. Bernard's *Rhythmica oratio*. The bass of the first stanza is compressed to form that for the shorter second one; the third verse reverts to the first bass, with a variant towards the end; and the final 'Amen' invokes the first few notes of this bass to create a new melody dominating the movement through several different keys, but always in the bass. 'Führwahr! Er trug unsere Krankheit'[4] is probably the finest piece in the last group, with its dramatic *sinfonia*, fine ensuing bass solo and chorus, and skilful development and repetition of this material in the rest of the work; another notable one is 'Ich halte es dafür'.[5] Many of the through-composed works are for a single voice, among which joyful ones such as 'Herr, wenn ich nur dich habe', 'Mein Herz ist bereit', and 'O fröhliche Stunden'[6] are pre-eminent: Buxtehude constantly writes effectively, with pleasantly varied phrase-lengths and harmony and with occasional nice surprises, so that the music is rarely predictable or merely conventional. Of the dialogues one might mention that between Christ and the Faithful Soul, 'Wo ist doch mein Freund geblieben',[7] part of whose appropriately joyful last movement is shown in Ex. 390. The concertatos of Böhm[8] are generally similar in style to Buxtehude's.

[1] References to sources given in n. 2 on p. 706 again apply.

[2] *Werke*, v, p. 29, vi, p. 14, and vii, p. 62, respectively; also ed. Grusnick (Kassel and Basle, 1957), Kiel (Hilversum, n.d.), and Johann Hedar (Copenhagen, 1954) respectively. Also see Jakoby, op. cit., p. 120, for 'Wie soll ich dich empfangen'.

[3] Ed. Dietrich Kilian (Berlin, 1961). On this work see Pirro, op. cit., pp. 202–5.

[4] Ed. Grusnick (Kassel and Basle, 1957); the *sinfonia* quoted complete in Pirro, op. cit., pp. 303–5.

[5] *Werke*, iii, p. 30; the final duet, 'Du gibest mir Ruh', is recorded in *The History of Music in Sound*, v.

[6] *Werke*, i, pp. 35 and 38 (two versions), i, p. 77, and ii, p. 74, respectively; the first ed. Grusnick (Kassel, 1941), the last two ed. Karl Matthaei (Kassel, 1929 and 1934 respectively).

[7] *Werke*, iii, p. 93.

[8] Examples in Böhm, op. cit., ii.

Ex. 390

(Thus the Soul and Jesus love each other constantly.)

FROM CONCERTATO TO CANTATA

The group of composers mostly born well within the second half of the seventeenth century and active until well into the eighteenth includes Bruhns, Johann Philipp Krieger, and Kuhnau. Beside their output may be placed the earliest works of J. S. Bach. The cantatas of Bruhns,[1] who worked in Schleswig-Holstein and Denmark, are to texts combining prose and free verses similar to those found in Buxtehude, with whom he studied. It is possible to see in his works,

[1] Several in Bruhns, *Gesammelte Werke*, ed. Stein, *Das Erbe deutscher Musik*, ii, *Landschaftsdenkmale: Schleswig-Holstein und Hansestädte*, 1–2 (Brunswick, 1937–9).

as in Buxtehude's, the emergence of the genuine church cantata including separate movements—recitatives, arias, choruses; but the well-integrated voices and instruments do not develop characteristic vocal and instrumental figures as in the later cantata. Two fine works by Bruhns are 'Die Zeit meines Abschieds ist vorhanden', which is entirely choral, and 'Hemmt eure Tränenflut', an Easter piece including solo parts;[1] sometimes his works seem to have been inspired by more ideas than he could control. Krieger's output, no less prolific than in other genres, ranges from simple old-fashioned strophic pieces such as 'Liebster Jesu, willst Du scheiden?'[2] (1687) to fully-fledged cantatas (dating from his later years) of the type to be discussed later and well represented by 'Rufet nicht die Weisheit',[3] a late work including a *da capo* aria (heard twice, sung by soprano and bass respectively) in which an idiomatic figure is developed in the instrumental bass. Kuhnau, Bach's immediate predecessor at Leipzig, was rather more conservative than Krieger in his later works, though he did write a few more forward-looking cantatas such as 'Wenn ihr fröhlich seid',[4] which includes a number of imaginative moments. Ex. 391 shows a characteristically bland passage from 'Ich freue mich im Herrn' (1718),[5] a single movement lasting for some 260 bars of 12/8 time.

Five 'cantatas' by J. S. Bach basically of the old concertato type date from his earliest years (up to about 1710): 'Gott ist mein König', BWV 71, a diffuse work composed for the inauguration of the Council of Mühlhausen in 1708; 'Nach Dir, Herr, verlanget mich', BWV 150; the wedding cantata 'Der Herr denket an uns', BWV 196; and two of his finest works—'Gottes Zeit', BWV 106, and 'Aus der Tiefe', BWV 131.[6] Practically all his subsequent cantatas are of the new type to be described in the next main section, (*k*), and for which alone the term 'cantata' is ideally best reserved. In 'Gottes Zeit', a funeral *actus tragicus* in two main movements, Bach reveals for the first time that insight into the profound mysteries of life and death that he was to develop to such an extraordinary degree in his later cantatas. It is manifest not so much in the treatment of individual words such as 'leben' ('live') or 'sterben' ('die') but much more fundamentally in the overall

---

[1] Ibid., i, p. 3, and ii, p. 115, respectively.

[2] Krieger, *21 ausgewählte Kirchencompositionen*, p. 37.

[3] Ibid., p. 275.

[4] *Knüpfer, Schelle, Kuhnau*, p. 292.

[5] Ibid., p. 321.

[6] In the original edition of the *Werke* the cantatas were published in groups of ten, in vols. i, ii, v(i), vii, x, xii(2), xvi, xviii, xx(i), xxii, xxiii, xxiv, xxvi, xxviii, xxx, xxxii, xxxiii, xxxv, xxxvii, and xli, in an order (by no means that of composition) subsequently adopted by Schmieder for his BWV numbering. In the *Neue Ausgabe* (Kassel and Basle, 1954–) they are ordered according to the liturgical purpose of their texts.

Ex. 391

(My delight is in the Lord, and my Soul rejoices in God.)

mood of a complete section, such as the alto and bass duet 'In deine Hände' and, still more so, the four-dimensional choral section 'Es ist der alte Bund' that precedes it. Here the lower, darker voices enunciate 'the old decree—Man, thou must die' over a 'relentless' bass line, while the sopranos sing words of comfort from Revelation and recorders play the chorale melody 'Ich hab mein Sach Gott heimgestellt' (to introduce a chorale in this way is, of course, quite different from basing all or much of a work on one): though they appear in one of his earliest works these fifty-five bars constitute one of Bach's most subtle, sublime, and deeply felt movements. In 'Aus der Tiefe' he interprets the words of Psalm 130 with the utmost power, without ever indulging in exaggeration. An early instance is heard in the agitated shouts of 'Herr, höre meine Stimme' ('Lord, hear my voice') in the Vivace which suddenly breaks in on the opening Adagio; here, too, the word 'Flehens' ('pleading') is set to broken and unbroken roulades and double echoes. In this work a chorale melody is again combined with another text—here it is, exceptionally, sung, whereas Bach's usual practice was to present it instrumentally (as in 'Gottes Zeit'); and another feature of his mature cantatas also appears—a fugue in triple counterpoint.

SOUTH GERMANY AND AUSTRIA

The twenty-six *Geistliche Konzerte* of Kerll,[1] written during his sojourn in Munich, are the most important south German contribution to the free concertato. The influence of his teacher Carissimi and his knowledge of Schütz's *Kleine geistliche Konzerte*[2] are plain from the snatches of Italianate melody—cf. Ex. 392, from 'Exsultate'[3]—and the rich, resonant scoring.

Ex. 392

---

[1] Kerll, *Ausgewählte Werke*, ed. Adolf Sandberger, *Denkmäler der Tonkunst in Bayern*, ii, 2 (Leipzig. 1901).

[2] Cf. ibid., p. lii.

[3] Ibid., p. 111.

(O most blessed virgin, with how much holiness, with how great brightness do you shine amid the angels!)

The concertatos of the Emperor Leopold I likewise boast rich textures, but with longer, more flowing phrases and more broken-up structures than Kerll's. Leopold's skill in handling large forces can clearly be seen in his 'Hymnus dedicatione ecclesiae'.[1]

(k) CANTATAS

INTRODUCTION

The gradual development of concertatos into true cantatas became more marked after 1700. From about the same time very few works were founded on a single chorale; in the present survey, therefore, no hard and fast division is made between chorale variations and freely composed cantatas (in many of which, of course, chorales are used in individual movements).

The evolution of the cantata, too, accelerated tremendously in the early eighteenth century. The principal musical feature distinguishing a cantata from a concertato is that its constituent parts—*sinfonie*, choruses, recitatives, ariosos, arias—are now individual movements in their own right, quite separated from each other. The influence of opera contributed to this change, thus producing a development parallel to

[1] Adler (ed.), *Musikalische Werke der Kaiser Ferdinand III., Leopold I. und Joseph I.*, p. 129.

that which led about the same time to the Passion oratorio. A large
number of lesser poets provided texts—one can almost call them
librettos—for composers to set, and some produced work of moderate
distinction, among them 'Picander' (whom we have already encountered as author of the newly written parts of the text of Bach's St.
Matthew Passion) and Erdmann Neumeister (1671–1756), who was a
pioneer in this field; among the others, however, were men of meagre
talent, who were both needed and willing to satisfy the constant demand
for new texts. Again as with Passion oratorios the texts are couched in
language that is often vivid in a rather sensational way and is a vehicle
for sentiments that rarely rise above sententious religiosity; but these
texts assuredly inspired composers—and not only J. S. Bach—to write
music far transcending them in quality. Compared with the fluidity of
many concertato texts, these so-called 'reform' texts also tend to be
somewhat rigid in structure—no doubt a consequence of the influence
of *opera seria*.

ZACHOW

Zachow, the earliest composer regularly to set cantata 'librettos' of
the reformed type, is the only one who did so before Bach.[1] His 'Herr,
wenn ich nur dich habe'[2] is based on a text still partly that of a psalm,
partly a paraphrase of it. The form is: a brief *sinfonia*; a long, very fine
chorus in which the homophonic opening acts as a ritornello; then four
free verses, in Zachow's settings of which—all in ternary form—the
third is a variation of the first and the fourth an almost exact repetition
of the second; and finally a restatement of the opening chorus. In his
German setting of the *Magnificat*[3] the liturgical text is confined, except
in the opening chorus, to brief unrepeated statements, which are
followed by free paraphrases or comments which Zachow develops at
length, so that the work belongs with the reform cantatas; there are one
or two close parallels between this work and J. S. Bach's setting,
BWV 10[4]. The Whitsuntide cantata 'Ruhe, Friede, Freud und Wonne'[5]
is an excellent example of a cantata whose entire text is a libretto of the
new type, depicting at first the plight of the sinner and his failure to be
aware of it. Quite early on there appears a self-contained bass aria,
'Ach und Weh!' ('Alas, woe is me'), and the sinner is brought to his
knees in a short recitative. In the text at this point there is an immediate
change of mood as the sinner resolves to reform. However, Zachow

---

[1] Examples in *Gesammelte Werke von Friedr. Wilh. Zachow*. See Thomas, op. cit.

[2] *Gesammelte Werke*, p. 25.

[3] Ibid., p. 104.

[4] Cf. *infra*, pp. 743–4.

[5] Ibid., p. 54. See Heuss, 'Friedrich Wilhelm Zachow als dramatischer Kantatenkomponist', *Zeitschrift der internationalen Musikgesellschaft*, x (1908–9), p. 228.

sacrifices drama to form by repeating his opening sonata before
establishing the new mood in an alto aria:

Ex. 393

(Begone, hellish night of sorrow.)

The rest of the cantata is given over to rejoicing and includes a large-
scale final chorus in ternary form. There is no concluding chorale, which
had yet to become the regular feature of the cantata that it became in
the bulk of Bach's output.

THE CANTATAS OF J. S. BACH:[1] INTRODUCTION

The two hundred or so cantatas of Bach, the majority of which date from the first few years after his arrival in Leipzig in 1723, include many of the 'reform' type outlined above, but some are still settings of century-old hymn verses. Historians have grouped these works in several different ways, none of them ideal. The following classification is by outward musical form, or the forces used, which, while having certain disadvantages, does at least provide a clear division between various types of choral and solo cantata. The BWV numbers at the end of each definition are references, by no means exhaustive, to important works of each type.

(1) Chorale cantatas, for chorus, in which the melody as well as the text occurs in all, or nearly all, movements. BWV 4, 93, 101, 113, 137.

(2) Chorale cantatas in which chorales are interposed between the freely composed parts, the two kinds of movement appearing in more or less equal proportions. BWV 10, 36, 80, 95, 122, 127, 140.

(3a) Cantatas which include chorale fantasias and generally a closing chorale, but in which all the rest of the music is free, although the texts may be hymns. BWV 5, 8, 16, 20, 21, 23, 41, 61, 62, 68 (also under 3b), 78, 91, 96, 97, 100, 114, 115, 116, 117, 125, 129, 130, 135.

(3b) Chorale cantatas which include a chorus in the old motet form with instruments *colla parte*. BWV 2, 28, 38, 68 (also under 3a), 144. These cantatas are different structurally from those in Groups 2 and 3a only by virtue of the nature of their motet choruses.

(4) Chorale cantatas which have no chorale fantasias and in which chorale melodies play little part in the structure of large movements or do not appear at all. BWV 6, 11, 19, 22, 30, 34, 39, 40, 43, 46, 47, 48, 50, 63, 65, 67, 75, 76, 79, 102, 104, 105, 108, 110, 119, 138, 146, 149, 171, 182, 190, 195.

(5a) Solo cantatas for a single voice. BWV 35, 51, 52, 54, 55, 56, 82, 169, 170, 199.

---

[1] The immense literature on Bach's cantatas includes the following: Charles Sanford Terry, *J. S. Bach: cantata texts* (London, 1926), Werner Neumann, *J. S. Bachs sämtliche Kantatentexte* (Leipzig, 1956), idem, *Handbuch der Kantaten Johann Sebastian Bachs* (3rd. ed., Leipzig, 1957), Terry, *Bach's Chorals*, ii (Cambridge, 1917), W. Gillies Whittaker, *The Cantatas of Johann Sebastian Bach*, 2 vols. (London, 1959), Dürr, 'Zur Chronologie der Leipziger Vokalwerke J. S. Bachs', *Bach-Jahrbuch*, xliv (1957), pp. 5–162, Paul Mies, *Die geistlichen Kantaten Johann Sebastian Bachs*, 2 vols. (Wiesbaden, 1959–60), Westrup, *Bach Cantatas* (London, 1966), Robert L. Marshall, 'Musical sketches in J. S. Bach's cantata autographs', *Studies in Music History: essays for Oliver Strunk*, ed. Harold S. Powers (Princeton, 1968), p. 405, Dürr, *Die Kantaten von Johann Sebastian Bach*, 2 vols. (Kassel and Basle, 1971), and Alec Robertson, *The Church Cantatas of J. S. Bach* (London, 1972). Schmieder, op. cit., gives a bibliography for each cantata, and addenda are given in *Bach-Jahrbuch*, xl (1953), pp. 139–40, xlv (1958), p. 134, and liii (1967), pp. 136–8. On the authors of the cantata texts, see Ferdinand Zander, 'Die Dichter der Kantatentexte Johann Sebastian Bachs: Untersuchungen zu ihrer Bestimmung', *Bach-Jahrbuch*, liv (1968), p. 9.

(5*b*) Solo cantatas for more than one voice (but ending with four-part chorales). BWV 13, 32, 57, 60, 81, 85, 86, 132, 151, 156, 159, 166, 167, 174, 188.

(6) Secular cantatas. BWV 198, 201, 202, 211, 212, 213, 214.

Not every movement in the listed cantatas is a masterpiece, but the level of invention and workmanship in these and in works not referred to here is on the whole astonishingly high; Bach unquestionably towers above all other composers of cantatas. Before embarkation on a detailed survey, two points (which also apply to similar works by other composers) should be emphasized. The cantatas were written primarily to illuminate the gospel of the day or occasionally to celebrate some municipal, political, or other secular event. And the chorale melodies and words which are used were so well known that simply to play the tunes on instruments would immediately bring the words to the listeners' minds.

BACH'S CHORALE CANTATAS

In his only example of chorale variations 'per omnes versus', 'Christ lag in Todesbanden', BWV 4 (1724),[1] Bach triumphed as no other composer did over the tendencies to tonal and thematic monotony inherent in this archaic form. He treats each of the seven verses of Luther's hymn distinctively. Although the chorale *canto fermo* is fully present in all of them, many vivid tone-pictures and an infinite variety of colours and textures within the narrow limits imposed by the setting of each verse in the tonic make this work one of the most moving of all the cantatas. Verse 1 is a chorale fantasia on a huge scale, and the voices here and in verses 2 and 7 are doubled by trombones; it finishes with a breathtaking 'Alleluia' in which the tempo is doubled and the long-note *canto fermo* abandoned in favour of a partly syncopated fugato on its last five notes. By contrast, verse 2 is a sombre duet for sopranos and altos, which underlines the text 'None could over death prevail' by means of poignant dissonances and a relentless *ostinato*. Verse 3 brings the even sharper contrast of a joyful trio for violins, tenor (who has the *canto fermo*), and continuo. Verse 4 is a four-part chorus with continuo (*canto fermo* in the alto), verse 5 an aria for bass in which the *canto fermo* is skilfully divided between the voice and first violin and in which there is an exceptional amount of word-painting. Verse 6 is a gigue for soprano, tenor, and continuo; the 'ambiguous' notation must be interpreted so that everything fits a 12/8 metre. The last verse is plainly but nobly harmonized.

[1] At any rate performed in Leipzig in that year. But Dürr (*Studien*, pp. 169 ff.) gives convincing arguments for an earlier date of composition: 1714 at latest and possibly as early as 1708.

Two other distinguished chorale cantatas date from 1724 and belong, like BWV 4, to the second 'cycle' for the church year; 'Nimm von uns, Herr, du treuer Gott', BWV 101, and 'Wer nur den lieben Gott lässt walten', BWV 93, have in common the somewhat unsatisfactory combination of free, moralizing recitative and *a tempo* chorale phrases in the same movements, two instances occurring in each. The examples in BWV 93 have extravagantly affective harmonies, figuration and tempo changes to interpret the words, perhaps to compensate for the lack of unity in the structure; those in BWV 101 are more restrained, but the chorale tune in the third verse is subjected to elaborate embellishment. The opening chorale fantasia in BWV 101, whose text prays for protection from war, pestilence, and famine, is more dissonant than anything else in the cantatas. The impression of modernity is fostered mainly by the use of a three-note chromatic appoggiatura figure, which is particularly strident when it is developed in the orchestral bass. The orchestra, apart from the doubling of the voices by the brass, is independent and consists of strings interlocking with three oboes:

Ex. 394

The *canto fermo* appears in instruments and voice in verse 4 (a bass aria with three oboes), a dramatic piece with many tempo changes. In verse 6 (a soprano and alto duet with flute and oboe da caccia) the melody is skilfully woven into both the instrumental and vocal lines, which, moreover, are charged with many arabesques. Both these verses are partly paraphrased. The soprano and alto duet in BWV 93 provides one of many, always effective instances in the cantatas of the playing of the *canto fermo* only in the middle of the texture; other examples include the soprano aria in BWV 31 and the alto aria in BWV 161.

BACH'S CANTATAS WITH INTERMITTENT CHORALES

These are the cantatas in the second category listed above. BWV 10, 80, 122, and 140 may be singled out as works that all have the chorales and free movements in some form of alternation, but they are vastly different in character. All the cantatas listed in this group here and above, with the exception of one or two movements in BWV 122, are of the highest quality. The seven-movement 'Meine Seel' erhebt den Herrn', BWV 10 (again 1724), is the German *Magnificat* already referred to in connection with Zachow's *Magnificat*;[1] verses 4–8 and the second half of verse 9 are colourfully paraphrased. This work presents many pictures inspired by individual words; these occur in quick succession in the tenor recitative 'Des Höchsten Güt und Treu' ('The highest's goodness and faithfulness') and, unusually, in the following bass aria, 'Gewaltige stösst Gott vom Stuhl' ('God casts down the mighty from their seat'), too. This aria is dominated by the continuo figure of the ritornello, which the opening sentence of the text explains:

Ex. 395

Over it the voice rapidly changes from tenderness for 'die Niedern' ('the humble') and cruelty for 'die Reichen' ('the rich'), whom God has left 'bloss und leer' ('destitute and empty'), to sympathetic chromaticism for 'die Hungrigen' ('the hungry'). The *Magnificat canto fermo* occurs three times: in the joyous opening movement (first in the soprano, then in the alto part); then trumpet and two oboes play it in unison in the

[1] Cf. *supra*, p. 738.

alto-tenor duet 'Er denket der Barmherzigkeit' ('He remembering his mercy'); and it is the melody of the closing, plainly harmonized chorale. The first movement is not a chorale fantasia; instead, voices and instruments develop throughout its course one or two figures independent of the *canto fermo*.

The great Reformation cantata 'Ein' feste Burg', BWV 80 (probably 1724, but partly based on an earlier work, BWV 80a, of 1716), uses Luther's tune and all four verses of the hymn, but words by the poet Salomon Franck are combined with Luther's second stanza and are freely set between the last three to provide necessary contrast to words and music of so stirring a character. Thus, for example, the gentle *siciliano* aria for soprano and continuo only, 'Komm in mein Herzens Haus' ('Come into my heart'):

Ex. 396

(Come into my heart, Lord Jesu, my longing.)

immediately precedes the fierce third stanza, 'Und wenn die Welt voll Teufel wär' ('And if the world were full of devils'), scored for three oboes, three trumpets, timpani, and strings, in which the chorale for S.A.T.B. in unison (the only example in all Bach's works of such writing throughout a movement) is combined with the first phrase of the *canto fermo* put into 6/8 time. The energy and astonishing resource with which the latter is developed throughout the 119 bars elevate the movement above all others of a similar character and purpose in the cantatas. The setting of verse 1 is a different sort of *tour de force*: an elaborately worked out 228-bar chorale fantasia of rather old-fashioned cast, for S.A.T.B., doubling instruments, and a free continuo is put into a gigantic framework consisting of a canon of the *canto fermo* between first trumpet (with oboes) and organ pedals (with 16-foot reed), strictly at a distance of one bar and at an interval of three octaves. In the chorale fantasia on 'Wachet auf', BWV 140, yet another work for the second cycle, antiphonal orchestral figures of an appropriately rousing character are independent of the voices. Between the chorale verses of this deservedly celebrated cantata come mystical love duets of great beauty such as evolved from the Hammerschmidt type of dialogue.

BWV 36, 95, and 127 each has its own peculiar structural features, both internal and external. For instance, in BWV 127, 'Herr Jesu Christ, wahr Mensch und Gott', for Quinquagesima 1725, Bach adopts an unusual type of fantasia: the first phrase of the chorale is seized upon as the idea that is to dominate not only the fugatos that precede or accompany each line of the text but practically every other bar of the movement too. In this fantasia another feature, subtle and also rare, is the introduction of the melody (without words) of another chorale suitable for the Sunday before Ash Wednesday, 'Christe du Lamm Gottes'; it is played by the orchestra in long notes from time to time during the movement. Apart from the plainly harmonized closing chorale, the *canto fermo* is nowhere else presented prominently, but in the bass recitative and aria 'Wenn einstens die Posaunen schallen' one of the two themes springs from it. The other idea in this movement provides one of the countless examples of Bach's power so to transform such conventionally affective figures as repeated semiquavers, quasi-tremolo, that they generate immense power and acquire a new significance.

BWV 95, 'Christus, der ist mein Leben' (1723), is one of the most beautiful of all the cantatas. Its form is original in that it contains stanzas from four different chorales, all bearing on the subject of death; these are separated by short recitatives and one long aria (the scoring of which is described below).[1] Each of the chorales is set simply. A gently syncopated figure, perhaps a death-lullaby, for orchestra accompanies the words of the first chorale, 'Christ, who is my life', whose second line is poignantly set:

[1] Cf. *infra*, p. 763.

Ex. 397

(Death is my reward.)

This figure, in triple time, punctuates each phrase of the recitative that immediately follows; as the recitative is by tradition in quadruple time, this makes some musical sentences of odd length. Next comes 'Mit

Fried' und Freud ich fahr dahin' ('In peace and joy I depart')—Luther's free versification of the *Nunc dimittis*—in which instruments (horn and two oboes in unison) treat the tune canonically in the manner of a chorale fantasia before each homophonic entry of the chorus. The vocal

Ex. 398

(i)

(Farewell will I give thee, thou wicked, false world.)

(ii)

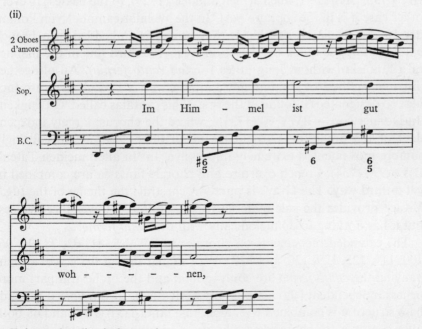

(It is good to live in heaven.)

49

lines are doubled by wind and lower strings, while first violins climb above the melody with a descant in which telling suspensions play a large part. A soprano recitative with a free text, having reproved the world for its falseness, after seventeen bars takes a wistful leave of it in the third chorale, 'Valet will ich dir geben' ('Farewell will I give thee'), set in triple time with continuo and an obbligato for two oboes d'amore. Here again is a very simple texture but also much colour; the opening and a later characteristic turn of harmony and embellishment of the melody are shown in Ex. 398.

The cantata closes with a fourth chorale, 'Weil du vom Tod erstanden bist' ('Because thou hast risen from the dead'), which is the fourth verse of 'Wenn mein Stündlein vorhanden ist' ('When my last hour is nigh'). This is harmonized plainly, but again the first violin is independent, perhaps representing the soul hovering over the body. Bach never seemed able to resist such treatment of these words and tune: there is another version in the last movement of BWV 31.

BACH'S CANTATAS INCLUDING CHORALE FANTASIAS

In all the cantatas listed above as class 3(a), except BWV 21 and 23, the chorale fantasia is the opening movement. In BWV 96, 'Herr Christ, der ein'ge Gottes-Sohn' (1724), the *canto fermo* is given to the altos, in BWV 21, 'Ich hatte viel Bekümmernis' (1723), to the tenors, and in BWV 135, 'Ach Herr, mich armen Sünder' (1724), to the basses; in every other case it is in the soprano part. In the Weimar cantata 'Nun komm, der Heiden Heiland', BWV 61, the chorale is embedded in a French *ouverture*, whose quick fugal section treats the third line in the manner of a fantasia (without long notes for the *canto fermo*). An altogether different method of combining a fantasia with a French overture (not here so designated) is found in the first of his cantatas called 'O Ewigkeit, du Donnerwort'—BWV 60 (1723)—where the chorus, largely independent of the orchestra, participates in all three sections; this fittingly sombre movement is extremely impressive. In 'In allen meinen Taten', BWV 97 (1734), French overture and chorale fantasia are combined in yet a third way. The Grave is purely orchestral; the theme of the fugal Vivace provides the sole material for the imitative lower three voices, but it has nothing to do melodically with the *canto fermo*.

The extended movements on chorales in BWV 5, 41, 62, 78, 91, 96, 100, 115, 125, 129, 130, and 135 are all similar in that the voices accompanying the *canto fermo* are contrapuntal and the orchestral part more or less independent (though possibly derivative). In BWV 78 a groundbass structure is combined with a chorale fantasia. BWV 8 and 68 both offer examples of chorales simply harmonized with an orchestral part developing independent ideas (as does BWV 113 among the chorale cantatas in the first category). BWV 5, 8, 20, 41, 61, 68, 78, 114, 115, 116, 130, and 135 are exceptionally well conceived throughout both as regards music and for consistently logical thought in the text. As an illustration let us consider 'Wo soll ich fliehen hin', BWV 5 (1724). The text is based on stanzas and paraphrases of Johann Heermann's hymn of the same title dating from 1630. The theme—the efficacy of even one drop of Jesus's blood to take away sin—is pursued consistently from the agitated first stanza to the confident prayer of the last one. Both text and music present the greatest possible variety. The fantasia is dominated by a four-note theme of repeated quavers deriving from the first, second, and third phrases of the *canto fermo* (the second is an inversion of the first). It is rich in instrumental themes, which are developed on the ritornello principle. The bass recitative that follows speaks of redemption through blood, leading logically to a beautiful aria for tenor with viola obbligato (the only one in the cantatas) in which voice and instruments develop the same theme—appropriately a flowing one:

Ex. 399

(Flow fully over me, thou heavenly spring.)

An alto recitative with oboe playing the *canto fermo* speaks mainly of comfort; the declamation is as free and expressive as if the fetters of the chorale were not present. A violent change of mood comes with the Vivace bass aria 'Verstumme, Höllenheer, du machst mich nicht verzagt!', which has a brilliant trumpet obbligato:

Ex. 400 (i)

(ii)

len - heer, ver - stum-me,   ver - stum-me,

(Be silent, host of hell.)

Yet this is merely another aspect of the same idea, for the third line of the text proclaims that the one drop of Christ's blood will immediately silence the forces of darkness. Musically this virtuoso aria provides the perfect contrast to what has gone before. A soprano recitative and plain chorale quickly bring the work to a conclusion.

Similarly satisfying are the musical structure and content of the early Advent cantata 'Nun komm, der Heiden Heiland', BWV 61, referred to above. Neumeister's text uses two chorales and a passage from the Bible. The French-overture setting of verse 1 of Luther's hymn is one of the most tightly symmetrical of forms as here adapted by Bach. The free texts which follow develop the various aspects of the coming of the Saviour. A tenor aria with obbligato violins and violas in unison sets 'Komm, Jesu, komm zu deine Kirche' ('Come, Jesu, come to thy church') in a gentle, slow 9/8, fittingly appealing in quality. The beauty of its seemingly endless melody derives in part from the subtle manner in which the dominant chord is prolonged and the final cadence postponed. A more personal approach to Advent is found in the simple yet highly ornamented soprano aria with continuo, 'Öffne dich mein Herz' ('Open thou my heart'), but before this comes the famous bass recitative ('Siehe, siehe! Ich stehe vor der Tür und klopfe an' ('Behold, I stand at the door and knock'), whose effect is enhanced by the staccato melisma on 'knock' and by the pizzicato treatment of the strings throughout. This concise and perfectly constructed cantata finishes aptly with the second half of the seventh verse of the chorale 'Wie schön leuchtet': 'Amen, komm, du schöne Freudenkrone' ('Amen, come, thou lovely crown of joy').

Although the text structure of BWV 78, the powerfully dramatic

'Jesu, der du meine Seele' (1724),[1] based on Rist's hymn of 1641, is similar to that of BWV 5, there are very strong emotional contrasts between the movements. Again, the use of a hymn, although partly paraphrased, gives the work structural coherence. The opening chorale fantasia has as the bass of its four-bar ritornello a chromatically descending ground-bass theme frequently found in baroque music (see the oboe parts in Ex. 401 below). The movement is virtually a chaconne, into which all the normal features of a fantasia are woven to create music of enormous power. The chromatic theme always forms the bass, vocal and instrumental, to the *canto fermo* in the soprano; it also appears in imitative counterpoint, inverted or otherwise, separating phrases of the *canto fermo*. It is particularly striking in its appearances in the middle of the orchestral texture and most of all when in stretto over a pedal:

Ex. 401

[1] See Joseph Kerman, *Opera as Drama* (New York, 1959), pp. 65–70.

The ensuing duet for soprano, alto, and continuo, 'Wir eilen mit schwachen, doch emsigen Schritten' ('We hasten with weak yet eager footsteps'), a charming Italianate piece with perpetual arco quavers on the cello and almost perpetual pizzicato crotchets on the violone depicting the hastening footsteps, could hardly stand in greater contrast to the chorus:

Ex. 402

(We hasten with weak yet eager footsteps, O Jesu, O Master.)

The recitatives for tenor (*secco*) and bass (*accompagnato*) both plumb the depths of grief in wide-flung modulations; the latter is more dramatic and leads to an arioso of exceptional beauty. The two solo arias stand in contrast to each other: the first, for tenor, flute, and pizzicato continuo, is, despite its limited resources, dramatic through the use of syncopation and quasi-*ostinato*; in the second, for bass, oboe, and strings, the concertante (oboe) and tutti features of the ritornello form are much in evidence. The cantata closes with a plain chorale that quotes the hymn text again.

BACH'S CANTATAS INCLUDING MOTET-LIKE CHORUSES

The type of chorus found in the cantatas of group 3(*b*) descends directly from the Renaissance motet in that there is a continuous web of polyphony consisting of fugatos on each successive line of the *canto fermo*. As in the Pachelbel type of organ chorale prelude, the highest voice does not participate in the imitation but has the *canto fermo* in long notes. Instruments, including brass, double the voices, but the continuo may be independent. All the motet choruses are of a very high order. That in 'Aus tiefer Noth', BWV 38 (1724), is characteristic: the chromaticisms and mounting syncopated suspensions which at times accompany the *canto fermo* express intense grief for sin and plead eloquently for forgiveness.

BACH'S FREE CANTATAS

The cantatas in group 4, whose choruses are not tied to a chorale *canto fermo*, vary much in form. Some kind of ritornello structure is evident in many of them (as well as in the arias). Often the bigger choruses combine this principle with fugue (the largest example of this in Bach is the opening movement of the Mass in B minor). Others, fewer in number, are purely fugal; they include the splendid double chorus 'Nun ist das Heil und die Kraft', which is all that survives of BWV 50.[1] BWV 105 provides another splendid example, as does BWV 67 of the first type. Considered as wholes, these cantatas are on a high level, and their solo movements provide good examples of the types of structure common by the first half of the eighteenth century. The opening movement of BWV 67, the Easter cantata 'Halt im Gedächtnis Jesum Christ' (1724), provides an interesting example of the transference of concerto form to church cantata; in fact the two main ideas in it correspond to the ritornello and concertante respectively. The formal scheme is as follows:

[1] Recorded in *The History of Music in Sound*, v.

Bars:	1–33	34–55	55–91	92–114	114–30
	Ritornello	Concertante	Ritornello	Concertante	Ritornello
	A1	B1	A2	B2	A3
	a – b1 – b2	Fugal exposition on new material plus A	a-link-b2 link-b1	Repetition of bars 41–55 modified at 10th bar ; extension by repetition for further 8 bars	a Repetition of bars 1–17
Keys:	I–V–V of V	I–VII minor	VII minor V–VI minor I–II minor	I–VI–I	I

In A and A3 there is an early turn towards the dominant key which is quickly contradicted; there is a corresponding move to V of V in A2. Aa is purely orchestral:

Ex. 403

Abl adds chorus, Ab2 shows an interchange of the voice parts of Abl. In A3 voices are added, mostly doubling orchestral lines. B is a fugue, with two genuine counter-subjects, on the main theme of A, the horn melody of Ex. 403, now set to 'Halt im Gedächtnis Jesum Christ' ('Hold in remembrance Jesus Christ'). B1 is accompanied only by continuo; B2 has doubling instruments and shows interchanges of the material in its last eight bars.

In the following tenor aria, 'Mein Jesus ist erstanden, allein was schreckt mich noch?' ('Jesus is risen, what can affright me now?'), 'erstanden' ('risen') and 'schreckt' ('affright') inspire different but complementary ideas, which are incorporated in a ritornello of six bars; this ritornello undergoes constant development to depict contrasts of mood, but it is never repeated in its entirety until the end. Much more clear-cut is the form of the aria (with chorus) 'Friede sei mit euch' ('Peace be unto you'), which is really a scena, in which Jesus breaks in suddenly with these words on the hubbub of the disciples' anxious chatter in the Upper Room on the Sunday after the first Easter Day. The form is:

Bars:	1–9	10–25		28–36	37–52	
	A1	B1		A2	B2	
	Orchestra (strings)	Solo voice and orchestra (woodwind)	2-bar link	A repeated with voices S.A.T. added	Solo voice and woodwind, repetition of 10–25 modified at 9th bar	4-bar link to IV
Keys:	I	I–V		I	I–VI	
Bars:	57–65	66–81		86–94	95–111	
	A3	B3		A4	B4	
	A repeated in IV, voices modified	Repetition of 10–25 in IV, modified at 8th bar to finish in III minor	4-bar link in which B is combined with A (voices and instruments)	Repetition of A, in I with voices added	Repetition in I of 10–25 altered at 9th bar to finish in I. Strings now double woodwind	

At the entrance of the solo voice 'the world and all its woes sink out of sight . . . in vain does the world rage round them again; [the disciples] sing through it all . . . "It is well with us; Jesus fights for us . . ." '.[1]

---

[1] Schweitzer, op. cit., p. 573; Eng. ed., ii, p. 192.

The first chorus of BWV 105, 'Herr, gehe nicht ins Gericht' (1723)—
'Lord, sit not in judgement on thy servant'—is in two sections, Adagio
and Allegro, it resembles a tightly-knit prelude and fugue and is full of
canonic devices. The Adagio is built on a ritornello establishing the
mood of the opening words. It consists of an orchestral section (eight-
and-a-half bars) and a related choral section (six-and-a-half bars, overlapping with the first eight-and-a-half); in the first four bars the two
highest parts are strictly canonic, and the vocal setting is also so closely
imitative as to give the effect of canon. The structural scheme is shown
below:

Bars
A1   1–9   orchestral ritornello in tonic
B1   9–15   choral fugato (new theme) leading to dominant chord
A2 15–23   orchestral ritornello (in dominant) with upper (canonic)
             parts interchanged
B2 23–29   choral fugato (still in the dominant) with parts inter-
             changed; orchestra independent with material derived
             from the vocal theme
B3 29–33   derivative link into which (bar 31) the choral fugato
             breaks, in the relative major
      34–42   A3+B3 continued; orchestral ritornello (as bars 1–9 in
             top—canonic—parts; modifications in viola and continuo)
             with development of vocal fugato, finishing with half-close
             on the dominant
      42–47   derivative orchestral canonic passage over a dominant pedal

An agitated fugue immediately follows, breaking in on the cadence. The
subject has three counter-subjects, making quadruple counterpoint,
which is used consistently until the closing few bars. The exposition
(voices and continuo only) is immediately followed by a full second
exposition doubled by orchestra, making eight appearances of the
subject and answer in strict succession. Then comes a six-bar episode
in the tonic followed by the subject (sopranos) and answer (altos) still
in tonic and dominant, presenting the quadruple counterpoint in yet
another interchange of position, which leads to a dramatic double echo,
with the subject in related keys. From this point onwards, one of the
voices breaks away from the quadruple counterpoint and freely develops
an idea from the second counter-subject. A two-bar episode, followed by
the subject (basses) in the tonic, a three-bar episode, and a final entry
(also basses) starting in the subdominant bring this most symmetrical
of movements to a conclusion. Throughout, the continuo is occasionally
independent, making a fifth voice.

The unfolding of the rest of the cantata affords wonderfully diverse examples of Bach's skill and imagination; it too is worth describing in detail as representing him at his finest. The mood of agitation continues in the next two numbers. The alto recitative even begins with a discord:

Ex. 404

(My God, cast me not away from thy presence, who bends before thee in humility.)

The soprano aria, no. 3, dispenses with continuo altogether, perhaps to reflect the lack of support that the text suggests: 'Wie zittern und wanken der Sünder Gedanken' ('How the sinner's thoughts tremble and totter'). The obbligato part, which is probably for oboe (no instrument is named), 'reels about above the quavering figures in the strings'.[1] This movement, which is particularly rich in thematic material and whose rhythm, harmony, declamation, and original texture give it extraordinary poignancy, is one of Bach's most sublime inventions:

Ex. 405

[1] Ibid., p. 571; Eng. ed., ii, p. 189.

The mood of the cantata changes with the accompanied recitative for bass, 'Wohl dem, der seinen Bürgen weiss' ('It is well for him who knows his surety'). Here tolling bells are heard in the perpetual pizzicato quavers of the continuo—a recurring feature in Bach, which nearly always suggests happiness or peace; three-part string chords in sixths flow comfortingly through the first half, but later the first violin manages to 'paint' several words without materially changing the shape of the opening theme. The exuberant *da capo* tenor aria 'Kann ich nur Jesum mir zum Freunde machen' ('If I only make Jesus my friend'), scored for horn and strings, makes extensive use of its eight-bar ritornello. In the closing chorale the thoughts of the whole work are recapitulated by the provision, unique in Bach, of a constantly varying type of rhythm in the independent accompaniment. This begins with throbbing semiquavers and, as the mood changes to one of confident hope, gradually slows down to peaceful crotchets in the last line.

BACH'S SOLO CANTATAS

These cantatas, and the secular cantatas too, include formal structures similar to those already described. The only surviving authentic cantata for tenor, 'Ich armer Mensch', BWV 55 (1726), has an exceptionally high tessitura; though little known, it is fully equal to the popular and very fine solo bass works 'Ich will den Kreuzstab', BWV 56 (dating from a month earlier), and 'Ich habe genug', BWV 82 (1727), and the soprano cantata with trumpet and strings, 'Jauchzet Gott', BWV 51 (1730). The opening of the alto cantata, 'Vergnügte Ruh'', BWV 170 (1726), shows Bach's melodic invention at its most sublime:

Ex. 406

(Contented rest, the soul's delight . . .)

and the first aria in BWV 54, 'Widerstehe doch der Sünde', is hardly less fine. Of the cantatas for more than one voice, 'Meine Seufzer, meine Tränen', BWV 13, includes two superb arias, for tenor (Ex. 407) and bass respectively:

Ex. 407

nicht zu zäh - len sein,

mei - ne

Seuf - zer, mei - ne Thrä - nen

(My sighs, my tears cannot be numbered.)

BACH'S SECULAR CANTATAS

Just as Bach's solo cantatas differ from his choral ones mainly by virtue of their smaller forces so do the handful of secular cantatas differ from the church cantatas mainly in the nature and purpose of the texts. (Although they properly belong not to this chapter but in Vol. VI, they can be most conveniently discussed here.) However, Bach's apparent custom of using the harpsichord as continuo in secular music and the organ for church music does provide a further practical distinction: the scoring of such a work as the great *Trauerode* for Queen Christiane Eberhardine of Poland, 'Lass, Fürstin, lass noch einen Strahl', BWV 198 (1727), in which two lutes are added to the continuo line, demonstrates this. As already mentioned,[1] several numbers from this funeral ode were used four years later for the now lost St. Mark Passion. No exception can be taken to any of the transferences whose music has survived: for instance, the text of the opening movement of BWV 198 asks the queen to let a beam of light shoot from Salem's starry vaults and to 'see how we with torrents of tears weep at thy memorial'; in the Passion the music for this bids Jesus 'go to thy agony, I will weep long for thee'. The similarity of emotion is almost as close between no. 3 of the ode and no. 49 of the Passion, and in the final movements the underlying mood of the outwardly different words is parallel enough for a seraphic *siciliano* to be perfectly fitting in both cases. The fourth movement of the *Trauerode* is the greatest of all Bach's 'death-knell' movements. The normal string band is enlarged by two gambas pizzicato and the two lutes already mentioned; to these are added two flutes, playing repeated notes, and two oboes, playing sustained notes. Bach produces the effect of a carillon starting with the smallest and finishing with the largest bell, and in the course of the movement's eleven bars some remarkable modulations also take place. There is no consistency of thought in this work, as there is in most of the church cantatas, and no quasi-operatic music as in some of the other secular ones (and indeed in the church cantatas); instead, various aspects of the queen's goodness and how she is mourned are expressed in music that is varied in style, colour, and texture.

The wedding cantata 'Weichet nur', BWV 202, for soprano solo, oboe, and strings, dating perhaps from Bach's years in Cöthen, is fervent and gay. The text is compact, with alternating recitatives and arias, and offers many charming ideas—relating to the countryside, the pleasures of love, and so on—which he sets to music of consistently high quality. At least half-a-dozen of the other secular cantatas would lend themselves well to stage production, for the music is often pointedly and wittily dramatic; such works include 'Schweigt stille, plaudert nicht',

[1] Cf. *supra*, p. 653.

BWV 211 (*c.* 1735; the so-called 'Coffee' Cantata), and 'Zerreisset, zersprenget, zertrümmert die Gruft', BWV 205 (1725), a real *dramma per musica*, written to celebrate a professor's birthday.

BACH'S CANTATAS: ORCHESTRATION AND TEXTURES

The originality of the instrumentation in Bach's cantatas[1] is such that they include sounds that have almost certainly not been produced by any other composer before or since; and there are countless other movements where the colours are unusual and are used with a new expressiveness.

In the eighteenth century orchestration was, as often at other times, based on associations; the difference in Bach's time was that these were systematized according to the doctrine of affections. The most memorable of his orchestral sounds are associated with death and involve the use of pizzicato. BWV 8, no. 1, has two wailing oboes, strings pizzicato, and a flute playing mainly quick high repeated notes, illustrating a text that asks when the hour of death will come; the haunting quality of this movement derives from all the elements used, but especially from the harmony and spacing. BWV 95, no. 5, likewise has strings pizzicato and two oboes d'amore, but there is no flute, and here the first violins suggest the ticking of a clock (which occasionally stops) by means of continuous semiquavers against a pattern of quavers and crotchets in other instruments: the text is 'Ach, schlage doch bald' ('Strike soon, blessed hour of death'). BWV 33, no. 3, has muted violins incessantly playing a single figure, with lower strings pizzicato.

Remarkable effects not using pizzicato include BWV 122, no. 3, where the brilliance of a soprano and three recorders (playing a Christmas chorale in three-part harmony) high above the continuo seems to fill the firmament with sound in accordance with the words of the text, and BWV 13, no. 5, where a solo violin and recorder in unison create a strangely plaintive effect. The third movement of the Michaelmas cantata, BWV 130, is one of several scored for trumpets, timpani and continuo alone (the others include BWV 119, no. 4, and BWV 172, no. 3); this aria, for bass, is a horrific picture of the 'old dragon' (Satan), burning with jealousy and devising new evils, but the same instrumentation in BWV 119 and 172 is used to represent municipal and divine power respectively.

Several features distinguish Bach's 'plain' harmonization of chorales from those of his contemporaries.[2] These include (*i*) the resonance

---

[1] See Terry, *Bach's Orchestra* (repr. London, 1958), *passim*.
[2] See Marshall, 'How J. S. Bach composed four-part chorales', *Musical Quarterly*, lvi (1970), p. 198.

achieved by scoring for the two middle voices high and close to the soprano's *canto fermo* line—often the tenors move with the top line in parallel sixths, with the alto in parallel thirds, a kind of writing that also produces harmonic richness in many other types of movement; (*ii*) the high proportion of stepwise movement, which makes possible (*iii*) an exceptional amount of passing dissonance; (*iv*) the careful preparation of all suspended discords; and (*v*) chromaticism, almost always arising from the text and always with a strong tonal purpose.

In taking over the Italian aria, Bach often made it a vehicle for counterpoint. There are, admittedly, a number of continuo arias and some with only one obbligato strand, and there are many in which homophony plays an important part. But probably the most characteristic type of aria is that in which voice, continuo, and obbligato instrument pursue a polyphonic texture closely related to the trio sonata, the three-part invention, and the fugue: that is, they employ to a greater or lesser extent the invertible counterpoint that is so prominent a feature of Bach's entire output from the simplest two-part pieces to large-scale choruses.

GRAUPNER, TELEMANN, AND OTHERS

There are a number of cantatas by Johann Ludwig Bach, a cousin of Johann Sebastian's who worked in Meiningen; eleven of them were copied out by J. S. Bach,[1] and seventeen or eighteen were performed by him in Leipzig in 1726. They are in the modern 'reform' style. As Karl Geiringer says:[2] '[This] is vigorous music, full of strength and inspiration, rich in variety and imbued with sensuous pleasure in tonal beauty. The treatment of the voices, particularly in the solo numbers, reveals a composer who has studied Italian models (for which the performances at the Meiningen court offered ample opportunities)'. This last feature is plainly seen in the soprano aria of 'Denn du wirst meine Seele', formerly attributed to J. S. Bach as BWV 15,[3] the common ancestry with Purcell giving it a turn of phrase that is in places strangely like the latter's music (see Ex. 408).

Outside his own family the leading composers of cantatas contemporary with Bach were Graupner and Telemann. Both were extremely prolific, highly esteemed in their own day, and preferred to Bach when the cantorship at St. Thomas's, Leipzig, became vacant on Kuhnau's death in 1722. Because of its sheer quantity, the output of both is

---

[1] See William H. Scheide, 'Johann Sebastian Bachs Sammlung von Kantaten seines Vetters Johann Ludwig Bach', *Bach-Jahrbuch*, xlvi (1959), p. 52, xlviii (1961), p. 5, and xlix (1962), p. 5.

[2] Geiringer, *The Bach Family* (London, 1954), p. 109.

[3] And published in J. S. Bach, *Werke*, ii, p. 135.

Ex. 408

(Up, rejoice my soul, thou art comforted, thy saviour has redeemed thee from death.)

inevitably uneven, but there are a number of distinguished cantatas by both. Christoph Graupner (1683–1760), who spent most of his life at Darmstadt, was an almost exact contemporary of Bach, whom he resembles in the form and sometimes the musical language of his cantatas, as can be seen from this representative excerpt from 'Die Krankheit, so mich drückt':[1]

Ex. 409

[1] Graupner, *17 äusgewählte Kantaten*, ed. Friedrich Noack, *Denkmäler deutscher Tonkunst*, li-lii (Leipzig, 1926), p. 1. Two cantatas also ed. idem (Darmstadt and Berlin, 1955). Among several writings by Noack see in particular *Christian Graupners Kirchenmusiken* (Leipzig, 1916).

(Break forth, O happy sea of tears.)

This extract is a good illustration of Graupner's rich melodic invention, which, with his rhythmic energy, is his most conspicuous quality. His recitatives often rise above the merely conventional and are at their best when most emotional, as in this one from 'Ach Gott und Herr':[1]

Ex. 410

[1] Graupner, *17 ausgewählte Kantaten*, p. 16.

ist nicht wei-ter mein. O Don-ner-wort,

O Her-zens-schlag, O Sün-den-angst,

O Jam-mer-tag! Wie werd ich doch be-steh'n?

(tacent)

Ich kann vor Schmerz_____ nichts wei-ter

spre-chen, die Wor-te sind ge-bro — — — chen,

und ich muss ver-geh'n.

(The soul feels the pains of hell: God is no longer mine. Oh word of terror, oh heartbeat, oh anguish of sin, oh day of lamentation. How shall I endure? Because of my pain I can speak no more, words are broken, and I must pass away.)

Graupner's favourite type of choral movement is the figured chorale, in which the choral parts are relatively simple and there is a consistent figure—often a *moto perpetuo*—in the orchestra. These movements, however, do not show Graupner at his best. For that we must turn to the chorale fantasias. 'O Mensch, wie ist dein Herz bestellt?',[1] for example, contains two, both on a big scale, besides a figured chorale at the end. The first is chromatic and in the form of an organ prelude. The second treats another chorale in an unusual way. It opens with a charming instrumental pastoral for strings and oboes, which provides material for the first vocal section; after this the non-derivative counterpoint is developed dramatically, and the instruments are entirely *colla parte*. This cantata also contains a powerful chorus whose effect is unusual because the four voices are in only two parts, sopranos with tenor and first violin parts, altos with bass and second violin parts, while viola and continuo are independent. 'Ihr Frommen richtet euch empor',[2] written in 1725, graphically describes the Day of Judgement by employing two texts simultaneously, each with their respective musical themes. Sopranos I and II and basses are the Saved—'O froher Ton, der uns zum Segen schallt!' ('O joyful sound, which peals for our blessing!'); altos and tenors I and II are the Damned—'Ihr Berge fallt, ach fallt, uns zu bedecken; O Angst, O Not, wer mag bestehen?' ('Ye mountains fall, ah, fall and cover us; O anguish, O misery, who can withstand you?'). It is interesting to compare this movement with Telemann's oratorio *Der Tag des Gerichts*[3] (1762), especially with the first chorus of Part II: Telemann does not allow the Wicked and the Righteous to appear together in the same movement (except in one recitative, and there they are juxtaposed, not combined). Graupner's imagination is perhaps seen at its best when he is not experimenting, as in the deeply expressive tenor aria that opens 'Es begab sich, dass Jesu in eine Stadt . . .',[4] with its

[1] Ibid., p. 123.
[2] Ibid., p. 77.
[3] Ed. Schneider, *Denkmäler deutscher Tonkunst*, xxviii (Leipzig, 1907), p. 1.
[4] Graupner, *17 ausgewählte Kantaten*, p. 198.

throbbing bass and bold modulations, or the opening chorus and duet (no. 3) of 'Ach stirb mein Herz'.[1]

Telemann's vocal writing has a Handelian strength emanating from rising sequences of runs and from melodies with a wide range. He excels in arias of a joyous or a dramatic nature. The choruses of his cantatas are mainly homophonic, and the textures here as well as in his arias are thin and bright. He does not overwork ideas that are in themselves not always very imaginative, but there are perhaps too many full *da capo* arias. However, his cantatas, which run to twelve cycles for the whole of the church's year, are—especially considering their quantity—generally of an extraordinarily high quality. The set of seventy-two solo works, published in 1725–6 as *Der Harmonische Gottesdienst*,[2] deserves close study and more than occasional performances, as a glance at the following movements will show: no. 1, final aria; no. 5, first aria; no. 64, first two arias (the first is quoted in Ex. 411); and no. 65, first aria, are examples of bright, energetic music.[3]

Ex. 411

[1] Ibid., p. 216.

[2] Ed. Gustav Fock, *Georg Philipp Telemann: Musikalische Werke*, ii–v (Kassel and Basle, 1953–7). For details of other modern editions of cantatas by Telemann see the excellent list in *Die Musik in Geschichte und Gegenwart*, xiii (1966), cols. 206–7. Four cantatas by Telemann were formerly attributed to Bach and appear as such in the latter's *Werke*, BWV 141, 160, 218, and 219.

[3] *Musikalische Werke*, ii, pp. 5 and 41, and v, pp. 520, 527, and 532 respectively.

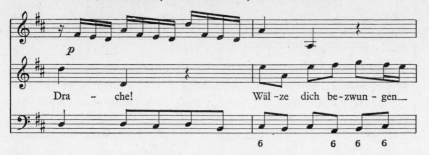

Dra — che! Wäl - ze dich be - zwun - gen__

fort, wäl — — — — — —

- ze dich, ge - lähm - ter Dra - che, wäl - ze dich be -

(Be gone, wounded dragon, heave thyself away!)

The last aria in no. 2 shows the same sort of energy combined with violently affective features; the first aria in no. 6 is an idyllic *siciliano*:

Ex. 412

(No, let thy patience, thy silence, incline me too to holy gentleness.)

and the first aria in no. 12 is a fine example of a more expressive type of movement.[1] Telemann's recitatives are fairly conventional, but he frequently shows his love of realism.

From among the choral cantatas, 'Gott sei mir gnädig'[2] is a typical reform-style work with a text whose contrasted moods are well reflected in the music, though it is in fact compounded of two originally separate works. The opening chorus is a concise, uneventful chorale fantasia of the Pachelbel type, faithfully setting a penitential text; the following soprano aria is a heartfelt cry for mercy in which a stepwise vocal part is accompanied by an incessant dotted-quaver pattern in the continuo, while violins pursue an independent line. After a *secco* recitative for bass, whose text is despairing and whose music only just falls short of fully expressing it:

Ex. 413

[1] Ibid., ii, pp. 15, 48, and 98 respectively.   [2] Ed. Fedtke (Stuttgart, 1963).

-damm-nis fort. Die Er-de möch-te wohl

mich zu verschlingen brech-en. Der Him-mel ist zu rein und

nimmt kein un-rein Her-ze ein.

(I have no comfort or counsel. My crime plagues me. Who will free and redeem me from the Evil One? The devil lurks in wait for a word that shall speak thy righteous wrath and send me to damnation. The earth would doubtless willingly open to swallow me up. Heaven is too pure and cannot accept an impure heart.)

there comes an exuberant soprano aria, much of which is in three parts only. The only other noteworthy feature is the alto recitative-arioso, during the course of which the words and tune of three lines of the chorale 'Was Gott tut, das ist wohlgetan' are quoted. At the end Telemann favours, as always, a very plain chorale harmonization. 'Machet die Tore weit'[1] which is found in Bach's handwriting, employs unusually full textures (violin I, viola I and II, two oboes—sometimes independent—and continuo). In the first movement, a powerful setting of four verses from Psalm 24, with the form A–B–A–C, the nineteen-bar quasi tremolando in section B for the strings which accompanies 'Er ist der Herr, stark und mächtig im Streit' ('It is the Lord, strong and mighty in battle') is particularly noteworthy. These German works show a more imaginative side of the composer than does, for example, the well-known Latin setting of Psalm 117,[2] which is somewhat foursquare, though not without charm.

There are some two dozen cantatas by Keiser, the solo cantatas among which are distinguished by bright textures and shapely melodies;

[1] Ed. idem (Stuttgart, 1963).　　　　　　　[2] Ed. Erich Valentin (Kassel, 1936).

and there are two notable ones by the minor composer Gottfried Kirchhoff (1685–1746),[1] who succeeded his teacher Zachow at Halle in 1713. There are also imaginative things in the cantatas of Johann Gottlieb Goldberg (1727–56),[2] a pupil of Bach, who wrote the Goldberg Variations for him to play. Other minor composers of cantatas at this period include Johann Friedrich Fasch (1688–1758),[3] Christoph Frauenholtz (1684–1754), Stölzel[4] and, perhaps the most interesting in this field, Christoph Förster (1693–1745), whose cantatas share with Telemann's a certain Handelian exuberance. But there can be no doubt that their cantatas, like those of all the other composers mentioned here, including Graupner and Telemann, are overshadowed by the tremendous achievement of J. S. Bach.

---

[1] *Gottfried Kirchhoff und Johann Gottlieb Goldberg: Kantaten*, ed. Dürr, *Das Erbe deutscher Musik*, xxxv (Kassel and Basle, 1957), pp. 1–20.

[2] Ibid., pp. 21–120.

[3] 'Siehe, dass deine Gottesfurcht', ed. A. Egidi (Berlin, 1930).

[4] Modern editions of cantatas by Stölzel include 'Liebster Jesu, deine Liebe', ed. J. Bachmair (Leipzig, 1926), 'Aus der Tiefe', ed. Adrio (Berlin, 2nd ed., 1957), and 'Kündlich gross ist das gottselige Geheimnis', ed. Hans Albrecht (Lippstadt, 1953).

BIBLIOGRAPHY

The bibliographies for Chapters III, IV, and VII have been compiled by James R. Anthony, for Chapter VIII by Peter Dennison, and for Chapter IX by Frederick Hudson; those for the other chapters have been compiled by the authors.

GENERAL

(i) *Modern Anthologies*

ABERT, ANNA AMALIE: *Die Oper: von den Anfängen bis zum Beginn des 19. Jahrhunderts* (*Das Musikwerk*, v) (Cologne, 1953; English ed., 1962).

DAVISON, ARCHIBALD T. and APEL, WILLI: *Historical Anthology of Music,* ii (Cambridge, Mass., 1950).

FERAND, ERNEST T.: *Die Improvisation in Beispielen aus neun Jahrhunderten abendländischer Musik* (*Das Musikwerk*, xii) (Cologne, 1956; English ed., 1961).

PARRISH, CARL: *A Treasury of Early Music* (New York, 1958).

PARRISH, CARL and OHL, JOHN F.: *Masterpieces of Music before 1750* (New York, 1951).

SCHERING, ARNOLD: *Geschichte der Musik in Beispielen* (2nd ed., Leipzig, 1955).

WOLFF, HELLMUTH CHRISTIAN: *Die Oper, I: Anfänge bis 17. Jahrhundert; II: 18. Jahrhundert* (*Das Musikwerk*, xxxviii–xxxix) (Cologne, 1971).

——*Originale Gesangsimprovisation des 16. bis 18. Jahrhunderts* (*Das Musikwerk*, xli) (Cologne, 1972).

(ii) *Books and Articles*

AMBROS, A. W.: *Geschichte der Musik,* iv, ed. H. Leichtentritt (Leipzig, 1909).

BROSSARD, SÉBASTIEN DE: *Dictionnaire de musique* (Paris, 1703; repr. Amsterdam, 1964).

BUKOFZER, MANFRED F.: *Music in the Baroque Era* (New York, 1947).

BURNEY, CHARLES: *A General History of Music,* 4 vols. (London, 1776–89); ed. F. Mercer, 2 vols. (London, 1935; repr. New York, 1957).

CARSE, ADAM: *The History of Orchestration* (London, 1925; repr. New York, 1964).

——*The Orchestra in the XVIIIth Century* (Cambridge, 1940; repr. 1950).

CLERCX, SUZANNE: *Le Baroque et la musique* (Brussels, 1948).

DAVAL, PIERRE: *La Musique en France au XVIIIe siècle* (Paris, 1961).

GREGOR, JOSEPH: *Kulturgeschichte der Oper* (Vienna, 1941).

GROUT, DONALD J.: *A Short History of Opera* (2nd ed., New York, 1965).

HAAS, ROBERT: *Aufführungspraxis der Musik* (Potsdam, 1931).

——*Die Musik des Barocks* (Potsdam, 1928).

HAWKINS, SIR JOHN: *A General History of the Science and Practice of Music,* 5 vols. (London, 1776); 2nd ed., 2 vols. (London, 1853; repr. New York, 1963).

KRETZSCHMAR, HERMANN: *Geschichte der Oper* (Leipzig, 1919).

LANG, PAUL HENRY: *Music in Western Civilization* (New York, 1941).

LOEWENBERG, ALFRED: *Annals of Opera* (2nd ed., Geneva, 1955).

MOSER, HANS JOACHIM: *Geschichte der deutschen Musik,* 3 vols. (5th ed., Stuttgart and Berlin, 1930).

PALISCA, CLAUDE V.: *Baroque Music* (Englewood Cliffs, 1968).

PROD'HOMME, JACQUES-GABRIEL: *L'Opéra (1669–1925)* (Paris, 1925; repr. Geneva, 1972).

ROBINSON, MICHAEL F.: *Opera before Mozart* (2nd ed., London, 1972),

ROUSSEAU, JEAN-JACQUES: *Dictionnaire de musique* (Paris, 1768; repr. Hildesheim, 1969).

WELLESZ, EGON: *Essays on Opera* (London, 1950).

CHAPTER I
ITALIAN OPERA FROM THE LATER MONTEVERDI TO SCARLATTI

(i) *Modern Editions*

(a) *Anthologies*

BENVENUTI, GIACOMO: *35 arie di vari autori del secolo XVII* (Milan, 1922).

GEVAERT, FRANÇOIS-AUGUSTE: *Les Gloires de l'Italie*, 2 vols. (Paris, 1868).

JEPPESEN, KNUD: *La Flora*, 3 vols. (Copenhagen, 1949).

LANDSHOFF, LUDWIG: *Alte Meister des Bel Canto*, 5 vols. (Leipzig, 1912–27).

PARISOTTI, ALESSANDRO: *Arie antiche*, 3 vols. (Milan, 1885–1900).

TORCHI, LUIGI: *Canzoni ed arie del XVII secolo* (Milan, 1893).

——'Composizioni ad una e più voci, secolo XVII', *L'arte musicale in Italia*, v (Milan, 1897).

(b) *Works by Individual Composers*

CAVALLI, P. F.: *L'Ormindo*, ed. R. Leppard (London, 1969).

——*Il Giasone* [Act I], ed. R. Eitner, *Publikationen älterer praktischer und theoretischer Musikwerke*, xii (Berlin and Leipzig, 1883).

CESTI, A.: *La Dori; Le disgrazie d'Amore; La Semiramis; La magnanimità d'Alessandro* [excerpts], ed. R. Eitner, *Publikationen älterer praktischer und theoretischer Musikwerke*, xii (Berlin and Leipzig, 1883).

——*Il pomo d'oro*, ed. G. Adler, *Denkmäler der Tonkunst in Österreich*, vi, viii (Jg. iii(2), iv(2)) (Vienna, 1896–7).

——*Orontea*, ed. W. C. Holmes, *The Wellesley Edition*, xi (Wellesley, 1973).

MONTEVERDI, C.: *Il ritorno d'Ulisse*, ed. G. F. Malipiero, *Tutte le opere*, xii (Asolo, 1930); ed. R. Haas, *Denkmäler der Tonkunst in Österreich*, lvii (Jg. xxix(1)) (Vienna, 1921).

——*L'incoronazione di Poppea*, ed. G. F. Malipiero, *Tutte le opere*, xiii (Asolo, 1931).

PALLAVICINO, C.: *La Gerusalemme liberata*, ed. H. Abert, *Denkmäler deutscher Tonkunst*, lv (Leipzig, 1916).

SCARLATTI, A.: *La Griselda*, ed. O. Drechsler (Kassel, 1962).

——*La Rosaura* [excerpts], ed. R. Eitner, *Publikationen älterer praktischer und theoretischer Musikwerke*, xiv (Berlin and Leipzig, 1885).

STEFFANI, A.: *Ausgewählte Werke* [excerpts from operas], ed. H. Riemann, *Denkmäler der Tonkunst in Bayern*, xii, 2 (Leipzig, 1912).

——*Alarico*, ed. H. Riemann, *Denkmäler der Tonkunst in Bayern*, xi, 2 (Leipzig, 1911).

——*Tassilone*, ed. G. Croll, *Denkmäler rheinischer Musik*, viii (Düsseldorf, 1958).

TORRI, P.: *Ausgewählte Werke* [excerpts from operas], ed. A. Junker, *Denkmäler der Tonkunst in Bayern*, xix–xx (Leipzig, 1920).

(ii) *Books and Articles*

(a) *General*

ABERT, ANNA AMALIE: 'Die Barockoper. Ein Bericht über die Forschung seit 1945', *Acta Musicologica*, xii (1969), pp. 121–64.

ABERT, ANNA AMALIE: 'Schauspiel und Opernlibretto im italienischen Barock', *Die Musikforschung*, ii (1949), pp. 133–41.

BAUER, ANTON: *Opern und Operetten in Wien. Verzeichnis ihrer Erstaufführungen in der Zeit von 1629 bis zur Gegenwart* (Graz and Cologne, 1955).

BEARE, MARY: *The German Popular Play 'Atis' and the Venetian Opera* (Cambridge, 1938).

DELLA CORTE, ANDREA: 'Tragico e comico nell' opera veneziana della seconda parte del seicento', *Rassegna musicale,* xi (1938), pp. 325–32.

DE' PAOLI, DOMENICO: *L'opera italiana dalle origini all'opera verista* (Rome, 1955).

Enciclopedia dello spettacolo, vi (Rome, 1959).

GALVANI, L. N.: *I teatri musicali di Venezia nel secolo XVII (1637–1700): memorie storiche e bibliografiche* (Milan, 1878).

GOLDSCHMIDT, HUGO: 'Francesco Provenzale als Dramatiker', *Sammelbände der internationalen Musikgesellschaft,* vii (1905–6), pp. 608–34.

——*Studien zur Geschichte der italienischen Oper im 17. Jahrhundert,* 2 vols., (Leipzig, 1901–4; repr. 1967).

KRETZSCHMAR, HERMANN: 'Beiträge zur Geschichte der venezianischen Oper', *Jahrbuch der Musikbibliothek Peters,* xiv (1908), pp. 71–81; xvii (1911), pp. 61–71; xviii (1911), pp. 49–61.

LANDSHOFF, LUDWIG: 'Über das vielstimmige Accompagnement und andere Fragen des Generalbassspiels', *Festschrift zum 50. Geburtstag Adolf Sandberger* (Munich, 1918), pp. 189–208.

MENESTRIER, C. F.: *Des Représentations de musique anciennes et modernes* (Paris, 1681).

NIETAN, HANNS: *Die Buffoszenen der spätvenezianischen Oper (1680–1710)* (Diss., Halle, 1925).

OSTHOFF, WOLFGANG: 'Maske und Musik. Die Gestaltwerdung der Oper in Venedig', *Castrum Peregrini,* lxv (1964), pp. 10–49.

PRUNIÈRES, HENRY: *L'Opéra italien en France avant Lulli* (Paris, 1913).

RICCI, CORRADO: *I teatri di Bologna nei secoli 17 e 18: storia aneddotica* (Bologna, 1888).

ROBINSON, MICHAEL F.: *Naples and Neapolitan Opera* (Oxford, 1972).

ROLLAND, ROMAIN: *Histoire de l'opéra en Europe avant Lully et Scarlatti* (Paris, 1895).

RUDHARDT, F. M.: *Geschichte der Oper am Hofe zu München,* 2 vols. (Freising, 1865).

SABBATINI, NICOLA: *Pratica di fabricar scene* (Ravenna, 1638; repr. 1955); ed. W. Flemming (Weimar, 1926).

TESSIER, ANDRÉ: 'La Décoration théâtrale à Venise à la fin du XVIIᵉ siècle', *La Revue de l'art ancien et moderne,* liv (1928), pp. 181–90, 217–34.

WEAVER, ROBERT L.: *Florentine Comic Operas of the 17th Century* (Diss., North Carolina, 1958, unpub.).

WEILEN, ALEXANDER VON: *Zur Wiener Theatergeschichte. Die vom Jahre 1629 bis zum Jahre 1749 am Wiener Hof zur Aufführung gelangten Werke theatralischen Charakters und Oratorien* (Vienna, 1901).

WELLESZ, EGON: 'Die Opern und Oratorien in Wien von 1660–1708', *Studien zur Musikwissenschaft,* vi (1919), pp. 5–138.

WIEL, TADDEO: *I codici contariniani del secolo XVII nella R. Biblioteca di S. Marco in Venezia* (Venice, 1888).

WOLFF, HELLMUTH CHRISTIAN: *Die Barockoper in Hamburg, 1678–1738,* 2 vols. (Wolfenbüttel, 1957).

——'Bühnenbild und Inszenierung der italienischen Oper, 1600–1700', *Claudio Monteverdi e il suo tempo* (Venice, 1968), pp. 109–15.

——'Der Manierismus in der barocken und romantischen Oper', *Die Musikforschung,* xix (1966), pp. 261–9.

——'Die Musik im alten Venedig', *Festschrift Heinrich Besseler zum sechszigsten Geburtstag* (Leipzig, 1961), pp. 291–303.

——'Das Opernpublikum der Barockzeit', *Festschrift Hans Engel zum siebzigsten Geburtstag* (Kassel, 1964), pp. 442–52.

WOLFF, HELLMUTH CHRISTIAN: *Oper, Szene und Darstellung von 1660 bis 1900*, *Musikgeschichte in Bildern*, iv, 1 (Leipzig, 1968).

——*Die venezianische Oper in der zweiten Hälfte des 17. Jahrhunderts* (Berlin, 1937).

WORSTHORNE, SIMON TOWNELEY: *Venetian Opera in the Seventeenth Century* (Oxford, 1954; repr. 1968).

(b) *Individual Composers*

Bontempi

ENGLÄNDER, RICHARD: 'Die erste italienische Oper in Dresden: Bontempis "Il Paride in musica" (1662)', *Svensk Tidskrift för Musikforskning*, xlii (1961), pp. 119–34.

Cavalli

GOLDSCHMIDT, HUGO: 'Cavalli als dramatischer Komponist', *Monatshefte für Musikgeschichte*, xxv (1893), pp. 105–11.

LEPPARD, RAYMOND: 'Cavalli's Operas', *Proceedings of the Royal Musical Association*, xciii (1966–7), pp. 67–76.

KRETZSCHMAR, HERMANN: 'Die venezianische Oper und die Werke Cavallis und Cestis', *Vierteljahrsschrift für Musikwissenschaft*, viii (1892), pp. 1–76.

POWERS, HAROLD: *'L'Erismena travestita'*, *Studies in Music History: Essays for Oliver Strunk* (Princeton, 1968), pp. 259–324.

PRUNIÈRES, HENRY: *Francesco Cavalli et l'opéra vénitien au XVIIᵉ siècle* (Paris, 1931).

WELLESZ, EGON: 'Cavalli und der Stil der venezianischen Oper von 1640–1660', *Studien zur Musikwissenschaft*, i (1913), pp. 1–103.

Cesti

HOLMES, WILLIAM C.: 'Giacinto Andrea Cicognini's and Antonio Cesti's *Orontea* (1649)', *New Looks at Italian Opera: Essays in Honor of Donald J. Grout* (Ithaca, N.Y., 1968), pp. 108–32.

KRETZSCHMAR, HERMANN: 'Die venezianische Oper und die Werke Cavallis und Cestis', *Vierteljahrsschrift für Musikwissenschaft*, viii (1892), pp. 1–76.

OSTHOFF, WOLFGANG: 'Antonio Cestis "Alessandro vincitor di se stesso"', *Studien zur Musikwissenschaft*, xxiv (1960), pp. 13–43.

PIRROTTA, NINO: 'Tre capitoli su Cesti', *La scuola romana: G. Carissimi, A. Cesti, M. Marazzoli*, A. Bruers, P. Capponi, N. Pirrotta and F. Schlitzer (Siena, 1953), pp. 27–79.

TESSIER, ANDRÉ: 'L'Orontée de Lorenzani et l'Orontea du Padre Cesti', *Revue musicale*, ix (1928), pp. 169–86.

Draghi

NEUHAUS, MAX: 'Antonio Draghi', *Studien zur Musikwissenschaft*, i (1913), pp. 104–92.

Lorenzani

TESSIER, ANDRÉ: 'L'Orontée de Lorenzani et l'Orontea du Padre Cesti', *Revue musicale*, ix (1928), pp. 169–86.

Marazzoli

WITZENMANN, WOLFGANG: 'Autographe Marco Marazzolis in der Biblioteca Vaticana (I)', *Analecta Musicologica*, vii (1969), pp. 36–86.

Monteverdi

ABERT, ANNA AMALIE: *Claudio Monteverdi und das musikalische Drama* (Lippstadt, 1954).

ARNOLD, DENIS: *Monteverdi* (London, 1963).

OSTHOFF, WOLFGANG: *Das dramatische Spätwerk Claudio Monteverdis* (Tutzing, 1960).

SCHRADE, LEO: *Monteverdi: the Creator of Modern Music* (New York, 1950; repr. 1964).

Pallavicino

ABERT, HERMANN: Introduction to Pallavicino, *La Gerusalemme liberata, Denkmäler Deutscher Tonkunst*, lv (Leipzig, 1916), pp. v–lx.

SMITH, JULIAN: 'Carlo Pallavicino', *Proceedings of the Royal Musical Association*, xcvi (1969–70), pp. 57–71.

Pasquini

CRAIN, GORDON F.: *The Operas of Bernardo Pasquini* (Diss., Yale, 1965, unpub.).

Pollaroli

TERMINI, OLGA: *Carlo Francesco Pollarolo: his Life, Time, and Music with Emphasis on the Operas* (Diss., Southern California, 1970, unpub.).

Scarlatti

DENT, EDWARD J.: *Alessandro Scarlatti: his life and works*, 2nd ed. Frank Walker (London, 1960).

——'The Operas of Alessandro Scarlatti', *Sammelbände der internationalen Musikgesellschaft*, iv (1902–3), pp. 143–56.

GROUT, DONALD J.: 'La "Griselda" di Zeno e il libretto dell'opera di Scarlatti', *Nuova rivista musicale italiana*, ii (1968), pp. 207–25.

JUNKER, HERMANN: 'Zwei "Griselda"-Opern', *Festschrift zum 50. Geburtstag Adolf Sandberger* (Munich, 1918), pp. 51–64.

LORENZ, ALFRED: *Alessandro Scarlattis Jugendoper*, 2 vols. (Augsburg, 1927).

SARTORI, CLAUDIO: 'Gli Scarlatti a Napoli', *Rivista musicale italiana*, xlvi (1942), pp. 374–90.

SARTORI, CLAUDIO and ZANETTI, EMILIA: 'Contributo a un catalogo delle opere teatrali di Alessandro Scarlatti', *Gli Scarlatti* (Siena, 1940), pp. 63–84.

WESTRUP, J. A.: 'Alessandro Scarlatti's Il Mitridate Eupatore (1707)', *New Looks at Italian Opera: essays in honor of Donald J. Grout* (Ithaca, N.Y., 1968), pp. 133–150.

Steffani

CROLL, GERHARD: *Agostino Steffani (1654–1728): Studien zur Biographie und Bibliographie der Opern und Turnierspiele* (Diss., Münster, 1961, unpub.).

——'Zur Chronologie der "Düsseldorfer" Opern Agostino Steffanis', *Festschrift Karl Gustav Fellerer zum sechszigsten Geburtstag* (Regensburg, 1962), pp. 82–7.

LUALDI, ADRIANO: 'Agostino Steffani diplomatico per forza', *Musiche italiane rare e vive* (Siena, 1962), pp. 129–43.

NEISSER, ARTHUR: *Servio Tullio. Eine Oper aus dem Jahre 1685 von Agostino Steffani* (Leipzig, 1902).

RIEMANN, HUGO: 'Agostino Steffani als Opernkomponist', *Denkmäler der Tonkunst in Bayern*, xii, 2 (Leipzig, 1912), pp. vii–xxiii.

Stradella

CATELANI, ANGELO: *Delle opere di Alessandro Stradella esistenti nell'archivio musicale della R. Biblioteca Palatina di Modena* (Modena, 1866).

GIANTURCO, CAROLYN: 'Caratteri stilistici delle opere teatrali di Stradella', *Rivista italiana di musicologia*, vi (1972), pp. 211–45.

——*The Operas of Alessandro Stradella* (Diss., Oxford, 1970, unpub.).

——'A possible date for Stradella's "Il Trespolo tutore" ', *Music and Letters*, liv (1973), pp. 25–37.

GIAZOTTO, REMO: *Vita di Alessandro Stradella (1645–1682)*, 2 vols. (Milan, 1962).

HESS, HEINZ: *Die Opern Alessandro Stradellas* (Leipzig, 1906).

JANDER, OWEN: *Alessandro Stradella and his Minor Dramatic Works* (Diss., Harvard, 1962, unpub.).

RONCAGLIA, GINO: 'Il "Trespolo tutore" di Alessandro Stradella, "la prima opera buffa" ', *Rivista musicale italiana*, lvi (1954), p. 326.

WESTRUP, J. A.: 'Stradella's "Forza d'amor paterno" ', *Monthly Musical Record*, lxxi (1941), pp. 52–9.

Torri

JUNKER, HERMANN: 'Zwei "Griselda"-Opern', *Festschrift zum 50. Geburtstag Adolf Sandberger* (Munich, 1918), pp. 51–64.

——'Pietro Torri als Opernkomponist', *Denkmäler der Tonkunst in Bayern*, xix–xx (Leipzig, 1920), pp. ix–lxv.

CHAPTER II

ITALIAN OPERA 1700–1750

(i) *Modern Editions*

(a) *Anthologies*

HABÖCK, FRANZ: *Die Gesangskunst der Kastraten* (Vienna, 1923).

KELLER, HERMANN: *Arien und Kanzonetten des 17. und 18. Jahrhunderts* (Kassel, 1960).

LEO, LEONARDO: *Delizie dell'opere*, 3 vols. (London, 1776).

PARISOTTI, ALESSANDRO: *Arie antiche*, 3 vols. (Milan, 1885–1900).

SCHMITZ, HANS-PETER: *Die Kunst der Verzierung im 18. Jahrhundert. Instrumentale und vokale Musizierpraxis in Beispielen* (Kassel, 1955).

(b) *Works by Individual Composers*

BONONCINI, G.: *Arias from the Venetian Operas*, ed. A. Ford, *The Baroque Operatic Arias*, i (London, 1971).

CALDARA, A.: *Dafne*, ed. C. Schneider, *Denkmäler der Tonkunst in Österreich*, xci (Vienna, 1955).

FUX, J. J.: *Costanza e fortezza*, ed. E. Wellesz, *Denkmäler der Tonkunst in Österreich*, xxxiii–xxxiv (Jg. xvii) (Vienna, 1910).

GRAUN, C. H.: *Montezuma*, ed. A. Mayer-Reinach, *Denkmäler deutscher Tonkunst*, xv (Leipzig, 1904).

HANDEL, G. F.: *Georg Friedrich Händels Werke,* lv–xciv, ed. F. Chrysander (Leipzig, 1858–1903).

——*Hallische Händel-Ausgabe. Serie II: Opern*, ed. Rudolf Steglich *et al.* (Kassel and Basle, 1958–   ).

HASSE, J. A.: *Arminio*, ed. R. Gerber, *Das Erbe deutscher Musik,* xxvii–xxviii (Mainz, 1957–66).

PERGOLESI, G. B.: *Opera omnia*, ed. F. Caffarelli (Rome, 1939–43).

——*Livietta e Tracollo (La finta polacca)*, ed. A. Toni (Milan, 1920).

——*L'Olimpiade*, ed. M. Zanon (Milan, 1915).

——*La serva padrona,* ed. H. Abert (Munich, 1910); ed. K. Geiringer (Vienna, 1925).

(ii) *Books and Articles*

(a) *General*

ABERT, ANNA AMALIE: 'Zum metastasianischen Reformdrama', *Gesellschaft für Musikforschung: Kongressbericht, Lüneburg, 1950*, pp. 138–9.

ABERT, HERMANN: 'Wort und Ton in der Musik des 18. Jahrhunderts', *Archiv für Musikwissenschaft*, v (1922–3), pp. 31–70; repr. in *Gesammelte Schriften und Vorträge* (Halle, 1929), pp. 173–231.

ALGAROTTI, FRANCESCO: *Saggio sopra l'opera in musica* (Leghorn, 1755); Eng. trans. in R. Northcott: *Francesco Algarotti* (London, 1917).

ANCONA, ALESSANDRO D': 'Federico il Grande e gli Italiani', *Nuova Antologia* (Rome, 1901), pp. 195–219, 417–49, 624–48.

ARIENZO, NICOLO D': 'Le origini dell'opera comica', *Rivista musicale italiana*, vi (1899), pp. 473–95.

ARTEAGA, STEFANO: *Le rivoluzioni del teatro musicale italiano dalle sue origini fino al presente*, 3 vols. (Bologna, 1783–8).

BAUER, ANTON: *Opern und Operetten in Wien. Verzeichnis ihrer Erstaufführungen in der Zeit von 1629 bis zur Gegenwart* (Graz and Cologne, 1955).

BECKER-GLAUCH, IRMGARD: *Die Bedeutung der Musik für die Dresdener Hoffeste* (Kassel, 1951).

CALZABIGI, RANIERO: 'Dissertazione su le poesie drammatiche del Sig. Abate Pietro Metastasio', in P. Metastasio, *Poesie*, i (Turin, 1757).

DELLA CORTE, ANDREA: *Il libretto e il melodramma* (Turin, 1951).

DENT, EDWARD J.: 'Ensembles and Finales in 18th-century Italian Opera', *Sammelbände der internationalen Musikgesellschaft*, xii (1910–11), pp. 112–38.

DOWNES, EDWARD O. D.: 'Secco Recitative in Early Classical Opera (1720–1780)', *Journal of the American Musicological Society*, xiv (1961), pp. 50–69.

——'The Neapolitan Tradition in Opera', *International Musicological Society: Report of the Eighth Congress, New York, 1961*, i (Kassel, 1961), pp. 277–84.

EBERT, ALFRED: *Attilio Ariosti in Berlin (1697–1703). Ein Beitrag zur Geschichte der Musik am Hofe Friedrichs I. von Preussen* (Leipzig, 1905).

FEHR, MAX: *Apostolo Zeno und seine Reform des Operntextes. Ein Beitrag zur Geschichte des Librettos* (Zürich, 1912).

FLORIMO, FRANCESCO: *La scuola musicale di Napoli e i suoi conservatorii*, 4 vols. (Naples, 1880–2).

FREEMAN, ROBERT S.: *Opera without Drama: Currents of Change in Italian Opera, 1675 to 1725, and the Roles Played therein by Zeno, Caldara and others* (Diss., Princeton, 1967, unpub.).

FUCHS, MARIANNE: *Die Entwicklung des Finales in der italienischen Opera buffa vor Mozart* (Diss., Vienna, 1932).

FÜRSTENAU, MORITZ: *Zur Geschichte der Musik und des Theaters am Hofe zu Dresden*, 2 vols. (Dresden, 1861–2).

GIAZOTTO, REMO: 'Apostolo Zeno, Pietro Metastasio e la critica del settecento', *Rivista Musicale Italiana*, xlviii (1946), pp. 324–60; xlix (1947), pp. 46–56; l (1948), pp. 39–65.

——*Il melodramma a Genova nei secoli XVII e XVIII* (Genoa, 1941).

——*Poesia melodrammatica e pensiero critico nel settecento* (Milan, 1952).

HABÖCK, FRANZ: *Die Kastraten und ihre Gesangskunst* (Stuttgart, 1927).

HADAMOWSKY, FRANZ: 'Barocktheater am Wiener Kaiserhof (1625–1740)', *Jahrbuch der Gesellschaft für Wiener Theaterforschung, 1951–2* (1955), pp. 7–117.

——*300 Jahre österreichisches Bühnenbild* (Vienna, 1960).

HILLER, JOHANN ADAM: *Über Metastasio und seine Werke* (Leipzig, 1786).

HOEGG, MARGARETE: *Die Gesangskunst der Faustina Hasse und das Sängerinnenwesen ihrer Zeit in Deutschland* (Diss., Berlin, 1931).

HUCKE, HELMUTH: 'Die neapolitanische Tradition in der Oper', *International Musicological Society: Report of the Eighth Congress, New York, 1961*, i (Kassel, 1961), pp. 253–77.

KRETZSCHMAR, HERMANN: 'Aus Deutschlands italienischer Zeit', *Jahrbuch der Musikbibliothek Peters*, viii (1901), pp. 47–58.

KUNZ, H.: 'Höfisches Theater in Wien zur Zeit der Maria Theresia', *Jahrbuch der Gesellschaft für Wiener Theaterforschung, 1953–4* (1958), pp. 3–113.

MANCINI, GIOVANNI BATTISTA: *Pensieri e riflessioni pratiche sul canto figurato* (Vienna, 1774); ed. by A. Della Corte as *Canto e bel canto* (Turin, 1933).

MARPURG, F. W.: *Kritische Briefe über die Tonkunst*, i–ii (Berlin, 1761–3).

784 BIBLIOGRAPHY

NEUMANN, F. H.: *Die Ästhetik des Rezitativs. Zur Theorie des Rezitativs im 17. und 18. Jahrhundert* (Strasbourg, 1962).

PIETZSCH, W.: *Apostolo Zeno und seine Abhängigkeit von der französischen Tragödie* (Leipzig, 1907).

PIRROTTA, NINO: 'Commedia dell'arte and Opera', *Musical Quarterly*, xliv (1955), pp. 305–24.

PISTORELLI, L.: *I melodrammi di Apostolo Zeno* (Padua, 1894).

PULVER, JEFFREY: 'The Intermezzi of the Opera', *Proceedings of the Musical Association*, xliii (1916–17), pp. 139–62.

RAGUENET, FRANÇOIS: *Parallèle des italiens et des françois en ce qui regarde la musique et l'opéra* (Paris, 1702).

ROBINSON, MICHAEL F.: *Naples and Neapolitan Opera* (Oxford, 1972).

ROLLAND, ROMAIN: 'Métastase, précurseur de Gluck', *Voyage musical au pays du passé* (Paris, 1919; Eng. trans., London, 1922).

SACHS, CURT: *Musik und Oper am kurbrandenburgischen Hof* (Berlin, 1910).

SCHIEDERMAIR, LUDWIG: *Bayreuther Festspiele im Zeitalter des Absolutismus* (Leipzig, 1908).

SCHNEIDER, LOUIS: *Geschichte des Berliner Opernhauses* (Berlin, 1852).

TARGOSZ-KRETOWA, KAROLINA: *Teatr dworski Władysława IV (1635–1648)* (Cracow, 1965).

TOSI, PIER FRANCESCO: *Opinioni de' cantori antichi, e moderni, o sieno osservazioni sopra il canto figurato* (Bologna, 1723; Eng. trans. as *Observations on the Florid Song*, London, 1742).

VETTER, WALTHER: 'Deutschland und das Formgefühl Italiens. Betrachtungen über die Metastasianische Oper', *Deutsches Jahrbuch für Musikwissenschaft 1959* (Leipzig, 1960), pp. 7–37.

——'Zur Stilproblematik der italienischen Oper des 17. und 18. Jahrhunderts', *Studien zur Musikwissenschaft*, xxvi (1962), pp. 561–72.

VIERTEL, KARL-HEINZ: *Untersuchungen zur Ästhetik und Aufführungspraxis der italienischen Opera seria des 18. Jahrhunderts unter besonderer Berücksichtigung der Affektenerkennung* (Diss., Leipzig, 1971, unpub.).

WESTRUP, J. A.: 'The Cadence in Baroque Recitative', *Natalicia Musicologica Knud Jeppesen* (Copenhagen, 1962), pp. 243–52.

——'The Nature of Recitative', *Proceedings of the British Academy*, xlii (1956), pp. 27–43; also issued separately (London, 1956).

WIEL, TADDEO: *I teatri musicali veneziani del settecento (1701–1800)* (Venice, 1891–7).

WIERZBICKA-MICHALSKA, KARYNA: *Teatr Warszawski za Sasów* (Wrocław, Warsaw, and Cracow, 1964).

WOLFF, HELLMUTH CHRISTIAN: *Die Barockoper in Hamburg (1678–1738)*, 2 vols. (Wolfenbüttel, 1957).

——'The Fairy-Tale of the Neapolitan Opera', *Studies in Eighteenth-Century Music: a tribute to Karl Geiringer on his seventieth birthday* (London, 1970), pp. 401–6.

——'Das Märchen von der neapolitanischen Oper und Metastasio', *Analecta Musicologica*, ix (1970), pp. 94–111.

——'Die Sprachmelodie im alten Opernrezitativ', *Händel-Jahrbuch*, 2nd ser., ix (1963), pp. 93–134.

——'Vom Wesen des alten Belcanto', *Händel–Konferenz–Bericht, Halle, 1959* (Leipzig, 1961), pp. 95–9.

ZUCKER, PAUL: *Die Theaterdekoration des Barock* (Berlin, 1925).

(b) Individual Composers

Bertali

LA ROCHE, C.: *Antonio Bertali als Opern- und Oratorienkomponist* (Diss., Vienna, 1919).

Giovanni Bononcini

HUEBER, KURT: *Die Wiener Opern Giovanni Bononcinis von 1697 bis 1710* (Diss., Vienna, 1955, unpub.).

——'Gli ultimi anni di Giovanni Bononcini: notizie e documenti inediti', *Accademia di Scienze, Lettere e Arti di Modena: Atti e Memorie,* ser. 5, xii (1954), pp. 1–21.

WOLFF, HELLMUTH CHRISTIAN: 'Bononcini—oder die Relativität historischer Urteile', *Revue belge de musicologie,* xi (1957), pp. 3–16.

Buini

DENT, EDWARD J.: 'Giuseppe Maria Buini', *Sammelbände der internationalen Musikgesellschaft,* xiii (1911–12), pp. 329–36.

Fux

KÖCHEL, LUDWIG VON: *Johann Josef Fux* (Vienna, 1872).

LIESS, ANDREAS: *Johann Joseph Fux* (Vienna, 1948).

WELLESZ, EGON: *Fux* (London, 1965).

Galuppi

BOLLERT, WERNER: *Die Buffoopern Baldassare Galuppis* (Diss., Berlin, 1935, unpub.).

Graun

MAYER-REINACH, A.: 'Carl Heinrich Graun als Opernkomponist', *Sammelbände der internationalen Musikgesellschaft,* i (1899–1900), pp. 446–529.

Handel

CHRYSANDER, FRIEDRICH: *G. F. Händel,* 3 vols. (2nd ed., Leipzig, 1919).

DEAN, WINTON: 'Handel and Keiser: Further Borrowings', *Current Musicology,* ix (1969), pp. 73–80.

——*Handel and the Opera Seria* (Berkeley, 1969).

——'Vocal Embellishment in a Handel Aria', *Studies in Eighteenth-Century Music: a tribute to Karl Geiringer on his seventieth birthday* (London, 1970), pp. 151–9.

DENT, EDWARD J.: 'Handel on the Stage', *Music and Letters,* xvi (1935), pp. 174–87.

——'The Operas', *Handel: a Symposium,* ed. G. Abraham (London, 1954), pp. 12–65.

DEUTSCH, OTTO ERICH: *Handel: a Documentary Biography* (London, 1955).

EISENSCHMIDT, JOACHIM: *Die szenische Darstellung der Opern Händels auf der Londoner Bühne seiner Zeit,* 2 vols. (Wolfenbüttel and Berlin, 1941).

HALL, JAMES S. and MARTIN V.: 'Handel's Graces', *Händel-Jahrbuch,* 2nd ser., iii (1957), pp. 25–43.

KIMBELL, DAVID: 'The Libretto of Handel's "Teseo" ', *Music and Letters,* xliv (1963), pp. 371–9.

LANG, PAUL HENRY: *George Frederic Handel* (New York, 1966).

LEWIS, ANTHONY: 'Handel and the Aria', *Proceedings of the Royal Musical Association,* lxxxv (1958–9), pp. 95–107.

REDLICH, HANS F.: 'Handel's *Agrippina* (1709): Problems of a Practical Edition', *Music Review,* xii (1951), pp. 15–23.

ROBINSON, PERCY: 'Handel, or Urio, Stradella and Erba', *Music and Letters,* xvi (1935), pp. 269–77.

SPITZ, CHARLOTTE: 'Die Opern "Ottone" von G. F. Händel (London, 1722) und "Teofane" von A. Lotti (Dresden, 1719); ein Stilvergleich', *Festschrift zum 50. Geburtstag Adolf Sandberger* (Munich, 1919), pp. 265–71.

STREATFEILD, R. A.: *Handel* (London, 1909).

TROWELL, BRIAN: 'Handel as a Man of the Theatre', *Proceedings of the Royal Musical Association,* lxxxviii (1961–2), pp. 17–30.

WOLFF, HELLMUTH CHRISTIAN: *Die Händel-Oper auf der modernen Bühnen, 1920–1956* (Leipzig, 1957).

Hasse

GERBER, RUDOLF: *Der Operntypus Johann Adolf Hasses und seine textlichen Grundlagen* (Leipzig, 1925).

ZELLER, BERNHARD: *Das Rezitativo accompagnato in den Opern J. A. Hasses* (Diss., Halle, 1911).

Leo

DENT, EDWARD J.: 'Leonardo Leo', *Sammelbände der internationalen Musikgesellschaft*, viii (1906–7), pp. 550–66.

REICHARDT, JOHANN FRIEDRICH: 'Leonardo Leo', *Musikalisches Kunstmagazin*, i (1782), pp. 39–41.

PASTORE, GIUSEPPE A.: *Leonardo Leo* (Galatina, 1957).

WOLFF, HELLMUTH CHRISTIAN: 'Leonardo Leo's Oper "L'Andromaca" (1742)', *Studi musicali*, i (1972), pp. 285–315.

Logroscino

KRETZSCHMAR, HERMANN: 'Zwei Opern Nicolò Logroscinos', *Jahrbuch der Musikbibliothek Peters*, xv (1908), pp. 47–68.

Lotti

SPITZ, CHARLOTTE: *Antonio Lotti und seiner Bedeutung als Opernkomponist* (Diss., Munich, 1918).

——'Die Opern "Ottone" von G. F. Händel (London, 1722) und "Teofane" von A. Lotti (Dresden, 1719); ein Stilvergleich', *Festschrift zum 50. Geburtstag Adolf Sandberger* (Munich, 1919), pp. 265–71.

Marcello

ANGELI, ANDREA D': *Benedetto Marcello* (2nd ed., Milan, 1946).

BUSI, L.: *Benedetto Marcello* (Bologna, 1884).

Paganelli

SCHENK, ERICH: *G. A. Paganelli* (Salzburg, 1928).

Pergolesi

RADICIOTTI, GIUSEPPE: *Giovanni Battista Pergolesi* (2nd ed., Milan, 1945; trans. and ed. A.-E. Cherbuliez as *Giovanni Battista Pergolesi. Leben und Werk*, Zürich and Stuttgart, 1954).

WALKER, FRANK: 'Pergolesiana' [letter], *Music and Letters*, xxxii (1951), pp. 295–6.

——'Two Centuries of Pergolesi Forgeries and Misattributions', *Music and Letters*, xxx (1949), pp. 297–320.

Porta

WESTERMANN, GERHARD VON: *Giovanni Porta als Opernkomponist* (Diss., Munich, 1921).

Porpora

ROBINSON, MICHAEL F.: 'Porpora's operas for London, 1733–1736', *Soundings*, ii (1971–2), pp. 57–87.

Rinaldo di Capua

SPITTA, PHILIPP: 'Rinaldo von Capua und seine Oper *Die Zigeunerin*', *Musikgeschichtliche Aufsätze* (Berlin, 1894), pp. 131–74.

Vinci

CALMUS, GEORGY: 'L. Vinci, der Komponist von *Serpilla e Bacocco*', *Zeitschrift der internationalen Musikgesellschaft*, xiv (1912–13), p. 114; see also O. G. Sonneck, ibid., pp. 170–2 and G. Calmus, ibid., pp. 172–3.

GEIRINGER, KARL: 'Eine Geburtstagskantate von Leonardo Vinci', *Zeitschrift für Musikwissenschaft*, ix (1926–7), pp. 270–83.

SILVESTRI SILVA, GIUSEPPE: *Illustri musicisti calabresi: Leonardo Vinci* (Genoa, 1935).

Vivaldi

KOLNEDER, WALTER: *Antonio Vivaldi, Leben und Werk, 1680–1743* (Wiesbaden, 1965; Eng. trans., London, 1970).

PINCHERLE, MARC: *Vivaldi* (Paris, 1955; Eng. trans., London, 1958).

RINALDI, MARIO: *Catalogo numerico tematico delle composizioni di Antonio Vivaldi* (Rome, 1945).

WOLFF, HELLMUTH CHRISTIAN: 'Vivaldi und der Stil der italienischen Oper', *Acta Musicologica*, xl (1968), pp. 179–86.

Zeno

BURT, NATHANIEL: 'Opera in Arcadia', *Musical Quarterly*, xli (1955), p. 145.

FREEMAN, ROBERT: 'Apostolo Zeno's Reform of the Libretto', *Journal of the American Musicological Society*, xxi (1968), pp. 321–41.

——'The Travels of *Partenope*', *Studies in Music History: Essays for Oliver Strunk* (Princeton, 1968), pp. 356–85.

OPERA IN SPAIN

(i) *Modern Editions*

(a) *Anthology*

PEDRELL, FELIPE: *Teatro lirico español anterior al siglo XIX* (Corunna, 1897–8).

(b) *Works by Individual Composers*

LITERES, A.: 'Si de rama en rama', *Accis y Galatea*, ed. R. Mitjana, *Encyclopédie de la musique*, ed. A. Lavignac and L. de La Laurencie, I, iv (Paris, 1920), pp. 2111–13.

HIDALGO, J.: *Celos aun del aire matan* [Act I only], ed. J. Subirá (Barcelona, 1933).

(ii) *Books and Articles*

(a) *General*

CHASE, GILBERT: *The Music of Spain* (2nd ed., New York, 1959).

COTARELO Y MORI, EMILIO: *Orígenes y establecimiento de la ópera en España hasta 1800* (Madrid, 1917).

HAMILTON, MARY N.: *Music in Eighteenth Century Spain* (Urbana, 1937).

LIVERMORE, ANN: 'The Spanish Dramatists and their Use of Music', *Music and Letters*, xxv (1944), pp. 140–9.

MITJANA, RAFAËL: 'Apparition de l'opéra italien'; 'La musique profane (XVIII⁰ siècle)', *Encyclopédie de la musique*, ed. A. Lavignac and L. de La Laurencie, I, iv (Paris, 1920), pp. 2123–8, 2150–80

SUBIRÁ, JOSÉ: *El teatro del Real Palacio* (Madrid, 1950).

——*Historia de la música teatral en España* (Barcelona, 1945).

——*Historia y anecdotario del Teatro Real* (Madrid, 1949).

——*La música en la casa de Alba* (Madrid, 1927).

——*La ópera en los teatros de Barcelona* (Barcelona, 1945).

——'Le style dans la musique théâtrale espagnole', *Acta Musicologica*, iv (1932), pp. 67–75.

——'Un manuscrito musical de principios del siglo XVIII: contribución a la música teatral española', *Anuario musical*, iv (1949), pp. 181–91.

(b) *Individual Composers*

Hidalgo

SUBIRÁ, JOSÉ: *El operista español d. Juan Hidalgo* (Madrid, 1934).

URSPRUNG, OTTO: '*Celos aun del aire matan*, Text von Calderón, Musik von Hidalgo, die älteste erhaltene spanische Oper', *Festschrift Arnold Schering zum sechzigsten Geburtstag* (Berlin, 1937), pp. 223–40.

Nebra

SOLAR-QUINTES, NICOLÁS: 'El compositor español José de Nebra', *Anuario musical,* ix (1954), pp. 179–206.

CHAPTERS III and IV
THE ORIGINS OF FRENCH OPERA
FRENCH OPERA FROM LULLY TO RAMEAU

(i) *Modern Editions*

(a) Anthologies

DELSARTE, FRANÇOIS: *Archives du chant,* i–xiii, xv–xviii, xx–xxii, xxiv, supplement (Paris, 1860–70).
——*Échos de France,* i–iv (Paris, 1909).
PRUNIÈRES, HENRY: *Les Maîtres du chant,* ii, iv, vi (Paris, 1924–7).

(b) Works by Individual Composers

BEAULIEU, LAMBERT DE: *Le Balet Comique de la Royne,* facsimile ed., ed. G. Gaula (Turin, 1965).
CAMBERT, R.: *Pomone; Les Peines et les plaisirs de l'amour;* ed. J. B. Weckerlin, *Les Chefs-d'oeuvre classiques de l'opéra français* (Paris, 1881).
CAMPRA, A.: *L'Europe galante,* ed. T. de Lajarte; *Les Fêtes vénitiennes,* ed. A. Guilmant; *Tancrède,* ed. A. Guilmant, *Les Chefs-d'oeuvre classiques de l'opéra français* (Paris, 1881).
——*Les Fêtes vénitiennes,* ed. M. Lütolf (Paris, 1971).
——*Operatic Arias,* ed. G. Sadler, *The Baroque Operatic Arias,* ii (London, 1973).
CHARPENTIER, M.-A.: *Prologues et intermèdes du Malade imaginaire de Molière,* ed. H. W. Hitchcock (Geneva, 1973).
COLASSE, P.: *Les Saisons; Thétis et Pélée;* ed. L. Soumis, *Les Chefs-d'oeuvre classiques de l'opéra français* (Paris, 1881).
DESTOUCHES, A. C.: *Les Eléments* [with Lalande]; *Issé; Omphale;* ed. V. d'Indy, *Les Chefs-d'oeuvre classiques de l'opéra français* (Paris, 1881).
LULLY, J.-B.: *Alceste; Amadis; Cadmus et Hermione; Œuvres complètes,* ed. H. Prunières, *Opéras, i–iii* (Paris, 1930–39).
——*Alceste; Armide; Atys; Bellérophon; Cadmus et Hermione; Isis; Persée; Phaëton; Proserpine; Psyché; Thésée;* ed. T. de Lajarte, *Les Chefs-d'oeuvre classiques de l'opéra français* (Paris, 1881).
——*Armide,* ed. R. Eitner, *Publikationen älterer praktischer und theoretischer Musikwerke,* xiii (Berlin and Leipzig, 1886).
RAMEAU, J.-P.: *Œuvres complètes,* ed. C. Saint-Saëns (Paris, 1895–1913).
——*Zoroastre,* ed. F. Gervais (Paris, 1964).

(ii) *Books and Articles*

(a) General

ANTHONY, JAMES R.: *French Baroque Music from Beaujoyeulx to Rameau* (London, 1973).
——'The French Opera-Ballet in the Early 18th Century: Problems of Definition and Classification', *Journal of the American Musicological Society,* xviii (1965), pp. 197–206.
BARNES, CLIFFORD R.: 'Instruments and Instrumental Music at the "Théâtres de la Foire"', *Recherches sur la musique française classique,* v (1965), pp. 142–68.
——'Vocal Music at the "Théâtres de la Foire"', *Recherches sur la musique française classique,* viii (1968), pp. 141–60.

BARTHÉLEMY, MAURICE: 'La Musique dramatique à Versailles de 1660 à 1715', *XVIIᵉ Siècle: Bulletin de la Société d'Étude du XVIIᵉ siècle*, xxxiv (1957), pp. 7–18.

——'L'Opéra français et la querelle des Anciens et des Modernes', *Lettres romanes*, x (1956), pp. 379–91.

BENOIT, MARCELLE: *Versailles et les musiciens du roi, 1661–1733* (Paris, 1971).

BJURSTRÖM, PER: *Giacomo Torelli and Baroque Stage Design* (Stockholm, 1961).

BLAZE, FRANÇOIS-HENRI-JOSEPH [called CASTIL-BLAZE]: *L'Académie Impériale de Musique* (Paris, 1856).

BONNET, GEORGES-EDGAR: 'La Naissance de l'opera-comique en France', *Revue musicale*, ii (1921), pp. 231–43.

BORLAND, JOHN E.: 'French Opera before 1750', *Proceedings of the Musical Association*, xxxiii (1906–7), pp. 133–57.

BORREL, EUGÈNE: 'L'Interprétation de l'ancien récitatif français', *Revue de musicologie*, xii (1931), pp. 13–21.

——'Remarques sur l'histoire de la musique au théâtre en France au XVIIᵉ siècle', *Revue de musicologie*, xxxix (1957), pp. 56–60.

BOYER, NOËL: *La Guerre des Bouffons et la musique française* (Paris, 1945).

BRICQUEVILLE, EUGÈNE DE: *Le Livret d'opéra de Lully à Gluck* (Paris, 1888).

BROSSARD, YOLANDE DE: 'La Vie musicale en France d'après Loret et ses continuateurs, 1650–1688', *Recherches sur la musique française classique*, x (1970), pp. 117–93.

CAHUSAC, LOUIS DE: *La Danse ancienne et moderne* (The Hague, 1754; repr. Geneva, 1971).

CAMPARDON, ÉMILE: *L'Académie Royale de Musique au XVIIIᵉ siècle* (Paris, 1884; repr. Geneva, 1970).

——*Les Comédiens du roi de la troupe italienne* (Paris, 1880).

——*Les Spectacles des Foires—depuis 1595 jusqu'à 1791* (Paris, 1877).

CARMODY, FRANCIS J.: *Le Répertoire de l'opéra-comique en vaudevilles de 1708 à 1764* (Berkeley, 1933).

CHRISTOUT, MARIE-FRANÇOISE: *Le Ballet de cour de Louis XIV, 1643–1672* (Paris, 1967).

COOPER, MARTIN: *Opéra-comique* (London, 1949).

CUCUEL, GEORGES: *Les Créateurs de l'opéra-comique français* (Paris, 1914).

——'Sources et documents pour servir à l'histoire de l'opéra-comique en France', *Année musicale*, iii (1913), pp. 247–82.

DACIER, ÉMILE: *Une Danseuse de l'opéra sous Louis XV: Mlle. Sallé (1707–1756)* (Paris, 1909; repr. Geneva, 1972).

DAVAL, PIERRE: *La Musique en France au XVIIIᵉ siècle* (Paris, 1961).

DEIERKAUF-HOLSBOER, WILMA: *Le Théâtre du Marais II: le berceau de l'Opéra et de la Comédie-Française, 1648–1673* (Paris, 1958).

DEMUTH, NORMAN: *French Opera: its Development to the Revolution* (Horsham, Sussex, 1963).

DU BOS, JEAN-BAPTISTE: *Réflexions critiques sur la poésie et la peinture* (Paris, 1719; 1770 ed. repr. Geneva, 1971).

DUCAUNNÈS-DUVAL, G.: 'L'Opéra à Bordeaux en 1748', *Revue de musicologie*, xviii (1937), pp. 82–3.

DUCROT, ARIANE: 'Les Représentations de l'Académie Royale de la Musique à Paris au temps de Louis XIV (1671–1715)', *Recherches sur la musique française classique*, x (1970), pp. 19–55.

DUFOURCQ, NORBERT: 'Nouvelles de la cour et de la ville (1734–1738); publiées par le Comte E. Barthélemy', *Recherches sur la musique française classique*, x (1970), pp. 101–6.

DUREY DE NOINVILLE, JACQUES-BERNARD-TRAVENOL: *Histoire du théâtre de l'Académie Royale de Musique* (Paris, 1757; repr. Geneva, 1972).

ÉCORCHEVILLE, JULES: *Corneille et la musique* (Paris, 1906).

——*De Lulli à Rameau, 1690–1730: l'esthétique musicale* (Paris, 1906; repr. Geneva, 1970).

FAVART, CHARLES-SIMON: *Théâtre de M. (et Mme.) Favart* (Paris, 1763–72; repr. Geneva, 1971).

FEUILLET, RAOUL-AUGER: *Choréographie, ou L'Art de décrire la danse par caractères, figures et signes démonstratifs* (Paris, 1700; repr. New York, 1968).

FONT, AUGUSTE: *Favart, l'opéra-comique et la comédie-vaudeville aux XVIIe et XVIIIe siècles* (Paris, 1894; repr. Geneva, 1970).

GASTOUÉ, AMÉDÉE: 'Les Notes inédites du Marquis de Paulmy sur les oeuvres lyriques françaises, 1655–1775', *Revue de musicologie*, special ser., i (1943), pp. 1–7.

GAUDEFROY-DEMOMBYNES, JEAN: *Les Jugements allemands sur la musique française au XVIIIe siècle* (Paris, 1941).

GENEST, ÉMILE: *L'Opéra-comique connu et inconnu* (Paris, 1925).

GEULETTE, THOMAS SIMON: *Notes et souvenirs sur le Théâtre Italien au XVIIIe siècle* (Paris, 1938).

GHERARDI, EVARISTO: *Le Théâtre Italien de Gherardi* (5th ed., Amsterdam, 1721).

GIRDLESTONE, CUTHBERT: *La Tragédie en musique considerée comme genre littéraire, 1673–1750* (Geneva, 1972).

GRIMAREST, JEAN: *Traité du récitatif* (Paris, 1707).

GROS, ÉTIENNE: 'Les Origines de la tragédie lyrique et la place des tragédies à machines dans l'évolution du théâtre vers l'opéra', *Revue d'Histoire littéraire de la France*, xxv (1928), pp. 161–93.

GROUT, DONALD J.: 'The Music of the Italian Theatre at Paris, 1682–1697', *Papers of the American Musicological Society*, xx (1941), pp. 158–170.

——*The Origins of the Opéra-Comique* (Diss., Harvard, 1939, unpub.).

——'Seventeenth-century Parodies of French Opera', *Musical Quarterly*, xxvii (1941), pp. 211–19, 514–26.

——'Some Forerunners of the Lully Opera', *Music and Letters,* xxii (1941), pp. 1–25.

HIRSCHBERG, EUGEN: *Die Encyclopädisten und die französische Oper im 18. Jahrhundert* (Leipzig, 1903).

ISHERWOOD, ROBERT: *Music in the Service of a King* (Ithaca, N.Y., and London, 1973).

JACQUOT, JEAN, ed.: *Le Théâtre des Jésuites (Dramaturgie et Société, ii)* (Paris, 1968).

JAPY, ANDRÉ: *L'Opéra royal de Versailles* (Versailles, 1958).

LACROIX, PAUL: *Ballets et mascarades de cour d'Henri III à Louis XIV* (Geneva, 1868–70; repr. Geneva, 1968).

LAJARTE, THÉODORE DE: *Bibliothèque musicale du Théâtre de l'Opéra: catalogue historique, chronologique, anecdotique* (Paris, 1878; repr. Geneva, 1969).

LA LAURENCIE, LIONEL DE: *Les Créateurs de l'opéra français* (Paris, 1930).

——'La Musique française de Lulli à Gluck', *Encyclopédie de la musique et dictionnaire du Conservatoire*, I, iii (Paris, 1925), pp. 1362–489.

——'L'Opéra français au XVIIe siècle: la musique', *Revue musicale*, vi (1925), pp. 26–43.

——'Les Pastorales en musique au XVIIe siècle en France avant Lully et leur influence sur l'opéra', *International Music Society, Report of Fourth Congress* (London, 1912), pp. 139–46.

LANCASTER, H. CARRINGTON: 'Comedy versus Opera in France, 1683–1700', *Essays and Studies in Honor of Carleton Brown* (New York, 1940), pp. 257–63.

LANG, PAUL HENRY: *The Literary Aspect of the History of Opera in France* (Diss., Cornell, 1935, unpub.).

LANGLOIS, ROSE-MARIE: *L'Opéra de Versailles* (Paris, 1958).

LA VALLIÈRE, LOUIS CÉSAR, DUC DE: *Ballets, opéras et autres ouvrages lyriques par ordre chronologique* (Paris, 1760; repr. London, 1967).

LAWRENCE, W. J.: 'The French Opera in London: a Riddle of 1686', *Times Literary Supplement* (London, 28 March 1936), p. 268.

LE BRUN, ANTOINE LOUIS: *Le Théâtre lyrique* (Paris, 1712).

LECERF DE LA VIÉVILLE, JEAN-LAURENT: *Comparaison de la musique italienne et de la musique française* (Brussels, 1705–6; repr. Geneva, 1972).

LE SAGE, ALAIN and D'ORNEVAL: *Théâtre de la Foire, ou L'Opéra comique* (Paris, 1724–37).

LESURE, FRANÇOIS: *L'Opéra classique français* (*Iconographie musicale*, i) (Geneva, 1972).

LEVINSON, ANDRÉ: 'Notes sur le ballet du XVIIe siècle: les danseurs de Lully', *Revue musicale*, vi (1925), pp. 44–55.

LORET, JEAN: *La Muze historique* (Paris, 1650–65; repr. Paris, 1877–8).

LOWE, ROBERT W.: 'Les Représentations en musique au collège Louis le Grand 1650–1688', *Revue d'histoire du théâtre*, xi (1958), pp. 21–34.

MANOIR, GUILLAUME DU: *Le Marriage de la musique avec la danse* (Paris, 1664); ed. J. Gallay (Paris, 1870).

MASSON, PAUL-MARIE: 'Le Ballet héroïque', *Revue musicale*, ix (1928), pp. 132-54.

——'Lullistes et Ramistes', *Année musicale*, i (1911), pp. 187–213.

——'Musique italienne et musique française', *Rivista musicale italiana*, xix (1912), pp. 519–45.

MAURICE-AMOUR, LILA: 'Les Musiciens de Corneille, 1650–1699', *Revue de musicologie*, xxxvii (1955), pp. 43–75.

McGOWAN, MARGARET M.: *L'Art du Ballet de cour en France, 1581–1643* (Paris, 1963).

MÉLÈSE, PIERRE: *Répertoire analytique des documents contemporains . . . concernant les théâtres à Paris sous Louis XIV* (Paris, 1934).

——*Le Théâtre et le public à Paris sous Louis XIV* (Paris, 1934).

MENESTRIER, CLAUDE FRANÇOIS: *Des ballets anciens et modernes* (Paris, 1682; repr. Geneva, 1972).

——*Des représentations en musique anciennes et modernes* (Paris, 1681; repr. Geneva, 1972).

NOUGARET, PIERRE JEAN-BAPTISTE: *De l'art du théâtre* (Paris, 1769; repr. Geneva, 1971).

NUITTER, CHARLES and THOINAN, ERNEST: *Les Origines de l'opéra en France* (Paris, 1886; repr. Geneva, 1972).

PACQUOT, MAURICE: *Les Étrangers dans les divertissements de cour de Beaujoyeulx à Molière, 1581–1673* (Paris, c. 1933).

PAILLARD, JEAN-FRANÇOIS: *La Musique française classique* (Paris, 1960).

PARFAICT, CLAUDE and FRANÇOIS: *Dictionnaire des théâtres de Paris* (Paris, 1756; repr. of 1767–70 ed., Geneva, 1971).

——*Histoire de l'ancien théâtre italien depuis son origine en France, jusqu'à sa suppression en l'année 1697* (Paris, 1753).

——*Mémoires pour servir à l'histoire des spectacles de la Foire* (Paris, 1743).

PRUNIÈRES, HENRY: *Le Ballet de cour en France avant Benserade et Lully* (Paris, 1914).

——'Lecerf de la Viéville et l'esthétique musicale classique au XVIIe siècle', *Bulletin français de la S.I.M.*, iv (1908), pp. 619–54.

——'Notes sur les origines de l'ouverture française', *Sammelbände der internationalen Musikgesellschaft*, xii (1910–11), pp. 565–85.

——*L'Opéra italien en France avant Lulli* (Paris, 1913).

PURE, MICHEL DE: *Idées des spectacles anciens et nouveaux* (Paris, 1668; repr. Geneva, 1972).

La Querelle des Bouffons [59 texts] (Paris and The Hague, 1752–4; repr. Geneva, 1971).

QUITTARD, HENRI: 'La première comédie française en musique', *Bulletin français de la S.I.M.*, iv (1908), pp. 378–96, 497–537.

RAGUENET, FRANÇOIS: *Défense du Parallèle des Italiens et des François en ce qui regarde la musique et les opéras* (Paris, 1705).

——*Parallèle des Italiens et des François en ce qui regarde la musique et les opéras* (Paris, 1702; Eng. trans., London, 1709, repr. London, 1968).

RAMEAU, PIERRE: *Le Maitre à danser* (Paris, 1725; Eng. trans., London, 1931).

Recueil général des opéras représentez par l'Académie Royale de Musique depuis son établissement (Paris, 1703–46; repr. Geneva, 1971).

RÉMOND DE SAINT-MARD, TOUSSAINT: *Réflexions sur l'opéra* (The Hague, 1741; repr. Geneva, 1972).

RICCOBONI, ANTOINE-FRANÇOIS: *L'Art du théâtre* (Paris, 1750; repr. Geneva, 1971).

RICCOBONI, LUIGI: *Réflections historiques et critiques sur les différens théâtres de l'Europe* (Paris, 1738; Eng. trans., London, 1741).

ROBERT, JEAN: 'Les Ranc d'Avignon, propagateurs de l'opéra à la fin du XVIIe siècle', *Recherches sur la musique française classique*, vi (1966), pp. 95–115.

ROLLAND, ROMAIN: 'Notes sur l'*Orfeo* de Luigi Rossi et sur les musiciens italiens à Paris, sous Mazarin', *Revue d'histoire et de critique musicales*, i (1901), pp. 225–236, 363–71.

——'La Représentation d'*Orfeo* à Paris et l'opposition religieuse et politique à l'opéra', *Revue d'histoire et de critique musicales,* i (1901), pp. 10–17.

SAINT-EVREMOND, CHARLES DE SAINT-DENIS: 'Sur les opéra'; 'Les Opéra (comédie); 'À Monsieur Lulli'; *Oeuvres meslées,* ii–iii (London, 1709).

SILIN, CHARLES I.: *Benserade and his Ballets de Cour* (2nd ed., Baltimore, 1970).

TESSIER, ANDRÉ: 'Berain, créateur du pays d'opéra', *Revue musicale*, vi (1925), pp. 56–73.

——'Giacomo Torelli a Parigi e la messa in scena delle *Nozze di Peleo e Teti* di Carlo Caproli', *Rassegna musicale*, i (1928), pp. 573–90.

TIERSOT, JULIEN: 'La Musique des comédies de Molière à la Comédie-Française', *Revue de musicologie*, iii (1922), pp. 20–28.

TITON DU TILLET, EVRARD: *Le Parnasse françois* (Paris, 1732–43; repr. Geneva, 1971).

VALLAS, LÉON: *Un Siècle de musique et de théâtre à Lyon* (Lyons, 1932; repr. Geneva, 1971).

VERCHALY, ANDRÉ: 'Les Ballets de cour d'après les recueils de musique vocale (1600–1643)', *Cahiers de l'Association Internationale des Études Français*, xi (1957), pp. 198–218.

VERLET, PIERRE: 'L'Opéra de Versailles', *Revue d'histoire du théâtre*, ix (1957), pp. 133–54.

WILD, NICOLE: 'Aspects de la musique sous la régence: Les Foires: naissance de l'opéra comique', *Recherches sur la musique française classique*, v (1965), pp. 129–41.

(b) Individual Composers

Cambefort

PRUNIÈRES, HENRY: 'Jean de Cambefort', *Année musicale*, ii (1912), pp. 205–26.

Cambert

FLOOD, W. H. GRATTAN: 'Quelques précisions nouvelles sur Cambert et Grabu à Londres', *Revue musicale*, ix (1928), pp. 351–61.

POUGIN, ARTHUR: *Les vrais créateurs de l'opéra français: Perrin et Cambert* (Paris, 1881).

TESSIER, ANDRÉ: 'Robert Cambert à Londres', *Revue musicale*, viii (December, 1927), pp. 101–2.

Campra

ANTHONY, JAMES R.: 'Printed Editions of André Campra's *L'Europe galante'*, *Musical Quarterly*, lvi (1970), pp. 54–73.

——'Some Uses of the Dance in the French Opera-Ballet', *Recherches sur la musique française classique*, ix (1969), pp. 75–90.

——'Thematic Repetition in the Opera-Ballets of André Campra', *Musical Quarterly*, lii (1966), pp. 209–20.

BARTHÉLEMY, MAURICE: *André Campra, sa vie et son oeuvre (1660–1744)* (Paris, 1957).

——'L'Orchestre et l'orchestration des oeuvres de Campra', *Revue musicale*, numéro spécial 226 (1955), pp. 97–104.

——'Le Premier divertissement connu d'André Campra', *Revue belge de musicologie*, xi (1957), pp. 51–3.

LA LAURENCIE, LIONEL DE: 'André Campra, musicien profane', *Année musicale*, iii (1913), pp. 153–205.

——'Notes sur la jeunesse d'André Campra', *Sammelbände der internationalen Musikgesellschaft*, x (1908–9), pp. 159–258.

——'*L'Orfeo nell'inferni* d'André Campra', *Revue de musicologie*, ix (1928), pp. 129–33.

MASSON, PAUL-MARIE: 'Les "Fêtes vénitiennes" d'André Campra (1710)', *Revue de musicologie*, xiii (1932), pp. 127–46, 214–26.

Charpentier

CRUSSARD, CLAUDE: *Un Musicien français oublié: Marc-Antoine Charpentier* (Paris, 1945).

HITCHCOCK, H. WILEY: 'Marc-Antoine Charpentier and the Comédie-Française', *Journal of the American Musicological Society*, xxiv (1971), pp. 255–81.

——'Problèmes d'édition de la musique de Marc-Antoine Charpentier pour *Le Malade imaginaire*', *Revue de musicologie*, lviii (1972), pp. 3–15.

LA LAURENCIE, LIONEL DE: 'Un Opéra inédit de M.-A. Charpentier: "La Descente d'Orphée aux enfers"', *Revue de musicologie*, x (1929), pp. 184–93.

LOWE, ROBERT W.: *Marc-Antoine Charpentier et l'opéra de collège* (Paris, 1966).

Collin de Blamont

MASSIP, CATHÉRINE: *François Collin de Blamont, musicien du roi* (Diss., Paris Conservatoire, 1971, unpub.).

Desmarest

ANTOINE, MICHEL: *Henry Desmarest (1661–1741): biographie critique* (Paris, 1965).

Destouches

BRENET, MICHEL: 'Destouches et son opéra d'*Issé*', *Le Courrier musical*, xi (1908), pp. 661–5.

CARLEZ, JULES: *La Sémiramis de Destouches* (Caen, 1892).

DULLE, KURT: *André Cardinal Destouches, 1672–1749* (Leipzig, 1909).

KIMBELL, DAVID R. B.: 'The "Amadis" Operas of Destouches and Handel', *Music and Letters*, xlix (1968), pp. 329–46.

MASSON, PAUL-MARIE: 'La "Lettre sur Omphale" (1752)', *Revue de musicologie*, xxvii (1945), pp. 1–19.

MASSON, RENÉE P.-M.: 'André Cardinal Destouches, surintendant de la musique du Roi, directeur de l'opéra, 1672–1749', *Revue de musicologie*, xliii (1959), pp. 81–98.

TESSIER, ANDRÉ: 'Correspondance d'André Cardinal des Touches et du Prince Antoine 1er de Monaco', *Revue musicale*, vii (1926), pp. 97–114; viii (1927), pp. 104–17, 209–24.

Gatti

BARTHÉLEMY, MAURICE: 'Theobaldo di Gatti et la tragédie en musique, "Scylla"', *Recherches sur la musique française classique*, ix (1969), pp. 56–66.

Guédron

LA LAURENCIE, LIONEL DE: 'Un Musicien dramatique du XVIIᵉ siècle: Pierre Guédron', *Rivista musicale italiana*, xxix (1922), pp. 445–72.

VERCHALY, ANDRÉ: 'Un Précurseur de Lully: Pierre Guédron', *XVIIᵉ Siècle: Bulletin de la Société d'Étude du XVIIᵉ siècle*, xxi-xxii (1954), pp. 383–93.

Lalande

BERT, HENRI: 'Un Ballet de Michel-Richard Delalande', *XVIIᵉ Siècle: Bulletin de la Société d'Étude du XVIIᵉ siècle*, xxiv (1957), pp. 58–72.

DUFOURCQ, NORBERT: 'Quelques réflexions sur les ballets et divertissements de Michel Delalande', *Cahiers de l'Association Internationale des Études françaises*, ix (1957), pp. 44–52.

DUFOURCQ, NORBERT and others: *Notes et références pour servir à une histoire de Michel-Richard Delalande* (Paris, 1957).

Lorenzani

PRUNIÈRES, HENRY: 'Paolo Lorenzani à la cour de France', *Revue musicale*, iii (August, 1922), pp. 97–120.

TESSIER, ANDRÉ: 'L'Orontée de Lorenzani et l'Orontea du Padre Cesti', *Revue musicale*, ix (1928), pp. 169–86.

Lully

BÖTTGER, FRIEDRICH: *Die 'Comédie-Ballet' von Molière-Lully* (Berlin, 1931).

BORREL, EUGÈNE: 'L'Interprétation de Lully après Rameau', *Revue de musicologie*, x (1929), pp. 17–25.

——'Jean-Baptiste Lully', *Euterpe*, vii (Paris, 1949).

CHAILLEY, JACQUES: 'Notes sur la famille de Lully', *Revue de musicologie*, xxxiv (1952), pp. 101–8.

CHAMPIGNEULLE, BERNARD: 'L'Influence de Lully hors de France', *Revue musicale*, xxvii (February-March, 1946), pp. 26–35.

CORDEY, JEAN: 'Lulli d'après l'inventaire de ses biens', *Revue de musicologie*, xxxvii (1955), pp. 78–83.

CUDWORTH, C. L.: 'Baptist's Vein: French Orchestral Music and its Influence', *Proceedings of the Royal Musical Association*, lxxxiii (1956–7), pp. 29–47.

DUCROT, ARIANE: *Recherches sur Jean-Baptiste Lully (1632–1687) et sur les débats de l'Académie Royale de Musique* (Diss., École des Chartes, 1961, unpub.).

ÉCORCHEVILLE, JULES: 'Lully gentilhomme et sa descendance', *Revue musicale de la S.I.M.*, v (1909), pp. 1–19; vi (1910), pp. 1–27; vii (1911), pp. 36–52.

ELLIS, HELEN MEREDITH: *The Dances of J. B. Lully* (Diss., Stanford, 1967, unpub.).

——'Inventory of the Dances of Jean-Baptiste Lully', *Recherches sur la musique française classique*, ix (1969), pp. 21–55.

——'The Sources of Jean-Baptiste Lully's Secular Music', *Recherches sur la musique française classique*, viii (1968), pp. 89–130.

EPPELSHEIM, JÜRGEN: *Das Orchester in den Werken J.-B. Lullys* (Tutzing, 1961).

HIBBERD, LLOYD: 'Mme de Sévigné and the Operas of Lully', *Essays in Musicology: a Birthday Offering for Willi Apel* (Bloomington, Indiana, 1968), pp. 153–63.

LA LAURENCIE, LIONEL DE: 'Une Convention commerciale entre Lully, Quinault et Ballard en 1680', *Revue de musicologie*, ii (1920–1), pp. 176–82.

——*Lully* (Paris, 1911).

NAGLER, ALOIS M.: 'Lully's Opernbühne', *Kleine Schriften der Gesellschaft für Theatergeschichte*, xvii (Berlin, 1960).

NOACK, FRIEDRICH: 'Musik zu der Molièrschen Komödie *Monsieur de Pourceaugnac* von Jean-Baptiste de Lully', *Musikwissenschaftliche Beiträge: Festschrift für Johannes Wolf* (Berlin, 1929), pp. 139–47.

NODOT: 'Le Triomphe de Lully aux Champs-Élysées', *Revue musicale*, vi (January, 1925), pp. 89–106.

PELLISSON, MAURICE: *Les Comédies-ballets de Molière* (Paris, 1914).

POUGIN, ARTHUR: 'Les Origines de l'opéra français: Cambert et Lully', *Revue d'art dramatique*, vi (1891), pp. 129–55.

PRUNIÈRES, HENRY: 'La Jeunesse de Lully', *Bulletin français de la S.I.M.*, v (1909), pp. 234–42, 329–53.

——'Lettres et autographes de Lully', *Revue musicale de la S.I.M.*, viii (1912), pp. 19–20.

——*Lully* (Paris, 1910).

——'Lully, fils de meunier', *Revue musicale de la S.I.M.*, viii (1912), pp. 57–61.

——'Les Premières ballets de Lully', *Revue musicale*, xii (June, 1931), pp. 1–17.

——'Recherches sur les années de jeunesse de Jean-Baptiste Lully', *Rivista musicale italiana*, xvii (1910), pp. 646–54.

——*La Vie illustre et libertine de Jean-Baptiste Lully* (Paris, 1929).

ROLLAND, ROMAIN: 'Notes sur Lully', *Musiciens d'autrefois* (Paris, 1908; Eng. trans., London, 1915).

STORZ, WALTER: *Der Aufbau der Tänze in den Opern und Balletts Lullys* (Göttingen, 1928).

Marais

BARTHÉLEMY, MAURICE: 'Les Opéras de Marin Marais', *Revue belge de musicologie*, vii (1953), pp. 136–46.

LAJARTE, THÉODORE DE: 'Transformations d'un opéra au XVIIIe siècle', *Chronique musicale* (15 April 1874).

Montéclair

BORREL, EUGÈNE: 'Notes sur l'orchestration de l'opéra *Jephté* de Montéclair (1733) et de la symphonie *Les Élémens* de J. F. Rebel (1737)', *Revue musicale*, numéro spécial 226 (1955), pp. 105–16.

CARLEZ, JULES: *Un Opéra biblique au XVIIIe siècle* (Caen, 1879).

MILLIOT, SYLVETTE: 'Le Testament de Michel Pignolet de Montéclair', *Recherches sur la musique française classique*, viii (1968), pp. 131–40.

VIOLLIER, RENÉE: 'Trois *Jephté*, trois styles' [abstract], *Revue de musicologie*, xliii (1959), pp. 125–6.

VOILLARD, ÉMILE: *Essai sur Montéclair* (Paris, 1879).

Mouret

BARTHÉLEMY, MAURICE: 'Les Divertissements de Jean-Joseph Mouret pour les comédies de Dancourt', *Revue belge de musicologie*, vii (1953), pp. 47–51.

VIOLLIER, RENÉE: *Jean-Joseph Mouret, le musicien des Grâces* (Paris, 1950).

——'La Musique à la cour de la Duchesse du Maine', *Revue musicale*, xx (1939), pp. 96–105, 133–8.

Rameau

BRENET, MICHEL: 'La Jeunesse de Rameau', *Rivista musicale italiana*, ix (1902), pp. 868–93; x (1903), pp. 62–85, 185–286.

CHARLIER, HENRI: *Jean-Philippe Rameau* (Lyons, 1955).

DACIER, ÉMILE: 'L'Opéra au XVIIIe siècle: les premières représentations du *Dardanus* de Rameau', *Revue d'histoire et de critique musicales*, iii (1903), pp. 163–73.

GARDIEN, JACQUES: *Jean-Philippe Rameau* (Paris, 1949).

GEOFFROY-DECHAUME, ANTOINE: 'Connaissance de Rameau', *Revue musicale*, numéro spécial 260 (1965), pp. 37–45.

GERVAIS, FRANÇOISE: 'La Musique pure au service du drame lyrique chez Rameau', *Revue musicale*, numéro spécial 260 (1965), pp. 21–35.

GIRDLESTONE, CUTHBERT: *Jean-Philippe Rameau: his Life and Work* (London, 1957; 2nd ed., Paris, 1962).

——'Voltaire, Rameau et *Samson*', *Recherches sur la musique française classique*, vi (1966), pp. 133–43.

KISCH, EVE: 'Rameau and Rousseau', *Music and Letters,* xxii (1941), pp. 97–114.

LA LAURENCIE, LIONEL DE: 'Quelques documents sur Jean-Philippe Rameau et sa famille', *Bulletin français de la S.I.M.,* iii (1907), pp. 541–614.

——*Rameau, biographie critique* (Paris, 1908).

——'Rameau et son gendre', *Revue musicale de la S.I.M.,* vii (1911), no. 2, pp. 12–23.

LALOY, LOUIS: 'Les Idées de Jean-Philippe Rameau sur la musique', *Bulletin français de la S.I.M.,* iii (1907), pp. 1144–59.

——*Rameau* (Paris, 1908).

LECLERC, HÉLÈNE: '*Les Indes galantes* (1735–1952): les sources de l'opéra-ballet, l'exotisme orientalisant, les conditions matérielles du spectacle', *Revue d'histoire du théâtre,* v (1953), pp. 259–85.

MALIGNON, JEAN: 'Zoroastre et Sarastro', *Recherches sur la musique française classique,* vi (1966), pp. 144–58.

MASSON, PAUL-MARIE: 'Les Deux versions du *Dardanus* de Rameau', *Acta Musicologica,* xxvi (1954), pp. 36–48.

——*L'Opéra de Rameau* (2nd ed., Paris, 1948).

——'Rameau and Wagner', *Musical Quarterly,* xxv (1939), pp. 466–78.

MIGOT, GEORGES: *Jean-Philippe Rameau et le génie de la musique française* (Paris, 1930).

QUITTARD, HENRI: 'Les Années de jeunesse de J.-P. Rameau', *Revue d'histoire et de critique musicales,* ii (1902), pp. 61–3, 100–14, 152–70, 208–18.

SEEFRID, GISELA: *Die Airs de Danse in den Bühnenwerken von Jean-Philippe Rameau* (Wiesbaden, 1969).

TIERSOT, JULIEN: 'Rameau', *Musical Quarterly,* xiv (1928), pp. 77–107.

VIOLLIER, RENÉE: 'Rameau vivant', *Recherches sur la musique française classique,* v (1965), pp. 185–91.

Rebel

DACIER, ÉMILE: 'Les Caractères de la danse: histoire d'un divertissement pendant la première moitié du XVIIIe siècle', *La Revue musicale,* v (1905), pp. 324–35, 365–7.

Rousseau

JANSEN, ALBERT: *Jean-Jacques Rousseau als Musiker* (Berlin, 1884; repr. Geneva, 1971).

MASSON, PAUL-MARIE: 'Les Idées de Rousseau sur la musique', *Revue musicale de la S.I.M.,* viii, No. 6 (1912), pp. 1–17; Nos. 7–8 (1912), pp. 23–32.

POUGIN, ARTHUR: *Jean-Jacques Rousseau musicien* (Paris, 1901).

TIERSOT, JULIEN: *Jean-Jacques Rousseau* (Paris, 1912).

——'La Musique de J.-J. Rousseau', *Revue musicale de la S.I.M.,* viii (1912), No. 6, pp. 32–56.

CHAPTER V
OPERA IN ENGLAND AND GERMANY
(*a*) ENGLAND

(i) *Modern Editions*

BLOW, J.: *Venus and Adonis,* ed. A. Lewis (Paris, 1939).

LOCKE, M. and GIBBONS, C.: *Cupid and Death,* ed. E. J. Dent, *Musica Britannica,* ii (2nd ed., London, 1965).

PURCELL, H.: *Dramatic Music, Parts 1–3,* ed. A. Gray, *Purcell Society Edition,* xvi, xx, xxi (London, 1906, 1916, 1917).

——*Dido and Aeneas,* ed. M. Laurie and T. Dart (London, 1961).

——*Dioclesian,* rev. M. Laurie, *Purcell Society Edition,* ix (London, 1961).

——*The Fairy Queen,* rev. A. Lewis, *Purcell Society Edition,* xii (London, 1968).

PURCELL, H.: *The Indian Queen*; *The Tempest*; ed. E. J. Dent, *Purcell Society Edition*, xix (London, 1912).

——*King Arthur,* rev. M. Laurie, *Purcell Society Edition,* xxvi (London, 1971).

(ii) *Books and Articles*

(a) *General*

DENT, EDWARD J.: *Foundations of English Opera* (Cambridge, 1928, repr. New York, 1965).

FISKE, ROGER: *English Theatre Music in the Eighteenth Century* (London, 1973).

LORD, PHILLIP: 'The English-Italian Opera Companies 1732-3', *Music and Letters,* xlv (1964), pp. 239–51.

NICOLL, ALLARDYCE: *A History of English Drama, 1600–1700* (4th ed., Cambridge, 1952).

SUMMERS, MONTAGUE: *The Playhouse of Pepys* (London, 1935).

WHITE, ERIC WALTER: *The Rise of English Opera* (London, 1951).

(b) *Individual Composers*

Blow

LEWIS, ANTHONY: 'Purcell and Blow's "Venus and Adonis"', *Music and Letters,* xliv (1963), pp. 266–9.

Eccles

LINCOLN, STODDARD: 'The First Setting of Congreve's "Semele"', *Music and Letters,* xliv (1963), pp. 103–17, 417–19.

Purcell

HOLLAND, A. K.: *Henry Purcell* (London, 1932).

LAURIE, MARGARET: 'Did Purcell set *The Tempest*?', *Proceedings of the Royal Musical Association,* xc (1963–4), pp. 43–57.

LEWIS, ANTHONY: 'Purcell and Blow's "Venus and Adonis"', *Music and Letters,* xliv (1963), pp. 266–9.

MOORE, ROBERT ETHERIDGE: *Henry Purcell and the Restoration Theatre* (London, 1961).

WESTRUP, J. A.: *Purcell* (2nd ed., London, 1937).

WHITE, ERIC WALTER: 'New Light on "Dido and Aeneas"', *Henry Purcell, 1659–1695: Essays on his Music,* ed. I. Holst (London, 1959), pp. 14–34.

Smith

MCCREDIE, ANDREW D.: 'John Christopher Smith as a Dramatic Composer', *Music and Letters,* xlv (1964), pp. 22–38.

(b) GERMANY

(i) *Modern Editions*

FRANCK, J. W.: *Die drey Töchter des Cecrops,* ed. G. F. Schmidt, *Das Erbe deutscher Musik,* ii, *Landschaftsdenkmale: Bayern,* 2 (Brunswick, 1938).

KEISER, R.: *Der hochmüthige, gestürtzte und wieder erhabene Croesus,* ed. M. Schneider, *Denkmäler deutscher Tonkunst,* Jg. xxxviii, 2nd ed. by H. J. Moser (Leipzig, 1958).

——*Der lächerliche Printz Jodelet,* ed. F. Zelle, *Publikationen älterer praktischer und theoretischer Musikwerke,* xviii (Berlin and Leipzig, 1892).

——*Die römische Unruhe, oder Die edelmüthige Octavia,* ed. M. Seiffert, *Händel-Gesamtausgabe,* supplement, vi (Leipzig, 1902).

KUSSER, J. S.: *Arien, Duette und Chöre aus Erindo, oder Die unsträfliche Liebe,* ed. H. Osthoff, *Das Erbe deutscher Musik,* ii, *Landschaftsdenkmale: Schleswig-Holstein und Hansestädte,* 3 (Brunswick, 1938).

SCHÜRMANN, G. C.: *Ludovicus Pius, oder Ludewig der Fromme,* ed. H. Sommer, *Publikationen älterer praktischer und theoretischer Musikwerke,* xvii (Berlin and Leipzig, 1890).

TELEMANN, G. P.: *Der geduldige Socrates,* ed. B. Baselt, *G. P. Telemann: Musikalische Werke,* xx (Kassel, 1967).

——*Pimpinone, oder Die ungleiche Heirat,* ed. T. W. Werner, *Das Erbe deutscher Musik,* i, *Reichsdenkmale,* 6 (Leipzig, 1936).

(ii) *Books and Articles*

(a) *General*

SCHULZE, WALTER: *Die Quellen der Hamburger Oper (1678–1738)* (Hamburg and Oldenburg, 1938).

WOLFF, HELLMUTH CHRISTIAN: *Die Barockoper in Hamburg (1678–1738),* 2 vols. (Wolfenbüttel, 1957).

(b) *Individual Composers*

Bontempi, Peranda

ENGLÄNDER, RICHARD: 'Zur Frage der *Dafne* (1671) von G. A. Bontempi und M. G. Peranda', *Acta Musicologica,* xiii (1941), pp. 59–77.

Franck

SQUIRE, W. BARCLAY: 'J. W. Franck in England', *Musical Antiquary,* iii (1911–12), pp. 181–90.

Keiser

DEAN, WINTON: 'Handel and Keiser: Further Borrowings', *Current Musicology,* ix (1969), pp. 73–80.

DEANE, BASIL: 'Reinhard Keiser: an Interim Assessment', *Soundings,* iv (1974), pp. 30–41.

Schürmann

SCHMIDT, GUSTAV F.: *Die frühdeutsche Oper und die musikdramatische Kunst Georg Caspar Schürmanns* (Regensburg, 1934).

Staden

EITNER, ROBERT: 'Das älteste bekannte deutsche Singspiel, *Seelewig,* von S. T. Staden, 1644', *Monatshefte für Musikgeschichte,* xiii (1881), pp. 53–147.

Telemann

OTTZEN, CURT: *Telemann als Opernkomponist* (Berlin, 1902).

CHAPTER VI

CHURCH MUSIC AND ORATORIO IN ITALY AND
CENTRAL AND EASTERN EUROPE

(a) ITALIAN ORATORIO AND PASSION

(i) *Modern Editions*

(a) *Anthology*

PANNAIN, GUIDO: *L'Oratorio dei Filippini e la scuola musicale di Napoli* (Istituzioni dell'arte musicale italiana, v) (Milan, 1934).

(b) *Works by Individual Composers*

CARISSIMI, G.: *Abraham et Isaac: vir frugi et pater familias,* ed. L. Bianchi (Rome, 1953).

CARISSIMI, G.: *Job*; *Ezechia*; ed. C. dall'Argine, F. Ghisi and R. Lupi (Rome, 1951).
——*Jonas*; *Jephte*; *Judicium Salomonis*; *Balthazar*; ed. F. Chrysander, *Carissimis Werke*, i: *Oratorien* (*Denkmäler der Tonkunst*, ii) (Bergedorf, 1869).
——*Jonas*, ed. L. Henry (London, 1872).
HASSE, J. A.: *La conversione di Sant'Agostino*, ed. A. Schering, *Denkmäler deutscher Tonkunst*, xx (Leipzig, 1905).

(ii) *Books and Articles*

(a) *General*

ALALEONA, DOMENICO: *Storia dell'oratorio musicale in Italia* (2nd ed., Milan, 1945).
BIANCHI, LINO: *Carissimi, Stradella, Scarlatti e l'oratorio musicale* (Rome, 1969).
CASIMIRI, RAFFAELE: 'Oratorii del Masini, Bernabei, Melani, Di Pio, Pasquini e Stradella, in Roma nell'Anno Santo 1675', *Note d'archivio*, xiii (1936), pp. 157–69.
GASBARRI, C.: *L'oratorio Filippino, 1552–1952* (Rome 1957).
HILLER, J. A.: *Über Metastasio und seine Werke* (Leipzig, 1786).
PASQUETTI, G.: *L'oratorio musicale in Italia* (Florence, 1906).
SCHERING, ARNOLD: *Geschichte des Oratoriums* (Leipzig, 1911; repr. 1966).
VATIELLI, FRANCESCO: *L'oratorio a Bologna* (Rome, 1938).
WEILEN, ALEXANDER VON: *Zur Wiener Theatergeschichte. Die vom Jahre 1629 bis zum Jahre 1740 am Wiener Hof zur Aufführung gelangten Werke theatralischen Charakters und Oratorien* (Vienna, 1901).
WELLESZ, EGON: 'Die Opern und Oratorien in Wien von 1660–1708', *Studien zur Musikwissenschaft*, vi (1919), pp. 5–138.

(b) *Individual Composers*

Bertali
LA ROCHE, C.: *Antonio Bertali als Opern- und Oratorienkomponist* (Diss., Vienna, 1919, unpub.).

Bonno
BREITNER, KARIN: *Giuseppe Bonno und sein Oratorienwerk* (Diss., Vienna, 1961, unpub.).

Caldara
KIRKENDALE, URSULA: *Antonio Caldara. Sein Leben und seine venezianisch-römische Oratorien* (Graz and Cologne, 1966).

Carissimi
BRENET, MICHEL: 'Les "Oratorios" de Carissimi', *Rivista musicale italiana*, iv (1897), pp. 461–83.
GHISI, FEDERICO: 'Die Oratorien von Giacomo Carissimi in der Hamburg Staats-bibliothek', *Gesellschaft für Musikforschung: Kongressbericht, Lüneburg, 1950*, pp. 103–7.
MASSENKEIL, GÜNTHER: *Die oratorische Kunst in den lateinischen Historien und Oratorien Giacomo Carissimis* (Diss., Mainz, 1952).
VOGL, EDITH: *Die Oratorientechnik Carissimis* (Prague, 1928).

Draghi
NEUHAUS, MAX: 'Antonio Draghi', *Studien zur Musikwissenschaft*, i (1913), pp. 104–92.

Fux
KÖCHEL, LUDWIG VON: *Johann Josef Fux* (Vienna, 1872).
WELLESZ, EGON: *Fux* (London, 1965).

Hasse
KAMIEŃSKI, LUCIAN: *Die Oratorien von J. A. Hasse* (Leipzig, 1912).

MÜLLER, WALTHER: *Johann Adolph Hasse als Kirchenkomponist* (Leipzig, 1911).

Leo

WOLFF, HELLMUTH CHRISTIAN: 'Un oratorio sconosciuto di Leonardo Leo', *Rivista italiana di musicologia*, vii (1972), pp. 196–213.

Lotti

HOPPE, R. H.: 'Antonio Lotti als Kirchenkomponist', *Musica sacra*, xx (1958), p. 46.

Marcello

ANGELI, ANDREA D': *Benedetto Marcello* (2nd ed., Milan, 1946).

BUSI, L.: *Benedetto Marcello* (Bologna, 1884).

Pergolesi

RADICIOTTI, GIUSEPPE: *Giovanni Battista Pergolesi* (2nd ed., Milan, 1945; trans. and ed. A.-E. Cherbuliez as *Giovanni Battista Pergolesi. Leben und Werk,* Zürich and Stuttgart, 1954).

Scarlatti

DENT, EDWARD J.: *Alessandro Scarlatti: his Life and Works* (2nd ed., by Frank Walker, London, 1960).

POULTNEY, DAVID: 'Alessandro Scarlatti and the Transformation of Oratorio', *Musical Quarterly*, lix (1973), pp. 584–601.

Stradella

ALLAM, EDWARD: 'Alessandro Stradella', *Proceedings of the Royal Musical Association*, lxxx (1953–4), pp. 29–42.

CATELANI, ANGELO: *Delle opere di Alessandro Stradella esistenti nell'archivio musicale della R. Biblioteca Palatina di Modena* (Modena, 1866).

DIETZ, HANNS-BERTHOLD: 'Musikalische Struktur und Architektur im Werke Alessandro Stradellas', *Analecta Musicologica*, ix (1969), pp. 87–111.

GIAZOTTO, REMO: *Vita di Alessandro Stradella (1645–1682)*, 2 vols. (Milan, 1962).

ROBINSON, PERCY: 'Handel, or Urio, Stradella and Erba', *Music and Letters*, xvi (1935), pp. 269–77.

RONCAGLIA, GINO: 'Le composizioni vocali di Alessandro Stradella', *Rivista musicale italiana*, xlv (1941), 133–49; xlvi (1942), 1–16.

(*b*) LITURGICAL MUSIC IN ITALY

(i) 1610–60

(i) *Modern Editions*

Works by Individual Composers

BENEVOLI, O.: *Festmesse und Hymnus,* ed. G. Adler, *Denkmäler der Tonkunst in Österreich*, xx (Jg. x(1)) (Vienna, 1903).

CARISSIMI, G.: 'Annunciate gentes', ed. N. M. Jensen (Egtved, 1967).

CAVALLI, P. F.: 'Laetatus sum', ed. R. Leppard (London, 1969).

——'Laudate Dominum', ed. R. Leppard (London, 1969).

——*Messa concertata*, ed. R. Leppard (London, 1966).

——'Salve Regina', ed. R. Leppard (London, 1969).

CRIVELLI, G. B.: 'O Maria mater gratiae', ed. J. Roche (London, 1968).

DONATI, I.: 'Alleluia, haec dies', ed. J. Roche (London, 1968).

GABRIELI, G.: *Opera Omnia*, ed. D. Arnold, *Corpus Mensurabilis Musicae*, xii, (Rome, 1956–   ).

GRANDI, A.: 'Anima Christi'; 'Hodie nobis de caelo'; ed. J. Roche, *Proceedings of the Royal Musical Association*, xciii (1966–7), pp. 44–50.

——*Drei konzertierende Motetten* ['Deus, qui nos in tantis periculis'; 'Plorabo die ac nocte'; 'Ave Regina coelorum'], ed. F. Blume, *Das Chorwerk*, xl (Berlin, 1936).

GRANDI, A.: 'Exaudi Deus', ed. J. Roche (London, 1968).
——'Veniat dilectus meus', ed. J. Roche (London, 1968).
MONTEVERDI, C.: *Tutte le opere*, ed. G. F. Malipiero, xv, xvi (Asolo, 1932, 1940).
——'Beatus vir', ed. J. Steele (London, 1965).
——'Laudate Dominum', ed. D. Arnold (London, 1966).
——*Magnificat, 1640*, ed. J. Steele and D. Stevens (London, 1970).
——*Missa a 4 voci, 1640*, ed. D. Arnold (London, 1962).
——*Missa a 4 voci, 1651*, ed. H. F. Redlich (London, 1952).
——*Missa a 6 voci*, ed. H. F. Redlich (London, 1962).
PRIULI, G.: 'Salvum me fac, Deus', ed. J. Roche (London, 1968).
ROVETTA, G.: 'Laudate Dominum', ed. J. Steele (London, 1966).
VIADANA, L. G. DA: *Cento concerti ecclesiastici (prima parte)*, ed. C. Gallico (Kassel and Basel, 1964).

(ii) *Books and Articles*

(a) *General*

ADRIO, ADAM: *Die Anfänge des geistlichen Konzerts* (Berlin, 1935).
ARNOLD, DENIS: 'The Monteverdian Succession at St. Mark's', *Music and Letters,* xlii (1961), pp. 205–11.
BANCHIERI, ADRIANO: *Conclusioni nel suono dell'organo* (Bologna, 1609; repr. Milan, 1934).
LEICHTENTRITT, HUGO: *Geschichte der Motette* (Leipzig, 1908).
ROCHE, JEROME: 'The Duet in Early Seventeenth-century Italian Church Music', *Proceedings of the Royal Musical Association*, xciii (1966–7), pp. 33–50.
——'Music at S. Maria Maggiore, Bergamo, 1614–1643', *Music and Letters,* xlvii (1966), pp. 296–312.

(b) *Individual Composers*

Grandi
ARNOLD, DENIS: 'Alessandro Grandi, a disciple of Monteverdi', *Musical Quarterly,* xliii (1957), pp. 171–86.

Monteverdi
ARNOLD, DENIS: *Monteverdi* (London, 1963).
ARNOLD, DENIS and FORTUNE, NIGEL, eds.: *The Monteverdi Companion* (London, 1968).
ROCHE, JEROME: 'Monteverdi: an interesting example of second thoughts', *Music Review*, xxxiii (1971), pp. 193–204.
SMITH BRINDLE, REGINALD: 'Monteverdi's G minor Mass: an experiment in construction', *Musical Quarterly*, liv (1968), pp. 352–60.

(ii) 1660–1750

(i) *Modern Editions*
(a) *Anthology*
NOVELLO, VINCENT, ed.: *The Fitzwilliam Music*, 5 vols. (London, 1825).

(b) *Works by Individual Composers*
CALDARA, A.: *Kirchenwerke,* ed. E. Mandyczewski, *Denkmäler der Tonkunst in Österreich*, xxvi (Jg. xiii(1)) (Vienna, 1906).
——'Stabat Mater', ed. P. Smith (London, 1972).

DRAGHI, A.: *Kirchenwerke*, ed. G. Adler, *Denkmäler der Tonkunst in Österreich*, xlvi (Jg. xxiii(1)) (Vienna, 1916).
LOTTI, A.: *Messen*, ed. H. Müller, *Denkmäler deutscher Tonkunst*, lx (Leipzig, 1930).
PERGOLESI, G. B.: *Opera Omnia*, ed. F. Caffarelli (Rome, 1939–42).
SCARLATTI, A.: 'Audi, filia', ed. J. Steele (London, 1968).
——'St. Cecilia' Mass, ed. J. Steele (London, 1968).
——'Stabat Mater', ed. F. Boghen (Milan, 1928).
STEFFANI, A.: *Ausgewählte Werke*, ed. A. Einstein and A. Sandberger, *Denkmäler der Tonkunst in Bayern*, vi, 2 (Leipzig, 1905).
——'Stabat Mater', ed. H. Sievers (Wolfenbüttel, 1956).
VIVALDI, A.: *Musica sacra*, ed. R. Fasano (Vienna, 1969–   ).
——*Gloria*, ed. M. Martens (North Hollywood, 1961).

(ii) Books and Articles

(a) General

BERGER, JEAN: 'Notes on some 17th-century Compositions for Trumpets and Strings at Bologna', *Musical Quarterly*, xxxvii (1951), pp. 354–68.
CAFFI, FRANCESCO: *Storia della musica sacra nella già Cappella Ducale di San Marco in Venezia*, 2 vols. (Venice, 1854–5; repr. Milan, 1931).
CELANI, ENRICO: 'I cantori della cappella pontificia nei secoli XVI-XVIII', *Rivista musicale italiana*, xvi (1909), pp. 55–112.
FELLERER, KARL GUSTAV: *Der Palestrinastil und seine Bedeutung in der vokalen Kirchenmusik des 18. Jahrhunderts* (Augsburg, 1929; repr. 1972).
FLORIMO, FRANCESCO: *Cenno storico sulla scuola musicale di Napoli* (Naples, 1869).
FRATI, LODOVICO: 'Per la storia della musica in Bologna nel secolo XVII', *Rivista musicale italiana*, xxxii (1925), pp. 544–65.
SCHNOEBELEN, ANNE: 'Cazzati vs. Bologna: 1657–1671', *Musical Quarterly*, lvii (1971), pp. 26–39.
——*The Concerted Mass at San Petronio in Bologna, ca. 1660–1730: a Documentary and Analytical Study* (Diss., Illinois, 1966, unpub.).

(b) Individual Composers

Bassani

HASELBACH, RICHARD: *Giovanni Battista Bassani* (Kassel, 1955).

Carissimi

MASSENKEIL, GÜNTHER: 'Über die Messen Giac. Carissimis', *Analecta Musicologica*, i (1963), pp. 28–37.

Marcello

ANGELI, ANDREA D': *Benedetto Marcello* (2nd ed., Milan, 1946).

Perti

BERGER, JEAN: 'The Sacred Works of Giacomo Antonio Perti', *Journal of the American Musicological Society*, xvii (1964), pp. 370–7.

Pergolesi

DEGRADA, FRANCESCO: 'Le messe di G. B. Pergolesi: problemi di cronologia e d'attribuzione', *Analecta Musicologica*, iii (1966), pp. 65–79.
WALKER, FRANK: 'Two Centuries of Pergolesi Forgeries and Misattributions', *Music and Letters*, xxx (1949), pp. 297–320.

The Scarlattis

DENT, EDWARD J.: *Alessandro Scarlatti: his Life and Works* (2nd ed., Frank Walker, London, 1960).
KIRKPATRICK, RALPH: *Domenico Scarlatti* (Princeton, 1953).

(c) CHURCH MUSIC IN CENTRAL AND EASTERN EUROPE

POLAND

(i) *Modern Editions*

(a) *Anthologies*

FEICHT, HIERONIM, ed.: *Muzyka staropolska* (Cracow, 1966).
SURZYŃSKI, JÓZEF, ed.: *Monumenta Musices Sacrae in Polonia*, 5 vols. (Poznan, 1885–96).
SZWEYKOWSKI, ZYGMUNT M., ed.: *Muzyka w dawnym Krakowie* (Cracow, 1964).

(b) *Works by Individual Composers*

GORCZYCKI, G. G.: *Completorium*, ed. J. Węcowski, *Źródła do historii muzyki polskiej*, vii (Cracow, 1963).
——'Laetatus sum' (Concerto *a* 9), ed. K. W. Świerczek, *Wydawnictwo dawnej muzyki polskiej*, xxxvii (Cracow, 1958).
——*Missa paschalis*, ed. A. Chybiński, *Wydawnictwo dawnej muzyki polskiej*, vii (3rd ed., Cracow, 1967).
——*Missa rorate*, ed. K. W. Świerczek, *Wydawnictwo dawnej muzyki polskiej*, lxv (Cracow, 1967).
PĘKIEL, B.: 'Audite mortales', ed. Z. M. Szweykowski, *Wydawnictwo dawnej muzyki polskiej*, iv (2nd ed., Cracow, 1968).
——'Magnum nomen Domini'; 'Resonet in laudibus'; ed. H. Feicht, *Wydawnictwo dawnej muzyki polskiej*, xix (3rd ed., Cracow, 1971).
——*Missa a 14*, ed. Z. M. Szweykowski, *Wydawnictwo dawnej muzyki polskiej*, lxix (Cracow, 1971).
——*Missa brevis*, ed. H. Feicht and K. W. Świerczek, *Wydawnictwo dawnej muzyki polskiej*, lxii (Cracow, 1966).
——*Missa paschalis*, ed. H. Feicht, *Wydawnictwo dawnej muzyki polskiej*, lviii (Cracow, 1965).
——*Missa pulcherrima*, ed. H. Feicht, *Wydawnictwo dawnej muzyki polskiej*, xvii (4th ed., Cracow, 1971).
——'Patrem na rotuły'; 'Patrem rotulatum'; ed. H. Feicht, *Wydawnictwo dawnej muzyji polskiej*, lii (Cracow, 1963).
RÓŻYCKI, J.: 'Confitebor', ed. Z. M. Szweykowski, *Wydawnictwo dawnej muzyki polskiej*, lx (Cracow, 1965).
——'Exultemus omnes', ed. Z. M. Szweykowski, *Wydawnictwo dawnej muzyki polskiej*, xl (2nd ed., Cracow, 1966).
——*Hymni ecclesiastici*, ed. A. Chybiński and B. Rutkowski, *Wydawnictwo dawnej muzyki polskiej*, iii (2nd ed., Cracow, 1947).
——'Magnificemus in cantico', ed. A. Chybiński, *Wydawnictwo dawnej muzyki polskiej*, xvi (2nd ed., Cracow, 1964).
STACHOWICZ, D.: 'Veni consolator', ed. Z. M. Szweykowski, *Wydawnictwo dawnej muzyki polskiej*, xiii (3rd ed., Cracow, 1966).
STAROMIEYSKI, M.: 'Fidelia omnia'; 'Suscepit Israel'; ed. T. Ochlewski, *Florilegium Musicae Antiquae*, xvi (Cracow, n.d.).
SZARZYŃSKI, S. S.: 'Ad hymnos, ad cantus', ed. Z. M. Szweykowski, *Wydawnictwo dawnej muzyki polskiej*, xxvi (2nd ed., Cracow, 1964).
——'Ave Regina', ed. Z. M. Szweykowski, *Wydawnictwo dawnej muzyki polskiej*, xxv (2nd ed., Cracow, 1964).
——'Jesu spes mea', ed. H. Feicht and Z. M. Szweykowski, *Wydawnictwo dawnej muzyki polskiej*, x (3rd ed., Cracow, 1971).
——'Pariendo non gravaris', ed. A. Chybiński, K. Sikorski and T. Ochlewski, *Wydawnictwo dawnej muzyki polskiej*, v (2nd ed., Cracow, 1960).

SZARZYŃSKI, S. S.: 'Veni sancte spiritus', ed. K. W. Świerczek, *Wydawnictwo dawnej muzyki polskiej*, 1 (Cracow, 1963).

ŻEBROWSKI, M.: *Magnificat*, ed. R. Heising, *Wydawnictwo dawnej muzyki polskiej*, lxiv (Cracow, 1968).

——'Salve regina', ed. R. Heising, *Wydawnictwo dawnej muzyki polskiej*, lxviii (Cracow, 1971).

(ii) *Books and Articles*

(a) *General*

BELZA, IGOR: *Istoriya polskoy muzïkalnoy kulturï*, i (Moscow, 1954).

CHYBIŃSKI, ADOLF: 'Z dziejów muzyki polskiej do 1800 roku', *Muzyka polska*, ed. M. Gliński (Warsaw, 1927).

FEICHT, HIERONIM: 'Muzyka w okresie polskiego baroku', *Z dziejów polskiej kultury muzycznej*, i, ed. Z. M. Szweykowski (Cracow, 1958).

JACHIMECKI, ZDZISŁAW: *Historja muzyki polskiej* (Warsaw, 1920).

——*Muzyka polska w rozwoju historycznym*, 2 vols. (Cracow, 1948, 1951).

SZWEYKOWSKI, ZYGMUNT M.: 'Some Problems of Baroque Music in Poland', *Musica Antiqua Europae Orientalis*, ed. Z. Lissa (Warsaw, 1966).

(b) *Individual Composers*

Gorczycki

FEICHT, HIERONYM: 'Do biografi G. G. Gorczyńskiego', *Polski rocznik muzykologiczny*, ii (1936).

Pękiel

FEICHT, HIERONYM: ' "Audite mortales" Bartłomieja Pekiela', *Kwartalnik muzyczny*, i, 4 (1929).

——'Bartłomiej Pękiel', *Przegląd muzyczny*, no. 10–12 (1925).

Różycki

CHYBIŃSKI, ADOLF: 'Jacek Różycki', *Przegląd muzyczny*, no. 1 (1911).

——'Nowe szczegóły do biografii J. Różyckiego', *Przegląd muzyczny*, no. 11 (1929).

——'Przyczynki biograficzne i bibliograficzne do dawnej muzyki polskiej, II. Jacek Różycki', *Przegląd muzyczny*, nos. 1, 4, and 5 (1926).

Stachowicz

CHYBIŃSKI, ADOLF: 'Przyczynki bio- i bibliograficzne do dawnej muzyki polskiej', *Przegląd muzyczny*, no. 2 (1929).

SZWEYKOWSKI, ZYGMUNT M.: 'Sylwetka kompozytorska Damiana Stachowicza', *Muzyka*, no. 1 (1962).

Szarzynski

CHYBIŃSKI, ADOLF: 'Przyczynki biograficzne i bibliograficzne S. S. Szarzyński', *Przegląd muzyczny*, no. 1 (1959).

SZWEYKOWSKI, ZYGMUNT M.: 'Niespodziewane zasoby sandomierskie S. S. Szarzyński', *Ruch muzyczny*, no. 14 (1959).

ITALO-POLISH INFLUENCE IN RUSSIA

Books and Articles

DILETSKY, NIKOLAY: *Gramatyka muzyczna*, ed. S. V. Smolensky (St. Petersburg, 1910; Ukrainian ed., Kiev, 1970).

FINDEIZEN, NIKOLAY: *Ocherki po istorii muzïki v Rossii*, i (Moscow and Leningrad, 1928).

KELDÏSH, YURY: *Russkaya muzïka XVIII veka* (Moscow, 1965).

LEVASHEVA, O., KELDÏSH, Y. and KANDINSKY, A.: *Istoriya russkoy muzïki*, i (Moscow, 1972).

LIVANOVA, TAMARA: *Ocherki i materialï po istorii russkoy muzïkalnoy kulturï* (Moscow, 1938).
SKREBKOV, S.: 'K voprosu o periodizatsii v istorii russkoy muzïki XVII-XVIII vekov', *Sovetskaya muzïka*, no. 7 (1946).

BOHEMIA

(i) *Modern Editions*

(a) *Anthologies*

POHANKA, JAROSLAV: *Dějiny české hudby v příkladech* (Prague, 1958).
Prager deutsche Meister, ed. T. Veidl, *Das Erbe deutscher Musik,* ii, *Landschafts-denkmale: Sudetenland, Böhmen und Mähren,* 4 (Reichenberg [Liberec], 1943).

(b) *Works by Individual Composers*

MICHNA, A.: *Missa Sancti Wenceslai,* ed. J. Sehnal, *Musica Antiqua Bohemica,* ser. II, i (Prague, 1966).
PLÁNICKÝ, J.: *Opella ecclesiastica,* ed. J. Sehnal, *Musica Antiqua Bohemica,* ser. II, iii (Prague, 1968).
TŮMA, F. I.: *Ausgewählte Chöre und Chorsätze,* ed. O. Schmid (Leipzig, 1900).
——*Passionsgesänge,* ed. O. Schmid (Leipzig, 1901).
——*Stabat mater,* ed. J. Plavec (Prague, 1959).
ZELENKA, J. D.: *Lamentationes Jeremiae prophetae.* ed. V. Bělský, *Musica Antiqua Bohemica,* ser. II, iv (Prague, 1969).
——'Salve Regina'; *Magnificat;* ed. F. Naue (Leipzig, n.d.).

(ii) *Books and Articles*

(a) *General*

BRANBERGER, JAN: 'Český hudební barok', *Československá vlastivěda,* viii (1935).
BELZA, IGOR: *Istoriya cheshkoy muïkalnoy kulturï,* i (Moscow, 1959).
NĚMĚCEK, JAN: *Nástin české hudby XVIII. století* (Prague, 1955).
NETTL, PAUL: *Musik-Barock in Böhmen und Mähren* (Brno, 1927).
RACEK, JAN: *Česká hudba* (Prague, 1958).
——*Duch českého hudebního baroku* (Brno, 1940).
SEHNAL, JIŘÍ: 'Die Musikkapelle des Olmützer Bischofs Karl Liechtenstein-Castelcorn in Kremsier', *Kirchenmusikalisches Jahrbuch,* li (1967), pp. 79–123.
TROLDA, EMILIÁN: 'Česká církevní hudba v období generálbasovém', *Cyril,* lx (1934); lxi (1935).

(b) *Individual Composers*

Černohorský
HNILIČKA, ALOIS: 'Bohuslav Černohorský', *Cyril,* xlii (1916).
TROLDA, EMILIÁN: 'B. M. Černohorský', *Cyril,* lx (1934).

Holan Rovenský
TICHÝ, F.: 'V. K. Holan Rovenský', *Cyril,* lxx (1944).

Michna
MUK, JAN: *Adam Michna z Otradovic, básník a skladatel českého baroku* (Jindřichův Hradec, 1941).
TROLDA, EMILIÁN: 'Adam Michna z Otradovic: svatováclavská mše', *Přehled,* xx (1930).
URBAN, OTMAR: *Sacra et litaniae Michny z Otradovic* (Brno, 1953).

Plánický
SCHOENBAUM, CAMILLO: 'Die *Opella ecclesiastica* des Joseph Anton Planicky (1691?–1732)', *Acta Musicologica,* xxv (1953), pp. 39–79.

TROLDA, EMILIÁN: 'Josef Antonín Plánický', *Cyril*, lix (1933).

Tůma

VANICKÝ, J.: 'František Ignác Tůma', *Hudební rozhledy*, vii (1954).

Zach

KOMMA, KARL MICHAEL: *Johann Zach und die tschechischen Musiker im deutschen Umbruch des 18. Jahrhunderts* (Kassel, 1938).

NĚMEC, A.: 'Život a dílo Jana Zacha', *Bertramka*, ii (1950).

Zelenka

HNILIČKA, ALOIS: 'J. D. Zelenka', *Cyril*, xli (1915).

TROLDA, EMILIÁN: 'O skladbách J. D. Zelenkových', *Cyril*, lv-lix (1929–33).

CHAPTER VII
CHURCH MUSIC IN FRANCE

(i) *Modern Editions*

(a) *Anthologies*

BORDES, C., ed.: *Anthologie des maîtres religieux primitifs des XVe, XVIe et XVIIe siècles* (Paris, 1893–8).

——*Meslanges: motets et dialogues choisis des maîtres français des XVIIe et XVIIIe siècles* (Paris, c. 1906).

GASTOUÉ, A., ed.: *Motets choisis des maîtres du XVe au XVIIIe siècle* (Paris, 1930). *Oeuvres françaises du temps de Richelieu et du XVIIe siècle*, ed. B. Loth *et al.* (Paris, 1950–). *Les Chefs-d'oeuvre religieuses de l'école classique Versaillaise*, ed. G. Roussel *et al.* (Paris, c. 1950–).

(b) *Works by Individual Composers*

BERNIER, N.: 'Confitebor tibi, Domine', ed. A. Cellier (Paris, 1954).

BOËSSET, A.: *Sanctus, Agnus Dei* (*Messe du 4e ton*), ed. J. Chailley, *Musique et liturgie*, i (1948).

BOËSSET, J.-B.: *Magnificat*; 'Domine, salvum fac'; ed. D. Launay, *Anthologie du motet latin polyphonique en France* (Paris, 1963).

BOUZIGNAC, G.: About 45 motets and 1 mass, ed. D. Launay, B. Loth, F. Raugel *et al.*, *Oeuvres françaises du temps de Richelieu et du XVIIe siècle* (Paris, various dates).

——Nine motets, ed. D. Launay, *Anthologie du motet latin polyphonique en France* (Paris, 1963).

——Five motets, ed. H. Quittard, *Sammelbände der internationalen Musikgesellschaft*, vi (1904–5), pp. 396–417.

BROSSARD, S. DE: Four motets, ed. R. Ewerhart, *Cantio sacra* (Cologne, n.d.).

——*Canticum eucharisticum pro pace facta anno 1697*, ed. F.-X. Mathias (Strasbourg, c. 1925).

——'Laudate Caeciliam', ed. F. Raugel (Strasbourg, 1955).

CAMPRA, A.: Eight motets, ed. R. Ewerhart, *Cantio sacra* (Cologne, n.d.).

——'Cantemus, exaltemus', ed. H.-A. Durand (Paris, c. 1960).

——*Missa quatuor vocibus, cui titulus Ad majorem Dei gloriam*, ed. H. Montagne (Paris, 1952).

——'Omnes gentes', ed. H.-A. Durand (Paris, c. 1960).

——'O Jesu mi dulcis', ed. A. Steck (Strasbourg, 1958).

——'Pange lingua', ed. H. Montagne (Paris, 1953).

——'Tota pulchra es', ed. C. Pineau (Paris, 1958).

CHARPENTIER, M.-A.: 'Ave Regina', ed. H. Expert, *Répertoire classique de musique religieuse et spirituelle* (Paris, 1913–14).

CHARPENTIER, M.-A.: 'In nativitate Domini nostri Jesu Christi canticum', ed. H. W. Hitchcock (St. Louis, *c*. 1959).
——*Judicium Salomonis*, ed. H. W. Hitchcock (New Haven, 1964).
——*Magnificat* (*a* 3), ed. C. Crussard, *Flores musicae* (Lausanne, n.d.).
——*Magnificat* in G, ed. A. Bichsel (St. Louis, 1960).
——*Mass for soloists, double chorus and orchestra*, ed. C. de Nys (London and New York, 1971).
——*Messe à 4 voix et instruments*, ed. H. Herman (Colorado Springs, 1958).
——*Messe du Samedy de Pâques*, ed. Guy-Lambert (Paris, 1949).
——*Messe de minuit pour Noël*, ed. H. W. Hitchcock (St. Louis, 1962).
——*Messe pour les trespasses*, ed. Guy-Lambert (Paris, n.d.).
——'Pie Jesu', ed. C. Crussard, *Flores musicae* (Lausanne, n.d.).
——'Pulchra es', ed. H.-A. Durand (Paris, 1962).
——'Serve bone', ed. H.-A. Durand (Paris, 1963).
——'Tantum ergo', ed. J. Gelineau (Paris, 1949).
——*Te Deum*, ed. W. Kolneder (Vienna, *c*. 1957).
——*Te Deum*, ed. D. Launay, *Le Pupitre* (Paris, 1969).
COSSET, F.: *Missa 'Cantate Domino'*; *Missa 'Exultate Deo'*; ed. H. Expert, *Anthologie de musique sacrée des maîtres anciens* (Paris, 1926).
COUPERIN, F.: *Oeuvres complètes*, ed. P. Brunold, xi–xii (Paris, 1932–3).
——*Neuf motets*, ed. P. Oboussier, *Le Pupitre* (Paris, 1972).
——'Adolescentulus sum', ed. J. Gallon (Paris, *c*. 1933).
——*Leçons de ténèbres* [nos. 1–3], ed. L. Vidal, *Le Pupitre* (Paris, 1968).
——'O vos omnes', ed. H. Expert, *Répertoire classique de musique religieuse et spirituelle* (Paris, 1913–14).
DU MONT, H.: *Les Messes royales de Henri Dumont*, ed. A. Gastoué (Paris, 1939).
——Six motets, ed. H. Expert, *Répertoire classique de musique religieuse et spirituelle* (Paris, 1913–14).
——Four motets, ed. D. Launay, *Anthologie du motet latin polyphonique en France* (Paris, 1963).
——'Desidero te', ed. R. Noël (Paris, 1957).
——'O felix Roma', ed. J. Bonfils (Paris, n.d.).
——'O vos omnes', ed. A. Steck (Strasbourg, 1967).
FORMÉ, N.: 'Ecce tu pulchra es', ed. D. Launay, *Anthologie du motet latin polyphonique en France* (Paris, 1963).
——*Sanctus, Agnus Dei* (*Mass for double chorus*), ed. A. Gastoué (Paris, 1939).
GILLES, J.: *Messe des morts*, ed. L. Boulay (Paris, *c*. 1956).
LALANDE, M.-R. DE: 'Cantemus Domino', ed. K. Huss (New York, 1971).
LALLOUETTE, J. F.: *Missa 'Veritas'*, ed. Abbé Delporte (St.-Laurent-sur-Sèvre, 1941).
LOCHON, J.-F.: 'Pastores', *Oratorio de Noël*, ed. G. Massenkeil (Cologne, 1970).
LULLY, J.-B.: Motets, ed. H. Prunières, *Œuvres complètes: Les motets*, i–iii (Paris, 1931, 1935, 1972).
——'Ave coeli', ed. C. Pineau (Paris, 1913).
——'Dies Irae', ed. G. Roussel (Paris, 1955).
——'Plaude laetare', ed. G. Roussel (Paris, 1954).
——'Salve Regina', ed. J. Chailley (Paris, 1954).
——*Te Deum*, ed. F. Raugel (Paris, 1949); ed. W. K. Stanton (London, 1955).
MAUDUIT, J.: 'Era verba dicite'; 'Est Deus pastor mihi'; ed. D. Launay, *Anthologie du motet latin polyphonique en France* (Paris, 1963).
MONDONVILLE, J.-J. C. DE: 'Jubilate'; 'Cantate Domino'; ed. E. Borroff (Pittsburgh, 1961).
MOULINIÉ, É.: *Missa pro defunctis*, ed. D. Launay (Paris, 1952).
——Five motets, ed. D. Launay, *Anthologie du motet latin polyphonique en France* (Paris, 1963).

MOULINIÉ, É.: 'Veni, sponsa mea', ed. D. Launay (Paris, 1954).

NIVERS, G.: 'Quam pulchra es', ed. C. Pineau (Paris, 1957).

PÉCHON, A.: 'Ecce panis', ed. F. Raugel (Paris, 1950).

——'Pange lingua', ed. A. Gastoué (Paris, 1927).

——'Si quis diligit me,' ed. D. Launay, *Anthologie du motet latin polyphonique en France* (Paris, 1963).

POITEVIN, G.: 'Introitus', 'Offertorium', 'Lux aeterna', (*Messe des morts*), ed. H.-A. Durand (Paris, 1962).

RAMEAU, J.-P.: *Œuvres complètes*, iv–v, ed. C. Malherbe (Paris, 1898–9).

ROBERT, P.: 'Deus noster refugium'; 'Quare fremuerunt gentes'; ed. H. Charnassé, *Le Pupitre* (Paris, 1969).

SIGNAC: Nine psalms, ed. H. Quittard, *Sammelbände der internationalen Musikgesellschaft*, xi (1909–10), pp. 497–507.

(ii) *Books and Articles*

(a) *General*

ANTHONY, JAMES R.: *French Baroque Music from Beaujoyeulx to Rameau* (London, 1973).

BENOIT, MARCELLE: *Musiques de cour: chapelle, chambre, écurie, 1661–1733* (Paris, 1971).

——*Versailles et les musiciens du roi, 1661–1733* (Paris, 1971).

BENOIT, MARCELLE and DUFOURCQ, NORBERT: *Dix années à la chapelle royale de musique, d'après une correspondance inédite, 1718–1728* (Paris, 1957).

——'La Vie musicale en Île de France sous la régence: douze années à la chapelle royale de musique d'après une correspondance inédite (1716–1728)', *Revue de musicologie*, xxxvii (1955), pp. 3–29, 148–85.

BERT, MARIE: 'La Musique à la maison royale Saint-Louis de Saint-Cyr', *Recherches sur la musique française classique*, iii (1963), pp. 55–71; iv (1964), pp. 127–31; v (1965), pp. 91–127.

BOULAY, LAURENCE: 'Les Cantiques spirituels de Racine, mis en musique au XVIIe siècle', *XVIIe siècle: Bulletin de la société d'étude du XVIIe siècle*, xxxiv (1957), pp. 79–92.

BOURGOING, FRANÇOIS: *Brevis psalmodi ratio . . .* (Paris, 1634).

BOURLIGUEUX, GUY: 'La Psallette de la cathédrale Saint-Pierre de Vannes: notes historiques et documents inédits', *Recherches sur la musique française classique*, ix (1969), pp. 115–31.

——'La Vie quotidienne à la psallette de la cathédrale de Rennes au XVIIIe siècle', *Recherches sur la musique française classique*, vii (1967), pp. 205–16; viii (1968), pp. 207–27.

BRENET, MICHEL: *Les Musiciens de la Sainte-Chapelle du Palais* (Paris, 1910; repr. Geneva, 1973).

——'La Musique dans les églises de Paris, de 1716 à 1738, d'après les almanachs du temps', *Tribune de Saint-Gervais* (1903), pp. 71–5.

——*La Musique sacrée sous Louis XIV* (Paris, 1899).

——'Notes sur l'introduction des instruments dans les églises de France', *Hugo Riemann zum sechzigsten Geburtstag* (Leipzig, 1909), pp. 277–86.

CHARTIER, FRANÇOIS: *L'Ancien chapitre de Notre-Dame de Paris et sa maîtrise* (Paris, 1897; repr. Geneva, 1971).

CLERVAL, J.-A.: *L'Ancienne maîtrise de Notre-Dame de Chartres* (Paris, 1899; repr. Geneva, 1972).

COLLETTE, AMAND-ROMAIN and BOURBON, A.: *Histoire de la maîtrise de Rouen* (Rouen, 1892; repr. Geneva, 1972).

DAVAL, PIERRE: *La Musique en France au XVIIIe siècle* (Paris, 1961).

DUFOURCQ, NORBERT: 'Les Chapelles de musique de Saint-Sernin et de Saint-Étienne de Toulouse dans le dernier quart du XVIIᵉ siècle', *Revue de musicologie*, xxxix-xl (1957), pp. 36–55.

——'Un Inventaire de la musique religieuse de la collégiale Notre-Dame d'Annecy', *Revue de musicologie*, xli (1958), pp. 38–59.

——'La Musique religieuse française de 1660 à 1789', *Revue musicale*, numéro spécial 222 (1953–4), pp. 89–110.

DURAND, HENRI-ANDRÉ: 'Les Instruments dans la musique sacrée au chapitre collégial Saint-Agricol d'Avignon', *Revue de musicologie*, lii (1966), pp. 73–87.

GARROS, MADELEINE: 'La Musique religieuse en France de 1660 à 1758', *Histoire de la musique*, ed. Roland-Manuel, i (1960), pp. 1591–1613.

GASTOUÉ, AMÉDÉE: *Le Cantique populaire en France* (Paris, 1926).

LAUNAY, DENISE: 'Les Motets à double choeur en France dans la première moitié du XVIIᵉ siècle', *Revue de musicologie*, xxxix-xl (1957), pp. 173–95.

——'La "Paraphrase des pseaumes" de Godeau et ses musiciens', *Revue de musicologie*, 1 (1964), pp. 30–75.

LEBEAU, ÉLISABETH: 'Un Fonds provenant du Concert spirituel à la Bibliothèque Nationale', *Revue de musicologie*, xxxvii (1955), pp. 187–91; xxxviii (1956), pp. 54–67.

LEBEUF, JEAN: *Traité historique et pratique sur le chant ecclésiastique* (Paris, 1741; repr. Geneva, 1972).

LE MOËL, MICHEL: 'La Chapelle de musique sous Henri IV et Louis XIII', *Recherches sur la musique française classique*, vi (1966), pp. 5–26.

LINDEN, ALBERT VAN DER: 'Inventaire de la musique de l'église Saint-Michel à Gand au XVIIIᵉ siècle', *Liber amicorum Charles van den Borren* (Antwerp, 1964), pp. 206–18.

MERSENNE, MARIN: *Harmonie universelle* (Paris, 1636–7; repr. Paris, 1963).

MORBY, JOHN E.: 'The Great Chapel-Chamber Controversy', *Musical Quarterly*, lviii (1972), pp. 383–97.

——*Musicians at the Royal Chapel of Versailles, 1683–1792* (Diss., California: Berkeley, 1971, unpub.).

PAILLARD, JEAN-FRANÇOIS: *La Musique française classique* (Paris, 1960).

PRIM, JEAN: '"Chant sur le livre" in French Churches in the 18th Century', *Journal of the American Musicological Society*, xiv (1961), pp. 37–49.

QUITTARD, HENRI: 'Un Recueil de psaumes français du XVIIᵉ siècle', *Sammelbände der internationalen Musikgesellschaft,* xi (1909–10), pp. 483–508.

RAUGEL, FÉLIX: 'Une Maîtrise célèbre au grand siècle: la maîtrise de la cathédrale d'Aix-en-Provence', *XVIIᵉ siècle: Bulletin de la société d'étude du XVIIᵉ siècle*, xxi-xxii (1954), pp. 422–32.

——'La Musique à la chapelle de Versailles sous Louis XIV', *XVIIᵉ siècle: Bulletin de la société d'étude du XVIIᵉ siècle*, xxiv (1957), pp. 19–25.

——'Notes pour servir à l'histoire musicale de la collégiale de Saint-Quentin depuis les origines jusqu'en 1679', *Festschrift Heinrich Besseler zum sechzigsten Geburtstag* (Leipzig, 1961), pp. 51–8.

ROBERT, JEAN: 'Maîtres de chapelle à Avignon, 1610–1715', *Revue de musicologie,* li (1965), pp. 149–69.

SAUVAL, H.: *Histoire et recherches des antiquités de la ville de Paris* (Paris, 1724; repr. Geneva, 1972).

SONNET, MARTIN: *Ceremoniale parisiense* (Paris, 1662).

VERCHALY, ANDRÉ: 'La Musique religieuse française de Titelouze à 1660', *Revue musicale*, numéro spécial 222 (1953–4), pp. 77–88.

Vie musicale dans les provinces françaises, i [Includes reprints of C. Gomart: *Notes historiques sur la maîtrise de Saint-Quentin*, 1851; A.-E. Prévost: *Histoire de la maîtrise de la cathédrale de Troyes*, 1906; J. Brosset: *Le Grand orgue, les maîtres de chapelle et musiciens du choeur, les organistes de la cathédrale Saint-Louis de Blois*, 1907; G. Durand: *La Musique de la cathédrale d'Amiens avant la Révolution*, 1922] (Geneva, 1972).

Vie musicale dans les provinces françaises, ii [Includes reprints of L. Royer: *Les Musiciens et la musique à l'ancienne collégiale Saint-André de Grenoble du XVᵉ au XVIIIᵉ siècle*, 1938; B. Populus: *L'Ancienne maîtrise de Langres*, 1930] (Geneva, 1972).

YVON-BRIAND, ANNE-MARIE: 'La Maîtrise de Notre-Dame aux XVIIᵉ et XVIIIᵉ siècles', *8ᵉ centenaire de Notre-Dame de Paris*, Congress, 1964 (Paris, 1967).

——*La Vie musicale à Notre-Dame de Paris* (Diss., École des Chartes, 1949).

(b) Individual Composers

Aux-Cousteaux

BLOCH-MICHEL, ANTOINE: 'Les Messes d'Aux-Cousteaux', *Recherches sur la musique française classique*, iii (1963), pp. 31–40.

REBOURD, RENÉ MARIE: 'Messire Arthus Aux-Cousteaux, maître de musique de la Saint-Chapelle au Palais', *XVIIᵉ siècle: Bulletin de la société d'étude du XVIIᵉ siècle*, xxi–xxii (1954), pp. 403–17.

Bernier

DUFOURCQ, NORBERT and BENOIT, MARCELLE: 'À propos de Nicolas Bernier (1667–1734)', *Revue de musicologie*, xxxix (1957), pp. 78–91.

NELSON, PHILIP: 'Nicolas Bernier: a Bibliographic Study', *Studies in Musicology: Essays . . . in Memory of Glen Haydon* (Chapel Hill, 1969), pp. 109–17.

——'Nicolas Bernier: a Résumé of his Work', *Recherches sur la musique française classique*, i (1960), pp. 93–8.

——*Nicolas Bernier: a Study of the Man and his Music* (Diss., North Carolina, 1958, unpub.).

J.-B. Boësset

DUFOURCQ, NORBERT: *Jean-Baptiste de Boësset, 1614–1685* (Paris, 1962).

Bouzignac

LAUNAY, DENISE: 'Bouzignac', *Musique et liturgie* (1951), pp. 3–8.

QUITTARD, HENRI: 'Un Musicien oublié du XVIIᵉ siècle français, G. Bouzignac', *Sammelbände der internationalen Musikgesellschaft*, vi (1904–5), pp. 356–417.

Brossard

BRENET, MICHEL: 'Sébastien de Brossard, prêtre, compositeur, écrivain et bibliophile, d'après ses papiers inédits', *Mémoires de la société de l'histoire de Paris et de l'Île de France*, xxiii (1896), pp. 72–124.

MATHIAS, FRANÇOIS-XAVIER: 'Le "Canticum eucharisticum pro pace facta anno 1697" de Sébastien de Brossard', *Revue de musicologie*, xii (1928), pp. 77–85.

Campra

BARTHÉLEMY, MAURICE: *André Campra* (Paris, 1957).

CASTLE, CONAN J.: *The Grands Motets of André Campra* (Diss., Michigan, 1962, unpub.).

DELPORTE, JULES: 'Le "Benedictus Dominus" d'André Campra', *Musique et liturgie*, xxii (1938), pp. 14–17.

DURAND, HENRI-ANDRÉ: 'Sur une prétendue Messe des Morts de Gilles et Campra', *Revue de musicologie*, xlv (1960), pp. 86–9.

LA LAURENCIE, LIONEL DE: 'Notes sur la jeunesse d'André Campra', *Sammelbände der internationalen Musikgesellschaft*, x (1908–9), pp. 159–258.

Charpentier

BARBER, CLARENCE: *The Liturgical Music of Marc-Antoine Charpentier* (Diss., Harvard, 1955, unpub.).

——'Les Oratorios de Marc-Antoine Charpentier', *Recherches sur la musique française classique*, iii (1963), pp. 90–130.

CRUSSARD, CLAUDE: *Un Musicien français oublié: Marc-Antoine Charpentier* (Paris, 1945).

DUNN, JAMES T.: *The Grands Motets of Marc-Antoine Charpentier* (Diss., Iowa, 1962, unpub.).

HITCHCOCK, H. WILEY: 'The Instrumental Music of Marc-Antoine Charpentier', *Musical Quarterly*, xlvii (1961), pp. 58–72.

——'The Latin Oratorios of Marc-Antoine Charpentier', *Musical Quarterly*, xli (1955), pp. 41–65.

MASSENKEIL, GÜNTHER: 'Marc-Antoine Charpentier als Messenkomponist', *Colloquium amicorum: Joseph Schmidt-Görg zum 70. Geburtstag* (Bonn, 1967), pp. 228–38.

Couperin

MELLERS, WILFRID: *François Couperin and the French Classical Tradition* (London, 1950; repr. 1968).

OBOUSSIER, PHILIPPE: 'Couperin Motets at Tenbury', *Proceedings of the Royal Musical Association*, xcviii (1971–2), pp. 17–29.

TIERSOT, JULIEN: 'François ii Couperin, compositeur de musique religieuse', *Revue de musicologie*, iii (1922), pp. 101–9.

Danielis

BOURLIGUEUX, GUY: 'Le mystérieux Daniel Daniélis, 1635–1696', *Recherches sur la musique française classique*, iv (1964), pp. 146–78.

Desmarest

ANTOINE, MICHEL: *Henry Desmarest (1661–1741)* (Paris, 1965).

Du Mont

QUITTARD, HENRI: *Un Musicien en France au XVIIe siècle: Henry Du Mont* (Paris, 1906).

Formé

LESURE, FRANÇOIS: 'Un Contrat d'exclusivité entre Nicolas Formé et Ballard, 1638', *Revue de musicologie*, 1 (1964), pp. 228–9.

QUITTARD, HENRI: 'Un Chanteur compositeur de musique sous Louis XIII: Nicolas Formé', *La Revue musicale*, iii (1903), pp. 362–7.

——'Une composition française du XVIIe siècle à deux choeurs', *La Revue musicale*, iv (1904), pp. 275–83.

Gantez

GANTEZ, ANNIBAL: *L'Entretien des musiciens* (Auxerre, 1643; repr. of 1878 ed., Geneva, 1971).

Gilles

HAJDU, JOHN H.: *The Life and Works of Jean Gilles* (Diss., Colorado, 1973, unpub.).

Lalande

BOULAY, LAURENCE: 'Notes sur quatre motets inédits de Michel-Richard Delalande', *Recherches sur la musique française classique*, i (1960), pp. 77–86.

DUFOURCQ, NORBERT: 'Retour à Michel-Richard Delalande', *Recherches sur la musique française classique*, i (1960), pp. 69–75.

DUFOURCQ, NORBERT and others: *Notes et références pour servir à une histoire de Michel-Richard Delalande* (Paris, 1957).

53

DURAND, HENRI-ANDRÉ: 'Notes sur la diffusion de M.-R. Delalande dans les chapitres provençaux au XVIIIe siècle', *Revue de musicologie*, xxxix (1957), pp. 72–3.

RICHARDS, JAMES E.: *The 'Grand Motet' of the Late Baroque in France as exemplified by Michel-Richard de Lalande* (Diss., Southern California, 1950, unpub.).

——'Structural Principles in the Grands Motets of de Lalande', *Journal of the American Musicological Society*, xi (1958), pp. 119–27.

TESSIER, ANDRÉ: 'La Carrière versaillaise de La Lande', *Revue de musicologie*, ix (1928), pp. 134–48.

THIBAULT, GENEVIÈVE: 'Le "Te Deum" de Lalande', *Fontes artis musicae*, xii (1965), pp. 162–5.

Lully

COLE, WILLIAM POWELL: *The Motets of Jean-Baptiste Lully* (Diss., Michigan, 1967, unpub.).

Montéclair

BRIQUET, M.: 'Deux motets inédits de Montéclair', *International Musicological Society: Report of the Seventh Congress, Cologne, 1958*, pp. 125–6.

Rameau

GIRDLESTONE, CUTHBERT: *Jean-Philippe Rameau: his Life and Work* (London, 1957; 2nd ed., Paris, 1962).

Robert

CHARNASSÉ, HÉLÈNE: 'Contribution à l'étude des grands motets de Pierre Robert', *Recherches sur la musique française classique*, iii (1963), pp. 49–54; iv (1964), pp. 105–20.

——'Contribution à l'étude du récitatif chez l'Abbé Pierre Robert', *Recherches sur la musique française classique*, i (1960), pp. 61–7.

——'Quelques aspects des "ensembles de récits" chez l'Abbé Pierre Robert', *Recherches sur la musique française classique*, ii (1961–2), pp. 61–70.

MASSON, PAUL-MARIE: 'Le Motet "Splendor aeternae gloriae" de Pierre Robert', *Musique et liturgie*, xxi (1938), pp. 57–8.

CHAPTER VIII

ENGLISH CHURCH MUSIC

(i) *Modern Editions*

(a) *Anthology*

DEARNLEY, CHRISTOPHER, ed.: *The Treasury of English Church Music*, iii: *1650–1760* (London, 1965).

(b) *Works by Individual Composers*

ARNE, T. A.: 'Help me, O Lord' (London, 1924).
——'Libera me', ed. A. Lewis (London, 1950).
BLOW, J.: *Coronation and Verse Anthems*, ed. A. Lewis and W. Shaw, *Musica Britannica*, vii (2nd, rev. ed., London, 1969).
——*Fourteen Full Anthems*, ed. H. D. Statham (London, 1925).
——'Be merciful unto me, O Lord', ed. H. D. Statham (London, 1956).
——'God is our hope and strength', ed. H. D. Statham (London, 1931).
——'I beheld and lo a great multitude', ed. W. Shaw (London, 1953).
——'In the time of trouble', ed. H. D. Statham (London, 1965).
——'Lift up your heads', ed. W. Shaw (London, 1970).
——'Look upon my adversity', ed. J. E. West (London, 1906).

BLOW, J.: *Magnificat* and *Nunc Dimittis* in the Dorian Mode, ed. H. D. Statham and W. Shaw (London, 1958).
——*Magnificat* and *Nunc Dimittis* in F, ed. W. Shaw (London, 1971).
——*Magnificat* and *Nunc Dimittis* in G, ed. W. Shaw (London, 1941).
——'My days are gone like a shadow', ed. H. D. Statham (London, 1955).
——'O God, wherefore art thou absent', ed. J. E. West (London, 1910).
——'O pray for the peace of Jerusalem', ed. W. Shaw (London, 1952).
——'Put me not to rebuke', ed. H. D. Statham (London, 1965).
——'Save, Lord, and hear us', ed. J. E. West (London, 1905).
——'Save me, O God', ed. J. E. West (London, 1905).
——'Sing we merrily unto God', ed. C. Macpherson (London, 1908).
BOYCE, W.: 'I have surely built thee an house', ed. V. Novello (London, n.d.).
——'O where shall wisdom be found' (London, n.d.).
——'Save me, O God' (London, 1906).
——'The king shall rejoice', ed. J. R. Van Nice, *Recent Researches in the Music of the Baroque Era*, viii (Madison, 1970).
——'The souls of the righteous', ed. J. R. Van Nice, *Recent Researches in the Music of the Baroque Era*, vii (Madison, 1970).
——'Turn thee unto me', ed. J. E. West (London, 1920).
CLARKE, J.: 'How long wilt thou forget me?', ed. J. E. West (London, 1906).
——'I will love thee', ed. V. Novello (London, n.d.).
CROFT, W.: 'Hear my prayer', ed. C. H. Stewart (London, 1925).
——'O Lord, rebuke me not', ed. C. H. Stewart (London, 1925).
——'O Lord, thou hast searched me out', ed. C. H. Stewart (London, 1925).
——'Put me not to rebuke', ed. J. E. West (London, 1906).
——*The Order for the Burial of the Dead*, ed. G. C. Martin (London, 1894).
——'Turn thee, O Lord' [excerpt from 'O Lord, rebuke me not'], ed. A. Carpenter (London, 1971).
GREENE, M.: 'Lord, let me know mine end', ed. E. Bullock (London, 1938).
——*Magnificat* and *Nunc Dimittis* in G, ed. H. D. Johnstone (London, 1966).
HANDEL, G. F.: *Funeral Anthem*; *Dettingen Te Deum*; *Te Deum and Jubilate*; *Psalms*; ed. F. Chrysander, *Georg Friedrich Händels Werke*, xi, xxv, xxxi, xxxiv-xxxvi (Leipzig, 1863–73).
HUMFREY, P.: *Complete Church Music*, ed. P. Dennison, *Musica Britannica*, xxxiv–xxxv (London, 1972).
JEFFREYS, G.: 'He beheld the city and wept', ed. P. Aston (London, 1969).
——'O Domine Deus', ed. P. Aston (London, 1969).
LOCKE, M.: 'Turn thy face from my sins', ed. A. Greening (London, 1968).
PURCELL, D.: *Magnificat* and *Nunc Dimittis* in E minor, ed. C. Dearnley (London, 1971).
PURCELL, H.: *Sacred Music, Part 1*, ed. G. E. P. Arkwright, *Purcell Society Edition*, xiiia (London, 1921).
——*Sacred Music, Part 2*, rev. P. Dennison, *Purcell Society Edition*, xiv (London, 1973).
——*Sacred Music, Part 3*, rev. N. Fortune, *Purcell Society Edition*, xvii (London, 1964).
——*Sacred Music, Part 4*, ed. A. Lewis and N. Fortune, *Purcell Society Edition*, xxviii (2nd ed., London, 1967).
——*Sacred Music, Part 5*, ed. A. Lewis and N. Fortune, *Purcell Society Edition*, xxix (2nd ed., London, 1967).
——*Sacred Music, Part 7*, ed. A. Lewis and N. Fortune, *Purcell Society Edition*, xxxii (2nd ed., London, 1967).
ROGERS, B.: 'Lord, who shall dwell in thy tabernacle?', ed. C. F. Simkins (London, 1967).

ROGERS, B.: *Magnificat* and *Nunc Dimittis*, ed. B. Rose (London, 1968).
ROSEINGRAVE, T.: 'Arise, shine', ed. P. M. Young (London, 1968).
WISE, M.: 'Christ rising again from the dead', ed. M. J. Smith (London, 1973).
——*Magnificat* and *Nunc Dimittis*, ed. S. H. Nicholson (London, 1932).

(ii) *Books and Articles*

(a) *General*

DEARNLEY, CHRISTOPHER: *English Church Music, 1650–1750* (London, 1970).
FELLOWES, EDMUND H.: *English Cathedral Music* (5th ed., rev. J. A. Westrup, London, 1969).
HARLEY, JOHN: *Music in Purcell's London* (London, 1968).
SCHOLES, PERCY: *The Puritans and Music in England* (London, 1934).

(b) *Individual Composers*

Blow

SHAW, H. WATKINS: 'Blow's Use of the Ground Bass', *Musical Quarterly*, xxiv (1938), pp. 31–8.
——'John Blow's Anthems', *Music and Letters*, xix (1938), pp. 429–42.
——'Tradition and Convention in John Blow's Harmony', *Music and Letters*, xxx (1949), pp. 136–45.

Clarke

TAYLOR, THOMAS F.: *The Life and Works of Jeremiah Clarke (ca. 1673–1707)* (Diss., Northwestern University, 1967, unpub.).

Greene

JOHNSTONE, H. DIACK: *The Life and Work of Maurice Greene (1696–1755)* (Diss., Oxford, 1968, unpub.).

Humfrey

DENNISON, PETER: 'The Church Music of Pelham Humfrey', *Proceedings of the Royal Musical Association*, xcviii (1971–2), pp. 65–71.
——*The Life and Work of Pelham Humfrey* (Diss., Oxford, 1970, unpub.).

Jeffreys

ASTON, PETER: 'George Jeffreys', *Musical Times*, cx (1968), pp. 772–6.
——*George Jeffreys and the English Baroque* (Diss., York, 1971, unpub.).
——'Tradition and Experiment in the Devotional Music of George Jeffreys', *Proceedings of the Royal Musical Association*, xcix (1972–3), pp. 105–15.

Locke

HARDING, ROSAMOND E. M.: *A Thematic Catalogue of the Works of Matthew Locke* (Oxford, 1971).
LEWIS, ANTHONY: 'Matthew Locke: a Dynamic Figure in English Music', *Proceedings of the Royal Musical Association*, lxxiv (1947–8), pp. 57–71.

Purcell

HARLEY, JOHN: *Music in Purcell's London* (London, 1968).
HOLST, IMOGEN, ed.: *Henry Purcell 1659–95: Essays on his Music* (London, 1959).
QUERVAIN, FRITZ DE: *Der Chorstil Henry Purcells* (Berne, 1935).
WESTRUP, J. A.: *Purcell* (2nd ed., London, 1968).
ZIMMERMAN, FRANKLIN B.: *Henry Purcell, 1659–1695: an Analytical Catalogue of his Music* (London, 1963).
——*Henry Purcell, 1659–1695: his Life and Times* (London, 1967).

Turner

FRANKLIN, DON: *The Anthems of William Turner (1651–1740): an Historical and Analytical Study* (Diss., Stanford, 1967, unpub.).

CHAPTER IX

GERMAN CHURCH MUSIC

(i) *Modern Editions*

AHLE, J. R.: *Johann Rudolf Ahles ausgewählte Gesangswerke*, ed. J. Wolf, *Denkmäler deutscher Tonkunst*, v (Leipzig, 1901).

——*Geistliche Chorwerke*, ed. H. Mönkemeyer, *Antiqua Chorbuch*, i/5 (Mainz, 1951–2).

——'Was mag doch diese Welt', *Nagels Männerchor-Blätter*, xvi (Kassel, n.d.).

BACH FAMILY: *Music of the Bach Family*, ed. K. Geiringer (Cambridge, Mass., 1955).

BACH, J. C.: *Altbachisches Archiv aus J. S. Bachs Sammlung von Werken seiner Vorfahren* (*Das Erbe deutscher Musik*, i, *Reichsdenkmale*, 1–2) (Leipzig, 1935).

——*Drei Motetten*, ed. A. Fareanu, *Die Kunst des Bachschen Geschlechts*, iv (Leipzig, 1924–8).

——'Ich lasse dich nicht', ed. K. Ameln and G. Wolters (Wolfenbüttel, 1950).

BACH, J. H.: *Altbachisches Archiv aus J. S. Bachs Sammlung von Werken seiner Vorfahren* (*Das Erbe deutscher Musik*, i, *Reichsdenkmale*, 1–2) (Leipzig, 1935).

BACH, J. L.: *Zwei Motetten*, ed. K. Geiringer, *Das Chorwerk*, xcix (Wolfenbüttel, 1963).

BACH, J. M.: *Altbachisches Archiv aus J. S. Bachs Sammlung von Werken seiner Vorfahren* (*Das Erbe deutscher Musik*, i, *Reichsdenkmale*, 1–2) (Leipzig, 1935).

BACH, J. S.: *Johann Sebastian Bach's Werke*, ed. M. Hauptmann *et al.*, Bach-Gesellschaft (Leipzig, 1851–99).

——*Neue Ausgabe sämtlicher Werke*, ed. Alfred Dürr *et al.* (Kassel and Leipzig, 1954–).

BERNHARD, C.: 'Christ unser Herr zum Jordan kam', *Johann Theile und Christoph Bernhard: zwei Kurzmessen*, ed. R. Gerber, *Das Chorwerk*, xvi (Wolfenbüttel and Berlin, 1932).

——*Eine Kurzmesse und eine Motette*, ed. O. Drechsler, *Das Chorwerk*, cvii (Wolfenbüttel, 1966).

——*Matthias Weckmann und Christoph Bernhard: Solokantaten und Chorwerke*, ed. M. Seiffert, *Denkmäler deutscher Tonkunst*, vi (Leipzig, 1901).

BIBER, H. I. F. VON: *Missa Sancti Henrici*, ed. G. Adler, *Denkmäler der Tonkunst in Österreich*, xlix (Jg. xxv (l)) (Vienna, 1918).

——*Requiem*, ed. G. Adler, *Denkmäler der Tonkunst in Österreich*, lix (Jg. xxx (l)) (Vienna, 1923).

BRIEGEL, W. C.: 'Und es erhub sich ein Streit'; 'Fahre auf die Höhe'; 'Wohl dem, dem die Übertretung vergeben ist'; 'Mache dich auf, werde Licht'; ed. E. and F. Noack, *Kirchenmusik der Darmstädter Meister des Barock*, iii–vi (Berlin, 1955–62).

BRUHNS, N.: *Gesammelte Werke*, ed. F. Blume, *Das Erbe deutscher Musik*, ii, *Landschaftsdenkmale: Schleswig-Holstein und Hansestädte*, 1: *Kirchenkantaten 1–7;* 2: *Kirchenkantaten 8–12* (Brunswick, 1937–9).

BUXTEHUDE, D.: *Werke*, ed. W. Gurlitt, G. Harms, H. Trede, D. Kilian *et al.* (Klecken, 1925–6, Hamburg, 1930–).

——*Abendmusiken und Kirchenkantaten*, ed. M. Seiffert, *Denkmäler deutscher Tonkunst*, xiv (Leipzig, 1903).

——'Conquassabit capita', ed. R. Eitner, *Cantaten des 17. und 18. Jahrhundert*, i/3 (Leipzig, 1886).

——*Fire Latinske Kantater* (*Samfundet til Udgivelse af Dansk Musik*, ser. 3, no. 138) (Copenhagen, 1957).

BUXTEHUDE, D.: *Geistliche Chorwerke*, ed. H. Mönkemeyer, *Antiqua Chorbuch*, i/5 (Mainz, 1951–2).

——*Kantaten* (*Veröffentlichungen der Institut für Musikforschung*, ser. 1) (Berlin, 1955–).

——'O Gott, wir danken deiner Güt'; 'Frohlocket mit Händen alle Völker'; 'Nun danket alle Gott'; 'Wie wird erneuet, wie wird erfreuet'; 'Jesu meiner Freuden Meister'; ed. S. Sørensen (Copenhagen, 1972).

CRÜGER, J.: *Geistliche Chorwerke*, ed. H. Mönkemeyer, *Antiqua Chorbuch*, i/5 (Mainz, 1951–2).

——*Neun geistliche Lieder,* ed. C. Mahrenholz, *Chor-Archiv* (Kassel, n.d.).

DEMANTIUS, C.: *Der 116. Psalm*, ed. A. Adrio, *Das Chorwerk*, xxxvi (Berlin, 1936).

——*Geistliche Chorwerke*, ed. H. Mönkemeyer, *Antiqua Chorbuch*, i/4 (Mainz, 1951–2).

——*Passion nach dem Evangelisten Johannes*, ed. F. Blume, *Das Chorwerk*, xxvii Berlin, 1934).

——*Vier deutsche Motetten*, ed. A. A. Abert, *Das Chorwerk*, xxxix (Berlin, 1936).

EBERLING, J. G.: *Geistliche Chorwerke*, ed. H. Mönkemeyer, *Antiqua Chorbuch*, i/5 (Mainz, 1951–2).

EBERLIN, J. E.: *Der blutschwitzende Jesus*; *Stücke aus anderen Oratorien*; ed. R. Haas, *Denkmäler der Tonkunst in Österreich*, lv (Jg. xxviii (1)) (Vienna, 1921).

——*Salzburger Kirchenkomponisten,* ed. K. A. Rosenthal and C. Schneider, *Denkmäler der Tonkunst in Österreich*, lxxx (Jg. xliii (1)) (Vienna, 1936).

ERLEBACH, P. H.: 'Der Herr hat offenbaret', ed. H. Albrecht, *Organum*, ser. 1, no. 33 (Leipzig, 1962).

——*Geistliche Chorwerke*, ed. H. Mönkemeyer, *Antiqua Chorbuch*, i/5 (Mainz, 1951–2).

FERDINAND III: *Kirchenwerke*; *Gesänge aus Oratorien und Opern*, ed. G. Adler, *Musikalische Werke der Kaiser Ferdinand III., Leopold I. und Joseph I.*, 2 vols. (Vienna, 1892–3).

FRAUENHOLTZ, C.: 'Der Herr gedenkt an uns'; 'Verbirg nicht deine Holden Strahlen'; ed. H. Albrecht, *Organum*, ser. 1, nos. 31, 30 (Leipzig, 1954).

FROMM, A.: *Actus musicus de Divite et Lazaro*, ed. H. Engel, *Denkmäler der Musik in Pommern*, v (Kassel, 1936).

——*Lazarus*, ed. H. Engel, *Drei Werke pommerscher Komponisten* (Greifswald, 1931).

FUNCKE, F.: *Matthäus-Passion für Solostimmen, 4stg. Chor und Instrumente,* ed. J. Birke, *Das Chorwerk*, lxxvii–lxxix (Wolfenbüttel, 1960).

FUX, J. J.: *Gesammelte Werke*, ed. H. Federhofer (Kassel and Graz, 1959–).

——*Geistliche Solomotetten*, ed. C. Schoenbaum, *Denkmäler der Tonkunst in Österreich*, ci–cii (Graz and Vienna, 1962).

——*Messen*, ed. J. E. Habert and G. A. Glossner, *Denkmäler der Tonkunst in Österreich*, i (Jg. i (1)) (Vienna, 1894).

——*Motetten*, ed. J. E. Habert, *Denkmäler der Tonkunst in Österreich*, iii (Jg. ii (1)) (Vienna, 1895).

GOLDBERG, J. G.: *Kantaten,* ed. A. Dürr, *Das Erbe deutscher Musik*, i, *Reichsdenkmale*, 35 (Kassel, 1957).

GRAUN, C. H.: *Das Mitleid:* 'Mitleid lebst du noch?', ed. R. Eitner, *Cantaten des 17. und 18. Jahrhunderts*, i/3 (Leipzig, 1886).

——*Drei lateinische Werke*, ed. F. Commer, *Cantica sacra*, i, nos. 10–11; ii, no. 8 (Berlin, n.d.).

——*Passionsmusik:* 'Nun darf ich mich nicht', ed. F. Commer, *Cantica sacra,* ii, no. 22 (Berlin, n.d.).

——*Vier Kantaten*, ed. F. Rochlitz, *Sammlung vorzüglicher Gesangstücke*, iii, nos. 25–28 (Mainz, Paris, and Antwerp, 1840).

GRAUPNER, C.: *Ausgewählte Kantaten*, ed. F. Noack, *Denkmäler deutscher Tonkunst*, li-lii (Leipzig, 1926; repr. with supplement, Wiesbaden and Graz, 1960).

——'Jesu, führe meine Seele'; 'Wie bald hast du gelitten', ed. F. Noack, *Kirchenmusik der Darmstädter Meister des Barock,* iii (Berlin, 1955).

HAMMERSCHMIDT, A.: *Ausgewählte Werke*, ed. H. Leichtentritt, *Denkmäler deutscher Tonkunst*, xl (Leipzig, 1910).

——*Dialogi*, ed. A. W. Schmidt, *Denkmäler der Tonkunst in Österreich*, xvi (Jg. viii (1)) (Vienna, 1901).

——*Geistliche Chorwerke*, ed. H. Mönkemeyer, *Antiqua Chorbuch*, i/5 (Mainz, 1951–2).

HANDEL, G. F.: *Passion nach dem Evangelisten Johannes*; *Passion nach B. H. Brockes*; *Lateinische Kirchenmusik*; 'Laudate pueri' [1st and 2nd settings]; 'Dixit Dominus'; 'Nisi Dominus'; 'Salve Regina'; ed. F. Chrysander, *Georg Friedrich Händels Werke,* ix, xv, xxxviii (Leipzig, 1860, 1863, Bergedorf, 1872).

——*Passion nach dem Evangelisten Johannes*, ed. K. G. Fellerer; *Passion nach B. H. Brockes,* ed. F. Schroeder; 'Dixit Dominus'; ed. E. Wenzel, *Hallische Händel-Ausgabe,* ser. 1, *Oratorien und grosse Kantaten*, ii, vii, ser. 3, *Lateinische Kirchenmusik*, i (Kassel and Leipzig, 1964, 1965, 1960).

HASSE, J. A.: *Ausgewählte Werke*, ed. O. Schmid, *Musik am sächsischen Hofe,* vii–viii (Leipzig, 1898).

——*Drei lateinische Werke*, ed. F. Rochlitz, *Sammlung vorzüglicher Gesangstücke*, iii (Mainz, Paris, and Antwerp, 1840).

——*Geistliche Gesänge*, ed. F. Commer, *Cantica sacra*, i, nos. 2, 3, 23 (Berlin, n.d.).

KEISER, R.: 'Bei kühler Abenddämmerung'; 'Mir wird bald heiss, bald kalt'; 'Deine Grossmut, deine Güte'; 'Lieben, leiden, bitten, flehen'; ed. R. Eitner, *Cantaten des 17. und 18. Jahrhunderts,* i/1 (Leipzig, 1884).

KERLL, J. C.: *Ausgewählte Werke*, ed. A. Sandberger, *Denkmäler der Tonkunst in Bayern,* ii/2 (Brunswick, 1901).

——*Missa cujus toni; Missa a 3 cori*; ed. G. Adler, *Denkmäler der Tonkunst in Österreich*, xlix (Jg. xxv (1)) (Vienna, 1918).

——*Requiem*, ed. G. Adler, *Denkmäler der Tonkunst in Österreich*, lix (Jg. xxx (1)) (Vienna, 1923).

KINDERMANN, J. E.: *Ausgewählte Werke*, ed. M. Schneider and F. Schreiber, *Denkmäler der Tonkunst in Bayern,* xiii, xxi, xxiv (Leipzig, 1913, Augsburg, 1924).

KIRCHHOFF, G.: *Kantaten*, ed. A. Dürr, *Das Erbe deutscher Musik,* i, *Reichsdenkmale,* 35 (Kassel, 1957).

KNÜPFER, S.: *Ausgewählte Kirchenkantaten*, ed. A. Schering, *Denkmäler deutscher Tonkunst*, lviii–lix (Leipzig, 1918).

KRIEGER, J. P.: *Ausgewählte Werke*, ed. M. Seiffert, *Denkmäler der Tonkunst in Bayern,* xviii (Leipzig, 1917).

——*21 ausgewählte Kirchenkompositionen*, ed. M. Seiffert, *Denkmäler deutscher Tonkunst,* liii–liv (Leipzig, 1916).

KUHNAU, J.: *Ausgewählte Kirchenkantaten*, ed. A. Schering, *Denkmäler deutscher Tonkunst,* lviii–lix (Leipzig, 1918).

——'Ich habe Lust abzuscheiden', ed. M. Seiffert, *Organum*, ser. 1, no. 14 (Leipzig, 1928).

KÜHNHAUSEN, J.: *Passion nach dem Evangelisten Matthäus*, ed. A. Adrio, *Das Chorwerk*, 1 (Berlin, 1937).

LEOPOLD I: *Kirchenwerke*; *Gesänge aus Oratorien und Opern*, ed. G. Adler, *Musikalische Werke der Kaiser Ferdinand III., Leopold I. und Joseph I.*, 2 vols. (Vienna, 1892–3).

REUTTER, G. [the younger]: *Kirchenwerke,* ed. N. Hofer, *Denkmäler der Tonkunst in Österreich*, lxxxviii (Vienna, 1952).

ROSENMÜLLER, J.: *Die Psalmen 138 und 134*, ed. F. Hamel, *Nagels Musik-Archiv*, lix, lxxxi (Hanover, 1930, 1932).

——'Domine ne in furore'; 'Laboravi', ed. F. Commer, *Cantica sacra*, ii, nos. 18, 20 (Berlin, n.d.).

——'In hac misera valle', ed. M. Seiffert, *Organum*, ser. 1, no. 24 (Leipzig, [1933]).

——*Lamentationes Jeremiae prophetae*, ed. F. Hamel, *Nagels Musik-Archiv*, xxvii–xxviii (Hanover, 1929).

SCHEIDT, S.: *Cantiones sacrae* (*1620*); *Geistliche Konzerte* (*1631*); *Geistliche Konzerte* (*1634*); *Geistliche Konzerte* (*1635*); *Geistliche Konzerte* (*1640*); *Lateinische geistliche Konzerte* (*1622*); ed. C. Mahrenholz, A. Adrio, and E. Gessner, *Werke*, iv, viii, ix, x–xi, xiv–xv (Hamburg, 1933, 1957, 1960, 1964, 1971).

——Seven motets, ed. C. Mahrenholz, *Chor-Archiv* (Kassel, 1939–55).

SCHELLE, J.: *Ausgewählte Kirchenkantaten*, ed. A. Schering, *Denkmäler deutscher Tonkunst*, lviii–lix (Leipzig, 1918).

SCHMELZER, J. H.: *Missa nuptialis*, ed. G. Adler, *Denkmäler der Tonkunst in Österreich*, xlix (Jg. xxv (1)) (Vienna, 1918).

SCHOP, J.: 'Vom Himmel hoch, da komm ich her', ed. A. Strube, *Nagels Musik-Archiv*, lxix (Hanover, 1930).

SCHULTZ, J.: *Musikalischer Lüstgarte*, ed. H. Zenck, *Das Erbe deutscher Musik*, ii, *Landschaftsdenkmale: Niedersachsen*, 5 (Wolfenbüttel, 1937).

SCHULTZE, C.: *Das bittere Leiden und Sterben unsers Herren und Erlösers Jesu Christi*, ed. J. Wolf, *Veröffentlichungen der Musik-Bibliothek Paul Hirsch*, x (Berlin, 1930).

SCHÜTZ, H.: *Sämmtliche Werke*, ed. P. Spitta, A. Schering, and H. Spitta (Leipzig, 1885–1927).

——*Neue Ausgabe sämtlicher Werke*, ed. K. Ameln *et al.* (Kassel, 1955–).

——*Stuttgart Schütz-Ausgabe*, ed. G. Graulich (Stuttgart, 1971–).

——*Die sieben Worte Jesu Christi*, ed. C. K. Scott (London, 1938); ed. P. Steinitz (London, 1961).

——*A German Requiem* (*Musikalische Exequien*), ed. A. Mendel (New York, 1957).

——*The St. Luke Passion*; *The Passion according to St. John*; *The Passion according to St. Matthew*; ed. P. Steinitz (London, 1956, 1963, 1965).

SEBASTIANI, J.: *Passionsmusiken*, ed. F. Zelle, *Denkmäler deutscher Tonkunst*, xvii (Leipzig, 1904).

SELLE, T.: *Johannes-Passion mit Intermedien*, ed. R. Gerber, *Das Chorwerk*, xxvi (Berlin, 1933).

——*Ausgewählte Kirchenmusik*, ed. K. Vetter (Stuttgart, 1963).

——*Zwei Kurzmessen*, ed. J. Birke, *Das Chorwerk*, xc (Wolfenbüttel, 1963).

STADLMAYR, J.: *Hymnen*, ed. J. E. Habert, *Denkmäler der Tonkunst in Österreich*, v (Jg. iii (1)) (Vienna, 1896).

STOBÄUS, J.: *Geistliche Chorwerke*, ed. H. Mönkemeyer, *Antiqua Chorbuch*, i/5 (Mainz, 1951–2).

——'Laudent Deum', ed. J. M. Müller-Blattau, *Musica Reservata* (*Meisterwerke der Musik des 16. und 17. Jahrhunderts*), i (Kassel, n.d.).

STÖLZEL, G. H.: *Gloria*, ed. F. Rochlitz, *Sammlung vorzüglicher Gesangstücke*, iii, no. 18 (Mainz, Paris, and Antwerp, 1840).

——'Lob und Dank', ed. H. Albrecht, *Organum*, ser. 1, no. 29 (Leipzig, 1954).

——*Weihnachtskantate*, ed. H. Albrecht, *Organum*, ser. 1, no. 28 (Leipzig, 1953).

STRAUSS, C.: *Requiem*, ed. G. Adler, *Denkmäler der Tonkunst in Österreich*, lix (Jg. xxx (1)) (Vienna, 1923).

TELEMANN, G. P.: *Musikalische Werke*, ed. G. Fock *et al.* (Kassel, 1950–).

——'Laudate Jehovam omnes gentes,' ed. E. Valentin, *Chor-Archiv* (Kassel, n.d.).

——*Vier Motetten*, ed. W. K. Morgan, *Das Chorwerk*, civ (Wolfenbüttel, 1966).

THEILE, J.: *Passionsmusiken*, ed. F. Zelle, *Denkmäler deutscher Tonkunst*, xvii (Leipzig, 1904).

——*Johann Theile und Christoph Bernhard: zwei Kurzmessen*, ed. R. Gerber, *Das Chorwerk*, xvi (Wolfenbüttel and Berlin, 1932).

TUNDER, F.: 'Ach Herr, lass deine lieben Engelein'; 'Ein' feste Burg'; 'Ein kleines Kindelein'; 'Wachet auf!'; ed. M. Seiffert, *Organum*, ser. 1, nos. 7, 15, 3, 13 (Leipzig, 1924, 1929, 1929, 1928).

——*Gesangswerke: Solokantaten und Chorwerke*, ed. M. Seiffert, *Denkmäler deutscher Tonkunst*, iii (Leipzig, 1900).

WECKMANN, M.: *Ausgewählte Werke*, ed. F. Blume, *Das Erbe deutscher Musik*, ii, *Landschaftsdenkmale: Schleswig-Holstein und Hansestädte*, 4 (Brunswick, 1942).

——*Matthias Weckmann und Christoph Bernhard: Solokantaten und Chorwerke*, ed. M. Seiffert, *Denkmäler deutscher Tonkunst*, vi (Leipzig, 1901).

——'Weine nicht!'; 'Wie liegt die Stadt'; 'Zion spricht'; ed. M. Seiffert, *Organum*, ser. 1, nos. 18, 1, 17 (Leipzig, 1929, 1924, 1929).

ZACHOW, F. W.: *Gesammelte Werke von Friedr. Wilh. Zachow*, ed. M. Seiffert, *Denkmäler deutscher Tonkunst*, xxi-xxii (Leipzig, 1905).

——'Herr, wenn ich nur dich habe', ed. M. Seiffert, *Organum*, ser. 1, no. 5 (Leipzig, 1924).

(ii) *Books and Articles*

(a) *General*

ADRIO, ADAM: *Die Anfänge des geistlichen Konzerts* (Berlin, 1935).

BLUME, FRIEDRICH: *Geschichte der evangelischen Kirchenmusik* (2nd ed., Kassel, 1965).

——*Das monodische Prinzip in der protestantischen Kirchenmusik* (Leipzig, 1925).

BRAUN, WERNER: *Die mitteldeutsche Choralpassion im 18ten Jahrhundert* (Berlin, 1960).

GERBER, RUDOLF: *Die deutsche Passion von Luther bis Bach* (Gütersloh, 1931).

HUDEMANN, H.: *Die protestantische Dialogkomposition in 17. Jahrhundert* (Freiburg im Breisgau, 1941).

KRUMMACHER, FRIEDHELM: *Die Überlieferung der Choralbearbeitungen in der frühen evangelischen Kantate* (Berlin, 1965).

LANGE, MARTIN: *Die Anfänge der Kantate* (Diss., Leipzig, 1938).

LEICHTENTRITT, HUGO: *Geschichte der Motette* (Leipzig, 1908).

LOTT, WALTER: 'Zur Geschichte der Passionskomposition von 1650–1800', *Archiv für Musikwissenschaft,* iii (1920), pp. 285–320.

MOSER, HANS JOACHIM: 'Aus der Frühgeschichte der deutschen Generalbass-Passion', *Jahrbuch der Musikbibliothek Peters*, xvii (1920), pp. 18–30.

——'Die Zeitgrenzen des musikalischen Barock', *Zeitschrift für Musikwissenschaft*, iv (1921–2), pp. 253–4.

PREUSSNER, EBERHARD: 'Die Methodik im Schulgesang der evangelischen Lateinschulen des 17. Jahrhunderts', *Archiv für Musikwissenschaft*, vi (1923), pp. 407–49.

RIEBER, K. F.: *Die Entwicklung der deutschen geistlichen Solokantate im 17. Jahrhundert* (Lörrach, 1932).

SANDER, H. A.: 'Beiträge zur Geschichte der Barockmesse', *Kirchenmusikalisches Jahrbuch*, xxviii (1933), pp. 77–129.

SCHERING, ARNOLD: 'Die Kantaten der Thomas-Kantoren vor Bach', *Bach-Jahrbuch*, ix (1912), pp. 86–123.

SCHILD, E.: *Geschichte der protestantischen Messkomposition im 17. und 18. Jahrhundert* (Elberfeld, 1934).

SCHULZ, W.: *Studien über das deutsche, protestantische monodische Kirchenlied des 17. Jahrhunderts* (Diss., Breslau, 1934).

SMALLMAN, BASIL: *The Background of Passion Music* (2nd ed., New York, 1970).

TREIBER, F.: 'Die thüringisch-sächsische Kirchenkantate zur Zeit des jungen Bach (1700–1723)', *Archiv für Musikforschung*, ii (1937), pp. 129–59.

URSPRUNG, OTTO: *Die katholische Kirchenmusik* (Potsdam, 1931).

WINTERFELD, CARL VON: *Der evangelische Kirchengesang und sein Verhältnis zur Kunst des Tonsatzes*, 3 vols. (Leipzig, 1843–47; repr. 1966).

(b) Individual Composers

Ahle

JOHNSON, JOHN P.: *An Analysis and Edition of Selected Sacred Choral Works of Johann Rudolf Ahle*, 2 vols. (Diss., Southern Baptist Theological Seminary, 1969, unpub.).

WOLF, JOHANNES: 'Johann Rudolph Ahle: eine bio-bibliographische Skizze', *Sammelbände der internationalen Musikgesellschaft*, ii (1900–1), pp. 393–400.

Bach Family

ALBRECHT, HANS AND BACH, A.: *Die Bache in Arnstadt. Mitteilungsblatt des Bach'schen Familienverbandes für Thüringen* (Arnstadt, 1938).

BORKOWSKY, E.: *Die Musikerfamilie Bach* (Jena, 1930).

FREYSE, CONRAD: *Die Ohrdrufer Bache in der Silhouette. Johann Sebastian Bachs ältester Bruder Johann Christoph und seine Nachkommen* (Eisenach and Kassel, 1957).

GEIRINGER, KARL: *Die Familie Bach* (Vienna, 1936).

GEIRINGER, KARL and IRENE: *The Bach Family: seven generations of creative genius* (London, 1954).

HELMBOLD, H.: *Bilder aus Eisenachs Vergangenheit* (Eisenach, 1928).

MÜLLER-BLATTAU, JOSEPH: *Genealogie der musikalischen Bachischen Familie* (Kassel, 1950).

OLEARIUS, J. G., ed. R. Eitner: 'Begräbnispredigt auf Heinrich Bach', *Monatshefte für Musikgeschichte*, vii (1875), pp. 178–9.

RAUSCHENBERGER, W.: *Die Familien Bach* (Frankfurt am Main, 1950).

ROLLBERG, FRITZ: 'Johann Ambrosius Bach', *Bach-Jahrbuch 1927*, xxiv (1927), pp. 133–52.

——'Johann Christoph Bach', *Zeitschrift für Musikwissenschaft*, xi (1928–9), pp. 549–61.

SCHÄFER, F.: *Der Organist J. Christoph Bach und die Eisenacher Münze* (Luginsland, 1929).

SCHEIDE, WILLIAM H.: 'Johann Sebastian Bachs Sammlung von Kantaten seines Vetters Johann Ludwig Bach', *Bach-Jahrbuch 1959*, xlvi, pp. 52–94; *1961*, xlviii, pp. 5–24; *1962*, pp. 5–32.

SCHNEIDER, MAX: 'Thematisches Verzeichnis der musikalischen Werke der Familie Bach', *Bach-Jahrbuch 1907*, iv, pp. 103–77.

SCHUMM, O.: *Hof- und Stadtorganist J. Christoph Bach zu Eisenach* (Luginsland, 1927).

TERRY, CHARLES SANFORD: *The Origins of the Family of Bach* (Oxford, 1929).

THIELE, G.: 'Die Familie Bach in Mühlhausen', *Mühlhäuser Geschichtsblätter* (1920–21).

WENNIG, E.: *Chronik des musikalischen Lebens der Stadt Jena* (Jena, 1937).

WHITTAKER, W. GILLIES: 'The Bachs and Eisenach', *Collected Essays* (London, 1940), pp. 151–63.

WIEGAND, F., ed.: *J. S. Bach und seine Verwandten in Arnstadt* (Arnstadt, 1950).

J. S. Bach

SCHMIEDER, WOLFGANG: *Thematisch-Systematisches Verzeichnis der musikalischen Werke von Johann Sebastian Bach* (Leipzig, 1950) [contains comprehensive bibliography].

——'Das Bachschrifttum 1945–1952', *Bach-Jahrbuch 1953*, xl, pp. 119–68.

——'Das Bachschrifttum 1953–1957', *Bach-Jahrbuch 1958*, xlv, pp. 127–50.

FRANKE, ERHARD: 'Das Bachschrifttum 1958–1962', *Bach-Jahrbuch 1967*, liii, pp. 121–169.

AMELN, KONRAD: 'Zur Entstehungsgeschichte der Motette *Singet dem Herrn ein neues Lied* von J. S. Bach (BWV 225)', *Bach-Jahrbuch 1961*, xlviii, pp. 25–34.

BITTER, CARL H.: *Johann Sebastian Bach*, 4 vols. (Berlin, 1881).

BULLIVANT, ROGER: 'Zum Problem der Begleitung der Bachschen Motetten', *Bach-Jahrbuch 1966*, lii, pp. 59–68.

DADELSEN, GEORG VON: *Bemerkungen zur Handschrift Johann Sebastian Bachs, seine Familie und seines Kreises* (Trossingen, 1957).

——*Beiträge zur Chronologie der Werke Johann Sebastian Bachs* (Trossingen, 1958).

DAVID, HANS T. AND MENDEL, ARTHUR: *The Bach Reader* (2nd ed., New York, 1966).

DÜRR, ALFRED: 'Beobachtungen am Autograph der Matthäus-Passion', *Bach-Jahrbuch 1963–4*, 1, pp. 47–52.

——'Verstümmelt überlieferte Arien aus Kantaten J. S. Bachs', *Bach-Jahrbuch 1960*, xlvii, pp. 28–42.

——'Zu den verschollenen Passionen Bachs', *Bach-Jahrbuch 1949–50*, xxxviii, pp. 81–99.

——'Zur Chronologie der Leipziger Vokalwerke J. S. Bachs', *Bach-Jahrbuch 1957*, xlvii, pp. 5–162 [published separately, Kassel, 1958].

——'Zur Echtheit der Kantate *Meine Seele rühmt und preist* (BWV 189)', *Bach-Jahrbuch 1956*, xlii, pp. 155.

FORKEL, J. N.: *J. S. Bach* (Leipzig, 1802; Eng. trans., London, 1920).

FRANKE, F. W.: *J. S. Bachs Kirchen-Kantaten*, 2 vols. (Leipzig, [1925]).

GECK, MARTIN: 'Zur Echtheit der Bach-Motette *Lobet den Herren, alle Heiden*', *Bach-Jahrbuch 1967*, liii, pp. 57–69.

GEIRINGER, KARL: *Johann Sebastian Bach: the culmination of an era* (New York, 1966).

GOJOWY, DETLEV: 'Zur Frage der Köthener Trauermusik und der Matthäuspassion', *Bach-Jahrbuch 1965*, li, pp. 87–134.

HAMEL, FRED: *Johann Sebastian Bach: geistige Welt* (Göttingen, 1951).

HERZ, GERHARD: 'Bach's Religion', *Journal of Renaissance and Baroque Music*, i (1946), pp. 124–38.

HEUSS, ALFRED: *Die Matthäuspassion* (Leipzig, 1909).

HUDSON, FREDERICK: 'Bach's Wedding Music', *Current Musicology*, vii (1968), pp. 111–20.

——'The St. Matthew Passion and Hans Brandts Buys', *Musical Times*, xcvi (1955), p. 95.

HUDSON, FREDERICK and DÜRR, ALFRED: 'An Investigation into the Authenticity of Bach's *Kleine Magnificat*', *Music and Letters*, xxxvi (1955), pp. 233–6.

JAUERNIG, REINHOLD: 'Zur Kantate *Ich hatte viel Bekümmernis* (BWV 21)', *Bach-Jahrbuch 1954*, xli, pp. 46–9.

KAST, PAUL: *Die Bach-Handschriften der Berliner Staatsbibliothek* (Trossingen, 1955).

KINSKY, GEORG: *Die Original-Ausgaben der Werke J. S. Bachs* (Vienna, Leipzig, and Zürich, 1937).

KRAUSE, PETER: *Handschriften der Werke J. S. Bachs in der Musikbibliothek der Stadt Leipzig* (Leipzig, 1964).

KREY, JOHANNES: 'Zur Bedeutung der Fermaten in Bachs Chorälen', *Bach-Jahrbuch 1956*, xliii, pp. 105–11.

MARSHALL, ROBERT: *The Compositional Process of J. S. Bach* (Princeton, 1972).

——'How J. S. Bach Composed Four-part Chorales', *Musical Quarterly*, lvi (1970), pp. 198–220.

——'Musical sketches in J. S. Bach's Cantata autographs', *Studies in Music History: essays for Oliver Strunk* (Princeton, 1968), pp. 405–27.

MELCHERT, HERMANN: 'Das Rezitativ der Kirchenkantaten J. S. Bachs', *Bach-Jahrbuch 1958*, xlv, pp. 5–83.

MOSER, HANS JOACHIM: *Johann Sebastian Bach* (2nd ed., Berlin, 1943).

NEUMANN, WERNER: *J. S. Bach: sämtliche Kantatentexte* (Leipzig, 1954).

——*J. S. Bachs Chorfuge. Ein Beitrag zur Kompositions-technik Bachs* (Borna and Leipzig, 1938).

——*Handbuch der Kantaten J. S. Bachs* (Leipzig, 1947).

——*Kalendarium zur Lebensgeschichte Johann Sebastian Bachs* (Leipzig, 1970).

NEUMANN, WERNER AND SCHULZE, HANS-J.: *Schriftstücke von der Hand J. S. Bachs, Bach-Dokumente*, i (Kassel, 1963).

——*Fremdschriftliche und gedruckte Dokumente zur Lebensgeschichte J. S. Bachs, Bach-Dokumente*, ii (Kassel, 1969).

PIRRO, ANDRÉ: *L'Esthétique de Jean-Sébastien Bach* (Paris, 1907).

——*J. S. Bach* (Paris, 1906; Eng. trans., London, 1957).

SCHERING, ARNOLD: *Johann Sebastian Bachs Leipziger Kirchenmusik. Studien und Wege zu ihrer Erkenntnis* (2nd ed., Leipzig, 1954).

——*Johann Sebastian Bach und das Musikleben Leipzigs im 18. Jahrhundert* (Leipzig, 1941).

——*Über Kantaten J. S. Bachs* (Leipzig, 1942).

SCHULZE, HANS-J.: 'Bemerkungen zu einigen Kantatentexten J. S. Bachs', *Bach-Jahrbuch 1959*, xlvi, pp. 168–70.

——*Dokumente zum Nachwirken Johann Sebastian Bachs, Bach-Dokumente*, iii (Kassel, 1972).

SCHWEITZER, ALBERT: *J. S. Bach le musicien-poète* (Leipzig, 1905; Ger. version, Leipzig, 1908; expanded Eng. version, London, 1911, 2nd ed., 1952).

SERAUKY, WALTER: 'Die *Johannes-Passion* von Joh. Seb. Bach und ihr Vorbild', *Bach-Jahrbuch 1954*, xli, pp. 29–39.

SIEGELE, ULRICH: 'Bemerkungen zu Bachs Motetten', *Bach-Jahrbuch 1962*, xlix, pp. 33–57.

SMEND, FRIEDRICH: *Bach in Köthen* (Berlin, 1951).

——*Joh. Seb. Bach. Kirchenkantaten*, 6 vols. (Berlin, 1947–9).

SPITTA, PHILIPP: *Johann Sebastian Bach*, 2 vols. (Leipzig, 1873, 1880; 5th ed., Wiesbaden, 1962; shortened version by W. Schmieder, Leipzig, 1935; Eng. trans., 3 vols., London, 1884–99).

STEGLICH, RUDOLF: *Johann Sebastian Bach* (Potsdam, 1935).

TERRY, CHARLES SANFORD: *Bach's Four-part Chorales*, 3 vols. (London, 1915–1921).

——*J. S. Bach—a Biography* (2nd ed., London, 1933).

——*J. S. Bach: Cantata Texts Sacred and Secular* (London, 1926).

THIELE, EUGEN: *Die Chorfugen J. S. Bachs* (Berne, 1936).

VOIGT, WOLDEMAR: *Die Kirchenkantaten J. S. Bachs* (Leipzig, 1928).

WERKER, W.: *Die Matthäus-Passion* (Leipzig, 1923).

WESTRUP, J. A.: *Bach Cantatas* (London, 1966).

WHITTAKER, W. GILLIES: *The Cantatas of J. S. Bach*, 2 vols. (London, 1959).
——'A Lost Bach Magnificat', *Music and Letters*, xxi (1940), pp. 312–18.
WOLFF, LEONHARD: *J. S. Bachs Kirchenkantaten* (Leipzig, 1930).
ZANDER, FERDINAND: 'Die Dichter der Kantatentexte J. S. Bachs. Untersuchungen zu ihrer Bestimmung', *Bach-Jahrbuch 1968*, liv, pp. 9–64.

Bernhard

STREETMAN, RICHARD D.: *Christoph Bernhard*, 2 vols. (Diss., North Texas State University, 1967, unpub.).

Biber

NETTL, PAUL: 'Heinrich Franz Biber von Bibern', *Studien zur Musikwissenschaft*, xxiv (1960), p. 61.

Böhm

WALDSCHMIDT, CARL: *Georg Böhm, his Life and Works* (Diss., Northwestern University, 1962, unpub.).
WOLGAST, JOHANNES: *Georg Böhm, ein Meister der Übergangszeit vom 17. zum 18 Jahrhundert* (Diss., Berlin, 1924).

Bollius

GOTTRON, ADAM: *Tausend Jahre Musik in Mainz* (Berlin, 1941).

Briegel

HIRSCHMANN, K. F.: *Wolfgang Carl Briegel 1626–1712* (Marburg, 1934).

Bruhns

KÖLSCH, H.: *Nicolaus Bruhns, Leben und Werke* (Diss., Kiel, 1938, unpub.).

Buxtehude

ASHFORTH, D.: *Dietrich Buxtehude: his life and contribution to the development of the Lutheran cantata* (Diss., Hull, 1964, unpub.).
BLUME, FRIEDRICH: 'Das Kantatenwerk Dietrich Buxtehudes', *Jahrbuch der Musikbibliothek Peters für 1940*, pp. 10–39; reprinted in idem: *Syntagma musicologicum: gesammelte Reden und Schriften*, i (Kassel, 1963), pp. 320–51.
——'Dietrich Buxtehude in Geschichte und Gegenwart', in idem: *Syntagma . . .* (as foregoing item), pp. 351–63.
BUKER, ALDEN: *Choralbearbeitung from Johann Walther to Dietrich Buxtehude* (Diss., Boston, 1953, unpub.).
BUSZIN, WALTER E.: 'Dietrich Buxtehude (1637–1707) on the Tercentenary of his Birth', *Musical Quarterly*, xxiii (1937), pp. 465–90.
GECK, MARTIN: 'Die Authentizität des Vokalwerks Dietrich Buxtehudes in quellenkritischer Sicht', *Die Musikforschung*, xiv (1961), pp. 393–415; xvi (1963), pp. 175–81.
——*Die Vokalmusik Dietrich Buxtehudes und der frühe Pietismus* (Kassel, 1965).
HAGEN, M. D.: *Dietrich Buxtehude* (Copenhagen, 1920).
KARSTÄDT, GEORG: *Thematisch-systematisches Verzeichnis der musikalischen Werke von Dietrich Buxtehude: Buxtehude-Werke-Verzeichnis (BuxWV)* (Wiesbaden, 1974).
MAXTON, WILLY: 'Mitteilung über eine vollständige Abendmusik Dietrich Buxtehudes', *Zeitschrift für Musikwissenschaft*, x (1928), pp. 387–96.
PIRRO, ANDRÉ: *Dietrich Buxtehude* (Paris, 1907).
SEIFFERT, MAX: 'Buxtehude-Händel-Bach', *Jahrbuch der Musikbibliothek Peters für 1903*, pp. 13–27.
SØRENSEN, SØREN: *Diderich Buxtehudes vokale kirkemusik: studier til den evangeliske kirkekantates udviklingshistorie* (Copenhagen, 1958).
STAHL, WILHELM: *Dietrich Buxtehude* (Kassel, 1937).
——'Franz Tunder und Dietrich Buxtehude', *Archiv für Musikwissenschaft*, viii (1925–6), pp. 1–77; also issued separately (Leipzig, 1926).

Crüger

BRODDE, O.: *Johann Crüger, sein Weg und sein Werk* (Leipzig, [1936]).

FISCHER-KRÜCKEBERG, E.: 'Zur Geschichte ... des Berliner Kantors Johann Crüger', *Jahrbuch für Brandenburgische Kirchengesang*, xxv (1930), p. 156.

Eberlin

HAAS, ROBERT: 'Eberlins Schuldramen und Oratorien', *Studien zur Musikwissenschaft*, viii (1921), pp. 9–44.

Erlebach

BASELT, BERND: 'Die Musikaliensammlung der Schwarzburg-Rudolstädtischen Hofkapelle unter Philipp Heinrich Erlebach (1657–1714)', *Wissenschaftliche Zeitschrift der Martin-Luther-Universität Halle-Wittenberg, Sonderband* (1963), pp. 105–34.

KINKELDEY, OTTO: 'Philipp Heinrich Erlebach, nebst einigen Bemerkungen zur Rudolstädter Hofmusik', preface to *Denkmäler deutscher Tonkunst*, xlvi–xlvii (Leipzig, 1914).

LEHN, EDGAR VOM: *The Sacred Cantatas of Philipp Heinrich Erlebach (1657–1714)* (Diss., North Carolina, 1958, unpub.).

Fasch

ENGELKE, BERNHARD: 'J. F. Fasch. Versuch einer Biographie', *Sammelbände der internationalen Musikgesellschaft*, x (1908–9), pp. 263–83; autobiography in F. W. Marpurg: *Historisch-Kritische Beiträge*, iii (Berlin, 1757), pp. 124 ff., and J. A. Hiller: *Lebensbeschreibungen berühmter Tonkünstler* (Leipzig, 1784).

Ferdinand III

ADLER, GUIDO: Preface to *Musikalische Werke der Kaiser Ferdinand III., Leopold I. und Joseph I.*, 2 vols. (Vienna, 1892–3).

SOMERSET, H. V. F.: 'The Habsburg Emperors as Musicians', *Music and Letters*, xxx (1949), pp. 204–15.

Christoph Förster

ENGELKE, BERNHARD: 'Die Rudolstädter Hofkapelle unter Lyra und Johann Graf', *Archiv für Musikwissenschaft*, i (1918–19), pp. 594–606.

HARTNUNG, A.: *Christoph Förster* (Diss., Leipzig, 1914).

Kaspar Förster

BAAB, JERROLD C.: *The Sacred Latin Works of Kaspar Förster (1616–73)* (Diss., North Carolina, 1970, unpub.).

WOLFFHEIM, WERNER: 'Gedenk-Säule Caspar Försters', *Archiv für Musikwissenschaft*, ii (1919–20), pp. 289–92.

Frauenholtz

VOGELEIS, M.: *Quellen und Bausteine zur Geschichte der Musik in Elsass* (Strasbourg, 1911).

WENNAGEL, R.: *Les Cantates strasbourgeoises du 18ᵉ siècle* (Diss., Strasbourg, 1948, unpub.).

Fux

BENN, F.: *Die Messkompositionen des J. J. Fux* (Diss., Vienna, 1931).

JEPPESEN, KNUD: 'Johann Joseph Fux und die moderne Kontrapunkttheorie', *Bericht über den I. Musikwissenschaftlichen Kongress der Deutschen Musikgesellschaft, Leipzig, 1925* (Leipzig, 1926), pp. 187–8.

KÖCHEL, LUDWIG VON: *Johann Josef Fux* (Vienna, 1872).

WELLESZ, EGON: *Fux* (London, 1965).

——'Die Opern und Oratorien in Wien von 1660–1708', *Studien zur Musikwissenschaft,* vi (1919), pp. 5–138.

Goldberg

DADDER, E.: 'Johann Gottlieb Goldberg', *Bach-Jahrbuch 1923*, xx, pp. 57–71.

RAUSCHNING, H.: *Geschichte der Musik und Musikpflege in Danzig* (Danzig, 1931).

Graun

PROUT, EBENEZER: 'Graun's *Passion-Oratorio* and Handel's Knowledge of it', *Monthly Musical Record*, xxiv (1894), pp. 97 ff., 121 ff.

Graupner

FALL, H. CUTLER: *The Passiontide Cantatas of Christoph Graupner* (Diss., California: Santa Barbara, 1971, unpub.).

NOACK, FRIEDRICH: *Christoph Graupner als Kirchenkomponist* (Leipzig, 1926).

——*Christoph Graupners Kirchenmusiken* (Leipzig, 1916).

——'Johann Sebastian Bach und Christoph Graupner: *Mein Herze schwimmt in Blut'*, *Archiv für Musikwissenschaft*, ii (1919–20), pp. 85–98.

Hammerschmidt

MUELLER, HAROLD: *The "Musicalische Gespräche über die Evangelia" of Andreas Hammerschmidt* (Diss., Rochester, N.Y., 1953, unpub.).

SCHÜNEMANN, GEORG: 'Beitrage zur Biographie Hammerschmidts', *Sammelbände der internationalen Musikgesellschaft*, xii (1910–11), pp. 207–12.

Handel

CLAUSEN, HANS DIETER: *Händels Direktionspartituren ("Handexemplare")*, *Hamburger Beiträge zur Musikwissenschaft*, vii (Hamburg, 1972) [The first catalogue of Handel's 'conducting scores' in the Staats- und Universitätsbibliothek, Hamburg].

LAM, BASIL: 'The Church Music', *Handel: a Symposium*, ed. G. Abraham (London, 1954), pp. 156–178.

LANG, PAUL HENRY: *George Frederic Handel* (New York, 1966).

MOSER, HANS JOACHIM: *Der junge Händel und seine Vorläufer in Halle* (Halle, 1929).

SASSE, KONRAD: *Händel Bibliographie* (Leipzig, 1963); *1. Nachtrag: 1962–1965* (Leipzig, 1967).

SEIFFERT, MAX: 'Buxtehude-Händel-Bach', *Jahrbuch der Musikbibliothek Peters für 1903*, ix, pp. 13–27.

——'Händels Verhältnis zu Tonwerken älterer deutscher Meister', *Jahrbuch der Musikbibliothek Peters für 1908*, xiv, pp. 41–57.

SERAUKY, WALTER: 'Georg Friedrich Händels lateinische Kirchenmusik', *Händel-Jahrbuch 1957*, iii, pp. 5–24.

SIEGMUND-SCHULTZE, WALTHER, ed.: 'Die Biographien Georg Friedrich Händels und Georg Philipp Telemanns aus Johann Matthesons *Grundlage einer Ehrenpforte'*, *Händel-Jahrbuch 1971*, xvii, pp. 89–115 [facs.].

SMEND, JULIUS: 'Händel und das deutsche Kirchenlied', *Monatschrift für Gottesdienst und kirchliche Kunst*, xxx (1925), pp. 240–4.

TAUT, KURT: 'Verzeichnis des Schrifttums über G. F. Händel', *Händel-Jahrbuch 1933*, vi, pp. 1–153.

WALKER, ARTHUR D.: *George Frideric Handel—The Newman Flower Collection in the Henry Watson Music Library* (Manchester, 1972).

Hasse

KAMIEŃSKI, LUCIAN: *Die Oratorien von J. A. Hasse* (Leipzig, 1912).

MÜLLER, WALTHER: *Johann Adolf Hasse als Kirchenkomponist* (Leipzig, 1911).

Keiser

KÜMMERLING, HARALD: 'Fünf unbekannte Kantaten in Reinhard Keisers Autograph', *Festschrift Max Schneider zum achtzigsten Geburtstag* (Leipzig, 1955), pp. 177–81.

MOE, DONALD G.: *The St. Mark Passion of Reinhard Keiser: A Practical Edition, with an Account of its Historical Background*, 2 vols. (Diss., Iowa, 1968, unpub.).
PETZOLD, R.: *Die Kirchenkompositionen und weltlichen Kantaten Reinhard Keisers* (Düsseldorf, 1935).

Kerll
ADLER, GUIDO: 'Zur Geschichte der Wiener-Messkomposition in der zweiten Hälfte des XVII. Jahrhundert', *Studien zur Musikwissenschaft*, iv (1916), pp. 5–45.
GIEBLER, ALBERT C.: *The Masses of Johann Caspar Kerll*, 2 vols. (Diss., Michigan, 1957, unpub.).

Kindermann
SAMUEL, HAROLD E.: *The Cantata in Nuremberg during the 17th Century* (Diss., Cornell, 1963, unpub.).
SCHREIBER, FELIX: Preface to *Ausgewählte Werke, Denkmäler der Tonkunst in Bayern*, xiii (Leipzig, 1913).

Kirchhoff
MITTAG, J. G.: *Hallische Schul-Historie*, iii (Halle, 1748).
SERAUKY, WALTER: *Musikgeschichte der Stadt Halle*, ii/1 (Halle and Berlin, 1939; repr. 1970).

Knüpfer
KANDMANN, O.: *Das Werk Sebastian Knüpfers im Überblick* (Diss., Leipzig, 1960, unpub.).
SCHERING, ARNOLD: *Musikgeschichte Leipzigs*, ii (Leipzig, 1926).

J. P. Krieger
EITNER, ROBERT: 'Johann Philipp Krieger', *Monatshefte für Musikgeschichte*, xxix (1897), pp. 114–17.

Kühnhausen
ADRIO, ADAM: 'Die Matthäus-Passion von J. G. Kühnhausen (Celle um 1700)', *Festschrift Arnold Schering zum sechzigsten Geburtstag* (Berlin, 1937), pp. 24–35.
LINNEMANN, G.: *Celler Musikgeschichte bis zum Beginn des 19. Jahrhundert* (Celle, 1935).

Kuhnau
MARTIN, JOHANNES C.: *Die Kirchenkantaten Johann Kuhnaus* (Borna-Leipzig, 1928).
RICHTER, B. F.: 'Verzeichnis von Kirchenmusiken J. Kuhnau's aus den Jahren 1707–1721', *Monatshefte für Musikgeschichte*, xxxiv (1902), pp. 176–81.
RIMBACH, EVANGELINE L.: *The Church Cantatas of Johann Kuhnau*, 2 vols. (Diss., Rochester, N.Y., 1966, unpub.).

Leopold I
ADLER, GUIDO: Preface to *Musikalische Werke der Kaiser Ferdinand III., Leopold I. und Joseph I.*, 2 vols. (Vienna, 1892–3).
SOMERSET, H. V. F.: 'The Habsburg Emperors as Musicians', *Music and Letters*, xxx (1949), pp. 204–15.

Mattheson
CANNON, BEEKMAN C.: *Johann Mattheson, Spectator in Music* (New Haven, 1947).
PETZOLDT, RICHARD: 'Johann Mattheson', *Die Musik*, xxiii (1930–1), pp. 887–90.
SCHMIDT, H.: *Johann Mattheson, ein Förderer der deutschen Tonkunst, im Lichte seiner Werke* (Leipzig, 1897).

Meder
BOLTE, JOHANNES: 'Nochmals Johannes Valentin Meder', *Vierteljahrsschrift für Musikwissenschaft*, vii (1891), pp. 455–8.
——'Johann Valentin Meder's Stammbuch', *Sammelbände der internationalen Musikgesellschaft*, i (1899–1900), pp. 530–4.

SMALLMAN, BASIL: 'A forgotten Oratorio Passion' [Meder's St. Matthew Passion], *Musical Times*, cxv (1974), pp. 118–21.

Pachelbel
EGGEBRECHT, HANS HEINZ: 'Johann Pachelbel als Vokalkomponist', *Archiv für Musikwissenschaft*, xi (1954), pp. 120–45.
KRUMMACHER, FRIEDHELM: 'Kantate und Konzert im Werk Johann Pachelbels', *Die Musikforschung*, xx (1967), pp. 365–92.
SEIFFERT, MAX: 'Pachelbel's musikalische Sterbensgedanken', *Sammelbände der internationalen Musikgesellschaft*, vi (1903–4), pp. 476–88.

Pfleger
NAUSCH, ANNE MARIE: *Augustin Pfleger. Leben und Werke* (Kassel, 1955).

Reutter, father and son
HOFER, NORBERT: *Die beiden Reutter als Kirchenkomponisten* (Diss., Vienna, 1915).
RAUGEL, FÉLIX: 'Les véritables auteurs d'oeuvres religieuses attribueés à Mozart', *Revue de musicologie*, xxxvi (1954), pp. 146–7.

Rosenmüller
HAMEL, FRED: *Die Psalmkompositionen Johann Rosenmüllers* (Strasbourg, 1933).
HORNEFFER, A.: *Johann Rosenmüller (ca. 1619–1684)* (Charlottenburg, 1898); summary in *Monatshefte für Musikgeschichte*, xxx (1898), p. 102.
SNYDER, KERALA J.: *Johann Rosenmüller's Music for Solo Voice* (Diss., Yale, 1970, unpub.).

Scheidt
ADRIO, ADAM: 'Zu Samuel Scheidts Vokalmusik', *Musik und Kirche*, xxiv (1954), pp. 145–52.
HÜNICKEN, R.: *Samuel Scheidt, ein althallischer Musikus. Sein Leben und Wirken* (Halle, 1934).
MAHRENHOLZ, CHRISTHARD: *Samuel Scheidt, sein Leben und sein Werk* (Leipzig, 1924).

Schelle
BASELT, BERND: 'Der "Actus Musicus auf Weyh-Nachten" des Leipzig Thomaskantors Johann Schelle', *Wissenschaftliche Zeitschrift der Martin-Luther-Universität Halle-Wittenberg*, Jg. xiv/5 (1965), pp. 331–4.
GRAUPNER, F.: *Das Werk des Thomaskantors Johann Schelle* (Wolfenbüttel and Berlin, 1929).
SCHERING, ARNOLD: 'Die Kantaten der Thomas-Kantoren vor Bach', *Bach-Jahrbuch 1912*, pp. 86–123.

Schmelzer
ADLER, GUIDO: 'Zur Geschichte der Wiener Messkomposition in der zweiten Hälfte des XVII. Jahrhundert', *Studien zur Musikwissenschaft*, iv (1916), pp. 5–45.
RIEDEL, F. W.: *Das Musikarchiv im Minoritenkonvent zu Wien* (Kassel, 1963), pp. 81ff.

Schop
KRÜGER, LISELOTTE: *Die Hamburgische Musikorganisation im 17. Jahrhundert* (Strasbourg, 1933).
STEPHENSON, KURT: *Johann Schop* (Diss., Halle, 1924).

Schultz
SIEBECK, R.: *Johannes Schultz* (Leipzig, 1913).

54

Schultze

BRAUN, WERNER: 'Der Kantor C. Schultze (1606–1683) und die "Neue Musik" in Delitzsch', *Wissenschaftlichen Zeitschriften der Martin-Luther-Universität Halle-Wittenberg*, Jg. x/4 (1961), pp. 1187–225.

Schütz

ABERT, ANNA AMALIE: *Die stilistischen Voraussetzungen der 'Cantiones Sacrae' von Heinrich Schütz* (Wolfenbüttel and Berlin, 1935).

AGEY, CALVIN B.: *A Study of the 'Kleine geistliche Concerte' and 'Geistliche Chormusik' of Heinrich Schütz*, 2 vols. (Diss., Florida State University, 1955, unpub.).

BITTINGER, WERNER, ed.: *Schütz-Werke-Verzeichnis* (Kassel, 1960).

EINSTEIN, ALFRED: *Heinrich Schütz* (Kassel, 1928).

GERBER, RUDOLF: *Das Passionrezitativ bei Heinrich Schütz und seine stilgeschichtlichen Grundlagen* (Gütersloh, 1929).

——'Wort und Ton in den *Cantiones sacrae* von Heinrich Schütz', *Gedenkschrift für Hermann Abert von seinen Schülern* (Halle, 1928), pp. 57–71.

KREIDLER, WALTHER: *Heinrich Schütz und der Stile concitato von Claudio Monteverdi* (Stuttgart, 1934).

MOSER, HANS JOACHIM: *Heinrich Schütz: sein Leben und Werk* (2nd ed., Kassel, 1954; Eng. trans., St. Louis, 1959).

——*Kleines Heinrich-Schütz-Buch* (3rd ed., Halle, 1952; Eng. trans., London, 1967).

PIRRO, ANDRÉ: *Heinrich Schütz* (Paris, 1913).

REITTER, L.: *Doppelchortechnik bei Heinrich Schütz* (Derendingen, 1937).

SCHNEIDER, MAX: 'Zum Weihnachtsoratorium von Heinrich Schütz', *Theodor Kroyer: Festschrift zum sechzigsten Geburtstage* (Regensburg, 1933), pp. 140–3.

SCHUH, WILLI: *Formprobleme bei Heinrich Schütz* (Leipzig, 1928).

SPITTA, FRIEDRICH: *Heinrich Schütz, ein Meister der Musica sacra* (Halle, 1925).

——*Die Passionen nach den vier Evangelien von Heinrich Schütz* (Leipzig, 1886).

——'Die Passionen von Schütz und ihre Wiederbelebung', *Jahrbuch der Musikbibliothek Peters für 1906*, xii, pp. 17–28.

Sebastiani

DAVIDSSON, ÅKE: *Musikbibliographische Beiträge* (Uppsala and Wiesbaden, 1954), pp. 62–5.

MAYER-REINACH, ALBERT: 'Zur Geschichte der Königsberger Hofkapelle in den Jahren 1578–1720', *Sammelbände der internationalen Musikgesellschaft*, vi (1904–5), pp. 67–75.

Selle

BIRKE, JOACHIM: *Die Passionsmusiken von Thomas Selle* (Diss., Hamburg, 1957).

GÜNTHER, S.: *Die geistliche Konzert-Musik von Th. Selle nebst einer Biographie* (Diss., Giessen, 1935).

Stadlmayr

DANIEL, F.: *Die konzertanten Messen J. Stadlmayers* (Diss., Vienna, 1928).

JUNKERMANN, HILDE H.: *The Magnificats of Johann Stadlmayr*, 2 vols. (Diss., Ohio State University, 1966, unpub.).

Stobäus

KAMIEŃSKI, LUCIAN: *J. Stobaeus* (Posen [Poznań], 1928).

Stölzel

BÖHME, E. W.: 'Gottfried Heinrich Stoeltzel in Gera', *Zeitschrift für Musikwissenschaft*, xiii (1930–1), pp. 333–4.

SIETZ, REINHOLD: 'Alte Meister: G. H. Stölzel', *Das Musikleben*, vi (1953).

Strauss

GANO, PETER W.: *The Masses of Christoph Strauss* (Diss., California: Santa Barbara, 1971, unpub.).

GEIRINGER, KARL: 'Christoph Strauss, ein Wiener Künstlerdasein am Beginn des 17. Jahrhunderts', *Zeitschrift für Musikwissenschaft*, xiii (1930–1), pp. 50–60.

Telemann

BASELT, BERND: 'Georg Philipp Telemann und die protestantische Kirchenmusik', *Musik und Kirche*, xxxvii/5 (1967), pp. 196–207.

FLEISCHHAUER, GÜNTER: 'Die Musik Georg Philipp Telemanns im Urteil seiner Zeit', *Händel-Jahrbuch 1967–8*, xiii–xiv, pp. 173–205.

HÖRNER, HANS: *G. Ph. Telemanns Passionsmusiken* (Leipzig, 1933).

RHEA, CLAUDE H., Jnr.: *The Sacred Oratorios of George Philipp Telemann (1681–1767)*, 2 vols. (Diss., Florida State University, 1958, unpub.).

Theile

MACKEY, ELIZABETH J.: *The Sacred Works of Johann Theile*, 2 vols. (Diss., Michigan, 1968, unpub.).

MAXTON, WILLY: *Johann Theile* (Diss., Tübingen, 1926).

Tunder

GUDEWILL, KURT: *Franz Tunder und die nordelbingsche Musikkultur seiner Zeit* (Lübeck, 1967).

HENNINGS, J.: 'Tunderiana', *Lübecksche Blätter*, lxxv (1934),

HENNINGS, J. AND STAHL, WILHELM: *Musikgeschichte Lübecks*, ii (Kassel, 1952).

SHARP, G. B.: 'Franz Tunder: 1614–1667', *Musical Times*, cviii (1967), pp. 997–9.

STAHL, WILHELM: 'Franz Tunder und Dietrich Buxtehude', *Archiv für Musikwissenschaft*, viii (1925–6), pp. 1–77; also issued separately (Leipzig, 1926).

WINZENBURGER, WALTER P.: *The Music of Franz Tunder* (Diss., Rochester, N.Y., 1965, unpub.).

Weckmann

ILGNER, G.: *Matthias Weckmann. Sein Leben und seine Werke* (Wolfenbüttel and Berlin, 1939).

SEIFFERT, MAX: 'Matthias Weckmann und das Collegium musicum in Hamburg', *Sammelbände der internationalen Musikgesellschaft*, ii (1900–1), pp. 76–132.

Zachow

BASELT, BERND: 'Friedrich Wilhelm Zachow und die protestantische Kirchenkantate', *Festschrift der 11. Händelfestspiele der DDR* (Halle, 1962), pp. 45–54.

HEUSS, ALFRED: 'Zachow als dramatischer Kantatenkomponist', *Zeitschrift der internationalen Musikgesellschaft*, x (1908–9), pp. 228–35.

THOMAS, GÜNTER: *Friedrich Wilhelm Zachow* (Regensburg, 1966).

WICKE, A.: *Die Kantaten Friedrich Wilhelm Zachows in ihrer geschichtlichen Stellung* (Diss., Humboldt University, Berlin, 1956, unpub.).

LIST OF CONTENTS OF
THE HISTORY OF MUSIC IN SOUND

VOLUME V

The History of Music in Sound is a series of volumes of gramophone records, with explanatory booklets, designed as a companion series to the *New Oxford History of Music*. Each volume covers the same ground as the corresponding volume in the *New Oxford History of Music* and is designed as far as possible to illustrate the music discussed therein. The records are issued in England by E.M.I. Records Ltd. (H.M.V.) and in the United States by R.C.A. Victor, and the booklets are published by the Oxford University Press. The editor of Volume V of *The History of Music in Sound* is J. A. Westrup.

The History of Music in Sound is available on LP records, and the side numbers are given below.

INDEX

Compiled by Frederick Smyth

Page numbers in *italic type* indicate the more important references. Operas and other stage works, and oratorios, are indexed under composers and librettists, the latter being identified as such.

55